THE INTERNATIONAL DIMENSIONS OF HUMAN RIGHTS

Dimensions internationales des droits
= de l'homme. English.

THE INTERNATIONAL DIMENSIONS OF HUMAN RIGHTS

Karel Vasak ed.
General Editor

Revised and edited for the English edition
by Philip Alston

Volume 1

GREENWOOD PRESS
WESTPORT, CONNECTICUT

UNESCO, PARIS, FRANCE

Library of Congress Cataloging in Publication Data

Dimensions internationales des droits de l'homme.
  English.
  The International dimensions of human rights.

  Translation of: Les dimensions internationales des
droits de l'homme.
  Bibliography: v. 2, p.
  Includes indexes.
    1. Civil rights (International law)—Addresses, essays,
lectures.   2. Civil rights—Addresses, essays, lectures.
I. Vasak, Karel.   II. Alston, Philip.   III. Unesco.
IV. Title.
K3240.6.D5513   341.48'1   81-22566
ISBN: 0-313-23394-2 (set)   AACR2
ISBN: 0-313-23395-0 (vol. 1)
ISBN: 0-313-23396-9 (vol. 2)

Library of Congress Catalog Card Number: 81-22566
Greenwood Press ISBN: 0-313-23394-2 (set)

Unesco ISBN: 92-3-101477-3

First published 1982 by the United Nations Educational, Scientific and Cultural
Organization, 7, Place de Fontenoy, 75700, Paris, France, and Greenwood Press,
a division of Congressional Information Service, Inc.
88 Post Road West, Westport, Connecticut 06881

Printed in the United States of America

10 9 8 7 6 5 4 3 2 1

Contents

Contents

Contents

Tables

Foreword

"Human rights are neither a new morality nor a lay religion and are much more than a language common to all mankind. They are requirements which the investigator must study and integrate into his knowledge, using the rules and methods of his science, whether this is philosophy, the humanities or the natural sciences, sociology or law, history or geography. In a word, the task is gradually to build up or promote a genuine scientific formulation of human rights."[1]

This work is a treatise intended to be of use in the teaching of human rights; it has been produced with this purpose in mind.

Since the Second World War, there has been a prodigious development of ideas, expressions, behaviour patterns, rules and institutions, the novelty of which lies not so much in its nature as in the scale on which it has occurred. This has resulted in what may truly be termed a "human rights phenomenon". True, this phenomenon has not arisen *ex nihilo*; it has derived from a past which is common to all mankind in that human rights have benefited from every major trend of thought. It is not our intention to demonstrate this again because Unesco, ever mindful to "give credit where credit is due" by tracing back to their origins the ideas which inspire and guide us, has already done so. In 1965, at the memorable Oxford Round Table, the philosophy and content of the Universal Declaration of Human Rights were examined in the context of the various religious traditions, ideologies, cultures and dominant values of various types of society.[2] Then the admirable work, *Birthright of Man*, although modestly described as a "selection of texts"[3], in fact provided a dazzling display of those fraternal bonds which cannot but unite all those who together constitute the human race. To make a summary here of these two fundamental publications would be to mutilate them, but they must be constantly referred to, if the inspiration and the very substance of this treatise are to be understood.

While the "human rights phenomenon" derives from the past, it is also tied in with the present, a present in the process of continual change. In the face of this contemporary phenomenon there is but one valid approach: that awareness from which the human rights phenomenon springs must, if it is not to lapse into a sterile romanticism or fall prey to an exclusive ideology, thereby giving rise to an irreversible wave of violence, be sustained by objective and impartial work. In other words, the specific manifestation of human rights in the latter half of the 20th century makes it mandatory that these rights be regarded as "subjects of scientific investigation" constituting a particular field of study, in order that respect for human rights be based upon scientific data rather than dictated by the express requirements of a dogma.

It is for this reason that the contemporary phenomenon of human rights demands that a genuine *science of human rights* be developed, the objectivity and rigour of which will vouch for the independence of human rights from any particular school of thought or any particular interpretation of reality.

Any science in the process of formation must start off by defining its subject and working out its method. This was one of the goals of the Nice Colloquium, organized on 5 and 6 March 1971, at the request of Unesco, by the International Institute of Human Rights, on the theme: "The Methodology and Teaching of the Science of Human Rights".

At the colloquium René Cassin, the principal drafter of the Universal Declaration of Human Rights, gave a *deductive* definition of the science of human rights: "The science of human rights is defined as a particular branch of the social sciences, the object of which is to study human relations in the light of human dignity while determining those rights and faculties which are necessary as a whole for the full development of each human being's personality".

On the basis of the study of the frequency of the terms to be found in national and international texts dealing with human rights, one can formulate a second, *inductive* definition. Conducted with the help of a computer which was fed with more than 50,000 terms relating to "human rights," this study has enabled me, by using those terms which were most frequently employed, to define the science of human rights as follows:

"The science of human rights concerns the individual person living within a state who, being accused of an offense or being the victim of a situation of war, benefits from the protection of the law, due to either the intercession of the national judge or that of international organizations (such as the organs of the European Convention on Human Rights), and whose rights, particularly the right to equality, are harmonized with the requirements of public order."

One cannot fail to be struck by the fact that in this second definition, which is more descriptive than teleological, it is the *law*, synonymous with freedom, which occupies the central place among the means of protecting human rights, and that it is equality which, among human rights, is given the leading place.

It is obvious, as suggested by the two definitions, that in the study of human rights all the human disciplines interconnect and enrich each other to form, with human rights, the equivalent of philosophy in the Middle Ages, the science of sciences. Even though some will balk at this "domination" of human rights over the other sciences, we shall certainly be quite prepared to draw the conclusion that there is a need for an *interdisciplinary* study of human rights.

Indeed, this is the only method which will make it possible to grasp the wealth
and variety of human rights as well as their relative and global character.[4]

This treatise is, however, primarily a legal treatise, intended first and
foremost to be of use in the teaching of human rights in Faculties of Law and in
Faculties of Political and Social Sciences. This juristic approach is not without
risks insofar as, in sociology, it will not provide any clear evidence of the fact
that human rights constitute one element among others of the structures of
society, and that, consequently, violations of human rights may be total and
not particularized, being the result of certain inherently unjust and inhumane
social structures. This danger of the study of human rights being thereby
deprived of some of its value is undeniable. However, this can be surmounted
by increasing the number of interdisciplinary research undertakings in the
field of human rights; Unesco will aid in this task in coming years, as is stressed
in its Medium-Term Plan.

The truth of the matter is that this first treatise on human rights is primarily
a legal treatise for practical reasons and because there is a need for such a work
in education. The language in which human rights are formulated is primarily
the language of law; it consequently falls to the jurist to be the first to gather
together the various scattered elements in this field and to provide a survey of
them. Thus, it was the Law Faculties throughout the world who were the first
to open the door to the scientific study of human rights. Today their teachers
and students demand teaching materials which will enable them to go beyond
general notions now taught everywhere in courses on constitutional law or in
those relating to public international law.[5] It is primarily for them that this
treatise is intended.

This "Unesco Treatise on Human Rights" is a collective work. Having had
the honour of overseeing its preparation, I have taken care not to modify its
collective character, and each author has been allowed complete freedom to
guarantee the independent nature of the treatise. No leading idea governs this
treatise, save that it should be of use in the teaching of human rights; it
expresses no particular ideology, even though it tends perhaps to reflect all
ideologies, owing to the choice of its authors.

Of course, this diversity is not without drawbacks. For example, after
reading this treatise, the reader will not know if the right to self-determination
is a genuine human right, if it is a necessary, but not sufficient, condition for
human rights, or if it is a so-called constitutional principle of human rights. All
these theses are formulated, explicitly or implicitly, in this work. In the final
analysis, the diversity of views presented constitutes an invitation to the
reader to exercise his own right as a human being to choose freely one or the
other of these theses or to propose his own.

The divergence may be even more fundamental. Thus, some of the authors
of the treatise support the thesis of the absolute sovereignty of the State and,
consequently, the absolute bearing of Article 2, paragraph 7, of the United
Nations Charter, being of the opinion that human rights are solely a matter of

domestic jurisdiction and that the international "protection" of human rights is in actual fact merely a particular form of co-operation between sovereign States. Other authors of the treatise are far from subscribing to this thesis. While not questioning the notion of sovereignty, they emphasize its limits and relative character and, most of all, they stress its subordination to international law, of which human rights form a part, particularly since human rights have been enshrined in several provisions in the United Nations Charter. In point of fact, the opinions differ only in regard to the extent to which sovereignty is, if not limited, at least determined in respect of its exercise, by the development of international law and, primarily, by international human rights law, the existence of which, in my opinion at least, is now difficult to deny.

Other examples of similarly conflicting views, and consequently of the same freedom of critical opinion, can be found in the pages of the treatise. Is this a defect? I do not think so, being of the opinion that all the theses deserve to be known provided, however, that they are set forth in a spirit of tolerance and of respect for others, as this treatise seeks to do. If, however, the treatise contains anything that gives offence, it does so unintentionally and, above all, unwittingly.

In concluding this foreword, I should like to thank my colleagues, all of whom have become my friends, who contributed to the preparation of this treatise:

Imre Szabo (Hungary), Professor at the University of Budapest; Director of the Institute for Legal and Administrative Sciences of the Hungarian Academy of Sciences;

Theodoor C. van Boven (Netherlands), former Director of the United Nations Division of Human Rights; former Member of the United Nations Sub-Commission on Prevention of Discrimination and Protection of Minorities;

Karl Josef Partsch (Federal Republic of Germany), Professor and former Rector of the University of Bonn; Member of the United Nations Committee on the Elimination of Racial Discrimination;

Vladimir Kartashkin (USSR), Special Assistant to the Legal Counsel of the United Nations; former Senior Researcher, Institute of Law and of the State;

Frank C. Newman (USA), Professor Emeritus and former Dean of the School of Law, University of California, Berkeley; Associate Justice of the Supreme Court of California;

Stephen P. Marks (USA), member of the Unesco Division of Human Rights and Peace; former collaborator of the International Institute of Human Rights, Strasbourg;

Egon Schwelb (United Kingdom), former Deputy Director of the United Nations Division of Human Rights, and former Lecturer in Law Emeritus, School of Law, Yale University, whose death in 1979 was a great loss to the cause of human rights;

Philip Alston (Australia), former member of the United Nations Secretariat; member of the United Nations Division of Human Rights;

Kamleshwar Das (India), former Deputy Director of the United Nations Division of Human Rights;

Nicolas Valticos (Greece), Assistant Director-General and Adviser for International Labour Standards, International Labour Organisation;

Hanna Saba (Egypt), former Assistant Director-General of Unesco;

Christian Dominicé (Geneva), Professor and former Dean, Faculty of Law, University of Geneva;

Héctor Gros Espiell (Uruguay), Secretary-General of OPANAL (Organization for the Abolition of Nuclear Weapons in Latin America); former Member of the United Nations Sub-Commission on Prevention of Discrimination and Protection of Minorities;

Boutros Boutros-Ghali (Egypt), Minister of State for Foreign Affairs of Egypt; former Director of the Department of Political Science, Cairo University;

Kéba M'Baye (Senegal), First President of the Supreme Court of Senegal; Judge at the International Court of Justice;

Birame Ndiaye (Senegal), Lecturer at the Faculty of Law and Economics of Dakar;

Hiroko Yamane (Japan), member of the Unesco Division of Human Rights and Peace.

It goes without saying that in a collective work such as this treatise, the merits are, above all, those of its authors. My colleagues and Unesco have honoured me in entrusting to me the formidable and exciting task of being general editor of this treatise. I crave the indulgence of the jury of readers for any defects and hope others will have the courage to undertake similar works in the future.

The General Editor
Karel Vasak*

Note concerning this English edition

This textbook was originally published in French by Unesco in 1978 under the title *Les dimensions internationales des droits de l'homme*. In the preparation of the present English version a considerable amount of revision and updating of the various contributions has been undertaken in order to maximize their usefulness and currency. In general, this has been done by, or in consultation with, the various authors. However, in some instances this has not proved possible and responsibility for any changes, all of which have been undertaken in the spirit of the original version, rests with the editors. As far as possible the information herein is that available as of January 1, 1982.

---

* Presently Legal Adviser to Unesco and formerly Director of the Unesco Division of Human Rights and Peace; at the time of the initial preparation of this volume, Secretary-General of the International Institute of Human Rights.

NOTES

1. Unesco, *Medium-Term Plan (1977-1982)*, Doc. 19 C/4, p. 7, para. 1122.

2. Round Table on Human Rights, Oxford, 11-19 November 1965. Three of the written communications presented to the Round Table have been published in the *International Social Science Journal*, Vol. XVIII (1966), No. 1, on "The Marxist approach" (M. Hirszowicz), "The liberal Western tradition of human rights" (D.D. Raphael) and "The Hindu and Buddhist traditions". Other communications related, *inter alia*, to "The problem of human rights in the Judeo-Christian tradition" (Rev. C. Fabro), "The problem of human rights in other Asian traditions" (M. Ito), "The problem of human rights in the Islamic tradition" (A.A.V. Wafi), "Human rights and negritude" (M.L. Diakhaté) and "The liberal tradition of human rights in the West" (R. Cassin).

3. Unesco, 1968, prepared under the direction of Jeanne Hersch.

4. See the demonstration of the interdisciplinary nature of human rights and the need for an appropriate method in "Méthodologie des droits de l'homme," Vol. IV of *Mélanges René Cassin*, Paris, 1972.

5. See the conclusion of the world survey on "The teaching of human rights in universities" published in the *Human Rights Journal*, Vol. VI, 1973, pp. 4-222; and the conclusions of the International Congress on the Teaching of Human Rights, Vienna, 12-16 September 1978, in "The Teaching of Human Rights", Paris, Unesco, 1980.

Preface

The action of Unesco in support of human rights is in accordance with the highest purpose of the Organization as defined by its Constitution:

"...to further universal respect for justice, for the rule of law and for the human rights and fundamental freedoms which are affirmed for the peoples of the world, without distinction of race, sex, language or religion, by the Charter of the United Nations."

In regard to the teaching of human rights, the United Nations Commission on Human Rights has recognized Unesco's specific role by requesting it to consider "the desirability of envisaging the systematic study and development of an independent scientific discipline of human rights, taking into account the principal legal systems of the world, with a view to facilitating the understanding, comprehension, study and teaching of human rights at university level and subsequently at other educational levels...". This treatise is the result of Unesco's efforts in the direction of universities. It has been produced under the auspices of Unesco at the initiative of the International Institute of Human Rights of Strasbourg.

Unesco wishes to express its warmest thanks to the General Editor and the authors of this treatise, who have managed to deal with the subject of human rights in a spirit of mutual co-operation and understanding. Of course, the opinions expressed in this work and the interpretation of the facts which it contains are the sole responsibility of the authors and thus do not commit Unesco,* although Unesco fully endorses the objectives shared by all the authors, namely, universal and effective respect for human rights and fundamental freedoms. Unesco hopes that this treatise will make a tangible contribution to the realization of this aspiration which, throughout the history of mankind, has been the aspiration of all.

*"The designations employed and the presentation of material throughout the publication do not imply the expression of any opinion whatsoever on the part of Unesco concerning the legal status of any country, territory, city or area or of its authorities, or concerning the delimitation of its frontiers or boundaries."

Abbreviations

AJIL	*American Journal of International Law*
ECHR Yearbook	*European Convention on Human Rights Year-book*
ECOSOC	Economic and Social Council
FAO	Food and Agriculture Organization
GA	General Assembly
HR	Human Rights: A Compilation of International Instruments (United Nations, 1978 ed.)
IBRD	International Bank for Reconstruction and Development (World Bank)
ICJ	International Court of Justice
ICLQ	*International and Comparative Law Quarterly*
ILO	International Labour Organisation
IMF	International Monetary Fund
NGO	Non-Governmental Organization
OAS	Organization of American States
OAU	Organization of African Unity
RCADI	*Recueil des cours de l'Académie de Droit International* (Collected Courses of the Hague Academy of International Law)
RDH/HRJ	*Revue des droits de l'homme/Human Rights Journal*
Recueil/Collected Texts	Collected Texts of the Decision of the European Commission of Human Rights
Res.	Resolution
RGDIP	Revue générale de droit international public
Sub-Commission	United Nations Sub-Commission on Prevention of Discrimination and Protection of Minorities

UN	United Nations
UNESCO	United Nations Educational, Scientific and Cultural Organization
UNTS	United Nations Treaty Series
WHO	World Health Organization

THE INTERNATIONAL
DIMENSIONS OF
HUMAN RIGHTS

1 Human Rights: As a Legal Reality

Karel Vasak

A modern expression of a long-established reality, human rights as a whole were for a long time of only moderate interest to the jurist.[1] Having strong political connotations, the subject of human rights was relegated to that uncertain zone where the disquieting shadows of politics eclipsed the light of pure law which provided the technique preferred by the jurist, familiar with the analysis of age-old codes of law.

Only the philosopher of law took an interest in human rights, behind which he sought to identify the aims of the political authorities. However, his intellectual approach was too isolated to have any effect on traditional attitudes.

This strange embarrassment on the part of the jurist in the face of the subject of human rights is in the process of disappearing at the domestic level. The "integration" of the political sphere into law has had the effect of causing the jurist to shed that which smacked excessively of the scholastic approach in his training in civil law. The gradual "positivization" of human rights has removed the programmatic character that the scholarly texts establishing them seemed to attribute to them by means of language that was perhaps forceful and even revolutionary, but definitely foreign to the style of classical law. Today, the declarations of rights which preface constitutions are increasingly becoming a source of law from which judges are tempted to draw the decisive argument which clinches a case.

Although at the present time there are few revolutions that are fought in the name of human rights (and this is perhaps regrettable), the number of proceedings instituted in order to have those rights respected are innumerable. This change in outlook demonstrates better than anything else the fact that human rights have become a reality in law.

In the context of day-to-day reality, however, the fate of human rights varies so much in terms of the geographical area under consideration that we are sometimes tempted, like the French revolutionaries of 1789, to erect here and there in the world frontier posts bearing the legend: "Here begins the land of freedom". But it is not our intention to examine the discrepancies which may exist in the different countries between regulations relating to human rights and their application, and to seek the causes. Such a study, as interesting as it might be, would serve only to bear out a commonplace observation, namely, that it is extremely rare for actual situations to be in conformity with the law. Let it be said, moreover, that such a discrepancy is not necessarily always to be condemned, since it may reveal that in reality man benefits from greater protection than that granted to him by legal texts.

Human rights may thus fail to correspond to the texts establishing them. However, before comparing the two, which necessarily involves a value judgment, should we not seek to ascertain the conditions in which human rights become a reality in law or how human rights, which have been merely *proclaimed*, even in solemn form, become established as *guaranteed* human rights? In other words, insofar as legal reality is synonymous with positive law (and for the jurist, this cannot but be the case), it is important to seek to establish guidelines for a *legal system of human rights* whereby the individual may really be ensured of his human rights and be able to enjoy them in his daily life. It is here that an essential, but often neglected preambular paragraph of the Universal Declaration of Human Rights should be recalled. And it is to be recalled all the more forcefully in that it provides, in the final analysis, the best justification for the work undertaken under the auspices of Unesco in this treatise:

"Whereas it is essential, if man is not to be compelled to have recourse, as a last resort, to rebellion against tyranny and oppression, that human rights should be protected by the rule of law...".

In order for human rights to become a legal reality, three requirements must be met:

- an organized society must exist in the form of a *de jure* State;

- within the State human rights must be exercised in a pre-established legal framework, which may nevertheless vary according to circumstances and according to the nature of the rights;

- lastly, those entitled to exercise human rights must be provided with specific legal guarantees and, in particular, recourse must be provided so as to ensure that those rights are respected.

1. FIRST REQUIREMENT: A *DE JURE* STATE

Man can be free only in a free State. It follows from this banal truth that human rights hinge directly on the ways in which the political institutions governing peoples are organized and that these rights therefore depend closely upon the legal system of society as *a whole*.

This first requirement in fact covers two requirements:

- for a State to be free, the people which composes it must be able freely to decide its fate (*self-determination*);

- the people must freely define, by means of general and impersonal laws, the legal system governing human rights (*the rule of law*).

(a). Self-determination

A great deal has been written on the self-determination of peoples, with reference to human rights. However, very often the authors involved, influenced by the prestige enjoyed by human rights in contemporary life, make self-determination into a genuine human right. This conception is also shared by the United Nations since the United Nations Covenants on Human Rights start off by declaring:

"All peoples have the right of self-determination. By virtue of that right they freely determine their political status and freely pursue their economic, social and cultural development".

The third paragraph of the same Article even defines the nature of the undertaking contracted since it stipulates:

"The States Parties to the present Covenant, including those having responsibility for the administration of Non-Self-Governing and Trust Territories, shall promote the realization of the right of self-determination, and shall respect that right, in conformity with the provisions of the Charter of the United Nations".

The fact that the self-determination of peoples has been able to be placed on the same footing as, and included among, human rights would seem to be due more to reasons of political expediency than to there being any substantive basis for so doing. Being able to be exercised only collectively, self-determination is to peoples what freedom is to individuals, that is to say, the very basis of their existence. While self-determination cannot be an individual human right, it is definitely the necessary condition for the very existence of human rights in the sense that, where it does not exist, man cannot be free since he is not allowed to liberate himself.

But while self-determination is the necessary condition for the respect of human rights, is it also a *sufficient* condition? No one would dare to affirm it so long as it is obvious that independence acquired through self-determination has not always been synonymous with the liberation of the community nor has it been necessarily followed by the liberation of individuals.

(b). The rule of law

Human rights become a reality in law only in a *de jure* State. Without entering into theoretical discussions, it may simply be said that a *de jure* State is one in which all the authorities and all individuals are bound by pre-established general and impersonal rules, in a word, by *law*. Such indeed was the prevailing conception at the time of the French Revolution, which, in this connection, merely made explicit an idea which had been subscribed to for a far longer time. Thus, it is stipulated in Article 4 of the Declaration of the Rights of Man and of the Citizen of 1789 that "the exercise of the natural rights of every man has no other limits than those which are necessary to secure to every other man the free exercise of the same right; *and these limits are determinable only by the law*".

Although in our time the law is hardly the expression of the general will, as Rousseau contended, it remains the most effective practical means for citizens to preserve the sphere of human rights from the executive, through the role which they play in choosing their legislative body. In other words, the law, insofar as it is the work of a parliament elected by the citizens, constitutes the sole possible legal basis for human rights. It is for this reason that human rights are bound to be more likely to exist in countries with a parliamentary tradition. Historically, it can be observed that parliamentarism and human rights have progressed in conjunction with each other, the former becoming the guarantee of the latter, while the latter became the basis for the former. Conversely, it is very difficult for human rights to gain acceptance in countries where the idea that the law should be the work of parliament is unknown, and where the parliament is regarded solely as a place where governmental decrees are recorded.

Thus, it is evident that through the medium of the law and the work of parliament links are established between human rights and a country's political system. Moreover, human rights are more likely to be achieved in a political, economic and social democracy. While it is necessary that a democratic system for human rights becomes a reality, conversely, democracy cannot be maintained in the absence of human rights.

2. SECOND REQUIREMENT: A SPECIFIC LEGAL FRAMEWORK

Human rights would be meaningless if they were not assigned a place within the social order in which they are to be exercised. This means that human rights, which are essentially individual in character, for they are meant to be enjoyed by individuals, constitute a *social phenomenon* by virtue of those for whom they are intended. We too frequently forget this last aspect of the problem, which leads us to set in opposition, human rights on the one hand, with the authorities on the other. No one—except perhaps out-and-out anarchists—would deny that life in society, which is the proper context of human rights, cannot dispense with political authority. Chesterton has rightly written that if there existed a society composed solely of Hannibals and Napoleons, it would be better, in case of surprise, for them not all to be in command at the same time. But are not human rights, which from the outset turn each one of us into Hannibals if not Napoleons, consequently bound to be in opposition to the political authority which springs from life in society? Starting from this opposition, a natural and mechanical one, the conclusion is reached that there can only be a balance between human rights and political power when the two parties involved are subject to real *limitations*. Such a conception, based upon a latent and potential conflict between human rights and political power, seems dangerous if human rights are to become a reality in law. For, as has been pointed out,[2] in a conflict situation human rights represent law without power, whereas, by contrast, the political authority only sometimes represents the law, but always represents power. Therefore, if there is a conflict, human rights will always be the losers.

(a). Human rights and the creation of a legal system for their protection

Going to the heart of the matter, it becomes clear, however, that the social purpose of human rights results less in their being limited than in their being promoted in society or, to use legal language, in the creation of a legal system for their protection. When the legislature orders that traffic will keep to one side of the highway, it does not restrict the freedom of traffic to move but on the contrary makes it possible. When, by nationalizing virtual monopolies or by imposing a highly graduated tax, the legislature attacks the right of property, this involves not so much limiting that right as making it possible for the greatest number to benefit. There are even many human rights which do not really exist until such time as the society through its political authority creates a place for them in the social order. The right to work may amount to no more than permission to die of hunger unless the State creates the conditions conducive to its exercise. The right to education would be but the right to ignorance for the great majority if the State did not provide the actual facilities necessary for the enjoyment of that right.

In the final analysis, it is apparent that the social purpose of human rights makes them, if not dependent on, at least related to, political power. Far from being in opposition, human rights and political power support each other. The political authority therefore cannot limit human rights, just as human rights should not be used as an arm against those in power.

It immediately becomes clear that this indispensable and reciprocal link will be difficult to maintain merely at the level of legal texts, established by the authorities with a view to the socially harmonious exercise of human rights. For, very easily, the political authority will in fact, after introducing the necessary laws for the protection of human rights, gradually start restricting them and will perhaps end up by purely and simply *suppressing* them.

(b). Grounds for the creation of a legal system for the protection of human rights

For human rights to become a reality in law, they have to be governed by a system of law established by the political authority. However, it is important that the sole purpose in establishing such a system be that of facilitating their exercise, taking into account three imperative factors: the human rights of "others", the life of the group regarded as an entity and the life of mankind as a whole.[3]

Without examining in detail these three grounds for the creation of such a legal system, we may simply note that their observance will result in human

rights becoming a reality in law, even though they may vary in accordance
with time, place and circumstances. Thus, for instance, legal provisions governing the freedom of the press cannot follow the same lines in a developed
country as in a developing country. For there can be no doubt that in a
country of the latter type the mere fact that the press is in the hands of
foreigners makes it necessary for there to be different provisions, not to
mention the considerations by which that State is bound arising from the
need to enable the people to overcome their economic under-development.
However, this relative character of human rights in legal reality should not
by any means call into question the principle of freedom, which is, and which
should remain, at the basis of human rights. In other words, the establishment of legal provisions, for whatever reason and whatever their scope, must
allow for the continued existence of human rights.

3. THIRD REQUIREMENT: EFFECTIVE GUARANTEES

Even when proclaimed by a free State and protected by legal provisions
established by the legislature, human rights would scarcely amount to much
if they were not effectively guaranteed or, in other words, if those entitled to
them were not provided with the means of obtaining redress for violations of
which they have been the victims. Such guarantees may be placed in two
categories: organized guarantees and unorganized guarantees.

(a). Organized guarantees

These guarantees exist within the framework of the State in the form of
procedures enabling the individual to obtain either the annulment of the
measures which constitute a violation of his human rights or, in cases where
this is impossible, financial compensation. There is no point in going into this
matter in detail, it being well-known. It is also unnecessary to emphasize the
superiority of legal procedures, especially those of a constitutional nature,
over procedures relating to non-legal bodies. At the international level organized procedures now exist both on a universal and regional basis and some of
these will be considered in the following pages, although the legal nature of
such procedures varies considerably from one system to another.

(b). Unorganized guarantees

Among unorganized guarantees of human rights, the right to refuse to obey
an unjust law seems to be engraved, if not in the positive law of every
country, at least in the minds of all men.

But it is resistance to oppression, when organized procedures are inadequate, which constitutes the supreme guarantee of human rights. Officially
enshrined in the Declaration of Independence of the United States of America of 4 July 1776, resistance to oppression acquired its real significance as a
guarantee of human rights under the French Revolution. Thus, the Déclara-

tion des droits de l'homme of 24 June 1793 proclaims: "Resistance to oppression is the consequence of other human rights". And it adds the following, much-quoted provision: "When the government violates the rights of the people, insurrection is for the people and for each section of the people the holiest of rights and the most indispensable of duties".

While the jurist cannot fall to recognize the value of this supreme guarantee of human rights, he will, as a man, hesitate before proposing that it be put into effect in the world of today. For although in the last century it was still possible for a small amount of damage to the municipal highroads, caused by barricades, to bring about the fall of an oppressive government, it has been shown on numerous occasions that the modern State, especially when it receives foreign assistance, is so well equipped that the most just of revolts runs the risk of ending in a blood-bath.

In the face of such odds should we conclude that resistance to oppression belongs to the romantic period of our common history and that, at the present time, human rights depend on the good will of the State? I personally would hesitate to answer in the negative to this terrible question.

And one is all the more embarrassed at having to reply in such a way, for earlier in this analysis, emphasis was placed on the need to make political power and human rights mutually interdependent in the interests of the latter. Unfortunately, we are compelled today to acknowledge the increasingly forceful hold that the State exercises over individuals and its increasingly numerous encroachments upon the sphere of individual freedom. Even those who, by virtue of their political choices, expect a great deal of the State, warn us against this modern Leviathan. Is it not symptomatic that a political leader has written in substance that the modern State, with its huge organizations, is, by essence, totalitarian and its natural tendency is towards despotism?[4] And another English author has expressed the same idea in a more colourful, and hence more striking way, by suggesting that whereas, "up to now, the machine-gun has been regarded as the symbol of modern tyranny, it could perhaps be contended that it has been supplanted by the telephone and the card index".[5]

What, then, should be done? The only way, inadequate as it may be, of emerging from the blind alley to which the omnipotence of the modern State seems to have relegated human rights, consists of stepping outside the narrow limits of the State in order to pose the problem of human rights at the international level. Whether this be within regional or world organizations, human rights should thus be treated as an international problem—the only real international problem.

It would, however, be puerile to think that the internationalization of human rights will provide the solution to all our difficulties. This illusion is all the more to be guarded against in that, at the present time, all international organizations, even those that are usually described as supra-national, are in fact no more than inter-State groups where power still rests with those same

States. The most striking illustration of this situation is supplied by the European Convention on Human Rights, an instrument which represents the most notable advance towards the international realization of human rights. When a State is judged by the European Court of Human Rights to be "guilty" of violating human rights, it falls to that particular State, according to Article 50, to draw the proper consequences, the decision of the Court not being directly enforceable. Only if the municipal law of the interested State allows reparation to be made for the consequences of the violation can the Court afford "just satisfaction" to the injured parties. In most cases, this turns out to be of a financial nature. What happens if the State does not give effect to the decision of the Court? The drafters of the Convention, trusting, naive or helpless, it matters little, have not provided for this eventuality. At the very most, it would then be possible, by invoking the Statute of the Council of Europe, to consider expelling the guilty State from the Organization. However, one does not necessarily improve the patient's health by breaking the thermometer.

The only way out of this new blind alley is to appeal to those who are the first to be concerned with the protection of human rights, that is, every one of us. For, in the last analysis, it is on ourselves, the people, that the State's observance of human rights depends. It is *public opinion*, especially when the nationals of several countries are involved, which alone is capable of forcing States to respect human rights. For in today's world, the only effective sanction against the violation of human rights remains, whether one likes it or not, public opinion. And it is for this reason that I should like with all my heart to express the wish that this treatise, which is intended to be used in university *teaching* and in the *training* of human rights teachers, will *also* become an instrument for *informing* the general public. On this hinges the success of Unesco's endeavour to develop understanding and protection of human rights.

NOTES

1. Karel Vasak: *La Convention européenne des droits de l'homme*, Libraire générale de droit et de jurisprudence, Paris 1964, 327 pages.

2. See G. Burdeau: *Les libertés publiques*, Presses universitaires de France, Paris 1961, p. 29.

3. Cf. Salvador de Madariaga: *Droits de l'homme ou relations humaines?* (Concerning the new Universal Declaration of Human Rights, Unesco, Paris 1949, p. 44).

4. R.H.S. Crossman: *Socialism and the New Despotism*, Fabian Tract 298, London 1956, p. 24.

5. Anthony Hartley: *A State of England*, Hutchinson, London 1963.

2 Historical Foundations of Human Rights and Subsequent Developments

Imre Szabo

1. HUMAN RIGHTS IN GENERAL

(a). *The notion of human rights*

The notion of human rights falls within the framework of constitutional law and international law, the purpose of which is to defend by institutionalized means the rights of human beings against abuses of power committed by the organs of the State and, at the same time, to promote the establishment of humane living conditions and the multi-dimensional development of the human personality.

This first general definition provides a basis on which to formulate at this point certain fundamental laws which will be analyzed in detail subsequently: i) that human rights constitute a juridical notion; ii) that in the legal system human rights are covered by two branches of law; iii) that human rights pertain to the citizen and to man; iv) and that, contrary to a mistaken conception which is commonly advanced, human rights protect an individual who is not in conflict with the State, since the State exists solely through its organs.

(b). *Historical background of human rights*

For some authors, the origins of human rights go back to Greek antiquity. They consider that human rights should come under natural law. The classic example, taken from Greek literature, is that of Antigone: according to Sophocles, when Creon reproaches Antigone for having buried her brother despite her having been forbidden to do so, Antigone replies that she has acted in accordance with the unwritten and unchanging laws of heaven.[1] In philosophy the general tendency is to view the problem of human rights—or more precisely that of man's natural rights (and it is to be noted that equating the one with the other obscures the problem at the level of theory)—in terms of the doctrine of stoicism.

It is more difficult to seek the origins of human rights in Roman law, although an attempt has been made to discover in Cicero's work certain ideas relating to this subject. On the one hand, Roman law postulated the existence of a natural law, that is to say, of man's natural rights:[2] according to Ulpian, natural law is that which nature teaches to all living beings. But, on the other hand, this natural law is linked to the *jus gentium*, which has at least two meanings. It signifies first of all the rights of those who are not Roman citizens, and thus refers to those rights to which men are entitled wherever they go; it also represents international law at the same time.[3]

It should not be forgotten, particularly when speaking of the present significance of human rights, that all that derives from the Graeco-Roman world relates to a system in which Aristotle recognized the legitimacy of slavery.[4] In that world it was considered to be perfectly natural (and therefore in conformity with natural law) that there should exist radical social differences which exclude *ab ovo* the central idea of human rights: that of the equality of men.

(c). The Middle Ages

The Middle Ages were favourable neither to the idea of human rights nor to their observance. Wholly under the influence of Aristotelian philosophy, Saint Thomas Aquinas regarded natural law as deriving from reason. Thus, the mediaeval philosophy of law, a characteristic element of which was, among other things, the recognition by Aquinas, in the manner of Aristotle, of slavery itself, did not recognize those human qualities that it did not understand. In particular, it did not seek to place the human personality at the centre of the concerns of law and social life. We would say today that that philosophy was not open to any type of thinking centred upon man.

The other branch of legal thinking in the Middle Ages, which developed considerably at the end of that period, focussed its research on the State, soon arriving at the major principle of the sovereignty of the State. This principle was subsequently to become one of the greatest obstacles to the international protection of human rights.

(d). The appearance of the idea of human rights: general conditions underlying that idea. The contract theory.

It would be a grave mistake to attempt to trace back the origins of human rights to social systems which were not familiar with its basic condition governing the existence of human rights, namely, the idea of freedom and equality. It is not possible to project a new institution upon social relations which have been superseded, and to which it does not correspond. In order for human rights to appear as the general rule in society and for them to be felt both as a need and as a reality, it was indispensable for there to be basic social changes in the relations of production (and, more precisely, in the relations of ownership) within the previous social system—feudalism. Everyone's rights had to be recognized as being, in principle, equal with regard to ownership and the acquisition and enjoyment of property. True, the right to property had previously been regarded as a natural right, or in other words, as a fundamental and inalienable right of man, first by Aquinas, then later, more explicitly, by Grotius, who set this right outside the universe of natural rights. Grotius had asserted that the right to property had been "introduced by human will" and, so that we should not be offended, he invited us to understand and to consider our property as corresponding to natural law.[5]

Two major ideas emerged from this line of reasoning, but both subsequently splintered off from their origins: these were the ideas of freedom and equality. The idea of freedom was that of free ownership, of the free possession of property, and to this was later added the idea of free enterprise, with all the other corollaries of freedom. But its origins should never be forgotten, for they account for its appearance and for its development.

As for the idea of equality, it too owes its origin, at least in part, to the appearance of a new type of ownership. It signified equality for all as regards the right to acquire property, but considering it more closely, its true origin turns out to be connected with the political idea of the State in the modern sense of the term. It also concerned equality in respect of participation in political life. Consequently, equality was, so to speak, a political idea and a political right, whereas freedom possessed an economic character, at least so far as its origins were concerned. According to modern political philosophy, every individual should possess equal rights in the life of the State. Subsequently, the notion of equality was made to apply to the whole of man, to all of man's abilities and all of his rights.

However, an important difference was to remain between freedom and equality: bound up with ownership, freedom was considered to be a right which the State could not restrict because it was an absolute right. This was not true of equality as it was regarded as a political right and, as such, it could be restricted by the State.[6]

(e). Origins at the level of positive law

By and large, the origins of human rights, in respect of positive law, are traced back to documents which appeared in recent centuries. According to this point of view—the upholders of which are few in number since the majority of authors consider human rights to be natural rights—human rights are contracts concluded by the State with the population and, first of all, with the nobility. These contracts are seen as preserving certain rights for men while preventing the State from interfering in the exercise of those rights. The legal force of these rights is seen as being founded (contrary to the conception of the theory of the contract founded on natural law) on the will of the State, or better still, in the circumstances of the period, on their recognition by the King.

The fact that human rights or agreements with a similar objective in view have been given the form of Charters, Bills or Petitions and, where appropriate, Declarations, has led to these documents being placed on the same theoretical footing, although they were produced at different periods and for different purposes. In particular, in the specialized literature, a whole discussion is to be found on the common or different nature of the Magna Carta, the Petition of Rights and the Bill of Rights, as well as of the Declaration of Virginia and the Bills which followed it, and the French Declaration of 1789. What, then, are the relations between these documents? Are they of the same social importance and significance? Are not the later documents the logical consequence, or a simple copy, of those which preceded them?

In Central Europe, George Jellinek's book on the declarations of human rights (1904) caused a turmoil by subscribing to the view that these documents followed on from each other and were consequently directly related to each other. Moreover, he was not the only one to express that opinion. As for the opposite view, it suffices to draw attention here to a note in Dicey's work in which the author points out that the British documents constitute, rather, "judicial condemnations of claims or practices on the part of the Crown"; as for the American declarations, he writes: "They have...the distinct purpose of legally controlling the action of the legislature by the Articles of the Constitution".[7]

Eventually, Jellinek found it necessary to observe, in the second edition of his book, that in the United States the Bill of Rights has represented the culminating point, whereas the French Declaration was the starting point, which in itself constitutes a radical difference. Jellinek indirectly acknowledges, at the level of the history of civilization and of philosophy, as well as from the social point of view, the importance of the Declaration adopted by the Constituent Assembly of 1789. We can leave the matter there. The starting point of human rights in the modern sense of the term is clearly to be found both in the "Declaration of the Rights of Man and of the Citizen", voted during the French Revolution, and in the social conditions underlying it.

(f). Conceptions based on "natural law"

According to the most traditional conception of human rights, at the time that men passed from the primitive state to the social state they concluded a contract between themselves (the idea of which was first posited long before Rousseau), and by this contract they renounced part of their natural rights, which they had enjoyed in their free state, while preserving certain basic rights: the right to life, freedom and equality. The rights thus preserved constituted eternal and inalienable rights that every social and State system was obliged to respect. As for the origin of these rights, however, there are various differences to be found in the way in which the conception founded on natural law is set forth. The theory of the social contract is the product of the school of natural law which made its appearance in the 15th and 16th centries. According to this school, human rights are bound up with man's basic nature from which they derive, and for which reason they constitute human rights.

According to another conception, which goes back to Locke and his *Letters on Tolerance*, the starting point was tolerance in respect of other religions or, in other words, the right to profess any religion. Again, what is involved is a conception referring to natural law.[8] Furthermore, this idea set the scene for the creation of the United States of America, considering that freedom of religion played an important part in this connection.

There do of course exist other conceptions of human rights, for instance that according to which human rights originated in human understanding. Conceptions of this kind were already subscribed to in the Middle Ages. Virtually all the feudal varieties of the natural law theory (which consider the omnipotence of the absolute monarch to be a matter of natural law) belong to this type of thinking, and the same is true of the Kantian theory of law, founded on reason. This theory, like all the others, is forced to start off from certain promises established *a priori* and from which it is possible to *deduce* human rights. We find these premises in the metaphysical character of the rights.[9]

In my opinion, human rights can be "deduced" solely from the social relations from which they have arisen. Putting it bluntly, I personally am hostile to any theory, any explanation, based on so-called natural law. Law founded on reason is pure fiction, as is the assumed existence of a social contract. On the other hand, the economic development, and, correlatively, the political development specific to the 15th and 16th centuries is by no means a fiction since it corresponds to the real development of society. It is this evolution which is at the root of the demand for freedom—above all, economic freedon— in the face of feudal bondage; it was by virtue of this evolution that freedom was postulated and, more particularly, that equality before the law was asserted, in the face of the system of feudal privileges. These needs on the part of society assumed the form of natural law as they were presented as eternal needs. On this account, the relations between natural law and positive law appeared to be the relations between needs and reality, that is to say, positive law as it was subsequently to be established.

(g). *The rights of man and of the citizen*

The French Declaration of the Rights of Man and of the Citizen of 1789 and other documents, which appeared subsequently, make a distinction between, on the one hand, the rights of man and, on the other, the rights of the citizen. Man in these texts appears as a being who is imagined to exist outside society, who is assumed to exist prior to society. As for the citizen, he is subject to the State's authority. On this account, the rights of man are natural and inalienable rights, while the rights of the citizen are positive rights, rights granted by positive law. Human rights are fundamental rights for the very same reason that they existed before the State, whereas the rights of the citizen are subordinate to and depend upon them.

Marx dealt with this question in one of his early studies ("On the Jewish question")[10] and reached the following conclusion:

"In man and in his rights, society postulates a selfish being, independent of everyone, who is the subject of property (private property) and whose freedom (free ownership) constitutes the legal form and the basic requirement: man is an abstract subject in relation to the State, while human rights are alleged to be natural rights, abstract natural rights. The citizen, on the other hand, has rights only as a member of the political society: these are rights whose value is limited. The rights of the citizen are neither absolute nor unconditional, they are not granted to man everywhere and at every moment: they are not innate rights."

According to this view, the rights of the citizen are subordinate to the rights of man, the citizen's state depends on man's state. Political organization and political rights appeared to serve man, selfish man, and private property; bourgeois society was reduced to the level of the servant of private property.

In the course of social, political and ideological development, this distinction, this hierarchy in respect of the appearance and existence of the rights of man and of the citizen has, to a certain extent, become blurred. As the distinction between the rights of man and the rights of the citizen has disappeared, the two categories have merged. Insofar as certain traces of this distinction have remained, it has assumed new forms and has come to appear as a criterion for differentiating between branches of law: all rights as a whole which are recognized by Constitutions are thus considered as belonging to the category of the rights of the citizen, whereas the rights of man are those covered by international law.

In this way, the problem of human rights has been entirely reduced to the question of the simple relationship between two branches of law, a relationship in which constitutional law seems to be subordinate to international law. A special situation consequently appears to exist in the relations between municipal law and international law: international law has annexed part of the province of constitutional law which has ceased to be the monopoly of municipal law.[11]

(h). Constitutional law

In national systems human rights re-appear in the form of citizens' rights in constitutional law. And what is more, it is in Constitutions that human rights are established. An example had been set by the French Constitution of 1791, the text of which is preceded by the Declaration of the Rights of Man and of the Citizen of 1789. The Constitutions which followed no longer provide a general formulation of these rights in their preambles but integrate them into the actual text as basic rights upon which the State is founded, in view of the fact that these rights determine, in the last analysis, the relations between the State and the citizen and define the domain in which the State does not intercede (negative domain). At the same time, human rights become affected by a specific bias in constitutional law in that they acquire a particular character, linked up with the State's internal structure.

The various Constitutions, strange to say, omit to define the effect of the rights listed. They do not explicitly state which of these rights have a direct effect on the basis of constitutional law, and which ones necessitate special laws in order for them to be put into effect, and in which cases, consequently, fundamental rights are provisions binding solely upon the legislature and are of no benefit to citizens except by this indirect channel (this has further contributed to the confusion which prevails in connection with the notion of human rights).

In the socialist countries there are different views as to the place that the citizen's fundamental rights should occupy in the Constitution—whether they should be formulated ahead of constitutional law or, on the contrary, be included in the actual text of the Constitution. This problem conceals a substantive question: do fundamental rights constitute, together with the political system of the State, the basis of the State, or, on the contrary, are they but attributes of the State, a particular feature peculiar to a State system? Affecting both the State and man's place within the State, are human rights essential elements of the Constitution, or are they but particular, and consequently secondary, aspects of it?

The reply to this question depends on the way in which these rights are interpreted. Are they considered to be really fundamental rights or merely relatively fundamental rights? Generally speaking, at the present time, the system of fundamental constitutional rights is confused. The rights of man and those of the citizen are "mixed together", as are the rights of appeal available to the citizen in the face of the organs of the State and political rights (right to vote, etc.), which are an expression of the individual's status as a citizen. In this heterogeneous mass certain rights, such as economic, social and cultural rights—which are developed in fact in socialist Constitutions—represent constitutive rights of the socialist State's system, and are bound to have a direct effect, owing to the force of the Constitution. Other rights, however, are no more than directives addressed to the legislature, and consequently do not represent constitutive rights, but merely secondary rights. These may just as well be included at the end of the Constitution.

There is consequently in constitutional law a particular mixture of human rights and citizens' rights. It falls to theory to re-establish the notion of human rights and to set them back in their place. But notwithstanding this confusion, constitutions contain, in practice, a hierarchical system of citizens' rights which constitutes the starting point of the system of human rights as it has been formulated by international law.

(i). Classification of the rights of the citizen

Applying various criteria from a Constitutional Law perspective, several categories of rights can be made out among the rights of the citizens. From the theoretical point of view, I shall distinguish, in the group of citizens' rights, only two categories of rights: individual rights and collective rights.

By and large, individual rights are regarded as constituting the starting point for citizens' rights. From this point of view, the emergence of the individual and his recognition by law triggered the entire process leading to the elaboration of those rights. This thesis is not without some basis of truth, but only on the condition that it is admitted that individualism itself was the product of other social forces and, above all, of changes which occurred in the sphere of production and which ensured the individual a new and central place. It was from this that came the political process corresponding to these social needs, a process which had been preceded by the formulation, in the context of natural law, of these rights as in the form of a declaration. It is possible to highlight, in this context, those rights which signified a departure from the feudal system and, above all, from its political methods: orders under the King's private seal, the arbitrariness of epistolatory censorship, searches, as well as religious intolerance. The first role of the Declarations was to free the new political State from these feudal practices and to define, in this field, the individual's freedoms and rights.

Individual rights deriving from the new political and State system then followed: man was not yet recognized as such, but merely the individual in isolation, as an autonomous legal entity. What was already involved at this stage were the individual rights of bourgeois society, which were held by individuals and which gave rise to the rights of the individual in the form of human rights.

A large proportion of these so-called individual rights, however, are not able to be exercised in an individual capacity, without other individuals. This exercise of rights in society does not, however, deprive the person involved of his individuality. Each right continues to be an individual right. Thus, the right of free association remains the individual's right, even though it is quite clear that an association cannot be founded by a single person.

Collective rights are those which can be exercised only with the co-operation of a group, if only in the form of a single other person (marriage) or, more generally, of several persons (freedom of the press, of information, freedom of assembly, etc.). What was involved here was a development which, historically, led, concomitantly with the development of society, to the extension of collective rights at the expense of individual rights. In other words, human life comprises an increasing number of elements which make it necessary for the individual to collaborate with his fellows. This phenomenon was naturally to have repercussions upon the quantitative development of citizens' rights and human rights, as was the case, for instance, with regard to the appearance of life-long education.[12]

Thus, after the First World War, on account of the appearance of new States on the map of Europe, the League of Nations included in its programme the protection of the rights of national minorities. This is a typical

case of collective legal protection. It was here too that the establishment of
an international legal system for the protection of human rights began. It was
certainly not on account of the failure of this international protection that the
United Nations practically abandoned until 1966 (cf. Article 27 of the International Covenant on Civil and Political Rights) these groups of men and
their specific rights. At all events, it is to be noted that, having started from
questions of constitutional law, we have, by considering this matter, come to
the field of international law.

(j). Economic, social and cultural rights

One fact that is not contested by any author writing on this subject is that,
with the socialist October revolution and the new situation to which it gave
rise, there appeared in the Soviet Union, and gradually through the entire
world, a new category of citizens' rights: economic, social and cultural rights.
These rights were formulated in the first Soviet Constitution of 1918. They
also appeared in 1917 in the Mexican Constitution and, in 1919, in the Weimar
Constitution. They were gradually included in all modern Constitutions.

The social and State-derived character of these rights is twofold. On the
one hand, they express the fact that the foundation of all other citizens' rights
and the guarantee of their effectiveness lies in a given economic situation, in
a particular state of material conditions, in relation, among other things, to
man's social and cultural situation. In this way, a sort of hierarchical relationship is established between the various rights of the citizen which, without
assuming a distinct form, indicates the general pattern of their genesis and of
their effective action. On the other hand, economic, social and cultural rights
come under citizens' rights, of which they form a particular category.

Some authors deny that economic, social and cultural rights belong to the
category of "human rights", arguing that they cannot be regarded as "rights"
in the proper sense. It is just this view which is defended by those who
interpret human rights strictly in terms of "natural law". The question could
indeed be raised as to where, from the point of view of natural law, the
foundation of economic, social and cultural rights is situated. Should their
origin be sought in rational law? The scepticism of the partisans of natural
law is understandable for these rights cannot be deduced from natural law.
On the other hand, those who understand that citizens' rights and human
rights are the product of positive law and of its development, as determined
by the development of society, readily acknowledge that human rights necessarily become more numerous as society progresses and takes in new spheres
of social life and human existence. At the same time, society has to contract
new obligations in order to promote the flowering of the individual's cultural
personality and the development of his economic and social integrity.

From the point of view of positive law, the list of human rights and citizens'
rights possesses two characteristic features. First of all, this list has continued to expand in a manner commensurate with social development, which has

also been under way since the French Declaration. Today we are inclined to think that far too great a number of human rights are being established. Secondly, it is a fact that citizens' rights do not come under a single social system but are to be found in the legal system of several social régimes; it could even be contended that their basic elements are already contained, in certain respects, in a very early legal system. While human rights are not eternal rights, they are nonetheless a living reality in several social systems. But naturally, they are to be found typically in bourgeois society. Now in our time bourgeois society already co-exists with the new system, the socialist system, which also recognizes human rights. It can be concluded from this fact that the narrow national limits of constitutional law are no longer sufficient for human rights which transcend national frontiers and thereby go beyond the limits of municipal public law, falling within the framework of international law. By the same stroke, they become formulated at a more general level.

By dint of this process, the very subject of human rights seems to have changed, for it would appear that the individual, as an independent person within the State, becomes the subject of human rights, whereas in actual fact this is not the case. And human rights may themselves consequently appear to differ from the rights of the citizen. At all events, a new quality appears, namely, man.

This results, once again, in enormous confusion at the level of ideas. What, ultimately, are human rights and citizens' rights? Are they identical, or, on the contrary, different? There is one single interpretation, founded on natural law, which is consonant both with the character of citizens' rights and with that of human rights. The interpretation which it provides of both of these rights is in fact identical. But, in my opinion, this interpretation is not well-founded.

2. THE EMERGENCE OF HUMAN RIGHTS AT THE INTERNATIONAL LEVEL

(a). Historical antecedents

In international law those rights which correspond to citizens' rights are called "human rights". Upon international recognition of those rights all States have the same duty to respect them (what are involved are the international duties of States) in their own legislation as citizens' rights under municipal law. So long as this is not the case, human rights constitute merely rules of international positive law, which, from the point of view of municipal law, represent but an obligation contracted by the State, a mere promise in respect of the citizen and affecting the future. For this reason, then, an attempt is made once again to explain human rights in terms of natural law, for natural law too in its time constituted the prerequisite for what was to become international positive law, as now seems to be still the case in respect of municipal law. It is on this account that the interpretation of (international) human rights in the spirit of natural law seems so attractive and straightforward. And yet, once again, this interpretation is not valid.

In the confused international situation which followed the First World War, two notions of human rights emerged. One was the notion of individual rights. However, at the time that President Wilson recommended that provision be made for religious equality in the Covenant of the League of Nations, no action was taken upon his proposal. The second notion was the protection of minorities, particularly in the States created in Central Europe, the system, which was based upon the notion of collective rights, having been institutionalized by the League of Nations. According to some authors it even contributed to the lack of success of the League.

Naturally, the appearance of human rights in international law also had social causes, as was the case for citizens' rights. But whereas the emergence of the rights of the citizen had in its time been the result of social progress (and, a short time before, a manifestation of new and forward-looking needs), the bursting of human rights upon the international scene had been the consequence of social phenomena which cannot by any account be regarded as positive ones. The ruthless and wholesale destruction of individuals and groups in the fascist States, the contempt in which the human being was held and the extreme deterioration of the relations between the State and man were factors which helped to raise human rights to the level of international law and to cause a certain protection of those rights to be sought therein.

The first premonitory signs of change appeared in the nineteen-twenties. Already at that time certain people had championed the idea, both within and outside the League of Nations, of the international protection of human rights. However, what was involved was, in the main, private proposals which could not be carried out because they were not "official".

What finally led to the "official" adoption of measures designed to ensure the international protection of human rights was the number of atrocities committed against humanity by the fascist powers during the Second World War. These acts aroused the unanimous indignation of all those in the world who believed in society's capacity for improvement. A wave of public opinion arose demanding the establishment of organized international protection for human rights and the condemnation, prohibition and repression of fascist policy in every form. Before and during the Second World War, numerous proposals and privately sponsored measures were introduced which resulted in a Universal Declaration of Human Rights. It is enough to point out in this connection that the commission instructed by the United Nations to prepare the Declaration in 1947 had at its disposal 18 official or semi-official drafts.[13]

Several documents or declarations contributed to this international guarantee of human rights, not only documents which had been prepared for the constitution of the United Nations Organization, but some which already

dealt with the problem of human rights. The prime example of this was
President Roosevelt's declaration of 26 January 1941 on the "four freedoms":
freedom of opinion and expression, freedom of worship, the right to be free of
material want and the guarantee of life without fear. It was this same line
which was followed by the Atlantic Charter, drawn up on 14 August 1941 by
Roosevelt and Churchill, and which included, to a certain extent, the "four
freedoms", adding to them, however, the need for economic progress and
social security. This "prehistory" finally came to an end with the Declaration
by the United Nations of 1 January 1942 (jointly made by 26 countries and
ultimately adhered to by 21 other countries), which employed the same terms
as the Atlantic Charter, and which at the same time raised the stipulations of
that Charter to the level of international rights and duties.

(b). The Charter of the United Nations

The task of the conference that met in October 1944 at Dumbarton Oaks was
to draft the constitution of an international organization which was to succeed
the League of Nations. In this projected United Nations organization, human
rights occupied a place which was admittedly still a minor one but which was
already clearly defined.

A decisive step was taken in April 1945 at the conference of San Francisco
when the representatives of the four major powers submitted various amendments to the draft Charter under study by the conference. The major human
rights features of these proposals were as follows: i) the Charter should
express all human rights more clearly and more emphatically; ii) economic,
social and cultural problems and rights should be included in the Charter; and
iii) it was necessary to set up the Commission on Human Rights as one of the
UN major commissions, and provide for its creation in the very text of the
Charter.

The Charter deals in seven instances with human rights (including the
Preamble and the provisions relating to the establishment of the trusteeship
system), but in each case what is involved is a general reference to fundamental human rights and to equality before the law. There were many who
regarded this way of tackling the problem as inadequate, and they reproached
the drafters of the Charter for not having clearly stated in the Charter itself
what these human rights were. But perhaps this was not the object of the
Charter, as the matter still called for further reflection. It is enough to note
that the very concepts employed were not yet clear: for instance, that which
is referred to in the English and Russian texts of the Charter as "international problems of a cultural character" is translated in French by the words
"intellectual" problems (Chapter I, Article 1, paragraph 3), a very different
conception of the question. Time was necessary in order to discuss these
problems and clarify notions and solutions. But, in the final analysis, the task
of drafting a special document fell to the UN. Its purpose was to interpret the
Charter from the point of view of human rights. What was involved was a

document which virtually forms an integral part of the Charter, and which defines the significance of the references to human rights, and the way in which they should be interpreted. This task was carried out for the first time in history by the adoption of the Universal Declaration of Human Rights. Thus began the real history of human rights at the level of international law.

3. THE UNIVERSAL DECLARATION OF HUMAN RIGHTS

The person most responsible for the draft of the Universal Declaration of Human Rights was René Cassin, the Nobel Peace Prize winner. Mr. Cassin, who had been one of the principal promoters of human rights and who is considered to be the true father of human rights, has compared the human rights structure in the United Nations to a triptych of which one of the panels, the central panel, is the Declaration, while the two side panels could be said to be formed by the various conventions and the covenants on the one hand and the implementation measures on the other, the latter being the most imperfect and the least developed. This comparison seems to me to be perfectly accurate. In any event, it is admitted today by virtually everyone that within the United Nations the Universal Declaration of Human Rights, adopted on 10 December 1948 by the General Assembly at its third session, constitutes the central document for the cause of human rights. Subsequently, that day was proclaimed by the United Nations to be "Human Rights Day",[14] and it has remained as such ever since on the international calendar.

It is not my intention here to present the whole of the Universal Declaration in detail but merely to give a general description of it and to point out the problems which it poses. The idea that the repeated references to human rights contained in the UN Charter needed to be clarified was admitted by everyone shortly after the adoption of the Charter: the elaboration of the Declaration was thus considered to be one of the principal tasks of the UN. The fact that what resulted was a declaration and not a convention (the decision was reached only after lengthy discussions) represented a compromise. Moreover, this was also true of the entire Declaration as finally adopted, for its content had to reconcile the most diverse theoretical considerations. But it would have been difficult for it to have been otherwise. One of the reasons for the compromise in respect of the form of the document was the fear that the majority of States would not accept being immediately bound by a convention, i.e. a document endorsing direct obligations to implement these human rights in their domestic legal systems. This fear was not without foundation.

Since the "Declaration" has become a recognized legal form at the UN it constitutes, in the final analysis a document whose force is slightly greater than that of a "recommendation". It might be considered to be a document which is not enforceable, and which has no binding power but merely a moral value. But, as was stressed by René Cassin, particularly in view of Article 56 of the Charter wherein the States pledge to work in co-operation to achieve respect for human rights, the legal value of the Declaration exceeds that of a simple recommendation.[15] It is to be noted that the American Declaration of Rights and Duties of Man, which preceded the Universal Declaration, having been adopted in 1948 at Bogotá, and which was included in an annex to the documents of the 9th International Conference of American States as a recommendation, does not have any real legal value in international law, and cannot be compared with the Universal Declaration. In a strict sense, the international legal value of the Universal Declaration is the same, and yet its importance and its international role are fundamentally different.

Although some States abstained from voting on the Declaration in the General Assembly, the Declaration has gradually come to command increasing authority throughout the world, and, despite its omissions, its importance sets it at the same level as the Charter. At the very least it is considered today to be one of the cornerstones of the United Nations structure. Some States go so far as to refer directly to it in the preamble to their Constitutions, and every international document, and even some national documents, which are concerned with human rights unfailingly start off from the Universal Declaration or lead logically to it.

Despite all the criticisms and all the value judgments, it can be asserted that the Declaration has been a success rarely encountered in the history of international law.

(a). Some features of the Universal Declaration

The drafters of the Declaration have often been reproached for the absence of a firmly established and homogeneous theoretical basis, and no doubt this reproach is valid. The absence of such a basis reveals itself, *inter alia*, in the following features:

i. In the Declaration the difference between human rights and citizens' rights is blurred, all these rights being placed together in the category of human rights. Certain rights of the citizen which the State is obliged, by virtue of its very existence, to guarantee are set on the same footing as rights which derive from a conception of the world centred upon man and which, being independent, or almost, of the State, are the products of a profoundly individualistic philosophy.

ii. The Declaration is not satisfactorily linked to the present, or more exactly, to the recent past. It does not refer to the phenomena which triggered the indignation of everyone and does not condemn the abuse of human rights with sufficient vigour. Nor does it bar the way to these rights being used in a manner which would be contrary to their essentially democratic purpose. Admittedly, Article 30 of the Declaration prohibits all acts which, on the authority of the Declaration, are aimed at the destruction of the rights and freedoms set forth therein, but this is a purely negative approach to the question.

iii. This means that the Declaration does not, in the final analysis, possess a definite political character; it does not occupy a clearly-defined position on the scale of political values. It was intended that this should be a particular feature of the document. Those who drafted it purposely sought to remove anything that gave it a clear-cut character; moreover, they wished to draw up a politically neutral document. But the basic question of the international problem of human rights is thus raised, for it is highly questionable whether it is possible to establish a declaration which is sound and effective without its possessing a clearly-defined political character.

iv. Although mention is made in the Declaration of economic, social and cultural rights, they are referred to only in passing, and they are not examined in a manner comparable to that of other rights (five articles out of the thirty contained in the Declaration). On this account, the balance of the Declaration is upset.

v. With the exception of a short paragraph 1 in Article 29, there is no reference in the Declaration to the counterpart of the rights of man, namely, the duties of man. In point of fact, the Declaration was not intended to fulfil such a purpose. But how can the State agree to assume obligations towards persons who, for their part, accept no obligation, no duty, in regard to the community and the State? As things stand at present the problem of duties is without solution in all of the fields in which we are interested, and there is no mention of it, or virtually none, in the first documents. It seems to be true that the relations between the State and the individual are not proportional or symmetrical relations: it is man, the citizen, and not the State, that is threatened. If certain rights need to be protected, they are those of the individual in regard to the State. But what necessarily emerges as a result of this situation is the idea of an evil, execrable, threatening State, a modern Leviathan, and not a democratic State, careful, by virtue of its nature, to respect human rights. In any case, the fact remains that the Declaration virtually overlooks the problem, whereas constitutional law has for a long time been beset by the question of the relations existing between the rights of man and the duties of man. However, to all intents and purposes, this problem is not dealt with in the field of international law.

(b). Sovereignty

The problem of sovereignty is not, strictly speaking, one that is posed by the Declaration, but at the time a fundamental question was raised, namely, what was the relation between the international protection of human rights and the sovereignty of States? Clearly, this is a key question in regard to the international protection of human rights.

The problem of sovereignty had in fact been raised at the time of the League of Nations. Since 1945, the matter has hinged upon Article 2, paragraph 7, of the Charter, according to which nothing contained in the Charter shall authorize any of the nations belonging to the United Nations to intervene in matters "which are essentially within the domestic jurisdiction of any state". One of the axioms of the modern theory of the State today is still the sovereignty of the State, both domestic and foreign. It is external sovereignty, exercised in the relations of States with other States and international organizations, which affects matters relating to the international protection of human rights.

The fact is that the recognition of human rights opens up a new area for international law at the United Nations, in which the question of sovereignty remains entirely open. Here, the State senses a threat on the part of the international community and, out of principle, takes a stand against the community. It is this fact which, both in the past and in the present, continues to underlie the lengthy discussions. In the nineteen-twenties, at the time of the League of Nations, the theory was generally admitted that by formally participating in an international organization, the State would limit itself, would limit its own sovereignty, by delegating its own rights, or part of them, to the international organization. This theory of "self-limitation" is as inflexible, fantastic and false as had been the theory that the State had originated in a contract under the terms of which the individual, just before he becomes a member of the State, gives over part of his rights to the community. In the present case, so the argument goes, the State, in becoming a member of the international community, hands over part of its rights to that community. This explanation is not scientifically founded. However, at the present time, it is the only theoretical explanation which is given of the internationally guaranteed protection of human rights.

The circumspection shown in this field by States, or at least by some States, is perfectly understandable. They are afraid that the UN or its organs, in order to protect human rights, might interfere in the State's domestic affairs, protected by Article 2, paragraph 7, of the Charter. This fear is not without foundation. It cannot be denied that the world today is divided, and that the unity of the world represented by the UN is the unity of conflicting social systems. How often have human rights served as a pretext for mutual attacks! How often, in fact, does the defence of human rights serve as a pretext for systematically fomenting international incidents!

In my opinion the solution to the problem of sovereignty should be sought in what René Cassin terms the third panel of the human rights structure, namely their implementation. For it is here that guarantees should be provided whereby all breaches of sovereignty can be prevented and methods can be developed which reduce problems to the level of individual cases and prevent them from being blown up into questions of principle which can be used as a basis for large-scale attacks. In the event of a State regularly violating human rights of a large number of individuals, other provisions of the Charter would have to be brought to bear and other United Nations organs would have to act.

(c). The rights included in the Declaration and the rights of the citizen

We have already observed that the rights covered by the Declaration are of a very mixed character. What is being referred to is not merely the confusion characterizing human rights and citizens' rights. Jacques Maritain reduces human rights to the common weal and speaks of the well-being of the greatest number, of their at once physical and, above all, spiritual unity.[16] We thus see how far the "mystification" of the subjects of human rights can lead. In the Declaration and in the conception on which it is founded, individuals who are imagined independently of the State and those who actually exist within the State, are mixed together, as are individual rights and collective rights.

With the creation of the category "human rights", a certain wholesale watering-down of concepts took place. For what does the concept of human rights represent? The opposition between "man" and society? The independence of "man" in regard to society? But is it really possible to imagine an abstract man, situated outside society, or at least outside the State, "man" considered in himself, who has only demands to make of the State? This would appear to be a utopian view, and it must be admitted that the Declaration itself is not devoid of a certain utopian and speculative character.

The question remains in no way changed. Does there exist, at the theoretical level, a relation between the rights of the citizen, in other words between those rights which are at present guaranteed by the State, on the one hand, and human rights on the other? Natural law immediately answers in the affirmative since, for the champions of natural law, what are involved are human rights regarded as an abstraction, man separate both from the State and from the international community, in other words, from those elements which ensure and guarantee these very rights. For natural law, the international community and the State are but the passive objects of rights. It is impossible for me to subscribe to this view, which is false, for it implies the existence of rights without either object or support, floating around somewhere in space. According to the conception of natural law, then, citizens' rights and human rights are in principle identical. The absurdity of this conception compels us to reject it out of hand.

From the angle of international positive law and constitutional law, and more broadly, in international politics on the basis of the *de facto* relations existing between the State and the international community, the question arises today quite differently. It is the State which is the subject of the international postulation of human rights, for it is held responsible by international law for taking certain measures, within its own framework, on behalf of the citizen. International law itself consequently resembles a sort of natural law and moral imperative, the rules of which are put into effect in the context of the public law of the State, thus losing their character as postulates and becoming realities. From this conception a number of conclusions can be deduced in respect not only of the mutual relations which exist between the different branches of law and the situation, within the national legal system, of a part of international law, but also of the conditions governing the existence of the international community.

But let there be no mistake. This conception by no means signifies that human rights do not, in the last analysis, constitute, in international law, genuine rights: a positive reality in law. It does not lend itself to the claim that these rights exist only as needs and that, from the point of view of human rights, international law exists only as an imperative.[17]

Human rights are a well-established institution of international positive law. They are a legal and, consequently, social reality, which means that human rights have a direct social and legal effect. This situation raises the question of the individual's status as a subject of the law at the international level, which will be dealt with later. What is involved here is the international effect of "human rights", irrespective of the rights and international duties of the State. This is a problem which is difficult at the theoretical level, but the practical solution is even more so.

4. THE INTERNATIONAL COVENANTS ON HUMAN RIGHTS

(a). The right to self-determination

Scarcely had the Economic and Social Council set up the Commission on Human Rights pursuant to Article 68 of the United Nations Charter, when it appeared necessary to draw up a draft convention on human rights which would complement the Declaration and by which States would expressly undertake to respect the rights thus defined within the spheres of their competence. The United Nations carried out a great deal of work to this end; the General Assembly, together with the other UN organs, has concerned itself with this matter on many occasions. Without wishing here to describe the whole process, it is to be noted that in 1966 the two Covenants were finally completed, one on economic, social and cultural rights, and the other on civil and political rights. To the Covenant on Civil and Political Rights was added an optional Protocol concerning the procedure to be followed regarding complaints by individuals.

The first article of the two Covenants define, in an identical text, the right of peoples to self-determination. By virtue of this right, peoples freely determine their political status and freely pursue their economic, cultural and social development (paragraph 1 of Article 1 of the Covenants). Lengthy discussions preceded and accompanied the inclusion of these articles in the Covenants.[18] In this connection, reference was rightly made to Articles 1 and 55 of the Charter of the United Nations which allude to the right of peoples to self-determination. The fact that the Covenants define this right more precisely and in greater detail is of great importance, even if it is true that the

United Nations had already dealt several times with the right of peoples to self-determination in a positive manner on other occasions.

During the discussions at the General Assembly the question was raised as to whether the right to self-determination was a legal right or, simply, a fundamental political principle, i.e., whether this right did indeed have a place in a convention on human rights.[19] In the end it was recognized that self-determination was indeed a human right, but it may reasonably be asked whether, on this account, its importance was increased or decreased.

A certain apprehension must be voiced in this connection. The Covenants deal with human rights. The right to self-determination, being without doubt the right of an entire people or of an ethnic group, therefore constituted a collective right which does not concern individuals separately, but the whole of the group. In point of fact, human rights are founded on the right to self-determination. On the other hand, the true content of the right to self-determination, its true political importance, consists in the right to found an independent State and to establish a political organization leading to the creation of a State. The State actually represents the context in which human rights are anchored and effectively achieved. Thus in actuality in the Covenants, the right to create the preconditions for the implementation of human rights is declared to be a human right. The right in question here is that of establishing conditions from whence human rights will subsequently emerge. One may consequently wonder whether, in the relentless search to find a place for the right to self-determination, it was appropriate to attach that right to human rights. More precisely, and without denying the importance of a more accurate definition, if the need to set forth this right in the Covenants can be questioned, it is because human rights of a different type are thus brought together.

(b). One Covenant or two Covenants?[20]

An examination of the historical background of UN debates indicates that initially it was generally recognized that economic, social and cultural rights were closely connected to civil and political rights, and therefore should be covered by the same document, a single convention. This principle was effectively and officially adopted by the General Assembly at its fifth session. It stated that "the enjoyment of civil and political freedoms and that of economic, social and cultural rights are interdependent", and that "in cases where the individual is deprived of his economic, social and cultural rights, he does not represent the human person who is considered by the Declaration to be the ideal of the free man".[21] In 1951, however, ECOSOC submitted a proposal to the General Assembly that the decision taken in 1950 be revised. It was then that the General Assembly decided to draft two conventions which would be adopted together and be open for signature by States on the same date. According to the decision of the Assembly, the same spirit should guide the two conventions which should contain as many identical provisions as possible.[22]

Thus, the organs of the UN have been greatly concerned with the problem of the unity and division of human rights. In point of fact, the reasons put forward in favour of two separate conventions were not substantial. It was said that the system for implementing them should be different. According to Article 2 of the Covenant on Economic, Social and Cultural Rights, the full realization of the recognized rights should be achieved progressively, whereas civil and political rights should be ensured *uno actu* but, in both cases, it is indispensable for the rights to be jointly guaranteed by States. This false and artificial distinction is made with a view to marking out a frontier between the two categories of rights. Instead of including economic, social and cultural rights in all of the human rights structure, they are by this means set outside it, ostensibly on account of their novelty. The other reason advanced, which is moreover in contradiction with the spirit of the decision of the General Assembly, is no more convincing: to say that States will thereby have greater latitude in adhering to one or the other Convention or to both at the same time does not hold water since the General Assembly considered them to form an interdependent pair, and so they turned out to be when the time came for them to be ratified.

(c). Generality and universality

Very early at the United Nations the idea emerged that, like the Declaration, the Covenants should have a general character, and thus cover in principle all fundamental human rights. Here, we must at once distinguish between generality, as a notion concerning the content and scope of human rights, and universality, which designates the field of operation of the rights in question. As its name indicates, the Declaration has at once a universal character (having a universal value and being of universal effect) and a general character; the same is true of the Covenants.

Like the Declaration, the Covenants cover all the rights of man, considered as a social being and as an individual. They include the rights of man regarded as a citizen and they cover the rights of certain groups and the rights of the individual as the member of a given group. The Covenants foreshadow this multilateral approach to the question while seeking at the same time to make out a relatively stable limit between the two groups of rights: it appears that in the case of economic, social and cultural rights, the subjects of the rights are persons, whereas for civil and political rights, they are individuals. The question remains as to whether, over and above words, this distinction possesses some importance, or whether, in the final analysis, it involves notions which amount to the same thing.

It is a fact that both the Declaration and the Covenants seek to encompass all possible and imaginable human rights. It is this which gives these instruments their general character. But at the same time efforts were made at the United Nations to gain recognition for the various rights considered separately, and various draft conventions have already been adopted with this in

view: the Slavery Convention, the Convention on the Prevention and Punishment of the Crime of Genocide, the Convention on the Elimination of All
Forms of Discrimination against Women, the International Convention on
the Elimination of All Forms of Racial Discrimination, the International
Convention on the Suppression and Punishment of the Crime of *Apartheid*,
constitute such partial conventions. Strictly speaking, the general conventions already cover these partial conventions but, in view of their importance, the need was also felt to deal with these human rights separately and
to draw up special conventions to protect them.

Nowhere is there any authoritative analysis of the relations which exist
between general conventions and partial conventions on human rights. The
fact is that the general conventions cover all the partial conventions. One
example illustrates the resulting confusion, the Convention on *apartheid*
adopted in 1973. This Convention condemns all policies similar to *apartheid*
(racial discrimination, genocide, slavery) which are already condemned by
other partial conventions and resolutions. At the same time the Convention is
nothing other than the concrete expression of one element in the universal
conventions. Seen from this angle, the approach of the United Nations is
neither clear nor consistent.

Universality constitutes in itself a particular notion of international law. In
the case referred to, it represents the intention to afford all States that so
desire the opportunity to accede to a particular convention.

It is true that the partial conventions drawn up by the UN also have this
character but, in the case of the major conventions which cover all human
rights, provision is made not only for universality but also, by virtue of their
content, for the general character of the rights. In the case of the Covenants
on Human Rights, what is involved is conventions possessing universal value,
and which are consequently binding, in principle, on all countries and on all
men.

Universality corresponds to the present world situation and is even a
reflection of it. Today the universal conventions represent the extent of the
agreement achieved by the countries belonging to the various social systems
whereby they have declared the field of human rights, understood in the
broadest sense, to be a protected domain. Universality is thus equally valid
for all States that currently exist and that co-exist peaceably, whatever their
social system, assuming of course that the convention in question has been
ratified by them.

(d). The regional conventions[23]

Two regional conventions on human rights currently exist. In the region of
the socialist countries there exists no multilateral convention at present, but
the bilateral agreements concluded between the States concerned have led to
the creation of a *de facto* situation characterized by a clearly-defined and
homogeneous interpretation and common practice of human rights. This is

particularly so in the field of culture, but also in other fields relating to social conditions, public health, justice, etc.

The two existing regional conventions are the European Convention on Human Rights (Rome Convention of 1950) and the American Convention on Human Rights (San José, 1969). What characterizes both of them, but particularly the European Convention, is that, compared with the Universal Declaration and the Covenants, they include only a small group of human rights. These Conventions do not supply any clear indications concerning the relations existing between the universal conventions and the regional conventions, or what a State should do that participates in both of them. An essential question presents itself, considering this limited content: do the regional conventions possess any significance, as compared with the universal conventions?

It will be seen later on that the regional conventions represent an effort by the States concerned to try out new methods of realizing human rights in practice, and that, from this point of view, they are justified. However, so far as the list of human rights is concerned, it must be acknowledged that the regional conventions have not introduced a single new element and have not created a single new right; from this point of view, they are covered by the documents possessing a universal character. It would not, of course, be unthinkable for a regional convention to add to the list of human rights enumerated in the universal documents. However, it has been in the realization of human rights alone that the regional conventions have gone further than the universal conventions.

Giving the matter further thought, one arrives, moreover, at the following fundamental thesis: human rights are, by virtue of their very nature, universal rights; only thus do they have any significance, and in their general character, they cannot but be universal. It is not possible to imagine a region which, in establishing protection for human rights, excluded from the list of human rights covered by its convention a right recognized by the universal conventions. The fundamental feature of human rights, be they established in the framework of the United Nations or of the specialized agencies, is indeed their universality, their validity *urbi et orbi*, as well as their generality, or in other words their coverage of all human rights.

On the basis both of experience to date and of theoretical thinking, it is justifiable to conclude that in the field of human rights a regional convention means something only if it adds a new element to the universal system for the protection of human rights, be it at the level of rights (new content) or at that of their implementation (new procedure). If such is not the case, the universality of human rights should be maintained and even reinforced, for it is this very feature which principally accounts for the moral force of human rights, even if other elements also contribute to their legal force.

(e). Relations between the Declaration and the Conventions

The legal nature of the Declaration and the Conventions differs substantially, and the same is naturally true of their binding force in regard to States. It has already been observed that the Universal Declaration has acquired a moral authority such that it has almost become legally binding. But in reality this is not the case. The Declaration is not binding upon States and constitutes merely a statement of United Nations thinking on human rights. Admittedly, States can attribute to a declaration of this nature an importance such that the rights included in it will have an almost binding force. States can also include the Declaration in the preamble to their Constitutions. But even with all that, the Declaration will not be mandatory for a given State, since even the preamble to its own Constitution is not mandatory (this question has given rise to a substantial number of works in the field of constitutional law and also in that of the theory of law).[24] This means that the Declaration has been taken into consideration in the Constitution, and that it is respected therein. No more can be asked of a declaration, even a universal one; even that much is significant. As is stated elsewhere, the Universal Declaration is more important than a simple recommendation.

(f). Conventions

Apart from the Universal Declaration, and not counting the various recommendations, conventions constitute the basic form in which human rights are established at the international level. These are multilateral instruments of international law, and upon ratification the States concerned expressly undertake to guarantee the rights included in them and to include in their municipal law the human rights which have been formulated or, in other words, to ensure to all inhabitants of the State concerned the enjoyment of the human rights set forth in those conventions. On this account, and in accordance with the system of the sources of international law, conventions constitute the form required by international public opinion, for they explicitly place obligations upon States.

Another recognized source of international law is custom. According to some authors, the Universal Declaration, as a source of law, has a value no greater than that of custom. It is suggested, however, that the value of the Declaration is greater than that of mere international custom.

There can be no doubt that, of these two sources of law, it is conventions which represent clearly-defined legal obligations, for the execution or non-execution of which States can be held directly responsible. However, the example of human rights in fact shows that certain changes occur in the system of the sources of international law. As an international legal institution, human rights are indeed the expression of certain situations which represent more than mere custom, without however attaining the legal form of international conventions. They become binding on the various States only at such time as those States have ratified the conventions drawn up for that purpose.

At the UN, as at the League of Nations, although to a lesser degree, a procedure was introduced according to which conventions on human rights have to be voted on by the General Assembly. These rights consequently cease to be, to a certain extent, mere custom, which was perhaps their status until their acceptance; they then pass into the realm of international positive law. The vote at the General Assembly still has to be followed by the signing of the convention by the State, then by the ratification procedure in the framework of that same State. The convention thus acquires its full international legal value. And yet it cannot be said, and it is precisely this that is new in international practice, particularly regarding human rights, that the various phases of the process, the vote and signature, have no significance, and that the convention voted at the UN remains a mere custom up until the time that it is ratified.

In actual fact, the accession of human rights to the level of international law is effected by a process in the course of which human rights gradually acquire international standing and are progressively transformed into international positive law. It is not appropriate to deal here with the repercussions of this process on the system of the sources of international law in general or to raise the question as to whether or not it affects, and in what way, other fields of law.

In any event, in the framework of the United Nations, the conventions on human rights are instruments on the basis of which it is possible to compel States to meet the obligations which they contain and to accept the responsibility when they are not carried out. But one cannot disregard the process whereby they are transformed into positive law, a process in the course of which human rights, which had previously belonged to customary or unwritten law, pass into written international positive law, and thus become binding on States who then have to take domestic measures. This last aspect of the question shall now be examined.

5. THE IMPLEMENTATION OF HUMAN RIGHTS

(a). The United Nations system[25]

Contrary to the Declaration and to recommendations, which are almost equivalent to it from the legal point of view, States undertake, by ratifying conventions on human rights to: respect the clauses they contain; take adequate measures to maintain or establish a state of affairs postulated by the conventions; and provide for a particular system of appeal for the benefit of citizens. These general terms are formulated in detail by the Covenants which, at the same time, prohibit all forms of discrimination among human beings.

What means does the UN have at its disposal to induce States to meet the obligations which they assume when they ratify a convention? A convention, it should be remembered establishes a relationship between the State and the international community, which concerns the individual. But what is important here is the obligation assumed by the State. The State has obligations by virtue of the fact that it is a member of the UN and has accepted of its own accord to respect human rights by submitting to the authority of certain organs of the UN. The Covenants and conventions deal specifically only with cases in which States fail to fulfil their obligations or act in a manner which is inconsistent with the obligations which they contracted under the terms of the conventions. For such cases a procedure has been established which might be said largely to constitute a game that is played within the UN. In René Cassin's opinion, this is the weakest point of the human rights system established by the UN. States are in fact obliged to submit from time to time (generally each year) a report to the competent UN organ: the Commission on Human Rights, or to a committee specially set up for that purpose (see, for instance, the 1966 Covenant on Civil and Political Rights). In its turn, the organ addresses a report to the higher bodies or to the Secretary-General, or perhaps directly to the General Assembly. In expressing its opinion, the General Assembly may approve or formulate reservations or recommendations. In my view, this system is too rigid and encumbered by red tape, which makes the matter lose much of its interest in the course of the procedure.

Two principles of international law stand in the way of the UN's working out a more flexible and more effective system for the international protection of human rights: the principle of State sovereignty and the exclusion of the individual as a subject of international law or, more accurately, the fact that in international law only the State can be a subject of the law. When W.J. Ganshof van der Meersch wrote that, with human rights, international law annexed part of constitutional law, which consequently ceased to be the monopoly of municipal law,[26] he was probably right from the point of view of substantive law. But constitutional law possesses completely different machinery for legal protection which allows individual grievances to be formulated in the framework of the State, at a level, it is true, which is never the highest level in the State. In the UN human rights system, States give up their sovereignty only insofar as they are obliged to submit a report to the international organization. Apart from this, and not without reason, they vigorously defend their sovereignty against intervention by other States, effected sometimes through the intermediary of the UN. Furthermore, in this system the substantive discussion concerning the alleged violation of human rights before a particular organ of the UN (the Commission on Human Rights, for instance) is initiated on the basis of a complaint by another State and, consequently, the accused State has to defend itself not so much against the charge levelled at it, but rather against the other State. Even if my judgment seems severe, it has to be admitted that the UN has proved to be incapable of loosening the stranglehold of sovereignty, even with the help of human rights, although it was just these rights that represented an area of international concern *par excellence*, calling for certain "interventionist" measures.

The UN does however possess a means, the only one it must be said, whereby it can disregard the second limiting principle of not recognizing the individual as a subject of international law. Thus, at the present time only States have the possibility of addressing a complaint or a request to the UN, and this holds true more particularly for human rights since it is not considered to be wise for a State to authorize its own citizens to lodge a complaint with the UN against it, for such procedure would probably be devoid of all objectivity.[27] It is not in the general conventions but in the convention on genocide, and later in the convention on apartheid that the United Nations has recognized the individual as a subject of international law. In both these cases, genocide and the policy of apartheid are described as international crimes. By these conventions, States undertake either to summon those responsible for such acts before their own tribunals or to accept the jurisdiction of the international tribunal. At the same time, they undertake not to allow such criminal acts to be shielded from national or international penal justice on the plea that they constitute "political crimes". This, the most stringent procedure ever adopted by the UN, applies only in two cases. However, it has yet to be applied, and it is doubtful whether it will be put into effect because States may not be prepared to yield to such international pressure. It will perhaps be necessary for an entirely new line of approach to appear in the development of international criminal law for the provisions of these Conventions to become effective.

It might thus be said that the UN arsenal contains both the meekest weapon and the most severe one. An instrument of common law which will lend itself to general use has not yet been discovered. It is, however, in this direction that both the UN and the various States should progress.

(b). The system of regional conventions

The leading innovation introduced by the regional conventions relates to the implementation of human rights. It is here that we find a significance, if there is one, in the concluding of such regional conventions.

This innovation consists in the individual being recognized as a subject of international law, in other words, in the possibility for the individual to lodge a complaint with a regional commission on human rights in the event that his human rights are violated. But it must be stressed at once that at present this possibility is hedged in with a whole series of guarantees under which the State concerned is very well protected. For the individual must first of all have exhausted all the national procedures of appeal available, and it is only then that he is afforded the possibility of having recourse to an international organ for the purpose of notifying it that a particular right, which concerns him directly, has been violated. In general he cannot apply to the international organ for the purpose of notifying it that a particular violation, which does not concern him directly, has occurred. Moreover, before the international organ, the procedure takes place in two phases: first the commission considers whether the complaint is admissible, and it is only if it is so judged that it examines the merits of the case.

The result of this is that the European Commission declares scarcely one per cent of individual complaints to be admissible.[28] Thus, it might seem from the outside that while a new and admirable procedure has been made available here for the international protection of human rights, this procedure is in fact impracticable. On the basis of the complaint, the European Commission can itself take certain measures. It can oblige the accused State to take the necessary steps, or it can apply to either the Committee of Ministers of the Council of Europe or to the European Court of Human Rights, as the supreme judicial body, before which only States and the Commission can institute proceedings. Here, too, what is impressive is the external aspect, far more than the protection that these institutions actually provide. In my opinion, the Council of Europe can show at most one or two examples of ways in which human rights can be interpreted and protected, but it does not provide them with effective protection. It cannot be claimed that human rights have been violated only in the small number of cases in which the Strasbourg organization has really acted. One is therefore inclined to speak rather of the effect produced by the *possibility* of such a procedure on the conduct of States, and generally speaking, on the self-limiting power of that procedure.

Whatever the case, what is involved here is a procedure to which thought had also been given at the UN. For the Optional Protocol to the 1966 Covenant on Civil and Political Rights provides for the introduction of the same system in the United Nations.[29] It grants to the Committee established by the Covenant the right to receive and consider individual complaints; the Committee has to submit its conclusions to the State concerned and include that State's reply in its report. It is true that the optional Protocol has not been adopted by many States, for they have confirmed themselves to ratifying the two Covenants. The procedure provided thus remains a possibility which will probably not be used often, although it makes for a fairly moderate solution and one which cannot but have a certain importance at the level of principle.

A certain contradiction exists between the basic conception of the European Convention on Human Rights and its implementation. As conceived, the Convention is aimed at establishing a system of collective protection for human rights[30] but the means for putting it into effect and, primarily, the new means constituted by individual complaints, are typical non-collective. The fact nevertheless remains that the European Convention should be considered in the field of human rights as an attempt to provide for the partial recognition of the individual in international law.

The fact is that a stable and lasting system designed to protect human rights has not yet emerged at the United Nations. In this connection, it can be neither forgotten nor denied that the very basis of the existence of the UN is the simultaneous presence of countries belonging to different social systems. Now whereas one of the groups of countries avails itself, as a general rule, of the system of human rights established by the UN to seek to identify injustices perpetrated against individuals in the established order of a State belonging to the other social system, the position adopted by the other group has been characterized by a collective interpretation of human rights which neither recognizes nor admits of intervention in a State's domestic affairs, nor even the mere adoption of a position by the UN, except in cases where the particular situation, for instance that of a minority, endangers peace and international security. Reciprocal caution in the face of possible provocation hinders the establishment, within the UN, of a system ensuring the effective protection of human rights.

Conclusion

With the introduction of the international protection of human rights there appeared an institution of international law capable of becoming the basis and the framework for the full development of man's personality, respect for his standing as a human being and the equality of citizens before the law within the various States.

The central idea of human rights, and of the citizens' rights which preceded them in the history of law, is equality before the law; in other words, the equality of citizens which, even if only a matter of form, nonetheless exercises certain effects. This equality of citizens before the law, which subsequently became, with human rights, the universal equality of all, constitutes the central institution of human rights. In its negative form it signifies the absolute prohibition of every kind of discrimination. This idea is already contained in the Charter of the United Nations. It now finds its way into all general or partial documents relating to human rights in that virtually all reiterate the prohibition against discrimination and define, where need be, the grounds for such prohibition. Such is the fundamental idea which dominates the entire human rights structure: a leading place is given to the equal prohibition against discrimination and this is followed by a prohibition against concrete forms of discrimination. It is understandable that, by virtue of its importance among human rights, equality is regarded as a virtue to be protected before any other. We thus come back to our starting point: it is only when the social conditions pertaining to general equality become a reality that the very idea of human rights as a social institution can arise.

At the present time the fundamental right of man is no longer so much an absolute freedom allowing for the creation of a specific field of action, free from all unwarrantable interference, but rather the equality of man which, in the past, however, was regarded as a political right. This is the consequence of an individualism being, to a certain extent, superseded at the social level, and of the development of society and the concept of man. Within the State it may be individual freedoms which remain the dominant rights (although in the socialist countries such is certainly not the case) but, in the international sphere of human rights, this predominance is tantamount to the idea of equality. In the last analysis, recourse is had to this idea everywhere; this is also the idea on which the international legal institution of human rights is founded.

The importance of human rights is such that it can truly be asserted that, with their emergence and with the first steps taken to realize them, human society took a qualitative leap forward. In any event, human rights represent a new element in the development of mankind, and in the life of human society, for they signify the end of a period and the beginning of a new era in international relations.

It is not surprising that, in view of the relative unity of our divided world, human rights law, which could be the foundation of the contemporary international community, is unable to develop sufficiently. This relative unity is to be seen not so much at the level of the very concept of human rights and their definition but at the level of implementation. The view can be held that even in the present world, which is characterized by the co-existence of mutually opposing social systems, it is nevertheless possible to develop an homogeneous and more effective system for the implementation of human rights at the international level. Such should be our ambition.

NOTES

1. Sophocles: *Antigone*, "The unwritten, unchanging laws of the gods".
2. Ulpian, D.1.1.1., p. 3.
3. Gaius, D.1.1.g.
4. Aristotle: *Politics*, Book One.
5. H. Grotius: *De belli ac pacis*, Liber I, Caput I.4.
6. T. Hobbes: *Leviathan*, Chapter 14.
7. A.V. Dicey: *Introduction to the study of the law of the Constitution.* 9th edition, Chapter 4. p. 200, Note. l.
8. John Locke: *Epistola de Tolerentia.* "Omnia illi tam humanitatis quam civitatis jura sancte conservanda", "Sed maxime cavere debent magistratus, ne civili utilitatis praetextu ad opprimendum alicujus libertatum abutantur".
9. "...die grössere Übereinstimmung der Verfassung mit Rechtsprinzipien versteht, als nach welchem zu strefen uns die Vernunft einen Kategorischen Imperativ verbindlich macht". Kant: *Metaphysik der Sitten*, Kirch, 1870. *Rechtslehre*, II. Teil, Das öffentliche Recht, pp. 49, 157.
10. Marx-Engels: *Werke*, Berlin, 1957, pp. 347-377.
11. W.J. Ganshof van der Meersch: *Organisations européennes*, Vol. 1, Sirey, Paris, 1966, p. 255.
12. Cf. I. Szabo: *A kulturalis jogok* (Cultural rights), Budapest, 1973, pp. 85 *et seq.*
13. A. Verdoodt: *Naissance et signification de la Declaration universelle des droits de l'homme*, Louvain, Paris, 1963, pp. 41-43.

14. G.A. res. 423 (v) of 4 December 1950.

15. René Cassin: La Déclaration universelle et la mise en oeuvre des droits de l'homme, *RCADI*, Vol. 2, p. 293.

16. Jacques Maritain: *Les droits de l'homme et la loi naturelle*, Paris, 1947, p. 14.

17. To show how vague this theory is in respect of the relations existing between the State and international law, I refer the reader to the work of the outstanding international jurist, Philip Jessup. On page 90 we read: "It is inherent in the concept of fundamental rights of man that these rights inhere in the individual and are not derived from the State." On page 92 we find: "The human rights to be defined and protected must be considered not in a vacuum of theory, but in terms of the constitutions and laws and practices of more than seventy states." Cf. P. Jessup: *A Modern Law of Nations*, New York, 1949. But, in this case, is the State included in the concept of human rights? Are human rights rights which depend on the State, and solely on the State, or are they not?

18. See UN doc. A/2929 (1955), chap. IV.

19. See also below, Chapter 4, Section 1.

20. UN doc. A/2929 (1955), chap. I.

21. G.A. res. 543 (vi).

22. *Ibid.*

23. See below, chaps. 15-21.

24. Cf. C. Varga: "The preamble: A question of jurisprudence", *Acta Iuridica*, Tomus XIII, Fasc. 1-2, Budapest, 1971.

25. See below, chap. 10.

26. Cf. above, note 11.

27. Editor's note: since this chapter was written the Optional Protocol to the International Covenant on Civil and Political Rights has entered into force and, as of January 1982, 28 States have ratified it, thereby giving their citizens the right of individual petition to the UN Human Rights Committee. Cf. also the UNESCO complaints procedure described in Chapter 13 below.

28. For a more detailed analysis, see below, chap. 16, section 1.

29. See below, chap. 16, section 2.

30. Cf. W. J. Ganshof van der Meersch, n. 11 above, p. 259.

Part I
Principles and Norms of Human Rights

3 Distinguishing Criteria of Human Rights

Theodoor C. van Boven

1. FUNDAMENTAL HUMAN RIGHTS—OTHER HUMAN RIGHTS

There is certainly a risk in classifying human rights on the basis of their relative weight or importance. Through the ages and depending on the various cultures and regions, the fundamental nature of certain rights has been a matter of different appreciation and evaluation. The right to property is a case in point. Whereas this right was considered inviolable in historic statements,[1] there has more recently been a strong and growing tendency to make it subject to the requirements of the general welfare of society. Differences of opinion regarding the concept and the nature of the right to property even resulted in its omission from the International Covenants on Human Rights, although it was included in the Universal Declaration of Human Rights (Article 17). Those favouring its inclusion in the Covenants contended that "to omit it might create the impression that it was not a fundamental human right".[2]

There is another argument against making a distinction between fundamental human rights and other human rights. Such a distinction might imply that there is a hierarchy between various human rights according to their fundamental character. However, in modern human rights thinking the indivisibility of human rights and fundamental freedoms[3] is prevalent. This idea of indivisibility presupposes that human rights form, so to speak, a single package and that they cannot rank one above the other on a hierarchical scale.

This may all be true, but there still remain weighty arguments which militate in favour of distinguishing fundamental human rights from other human rights. Such fundamental rights can also be called elementary rights or supra-positive rights, i.e. rights whose validity is not dependent on their acceptance by the subjects of law but which are at the foundation of the international community. It would seem that the United Nations Charter recognizes this concept inasmuch as, in its preamble, the peoples of the United Nations are determined "to reaffirm faith in fundamental human rights, in the dignity and worth of the human person...etc." This reaffirmation cannot but refer to fundamental human rights norms which were already part of the law of the international community as constituted at that time.

Although it is more appropriate to analyze present human rights law in order to indicate what human rights might be considered as fundamental, it is nevertheless of interest to draw upon historical sources in order to place the Charter's reaffirmation of faith in fundamental human rights in proper perspective. Reference may be made in this connection to the minimum standard rules of treatment of aliens,[4] as well as to the theory of humanitarian intervention which considered large-scale violation of very elementary rights under certain conditions a legitimate ground for armed intervention. At the beginning of this century, an authoritative writer called these very elementary rights, whose violation might justify humanitarian intervention, "droits humains". He included in this category: "droit à la vie, droit à la liberté (physique et morale) et droit à la légalité".[5]

Under the League of Nations system for the international protection of minorities, respect for certain essential human rights was provided for in the minorities treaties and declarations, not only for the benefit of minority elements, but for all the inhabitants of the countries concerned. Among these essential rights were the right to life and liberty and freedom of religion and conscience.[6] Whereas these rights were guaranteed to all inhabitants, other rights such as the right to equality before the law, the enjoyment of other civil and political rights without discrimination, and special rights regarding the use of language and the establishment and maintenance of religions, charitable and social institutions were accorded to smaller circles of persons such as nationals or members of racial, linguistic or religious minorities. In fact, it would seem that the minorities system, though a human rights obligation for a limited number of States only, was again one of the constituent elements at the basis of the human rights "reaffirmation" of the UN Charter.

If the foregoing might justify the tentative conclusion that the community of nations as constituted at the end of the Second World War was at least bound by some supra-positive human rights norms, such as the right to life, the right to liberty and freedom of conscience and religion, it should nevertheless be emphasized that the content, the value and the weight of these fundamental human rights norms are in a constant process of development. Even the right to life, the most elementary of all human rights, is subject to changing opinions on the beginning and the end of life. Another cogent example of this process of development is the "upgrading" of the principle of non-discrimination,[7] notably racial non-discrimination, on the hierarchical scale of human rights norms, in so far as there is any such scale.

It is fair to say that in the practice and activities of the United Nations no human rights principle has received such a prominent position as the elimination of racism and racial discrimination. Machinery has been established (Special Committee on Apartheid, Ad Hoc Working Group of Experts, Committee on the Elimination of Racial Discrimination), campaigns launched (Decade of Action to Combat Racism and Racial Discrimination) and, last but not least, norms elaborated (Declaration and Convention on the Elimination of All Forms of Racial Discrimination, Convention on the Suppression and Punishment of the Crime of Apartheid) which go, in their purport and nature, beyond other action (and inaction) of the United Nations in the field of human rights. The intensity of the prevailing sentiments against racism and racial discrimination, the awareness of urgency and the political climate have made the principle of racial non-discrimination one of the foundations of the international community as represented in the UN. Members of this community are bound by this principle on the basis of the UN Charter, even if they do not adhere to the various international instruments specifically aimed at the elimination of racial discrimination and apartheid. This view was notably expressed by the International Court of Justice in its 1971 Advisory Opinion on the Legal Consequences for States of the Continued Presence of South Africa in Namibia.[8]

There is also a great deal of law in humanitarian conventions and in international human rights instruments supporting the existence of very fundamental human rights. This is that part of human rights law which does not permit any derogation even in time of armed conflict or in other public emergency situations threatening the life of the nation. The common article 3 of the four Geneva Conventions of 1949, setting out a number of minimum humanitarian standards which are to be respected in cases of conflict which are not of an international character, enumerates certain acts which "are and shall remain prohibited at any time and in any place whatsoever." The following acts are mentioned: "(a) violence to life and person, in particular murder of all kinds, mutilation, cruel treatment and torture; (b) taking of hostages; (c) outrages upon personal dignity, in particular, humiliating and degrading treatment; (d) the passing of sentences and the carrying out of executions without previous judgment pronounced by a regularly constituted court, affording all the judicial guarantees which are recognized as indispensable by civilized nations." The universal validity of these fundamental prescriptions is underlined by the words "at any time and in any place whatsoever" in this common article 3 of the four 1949 Geneva Conventions.

The International Covenant on Civil and Political Rights enumerates in article 4, para. 2, the rights from which no derogation is allowed in time of public emergency,[9] viz. the right to life (article 6), the right not to be subjected to torture or to cruel, inhuman or degrading treatment or punishment (article 7), the right not to be held in slavery or servitude (article 8, paras. 1 and 2), the right not to be imprisoned merely on the ground of inability to fulfil a contractual obligation (article 11), the prohibition of retroactive application of criminal law (article 15), the right to recognition everywhere as a person before the law (article 16) and the right to freedom of thought, conscience and religion (article 18). Regional human rights conventions contain a similar clause enumerating provisions from which no derogation may be made[10].

The fact that in a number of comprehensive human rights instruments at the worldwide and the regional level, certain rights are specifically safeguarded and are intended to retain their full strength and validity notably in serious emergency situations, is a strong argument in favour of the contention that there is at least a minimum catalogue of fundamental or elementary human rights.

Other arguments can also be used to support this contention. It was stated above that in the present theory and practice of the United Nations the principle of racial non-discrimination is a fundamental principle of the world organization. Similarly, other international organizations have come to recognize that certain human rights values are of such fundamental significance in relation to the work and purposes of those organizations that they have developed special procedures or established special machinery in order to promote or to protect these fundamental human rights values, even in the absence of conventional obligations. A case in point is the special procedure of the International Labour Organisation relating to Freedom of Association. This procedure, in which the ILO Governing Body Committee on Freedom of Association plays a central role, may be invoked even against States which are not formally bound by the ILO conventions on freedom of association (Nos. 87 and 98). Against the objection that obligations of Member States derive solely from ratified conventions and accepted recommendations, the Governing Body Committee argued, *inter alia*, that "the principle of freedom of association is among the aims of the ILO, as mentioned in the preamble to its Constitution. Moreover, the Declaration of Philadelphia relating to the aims and objectives of the ILO, which is an integral part of the Constitution, reaffirms the importance of freedom of expression and of association," etc.[11] In other words, freedom of association is a constitutional principle of the ILO and as such must be respected by the whole membership of the Organization. For this reason the basic concepts of the freedom of association conventions have to be considered in direct relationship with the Constitution of the ILO, including the Declaration of Philadelphia in particular, and are therefore fundamental principles of the Organization and binding upon its members.

Another example, taken from the practice of the Organization of American States, and in particular the Inter-American Commission on Human Rights, militates in favour of singling out certain human rights of a fundamental nature. The Second Special Inter-American Conference (Rio de Janeiro, 1965) requested the Commission to give particular attention to observance of the following human rights embodied in the American Declaration of the Rights and Duties of Man: the right to life, liberty and personal security (Article I); the right to equality before the law (Article II); the right to religious freedom and worship (Article III); the right to freedom of investigation, opinion, expression and dissemination (Article IV); the right to a fair trial (Article XVIII); the right to protection from arbitrary arrest (Article XXV); and the right to due process of law (Article XXVI). The

Commission established a special procedure for the handling of the communications charging the violation of any of the above-mentioned rights.[12] These rights were apparently considered of such fundamental importance, that they justified special attention by the Inter-American Commission on Human Rights as well as special powers and procedures in case of their alleged violation.

The character of some humanitarian norms may also be deduced from international penal law and from the rapidly developing law in relation to the "question of the violation of human rights and fundamental freedoms in any part of the world, with particular reference to colonial and other dependent countries and territories".[13] The Convention on the Prevention and Punishment of the Crime of Genocide provides the most forceful indication of fundamental norms which are to be considered as supra-positive. This was confirmed by the International Court of Justice when it said that "the principles underlying the Convention are principles which are recognized by civilized nations as binding on States, even without any conventional obligation."[14] Furthermore, attention should be drawn to the Convention on the Non-Applicability of Statutory Limitations to War Crimes and Crimes against Humanity. This Convention aims at affirming in international law the principle that there is no period of limitation for war crimes and crimes against humanity. It too conveys the idea that certain norms are so basic to humanity and to the international community that grave infringements of these norms, by contrast with infringements of other humanitarian norms, in no way lose their criminal character through the passage of time.

Finally, it is submitted that the UN Commission on Human Rights and its Sub-Commission on Prevention of Discrimination and Protection of Minorities have obtained since 1967 a mandate relating to violations of human rights that reflect not only upon the quantity of the violations but also upon the moral quality of the rights. In its resolution 1235 (XLII) of 6 June 1967, the Economic and Social Council authorized the Commission and the Sub-Commission "to examine information relevant to gross violations of human rights and fundamental freedoms, as exemplified by the policy of apartheid as practised in the Republic of South Africa and in the Territory of South West Africa..., and to racial discrimination as practised notably in Southern Rhodesia, contained in the communications listed by the Secretary-General pursuant to Economic and Social Council resolution 728 F (XXVIII) of 30 July 1959." Furthermore, ECOSOC resolution 1503 (XLVIII) of 27 May 1970, contains a detailed procedure for dealing with communications relating to violations of human rights and fundamental freedoms, especially in so far as those communications indicate the existence of "particular situations which appear to reveal a consistent pattern of gross and reliably attested violations of human rights requiring consideration by the Commission." It would seem that the powers of the Commission and its Sub-Commission in the matters of violations of human rights not only relate to the massive character of the violations, but also to the intensity and to the fundamental nature of the human rights norms involved. At least the policy of apartheid and racial discrimination in Southern Africa, explicitly mentioned as an example in ECOSOC resolution 1235 (XLII), provides some necessary guidance on the consistent pattern or massive character of the violations and on the fundamental nature of the human rights values at stake.

In the foregoing much has been said about fundamental human rights and every little about "other" human rights. This approach finds its explanation in the fact that this chapter deals with distinguishing criteria for fundamental human rights as distinct from "other" human rights recognized in national and international law. In conclusion, it might be useful to recapitulate some of the characteristics of fundamental human rights. These rights lie at the foundation of the international community as presently represented in the United Nations and, in a more limited sense, in other important worldwide and regional organizations. The membership of these organizations is bound to respect these fundamental rights and the international organizations are entitled to take action where there exists *prima facie* evidence of serious violations of these rights. These fundamental rights have a supra-positive character inasmuch they are binding on States, even in the absence of any conventional obligation or of any express acceptance of comment. Furthermore, such fundamental rights are considered to be valid under all circumstances, irrespective of time and place, and no derogation is allowed.

2. CIVIL AND POLITICAL RIGHTS; ECONOMIC, SOCIAL AND CULTURAL RIGHTS

Recent international instruments relating to the general promotion and protection of human rights contain either a comprehensive enumeration of civil and political rights together with economic, social and cultural rights, or deal separately with civil and political rights on the one hand and economic, social and cultural rights on the other. The Universal Declaration of Human Rights and the American Declaration of the Rights and Duties of Man are examples of the former type of instrument,[15] while the International Covenant on Civil and Political Rights, the International Covenant on Economic, Social and Cultural Rights, the European convention on Human Rights and the European Social Charter, as is evident from their respective titles, adopt the approach of two separate and distinct catalogues of rights.

Among the civil and political rights there are first of all the rights designed to protect the liberty, security and physical and spiritual integrity of the human person. Such rights are: the right to life; the right not to be subjected to torture or to cruel, inhuman or degrading treatment or punishment; the right not to be held in slavery or servitude; the right to liberty and security of person, including the right to a fair trial; the right to privacy, home and correspondence; and the right to freedom of thought, conscience and religion. Political rights include: the right to freedom of opinion and expression; the right to freedom of assembly and of association; the right to take part in the conduct of public affairs, including the right to vote and to be elected. The economic, social and cultural rights include: the right to work, including the right to just and favourable conditions of work; trade-union rights; the right to social security; the right to adequate food, clothing and housing; the right to an adequate standard of living; the right to health; the right to education; and rights relating to culture and science.[16]

The concept of human rights is very much the product of history and of human civilisation and as such is subject to evolution and change. In fact, the development of human rights has gone through various stages[17] and the concept of human rights started off as a political concept, i.e. it meant respect for a sphere of freedom of the human person from the State. In other words, the State was bound not to intervene in this sphere of "civil rights" or "freedom rights" or, as was stated in the previous paragraph, the rights which attempt to protect the liberty, the security and the physical and spiritual integrity of the human person. These rights are by and large of an individualistic character. In the next stage man is not placed in opposition to the State but he is the person who takes part in the political structuring of society of which he is a member. This is done through the exercise of political rights within the State. Finally, the emergence of the idea of economic, social and cultural rights as a distinct group of rights is a more recent phenomenon. These rights are to be realized through or by means of the State. In this concept the State acts as the promoter and protector of economic and social well-being. Whereas in earlier stages the State was mainly an authority for the protection and maintenance of public order and security of society, the modern State is (or should be) an instrument for the benefit of all persons within its jurisdiction in order to enable them to develop to the maximum their faculties, individually and collectively. The role of the State in the matter of human rights has changed considerably, and it should be realized that the enlarged function of the State is not only relevant in relation to social rights but also with respect to the whole field of human rights, insofar as the public authorities have also the duty to guarantee civil and political rights against intrusions by power elements which may have large economic, technological and scientific potentials at their disposal. It is sometimes contended that in view of this changed function of the State with respect to the promotion and protection of human rights, the difference between "social rights" and "civil rights" is in the process of disappearing. This may very well be true, but it should also be emphasized that in matters of human rights the main focus should not be the function of the State but rather the human existence and human personality on the individual and collective level. The indivisibility or the unity of the human person in the physical, intellectual and spiritual sense might be a more solid basis for approaching the question of the interconnection between civil and political rights, and economic, social and cultural rights.

During the early period of the drafting of the International Covenants on

Human Rights there was much discussion as to whether there should be one or two covenants. The arguments put forward in favour of either solution reflect clearly the various opinions regarding civil and political rights and their relation to economic, social, and cultural rights and vice-versa. These arguments, which will be noted below can be found in the Annotations prepared by the Secretary-General of the UN on the text of the draft International Covenants on Human Rights.[18] Those who were in favour of drafting a single covenant maintained that human rights could not be clearly divided into different categories, nor could they be so classified as to represent a hierarchy of values. All rights should be promoted and protected at the same time. Without economic, social and cultural rights, civil and political rights might be purely nominal in character; without civil and political rights, economic, social and cultural rights could not be long ensured.

However, those who favoured the drafting of two separate instruments argued that civil and political rights were enforceable, or justiciable, and immediately applicable, while economic, social and cultural rights were to be progressively implemented. They contended that, generally speaking, civil and political rights were rights of the individual "against" the State, that is, against unlawful and unjust action of the State, while economic, social and cultural rights were rights which the State would have to take positive action to promote. Those who stressed the difference between the two categories of rights also drew the attention to the fact that civil and political rights, being "legal" rights, required different means and methods of implementation (namely through complaints procedures) than economic, social and cultural rights, which were "programme" rights and could best be implemented through a system of periodic reports.

Although it was finally decided to have two separate covenants, there was wide agreement on the pronouncement in General Assembly resolution 421 (V), and reaffirmed in resolution 543 (VI), that "the enjoyment of civil and political freedoms and of economic, social and cultural rights are interconnected and interdependent" and that "when deprived of economic, social and cultural rights man does not represent the human person whom the Universal Declaration regards as the ideal of the free man." It should be noted that the third preambular paragraphs of both Covenants reflect this ideal of the free man in the light of the interconnection and interdependence of both groups of rights. As the Annotations of the Secretary-General point out, these paragraphs were intended to underline the unity of the two covenants while, at the same time, maintaining the distinctive character of each.[19] In recent years more emphasis has been laid on the unity than on the distinctive character of "civil rights" and "social rights". It has been pointed out that the UN Charter denotes a global concept of human rights and places the promotion of universal respect for, and observance of, human rights and fundamental freedoms in the context of international economic and social co-operation (article 55) and in relation to the purpose of achieving "international co-operation in solving international problems of an economic, social, cultural, or humanitarian character" (article 1, para. 3).[20] The idea of unity also finds clear expression in article 13 of the Proclamation of Teheran,[21] the terms of which were specifically endorsed by the UN General Assembly in 1977. In its resolution 32/130 the Assembly decided that the approach to the future work within the UN system with respect to human rights questions should take into account the following concepts: "(a) All human rights and fundamental freedoms are indivisible and interdependent; equal attention and urgent consideration should be given to the implementation, promotion and protection of both civil and political, and economic, social and cultural rights; (b) 'The full realization of civil and political rights without the enjoyment of economic, social and cultural rights is impossible; the achievement of lasting progress in the implementation of human rights is dependent upon sound and effective national and international policies of economic and social development', as recognized by the Proclamation of Teheran of 1968; . . . "

In spite of this trend emphasizing the idea of unity, the International Covenants on Human Rights as well as the European Convention on Human Rights and the European Social Charter—all these international instruments representing to a large extent Western human rights thinking—underline the different character of both categories of rights as far as the general obligations of States are concerned. While under the Covenant on Civil and Political Rights each State Party undertakes, in accordance with the concept of "legal" rights or directly enforceable rights, from the time of ratification or accession, to respect and to ensure to all individuals within its territory and under its jurisdiction the rights recognized in that Covenant, the States Parties to the Covenant on Economic, Social and Cultural Rights, in accordance with the concept of "programme" rights, undertake to take steps to the maximum of their available resources with a view to achieving progressively the full realization of the rights recognized in that Covenant (article 2, para. 1, of both Covenants). The aforementioned regional European instruments also make a distinction between human rights of immediate application and human rights of a promotional nature, and consequently the Contracting Parties are obliged under the Convention to "secure to everyone within their jurisdiction the rights and freedoms defined" and under the Social Charter "to accept as the aim of their policy, to be pursued by all appropriate means the attainment of conditions in which the following rights and principles may be effectively realized." It would indeed seem that a great deal of authoritative opinion endorses the idea that, on the basis of the relevant international instruments, economic, social and cultural rights are rights of progressive realization and civil and political rights are to be respected and guaranteed as an immediate obligation.[22]

The distinction on the basis of the notion of immediacy with regard to "civil rights" and of progressiveness in relation to "social rights" cannot be taken too categorically. First of all, the implementation approach of the Covenant on Civil and Political Rights at the national and international levels assumes the possibility of progressive realization of those rights. Article 2, para. 2, introduces on the national level "a certain degree of elasticity to the obligations imposed on the States by the covenant, since all States would not be in a position immediately to take the necessary legislative or other measures for the implementation of its provisions".[23] The same idea is an underlying element of the international implementation system of the Covenant on Civil and Political Rights inasmuch as reporting is the only obligatory means of implementation, and States Parties undertake, according to article 40, to report *inter alia* on the progress (again the notion of progressiveness) made in the enjoyment of the rights recognized in the Covenant.

Apart from these general indications which tend to blur the dividing line between "civil rights" and "social rights", a number of rights included in each of the International Covenants can be classified as falling outside the proper scope of each covenant. Article 23, para. 4, of the Covenant on Civil and Political Rights, which provides that States Parties shall take appropriate steps to ensure equality of rights and responsibilities of spouses to marriage, during marriage and at its dissolution, and article 24, para. 1, under which every child shall have the right to measures of protection on the part of his family, society and the State, are promotional provisions rather than rules of immediate application.[24] On the other hand, the Covenant on Economic, Social and Cultural Rights contains a good many provisions that are capable of immediate application. Among these can be mentioned the right to form and join trade unions, including the right to strike (article 8, para 1), the rule that marriage must be entered into with the free consent of the intending spouses (article 10, para. 1, last sentence), the prohibition of employment of children in harmful work (article 10, para. 3, third sentence), the respect of the liberty of parents to choose for their children schools other than those established by the public authorities (article 13, para. 3) and the undertaking to respect the freedom indispensable for scientific research and creative activity (article 15, para. 3).[25] The "double" or "mixed" nature of some rights can best be illustrated by the trade union rights. These rights clearly have economic and social aspects insofar as they are essential for the promotion and protection of economic and social interests, such as the right to work and the enjoyment of just and favourable conditions of work, the right to an adequate standard of living, the right to rest and leisure, etc. In this respect the right to form and join the trade union of one's choice is rightly included in instruments which aim at the realization of economic and social rights, such as the International Covenant on Economic, Social and Cultural Rights and the European Social Charter. On the other hand, trade union rights are a species of the right to freedom of peaceful assembly and association and as such recognized among the civil and political rights in the International Covenant on Civil and Political Rights, the European Convention on Human Rights and the American Convention on Human Rights. In fact, the ILO has emphasized time and again the particular relevance of respect for basic civil liberties for the exercise of trade union freedoms.[26]

On the basis of the foregoing paragraphs, the conclusion is justified that the difference between "civil rights" and "social rights" is not a clear-cut one but rather a question of gradation. The realization of "social rights" is very much dependent upon the use of available resources and the introduction of certain structural and institutional changes. The Secretary-General of the UN has stated: "Their effective transformation into directly applicable and enforceable legal rights may require time".[27] This statement implies that social rights principles as contained in legal instruments can be given concrete form and in due time can be converted into subjective and justiciable rights. It is interesting to note that this idea of the gradual conversion of principles in the social rights field into directly applicable and enforceable legal rights, also finds much support, particularly in developing countries, in respect to civil rights. This line of thinking was clearly expressed when the implementation machinery of the International Covenant on Civil and Political Rights was discussed at the twenty-first session of the General Assembly. The views of many representatives were reflected as follows: "The governments of several developing countries also feared that their real difficulties in securing forthwith some of the rights recognized in the Covenant might be misconstrued as bad will. . . . However, as all such difficulties would gradually disappear, an increasing number of States Parties would no doubt accept the optional clause . . . and thereby give full effect to the system of implementation of the Covenant." Viewed in a global perspective, the notion of gradual progress[28] seems to prevail in the whole of the human rights area, without a sharp distinction being made between "civil rights" and "social rights". The question remains whether history and the present state of affairs in the world can justify the supposition of gradual progress and advancement under any circumstances and whether decline in political, economic and social conditions is not a recurring phenomenon or risk affecting the quality of life and basic human rights. In such adverse situations, respect for the dignity and worth of the human person tends to lessen, and therefore the notion of human rights—and this would again apply to civil and political rights as well as to economic, social and cultural rights—is even more crucial in order to preserve human values, especially freedom from fear and want for every person and for the whole community in which he or she lives.

3. INDIVIDUAL RIGHTS; COLLECTIVE RIGHTS

The distinction between the rights of the individual and the rights of the group or community is also one which should not be taken in too categorical a way. It is, after all, within the community that the individual can develop fully his personality, as is pointed out in article 29, para. 1, of the Universal Declaration.[29] When a distinction is made between individual rights and group rights, this distinction should not be viewed in terms of a contradistinction. This does not diminish the fact that certain rights are of an individualistic nature, such as the rights to privacy, freedom of thought and conscience and the right to liberty and security of person; while other rights are by their nature collective rights, such as most economic and social rights. There are also rights which present individual and collective aspects. Freedom of religion and freedom of expression are cases in point.

It is, however, undeniable that the general orientation and outlook of the Universal Declaration of Human Rights is towards the individual person. The same is to a large extent true for the International Covenants on Human Rights. Most provisions of the Universal Declaration begin with the words "everyone has the right..." In fact, the Universal Declaration puts the individual and his personality on an elevated level in the national and international sphere. The basic idea is that every human being should have a full and equal chance to develop his personality, with due regard to the rights of others and to the community as a whole. As a corollary, respect for the individual person means respect for the unique and diverse character of every human person. This implies a large degree of tolerance within a plural society. It would furthermore seem that such an individualistic approach to human rights takes account of the creative role of the non-conformist in society. Recognition of the individual's right of recourse at the national level, and in view of various recently created procedures,[30] at the international level, also finds expression in the right of petition. This right of petition signifies the individualistic character of the human rights concept.

Before attention is paid to the rights of groups or collectivities, the social functioning or the social relationships of the individual must not be overlooked. Article 1 of the Universal Declaration, in summarising the three great principles of the French Revolution, states *inter alia* that "all human beings...should act towards one another in a spirit of brotherhood." The social order and the community, to which the individual belongs, are also put in a proper human rights perspective in articles 28 and 29 of the Universal Declaration and in the fifth preambular paragraph of the International Covenants on Human Rights. In fact, the International Bill of Human Rights[31] in its entirety places the human person in various social relationships of which he is an integral part, e.g. his family, his religious community, his employment, and the local, national and international order. In this manner human life in its manifold social relationships finds recognition and expression under the aegis of the promotion and protection of human rights.

While in the preceding paragraphs emphasis was put on the rights of the individual in the sense of the individual as a unique human being or as a person forming part of various social relationships, attention will now be paid to rights of groups or collectivities. No effort will be made to define a "group" or "collectivity", but for the sake of the distinction between individual rights and group rights, a group should be taken as a collectivity of persons which has special and distinct characteristics and/or which finds itself in specific situations or conditions. Those special and distinct characteristics, may be of a racial, ethnological, national linguistic or religious nature. The specific situations or conditions could be determined by political, economic, social or cultural factors. Taking into account these characteristics, which are inherent in a group, or the situations or conditions which are of an accidental nature, international human rights law aims either at protecting or preserving the characteristics of the group or tries to bring about change in those situations or conditions affecting the group which are intolerable under accepted international human rights standards. Not only whole peoples or minorities, whose right of self-determination is at stake, come within this purview, but also groups whose economic and social level of living is below minimum standards and groups who are victims of gross and large scale violations of human rights, including discrimination.

Collective rights *par excellence* are the rights of minorities with a view to preserving and developing their characteristics and the right of peoples to self-determination, viz. the right freely to determine their political status and freely to pursue their economic, social and cultural development. Under the League of Nations there existed an elaborate system for the protection of minorities, imposing obligations upon a number of countries which had fought in the First World War on the side of Germany.[32] The minorities treaties and declarations contained four elements: (a) principles of equality or non-discrimination; (b) guarantee of general human rights; in particular guarantees concerning the use of language or the maintenance of certain minority institutions; (d) guarantee of general or special autonomy or of traditional rights. While the first two categories of rights were of an individual nature and were to be assured to all inhabitants and all citizens of the countries in question,[33] the two latter categories were formulated either as rights of persons belonging to minorities[34] or as rights of the minorities themselves,[35] and as such collective rights. Under the United Nations the protection of minorities was never able to take a high profile;[36] the original orientation and outlook in the UN being in the direction of the rights of the individual. Due to the growing influence in the UN of the countries of the Third World, which received strong support in this matter from the East European countries, a great deal of emphasis has shifted from individual rights to collective rights, notably the right of peoples to self-determination, the right of under-privileged peoples and groups of persons to a fair and equitable share in the world's resources, the right of racially discriminated groups to equality before the law, notably in the enjoyment of human rights, and most recently, the right to development and the right to peace.

It is interesting to note that the very first article of both the International Covenants on Human Rights sets out a collective right, viz. the right of all people to self-determination. By virtue of this right, all peoples "freely determine their political status and freely pursue their economic, social and cultural development." The second paragraph of the same article deals with the economic counterpart of this right, viz. the question of permanent sovereignty over natural resources.[37] It reads: "All peoples may, for their own ends, freely dispose of their natural wealth and resources without prejudice to any obligations arising out of international economic co-operation, based upon the principle of mutual benefits and international law. In no case may a people be deprived of its own means of subsistence." One of the arguments raised against this article was that a collective right of this character was out of place in an international instrument on human rights, the more so as the notion of "people" was extremely vague. On the other hand it was stated that the collective right attached to all peoples, and that, if denied that right, no people, let alone individual members of that people, were free. In this line of thinking, the right to self-determination was considered the most fundamental of all human rights.[38] The right to self-determination has played an enormous role in the whole decolonization movement of the United Nations. The Declaration on the Granting of Independence to Colonial Countries and Peoples[39] and its implementation machinery became instrumental in this decolonization movement. This Declaration states unequivocally that "the subjection of peoples to alien subjugation, domination and exploitation constitutes a denial of fundamental human rights" (article 1) and affirms in more cogent and ultimate language than article 1 of the Covenants, the relevance of the right to self-determination for the enjoyment of other basic human rights and freedoms.[40]

The UN Secretary-General pointed out in his preliminary study of issues relating to the realization of economic and social rights that these rights are by their very nature collective rights.[41] Articles 55 and 56 of the UN Charter, which contain a pledge by the members of the UN to take joint and separate action to promote higher standards of living, full employment, and conditions of economic and social progress and development, together with the similar pledge to promote universal respect for, and observance of, human rights and fundamental freedoms for all, form the foundation for the efforts to attain a more just and equitable world economic and social order. In this regard the 1979 report of the UN Secretary-General on "the international dimensions of the right to development" is worthy of note. The report states that "enjoyment of the right to development necessarily involves a careful balancing between the interests of the collectivity on one hand, and those of the individual on the other. It would be a mistake, however, to view the right to development as necessarily attaching only at one level or the other. Indeed there seems no reason to assume that the interests of the individual and those of the collectivity will necessarily be in conflict. A healthy regard for the right of the individual to pursue his self-realization, manifested by respect for this right within collective decision-making procedures which permit the full participation of the individual, will contribute to, rather than weaken, the efforts of the collectivity to pursue its right to development. In addition, individual development and fulfilment can be achieved only through the satisfaction of collective prerequisites".[42] In 1979 the General Assembly, in resolution 34/46, emphasized that "the right to development is a human right and that equality of opportunity for development is as much a prerogative of nations as of individuals within nations".

A notable landmark in the development of the trend of a collectivist approach to human rights was the Proclamation of Teheran of 1968. The Proclamation repeatedly refers to gross and massive denials of human rights, particularly under the policy of apartheid and other policies and practices of racial discrimination, as a result of colonialism, arising out of aggression or any armed conflict, and arising from discrimination on the grounds of race, religion, belief or expressions of opinion.[43] It also refers to the widening gap between the economically developed and developing countries as an impediment to the realization of human rights in the international community, and such other urgent questions as large scale illiteracy and discrimination against women.[44] In fact, the proclamation reflects the current approach to relate human rights to urgent and serious worldwide political and economic problems of today, bringing to the forefront massive denials of human rights. Whereas the Universal Declaration of Human Rights of 1948 makes the individual the central figure in a variety of social relationships, the proclamation of Teheran focuses very much on the group as the massive victim of denials of human rights. This is, at least at the global level, a most striking development in two decades from the individualist to the collectivist approach to human rights.

NOTES

1. See for instance the French Declaration of the Rights of Man and of the Citizen, 1789, Article 17.

2. UN doc. A/2929, Annotations on the text of the draft International Covenants on Human Rights, Chapter VI, para. 198.

3. See especially General Assembly resolution 32/130 (1977).

4. See John P. Humphrey, "The International Law of Human Rights in the Middle Twentieth Century", in *The Present State of International Law and Other Essays*, International Law Association, 1973, pp. 75 ff.

5. Rougier, *La théorie de l'intervention d'humanité*, 17 RGIDP (1910), pp. 472 ff.

6. See for instance Article 2 of the Treaty of 28 June 1919 concluded with Poland.

7. See in particular E.W. Vierdag, *The Concept of Discrimination in International Law, with Special Reference to Human Rights*, Martinus Nijhoff, The Hague, 1973.

8. The Court stated: "Under the Charter of the United Nations, the former mandatory had pledged itself to observe and respect, in a territory having an international status,

human rights and fundamental freedoms for all without distinction as to race. To establish instead, and to enforce, distinctions, exclusions, restrictions and limitations exclusively based on grounds of race, colour, descent or national or ethnic origin which constitute a denial of fundamental human rights is a flagrant violation of the purposes and principles of the Charter", Sohn and Buergenthal, *International Protection of Human Rights*, Bobbs-Merrill, New York, (1973), p. 479. It is noteworthy that the Court established a direct link between the language of Articles 56 and 55 of the UN Charter and the terms of Article 1, para. 1, of the International Convention on the Elimination of All Forms of Racial Discrimination. See also E. Schwelb, "The International Court of Justice and the Human Rights Clauses of the Charter", 66 *AJIL*, p. 337 (1972), and Frank C. Newman, "Interpreting the Human Rights Clauses of the UN Charter", 5 *HRJ*, pp. 288-289 (1972).

9. The German language uses for this purpose the clear term "notstandsfest".

10. Article 15, para. 2, of the European Convention on Human Rights, prohibiting derogation from the right to life (Article 2), the right not to be subjected to torture or to inhuman or degrading treatment or punishment (article 3), the right not to be held in slavery or servitude (article 4, para. 1), the prohibition of retroactive application of criminal law (article 7). Article 27, para. 2, of the American Convention on Human Rights makes the following listing of articles which may not be suspended in time of war and other emergency situations: article 3 (right to juridical personality), article 4 (right to life), article 5 (right to humane treatment), article 6 (freedom from slavery), article 9 (freedom from *ex post facto* laws), article 12 (freedom of conscience and religion), article 17 (rights of the family), article 18 (right to a name), article 19 (rights of the child), article 20 (right to nationality), article 23 (right to participate in Government). See also Chapter 8, *infra*.

11. Governing Body Committee on Freedom of Association, 129th report, paras. 140 ff.

12. See report of the Organization of American States to the International Conference on Human Rights, Teheran, 1968, Chapter IV.D.

13. This and other related titles are now permanent features on the agenda of the UN Commission on Human Rights.

14. Advisory Opinion on Reservations, ICJ Reports, 1951, pp. 15 ff.

15. The American Convention on Human Rights contains an elaborate and detailed chapter on civil and political rights, consisting of no less than 23 articles, but it refers only very briefly in one article to economic, social and cultural rights (article 26). See in a critical sense Pedro Pablo Camargo, "The American Convention on Human Rights", 3 (1970) *HRJ*, pp. 333 ff.

16. This enumeration of rights is illustrative but by no means exhaustive.

17. See in particular Norberto Bibbio, "Human rights," in *Proceedings of the Italian Conference on Human Rights*, p. 23, Cedam, Padua, 1968. E. W. Vierdag, op. cit., pp. 74-78; and UN doc. E/CN. 4/988, para. 16 *et seq.*

18. UN doc. A/2929 (1955), chapter II, paras. 4-12.

19. *Ibid.*, chapter III, para. 8.

20. UN doc. E/CN.4/988, paras. 48 ff.

21. See *Final Act of the International Conference on Human Rights*. Teheran, UN Sales No. E. 68.XIV.2. See *ibid.*, resolution. XVII on "Economic Development and Human Rights."

22. See in particular Egon Schwelb, "The Nature of the Obligations of the States Parties to the International Covenant on Civil and Political Rights", in René Cassin, *Amicorum Discipulorumque Liber I*, Ed. Pédone, Paris, 1969, pp. 301 ff. See also International Labour Office, "Comparative Analysis of the International Covenants on Human Rights and the International Labour Conventions and Recommendations", *Official Bulletin*, vol. LII, 1969, no. 2, paras. 10 and 100.

23. UN doc. A/2929, chapter V, para. 8.

24. See Schwelb, note 22; see Chapter 10, *infra*.

25. UN doc. E/CN.4/988, para. 76.

26. See G. Caire, *Freedom of Association and Economic Development* (Geneva, ILO, 1977) and references therein.

27. UN doc. E/CN.4/988, para. 75, and paras. 31 and 154.

28. See article 2, para. 1, of the Covenant on Economic, Social and Cultural Rights: "...with a view to achieving progressively the full realization of the rights...."

29. See René Cassin, "De la place faite aux devoirs de l'individu dans la Déclaration universelle des droits de l'homme", *Mélanges Modinos*, Ed. Pédone, Paris, 1968, pp. 478 ff.; and UN doc. E/CN.4/SUB.2/432 and Adds. (1980).

30. See the Optional Protocol to the Covenant on Civil and Political Rights; article 14 of the International Convention on the Elimination of All Forms of Racial Discrimination; article 25 of the European Convention on Human Rights; article 44 of the American Convention on Human Rights; resolution 1503 (XLVIII) of the ECOSOC containing a procedure for dealing with communications relating to violations of human rights and fundamental freedoms.

31. The International Bill of Human Rights comprises: the Universal Declaration, the two International Covenants, and the Optional Protocol to the International Covenant on Civil and Political Rights.

32. See "The International Protection of Minorities under the League of Nations," UN doc. E/CN.4/Sub.2/6.

33. See articles 2 and 7 of the treaty of 28 June 1919 concluded with Poland.

34. See articles 8 and 9, para. 1, of the same treaty.

35. See article 9, para. 2, of the same treaty.

36. No provision on minorities was included in the Universal Declaration of Human Rights and the International Covenant on Civil and Political Rights contains an article on minorities of a limited scope (article 27). See *Study on the Rights of Persons Belonging to Ethnic, Religious and Linguistic Minorities*, by Francesco Capotorti, UN Sales No. 78.XIV.1 (1979).

37. See also General Assembly resolution 1803 (XVII) (1962) containing a declaration on "Permanent sovereignty over natural resources".

38. UN document A/2929, chapter IV, paras. 3-4.

39. General Assembly resolution 1514 (XV) of 14 December 1960.

40. See also the Declaration on Principles of International Law Concerning Friendly Relations and Co-operation Among States in Accordance with the Charter of the United Nations (General Assembly resolution 2625 (XXV) of 24 October 1970), notably the description of the principle of equal rights and self-determination of peoples.

41. UN doc. E/CN.4/988, para. 21.

42. UN doc. E/CN.4/1334 (1979), para. 85.

43. See *Final Act*, note 21 *supra*, paras. 7-11.

44. *Ibid.*, paras. 12, 14 and 15.

4 Fundamental Principles of Human Rights: Self-Determination, Equality and Non-Discrimination

Karl Josef Partsch

Three principles will be dealt with in this chapter* which are of fundamental importance for the protection of human rights. The import of each is of a different nature from that of the others. There can be no doubt that *equality of human beings before the law* is one of the most important of human rights and that it may be regarded as fundamental in the sense that it is the basis for the development of guarantees of specific human rights. Whether specific guarantees for equal protection by courts, equal pay for equal work, equal access to professions, to other economic activities or to the civil service, or the right of participating equally in the political process by voting or otherwise are expressly contained in a catalogue of human rights or not is not decisive as long as equality before the law is guaranteed in a general way. Courts and other state authorities may develop such guarantees from the basic norm. Equality has in this way the function of a general human right, offering a basis to a greater number of specific human rights which may after some time be incorporated into the catalogue but would also be applied by courts if this should not be the case. The guarantee of equality before the law has a function comparable only to the guarantee of the right to free development of the personality. It is a dynamic right which may form the basis for a great number of other rights.

Quite different is the character of the *principle of non-discrimination*. It is not a separate human right—however important this principle may be—but only a corollary to the right of equal protection before the law. In this framework it prevents certain criteria from being used and it broadens the application of the basic norm. If equality before the law is understood as the principle according to which equal facts should be treated equally and unequal facts may be treated in accordance with the special circumstances of the case, the principle of non-discrimination prohibits a differentiation in some respects. For instance, distinctions of race, colour, sex, language, religion, political or other opinion, national or social origin, property, birth or other status are not

*Written by the author in 1976 and updated by Unesco.

permissible though they may be regarded as legitimate criteria under the principle of equality before the law. It may therefore be said that the principle of non-discrimination determines the field of application of equality, without adding a further human right to the catalogue.

Self-determination presents more difficulties than the two other principles: Is the principle of self-determination as such one of the human rights or is it perhaps—as frequently alleged—the essential condition for all human rights?

The first theory—that self-determination is a human *right*—is true only if the principle is also a legally binding right in the sense which is given to this concept by the doctrine of the sources of international law. Furthermore the question is raised whether it is a *human* right. Both questions are controversial according to the opinions of learned scholars and also according to the practice of States and of international organizations. Both of these questions may be answered only after considering what "self-determination" means at present and how its understanding has been developed.

1. SELF-DETERMINATION[1]

(a). The Wilsonian approach

Without referring to achievements in former times and to its formulation by philosophers and politicians until the 19th century, it may be stated that this principle gained world wide importance during the First World War. The American President, Wilson, on January 8, 1918 announced fourteen points as a proposed basis for peace. He emphasized *inter alia*, the principle "that in determining all such questions of sovereignty the interests of the populations concerned must have equal weight with the equitable claims of the government whose title is to be determined".[2]

Later he defined this point more precisely: "The central principle that we have struggled for in this war is that no government or group of governments has the right to dispose of the territory or to determine the political allegiance of any free people." In implementation of this principle a great number of nations in Central and Eastern Europe gained independence; and the former German colonies and considerable parts of the Ottoman Empire were brought under the Mandate System of the League of Nations.[3] However, similar control was not established with regard to the colonial empires of the Allied and Associated powers themselves. In the peace treaties careful attention was given to the protection of ethnic minorities. One of the main methods of realizing the principle was plebiscites held in some territories in order to ascertain the ethnological and economic basis of the claims of the inhabitants.[4]

This "central principle" has certainly not been applied universally,[5] but rather in accordance with political expediency and taking into account strategic, economic and other political considerations. It was not regarded as a legally binding right but as a mere political principle which, according to the case in question, might or might not be applied. President Wilson's draft of the Covenant, however, again clearly expressed the relationship between self-determination—as understood at that time—and the principles of political independence and territorial integrity: self-determination may in certain cases prevail. The principle is proclaimed in universal terms and relates mainly to ethnic minorities living together in a certain territory inside a pre-existing state or empire.

Art. 3 of Wilson's draft for the Covenant of the League of Nations stipulated: "The Contracting Parties unite in guaranteeing to each other political independence and territorial integrity but it is understood between them that such territorial adjustments, if any, as may in future become necessary by reason of changes in present racial and political relationships, pursuant to the principle of self-determination, and also such territorial adjustments as may in the judgment of three-fourths of the delegates be demanded by the welfare and manifest interest of the people concerned, may be effected if agreeable to those peoples; and that territorial changes may in equity involve material compensation. The Contracting Powers accept without reservation the principle that the peace of the world is superior in importance to every question of political jurisdiction or boundary."

This provision was omitted in the final text; and in the Covenant of the League of Nations no express mention of self-determination was to be found. The principle however has dominated history between the two World Wars. It is sufficient to mention the case of Bohemia where first self-determination was denied to a substantial ethnic minority and later a flagrant violation of the same principle with regard to the majority was committed.

Between the two World Wars "self-determination" was understood as a political principle which applied to all kinds of "peoples" without distinction. The term was used in the following instances:

- "peoples" living entirely as minority (or even as majority) groups inside a state ruled by another "people" (as the Irish before 1919 and the Mongols before 1911/1921);

- "peoples" living as minority groups in more than one state without their own statehood (as Poles in Russia, Austria and Germany before 1919);

- a "people" living as minority group in a state but understanding itself as part of the people of a neighbouring state (Mexicans in California and Hungarians in Romania);

- "peoples" or "nations" forced by external influences to live in separate states (as the German nation within several states);

- a " people" living as the majority (or also a a minority group) inside a territory with a special status under foreign domination (main example: colonial regimes).

In all five cases it was required that the respective "peoples" settle in certain parts of the country where they at least formed the majority of the population. Groups of immigrants dispersed all over the country—such as Blacks and also non-English-speaking Europeans in the United States of America—were not regarded as "peoples".[6] Implementation of the principle took different forms: international protection of minorities, regional autonomy, statehood within a federal state or within a commonwealth of nations, and finally national independence.

(b). The Atlantic Charter

During the Second World War two major aspects of self-determination were emphasized in the Atlantic Charter of 14 August 1941: "*Second,* they desire to see no territorial changes that do not accord with the freely expressed wishes of the peoples concerned. *Third,* they respect the right of all peoples to choose the form of government under which they will live; and they wish to see sovereign rights and self-government restored to those who have been forcibly deprived of them." This text is still conceived in the spirit of the pre-war period and the question may be raised whether the provision in the Charter of the United Nations, where its purposes are defined, should not be read with the same understanding. Such purposes are: "2. To develop friendly relations among nations based on respect for the principle of equal rights and self-determination of peoples..." (Art. 1, para. 2).

The principle of self-determination is here not only combined but even identified with the principle of equal rights, using the word "principle" in the singular, whereas the "respect for human rights and for fundamental freedoms" only appears in the following paragraph. This strange combination led a distinguished early commentator on the Charter to the conclusion that "self-determination of peoples" in Art. 1, para. 2 can only mean "sovereignty of the states" and "that the formula of Art. 1, para. 2 has the same meaning as the formula of Art. 2, para. 1 where the principles of sovereignty and equality are combined in a rather ambiguous way into one principle: that of "sovereign equality".[7]

This strange inversion of the traditional meaning of the concept of self-determination has not been followed by other authors.[8] When published, Kelsen's opinion appeared isolated. Only in retrospect, thirty years later, does his opinion seem to reflect the fundamental changes which have taken place.

This change from a first period in which self-determination has come to a substantial measure of acceptance to the second period, following the Second World War, has been ably described: Wilson "proclaimed the right in universal terms, but for practical purposes he concentrated on the European territorial settlement following the war." The peoples involved during this period "were ethnic communities, nations or nationalities primarily defined by language and culture." "In the second (period) the focus of attention has been the disintegration of the overseas empires, which had remained effectively untouched in the round of Wilson's self-determination."..."In the present era of decolonization ethnic identity is essentially irrelevant, the decisive, indeed, ordinarily, the sole consideration being the existence of a political entity in the guise of a colonial territory."[9]

This development began soon after United Nations organs became active in the field of the international protection of human rights and met with considerable criticism from the side of those who still followed the ideas of Woodrow Wilson.[10]

The new doctrine abandoned the concept that groups, formed as "peoples" on the basis of political consciousness but living under foreign rule, are entitled to claim self-determination, that this principle applies universally and that the claim to self-determination could be fulfilled in various ways, either by conceding a certain degree of cultural or political autonomy within the State, by integration into or association with a State, or by secession in order to form a new State or to unite with another State.

According to the new concept only territories under colonial rule shall have the right to self-determination which involves accession to independent statehood. It does not matter how the population of such territory is ethnically composed. As soon as independent statehood is reached, the territorial integrity of the country is protected against any attempt aimed at the partial or total disruption of the national unity, even by one ethnic group which in this way is brought under alien domination. This new right of self-determination may also be exercised by the use of force and with the help of other powers.

(c). The Declaration on Decolonisation (1960)

These principles have been summarized in the Declaration on the Granting of Independence to Colonial Countries and Peoples, adopted by the UN General Assembly in Resolution 1514 (XV) on 14 December 1960, where an attempt is made to link the evolution of the field of human rights to the right of self-determination. This is already done in the preamble where a close connection between the principles of self-determination and of respect for human rights is established (para. 2); and also in the operative part which begins with the declaration that "the subjection of peoples to alien subjugation, domination and exploitation (i.e. the denial of self-determination) constitutes a denial of fundamental human rights . . ." (sub-para. 1). Though it is emphasized that "all peoples have the right to self-determination" (sub-para. 2), the effect of the preamble, where the desire to end colonization is mentioned not less than four times, is that self-determination is regarded to be a legal principle only as far as it is claimed by peoples under colonial rule.

This is confirmed under sub-para. 5: "In Trust and Non-Self-Governing Territories . . . immediate steps shall be taken to transfer all powers to the peoples of those territories . . . in order to enable them to enjoy complete independence and freedom." For these territories the following provision of sub-para. 6 states that "any attempt aimed at the partial or total disruption of the national unity and the territorial integrity of a country" is illegal.

In this Declaration of 1960 no attempt was made to bridge the apparent contradiction between the established right of secession and the guarantee of national unity. This was only done ten years later in the "Declaration on Principles of International Law Concerning Friendly Relations and Co-operation Among States in Accordance with the Charter of the United Nations",[11] with the development of the theory that "the territory of a colony or other non-self-governing territory has, under the Charter, a status separate and distinct from the territory of the State administering it." Under this assumption the guarantee of national unity applies to each colonial unit separately.

Both Declarations are drafted in the form of authoritative interpretations of the Charter, not as amendments thereof. If Art. 1, para. 2 of the Charter establishes only a political principle of self-determination, this apparently cannot be changed by Resolutions of the General Assembly.

In order to promote the process of decolonization, special bodies have been established by the General Assembly: first, a Committee on information relating to non-self-governing territories, later the Special Committee of 24 members (now 25). These subsidiary organs are not only to observe the conditions in non-self-governing countries and to inform the General Assembly thereon. A large part of their activity consists of influencing and encouraging liberation movements, in accordance with the Declaration on the Granting of Independence, under which these movements can enjoy special privileges. In order not to be limited to the sources of information provided by the administering States, these Committees receive petitions from the inhabitants of these territories. They tend to exercise a control similar, as far as possible, to the international Trusteeship System provided for in Chapters XII and XIII (articles 75–92) of the Charter.

When the legal effect of the abovementioned Declarations is evaluated, the practice established for several years has to be taken into account. Those who take the practice in this area into account when interpreting the content and importance of the relevant legal provisions must admit that in this field an important development has taken place.[12]

With the establishment of a procedure inside the Organization of the UN in favour of certain beneficiaries of the right to self-determination and with the definition of the content of this right, the legal character of the original principle has changed—but only within the limits of application of this new practice.

This would lead to the result that there exists a legal right to anti-colonial self-determination, a privilege for a relatively small part of the world population (from about 130 million in 1961 only about 3 million are left in 1981). The practice established in favour of these beneficiaries has, however, no effect for other peoples under foreign domination. With respect to them the legal situation under the Charter remains unchanged. The principle of self-determination under the Charter continues to be valid for them—as a principle whose realization may depend on political expediency and other circumstances, but without conferring on them a right to secession and to full independence.[13]

(d). Covenants on Human Rights

The International Covenants on Human Rights both contain in their common article 1 a guarantee of the right of self-determination without defining the beneficiaries or the content, and without establishing a procedure for its realization. Even though the Covenants came into force in 1976, little clarification has emerged.[14]

The following questions have to be answered: Can the principle of, or right to, self-determination be regarded as a "human right" in the technical sense; and how should the relations between these two principles be otherwise defined?

Without any doubt the ideological bases of both principles have much in common: both go back to the ideas of the French Revolution, when the concepts of human dignity, of the sovereignty of the people, and of the active role of the citizen in the political process were developed in opposition to the doctrines of the omnipotent State, of the sovereignty of princes and of the passive role of the obedient subject.

Both principles set limits on the powers of the State but in different forms: the protection of human rights secures a personal sphere of activity to the citizen who remains inside the frontiers of the State and in this way is enabled to live in freedom and dignity in his State. This protection may therefore be qualified as a positive contribution to the relations between individuals and the public authority. The principle of self-determination on the other hand has a negative character in relations between the entities concerned if a group of former citizens secedes. If an ethnic group gains a certain autonomy either as a State in a Federation or even as a self-administered unit in a decentralized unitarian State, a negative element exists. The main difference, however, is that the protection of human rights is assigned to individuals as such. The subject of the principle of self-determination is always a group which only collectively can make use of the powers, rights or possibilities offered by it.

The argument has been put forward that there are also other human rights which may only be exercised collectively, such as freedom of association and the right to join labour unions. It is true that there exists a collective element in these rights but besides this element there is in all such cases an individual element: the decision to join the association or the union. Such an individual element is hardly to be found in the exercise of self-determination, except perhaps in the decision to participate or not to participate in a possible plebiscite. Obviously, this weak individual element exists with regard to the old concept of self-determination of the Wilsonian period; it appears still weaker in the new concept. For all these reasons the principle of self-determination cannot be regarded as a "human right", although it has been inserted into the two Covenants of the United Nations against the opposition of some Member states.

How can the relationship between these two principles be defined correctly? In many resolutions of the General Assembly the formula is used that self-determination is a pre-requisite of the effective exercise of all human rights. This formula immediately raises objections to the extent that it is used as a political postulate.

Respect for human rights, irrespective of their common ideological bases already mentioned above, can satisfy the desires of those who wish to utilize the principle of self-determination: if freedom of speech is respected, if freedom of religion is safeguarded, together with freedom of assembly and of association, the temptation to leave a multinational or multiracial State is certainly less strong, and the possibility of integrating the minority group into the nation is higher. On the other hand, the principle of self-determination can be entirely realized only by granting certain privileges to an autonomous group: use of their own language by public authorities and in publicly financed schools, and a certain preferential treatment in election laws, to mention only some fields.

A proper definition of the relations between the two principles may perhaps be that respect for one is a pre-requisite for respect for the other.

2. EQUALITY

(a). Equality and non-discrimination

"Ever since the French Revolution, the principle that all human beings are equal before the law has found expression, either in this or in a similar wording, in a large number of European and non-European constitutions. However, within Europe it is only in Switzerland, Germany, Austria and Italy that it has developed into a genuine constitutional principle, i.e., into a principle which is recognized not only in administrative and civil law and in the procedural rules of the courts, but also in constitutional law, and is protected by specialized constitutional courts."

With these words, a well-known constitutionalist introduces *an essay* on the principle of equality.[15] The author certainly did not intend to place the legal order of the countries mentioned on a higher level than the legal order of other countries. Certainly he only wanted to explain the different approach to an important political problem—the limitation of discretionary power—in different legal systems. The four countries mentioned by him—and possibly others may have been added in the meantime—try to limit the powers not only of the executive and of the judiciary but also of the legislature by introducing the concept of equality before the law into the constitution, and by providing for a judicial control of formal and of substantive equality by constitutional courts. "Formal legal equality precludes intrinsically contradictory measures in either the legislative or the administrative field".[16] Substantive legal equality "demands that the same standard of rights and obligations be applied to all men. According to this conception, the factual peculiarities and differences should be taken into consideration. They must be respected not only by the authorities carrying out the law but, above all, by the law-making bodies."[17]

This is acceptable only for a legal system which—following the doctrine of the separation of powers—is ready to limit the powers of parliament by establishing certain constitutional limits for its work and by entrusting the enforcement of those limits to the courts. It is unacceptable for those countries which adhere to the principle according to which "the great exception—from the limitations of discretionary powers—is the unlimited discretion of the legislature."[18] This is not only true for the systems of absolute power of parliament, in the British tradition, but also for Socialist States.

From this comparison it can be seen that the principle of equality before the law has a different meaning in the national legal and constitutional orders. There exist among the three main legal traditions—Anglo-Saxon law, Socialist law, and continental European law based on Roman traditions—entirely different concepts.

The close relationships between the principle of equality before the law and the constitutional structure of a given State, the differences between legal systems when the values have to be defined which determine whether an act has to be regarded as "arbitrary" or "socially unjust", and finally, the extremely broad field of application of this principle make it impossible to define it in a manner valid for all national legal systems and for the formation of a sound basis for its universal application.

In order to avoid these uncertainties and to establish criteria for deciding which facts should be regarded as conforming to the principle of equality, the negative formulation of this principle has progressively gained importance in many national legal systems as well as in international law: with the proscription of *discrimination*.

The basic consideration in favour of this negative approach is to achieve a higher degree of clarity and certainty in arriving at equality. The non-discrimination clause is not limited to the claim that equality should be reached, but indicates also the notion of what should be equal, and according to what criteria. The abstract notion of equality is replaced by a concrete indication of the field of application and of criteria such as race, colour or descent. It should, however, be mentioned that the use of the negative approach does not solve all problems. If discrimination on the basis of sex is prohibited, does this mean that men and women must be treated without differentiation with regard to facts or circumstances connected with biological differences (as motherhood)? Or is only arbitrary discrimination excluded? Is only a detrimental differentiation excluded or also a preferential treatment with an indirect discriminatory effect? Is a discriminatory intention required or is a discriminatory effect sufficient?

Not all of the questions raised are answered by the numerous definitions of the term: only one of them is reproduced here as a model:

"The term discrimination. . .is generally used to connote unequal treatment of equals either by the bestowal of favours or imposition of burdens. Therefore, whenever discrimination is referred to in the context of international law, there is an implicit assumption of its relation to a norm, or sets of norms, prescribing equality of treatment. In addition, discrimination generally carries with it the idea of unfairness."[19]

(b). Relevant texts

In the light of these general remarks it is not surprising that in these instruments more attention is given to non-discrimination than to the principle of equality before the law.

(i). THE CHARTER OF THE UNITED NATIONS

The principle of non-discrimination appears three times in the operative part of the Charter: in art. 1 para. 3, in art. 55 para. 6, and in art. 76 (c). An express reference to "the equal rights of men and women" is to be found only in the Preamble. Implicitly, however, equality before the law is included in all the references to the protection of human rights.

(ii). THE UNIVERSAL DECLARATION OF HUMAN RIGHTS

The Preamble recalls the reference in the Preamble of the Charter to "the equal rights of men and women"; furthermore, art. 1 begins in a preambular style with the statement: "All human beings are born free and equal in dignity and rights." This sounds retrospective. One may find in these words an indication of the principles on which the rights are later enumerated,[20] a tribute to the important role the principle of equality played in former times when specific and more detailed rights had been derived from it. Such a dynamic role, however, does not seem to be expected on the international level, where "a common understanding of these rights and freedoms"[21] shall be the basis—and also the limit—of the undertaking to be achieved. The international protection of human rights is therefore extended only to the rights and freedoms universally recognized and expressly inserted into the catalogue. There is no room for a general clause as the basis for the development of additional rights.

The catalogue of the Universal Declaration begins then with the principle of non-discrimination:

Art. 1: "Everyone is entitled to all the rights and freedoms set forth in this Declaration, without distinction of any kind, such as race, colour, sex, language, religion, political or other opinion, national or social origin, property, birth or other status."

The rule is thus established as such without reference to equality before the law. This circumstance may be used as an argument that it has to be understood as a "strict" rule, i.e., that any distinction, whether arbitrary or not, is excluded and that no further qualifications may be required. The field of application of the rule is, however, limited to "the rights and freedoms set forth in this Declaration"; thus the rule of non-discrimination is not established absolutely. In a second paragraph the rule of non-discrimination is expressly confirmed for all countries subjected to any limitation of sovereignty. Only in article 7 do equality before the law and the equal protection of the law "without any discrimination" appear. Here no reference to the rights and freedoms set forth in the Declaration is added. The broader principle of general equality seems to have a wider field of application than the rule of non-discrimination. Whenever arbitrary discrimination outside the field covered by the rights and freedoms of the Universal Declaration occurs, may it then be regarded as a denial of equality, though it is not covered by article 2? Is the person affected entitled to equal protection by the law? The answer is given in the second sentence of article 7: protection against discrimination is to be guaranteed only if it has been committed "in violation of this Declaration." Nevertheless, a denial of the principle of equality before the law may have been committed, but sanctions against this denial have not been foreseen.[22]

It may be argued that such a legalistic interpretation of the Universal Declaration—an instrument not legally binding—is not appropriate and that it should be left to the Covenants to clear up such divergencies. This argument should be accepted. If, however, the Declaration is understood as an authoritative guide to the interpretation of the Charter, it is at least remarkable that in the Declaration the reciprocal relations between the broader and more general principle of equality before the law and the rule of non-discrimination have been reversed.

While the rule of non-discrimination—at least historically—had the value of a corollary to the principles of equality and of equal protection of the law, the latter now appears only as a method of applying, in theory and in practice, the rule of non-discrimination. Apparently political considerations have influenced the concept in a dogmatic way.

The first attempt to translate the Universal Declaration into positive international law on a regional basis should be mentioned here. The European Convention on Human Rights totally eliminated any reference to the right of equality before the law and contains solely an article regarding non-discrimination in the final provisions which follows the catalogue of human rights and freedoms. An attempt to include a guarantee for the protection of a general right to equality before the law in later years failed.[23] The main objections to this attempt were that it seemed inadvisable to include a general rule which could endanger the system of a restrictive enumeration of human rights in an international instrument.

(iii). THE COVENANTS

In the two Covenants the tradition of the Universal Declaration is followed, at least in the beginning. Part II of the two Covenants contains a rule of non-discrimination which largely follows article 2 of the Universal Declaration. In addition, article 3 introduces the undertaking to ensure the equal right of men and women in the enjoyment of all rights set forth in the respective Covenants.

A substantive difference from former instruments can be found in article 26 of the Covenant on Civil and Political Rights, concerning the relations between the rule of non-discrimination and the principles of equality before the law and equal protection of the law. In an earlier draft[24] the rule and the principles were mentioned side by side without establishing or defining the mutual relations between both of them. In the Third Committee of the General Assembly in 1961 the rule of non-discrimination was introduced into the guarantee of equality before the law. A vigorous reaction followed, aiming at a clear distinction between both principles. The result was a strange compromise: equality before the law and the equal protection of the law are guaranteed as such. The rule of non-discrimination, however, is subordinated to these two principles. This subordination has the practical consequences that no strict rule of non-discrimination is established. By this subordination the guarantee of non-discrimination is certainly weakened. It may be asked whether this weakening is actual. In any case one cannot say that the rule of non-discrimination, by its subordination to the principle of equality before the law, has lost any normative effect. When unacceptable criteria for differentiation are mentioned, this at least has the effect of reversing the burden of proof concerning the arbitrary character of the distinction.

The compromise achieved has the advantage of dogmatic clarity. Whether the practical political disadvantages[25] are considerable is open to doubt. With the Covenants, the history of general provisions regarding the guarantees of equality and non-discrimination is concluded. When reviewing later developments in special fields, it may appear that further progress has been achieved.

3. NON-DISCRIMINATION

(a). The catalogue of criteria

The practical importance of the rule of non-discrimination is largely determined by the addition of certain criteria and it has now to be asked *what* criteria are selected, *why*, and *how* the relations between them have to be determined.

Whereas the Charter of the United Nations expressly mentions only four criteria in its clauses on non-discrimination—i.e., race, sex, language and religion,[26] this catalogue has been considerably enlarged since the Universal Declaration on Human Rights in 1948. In addition to "race", "colour" also appears. Furthermore, political or other opinions, national or social origin, property, birth or other status (art. 2 (1)) are added. The Covenants of 1966 have taken over this catalogue verbatim and it has also been copied by regional human rights instruments and by a number of State Constitutions drafted after 1948.

Though this catalogue is not exhaustive ("distinction of any kind, such as...."), it may be asked why only these criteria have been selected and not others. In some cases, corresponding rights and freedoms set forth in the Universal Declaration can be found, such as

sex: equality of men and women (Art. 16)
religion: freedom of religion (Art. 18)
political or other opinions: freedom of thought and opinion (Art. 18/19)
property: right to own property (Art. 17)

For other criteria, such as "race ", this is not the case. Apparently there is no answer to the question from a systematic point of view. Listed are just those criteria which, according to experience, have led to unlawful discrimination. The catalogue is based on historical experience and reflects values which are prized at present. A hundred years ago the list would have been composed in a different way and might have included such items as honour and dignity. It is likely that in the year 2080 some items may have disappeared and others added.

As to the relations between the different criteria, it may be said that some are more important than others. That the four criteria mentioned in the Charter are more important than the other ones is already recognized by the fact that article 4 of the Covenant on Civil and Political Rights regarding the derogations of fundamental rights only requires that discrimination not be based on the grounds of race, colour, sex, language, religion or social origin. The other criteria are not mentioned. It is not possible to define a single criterion fixing its limits precisely. On the basis of article 1 of the International Convention on the Elimination of all Forms of Racial Discrimination, "race" includes colour, descent, national or ethnic origin. Ethnic origin relates to language, social origin and even religion. Political and other opinions are closely connected to national and social origin, to birth and other status. Certain criteria overlap. Hardly any of them can appear alone without affecting others.

In the following, only the three important criteria of discrimination are reviewed, namely, sex, race and religion.

(b). Discrimination based on sex

"It is a fundamental principle...that Parliament can do everything but make a woman a man, and a man a woman".[27] With this "grotesque expression which has almost become proverbial",[28] one of the problems of the legal equality between men and women is caught in a slogan: men and women are human beings who are biologically different from each other. This difference cannot be removed by the legal order. From this difference, however, it does not necessarily follow that their legal position is different. Both can be entitled to equal rights. This is the target that human rights instruments try to reach. They do it with care and precaution.

(i). THE CHARTER AND THE UNIVERSAL DECLARATION

In the Charter, faith is affirmed "in the equal rights of men and women" (Preamble). Non-discrimination as to sex with respect to human rights is stated twice (art. 1 (3); 55 (c) Charter), not as an independent rule but as the modality for the fulfillment of other rules. In the internal sphere of the UN, equality is established (art. 8). In the *Universal Declaration* no general rule is to be found stating that men and women shall have equal rights. The non-discrimination clause of the Charter is repeated (art. 2 (1)), equal rights in a limited field (as to marriage, during marriage and at its dissolution) are stated, but otherwise the equality of men and women is only indirectly expressed by using "everyone" or "all" as beneficiaries of the rights set forth.

(ii). UNITED NATIONS ACTIVITIES

Considerable activity has occurred in United Nations organs, as if a general rule has already been established that it is their task to eliminate, as far as possible, existing legal differences between man and woman. This activity is dedicated to the political rights of women, to those of nationality, civil law matters (especially marriage), education and economic and social life. A great number of Conventions have been concluded, and many decisions or recommendations have been adopted either by the General Assembly, by the International Labour Organization or by Unesco.[29]

(iii). COVENANTS ON HUMAN RIGHTS

Developments in special fields must be considered in order to show the context in which progress has been made towards a general guarantee. Both Covenants, adopted by the General Assembly 18 years after the Universal Declaration, provide in Part II, which contains the general provisions, an article 3 which reads in almost identical terms:

"The States Parties to the Present Covenant undertake to ensure the equal right of men and women to the enjoyment of all civil and political (all economic, social and cultural) rights set forth in the present Covenant."

This article 3 is apparently not a fundamental right of individuals—as results from a comparison with the manner in which such rights are drafted in Part III of the Covenant on Civil and Political Rights—but a State obligation. Furthermore, the principle of equality between men and women is not established as such and in an absolute manner but in relation to the enjoyment of the other rights set forth in the Covenants.

It may nevertheless be called a step forward in comparison to the non-discrimination clause of art. 2 (1). Such a clause is of a limitative character, while art. 3 indicates a positive aim to be achieved.

(iv). THE DECLARATION AND CONVENTION ON THE ELIMINATION OF DISCRIMINATION
AGAINST WOMEN

One year later—in 1967—an instrument was adopted by the General Assembly which summed up the progress made in the last twenty years and also contributed to a further development: The Declaration on the Elimination of Discrimination against Women.[30] This Declaration is unique in the drafting history of United Nations instruments.

The normal procedure is that a Declaration precedes a Convention as in the case of the Universal Declaration and the Covenants. There are also cases in which the organs of the United Nations have taken only the first step of adopting a Declaration without continuing to prepare also a Convention; the main examples are the Declaration on Granting of Independence to Colonial Countries and Peoples, and the Declaration on Principles of International Law concerning Friendly Relations and Co-operation among States. Here, however, a number of Conventions had already been adopted by the United Nations Organization or their specialized agencies and a declaration followed only afterwards, in order to present a systematic review of the progress achieved and to add new claims for further progress.

More recently, in December 1979, the General Assembly adopted the Convention on the Elimination of All Forms of Discrimination against Women which is considered in detail in Chapter 10 below.

(v). CONCLUSIONS

In order to summarize the result of this investigation it seems apparent that the best results have been achieved in the political field. In the field of education and labour relations a degree of progress has been achieved with the active help of the competent specialized agencies. The greatest lacunae are to be found in the field of civil and private law. This may be partly due to the lack of sufficiently vigorous and organized pressure from those interested.

(c). Racial discrimination

(i). THE CHARTER

"Distinction as to race" holds a predominant place in the United Nations *Charter*. It appears in the first article and as the first of the four banned grounds for distinction: "race, sex, language or religion".

It is certainly for historical reasons that the "race" question is thus privileged. It recalls the holocaust in which millions died only because they belonged to a certain race. In the meantime the problem of the conflict between whites and coloured, between colonial powers and colonized peoples has gained increasing importance. The race question is even more serious when seen from the viewpoint of decolonization and of the elimination of the remnants of colonial rule, especially in South Africa.

(ii). THE INTERNATIONAL COURT OF JUSTICE

The importance of this problem is also marked by another fact: with respect to racial discrimination the *International Court of Justice* has stated that the provisions of the Charter regarding the promotion of human rights are, under certain conditions, legally binding on States Parties:

"To establish. . .and to enforce distinctions, exclusions, restrictions and limitations exclusively *based on grounds of race*, colour, descent or national or ethnic origin which constitute a denial of fundamental human rights *is a flagrant violation of the purposes and principles of the Charter.*" (Opinion on the presence of South Africa in Namibia I.C.J. Reports, 1971, para. 131).

In no other case has the Court stated so clearly that the denial of fundamental rights may constitute a violation of the Charter and therefore be illegal.

(iii). RACE AND OTHER CRITERIA OF DISCRIMINATION

Before discussing what "race" is and how it may be defined, one element should be mentioned which enables the rule of non-discrimination to be *distinguished from other criteria*. Invidious discrimination on the grounds of sex, language or religion can be eliminated by the full realization and implementation of specific human rights. If equality between men and women in their mutual relations, if linguistic freedom, if freedom of religion and belief are fully guaranteed and if these guarantees are also implemented, discrimination on these grounds should disappear. There is a correlation between these *specific freedoms* and the possibility of discriminatory acts. In respect of "race" no such specific freedom exists. Racial discrimination will only disappear if full equality—in its broadest sense—is achieved. One could even say that to this end all of the fundamental human rights have to be implemented. The relations between fundamental human rights and racial discrimination will be further defined later.

(iv). DEFINITION OF "RACE"

The *definition* of "race" and "racial discrimination" presents many problems. A vast literature has been written by anthropologists, biologists, social scientists and lawyers. Only the definition given by sociologists can be used for legal purposes: "a human group that defines itself and/or is defined by other groups as different from other groups by virtue of innate and immutable physical characteristics".[31]

Important is the subjective element: "a group that is defined by other groups as different. . ." It is Unesco which has more systematically considered the racial question using an interdisciplinary approach. It has always endeavoured to associate in its work biologists, anthropologists, sociologists, jurists, ethnographers, historians and geneticians, as well as representatives of other scientific disciplines. Four Unesco Declarations[32] constitute landmarks on the road leading to the study of race and racism:

1. Declaration on Race, July 1950
2. Declaration on Race and Racial Differences, June 1951
3. Proposals on Biological Aspects of the Racial Question, August 1964
4. Declaration on Race and Racial Prejudices, September 1967

These four declarations constituted the basis for the preparation of the very significant Declaration on Race and Racial Prejudice, adopted by the Unesco General Conference in 1978. The significance of this declaration is considered in Chapter 13 below.

The most important legal definition in this general area is contained in the International Convention on the Elimination of All Forms of Racial Discrimination (1965),[33] which (in article 1(1)) includes besides race, also colour, descent, and national and ethnic origin. As mentioned above, "race" refers to a group that is socially defined on the basis of physical criteria. "Colour" is only one of these criteria. "Descent" means a social group defined on the basis of language, culture or history. National and ethnic origin is mainly determined on the basis of consciousness. In all these cases it is not an objective but a subjective definition which, however, refers to different criteria. The important question is always whether a person is held to be physically, socially or culturally different by others, whether this is true or not. In general it is another person who determines the "race" of a person.

It results from this definition that the concept of "race" is very broad and covers a multitude of cases of varying intensity and importance. The relationship between Bantus and Afrikaaners in South Africa is included as well as the relationship between Pakistani and British workers in an English factory or between Italian workers from Verona and colleagues in a Bavarian factory, though both may be of the same Langobardian "descent", but speaking two different languages and adhering to different ethnic traditions.

It has been asserted that a substantial difference exists between "race relations" and the relations between ethnic groups: a solution of race problems is only conceivable on the basis of complete equality and integration, while an ethnic group had a legitimate interest to reach a certain autonomy on the basis of special privileges.[34] Certainly different opinions exist about adequate solutions of these group problems. These should, however, not be introduced into the definition of theoretical concepts. According to positive law, national or ethnic groups can also be the object of "racial discrimination".[35]

The question of "nationality", in the sense of "citizenship" (Article 1 (3) of the above mentioned convention), is not connected to "race". The foreigner may be treated on another basis than the co-national. It is not even required that all foreigners should be treated on the same basis. There is room for *most-favoured* treatment for the nationals of certain States as for instance within the European Community. If an Italian or French worker is admitted to work without a work permit in other member States of the Community, this does not constitute racial discrimination with respect to workers from outside the Community as for instance Yugoslavs.

Religion is not one of the criteria which would be relevant in order to distinguish a racial group from another group. It is, however, possible that the consciousness to constitute a "people" is based on religious tradition. In this way, for instance, the Jewish people acquired the quality of an ethnic group. The antagonism between Israel and Muslim Arab countries is a racial problem in the sense of Article 1 of the Convention. It may be questioned whether the same applies in the case of relations between Jews in other countries and the dominant national group or groups in these countries.

(v). DEFINITION OF RACIAL DISCRIMINATION

The *concept* of "discrimination" in general has been discussed above. In the special case of "racial discrimination" it is required that:
- there take place a certain action or omission described as distinction, exclusion, restriction or preference;
- that the act or omission be based on certain grounds;
- that the action must have a certain effect: that of nullifying or impairing the recognition, enjoyment or exercise of human rights and fundamental freedoms in certain fields.

All three requirements have to be fulfilled.[36]

(vi). RELATION TO HUMAN RIGHTS

Relations between racial discrimination and the *protection of human rights* exist in two directions: racial discrimination takes place if the enjoyment of human rights is denied (cf. Article 5 of the Convention). Human rights for this reason are listed in the Convention. This catalogue, however, is not limitative but only exemplary. It does not exclude the possibility that racial discrimination may occur where the general rule of equality is not respected.

The respect for human rights may also limit the non-discrimination rule and its consequences. This is shown by Article 4 of the Convention which stipulates that certain kinds of dissemination of ideas are punishable offences and are to be declared illegal, and that the prohibition of certain organizations is made dependent on whether their activities are or are not carried out in conformity with the guarantees of human rights. In this way a conflict between two elements of the legal order arises. The guarantees of human rights may, in the interest of freedom, limit the possibility of prohibiting acts of racial discrimination. Consequently, it should not be argued that all human rights may be limited (according to Article 29 of the Universal Declaration) by the just requirements of public order (to which also belongs the rule of non-discrimination as to race), because Article 30 of the Declaration—on the other hand—protects all rights and freedoms against destruction. This disposition clearly restricts the possibility of limiting such rights and freedoms, preventing their essential content from being undermined.

(vii). INTERNAL MEASURES OF IMPLEMENTATION

States parties are obliged to take all legislative, judicial and administrative measures in order to prevent, to prohibit and eradicate all forms of racial discrimination *within their own territories*. This implies that the *constitutional order* of the States provides for full equality of all citizens and that a special provision is included in order to oblige legislative, judicial and administrative organs to take the necessary measures to avoid any discrimination based on race. A general rule which provides for equality before the law is not sufficient (cf. the Convention, Article 2(1) preamble and litera (a) and (b)). The States are also obliged to review existing laws and regulations (lit.(c)) and to ensure effective legal protection and remedies against discriminatory measures taken by State organs as well as by private organizations or individuals (Article 2(d) combined with Article 6).

Special emphasis is made in declaring illegal and prohibiting organizations which promote and incite racial discrimination (Article 2(d) and Article 4(b)). Here the question is raised whether prohibition is in all cases an appropriate measure. The Convention requires appropriate means as required by circumstances. Does this mean that the Member State is obliged to take repressive measures when it may be foreseen that they increase the danger of forcing such organizations to go underground? It is, on the other hand, expressly stated that the States parties dispose of a certain discretion (see Article 2(2): "when the circumstances so warrant") with regard to special temporary measures in favour of certain racial groups.

Administrative measures are also foreseen in the fields of *teaching education, culture and information* with a view to combating racial prejudices and to promoting understanding, tolerance and friendship among racial or ethnic groups (Article 7). This opens up a vast field of activities. It is not limited to purely verbal propaganda or statements but comprises also the establishment of mechanisms for conciliation and other preventive measures. If one recalls that the concept of "race" is based largely on the prejudiced view that another social group is different and for this reason inferior in value, the importance of such precautionary arrangements is evident. Some States with racial problems lay considerable stress upon such activities and have reached remarkable results. The work of the Race Relations Boards and Community Councils in the United Kingdom should be mentioned as an interesting example.[37]

In this field, however, not too much should be expected from direct and official State activity. Such efforts decidedly need the initiative from social groups in order to be effective.

Among the measures to be taken in the internal order, penal prosecutions are only mentioned here as a last resort. Though in certain extreme cases repression by drastic remedies cannot be avoided, it will often only have an external effect without going to the crux of the problem. One should not forget that racial discrimination is a kind of social disease and that the results of fighting other social diseases by punishments are not very encouraging.

The Convention goes very far in obliging States parties to declare all kinds of discriminatory acts as offences punishable by law. Although incitement to acts of violence is in general punishable without respect to motivation, incitement to racial discrimination as such and its constituent elements are difficult to prove. The punishment of the simple dissemination of ideas based on racial superiority is hardly compatible with the freedom of thought and of opinion, and does not promise positive results. It seems hopeless to fight against ideas with penalties. They are better fought with arguments.

(viii). INTERNATIONAL MEASURES OF IMPLEMENTATION

Since racial discrimination ignores State boundaries, internal measures are not sufficient. They have to be complemented by measures on the international level. The first step towards an international consensus regarding this evil has been made. In conformity with the basic pronouncement of the Charter, the States parties to the Convention have expressly *condemned* racial discrimination as such (Article 2(1)), and two of its forms: racial segregation and apartheid. They have undertaken to eradicate all practices of this nature in territories under their jurisdiction (Article 3). This territorial limitation pays tribute to the principle of domestic jurisdiction (Article 2(7) Charter).

The establishment of the Committee for the Elimination of Racial Discrimination (CERD) with machinery to supervise the observance of the Convention has the effect of installing a pillory at which States parties have to confess what they do inside their territories. The Committee has at the same time the task of acting as a conciliator in controversial situations (Article 11–13). It may be authorized by special declarations to examine *petitions* of individuals in order to seek redress (Article 14).

A step towards declaring extreme forms of racial discrimination—specifically apartheid—to be crimes under international law was taken with the adoption by the General Assembly in 1973 of the International Convention on the Suppression and Punishment of the Crime of Apartheid.[38]

Since its first Session in 1946, the General Assembly has been concerned with the race conflicts in southern Africa. All kinds of methods and procedures available have been employed by the UN in its struggle against racial discrimination and apartheid in this country. By different means UN organs have tried to isolate South Africa politically, culturally and economically.[39] When it appeared that strenuous efforts over thirty years had met with no decisive success, the General Assembly in 1974 excluded the delegates of South Africa from its deliberations. This is not the place to discuss whether this measure was taken in conformity with the Charter, which, in Article 6, requests a recommendation of the Security Council before the General Assembly may expel a Member "which has persistently violated the Principles" of the Charter. The question only arises as to whether such a measure is appropriate to enforce the rule of non-discrimination. Doubts expressed are similar to those expressed with regard to the question whether penal punishment is appropriate to heal the evil of racial discrimination. With the exclusion of a State, the Organization renounces its possibilities of control. Isolation is likely to create obstinacy and embitter conflicts. Has not the Organization of United Nations been created in order to solve conflicts and not to aggravate them?

At the end of this study regarding racial discrimination an appraisal is expected. Can it be said that all the measures introduced in order to limit racial discrimination have had a positive effect? Certainly at present one is better informed on existing problems and States have been induced to pay more attention to them. Some have even revised their policy. Public opinion is more vigilant. This is not negligible.

(d). Religious discrimination

At the end of this chapter some remarks about the tendency to eliminate "religious intolerance" in protecting any human being against discrimination on the ground of religion or beliefs are appropriate.

(i). HISTORY

Some authors are of the opinion that the idea of the protection of human rights and freedoms as a whole had first been developed in the field of religious freedom. In so far as they refer to attempts made at the beginning of the Modern Age to destroy the unity of the Roman Catholic Church, this thesis seems problematic. Reformers such as Luther, Calvin, Zwingli or the Founders of the Church of England did not seek an absolute freedom of the individual, as such, but tried to replace an existing hierarchy by a new one. It is, however, true that they largely based their struggle against the traditional ecclesiastic rulers on theories developed during the Italian Renaissance which recognized, for the human being as such, authentic and autonomous rights not derived from divinity. A long time elapsed before constitutional rights were guaranteed to individuals.

(ii). RELIGION AND RELIGIOUS FREEDOM

Besides the problem of historical legitimacy, there are much more difficult ones of an intrinsic character. There is a multitude of religions and not all of them consider the concept of tolerance as an element of their doctrine.[40] If a religion demands that its followers spread its own faith and win new adherents there may ensue a situation in which the rules of this religion come into collision with the principle of religious tolerance. This problem has been formulated in the following extreme terms: "Freedom of religion and conscience does not only imply the right to profess one's own religion, but also the right to engage in convincing others that its own doctrines are 'right'—it includes the right of dogmatic intolerance" (W. Kaegi). The author apparently has in mind what certain religions may expect from their followers instead of asking himself what a free society is willing to concede to them: the individual right to profess a certain religion, to exercise this religion, to abandon a religion or confession and to be protected against any discrimination by public organs as well as by other citizens on grounds of religion or belief. He is silent on the limits which this guarantee attaches to religious activities: i.e. respect for the religions of others. His formulation is, however, illustrative of the possible collision between the freedom of religion and religion itself. The same may occur with regard to agnostic or atheistic beliefs. Where the same existence of transcendental beliefs is denied categorically, there is no room for the respect of theistic thoughts and religion.

(iii). PROTECTION AGAINST INDIVIDUALS

Another problem is created by the fact that freedom of religion and conscience have to be protected not only against the State and those who exercise public power but also against interference by other individuals or private groups.

(iv). STATE AND RELIGION

Nearly all Constitutions of modern States contain more or less elaborate guarantees for freedom of religion and conscience, and for protection against discrimination on grounds of religion or belief. They vary according to the position the religious community or communities hold in the State and in its society. There are still States where a "State religion" exists and certain positions in public life are only accessible to its true followers. There are States which, though giving a certain preference to one religion or confession, nevertheless tolerate others. There are totally neutral States which treat all theistic and also non-theistic or atheistic beliefs on an equal basis, and finally there are many States where atheism is officially favoured and where theistic religious communities are in danger of finding themselves in difficult situations.

(v). INTERNATIONAL GUARANTEES

In view of these divergent situations it is not surprising that the idea of an international guarantee for the principle of religious tolerance gained recognition in this century.

1) In the Peace Treaties ending the First World War the question of religious freedom appeared predominantly in connection with the protection of national minorities—which often were also at the same time religious minorities. The Covenant of the League of Nations mentioned this problem, however, only in connection with the responsibility of Mandatories in African countries, "under conditions which will guarantee freedom of conscience or religion, subject only to the maintenance of public order or morals, the prohi-

bition of abuses such as slave trade ..." (cf. Article XXII, para. 5 and 6). This mention appears rather marginal.[41]

2) During and after the Second World War the problem became of greater importance after religious groups—the Jewish communities among others— had been persecuted by National Socialists. In the joint Declaration by the United Nations of January 1, 1942, the principle of religious freedom—not only of the protection of religious minorities—has a predominant place:

"that complete victory over their enemies is essential to defend...religious freedom, and to preserve human rights and justice in their own lands as well as in other lands,..."

In this formulation a positive approach apparently prevails, directed to the active defence of religion.

3) This positive approach has not been incorporated into the United Nations Charter. Though proposals to do so were presented, the Charter as adopted refers only to "human rights and fundamental freedoms" in general, leaving it open whether the freedom of religion is such a fundamental right. It is added, however, that the respect for these rights is incompatible with "distinctions" also "as to religion".[42] From this reference alone it cannot be concluded that the freedom of religion is presupposed. If one compares the three other criteria: race, sex and language, there is also no corresponding "freedom" as regards "race".

4) The Universal Declaration of Human Rights, adopted on 10 December 1948 by the General Assembly as "a common standard of achievement for all peoples and all nations", without creating legal obligations,[43] contains a right to freedom of religion—together with the rights to freedom of thought and conscience (Article 18). It is guaranteed "without distinction of any kind such as...religion" (Article 2(1)). It has been noted that the relations between this right and the prohibition of religious discrimination raise special problems.[44] For one who is enjoying freedom of religion and exercising this right may easily come into a situation where he neglects the freedom of those who follow other creeds or beliefs.[45]

5) When the Declaration was transformed into a binding legal instrument, namely the International Covenant on Civil and Political Rights of 1966,[46] the problem of these precarious relations was taken care of. The guarantee in Article 18(1) of the Covenant clearly states that "this right shall include freedom to have and to adopt a religion or belief of his choice", not only, as according to Article 18 of the Declaration, "to manifest his religion or belief". Here a positive approach, as in 1942, appears again. The right to have or to adopt a religion or belief is no longer subjected to limitations. Only "the freedom to *manifest* one's religion or beliefs may be subject... to... limitations" and the law may prescribe such limitations only if they are *necessary* to protect certain interests. On the other hand, the clause regarding prohibited discrimination (Article 2(2)) does not refer to the substance of the guaranteed

rights and freedoms as such, but to their *exercise*. The result is that manifestations of religion or belief have to be exercised in a manner which does not discriminate against the followers of other religions or beliefs.

The field in which religious freedom may come into conflict with non-discrimination on grounds of religion has become narrower. It does not extend to the formulation of the doctrine but is limited to acts of the followers when manifesting their creed in relation to others. Here tolerance has to be respected. In extreme cases this rule is sanctioned: "Any advocacy of...religious hatred, that constitutes incitement to discrimination, hostility or violence shall be prohibited by law" (Article 20).

6) Even before the Covenants got their final form the project was taken up in the organs of the United Nations in 1962 with the view to elaborating a special Declaration and Convention "on the Elimination of All Forms of Religious Intolerance", distinct from the Declaration and Convention on the Elimination of All Forms of Racial Discrimination. This separation of religious and racial discrimination was apparently motivated by political considerations: the conflict between Arab Countries and Israel should not come under the instruments regarding racial discrimination.[47] Separate instruments regarding these two matters are, however, also justified for reasons of substance apart from political considerations. Religion as such is based on positive values, race is not. Even if there is consensus that intolerance based on race as well as on religion should be eliminated in the interest of the international community, the situation with regard to these two phenomena differs. Religious strictness is a counter value to religious tolerance. Racism is merely based on a prejudice, on a bias and is not based on a value which has to be brought into balance with racial tolerance.

This fundamental difference between the two problems may explain why nearly twenty years have been spent by the General Assembly and its Third Committee, by ECOSOC, the Commission on Human Rights and the Sub-commission on Prevention of Discrimination and Protection of Minorities in discussing the Declaration and Convention on Religious Discrimination, while the Racial Declaration and Convention were drafted and accepted in less than six years. In 1981 the Declaration was finally adopted by the General Assembly.[48] This delay is due only in part to controversies about procedure. For some time work continued simultaneously on drafting the Declaration as well as the Convention, until the General Assembly decided at its twenty-seventh Session (by Resolution 3027) to give priority to the completion of the Declaration before resuming consideration of the draft Covenant.[49]

NOTES

1. See, generally, Rosalyn Higgins: *The Development of International Law through the Political Organs of the United Nations*, Oxford University Press, London (1963); Rupert Emerson: *Self-Determination Revisited in the Era of Decolonization*, 9 Occasional Papers

in International Affairs, Harvard University, Cambridge, Massachusetts (1964); Harold S. Johnson: *Self-Determination within the Community of Nations*, A.W. Sijthoff, Leyden (1967); S. Calogeropoulos-Stratis: *Le droit des peuples à disposer d'eux-mêmes*, Etabl. Emile Bruyant, Bruxelles (1973); A. Rigo-Sureda: *The Evolution of the Right of Self-Determination—A Study of the United Nations Practice*, A.W. Sijthoff, Leyden (1973); and UN docs. E. 1979. XIV.5 and E/CN 4/sub. 2/406/Rev./(1979).

2. Foreign Relations of the United States, Washington, 1918, Supp. 1, Vol. 1, 12 and C.C. Hyde: *International Law, Chiefly as Interpreted and Applied by the United States*, 2nd. ed., Boston, Little Brown and Company (1947) p. 367.

3. Cf. Art. 22 of the Covenant of the League of Nations.

4. Cf. Sarah Wambaugh: *Plebiscites since the World War, with Collection of Official Documents*, Washington 1933.

5. Cf. Harold Nicolson: *Peace making 1919* (1933), p. 193.

6. For examples, see Alfred Cobban, *National Self-Determination*, 2nd edition, University of Chicago Press, Chicago, 1947.

7. Hans Kelsen: *The Law of the United Nations*, London, Stevens and Sons Ltd. (1951), p. 52 seq.

8. Cf. the abundant documentation delivered by Hu Chou-Young: *Das Selbstbestimmungsrecht als eine Vorbedingung des völligen Genusses der Menschenrechte*, 52 Zürcher Studien zum internationalen Recht, Polygraphischer Verlag, Zürich (1972), pp. 112-216.

9. Rupert Emerson: "Self-determination" 65 AJIL (1971), p. 463.

10. Cf. Clyde Eagleton: "Excesses of Self-Determination", *31 Foreign Affairs* (July 1953), p. 592; Joseph L. Kunz: "The principle of self-determination of peoples, particularly in the practice of the United Nations", in: Kurt Rabl (ed.): *Inhalt, Wesen und gegenwärtige praktische Bedeutung des Selbstbestimmungsrechts der Völker*, Verlag Robert Lerche, Munich, (1964), pp. 128-170.

11. Adopted 24 October 1970—cf. Annex to Resolution 2625 (XXV).

12. This is neglected by Karl Doehring: The Right of Self-Determination in International Law, *14 Berichte der Deutschen Gesellschaft für Völkerrecht*, C.F. Müller, Karlsruhe (1973).

13. With regard to the important case of Bangladesh cf. Ved. P. Nanda: "Self-determination in international law: the tragic tale of two cities—Islamabad (West-Pakistan) and Dacca (East Pakistan)", 66 AJIL (1972) pp. 321-336 and Commission Internationale des Juristes: *Bangladesh: A study in International Law* (1972).

14. Cf. A Cassese: Self-determination of Peoples, para 7 in: L. Henkin (ed.): *International Bill of Rights—The Covenant on Civil and Political Rights*, Columbia University Press, New York (1981).

15. Gerhard Leibholz: "Equality as a principle in German and Swiss constitutional law", in: *Politics and Law*, A.W. Sijthoff, Leyden (1965), p. 302.

16. *Ibid*, p. 303.

17. *Ibid*, p. 304.

18. J.D.B. Mitchell: *Constitutional Law*, 2nd ed., W. Green & Son Ltd. Edinburgh (1968) p. 56.

19. Hyder: *Equality of Treatment and Trade Discrimination in International Law*, The Hague (1968), p. 14.

20. N. Robinson: *The Universal Declaration of Human Rights*, Institute of Jewish Affairs—World Jewish Congress, New York (1958) p. 104; René Cassin: "La Déclaration universelle et la mise en oeuvre des droits de l'homme", RCDAI (1951) p. 277.

21. Last para. of the Preamble.

22. Cf. N. Robinson: op. cit. (note 20) p. 110.

23. Cf. K.J. Partsch: *Die Rechte und Freiheiten der Europäischen Menschenrechtskonvention*, Duncker e.Humblot, Berlin (1966) p. 90, Note 295; Jean de Meyer: *La Convention européenne des droits de l'homme et le Pacte international relatif aux droits*

Karl Josef Partsch

civils et politiques, Centre international d'études et de recherches européennes, Cours 1968 Edition Zega-Henle, Belgique (1969) p. 26.

24. The drafting history is reported in detail by Egon Schwelb: "The International Convention on the Elimination of All Forms of Racial Discrimination", 15 *ICLQ* (1966) p. 997 (1018); see also Wilhelm Kewenig: *Der Grundsatz der Nicht-Diskriminierung im Völkerrecht der internationalen Handelsbeziehungen*, Band 1, Athenäum Verlag, Frankfurt/M, (1972); and E.W. Vierdag: *The Concept of Discrimination in International Law*, Martinus Nijhoff, The Hague (1973) p. 120.

25. Cf. Egon Schwelb: op. cit. (note 24), p. 109.

26. In Art. 1(3), 13(2)b, 55(c) and 76(c).

27. De Lolme, *Constitution de l'Angleterre*, Amsterdam 1778.

28. A.V. Dicey, *Law of the Constitution*, 3rd edition, London 1889.

29. Cf. the exhaustive documentation in: *United Nations Action in the Field of Human Rights*, 2nd. ed. 1980 (Sales No. E.79 XIV 6).

30. GA Res. 2263 (XXII) (1967).

31. Cf. Pierre van den Berghe: *Race and Racism, a comparative perspective*, New York (1967), p. 9.

32. See texts of these Declarations and that adopted in 1978 in *Declaration on Race and Racial Prejudice* (Paris, Unesco, 1979).

33. E. Schwelb, op. cit. (note 24), p. 996 seq.; N. Lerner: *The UN Convention on the Elimination of All Forms of Racial Discrimination*, 2nd ed., Sijthoff and Noordhoff, Alphen aan den Rijn (1980), pp. 25-33.

34. J. Delbrück: *Die Rassenfrage als Problem des Völkerrechts und nationaler Rechtsordnungen*, Athenäum Verlag, Frankfurt (1971) p. 18.

35. Cf. Article 1(1) of Racial Discrimination Convention.

36. Cf. E. Schwelb, op.cit. (note 24) p. 1001.

37. See S. Abbot (ed.), *The Prevention of Racial Discrimination in Britain*, Oxford 1971.

38. See Article XV(1) of the Convention. For more details, see Part II, sub-section I, Chapter 11.

39. See chapter 10 *infra*.

40. A. Krishnaswami: *A Study of Discrimination in the matter of Religious Rights and Practices*, United Nations (Sub-Commission on Prevention of Discrimination and Protection of Minorities), New York (1960) Introduction (Sales No. 60 XIV.2).

41. E. Luard (ed.): *The International Protection of Human Rights*, New York/Washington, D.C. (1967) pp. 22-38.

42. A. Krishnaswami, op. cit. (note 40) p. 12—An express reference to "religion"—always in connection with the "without discrimination clause" is to be found in article 1(3), 13(1)b, 55(c) and 76(c) of the Charter.

43. Cf. M. Ganji: *International Protection of Human Rights*, Geneva/Paris (1962), p. 165.

44. A. Krishnaswami, op. cit. (note 40) p. 15.

45. Cf. Article 29(2) of the Declaration.

46. It came into force on 23 March 1976.

47. Cf. supra under para. 72.

48. Cf. the drafting history in: *United Nations Action in the field of Human Rights*, 2nd. ed. (1980); and UN doc. E/CN-4/1145 (1973), A/9322 (1975), E/CN-4/1305 and Add. 1-3, and E/CN-4/1337. The Declaration on the Elimination of All Forms of Intolerance and Discrimination Based on Religion or Belief was proclaimed by the General Assembly in December 1981 in resolution 36/55

49. See Chapter 10, *infra*.

5 Survey of the Positive International Law of Human Rights

Theodoor C. van Boven

INTRODUCTION: DIVERSITY OF SOURCES

Since the Second World War international human rights law has been developing in an unprecedented way and has become a very substantive part of international law as a whole. International organizations, whose concern is directed at the promotion of the well-being of the human person (groups as well as individuals) or certain categories of human persons, have been most instrumental in this respect. Very prominent is of course the United Nations, but much credit should also be given to its Specialized Agencies, notably the ILO and Unesco. Regional intergovernmental organizations, such as the Council of Europe and the Organization of American States, have also greatly contributed to the development of international human rights law. Membership, political climate and the particular field of competence of the various organizations concerned have an important bearing upon the content and nature of the human rights instruments elaborated by these organizations.

This development of positive international human rights law, has been inspired by, among other factors, the desire to establish a comprehensive system for the promotion and protection of human rights. This idea was reflected in the mandate extended in 1946 to the UN Commission on Human Rights to prepare an international bill of rights, which led eventually to the adoption of the Universal Declaration of Human Rights in 1948 and of the International Covenants in 1966. Other comprehensive instruments, covering a large number of human rights, have been drawn up at the regional level. They are the American Declaration of the Rights and Duties of Man of 1948, the American Convention on Human Rights of 1969, the European Convention on Human Rights of 1950 with its Five Protocols, and the European Social Charter of 1961.

It should also be noted that a number of specific and separate human rights instruments, inasmuch as they are interlinked and subject to a unified implementation system, may be considered to form, *in toto*, a comprehensive and consistent body of law and to come close to the concept of one general instrument. The international conventions and recommendations of the ILO are a case in point. They represent, in their totality, what is considered a *corpus juris* of social justice.

The other approach, prevalent in developing positive international human rights law, consists of the elaboration of human rights instruments with a more specific or limited purview. Certain categories of persons may need special attention as is reflected in specific international instruments aiming at the protection of refugees, stateless persons, migrant workers, children, disabled persons, etc. Specific instruments may also be drawn up with a view to defining and safeguarding certain rights in a more elaborate manner, e.g. the right to freedom of association or the right to education. Other specific instruments seek to eliminate or prevent focus on one specific form of discrimination, such as race or sex, and aim at the elimination of that special type of discrimination in relation to the whole field of human rights. The UN Declaration and the International Convention on the Elimination of All Forms of Racial Discrimination and the Declaration and Convention on the Elimination of Discrimination against Women are such instruments. Non-discrimination instruments may also focus on one particular human right in order to guarantee the exercise of that right without discrimination as to race, colour, sex, language, religion, political or other opinion, national or social origin, economic condition. The ILO Convention (No. 111) concerning Discrimination in Respect of Employment and Occupation and the Unesco Convention against Discrimination in Education are pertinent examples.

Whereas general human rights instruments result from a comprehensive and systematic approach and reflect a human rights concern in the wider sense, specific human rights instruments may result from the work of organizations or agencies with a competence or a responsibility in a particular area. Such specific instruments may also constitute a reply to political or social concerns of an urgent and widely-felt character.

In order to meet urgent demands of large parts of the international community a wide practice has developed, particularly in the UN of incorporating human rights norms in declarations or resolutions. Such instruments may also prove, depending upon circumstances and conditions, to be important sources of international human rights law. Some such instruments have become extremely important and may have more influence than conventions. The Universal Declaration of Human Rights and the Declaration on the Granting of Independence to Colonial Countries and Peoples are typical examples. In these days of law-making as a collective undertaking in international organizations, it is practically impossible to describe positive international human rights law on the basis of a separation between conventional instruments and other instruments, such as declarations.

The following paragraphs do not purport to give a full treatment of substantive human rights law. They are intended as an outline, showing various sources of the international law of human rights. In this respect, attention will be paid to general and specific instruments, drawn up in the form of conventions or declarations, and briefly to such other sources of human rights law as customary law, general principles of law, and decisions of international organs. It should be taken into account that these various sources are not necessarily watertight and separate categories. In many instances their effects are cumulative.

Such cumulation of sources can be found in relation to the Universal Declaration of Human Rights, which as a declaration is perhaps not binding in the same sense as a treaty or convention, but which, through a process of development by practice and custom, contains a great deal of law generally recognized as binding upon members of the international community. Moreover, many of the rights and freedoms enshrined in the Universal Declaration have been converted into treaty law in later international instruments.

1. GENERAL INSTRUMENTS

The most basic instrument laying the foundation of international human rights law is the Charter of the United Nations. The various human rights clauses of the UN Charter speak in terms of "promoting and encouraging respect for human rights and for fundamental freedoms for all without distinction as to race, sex, language, or religion". Particularly important is article 56, containing a "pledge" and as such an obligation for UN members with regard to the achievement of the purposes set forth in the preceding article, which includes a human rights clause along the lines of the formula cited above. It must be conceded that the term "human rights and fundamental freedoms" is not defined in the Charter, but it would be inconceivable if this frequently used term of the Charter had no meaning. It must therefore be assumed that this term stands for elementary human rights norms as discussed above in Chapter 3. It should be noted in this context that in case of a conflict between obligations undertaken under the UN Charter and obligations arising from other international instruments, the obligations under the Charter shall prevail (article 103 of the UN Charter).

The elaboration of the generally-worded human rights clauses of the UN Charter took the form of the International Bill of Human Rights, which encompasses (1) the Universal Declaration of Human Rights, (2) the International Covenant on Economic, Social and Cultural Rights, (3) the International Covenant on Civil and Political Rights, (4) the Optional Protocol to the International Covenant on Civil and Political Rights. This International Bill of Human Rights and its component parts (except the Optional Protocol which deals with a method of international implementation) are general instruments of substantive international human rights law. They present, with a view to establishing a world-wide system for the promotion and protection of human rights, a comprehensive enumeration of a wide variety of human rights and fundamental freedoms, in the recognition that "the inherent dignity and the

equal and inalienable rights of all members of the human family is the foundation of freedom, justice and peace in the world" (para. 1 of the preambles of
these instruments).

On the regional level, the American Declaration of the Rights and Duties of
Man and the American Convention on Human Rights, both elaborated within
the Organization of American States, as well as the European Convention for
the Protection of Human Rights and Fundamental Freedoms and the European Social Charter, drawn up within the framework of the Council of Europe, form the counterparts of the universal instruments noted above.

A close examination of these world-wide and regional instruments for the
promotion and protection of human rights reveals much similarity between
the texts and also striking examples of identity in some respects. This is due
to the fact that the authors of the European Convention and of the American
instruments paid a great deal of attention to the drafting work performed in
the United Nations. It should, moreover, be taken into account that in the
early days of the UN, when a great deal of drafting work was carried out, the
majority views were determined by (Western) European and American representatives. It is therefore no surprise that, by and large, the points of
similarity exceed the differences as between the world-wide and regional
general instruments, in particular as far as the orientation and formulation of
substantive human rights law is concerned.

The general instruments deal with three categories of human rights. First
are the rights which aim at protecting the liberty and the physical and moral
integrity of the human person, including: the right to life; freedom from
slavery, servitude and forced labour; freedom from torture or from cruel,
inhuman or degrading treatment or punishment; the right to freedom from
arbitrary arrest and detention; the right to a fair trial; the right to privacy;
and the right to freedom of thought, conscience and religion. The second
group includes political rights, in particular: the right to freedom of opinion
and expression; the right to peaceful assembly and to freedom of association;
the right to take part in the conduct of public affairs; and the right to vote, to
be elected and to have access to public service. The final category contains
economic, social and cultural rights such as: the right to work, to free choice
of employment and to just and favourable conditions of work; the right to
form and join trade unions, including the right to strike; the right to social
security; the right to rest and leisure; the right to an adequate standard of
living, including food, clothing, housing, medical and social services; the right
to education; and the right to participate in cultural life and to enjoy the
benefits of scientific progress.

The general human rights instruments have certain common features which
are very much part of human rights law. First the principle of equality or
non-discrimination which is in fact a guiding element of all the instruments
and which represents the idea of justice in human rights law. Another common feature is that of limitations which may be applied in relation to the

exercise of rights and freedoms. Some instruments, in particular the Universal Declaration and the American Declaration as well as a "promotional" instrument like the International Covenant on Economic, Social and Cultural Rights, contain a general limitation clause in relation to the instrument as a whole. The limitation clause mentions such factors as respect for the rights of others, the just requirements of morality, public order and the general welfare in a democratic society. On the other hand, the instruments which deal mainly or exclusively with civil and political rights—the International Covenant on Civil and Political Rights as well as the European and American Conventions—are more precise and have special and differentiated limitation clauses in connection with individual articles. These instruments contain, however, also a general limitation clause, allowing States parties to derogate from their obligations in time of public emergency, with the proviso that, from certain elementary rights, no derogation is allowed under any circumstances.

A third common feature is the notion of duties or responsibilities. This notion is particularly well developed in the American Declaration on the Rights and Duties of Man, which outlines the duties of every person in no less than ten articles. Other instruments are less explicit in this respect and contain in the preamble (the International Covenants) or in a special provision (the Universal Declaration and the American Convention) a reference to the duties of every person to the community in which alone—as the Universal Declaration puts it (article 29, para. 1)—the free and full development of the human personality is possible.

It should also be noted that the general human rights instruments—insofar as they are drawn up in the form of conventions—contain machinery for international implementation. The various institutions and procedures are described elsewhere. Only a few brief remarks may be made here. Whereas the functions to be carried out by institutions based on world-wide conventions are mainly concerned with information, conciliation and recommendation, the tasks to be performed by the organs provided for in the European and American Conventions are more in the nature of legal adjudication. Inasmuch as such institutions or organs are instrumental in interpreting and developing substantive human rights law, the world-wide institutions are more likely to perform work of a diplomatic or political character while, as is borne out by the practice of the European Commission and Court, the regional organs tend to follow a judicial approach.

The Universal Declaration and the American Declaration do not contain special implementation machinery, which has not prevented them from playing a dynamic role in the development of international human rights law. These declarations have not only been of great significance as reference material for the drafters of later international instruments, but have also been used as guiding standards of a moral and political character by many organs of the international society. The Universal Declaration is functioning in that sense in the work of the UN Commission on Human Rights and other UN organs, while the American Declaration is still the main standard of reference for the Inter-American Commission on Human Rights.

Noting the various human rights instruments, it would seem that neither the form in which they are embodied (conventions or declarations) nor the fact that they include special implementation machinery have, *per se*, been decisive factors in terms of their law-creating or law-developing functions. Only an analysis of the actual impact of such instruments on the international and national levels can shed more light on this question.

2. SPECIFIC INSTRUMENTS

(a). The protection of the human being in his very existence

Still under the shock of the extermination of large groups of human beings during the Second World War, the UN General Assembly adopted, on 11 December 1946, resolution 96 (I) on the crime of genocide and stated in the first paragraph of that resolution: "Genocide is a denial of the right of existence of entire human groups, as homicide is the denial of the right to live of individual human beings; such denial of the right of existence shocks the conscience of mankind, results in great losses to humanity in the form of cultural and other contributions represented by these human groups, and is contrary to moral law and to the spirit and aims of the United Nations." The same resolution requested the elaboration of a draft convention on the crime of genocide. Two years later, the Assembly approved in resolution 260 A (III) (1948) the Convention on the Prevention and Punishment of the Crime of Genocide. This crime under international law is defined as follows in the Convention: "Genocide means any of the following acts committed with intent to destroy, in whole or in part, a national, ethnical, racial or religious group, as such: (a) killing members of the group; (b) causing serious bodily or mental harm to members of the group; (c) deliberately inflicting on the group conditions of life calculated to bring about its physical destruction in whole or in part; (d) imposing measures intended to prevent births within the group; (e) forcibly transferring children of the group to another group." The Convention provides that, in addition to genocide, conspiracy, direct and public incitement and attempts to commit genocide, as well as complicity in genocide, shall also be punishable.

In the Convention on the Non-Applicability of Statutory Limitations to War Crimes and Crimes against Humanity, adopted by the United Nations General Assembly by resolution 2391 (XXIII) (1968), the crime of genocide is mentioned among the crimes against humanity to which no period of limitation applies.

The Convention on the Prevention and Punishment of the Crime of Genocide was in many respects a frame of reference for the drafters of the International Convention on the Suppression and Punishment of the Crime of *Apartheid*, adopted by General Assembly resolution 3068 (XXVIII) (1973). In this convention States parties declare that *apartheid* is a crime against humanity and that inhuman acts resulting from the policies and practices of *apartheid* and similar policies and practices of racial segregation and discrimination are crimes violating the principles of international law. The convention defines the crime of *apartheid* by listing a number of inhuman acts committed for the purpose of establishing and maintaining domination by one racial group of persons over any other racial group of persons and systematically oppressing them. Among the inhuman acts is mentioned denial to a member or members of a racial group or groups of the right to life and liberty of person. The further elaboration is in terms very similar to the genocide convention. Also the deliberate imposition on a racial group of living conditions calculated to cause its physical destruction in whole or in part appears in practically identical terms in both conventions. For the rest, however, the Convention on the Suppression and Punishment of the Crime of *Apartheid* goes far beyond the genocide convention in its enumeration of punishable acts.

(b). The elimination of racial discrimination

Hardly any other human rights concern has been so much in the forefront in recent times as the effort towards the elimination of racial discrimination. Racial prejudice and racism were clear features of nazism and led to barbarous acts in recent history. Policies and practices based on racial superiority and racial hatred jeopardize relations among individuals, people and nations. Racism and racial discrimination constitute a denial of fundamental human rights and affect the dignity of human beings. The international community has reacted strongly against that persistent and flagrant form of racism and racial discrimination, which is manifest in South Africa in the policy and practice of *apartheid* and similar types of racial discrimination and segregation. The evil of racial discrimination is, however, not confined to that region of the world. In no other field has the development of international human rights standards attained such dimensions as in the sphere of the elimination of racial discrimination. Examples of far-reaching types of international legislation are the International Convention on the Elimination of All Forms of Racial Discrimination of 1965 and the International Convention on the Suppression and Punishment of the Crime of *Apartheid* of 1973. Outstanding examples of international case law relating to racial discrimination are the 1971 Advisory Opinion of the International Court of Justice on Namibia, in particular the interpretation of the human rights clauses of the UN Charter (see chapter 3, note 8, above), and an opinion of the European Commission of Human Rights which considers that "discrimination based on race could, in certain circumstances, of itself amount to degrading treatment within the meaning of article 3 of the European Convention" ("East African Asians", I, decision on the admissibility of 10 October 1970).

The prohibition of discrimination on the ground of race is contained in most of the leading international instruments in the field of human rights. In 1962, the UN General Assembly requested the preparation of specific instruments on racial discrimination, viz. a Declaration and a Convention on the Elimination of All Forms of Racial Discrimination and, in addition to that, a Declaration and a Convention on the Elimination of All Forms of Religious Intolerance (resolutions 1780 (XVII) and 1781 (XVII)). While the former instruments were adopted in 1963 and 1965, the general climate was less propitious for reaching agreement on the content of the instruments relating to elimination of religious intolerance and, as a result, it was not until December 1981 that the Declaration on the Elimination of All Forms of Intolerance and of Discrimination Based on Religion or Belief was adopted by the General Assembly (resolution 36/55).

The United Nations Declaration on the Elimination of All Forms of Racial Discrimination, proclaimed by the General Assembly in 1963 (res. 1904 (XVIII)), can be considered as a comprehensive statement of UN philosophy and policy in regard to discrimination on the grounds of race, colour or ethnic origin. However, its significance was overshadowed by the adoption, two years later, of the International Convention on the Elimination of All Forms of Racial Discrimination (res. 2106 A (XX)(1965). In terms of human rights law, and in view of the inclusion in the convention of a special and comprehensive implementation machinery with the Committee on the Elimination of Racial Discrimination as its central organ, this convention was a major achievement on the world-wide level prior to the adoption of the two International Covenants. Closely following the definition of discrimination in the Discrimination (Employment and Occupation) Convention of the ILO (1958), and in the UNESCO Convention against Discrimination in Education (1960), the UN convention defines racial discrimination as "any distinction, exclusion, restriction or preference based on race, colour, descent, or national or ethnic origin which has the purpose or effect of nullifying or impairing the recognition, enjoyment or exercise, on an equal footing, of human rights and fundamental freedoms in the political, economic, social, cultural or any other field of public life".

The States parties undertake to amend, rescind or nullify any laws and regulations which have the effect of creating or perpetuating racial discrimination wherever it exists. They undertake not only not to engage in any act or practice of racial discrimination themselves, but also to prohibit and bring to an end racial discrimination by any person, group or organization. Much discussed in relation to freedom of expression and freedom of association were the provisions, whereby States parties undertake: (a) to declare as an offence punishable by law all dissemination of ideas based on racial superiority or hatred and also any incitement to racial discrimination; and (b) to declare illegal and prohibit organizations and propaganda activities which promote and incite racial discrimination, and to recognize participation in such organizations as an offence punishable by law. The Convention contains a long list of rights and freedoms in the enjoyment of which racial discrimination shall be prohibited and eliminated. The list contains not only most of the political, civil, economic, social and cultural rights embodied in the Universal Declaration of Human Rights, but also other rights on which the Universal Declaration does not contain express provisions, notably the right of access to any place or service intended for use by the general public, such as transport, hotels, restaurants, cafés, theatres and parks. It is clear that the latter provision is of considerable significance in view of discriminatory practices with regard to such facilities.

Taking into account the purpose and scope of the Convention, it may be assumed that it does not, in itself, guarantee the enjoyment of the various rights listed. It only requires the respect and exercise of the right of everyone to protection against racial discrimination and to equality before the law in the enjoyment of these human rights. Neither does the Convention in itself preclude possible restrictions on the exercise of these rights, but it does preclude and prohibit restrictions which are based on race, colour, descent, or national or ethnic origin. The Convention has now been ratified by a large number of States and can be considered an important part of international human rights law.

(c). The protection of women

The United Nations Charter refers in its preamble to equal rights of men and women and all human rights provisions of the Charter explicitly mention "sex" as one of the non-discrimination grounds. Many other international instruments, albeit not specifically aimed at the protection of women, have an important bearing upon the status of women. These include the Universal Declaration, both International Covenants on Human Rights, many conventions and recommendations of the ILO and conventions on prevention of discrimination such as the Unesco Convention against Discrimination in Education.

A number of international instruments have been drawn up with the special purpose of eliminating discrimination against women and promoting the emancipation of women. In this respect the UN Commission on the Status of Women has been instrumental since its inception in 1946. The Declaration on the Elimination of Discrimination against Women, prepared by the Commission, was proclaimed by the UN General Assembly in 1967 (res. 2263 (XXII)). It states that discrimination against women, leading to the denial or limitation of equal rights between men and women, is fundamentally unjust and constitutes an offence against human dignity. The Declaration calls for the abolition of existing laws, customs, regulations and practices which discriminate against women and provides for the establishment of adequate legal protection for equal rights of men and women. The Declaration contains the principle of equality of men and women in the field of political rights, stressing women's equal right to vote, to be eligible for election, and to hold public office and exercise public functions. It proclaims that women shall have the same rights as men with regard to the acquisition, change and retention of nationality. Furthermore, the Declaration deals with a number of questions relating to equal rights of women, married or unmarried, in the field of civil law and mentions, in particular, property rights and legal capacity, as well as the movement of persons. It also stresses the principle of equality of status of husband and wife in the family and it seeks to prohibit child marriage and the bethrothal of young girls before puberty. Of great importance are the provisions to ensure equal rights with men in education and in the field of economic and social life. The relevant article on education deals with various aspects of this equality as regards access to educational institutions; curricula, examinations, teaching staff, school premises and equipment; scholarships and study grants; continuing education; and it is concerned with the access to educational information to help in ensuring the health and well-being of families. With regard to various aspects of the status of women in economic and social life, the Declaration deals with the right of women to work without discrimination on any grounds and with the rights of women workers. It also contains a provision which is specifically aimed at preventing discrimination against women on account of marriage or maternity, and it deems measures taken to protect women in certain types of work, for reasons inherent in their physical nature, not to be discriminatory.

However, the most significant and comprehensive instrument in this field is the Convention on the Elimination of All Forms of Discrimination against Women, adopted by the General Assembly in 1979 (res.34/180). In the Convention, the term "discrimination against women" is defined to include "any distinction, exclusion or restriction made on the basis of sex which has the effect or purpose of impairing or nullifying the recognition, enjoyment or exercise by women, irrespective of their marital status, on a basis of equality of men and women, of human rights and fundamental freedoms in the political, economic, social, cultural, civil or any other field". The substantive provisions of the Convention are surveyed below in Chapter 10 and its procedural provisions are considered in Chapter 11.

A number of the issues covered by this Convention are also the subject of more specific international instruments relating to the status of women.

The Convention on Political Rights of Women of 1952 provides that women shall be entitled to vote on equal terms with men without any discrimination; that women shall be eligible for election to all publicly elected bodies, established by national law, and shall be entitled to hold public office and to exercise all public functions, established by national law, on equal terms with men and without any discrimination.

Under the Convention on the Nationality of Married Women of 1957, the

Contracting Parties agree that neither the celebration nor the dissolution of marriage between one of their nationals and an alien shall automatically affect the nationality of the wife. Neither shall any change of nationality by the husband during marriage affect the nationality of the wife. In other words, no change may be made in the nationality of the wife without an expression of desire on her part for such change. The Convention also provides that the alien wife of one of the nationals of a Contracting State may, at her request, acquire the nationality of her husband through specially privileged naturalization procedures.

The Convention on Consent to Marriage, Minimum Age for Marriage and Registration of Marriages of 1962 is aimed at the abolition of customs and practices of child marriages and the bethrothal of young girls. It provides that no marriage shall be legally entered into without the full and free consent of the partners, that a minimum age for marriage shall be specified (the Recommendation of 1965 adopted by the General Assembly on this subject (res. 2018 (XX)), states that the minimum age shall in any case not be less than fifteen years) and that all marriages shall be registered in an official register by the competent authority.

Finally, reference should be made to the Convention for the Suppression of the Traffic in Persons and of the Exploitation of the Prostitution of Others of 1950. The international law on this question dates back to the beginning of the twentieth century, and in particular to the efforts of the League of Nations to suppress the white slave traffic. The States parties to the 1950 Convention agree to punish any person who, to gratify the passions of another, procures, entices or leads away, for purposes of prostitution, another person or exploits the prostitution of another person, even with the consent of that person. The Convention asks also for the punishment of any person who keeps or manages a brothel or similar places.

(d). The protection of children

The need for special protection of children and youth in general is widely recognized in international human rights law. The Universal Declaration of Human Rights states that motherhood and childhood are entitled to special care and assistance and that all children, whether born in or out of wedlock, shall enjoy the same social protection (article 25, para. 2). The International Covenant on Civil and Political Rights forbids the imposition of death sentences on persons below eighteen years of age (article 6, para. 5); and it contains special rules for accused juvenile persons and juvenile offenders (article 10), and in relation to criminal procedure (article 14, para. 4). The same covenant has a special article on the right of every child to protection on the part of his family, society and the State. This article states also that every child shall be registered immediately after birth and shall have a name as well as the right to acquire a nationality (article 24). In the Genocide Convention the enumeration of acts which amount to genocide, include the forcible transfer of children of one group to another group (article 2(e)). The International Covenant on Economic, Social and Cultural Rights prescribes special measures of protection and assistance for all children and young persons in the economic and social field, in particular by forbidding child labour and employment harmful to morals or health or dangerous to life (article 10). The ILO has adopted a great number of texts fixing a minimum age for admission to employment, prohibiting night work of young persons, providing for more favourable conditions, guidance, apprenticeship and vocational training. Furthermore, the Geneva Convention relative to the Protection of Civilian Persons in Time of War (Convention IV) provides for special measures of protection and care for children under fifteen, who are orphaned or separated from their families as a result of the war (article 24), while the same convention has also a protection article for children in occupied territories (article 50).

The need for special safeguards and care for children is the principal motivation of the Declaration of the Rights of the Child, proclaimed by the General Assembly in 1959 (res. 1386 (XIV)). It sets forth, in the form of ten principles, a code for the well-being of every child without any exception whatsoever and without any discrimination. The Declaration provides that the child shall be given opportunities and facilities by law and by other means to enable him to develop physically, mentally, morally, spiritually and socially in a healthy and normal manner and in conditions of freedom and dignity. The best interests of the child shall be the paramount consideration in the enactment of laws for this purpose. The child shall be entitled from his birth to a name and a nationality. The Declaration also deals with the enjoyment by the child of the benefits of social security and the right to adequate nutrition, housing, recreation and medical services. A special provision deals with physically, mentally[1] or socially handicapped children. The Declaration proclaims that the child is entitled to receive education which will be free and compulsory, at least at the elementary stages. The child shall be protected against all forms of neglect, cruelty and exploitation and shall not be the subject of traffic in any form. Furthermore, a child shall not be admitted to employment before reaching an appropriate minimum age nor be permitted to engage in any occupation or employment which would prejudice his health or education or interfere with his physical, mental or moral development. Finally, the Declaration states that the child shall be protected from practices which foster racial, religious or any other form of discrimination and shall be brought up in a spirit of understanding, tolerance, friendship among peoples, peace and universal brotherhood. The latter aspect of care for children and young persons has been further developed in the Declaration on the Promotion among Youth of the Ideals of Peace, Mutual Respect and Understanding between Peoples, proclaimed by the UN General Assembly in 1965 (res. 2037 (XX)). Pursuant to a proposal submitted by Poland in 1978, the Commission on Human Rights began considering a draft convention on the Rights of the Child (Commission resolutions 20 (XXXIV), 19 (XXXV), 36 (XXXVI) and 6

(XXXVII) and the General Assembly requested it to give the highest priority to completing the draft in 1982 (res. 36/57).

(e). The protection of the worker

Since 1919, the International Labour Organisation has drawn up a great many Conventions and Recommendations which have come to be known as the "International Labour Code". This code is also called an international *corpus juris* of social justice. These international instruments deal with conditions of work and life, such as hours of work, protection of women and young workers, occupational safety and hygiene, social security and wages. They also deal with the basic machinery of labour administration, such as inspection, employment services and minimum wage fixing. A further group of international instruments lays down the fundamental human rights to which all workers should be entitled: freedom of association, freedom from compulsory labour, equal opportunity and treatment in their employment and occupation. The protection of the worker and the international instruments drawn up by the ILO for this purpose can be indicated on the basis of four principal objectives (freedom, equality, economic security and dignity) which were stated by the Declaration concerning the Aims and Purposes of the ILO (Philadelphia, 1944) in the following terms: "All human beings, irrespective of race, creed or sex, have the right to pursue both their material well-being and their spiritual development in conditions of freedom and dignity, of economic security and equal opportunity."

Of particular relevance to workers' rights are freedom of association and collective bargaining. In fact, freedom of association being a political right as much as an economic and social right, is one of the basic concerns of the ILO. There are two leading conventions in this area, viz. the Freedom of Association and Protection of the Right to Organise Convention (No. 87), adopted in 1948, and the Right to Organise and Collective Bargaining Convention (No. 98) of 1949. The first convention provides that workers and employers, without distinction whatsoever, shall have the right to establish and, subject only to the rules of the organization concerned, to join organizations of their own choosing without previous authorization. It also provides for certain rights and guarantees permitting these organizations, and any federations or confederations they may establish, to draw up their own constitutions and rules, to organize their administration and activities, and to formulate their programmes, without any interference from the public authorities which would restrict this right or impede its lawful exercise. The 1949 convention contains provisions to protect workers against anti-union discrimination, and also to afford workers' and employers' organizations adequate protection against acts of interference by each other or each other's agents or members in their establishment, functioning, or administration.

The concept of freedom of labour finds clear expression in the Abolition of Forced Labour Convention of 1957 (No. 105). This convention provides for

the immediate and complete abolition of forced or compulsory labour for
political purposes, as a method of mobilizing and using labour for purposes of
economic development, as a means of labour discipline, as a punishment for
having participated in strikes and as a means of racial, social, national or
religious discrimination. The right to freedom of choice of employment is also
recognized in the Employment Policy Convention of 1964 (No. 122), which
stipulates that States should pursue an active policy designed to promote full,
productive and freely chosen employment.

The elimination of inequality of treatment and the promotion of equal
opportunity are also basic elements of social justice. Prominent among the
international labour standards on this subject is the Discrimination (Employment and Occupation) Convention of 1958 (No. 111). The aim of this convention is to eliminate any distinction, exclusion or preference made on the basis
of race, colour, sex, religion, political opinion, national extraction or social
origin, or such other distinction, exclusion or preference, which has the effect
of nullifying or impairing equality of opportunity or treatment in employment
or occupation. This includes such labour conditions or preconditions as access
to vocational guidance and placement services, vocational training, access to
employment and to particular occupations, advancement, security of tenure
of employment, remuneration for work of equal value, hours of work, rest
periods, annual holidays with pay, occupational safety and health, social security and welfare in connection with employment.

Of particular importance are the efforts to eliminate discriminatory measures based on sex and on nationality. As regards discrimination based on
sex, the Equal Remuneration Convention of 1951 (No. 100) requires the
application of the principle of equal remuneration for men and women workers
for work of equal value. Equality of treatment for non-nationals is the objective of various ILO conventions, in particular the Migration for Employment
Convention (Revised) of 1949 (No. 97). Under this convention, immigrants
lawfully within the territory of a country are to be treated no less favourably
than nationals in respect of a number of matters, including conditions of
employment, training, trade union membership, and the enjoyment of the
benefits of collective bargaining and accommodation.

Many international standards were developed in order to safeguard the
economic security of the worker and to promote adequate conditions of work
and life. Of all the relevant instruments two important conventions will be
mentioned. First, the Employment Policy Convention of 1964 (No. 122),
which is of basic significance with respect to the right to work. The exercise
of this right is essential to the full development of man's personality, as well
as to his economic security. The convention requires that Members declare
and pursue, as a major goal, an active policy designed to promote full, productive and freely chosen employment. The convention acknowledges the
close interaction of economic policy and employment policy. The other convention relates to the right to social security. This Social Security (Minimum

Standards) Convention of 1952 (No. 102) consists of a number of parts, each dealing with a particular branch of social security: medical care; sickness, unemployment, old age, employment injury, family benefit; maternity, invalidity and survivors' benefit.

(f). The protection of refugees and stateless persons

The status of refugees and of stateless persons, in other words persons who for good reasons are unwilling or unable to avail themselves of the protection of the government of their own country, is a matter of particular international concern. The Office of the United Nations High Commissioner for Refugees has, since its establishment in January 1951, been charged with the international protection of these persons. Specific international instruments have been elaborated in order to assure for refugees and for stateless persons the widest possible exercise of human rights and fundamental freedoms. Two principles are the basis of these international instruments, in particular the Convention relating to the Status of Refugees of 1951 and the Convention relating to the Status of Stateless Persons of 1954: first, that there should be as little discrimination as possible between nations, on the one hand, and refugees or stateless persons on the other; second, that there should be no discrimination based on race, religion or country of origin among refugees and among stateless persons.

According to the Convention relating to the Status of Refugees, the term "refugee" shall apply to any person who "as a result of events occurring before 1 January 1951 and owing to well-founded fear of being persecuted for reasons of race, religion, nationality, membership of a particular social group or political opinion, is outside the country of his nationality and is unable or, owing to such fear, is unwilling to avail himself of the protection of that country; or who, not having a nationality and being outside the country of his former habitual residence as a result of such events, is unable or, owing to such fear, is unwilling to return to it." A Protocol relating to the Status of Refugees, which entered into force in 1967, was drawn up in order to remove the dateline of 1 January 1951 so that, *vis-à-vis* the States parties to the protocol, the scope of the convention is extended to persons who became refugees as a result of subsequent events. The Convention requires "national treatment", i.e. treatment at least as favourable as that accorded to their own nationals with regard to certain rights, such as freedom of religion, access to courts, elementary education and public relief. With regard to such other rights, as wage-earning, employment and the right to association, refugees are entitled to most-favoured-nation treatment, i.e. the most favourable treatment accorded to nationals of a foreign country. In other respects, e.g. self-employment and education other than elementary education, refugees receive treatment as favourable as possible and, in any event, not less favourable than that accorded to aliens in general. Of particular importance for refugees is the principle of *non-refoulement*, i.e that refugees may not on any account whatsoever be expelled or returned to a country where their life or freedom would be threatened. This provision may, however, not be invoked in the case of a refugee who has been convicted by a final judgment of a particularly serious crime or who constitutes a danger to the security of the country. This principle of *non-refoulement* is also included in the 1951 Convention. There is one human right which is of essential importance for refugees, viz. the right to asylum. The Universal Declaration of Human Rights proclaims that everyone has the right to seek and to enjoy in other countries asylum from persecution and this right to territorial asylum (which should be distinguished from diplomatic asylum) is further elaborated in the Declaration on Territorial Asylum, adopted by the UN General Assembly on 14 December 1967 (resolution 2312 (XXII)).

Among the regional organizations, the Organization of American States has dealt with the matter of refugees and aliens by drafting numerous instruments concerning them, such as: the Havana Convention on Asylum (1928), supplemented by the Montevideo Convention on Political Asylum (1933) and, more recently, by two Caracas conventions of 1954, one on diplomatic asylum and the other on territorial asylum.

The UN Convention relating to the Status of Stateless Persons of 1954 applies to "a person who is not considered as a national by any State under the operation of its law". As regards most matters, the treatment to be accorded to stateless persons is the same as that accorded to refugees under the Convention relating to the Status of Refugees. With respect to certain rights, however, the Stateless Persons Convention places stateless persons in a position less favourable than that assured for refugees, e.g. with regard to wage-earning employment and the right of association, stateless persons enjoy treatment not less favourable than that accorded to aliens generally and they are not entitled to most-favoured-nation treatment. In view of the fact that the status of statelessness is, generally speaking, an undesirable situation for persons having such status and taking into account the provision of the Universal Declaration on Human Rights that everyone has the right to a nationality, a Convention on the Reduction of Statelessness was adopted in 1961. This convention contains provisions for attributing a nationality to persons who would otherwise be stateless and it prohibits, subject to certain exceptions, the deprivation of nationality if such deprivation would render persons stateless.

(g). The protection of combatants, war victims and civilian populations

The body of international humanitarian law applicable in armed conflicts is contained in a large number of international instruments. The most important documents are the Fourth Convention concerning the Laws and Customs of War on Land (The Hague, 1907) and the Annex to this Convention, and the four Geneva Conventions of 1949. The "Law of the Hague" governs the rules to be observed between belligerents. These rules can be summarized in one overriding principle: belligerents do not have unlimited choice in the means of inflicting damage on the enemy. The "Law of Geneva" relates to the status and protection of specific categories of persons in armed conflicts: the wounded and sick in armed forces in the field; wounded, sick and ship-wrecked members of armed forces at sea; prisoners of war; and civilians. The predominant principle of the "Law of Geneva" is that persons placed *hors de combat* and those not directly participating in hostilities shall be respected, protected and treated humanely.

In 1968 the General Assembly unanimously adopted a resolution, which the basic humanitarian principles applicable in all armed conflicts were restated (res. 2444 (XXIII)). It affirmed the following principles for observance by all governmental and other authorities responsible for action in armed conflicts: (a) that the right of the parties to a conflict to adopt means of injuring the enemy is not unlimited; (b) that it is prohibited to launch attacks against civilian populations as such; (c) that distinction must be made at all times between persons taking part in the hostilities and members of the civilian population to the effect that the latter be spared as much as possible. It should be noted that these basic humanitarian principles were held applicable in all armed conflicts, whether of an international or of a non-international character.

The four Geneva Conventions of 1949 contain a common article 3, setting out basic rules which shall apply "to armed conflicts not of an international character occurring in the territory of one of the High Contracting Parties". In such cases each Party to the conflict shall be bound to apply, as a minimum, the rule that "persons taking no active part in the hostilities, including members of armed forces who have laid down their arms and those placed *hors de combat* by sickness, wounds, detention, or any other cause, shall in all circumstances be treated humanely, without any adverse distinction founded on race, colour, religion or faith, sex, birth or wealth, or any other similar criteria". The article also prohibits specifically: (a) violence to life and person, in particular murder of all kinds, mutilation, cruel treatment and torture; (b) taking of hostages; (c) outrages upon personal dignity, in particular humiliating and degrading treatment; (d) the passing of sentences and the carrying out of executions without previous judgment pronounced by a regularly constituted court, affording all the judicial guarantees which are recognized as indispensable by civilized peoples. These norms are so basic that they are applicable at any time and in any place (see also Part I, Introd., para. 9). This common article 3 constitutes, in fact, a human rights convention in itself within the framework of the Geneva Conventions.

With the exception of the common article 3, laying down minimum guarantees applicable under all circumstances, the provisions of the Geneva Conventions are drawn up for all cases of declared war or of any other armed conflict which may arise between two or more of the High Contracting Parties (common article 2).

Conventions I and II deal with the protection of the wounded, sick and shipwrecked as well as the medical and religious personnel. Convention III contains provisions on the treatment of prisoners of war. Article 4 of that convention defines the persons having a right to be treated as prisoners of war. These include: the regular armed forces, the militia and volunteer corps not part of the regular army, including resistance fighters, provided they fulfill the conditions of having a responsible commander, having a fixed distinctive sign, carrying arms openly and conducting their operations in accordance with the laws and customs of war. Prisoners of war have a right to humane treatment in all circumstances and to respect for their persons and honour, and they retain their full civil capacity (articles 13 and 14). The convention lays down detailed provisions on such matters as the beginning of captivity, conditions in internment camps, relations with the exterior and with the authorities, penal and disciplinary sanctions, termination of captivity and release and repatriation.

An innovation in 1949 was Convention IV relating to the protection of civilian persons, who find themselves in the hands of a Party to the conflict or an occupying power of which they are not nationals. They are protected against abuses of power by the enemy authorities. Part II of the Convention entitled "general protection of populations against certain consequences of war" deals with safety zones (areas of protection where certain elements of the population especially meriting protection—the sick, children, aged persons, expectant mothers—can find a refuge). This part also contains provisions for the protection of wounded and sick civilians and concerning free passage through blockades.

Part III, entitled "Status and treatment of protected persons", contains provisions common to the territories of the parties to the conflict and to occupied territories. These provisions have a basic character, to be respected in all circumstances. They require respect for the person, in particular his physical and spiritual integrity, the prohibition of coercion, torture, collective penalties and reprisals, and the taking of hostages. Part III also contains a special section relating to the status of aliens in the territory of a Party to the conflict and another, very elaborate, section on the treatment of the population in occupied territories. The latter section deals, *inter alia*, with such matters as the prohibition of deportations, ensuring food and medical supplies, law enforcement, in particular respect for the general laws in force and for judicial guarantees. Another section is devoted to the treatment of internees which is in many respects very similar to the treatment to be accorded to prisoners of war in conformity with Convention III.

There is in recent years a definite tendency towards providing greater protection for peoples who struggle against colonial and alien domination and against racist regimes for the implementation of their right to self-determination and independence. Two principal issues are at stake: the question of the international status of the liberation movements, and the treatment to those engaged in armed conflicts in connection with them. Many resolutions have been adopted by the General Assembly on this subject. Of particular importance is resolution 3103 (XXVIII) (1973) containing "basic principles of the legal status of the combatants struggling against colonial and alien domination and racist regimes" (adopted by a divided vote: 83 in favour, 13 against and 19 abstentions). The two issues, mentioned above, find expression in paragraph 3 of this resolution: "the armed conflicts involving the struggle of peoples against colonial and alien domination and racist regimes are to be regarded as international armed conflicts in the sense of the 1949 Geneva Conventions and the legal status envisaged to apply to the combatants in the 1949 Conventions and other international instruments are to apply to the persons engaged in armed struggle against colonial and alien domination and racist regimes". The question of bringing this type of armed conflict within the purview of rules applicable in international armed conflicts was the main controversial issue at the first session of the Diplomatic Conference on the Reaffirmation and Development of International Humanitarian Law (Geneva, 1974). The task of this conference—which held four sessions between 1974 and 1977—was to work out, on the basis of two draft protocols to the Geneva Conventions prepared by the International Committee of the Red Cross, additional rules in order to ensure better protection of victims of international and non-international armed conflicts. These two protocols were adopted in June 1977.[2]

3. CUSTOMARY LAW AND GENERAL PRINCIPLES OF LAW

According to traditional international law, the relations between a State and its own nationals were usually considered as being essentially within the exclusive sphere of interest of that State. With regard to aliens, however, a series of rules was developed in State practice and international judicial decisions in order to guarantee certain fundamental rights to these people, although these rights were not considered as subjective rights of the individual but rather as rights inherent in the capacity of each State to make claims against another State, in particular for the respect of certain rules of international law with regard to its own nationals. Thus minimum standards for the treatment of aliens became part of customary law. It would not be incorrect to say that this international minimum standard of just treatment of aliens included what was later reaffirmed in the United Nations Charter as fundamental human rights inherent in the dignity and worth of the human person, whatever his nationality or domicile. Mention should also be made here of the inviolability of the human person, of his life, physical liberty and security, of his freedom of conscience and belief, and of his right to compensation in case of manifest denial of justice. This minimum standard for the treatment of aliens may be considered as a sort of precursor to the International Bill of Human Rights adopted by the United Nations. It should not be forgotten

that the idea of a minimum standard for the treatment of aliens was advanced
by the developed countries of Western Europe and North America but strongly
contested by other States, in particular those of Latin America which were of
the opinion that a State whose nationals resided within the territory of another State could not expect better treatment for them than is given to the
nationals of the State of residence. This controversy of minimum standard vs.
equality of treatment has now faded away because, as a result of the development of international human rights through the United Nations Charter
and other later international instruments, nationals and aliens are entitled to
the same human rights and the same fundamental freedoms.

Inasmuch as most of the international human rights law has developed
since World War II as part of a collective process through international
organizations, "international custom, as evidence of a general practice accepted as law" (article 38, para. 1(b) of the Statute of the International Court
of Justice) can particularly be identified today as a source of human rights law
in the light of the collective practices of these organizations. Such collective
practices should, however, in order to become custom-generating, reflect
widely held opinions and represent a broad consensus with regard to the
content and the applicability of certain substantive norms. As was convinc-
ingly argued by Judge Tanaka, who in his dissenting opinion in relation to the
1966 judgment of the International Court of Justice on South West Africa
(Namibia) stressed the collective character of the law-making process, the
practice of the UN through the years sufficiently warrants considering that
the norm of non-discrimination or non-separation on the basis of race has
become a rule of customary international law. The question arises whether
not only the general norm of non-discrimination but also a whole range of
more specific human rights norms may also have become part of customary
international law. The UN Secretariat, when requested by the Commission
on Human Rights in 1962 to give an opinion regarding the difference between
a "declaration" and a "recommendation", touched upon this question in an
affirmative way. It stated, *inter alia*, that "... in view of the greater solem-
nity and significance of a 'declaration', it may be considered to impart, on
behalf of the organ adopting it, a strong expectation that members of the
international community will abide by it. Consequently, insofar as the expectation is gradually justified by State practice, a declaration may by custom
become recognized as laying down rules binding upon States" (E/CN.4/L.610).
It may be arguable whether the Universal Declaration of Human Rights in
its totality qualifies in this sense. But one can safely say that this declaration
has over the years been invested by the international community, as represented by the United Nations, with such authority that no responsible member of the international community may disregard an appeal to the rights
enshrined in it. In this respect, the legally enforceable character of these
rights seems to be less important than their moral and political relevance and
weight. Customary human rights law would seem to have a wider meaning

than law whose compliance is to be sought before national or international tribunals. It is foremost the law which is to be invoked before the international or national public fora, such as political organs of the United Nations and national parliaments.

The concept of "the general principles of law recognized by civilized nations" (article 38, para. 1(c) of the Statute of the International Court of Justice) is often used to denote general principles of municipal law, in particular in the field of private law, shared by a fair number of nations. A few observations may be made in order to indicate developments in the approach to this concept. It would seem that a restriction of this concept to private law principles is no longer valid. The International Court of Justice certainly assumed that the concept had a wider meaning when it stated in the Reservations to the Genocide Convention Case (I.C.J. Reports, 1951, p. 23) "that the principles underlying the Convention are principles which are recognized by civilized nations as binding on States, even without any conventional obligation". Fundamental human rights as described above in connection with the distinguishing criteria (see Chapter 3) would certainly fall under the general principles notion. They constitute peremptory norms of general international law (*jus cogens*) and are, as was pointed out earlier, part of a dynamic process. In such a process new peremptory norms may emerge (see article 64 of the Vienna Convention on the Law of Treaties).

It is, in terms of human rights law, difficult to draw a dividing line between the concepts of customary law and of general principles of law. It would seem that they substantially overlap, though the former is more reflected and affirmed by consistent practices of international organization and States, while the latter denotes fundamental or suprapositive norms which lie at the basis of the whole human society. In this connection a remark should be made about the qualifying phrase "recognized by civilized nations". The term "civilized nations"—and its predecessor "Christian nations"—derives from a period when the community of nations was constituted by a select group of States which pretended to represent human civilization. Since the international community, in the form of the UN, has now virtually reached universality, the notion of exclusiveness which was inherent in the term "civilized nations" is out of place and consequently the term should be avoided. General recognition of human rights and fundamental freedoms cannot be achieved unless pretentions of exclusiveness and notions of inequality disappear.

4. DECISIONS OF INTERNATIONAL ORGANS

Numerous international organs make decisions in human rights matters. One can roughly distinguish political organs, quasi-judicial organs and judicial organs. Political organs are, as a general rule, composed of officially designated representatives. Their proceedings are usually conducted in public meetings. Inasmuch as these political organs function in the framework of inter-governmental organizations, their decisions reflect, to a large extent, the views and interests of governments. Both on national and international levels, representative political organs have an important law-creating and law-developing function, in the sense that they act as (quasi-) legislators. Generally applicable norms, thus created or developed, ideally have their roots in the public opinion of the peoples ("We the Peoples of the United Nations . . ."). International instruments relating to human rights adopted by political organs, whether in the form of conventions—which need, however, to be ratified by States parties in order to become operative—or in the form of declarations, and even recommendations, are or become, by consistent affirmation and practice, part of international human rights law.

The very same law-creating or law-developing political organs or sub-organs, or, in matters of international peace and security, the Security Council as the appropriate organ, may also be called upon to make decisions relating to specific human rights situations which touch upon actual policies and practices of governmental authorities. In such concrete cases of application (or non-application) of human rights norms, the political factor is prevalent. It is certainly not suggested here that, in view of the prevailing political considerations, the pertinent decisions, whether they concern the *apartheid* policy or gross violations of human rights by a military *junta*, do not represent a very legitimate human rights concern. It is, however, admitted that such decisions are very much conditioned by political interests and views regarding the specific situation and that this does not mean that similar decisions would logically follow in relation to other cases when human rights are equally violated in a consistent manner. In other words, where the political organs make decisions in concrete human rights cases, political expediency will be much more decisive than such judicial categories as the force of law or legal precedents. This holds true for most of the organs of the United Nations, including the Security Council, the General Assembly, the Trusteeship Council, the Economic and Social Council, the Commission on Human Rights, etc. Decisions of such organs regarding concrete situations may be considered as political interventions on humanitarian grounds or, to put it another way, humanitarian interventions on political grounds.

Quasi-judicial organs usually deal with concrete situations or cases involving human rights. They are, as a general rule, not called upon to take legally binding decisions but rather to perform functions of inquiry or investigation and of conciliation. They may also express opinions or formulate recommendations. A whole range of such quasi-judicial organs has become part of the present-day international human rights structure, either as organs of a permanent character or as *ad hoc* bodies. Prominent among the permanent bodies are the European Commission of Human Rights, the Inter-American Commission on Human Rights, the Committee on the Elimination of Racial Discrimination, and the Freedom of Association Committee of the Governing Body of the ILO. Of the *ad hoc* bodies the *Ad Hoc* Working Group of Experts of the UN Commission on Human Rights (whose mandate has now repeatedly been extended) and Commissions of Inquiry established under article 26 of the ILO Constitution may be cited.

These quasi-judicial organs are called upon to apply international human rights standards, either as part of the implementation machinery of a convention or as a subsidiary organ of an international organization. Their task is to draw up a report embodying their findings of the relevant facts as well as their conclusions and recommendations, which might be directed to one or more governments concerned, to political organs or to judicial organs for further action. Some of these quasi-judicial organs, notably the European Commission of Human Rights and the Freedom of Association Committee of the ILO, have developed a large body of case law by interpreting and applying international standards. They often make reference to decisions which they have taken in previous cases, so that a certain continuity is developed as regards the criteria employed and the standards applied. In some instances they contribute to a progressive development of these standards even beyond the literal scope of the relevant international instruments. An example is the practice of the ILO Freedom of Association Committee with regard to the right to strike. Although this right is not included in the pertinent ILO Conventions on Freedom of Association, the Committee has repeatedly and consistently taken the view that allegations relating to this right are within its competence and that the right to strike by workers and their organizations is generally recognized as a legitimate means of defending their occupational interests. Although decisions of quasi-judicial organs are generally not legally binding, their impact as instructions directed to governments or to political or judicial organs is considerable. The actual practice of these quasi-judicial organs and their potential are of great value for the application and further development of international human rights law.

It would seem that, in the present state of international relations, quasi-judicial organs have more favourable prospects of becoming effective instruments for the promotion and protection of human rights than judicial organs like the European Court of Human Rights and the International Court of Justice which, in contentious cases, render legally binding decisions. In terms of actual practice the role of these courts is relatively limited in comparison with that of political organs and quasi-judicial organs dealing with human rights. It is on the other hand true that decisions of judicial organs, though rendered in respect of particular cases in the light of prevailing circumstances, carry great weight in providing authoritative interpretation of the law. In this respect decisions of judicial organs constitute reliable reference sources for use and application by the numerous organs of the national, regional and international communities that are concerned with the promotion and protection of human rights and fundamental freedoms.

5. DOCTRINE

There is no doubt that, given the development of a body of positive international human rights law, particularly in general and specific instruments, be they conventions or declarations, doctrine may only constitute a subsidiary source of law for determining the content and meaning of human rights. It may nevertheless be useful not to limit doctrine in this field to the writings of publicists but to take into account as well the reports or publications from persons, groups, associations or international organizations having a particular interest or competence in this field. Thus for example studies undertaken by special rapporteurs of the UN Commission on Human Rights or of its Sub-Commission may be of considerable importance in determining the field of application and the meaning of human rights law in a given area and may influence the further development of this law. Furthermore, studies and statements by non-governmental organizations and institutions (such as Amnesty International, the International Commission of Jurists, the International Institute of Human Rights) undeniably carry considerable authority. In fact, one of the specific traits of international human rights law is that this branch of international law extends well beyond the domain of international judicial decisions and inter-governmental practice, as well as the interests of the academic world. International human rights law is of interest to very many bodies in the national and international community and it would not be bold to affirm that the writings and acts of all who are concerned have a direct or indirect influence on the doctrine of human rights.

NOTES

1. The UN General Assembly proclaimed on 20 December 1971 a Declaration on the Rights of Mentally Retarded Persons (resolution 2856 (XXVI)).

2. See *infra*, Chapters 8 and 14.

6 Economic, Social and Cultural Rights

Vladimir Kartashkin

Economic, social and cultural rights now occupy an increasingly important place in the legal systems and political aspirations of different countries of the world. They are given much attention in the activities of the United Nations and other international organizations.

Constitutions and legislative acts adopted in the 18th and 19th centuries chiefly enumerated civil and political rights. Economic and social rights were considered at that time as a by-product of the development of civil and political rights. Only in the beginning of the 20th century did the constitutions of a number of States begin to place an increasingly greater emphasis on socio-economic rights. We may refer to such instruments as the Constitution of the United States of Mexico of 1917, the Declaration of Rights of the Working and Exploited Peoples of 16 January 1918 which was incorporated in the Constitution of the Russian Soviet Federative Socialist Republic adopted on 10 July 1918, the Weimar Constitution of Germany of 1919, the Constitution of the Spanish Republic of 1931, the Constitution of the USSR of 1937, and the Constitution of Ireland of 1937. Since the Second World War, largely under the impact of the Universal Declaration of Human Rights, the constitutional recognition of both civil and political rights and of economic, social and cultural rights has become a very widespread practice.[1] The precise legal effect of such constitutional guarantees admittedly varies considerably from judicially enforceable rights to mere statements of objectives of State policy.

In 1969 the UN Commission on Human Rights noted "the significant practical and theoretical contribution of Lenin, prominent humanist, to the development and realization of economic, social and cultural rights..." and "the historical influence of his humanistic ideas and activity" in this field (res. 16 (XXV)).

In the late 19th and early 20th centuries, the first international agreements in the field of regulating labour relations were concluded. Thus a beginning was made in the international regulation of the set of rights under review in this chapter.

Member States of the League of Nations undertook to "endeavour to secure fair and humane conditions of labour" (Art. 23 of the Covenant of the League of Nations). The Constitution of the International Labour Organization (ILO), a part of the Versailles Peace Treaty, stressed that all industrial communities should endeavour to apply the following methods and principles for regulating labour conditions: labour should not be regarded as a commodity or article of commerce; recognition of the right of association of the employed as well as of employers; payment of a wage sufficiently adequate to maintain a reasonable standard of life; adoption of an eight-hour working day or a forty-eight-hour working week; weekly rest of at least twenty-four consecutive hours; abolition of child labour and imposition of limitations on the labour of young persons to permit continuation of their education and to assure their physical development; men and women should receive equal remuneration for work of equal value; equitable economic treatment in each country of all workers lawfully resident therein; provision for a system of inspection to ensure enforcement of the laws and regulations for the protection of the employed.

From 1919 onwards, the ILO adopted a considerable number of conventions on various aspects of labour relations and working conditions.

The adoption of the UN Charter marked the beginning of a new stage in international law regulation of economic, social and cultural rights. Chapter IX of the Charter, entitled "International Economic and Social Co-operation", states that one of the primary goals of the United Nations is "higher standards of living, full employment, and conditions of economic and social progress and development; solutions of international economic, social, health and related problems; and international cultural and educational co-operation..." (Art. 55 (a) and (b)).

The Universal Declaration of Human Rights adopted in 1948 contains an extended and specific list of economic, social and cultural rights (Art. 22-27). These rights are regulated more fully in the International Covenant on Economic, Social and Cultural Rights whose provisions, as distinct from the Declaration, are designed to create binding obligations for States parties to the Covenant.

Although the General Assembly decided upon the adoption of two distinct Covenants—one dealing with economic, social and cultural rights, the other with civil and political rights—it did so essentially because of the different nature of the implementing measures which would generally be involved, and not so as to imply any divisibility or hierarchy among the rights concerned. Both Covenants, in their preambles, expressly recognize that the ideal of free human beings can be achieved only in conditions where the enjoyment both of economic, social and cultural rights and of civil and political rights is ensured.

At the level of regional organizations there has also been an increasing tendency to supplement universal human rights standards by regional instruments and institutions. Among instruments relating to economic, social and cultural rights, mention may be made of: the European Social Charter (1961) and the European Code of Social Security (1964); the American Declaration of the Rights and Duties of Man and the Inter-American Charter of Social Guarantees (both of 1948); the American Convention on Human Rights (1969) which, although dealing primarily with civil and political rights, also provides for the progressive realization of economic, social, educational, scientific and cultural standards set forth in the Charter of the Organization of American States; the Arab Labour Standards Convention (1967); and the Arab Social Security Standards Convention (1971).

International legal regulation of economic, social and cultural rights does not aim at codifying the legislation of different countries by passing laws which would establish a uniform legal system ensuring those rights. In view of the existence of States with different social systems, levels of economic development, class and national structures and historical traditions, such a goal would not be practicable. The international standards, however, establish a minimum level of social protection and welfare whose attainment should be sought by all States, whatever their systems or circumstances, even if—as in the case of the Covenant on Economic, Social and Cultural Rights—the full realization of the rights concerned is envisaged as a result of the progressive development of national policies, legislation and practical action.

The standards established by the Covenant on Economic, Social and Cultural Rights are frequently couched in general terms which do not delimit the exact scope of the rights concerned. However, among forms of international action aimed at its implementation, the Covenant provides for the conclusion of Conventions and the adoption of Recommendations. More detailed standards adopted under the auspices both of the United Nations and of the Specialized Agencies may thus constitute a valuable source for spelling out in greater detail what is required for the realization of the rights guaranteed by the Covenant. For instance, the Covenant recognizes the right of everyone to social security. To determine the substantive content of this right, it is appropriate to refer to the conventions in the field of social security adopted by the International Labour Organisation. They define the contingencies against which social security schemes should provide protection, the persons to be covered in respect of each of those contingencies, and the minimum level at which benefits should be provided. At the same time, they provide guidelines for the financing of social security schemes.

In some instances, a corresponding range of more detailed international standards does not exist. This appears to be the case, for example, as regards the right to an adequate standard of living, including adequate food, clothing and housing. In such cases, the supplementary standard-setting envisaged by the covenant may represent an important future task for the international community.

The implementation of economic, social and cultural rights depends to a large extent not on legislation but on the social and economic policies of

States. The inadequate level of economic development and shortage of resources of many countries thus represent a serious obstacle to the realization
of such rights. In these circumstances, as was stressed at the UN Seminar on
the Realization of Economic and Social Rights (Lusaka, Zambia, 1970), developing countries in particular find it necessary to establish priorities in the
realization of economic, social and cultural rights. However, even a high level
of economic development and an elaborated legal system are not an adequate
safeguard of human rights which requires, above all, a just socio-economic
structure.[2]

Some scholars have considered that the Covenant on Economic, Social and
Cultural Rights does not lay down binding legal obligations for States parties
to it.[3] Professor A.H. Robertson, for example, believes that the Covenant
establishes only standards which States should seek to attain.[4] Such a conclusion is made with reference to Article 2 of the Covenant which binds States
"to take steps...to the maximum of available resources, with a view to
achieving progressively the full realization of the rights recognized in the
present Covenant by all appropriate means, including particularly the adoption of legislative measures". However, some provisions of the Covenant
introduce a more specific timetable for their implementation. This is particularly true of the provisions concerning the introduction of compulsory free
education contained in Article 14. Even here, difficult choices may have to be
made with regard to priorities among measures to improve existing facilities,
so as to enable them to make an effective contribution to both spiritual
development and improvement of living standards, and the quantitative extension of facilities, so as to make educational opportunities available to all.[5]
On the other hand, since the concept of progressive implementation of economic, social and cultural rights is related to the availability of resources,
there would be less justification for deferring the recognition of rights whose
realization is not dependent on the allocation of resources, such as the trade
union rights provided for in Article 8 of the Covenant or the right to respect
for the freedom indispensable for scientific research and creative activity
guaranteed in Article 15. These considerations would also be relevant to the
implementation of the non-discrimination provisions in Articles 2 and 3 of the
Covenant.

As stressed in the UN study on the realization of economic, social and
cultural rights, "the Covenant provides the immediate basis for action at
international and regional levels, as well as for the translation of its standard
into national reality...Its only drawback is that in most of the less developed
countries its provisions can only be implemented progressively, according to
their level of development, availability of resources and size of population".[6]

The Covenant on Economic, Social and Cultural Rights regulates a large
number of economic, social and cultural rights, which will be reviewed below
in the order in which they are dealt with in that instrument.

1. THE RIGHT TO WORK

This right is one of the fundamental rights in the whole system of human rights and freedoms. Its realization is necessary not only for the material well-being of the individual but also for the harmonious development of his personality. Moreover, equitable labour conditions are also important to the maintenance of world peace. Thus the ILO Constitution notes that: "conditions of labour exist involving such injustice, hardship and privation to large numbers of people as to produce unrest so great that the peace and harmony of the world are imperilled" (Section I, Preamble).

According to the Covenant, the right to work "includes the right of everyone to the opportunity to gain his living by work which he freely chooses or accepts..." (Art. 6, para. 1). The right to free choice of work presumes the prohibition of forced or compulsory labour, as provided for in the Covenant on Civil and Political Rights (Art. 8, para. 3), as well as the absence of any discrimination in access of employment, opportunities for promotion or termination of employment (which would also be contrary to the non-discrimination provisions in Article 2 of the Covenant on Economic, Social and Cultural Rights).

The actual implementation of the right to work lies in the provision of work to all who want it and the protection of everyone from unemployment. The International Convention on the Elimination of All Forms of Racial Discrimination specially stresses that the States parties are under an obligation to ensure equality of everyone with respect to the realization of the right to work, including protection against unemployment (Art. 5 (i)). The right of everyone to work and protection against unemployment is also recognized in Article 23 of the Universal Declaration of Human Rights. The Charter specifically states that one of the objectives of the UN is to promote higher standards of living and "full employment" (Art. 55 (a)). The ILO Employment Policy Convention of 1964 (No. 122) requires that, with a view to "overcoming unemployment and underemployment, each Member shall declare and pursue, as a major goal, an active policy designed to promote full, productive and freely chosen employment" (Art. 1). This policy, according to the Convention, should be aimed at ensuring employment to everyone who seeks employment and is ready to accept it. The Discrimination (Employment and Occupation) Convention of 1958 (No. 111) provides for the declaration and pursuit of a national policy designed to promote equality of opportunity and treatment in respect of employment, with a view to eliminating any discrimination on the basis of race, colour, sex, religion, political opinion, national extraction or social origin. As regards termination of employment, these provisions are reinforced by the Termination of Employment Recommendation of 1963 (No. 119) which—in addition to excluding termination of unemployment on various specified grounds—establishes the general principle that a worker's employment should not be terminated by an employer unless there is a valid reason connected with the worker's capacity or conduct or based on the operational requirements of the enterprise. The fact that an employer's right to terminate an employment relationship is limited in this way provides no justification for restricting the worker's right to leave a job; on the contrary, the right of a worker to terminate a contract of employment of indefinite duration by notice of reasonable length constitutes an essential aspect of the right to free choice of employment.

The Covenant on Economic, Social and Cultural Rights provides that, with a view to full realization of the right to work, States parties should take appropriate steps, including technical and vocational guidance and training programmes, to achieve steady economic, social and cultural development and ensure full and productive employment (Art. 6, para. 2). It should, however, be borne in mind that the growth of economic potential does not always entail an increase of productive employment. Accompanied by mechanization and automation of production, it can sometimes bring about adverse results. It is therefore important that the employment implications of technological developments should be kept under constant review and that adequate guidance and training facilities should be made available to enable both entrants to the labour force and those already working to adapt to changing conditions and opportunities. In 1975 the ILO adopted comprehensive standards concerning vocational guidance and vocational training in the Human Resources Development Convention (No. 142) and Recommendation (No. 150) of 1975.

2. THE RIGHT OF EVERYONE TO JUST AND FAVOURABLE CONDITIONS OF WORK

Availability of jobs and safeguards of employment should be supplemented, in accordance with the Covenant, by the guarantee of the right to just and favourable conditions of work. According to Article 7 of the Covenant, this right includes:

(a) remuneration which provides all workers with fair wages and equal remuneration for work of equal value without distinction of any kind and a decent living;

(b) safe and healthy working conditions;

(c) equal opportunity for everyone to be promoted in his employment to an appropriate higher level, subject to no consideration other than those of seniority and competence;

(d) rest, leisure and reasonable limitation of working hours and periodic holidays with pay, as well as remuneration for public holidays.

The ILO has adopted a considerable number of conventions and Recommendations which spell out the above-mentioned aspects of the right to just and favourable working conditions. Provisions for the operation of minimum wage-fixing machinery in industry and commerce had been made in instruments adopted in 1938, while corresponding provisions for agriculture were embodied in instruments of 1951. More recent standards, with particular reference to developing countries, have been laid down in the Minimum Wage-Fixing Convention (No. 131) and Recommendation (No. 135), respectively of 1969 and 1970. They provide for creation or maintenance of machinery for the fixing of binding minimum wages, in full consultation with representative organizations of employers and workers, and define the element to be taken into consideration in determining the level of minimum wages.

Provisions for the implementation of the principle of equal remuneration for men and women workers for work of equal value have been laid down in the Equal Remuneration Convention of 1951 (No. 100). It should be noted that the Discrimination (Employment and Occupation) Convention, to which reference has already been made in connection with the right to work, would require elimination of discrimination on the basis of race, colour, sex, religion, political opinion, national extraction or social origin, in respect not only of remuneration but also of conditions of work in general, and the International Convention on the Elimination of All Forms of Racial Discrimination provides for the prohibition of racial discrimination in respect of all these matters.

Many ILO Conventions regulate matters of occupational safety and health. Standards laid down in these Conventions relate to safety conditions in particular sectors or occupations—such as the Safety Provisions (Building) Convention of 1937 (No. 62), the Hygiene (Commerce and Offices) Convention of 1964 (No. 120) and the Prevention of Accidents (Seafarers) Convention of 1970 (No. 134)—and to protection against particular hazards—such as the Radiation Protection Convention of 1960 (No. 155), the Guarding of Machinery Convention of 1963 (No. 119), the Occupational Cancer Convention of 1974 (No. 139) and the Working Environment (Air Pollution, Noise and Vibration) Convention of 1977 (No. 148).

Equal opportunity for everyone to be promoted in his employment, subject to no considerations other than those of seniority and competence, provided for by the Covenant, has also received legal recognition in international instruments which ban discrimination.

A series of ILO Conventions regulate matters of working hours, rest and paid leaves. As far back as 1919, ILO adopted the Hours of Work (Industry) Convention (No. 1), which laid down the standard of the eight-hour day and forty-eight hour week in industrial enterprises. In 1935 the ILO adopted the Forty-Hour Week Convention (No. 47), which provides for application of the principle of a forty-hour week in such a manner as not to entail a reduction in the standard of living. The Reduction of Hours of Work Recommendation of 1962 (No. 116), while laying down the maximum limit of 48 hours a week, calls on Member States of the ILO to formulate and pursue a policy aimed at a progressive reduction of working hours with a view to attaining a forty-hour week.

The ILO has also adopted a number of Conventions on weekly rest and annual paid leaves, such as the Weekly Rest (Industry) Convention of 1921 (No. 14), the Weekly Rest (Commerce and Offices) Convention of 1957 (No. 106), the Holidays with Pay Convention (Revised) of 1970 (No. 132) and the Hours of Work and Rest Periods (Road Transport) Convention of 1979 (No. 153).

3. TRADE UNION RIGHTS

In accordance with Article 8(1) of the Covenant, the States parties undertake to ensure:

"(a) the right of everyone to form trade unions and join the trade union of his choice for the promotion and protection of his economic and social interests...;
(b) the right of trade unions to establish federations or confederations and the right of the latter to form or join international trade union organizations;
(c) the right of trade unions to function freely...;
(d) the right to strike provided that it is exercised in conformity with the laws of the particular country."

Under the terms of the Covenant, the right to form and join trade unions and the right of trade unions to function freely may be made subject only to such limitations as are prescribed by law and necessary in a democratic society in the interests of national security, public order, or for the protection of rights and freedoms of others. The Covenant does not prevent the imposition of lawful restrictions by States on the exercise of the rights listed in Article 8 by members of the armed forces, the police or the administration of the State (Art. 8, para. 2).

The right of everyone to form trade unions and to join them for the protection of his interests is also recognized in the Universal Declaration of Human Rights (Art. 23, para. 3) and in the International Covenant on Civil and Political Rights (Art. 22, para. 1). Trade union rights are defined in greater detail in various ILO Conventions, most notably the Freedom of Association and Protection of the Right to Organize Convention of 1948 (No. 87), the Right to Organize and Collective Bargaining Convention of 1949 (No. 98) and the Workers' Representatives Convention of 1971 (No. 135).

Convention No. 87 guarantees to workers and employers, without any distinction whatsoever, the right to establish and to join organizations of their choosing without previous authorization (Art. 2); it recognizes the right of organizations to draw up their constitutions and rules, to elect their representatives in full freedom, to organize their programme without any interference on the part of public authorities (Art. 3); organizations of workers and employers are not to be subject to dissolution or suspension by administrative authority (Art. 4). The right to establish and join federations and confederations and to affiliate with international organizations of workers and employers is also recognized (Art. 5 and 6). In exercising the rights listed in the Convention workers, employers, and their organizations should respect the law of the land, but the law of the land should not impair, or be applied to impair, the guarantees provided for in the Convention (Art. 8). National legislation should determine the extent of the application to the armed forces and the police of the guarantees provided for in the Convention (Art. 9).

Convention No. 98, which supplements these rules, contains provisions regarding the protection of workers against acts of anti-union discrimination, in particular in regard to employment and dismissal (Art. 1), and the protection of organizations of employers and workers from mutual interference in the activities of the organizations and their administration (Art. 2).

Convention No. 135 makes provision for protecting and affording facilities to workers' representatives in enterprises.

As can be seen from the above indications, whereas the Covenant authorizes ratifying States to impose restrictions on the exercise of trade union rights by members of the armed forces, the police and the administration of the State,[7] ILO Convention No. 87 leaves a similar possibility only in respect of the armed forces and the police.[8] Workers employed in the administration of the State are entitled to the enjoyment of all the rights provided for in Convention No. 87, without distinction whatsoever. Furthermore, under this Convention, the right of international affiliation is guaranteed not only to federations and confederations of workers' or employers' organizations (as is the case under the Covenant) but also to the primary organizations themselves. These provisions are further elaborated upon in the Labour Relations (Public Service) Convention of 1978 (No. 151).

ILO supervisory bodies and the International Labour Conference have recognized the close relationship which exists between the exercise of trade union rights and the effective enjoyment of civil liberties, such as freedom and security of person and freedom from arbitrary arrest, freedom of opinion and expression, freedom of assembly, the right to a fair trial, and the right to protection of the property of trade union organizations.[9] In a resolution on this question adopted in 1970, the International Labour Conference affirmed that the absence of the civil liberties enunciated in the Universal Declaration of Human Rights and the Covenant on Civil and Political Rights removes all meaning from the concept of trade union rights.

There are no ILO Conventions which define the scope of the right to strike. ILO supervisory bodies have, however, recognized that the right to strike is one of the essential means through which workers and their organizations may promote and defend their occupational interests and that a general denial of the possibility of recourse to this means is inconsistent with the rights guaranteed by Convention No. 87. These bodies have enunciated a number of principles regarding the circumstances in which restrictions may be imposed on the exercise of the right to strike, the categories of workers who, on account of the special characteristics of their employment, may be prohibited from striking, and the compensatory guarantees which should be provided for the settlement of disputes affecting these categories of workers.[10] These internationally recognized principles may provide a significant source of reference for determining the scope of the right to be provided for under the Covenant.

Another international instrument which makes provision for the right to strike is the European Social Charter. The conclusions regarding the scope and implementation of that provision reached by the Committee of Independent Experts on the European Social Charter may provide another useful source of reference when considering the precise implications of the Covenant provisions relating to strikes.[11]

4. THE RIGHT OF EVERYONE TO SOCIAL SECURITY, INCLUDING SOCIAL INSURANCE

The right to social security, including social insurance, is provided for in the Covenant on Economic, Social and Cultural Rights in general terms. As previously noted, it is appropriate to turn to ILO instruments in this field to determine more precisely the scope of this right.

Comprehensive guidelines on the matter were adopted in 1944 in the Income Security Recommendation (No. 67) and in the Medical Care Recommendation (No. 69). The former advocates the provision of protection, by means of compulsory social insurance, in respect of all contingenicies in which an insured person is prevented from earning his living, whether by inability to work or inability to obtain remuneration for his work, or in case of death of the insured party leaving a dependent family, and the provision of social assistance to meet needs not covered by social insurance, particularly as regards dependent children, invalids, aged persons and widows. The Medical Care Recommendation relates to the provision of comprehensive medical care covering all members of the community.

These standards have been further developed in a series of subsequent Conventions and Recommendations. Minimum standards—regarding the persons to be protected and the range and level of benefits—were laid down in the Social Security (Minimum Standards) Convention of 1952 (No. 102) in respect of medical care and benefits in case of sickness, unemployment, old age, employment injury, maintenance of children, maternity, invalidity, and death of a breadwinner. The obligations of the Convention must be accepted in respect of at least three of these contingencies, with the possibility of accepting further parts subsequently. For most of the contingencies, Conventions establishing a higher level of protection have also been adopted, namely the Maternity Protection Convention of 1952 (No. 103), the Employment Injury Benefits Convention of 1964 (No. 121), the Invalidity, Old Age and Survivors' Benefits Convention of 1967 (No. 128) and the Medical Care and Sickness Benefits Convention of 1969 (No. 130); each of these Conventions is supplemented by a Recommendation advocating further enlargement of the protection to be granted. Unemployment benefits had been the subject of an earlier instrument, the Unemployment Provision Convention of 1934 (No. 44), but its provisions are no longer adapted to present needs and further ILO standards on this question are contemplated. A separate series of Conventions dealing with social security for seafarers has also been adopted.

The European Code of Social Security and its Protocol, adopted by the Council of Europe, are based on ILO Convention No. 102 but require acceptance of a higher level of obligations.

The various ILO and regional standards relating to equality of treatment of aliens as regards social security are considered in section 10 of the present chapter.

5. THE RIGHT TO PROTECTION OF AND ASSISTANCE TO THE FAMILY, MOTHERS AND CHILDREN

In accordance with Article 10 of the Covenant, this right includes protection of the family and assistance to it, the right of free consent to marriage, special protection and assistance to mothers during a reasonable period before and after childbirth, special protection and assistance to children and young persons and their protection from economic and social exploitation. The Covenant provides for the prohibition of the employment of children and young persons in work harmful to their morals or health or dangerous to life or likely to hamper their normal development. It also provides for the setting of age limits below which paid employment of children is to be prohibited and punishable by law.

The right to protection of and assistance to the family, mothers and children is regulated in the Covenant in much greater detail than in the Universal Declaration of Human Rights which says only that "maternity and childhood are entitled to special care and assistance" (Art. 25, para. 2).

The Universal Declaration also recognizes (in Art. 16) the right of men and women of full age to marry and found a family and provides that marriage should be entered into only with the free and full consent of the intending spouses. More detailed guarantees on these questions have been laid down in the Convention on Consent to Marriage, Minimum Age for Marriage and Registration of Marriages adopted by the UN.

The Declaration of the Rights of the Child adopted by the United Nations General Assembly on 20 November 1959 (Resolution 1386 (XIV)) states that "the child shall enjoy special protection, and shall be given opportunities and facilities, by law and by other means, to enable him to develop physically, mentally, morally, spiritually and socially in a healthy and normal manner and in conditions of freedom and dignity. In the enactment of laws for this purpose, the best interests of the child shall be the paramount consideration" (Principle 2).

A number of ILO Conventions expand on some aspects of the matters dealt with in Article 10 of the Covenant. The Maternity Protection Convention (Revised) of 1952 (No. 103) provides for a 12-week leave for women workers before and after confinement with at least six weeks for the post-confinement period, and for the right to cash benefits and medical care during the maternity leave. It is prohibited to dismiss women during pregnancy and confinement leaves. This Convention applies to women employed in industrial enterprises, commerce and agricultural occupations.

The Social Security (Minimum Standards) Convention of 1952 (No. 102) makes provision for the payment of family allowances in respect of children.

A series of ILO standards has been promulgated relating to the occupational safety and health of women workers concerning the danger which certain forms of work or substances may involve, both for their own health and for that of any children they may bear.

A number of ILO instruments deal with the protection of children and young persons. A series of Conventions relating to the minimum age for employment in different sectors of activity was revised by a Minimum Age Convention (No. 138) in 1973. This Convention calls for the pursuit of a national policy aimed at the abolition of child labour, through the adoption of a minimum working age of not less than 15 years (or, in less developed countries, initially 14 years), with higher minimum age (normally not less than 18 years) for work involving danger to health, safety or morals. Various limited exceptions to these standards are permitted.

The Night Work of Young Persons (Industry) Convention (Revised) of 1948 (No. 90) and the Night Work of Young Persons (Non-Industrial Occupations) Convention of 1946 (No. 79) prohibit the employment of persons under 18 years of age at night in the sectors concerned. Other ILO Conventions provide for medical examination and periodic re-examination of persons under 18 years (and, in certain occupations, of persons under 21 years).

6. THE RIGHT TO AN ADEQUATE STANDARD OF LIVING

According to Article 11 of the Covenant, the right to an adequate standard of living includes adequate food, clothing and housing. The same article also provides for recognition of the right to the continuous improvement of living conditions. The Covenant, recognizing "the fundamental right of everyone to be free from hunger", provides that States parties should, individually and through international co-operation, take appropriate measures to improve methods of production, conservation and distribution of food so as to achieve the most efficient development and utilization of natural resources and also to ensure an equitable distribution of world food supplies in relation to need.

Various international statements have elaborated upon these rights, particularly as regards the right to adequate food. Thus, the Programme of Action on the Establishment of a New International Economic Order adopted by the General Assembly of the United Nations at its Sixth Special Session in 1974 (Resolution 3202 (S-VI)) contains a special section on measures to secure adequate supplies of food. The World Food Conference, held in November 1974, adopted the Universal Declaration on the Eradication of Hunger and Malnutrition, as well as a series of resolutions on specific aspects such as objectives and strategies of food production, priorities for agricultural and rural development, policies and programmes to improve nutrition, the achievement of a desirable balance between population and food supply, the establishment of an International Fund for Agricultural Development, improved policies for food aid, and international trade stabilization and agricultural adjustment. At its 29th Session, the General Assembly of the United Nations endorsed these decisions and, in accordance with a further recommendation of the World Food Conference, established a World Food Council as an organ of the United Nations. This organ has adopted a number of recommendations directed at the eradication of hunger and malnutrition, such as the Manila Communiqué (UN doc.A/32/19). Among instruments adopted by the Food and Agricultural Organization of the United Nations, reference may be made to the Principles and Guiding Line for the Disposal of Agricultural Surpluses and the International Undertaking on World Food Security adopted by the Council of FAO in 1974. The World Food Programme, jointly established by the UN and FAO, is designed to provide food as an instrument of development and to assist in the realization of the right of everyone to be free from hunger.

The guarantee of an adequate standard of living and its continuous improvement is also the aim of most ILO Conventions which have already been referred to in connection with the consideration of other economic and social rights. The Social Policy (Basic Aims and Standards) Convention of 1962 (No. 117) provides more generally for policies and measures for the improvement of standards of living and states, *inter alia*: that "in ascertaining the minimum standards of living, account shall be taken of such essential family needs of the workers as food and its nutritive value, housing, clothing, medical care and education".

Other ILO instruments which may be mentioned in this connection are the Workers' Housing Recommendation of 1961 (No. 115), the Co-operatives (Developing Countries) Recommendation of 1966 (No. 127) and the Tenants and Sharecroppers Recommendation of 1968 (No. 132).

The right to continuous improvement of living conditions is a very broad concept. This right is ensured, first of all, by the absence of unemployment and inflation, growth of production and real wages, improvement of social security, etc. The improvement of living conditions depends chiefly on an appropriate economic policy of the State. However, it should be recalled that the Covenant stresses the need for international co-operation in this connection and requires ratifying States to ensure an equitable distribution of world food supplies in relation to need. The United Nations Declaration on the

Establishment of a New International Economic Order adopted on 1 May 1974 (Resolution 3201 (S-VI)) likewise establishes the principle that the new international economic order should be founded, among other things, on "the broadest co-operation of all the States Members of the international community, based on equity, whereby the prevailing disparities in the world may be banished and prosperity secured for all". It is thus clear that the striving for improved standards of living cannot be viewed solely within national limits but must have regard to the interests of the world community as a whole.

7. THE RIGHT OF EVERYONE TO THE HIGHEST ATTAINABLE STANDARD OF PHYSICAL AND MENTAL HEALTH

According to Article 12 of the Covenant, this right should be ensured by the State: through the reduction of the stillbirth rate and infant mortality and the healthy development of the child; improvement of all aspects of environmental and industrial hygiene; prevention, treatment and control of epidemic, endemic, occupational and other diseases; creation of conditions which would assure to all, medical service and medical attention in the event of sickness.

In connection with this right, reference should be made in the first place to the work of the World Health Organization. The Constitution of WHO, adopted in 1946, proclaimed that "the enjoyment of health is one of the fundamental rights of every human being without distinction of race, religion, political belief, economic or social condition". Although the Constitution of WHO provides for the possibility to adopt conventions or agreements, this power has not so far been used. The Organization has, however, adopted various regulations designed to prevent the international spread of disease and dealing with nomenclature with respect to diseases, causes of death, etc. The World Health Assembly has also adopted several resolutions on subjects related to the realization of rights provided in the Covenant, such as nutrition, family health and medical research.[12]

The realization of the right to the highest attainable standard of health is indissolubly linked with the realization of the right to fair and favourable conditions of work, to social security, an adequate living standard and its continuous improvement. Numerous studies carried out in a number of countries have established the relation between the level of income and death rate. Food, housing conditions environment, adequate medical service—all these factors have an impact on the health standard of everyone. It is therefore appropriate to bear in mind the various ILO Conventions to which reference has been made in connection with the right to fair and favourable conditions of work and the right to social security.

In recent years, international co-operation in the sphere of proper conservation of the environment has acquired increasing importance. The consequences of various activities harmful to the environment, such as pollution of the atmosphere, of international rivers and of the oceans, are of global nature and affect the interests and health of everyone wherever he may live. Concern with problems of rational use and conservation of natural resources of the biosphere and improvement of the environment led to the convening of a special United Nations Conference on the Problem of Man and his Environment in Stockholm in June 1972 and to the subsequent establishment of the United Nations Environment Programme. A large variety of international standards has been adopted in this field in the last decade.[13]

8. THE RIGHT OF EVERYONE TO EDUCATION

According to Article 13 of the Covenant, the full realization of this right envisages compulsory and free primary education for all, accessibility to secondary general education, including technical and vocational secondary education and higher education with progressive introduction of free education and liberty for parents to choose schools for their children. Free compulsory primary education should be progressively introduced in all colonial and dependent territories (Art. 14). It is also stressed in Article 13 of the Covenant that "education shall be directed to the full development of the human personality and the sense of its dignity, and shall strengthen the respect for human rights and fundamental freedoms... Education shall enable all persons to participate effectively in a free society, promote understanding, tolerance and friendship among all nations and all racial, ethnic or religious groups, and further the activities of the United Nations for maintenance of peace."

A series of international instruments has been adopted within the Unesco framework: the Convention against Discrimination in Education and an appropriate Recommendation of 1960; Recommendation concerning Technical and Vocational Education (1962) which was revised in 1974; Recommendation concerning the Status of Teachers (1966); Recommendation concerning Education for International Understanding, Co-operation and Peace and Education relating to Human Rights and Fundamental Freedoms (1974); and Recommendation on the Development of Adult Education (1976).

The Convention against Discrimination in Education was adopted by the General Conference of Unesco in 1960 and entered into force in 1962.[14] It is described in some detail in chapter 13 below.

In the field of technical and vocational education, the General Conference of Unesco adopted a recommendation in 1962. The International Labour Conference has also adopted a number of instruments on this subject, particularly the Vocational Guidance Recommendation (1949), the Vocational Training (Agriculture) Recommendation (1956), and the Vocational Training Recommendation (1962). Having these instruments in mind, the General Conference of Unesco adopted in 1974 the Revised Recommendation concerning Technical and Vocational Education, which sets forth general principles, goals and guidelines to be applied according to the needs and resources of each country.

According to this Recommendation, technical and vocational education should "contribute to the achievement of society's goals of greater democratization and social, cultural and economic development" (Part II, para. 5 (a)), *inter alia*, by "abolishing barriers between levels and areas of education, between education and employment and between school and society" (II, 6 (a)). Among the principles enunciated in the Recommendation are equality of access for women and men (II, 7 (f)), special forms of education for disadvantaged and handicapped persons (II, 7 (g)), participation of representatives of various segments of society in policy formulation on the national and local levels (III, 12), and equal standards of equality in order to exclude possible discrimination between the different educational channels (III, 14).

Principles relating to technical and vocational education as part of general education, as preparation for an occupational field and for continuing education are set out in some detail, as are goals relating to methods and materials and staff.

Another important instrument establishing or reaffirming international standards relevant to the right to education is the Recommendation concerning Education for International Understanding, Co-operation and Peace and Education relating to Human Rights and Fundamental Freedoms, which was adopted by the General Conference of Unesco in 1974. All stages and forms of education should be guided by the principles set forth in this Recommendation, which may be considered as an elaboration of the aims of education specified in Article 26, paragraph 2 of the Universal Declaration. These principles stress international solidarity and a global perspective for education, which should develop a sense of social responsibility and contribute to strengthening world peace. Member States are encouraged to ensure that the principles of the Universal Declaration and of the Convention on the Elimination of All Forms of Racial Discrimination are applied in the daily conduct of education; that every person is familiarized with the operation of local, national and international institutions in order to participate in the solving of problems of the community and the world; that education is linked with action wherever possible. Certain methods, equipment and materials and approaches to issues are recommended for different levels and types of education, both in school and out-of-school, as well as teacher training and research and development. Under international co-operation, States should develop international education, receive foreign students, research workers, teachers and educators, provide for exchange programmes and dissemination of information, without intervening in matters essentially within the domestic jurisdiction of any other State.

When adopting the Recommendation concerning the development of adult education, the General Conference of Unesco stated that "...the access of adults to education, in the context of life-long education, is a fundamental aspect of the right to education and facilitates the exercise of the right to participate in political, cultural, artistic and scientific life". The instrument defines a strategy for developing this type of education, indicating its contents, methods, means and structures in a perspective of democratization and international co-operation.

With these international instruments in mind, a few more general remarks may be made about the nature of the right to education. As the drafters of Article 26 of the Universal Declaration were well aware, education can only be established as a right of everyone in society if the means are available for generalizing elementary instruction, as well as technical and vocational schooling.[15] At that time, great emphasis was placed on the right of parents to choose the type of education of their children and this has proved to be a delicate and complex problem for implementation. The various aspects of the right to instruction and to education and the social and political problems to which its protection gives rise have been dealt with in a book published in Budapest.[16] This work contains an interesting discussion on the extent to which the right to education includes such notions as the right to adult education as part of the right to institutional formation, which includes out-of-school instruction. The author points out, moreover, that the Constitution of Unesco refers to two aspects of the right to education, namely advancing equality of educational opportunity and giving a "fresh impulse to popular education" (Art. 1, para. 2). As may be seen from the analysis above, the institutional and legislative developments over the past few decades have tended to transform these notions from the realm of objectives pursued through international co-operation to rights set out in international instruments.

9. CULTURAL RIGHTS

Generally speaking, cultural rights refer to a variety of aspects of the rights to education, to participation in cultural life, to communications and to information. They are therefore essential to the relationship between people and their society and to the question of whether one is able to develop his or her full human potential within that of society. They are, moreover, all interdependent and closely connected to other economic and social rights, as well as to certain civil and political rights. For the purposes of the present chapter, we shall evoke briefly certain aspects of cultural rights other than the right to education which has been dealt with above. These concern the possibility for writers, artists, etc. to create and transmit their works and the access of the public to their works so as to allow for participation in cultural life and the cultural identity of peoples.

The first two of these dimensions of cultural rights are considered together in the International Covenant on Economic, Social and Cultural Rights. Article 15 stipulates that everyone has the right to take part in cultural life, to enjoy the benefits of scientific progress and its applications and to benefit from the moral and material interests resulting from scientific, literary or artistic production.[17] Furthermore the States parties undertake to respect the freedom indispensable for scientific research and creative activity and to take the steps necessary for the conservation, the development and the diffusion of science and culture. They also recognize the importance of encouraging and developing international contacts in these areas.

A meaningful participation in cultural life and use of the benefits of scientific progress is possible only if there is effective protection of copyright and preservation of cultural heritage. The moral and material interests in intellectual production are protected, *inter alia*, by the Universal Copyright Convention of 1952, as revised in Paris in 1971, and by more specialized conventions relating to the protection of performers, producers of phonograms and broadcasting organizations (1961), protection against unauthorized duplication of phonograms (1971) and prohibiting and preventing the illicit import, export and transfer of ownership of cultural property (1970). A series of conventions relating to the protection of intellectual property and copyright has been adopted within the framework of the World Intellectual Property Organization, whose responsibilities relate to rights over literary, artistic and scientific work and inventions and scientific discoveries.[18] Mention should also be made of the Recommendation on the Status of Scientific Researchers, adopted on 20 November 1974 by the General Conference of Unesco at its 18th Session.

As regards the protection of cultural property, particular attention has been given to preserving certain monuments, sights, buildings, manuscripts and collections of books or archives from destruction or damage in time of armed conflict, as well as from theft, pillage or vandalism. The Convention of the Hague for the Protection of Cultural Property in the Event of Armed Conflict and Protocol for the Execution of the Convention, both of 1954, contain detailed principles and regulations of the type found in the Geneva Conventions for the Protection of Victims of War of 1949, including special protection for internationally registered property (for which there is an "International Register of Cultural Property under Special Protection"). There are provisions for their control with the assistance of special commissioners-general, for their safe transport, as well as others aimed at preserving treasures belonging to the cultural heritage of mankind.[19]

The international community is now increasingly concerned with attaining the general objective of ensuring for everyone the right to participate freely in the cultural life of society laid down in the Charter of the United Nations, the Universal Declaration of Human Rights and the Covenant on Economic, Social and Cultural Rights.

In this spirit, in 1973, the UN General Assembly urged governments "to make cultural values, both material and spiritual, an integral part of development efforts" and to promote "involvement of the population in the elaboration and implementation of measures ensuring preservation and future development of cultural and moral values" (res. 3148 (XXVIII)).

At its nineteenth session (Nairobi, 1976), the General Conference of Unesco adopted a Recommendation on Participation by the People at Large in Cultural Life and their Contribution to It. This Recommendation is a detailed instrument containing 25 preambular paragraphs and a series of principles and norms which are to be implemented in accordance with the constitutional practice of each State. They cover definitions, legislation and administration, technical, administrative, economic and financial measures and international co-operation. The Recommendation stipulates, *inter alia*, that States should guarantee cultural rights as human rights, guarantee equality of cultures, provide access to the treasures of national and world culture without discrimination, protect and develop authentic forms of expression, and a number of other policies relating to the status of persons participating in the creative processes, mass communication media, education, leisure, etc. Certain measures are recommended in order to make these policies operationally effective, such as: decentralizing facilities, activities and decision-making; utilizing non-institutionalized and non-professional initiatives and advisory structures; making wide use of information media, diversification of programmes; and granting subsidies and awarding prizes for cultural activities.

Cultural identity constitutes a preoccupation not only for countries engaged in the process of liberation from foreign domination—which always includes a cultural component—but also for countries where the problem is posited in terms of alienation. In this respect, the notion of participation should be stressed in the sense of active participation of the community in artistic events, which is a feature of the cultural life of countries, such as the African ones, where culture is rooted in the people and the community.[20] Democratization and decentralization are imperative in these countries as essential aspects of cultural policy. Countries under colonial domination are intensely aware of the need to establish and assert a national identity on the basis of cultural values which often need to be revised and adapted to present conditions. Cultural identity contributes to liberation, for it provides a justification for independence movements and resistance to colonialism. Since the Bandung Conference of 1955, the importance of cultural identity has been reflected in international declarations and meetings and the promotion of cultural identity is a recognized objective within the context of global development strategy, among individuals, groups, nations and regions. In 1966, the General Conference of Unesco adopted the Declaration of Principles of International Co-operation which proclaims in Article I:

"1. Each culture has a dignity and value which must be respected and preserved.

2. Every people has the right and the duty to develop its culture.

3. In their rich variety and diversity, and in the reciprocal influences they exert on one another, all cultures form part of the common heritage belonging to all mankind."

The Intergovernmental Conference on Cultural Policies in Africa, organized by Unesco with the co-operation of the OAU (Accra, 27 October-6 November 1975), expressed the principles relating to cultural identity in the following way:

"32. The assertion of cultural identity was considered to be an act of liberation, a weapon in the fight for effective independence and the best means of achieving the self-fulfilment of individuals and the harmonious development of societies. It was, moreover, the first prerequisite for the advent of a new world order, based on the inalienable right of nations to dispose of themselves and on recognition of the absolute equality and dignity of all cultures.

33. However, the assertion of cultural identity presupposed resolution and deliberate action to remove the element of alienation inherent in forms of thought and action which were foreign to African reality, and the abandonment of undue susceptibility to outside influences which still too often characterized certain kinds of behaviour. There could be no genuine independence without cultural decolonization."

These principles are continually being updated and reaffirmed to give greater weight to this essential component of cultural rights.

10. EQUALITY IN THE ENJOYMENT OF ECONOMIC, SOCIAL AND CULTURAL RIGHTS

The Universal Declaration of Human Rights proclaims, in Article 2, paragraph 1, that "everyone is entitled to all the rights and freedoms set forth in this Declaration without distinction of any kind such as race, colour, sex, language, religion, political or other opinion, national or social origin, property, birth or other status". These words are echoed in Article 2, paragraph 2 of the Covenant on Economic, Social and Cultural Rights. The Covenant, however, goes on to provide, in Article 2, paragraph 3, that "developing countries, with due regard to human rights and their national economy, may determine to what extent they would guarantee the economic rights recognized in the present Covenant to non-nationals". It should be noted that this limitation is confined to developing countries and applies only to economic rights, as distinct from social and cultural rights. It appears from the preparatory work that its purpose was to prevent non-nationals from monopolizing the economy of developing countries, and to safeguard the right of these countries to the enjoyment and disposal of their natural wealth and resources.[21]

It should be noted that the right to property, which had been provided for in Article 17 of the Universal Declaration of Human Rights, has not been included in the Covenants, and hence nothing in the positive provisions of the Covenants would prevent the assertion of control over a country's economy and resources.

One of the main problems which remains is the possibility for States to regulate the employment of foreigners and to be able to pursue policies designed to promote the employment of their own nationals at all levels of responsibility.

In this connection, it may be noted that Article 2, paragraph 2 of the Covenant on Economic, Social and Cultural Rights rules out discrimination on grounds of national origin, but this is not the same as distinctions based on nationality. A similar approach was adopted in the ILO's Discrimination (Employment and Occupation) Convention of 1958 (No. 111), it being understood that States would retain the possibility of regulating the employment of alien labour (which may, of course, be the subject of special bilateral or multilateral arrangements). It should, however, be noted that the ILO's recently adopted Migrant Workers (Supplementary Provisions) Convention of 1975 (No. 143) does within the framework of a policy to promote equality of opportunity and treatment in employment and occupation of migrant workers lawfully resident in the national territory, permit restrictions on free choice of employment during a limited period as well as in certain categories of employment where required in the interests of the State.[22]

Leaving aside the special considerations mentioned above, there is no reason why the greater part of the rights provided for in the Covenant should not be accorded to aliens lawfully residing within the national territory, such as the right to fair remuneration, safe and healthy working conditions, social security coverage, medical care, etc. Indeed, the failure to accord equality of treatment to aliens in regard to such rights would be likely to lead to the very forms of exploitation of migrant labour which the international community has been seeking to combat. In that connection, it should be noted that most international labour Conventions, even those not containing any specific provision for equal treatment of aliens, apply to all persons falling within their scope, without distinction as to nationality, and that it would therefore not be open to a State, which ratified any such Convention, to exclude aliens from its application. This would be the case, for example, as regards Conventions relating to wages, hours of work, weekly rest, holidays with pay, the employment of women and young persons, industrial health and safety, the abolition of forced labour or trade union rights, freedom of association and social security.

Several ILO Conventions have as their main object the protection and equality of treatment in employment of alien workers, such as the Migration for Employment Convention (Revised) of 1949 (No. 97), the Equality of Treatment (Social Security) Convention of 1962 (No. 118), and the Migrant Workers (Supplementary Provisions) Convention of 1975 (No. 143). The last-mentioned, in addition to providing for measures to combat migration in abusive conditions, provides for the declaration and pursuit of national policy to promote and guarantee equality of opportunity and treatment in respect of employment and occupation, social security, trade union and cultural rights, and of individual and collective freedoms for migrant workers and their families lawfully residing within the national territory.

A series of instruments concerning equal treatment of migrant workers in the field of social security has also been adopted at the regional level under the auspices of organizations such as the European Economic Community, the Council of Europe, the Organization of Central American States, and the Common African, Malagasy and Mauritian Organization.

An analysis of the economic, social and cultural development of many countries shows that their achievements are still far from the standards recognized in the Covenant and other international instruments. For a fair and comprehensive realization of economic, social and cultural rights, it is very important that each State implements the principles and aims of the Declaration on Social Progress and Development adopted by the United Nations General Assembly.[23] The Declaration calls for the realization of a number of national and international programmes which comprise a basis of the policy of social development and progress. Particularly important for the realization of economic, social and cultural rights are the following aims and principles proclaimed in the Declaration: elimination of all forms of discrimination, inequality, colonialism, racism, nazism, *apartheid* and exploitation of the peoples and individuals; respect for national sovereignty and territorial integrity of States and non-interference in their domestic affairs; the implementation of agrarian reforms as a result of which systems of land ownership and land tenure would best serve the goals of social justice and economic development; the adoption of measures for continuous and comprehensive industrial and agricultural growth and assurance of the right to work to all; fair and equitable distribution of national wealth and income among all members of society; elimination of inequality, poverty, hunger and undernourishment, as well as assurance of adequate housing to all; establishment of comprehensive systems of social security and insurance; achievement of high standards of medical care and protection of health and medical service free whenever possible; eradication of illiteracy with free education at all levels and general access to culture; elaboration of measures for the protection and improvement of the environment; development of international co-operation with the aim of international exchange of information, knowledge, experience in the field of social progress and development; and the achievement of general and complete disarmament and channelling of the resources released to the needs of economic and social progress and well-being of all nations.

NOTES

1. See *United Nations Actions in the Field of Human Rights*, 2nd ed., UN doc., Sales No. E.80.XIV.3.

2. ST/TAO/HR/40, para. 47.

3. A.P. Movchan, *Mezhdunarodnaya zashchita prav cheleveka* [International Protection of Human Rights], p. 91, Moscow, Gosjurizdat, 1958. A.H. Robertson, *Human Rights in the World*, p. 35, Manchester, University Press, 1972.

4. Ibid., p. 35.

5. See Report of the Joint ILO/Unesco Committee of Experts on the Application of the Recommendation concerning the Status of Teachers, Second Session, Paris, April-May 1970, paras. 304 and 365.

6. *The Realization of Economic, Social and Cultural Rights: Problems, Policies, Progress*, by M. Ganji (UN Sales No. E.75.XIV.2)

7. The European Convention for the Protection of Human Rights and Fundamental Freedoms in this respect follows the wording of the Covenant.

8. The European Special Charter and the American Convention on Human Rights also permit restrictions on the right to organize only of members of the armed forces and the police.

9. See *Freedom of Association—Digest of Decisions of the Freedom of Association Committee of the Governing Body of the ILO*, Geneva, 1972, paras. 305-328, and *Trade Union Rights and their Relation to Civil Liberties*, Report VII, International Labour Conference, 54th Session (1970).

10. See *Freedom of Association and Collective Bargaining, General Survey by the Committee of Experts on the Application of Conventions and Recommendations*, Report III (Part 43), International Labour Conference, 58th Session (1973), and *Freedom of Association—Digest of Decisions of the Freedom of Association Committee of the Governing Body of the ILO*, Geneva, 1972, paras. 240-292.

11. The question might merit examination, for example, whether—following the practice adopted in regard to parallel provisions in the European Social Charter—national laws regulating the exercise of the right to strike should be viewed in the light of the principle, laid down in Article 4 of the Covenant, that limitations on rights recognized by the Covenant must be compatible with the nature of these rights and be imposed solely for the purpose of promoting the general welfare in a democratic society.

12. See also *Health Aspects of Human Rights, with Special Reference to Developments in Biology and Medicine*, Geneva, WHO, 1976.

13. A register of these is contained in UN doc A/35/359(1980).

14. On the functioning of this Convention, see Pierre Mertens, "L'application de la convention et de la recommandation de l'Unesco concernant la lutte contre la discrimination dans le domaine de l'enseignement: un bilan provisoire", *RDH/HRJ*, vol. I, no. 1, 1968, pp. 91-108.

15. See the analysis of the discussion on this Article in A. Verdoodt, *Naissance et signification de la Déclaration universelle des droits de l'homme*, pp. 241-252, Louvain-Paris, Editions Nauwelaerts, 1964.

16. Imre Szabo, *Cultural Rights*, pp. 11-42, Budapest, Akadémiai Kiado, 1974.

17. See also Article 27 of the Universal Declaration of Human Rights.

18. The basic international instruments relating to these matters are the Paris Convention of 1883 for the Protection of Industrial Property, revised in 1967, the Berne Convention of 1886 for the Protection of Literary and Artistic Work and the Universal Copyright Convention, signed in Geneva in 1952.

19. See generally UN doc. A/35/349 (1980).

20. See Intergovernmental Conference on Cultural Policies in Africa, Accra, 27 October-6 November 1975, Final Report, Part II (Report of Commission I), para. 8, Unesco, 1975.

21. See International Provisions Protecting the Rights of Non-Citizens, UN, New York, 1980 (Sales No. E.80.XIV.2).

22. In 1980 a working group of the General Assembly began work on the elaboration of an international convention on the protection of the rights of all migrant workers and their families. See GA res. 34/172 (1979).

23. GA res. 2542 (XXIV) (1969).

7 Civil and Political Rights

Frank C. Newman and Karel Vasak

1. PROBLEMS IN THE APPLICATION AND INTERPRETATION OF CIVIL AND POLITICAL RIGHTS by Frank C. Newman

In this section, we shall show on the one hand, that innumerable international instruments relate to human rights and, on the other, that these instruments are implemented and enforced to varying degrees. The question thus arises as to exactly what these instruments prescribe in the field of civil and political rights.

This basic question leads to subsidiary questions:

Which human rights are "civil and political"?
What international documents contain civil and political rights?
Where do we find the official interpretation of these documents?
What about "moral" rights (compared with "legal")?
Are precedents created when human rights laws are violated?

Before replying to these five questions, it may be useful to delimit the subject matter of this section through examples. The "right to vote"—an important political right—is a good example to start with. The International Bill of Human Rights[1] has the following provision relating to the right to vote (Article 25 of the International Covenant on Civil and Political Rights):

"Every citizen shall have the right and the opportunity, without any of the distinctions mentioned in Article 2 and without unreasonable restrictions: a) to take part in the conduct of public affairs, directly or through freely chosen representatives; b) to vote and to be elected at genuine periodic elections which shall be by universal and equal suffrage and shall be held by secret ballot, guaranteeing the free expression of the will of the electors..."

We shall not deal here with the "distinctions mentioned in Article 2" namely discrimination based on race, sex, religion, etc., which are dealt with elsewhere in this book.[2] Nor shall we examine "general" limitations which may be made on the right to vote. These are, for example, the restrictions applied in case of public emergency and the various derogation clauses dealt with later.

What then? The terms of Article 25 of the Covenant on Civil and Political Rights just quoted are very ambiguous and raise many questions such as:

> When are the restrictions on the right to vote "unreasonable"?
> When are representatives "freely chosen"?
> What are "genuine periodic elections"?
> When is suffrage "universal and equal"?
> What is meant by "secret ballot"?
> Who should be considered a "citizen"?

One of the main purposes of this section is to make it possible to answer such questions.

The term "genocide" is a different type of example. The human right at stake is the right not to be threatened by or become a victim of genocide. Article 6 of the Covenant on Civil and Political Rights refers to the 1948 Convention on The Prevention and Punishment of the Crimes of Genocide and stipulates that the death penalty shall not be "contrary to the provisions" of the Convention. According to the definition given therein, genocide means "any of the following acts committed with intent to destroy, in whole or in part, a national, ethnical, racial or religious group, such as: a) killing members of the group; b) causing serious bodily or mental harm to members of the group; c) deliberately inflicting on the group conditions of life calculated to bring about its physical destruction in whole or in part; d) imposing measures intended to prevent births within the group; e) forcibly transferring children of the group to another group."

This definition seems reasonably clear. It applies to any "national, ethnical, racial or religious" group but not to purely "political" groups. The glaring disparity between legal definitions and rhetoric about this term comes out in the following:

"(An alleged oppressor)...was clever enough not to concentrate on individuals who opposed the regime but to crush the soul and pride of the nation as a whole. This is spiritual genocide." (*The New York Times*, 23 September 1972, p. 29).

"Urgently request UN mission to visit territory and examine unjust and iniquitous land laws designed to deprive illiterate indigenes of their land. Stop. Such deprivation amounts to genocide as indigenes have no other resource." (A/AC.109/PET.1122, 29 December 1969.

(Paragraph 30 . . . (in UN Doc. E/CN4/Sub.2/L.582) appeared to be inspired by tendentious propaganda based on racial and religious hatred. The Special Rapporteur *had confused the specific characteristics of the crime of genocide with the normal consequences of wars*. However, in a study which was intended to be scientific, it was inadmissible that a distorted picture of certain past events should be included Indeed, it would merely complicate the Commission's work in its search for an exact definition of the crime of genocide." (E/CN.4/SR.1286, 8 March 1974, p. 3—emphasis added).

"The United Nations heard charges today that 'North American imperialists' were embarked on a 'plan of genocide' in Puerto Rico that has led to sterilization of 200,000 women, or 35 percent of those of childbearing age." (*The New York Times*, 31 October 1974, p. 10).

"There have been allegations that school busing, birth control clinics, lynching, police actions with respect to the Black Panthers, and the incidents at My Lai constitute genocide. The Committee wants to make clear that . . . none of these and similar acts is genocide unless the intent to destroy the group as a group is proven. Harassment of minority groups and racial and religious intolerance generally, no matter how much to be deplored, are not outlawed *per se* by the Genocide Conventions." (U.S. Sen. Ex. Rep. 93-5, 6 March 1973, p. 6).

The indications provided in this section regarding interpretation may be useful to all who, at the political or practical level, must reply to accusations of genocide so often made by the press and other media.

(a). Which human rights are "civil and political"?

Here we differentiate "civil and political" from "economic, social and cultural". For exact definitions, we use the Universal Declaration of Human Rights and the two UN Covenants. Even in that unique compilation there are a few overlappings and inconsistencies.

This chapter excludes civil and political rights that are discussed elsewhere in this book. An example is freedom from discrimination on grounds of race, colour, sex, language, religion, political or other opinion, national or social origin, property, birth or other status (Art. 2 of each Covenant). See also these words in Article 27 of the Civil and Political Covenant:

"In those States in which ethnic, religious or linguistic minorities exist, persons belonging to such minorities shall not be denied the right, in community with the other members of their group, to enjoy their own culture, to profess and practice their own religion, or to use their own language."

Some jurists try to list or classify civil and political rights. In Article 5 of the United Nations Convention on the Elimination of All Forms of Racial Discrimination, for instance, this catalogue appears:

"a) The right to equal treatment before the tribunals and all other organs administering justice;

b) The right to security of person and protection by the State against violence or bodily harm, whether inflicted by Government officials or by any individual, group or institution;

c) Political rights, in particular the rights to participate in elections, to vote and to stand for election—on the basis of universal and equal suffrage, to take part in the Government as well as in the conduct of public affairs at any level and to have equal access to public service;

d) Other civil rights, in particular:

   (i) the right to freedom of movement and residence within the border of the State;

   (ii) the right to leave any country, including one's own, and to return to one's country;

   (iii) the right to nationality;

   (iv) the right to marriage and choice of spouse;

   (v) the right to own property alone as well as in association with others;

   (vi) the right to inherit;

   (vii) the right to freedom of thought, conscience and religion;

   (viii) the right to freedom of opinion and expression;

   (ix) the right to freedom of peaceful assembly and association."

A less formal list, describing for schoolchildren the relevant articles of the American Declaration on the Rights and Duties of Man, reads as follows:

"Every human being has the right to be treated as a brother.

The Articles of this Declaration are applicable to all peoples, no matter who they are, what they do, what they believe, or where they live.

Every human being has the right to live peacefully.

No one is compelled to work as a slave.

No one should be treated inhumanly.

Every person, everywhere, under all circumstances, is deserving of his rights.

All persons have the right to equality before the law.

No one may be punished for a crime or offence he did not commit.

Every person has the right to defend himself before a previously established court.

Every person has the right to be considered innocent until he is proved guilty.

Every person has the right to establish a residence and to freedom of movement.

Any person who is persecuted in one country has the right to change his residence to another.

Every person has the right to the inviolability of his home.

Every person has the right to own property and to preserve it.

Every person has the right to the freedom of religion and worship.

Every person has the right to hold his own ideas and to express them.
Every person has the right to vote for the candidates of his choice, by secret
    ballot, and in honest elections.
Every person has the right to be a member of any association permitted by
    law...
Every child has the right to determine his paternity.
Every person has the right to assemble peaceably with others.
Every person should endeavor, whenever possible, to aid others to ensure
    these rights".[3]

Here we will attempt no list, classification or catalogue. Instead we will
stress words, especially the words in the Universal Declaration of Human
Rights (its first 21 articles, also Articles 28 to 30) and in the Civil and Political
Covenant (Parts II and III). They are the instruments which are essential for
human rights. This chapter should be read along with a copy of those two
documents which must be studied with care. Almost every word that sur-
vived the drafting disputes during the UN deliberations will merit scholarly
analysis.[4]

(b). What international documents contain civil and political rights?

Obviously, the provisions of the Universal Declaration and the Covenant on
Civil and Political Rights are only the starting point for our search. Countless
other international instruments also contain relevant provisions.

It should be kept in mind that a government may be bound not only by
human rights treaties to which it is a signatory or a party but also by some
treaties it has not signed, ratified or acceded to, and some instruments that
are not treaties. This results in part from the substance of international law
which includes, as illustrated by the famous words of Article 38, paragraph 1,
of the Statute of the International Court of Justice, "custom" and "general
principles". What is still more important is that numerous treaties and other
documents authoritatively interpret the human rights clauses of the UN
Charter by which practically every State is bound. This is clearly the case
with the International Bill of Human Rights; and a parallel interpretative
impact of the UN Convention on Racial Discrimination, the Declaration on
the Granting of Independence to Colonial Countries and Peoples, the 1949
Geneva Conventions and many other documents is now well-established.[5]

To illustrate: exactly what are the obligations of governments regarding
torture? All UN Member States pledged themselves, in Article 56 of the
Charter, "to take joint and separate action in co-operation with the Organization for the achievement of the purposes set forth in Article 55"; and those
purposes set forth in Article 55 include promotion of "respect for, and observance of, human rights". *When a government condones torture, is its
action consistent with the promotion of respect for, and observance of,
human rights?*

Yet may a government's officials contend that its obligation under the Charter is really too ephemeral, too vague? Fortunately, many other documents, in detail, spell out the world's proscriptions of torture. For example:

Universal Declaration of Human Rights
No one shall be subjected to torture or to cruel, inhuman or degrading treatment or punishment (Art. 5).
Covenant on Civil and Political Rights
No one shall be subjected to torture or to cruel, inhuman or degrading treatment or punishment. In particular, no one shall be subjected without his free consent to medical or scientific experimentation (Art. 7).
All persons deprived of their liberty shall be treated with humanity and with respect for the inherent dignity of the human person (Art. 10.1).
European Convention on Human Rights
No one shall be subjected to torture or to inhuman or degrading treatment or punishment (Art. 3).
American Declaration of the Rights and Duties of Man
Every individual who has been deprived of his liberty...has the right to humane treatment during the time he is in custody (Art. XXV).
Every person accused of an offense has the right...not to receive cruel, infamous or unusual punishment (Art. XXVI).
American Convention on Human Rights
No one shall be subjected to torture or to cruel, inhuman, or degrading punishment or treatment. All persons deprived of their liberty shall be treated with respect for the inherent dignity of the human person (Art. 5.2).
1949 Geneva Conventions on the Wounded, Prisoners of War, Civilians
The following acts are...prohibited...
a) violence to...person, in particular...mutilation, cruel treatment and torture;...
b) outrages upon personal dignity; in particular, humiliating and degrading treatment...(Art. 3.1).
UN Standard Minimum Rules for the Treatment of Prisoners
Corporal punishment, punishment by placing in a dark cell, and all cruel, inhuman or degrading punishment shall be completely prohibited as punishment for disciplinary offenses (Art. 31).

What should a government's legal advisors and other lawyers advise regarding all these words? Every nation in the world, we submit, is bound, as to torture, by all those clauses in the UN Charter, the Universal Declaration, the Covenant on Civil and Political Rights, the Geneva Conventions of 1949, and the Standard Minimum Rules.[6] Every individual in the world is entitled to the protections afforded by "the best words" of all those documents. The European Convention because of its stingy wording does not add to the substantive law; yet its procedural protections could be crucial. The two American texts, differing as they do slightly from the UN texts, might be supplementary in borderline cases; they too, of course, could be the basis for procedural protection.

Torture exemplifies many problems of human rights in which, to find the relevant provisions of substantive law, we must examine whole sets of documents. The fact that one document seems clearly to apply to a situation is *never* sufficient reason for assuming that greater protection may not be accorded by other documents.

(c). Where do we find the official interpretation of these documents?

In many nations, the most official and most influential interpretations are found in the decisions of courts and tribunals. Only sporadically, however, do domestic courts and tribunals deal with international human rights law. On their part, international decision-making organs are even more rarely concerned. Therefore, we are not normally instructed by the lessons of adjudicated cases.

International precedents relating to civil and political rights are mostly due to the efforts of diplomats and other non-judges, and of bodies whose powers are analogous to those of an *ombudsman* in that their functions are investigative, reportive, recommendatory and censurial rather than adjudicative.

The practice of legislative bodies and of other quasi-legislative bodies is relevant. There are, of course, some doubts as to when that practice truly does interpret or apply international law. Yet it is legislative practice, for example, that seems to have abolished any juridical distinction between "human rights" and "fundamental freedoms". The UN Charter, which mentions "human rights and fundamental freedoms", could have been interpreted to create distinctions.[7]

How should we approach the international case law and practice that affect civil and political rights? Traditionally, jurists have been most comfortable at that kind of task when they take the words of a treaty or other document and then line up the precedents that seem to interpret, apply or in other ways concretize those words. They then decide which precedents seem most correct, most authoritative, most persuasive for whatever reasons.

That process can be and is employed in international human rights law. By examining, for instance, the Secretariat's *Repertory of Practice of UN Organs* and also *Charter of the United Nations: Commentary and Documents* (Goodrich, Hambro and Simon, 3rd edition, 1969), we can find citations that concern each human rights clause of the UN Charter.[8]

By examining the works of Fawcett, Partsch and others and the *Digest of Case-Law Relating to the European Convention on Human Rights 1955-1967*, we are able to identify cases and practices regarding each clause of the European Convention on Human Rights.[9] These volumes are notable among hundreds that might usefully guide us.

(d). What about "moral" rights (compared with "legal" rights)?

Our attention is focused here on legal rights. The question "Have human rights been violated?" here means, "Has human rights law been violated?". Further, we here postulate a violator, whether governmental or non-governmental.

To illustrate: starvation often violates individuals' human rights. In this case there are two inquiries: "Where legal norms violated?" and "Was there a violator?". Governments and non-governmental persons may have moral, not always legal, duties to help prevent starvation, but moral duties are not here our concern.

(e). Are precedents created when human rights laws are violated?

We here presume that legal rights exist whether or not there are remedies. That does not mean we ignore or condone violations which persist unremedied. That they do persist, however, hardly transforms them into precedents. International human rights law still is new law. Traditional doctrines such as desuetude seem inapt. A distinguished scholar and statesman has reminded us that "a model for behaviour can remain a legal norm (even) if it is not universally respected" and that "it ceases to be a norm, and becomes a dream, (only) when it no longer corresponds to the generality of practice and society abandons any attempt to vindicate or protect it."[10] By no means has our society yet abandoned its vigorous attempts to vindicate and protect human rights law.

2. ANALYTICAL EXAMINATION OF CIVIL AND POLITICAL RIGHTS by Karel Vasak

In order to carry out an analytical examination of civil and political rights, it is fitting to refer to those legal instruments whose very purpose is either to proclaim those rights or to guarantee them. These are the Universal Declaration of Human Rights (Articles 3-21) and the International Covenant on Civil and Political Rights, then the regional Conventions, namely the European Convention on Human Rights and its Additional Protocols Nos. 1 and 4, the American Declaration of the Rights and Duties of Man (Articles 1 to 10, 17 to 28), and the American Convention on Human Rights, together with a number of specific instruments concerning particular civil or political rights such as, for instance, the Convention on the Prevention and Punishment of the Crime of Genocide.

It is primarily in connection with treaties relating to civil and political rights that the question arises as to whether their provisions are "self-executing"[11] or, in other words, whether they are directly and immediately applicable under the municipal law of States that have ratified them or, in order for them to be applied, they necessitate national measures of implementation. It is to be noted that this question arises only for those States in which a treaty, once ratified becomes an integral part of its municipal law; for other States, this same treaty will remain a simple inter-State commitment that will have to be executed by the State under its municipal law by means of legislative and other measures of its choice.

In the doctrine, the self-executing character of both the Covenant on Civil and Political Rights and the European Convention on Human Rights[12] has been much debated, but the problem does not seem to have been discussed in regard to the other treaties mentioned above. In the case of the Covenant, it has been contended that paragraph 2 of Article 2, in particular, allows one to conclude that the Covenant does not oblige States to put it immediately into application since it stipulates: "Where not already provided for by existing legislative or other measures, each State Party to the present Covenant undertakes to take the necessary steps, in accordance with its constitutional processes and with the provisions of the present Covenant, to adopt such legislative or other measures as may be necessary to give effect to the rights recognized in the present Covenant." Conversely, it has been stressed that "the obligations undertaken by the parties to the International Covenant on Civil and Political Rights are, by and large, meant to be implemented immediately upon ratification, and the rights set forth in the International Covenant on Economic, Social and Cultural Rights are to be implemented progressively".[13]

Without taking sides in this controversy the importance of which is not merely theoretical, I must point out that in those countries which consider the treaties on human rights to be self-executing, these treaties can consequently be directly invoked before the national authorities and, first of all, before the courts. Thus, there will be a *national* case-law and practice interpreting the provisions of these treaties alongside an *international* case-law and practice which will be the work of organs responsible for international implementation, with the first, however, not having the same authority as the second. Although this case-law and practice, both national and international, is as yet in an embryonic state for the universal treaties[14]—the Covenant only entered into force in 1976—their volume is already considerable in the case of the regional treaties and, primarily, the European Convention on Human Rights.[15] Insofar as the treaties protecting civil and political rights contain identical or largely similar provisions—in this respect there are a far larger number of equivalent provisions than of divergent ones—national and international case-law and practice in regard to a treaty may serve, if not as legal precedents, at least as elements of reference or inspiration for the interpretation of the provisions of another treaty. In the following pages, I shall, for lack of space, make do with giving merely a few very general guidelines; a comparative and truly exhaustive analytical study still unfortunately remaining to be carried out.

The civil and political rights set forth in the different instruments on human

rights are aimed at protecting man's personal integrity (a), his freedom (b),
his right to the proper administration of justice (c), his family and his privacy
(d), his intellectual activity (e), his political and trade union activity (f), and
his economic activity (g); but the rights thus guaranteed are also subject to
several restrictions (h), and to the principles of equality and non-discrimination,
dealt with above,[16] which govern their application and their interpretation.

(a). Protection of the integrity of the human person

(i). THE RIGHT TO LIFE

The right to life is the first right of man. All the international instruments
proclaim that right in largely similar terms.[17] The death penalty, however, is
not prohibited, although its abolition seems to be desired by the Covenant, in
particular in paragraph 6 of Article 6. According to the Covenant, no one
shall be "arbitrarily" deprived of his life, or only in cases specifically enumerated by the regional Conventions. Protection must be provided against the
death sentence in Member States of the international community with regard, in particular, to persons under 18 years of age and pregnant women;
furthermore, all ways and means of avoiding capital punishment must be
preserved (pardon, commutation of sentence, amnesty).

While it falls to the national legislature to establish the violation of the
right to life as a crime and to take all the necessary measures, such violations,
when directed, in whole or in part, against the right to life of a national,
ethnic, racial or religious group, are referred to as genocide—a crime which
the international community has made the subject of a specific Convention,
namely the Convention on the Prevention and Punishment of the Crime of
Genocide of 9 December 1948.[18] The crime of genocide, like other crimes
against humanity, together with war crimes, is not subject to statutory limitation under the terms of the Convention on the Non-Applicability of Statutory Limitations to War Crimes and Crimes against Humanity of 26 November
1968, the equivalent of which exists in Europe in the form of the Council of
Europe Convention on the Non-Applicability of Statutory Limitations to War
Crimes and Crimes against Humanity of 25 January 1974.

In recent years the question, which has most frequently been brought
before both national tribunals[19] and international organs for the implementation of human rights,[20] is that of the compatibility of abortion and certain
other means of birth control with the right to life.

(ii). RECOGNITION OF JURIDICAL PERSONALITY AND THE RIGHT TO NATIONALITY

Everyone has the right to recognition everywhere as a person before the
law;[21] "civil death", whatever its form, consequently is not permitted by the
international community.

It is here that the question arises as to whether and to what extent the
human rights recognized by the international instruments benefit *both* natu-

ral persons and legal persons. The question is not always settled in the clearest terms, although the general tendency is to recognize that legal persons enjoy those human rights that are compatible with their nature. But hesitations are still allowed, particularly in the case of the Covenant.[22]

Whereas the Universal Declaration proclaims in its Article 15 that "everyone has the right to a nationality" and that "no one shall be arbitrarily deprived of his nationality nor denied the right to change his nationality", the Covenant confines itself to stipulating in its Article 24, paragraph 3, that "every child has the right to acquire a nationality".[23] Specific conventions designed to settle the problems of double nationality, to guard against statelessness and to facilitate the exercise of human rights by refugees and stateless persons have been drawn up by the UN. These are: the Convention on the Nationality of Married Women of 29 January 1957, the Convention on the Reduction of Statelessness of 30 August 1961, the Convention relating to the Status of Stateless Persons of 28 September 1954, the Convention relating to the Status of Refugees of 28 July 1951 and the Protocol relating to the Status of Refugees of 31 January 1967.[24]

(iii). THE PROHIBITION OF TORTURE, CRUEL, INHUMAN OR DEGRADING TREATMENT OR PUNISHMENT AND MEDICAL OR SCIENTIFIC EXPERIMENTATION

The prohibition of torture, cruel, inhuman or degrading treatment or punishment and medical or scientific experimentation without the free consent of the person concerned is most strikingly revealed by the international community's concern to defend and preserve the physical and moral integrity of the human being. Not only is this prohibition included in all the instruments on human rights[25] but, in addition, there can never be any derogation from it, even in the event of public emergency.[26]

The General Assembly reacted against the spread of torture by adopting at its 30th session in 1975, by Resolution 3452 (XXX), the Declaration on the Protection of All Persons from Being Subjected to Torture and Other Cruel, Inhuman or Degrading Treatment or Punishment. In that Declaration torture is defined, in Article 1, as follows:

"1. For the purpose of this Declaration, torture means any act by which severe pain or suffering, whether physical or mental, is intentionally inflicted by or at the instigation of a public official on a person for such purposes as *obtaining* from him or a third person information or confession, punishing him for an act he has committed or is suspected of having committed, or intimidating him or other persons. It does not include pain or suffering arising only from, inherent in or incidental to, lawful sanctions to the extent consistent with the Standard Minimum Rules for the Treatment of Prisoners.
2. Torture constitutes an aggravated and deliberate form of cruel, inhuman or degrading treatment or punishment."

Since the adoption of the Declaration many States have made unilateral declarations in conformity with the principles contained therein (See UN doc.

A/35/370 (1980)). The drafting of a Convention against Torture and Other Cruel, Inhuman or Degrading Treatment or Punishment was begun by the Commission on Human Rights in 1978 but had not been completed as at February 1981.

Moreover, the question of torture has been raised on numerous occasions before several organs of the United Nations and in particular the Commission on Human Rights, in connection with different territories in southern Africa (Namibia, Rhodesia, South Africa), territories occupied by Israel and, more recently, Chile. The matter has also been brought before the regional institutions on human rights: the Inter-American Commission on Human Rights deals with allegations of torture in nearly all its reports;[27] the European Commission on Human Rights has had to concern itself with torture in the inter-State cases—*Greece v. United Kingdom; Denmark, Norway, Sweden and the Netherlands v. Greece* (the "Greek case"); *Ireland v. United Kingdom* and *Cyprus v. Turkey*, as well as in a great number of individual applications brought by prisoners who complained not so much of being tortured as of being ill-treated (*Kornman v. Federal Republic of Germany; Simon-Herald v. Austria*, etc.).

The prohibition of medical or scientific experimentation, practised on human beings in conditions contrary to human rights, was one of the after-effects against Nazism which had practised it on a large scale. While the so-called Nuremberg rules[28] define the limits and conditions for authorizing experimentation, they have not resolved all the problems arising in this area, which has again become topical in the last few years. "Patients' Bills of Rights" have been adopted in some States while, at the international level, the UN General Assembly again considered in 1980 a Draft Code of Medical Ethics, drafted by the World Health Organization with a view to protecting persons subjected to any form of detention or imprisonment, against torture and other cruel, inhuman or degrading treatment or punishment.[29]

(iv). PROHIBITION OF SLAVERY, SERVITUDE AND FORCED AND COMPULSORY LABOUR

Slavery and servitude, too, are absolutely prohibited, everywhere and at all times, by all the human rights instruments.[30] Specific conventions further reinforce this prohibition by defining, in particular, slavery: these are the Slavery Convention signed at Geneva on 25 September 1926 and the Protocol of 7 December 1953, which amends it, together with the Supplementary Convention on the Abolition of Slavery, the Slave Trade, and Institutions and Practices Similar to Slavery of 4 July 1957. In the same vein of thought, mention should be made of the Convention for the Suppression of the Traffic in Persons and of the Exploitation of the Prostitution of Others of 21 March 1950 which incorporates several instruments, adopted before the Second World War, aimed at the same objective.[31]

While, under the terms of the human rights instruments,[32] no one can be obliged to perform forced or compulsory labour, certain cases, limitatively enumerated, are not regarded as "forced or compulsory labour". These are: work by a person under detention; by a soldier; or by a conscientious objector where civic service is required in the interest of the community. Here too the prohibition of forced labour is reinforced by two international labour conventions: the ILO Convention Concerning Forced or Compulsory Labour of 1930 (No. 29) and the ILO Convention Concerning the Abolition of Forced Labour of 25 June 1957 (No. 105).

The question of forced or compulsory labour, after being the subject of discussions both at the United Nations and at the ILO, has been the theme of several proceedings instituted before international institutions responsible for implementing human rights. First, in the *Ghana v. Portugal* case in which the question to be answered was whether ILO Convention No. 105 had been violated in the African territories which at that time were Portuguese colonies;[33] then in the *Portugal v. Liberia* case, in which the question of forced labour in Liberia was raised in regard to ILO Convention No. 29.[34] In the framework of the European Convention on Human Rights, the two best-known cases are *Iversen v. Norway*, concerning compulsory service imposed on a dentist required to exercise his profession in the northern part of the country, and *Gussenbauer v. Austria*, which concerned the compulsory and free assistance of accused persons by lawyers and resulted in a friendly settlement through the reform of the Austrian system of legal assistance.

(b). Protection of freedom

(i). FREEDOM OF MOVEMENT

The recognized rights of everyone

What is involved here is first of all the right to *freedom of movement* within the territory of a State and *freedom to choose one's residence* for all who are lawfully within that territory.[35] The requirement concerning the *lawfulness* (Covenant and American Convention) or *regularity* (European Convention) of residence within the territory of a contracting State immediately rules out those who do not respect the administrative regulations governing entry and residence within the territory of a State and, in particular, aliens who have entered the country clandestinely. This provision constitutes, to a certain extent at least, a tautology since its result is to protect freedom of movement within the national territory for those who previously have been allowed by the State to exercise that same freedom.

In addition, everyone is free to leave any country, including his own.[36] The terminology employed recalls that of the Universal Declaration; in the case of the European Convention, the authors of the Protocol to that Convention proposed to give "the broadest possible meaning to the freedom to leave any region whatsoever, regardless of whether it is or is not a State".

These two recognized rights of all persons may be subject to certain restrictions *limitatively* but in fact, fairly broadly, enumerated in the paragraphs following the provisions protecting them. These are, firstly, the restrictions which, provided for by law, constitute measures "necessary to protect national security, public order (*ordre public*), public health or morals or the rights and freedoms of others".[37] It will be noticed (and the matter was amply discussed in Europe at the time of the preparation of Protocol No. 4 to the European Convention on Human Rights) that no restriction is admissible according to the Covenant if it is motivated by the requirements of the "economic welfare of the country" or, as was proposed at the time of the preparation of Protocol No. 4 to the European Convention, by the "requirements of economic prosperity". For various reasons, and partly because the notion of "*ordre public*", as it is understood in French, covers at least some of the aspects of the need to ensure the country's economic prosperity, it was decided not to include this factor among those governing the admissibility of a restriction.

The recognized rights of nationals

Under the terms of the European Convention and the American Convention on Human Rights,[38] only nationals are protected against *expulsion*, by means either of an individual or a collective measure, from the territory of the State of which they are nationals. The problem here is less that of protecting this right than that of enforcing it against the authority of the State, which is free to define who its nationals are. For a State might be tempted to get around the prohibition against the expulsion of nationals by depriving those concerned of their status as nationals.[39] This question, however, is not settled by the conventions on human rights, although general international law does contain certain elements limiting the right of the State to deprive persons of their status as nationals.

The Covenant, for its part, provides that no national shall be arbitrarily deprived of the right to enter "his own country".[40] In the regional conventions on human rights, the "country" referred to is identified with the State of which the person in question is a national. Here, too, there still remains a risk that a State might define its nationals in such a way as in fact to deprive certain categories of persons of the right to return to what is in reality "their own country", for instance, their country of permanent residence.[41]

The recognized rights of aliens

Of signal importance for aliens, the *right not to be expelled* from the territory of the State where they permanently reside is protected by the Covenant[42] in Article 13 which stipulates:

"An alien lawfully in the territory of a State Party to the present Convention may be expelled therefrom only in pursuance of a decision reached in accordance with law and shall, except where compelling reasons of national security otherwise require, be allowed to submit the reasons against his expulsion and to have his case reviewed by, and be represented for the purpose before, the competent authority or a person or persons especially designated by the competent authority."

In actual fact, the text contains so many loopholes that the principle alone seems to remain, the rule being submerged by countless exceptions.

In the regional conventions on human rights, the *collective expulsion of aliens* is prohibited.[43] This provision has a fairly unusual character in conventions protecting individual rights in that it concerns a group of individuals and no longer merely individuals in isolation. Its historical origin is obvious: it provides at least partial protection against the temptation for a State to denationalize a minority group, in order to transform its members into aliens, and subsequently to expel them.

(ii). RIGHT OF ASYLUM

Vigorously proclaimed in the Universal Declaration of Human Rights (Art. 14), the right of asylum was not provided for by the drafters of the Covenant, nor indeed by the European Convention on Human Rights.[44] The American Convention alone protects asylum in the form, both of the right to seek and be granted asylum and the right not to be deported to a country where the person concerned would fear for his life or freedom ("principle of non-deportation").

At the United Nations, the right to asylum was the subject of a Declaration adopted on 14 December 1962.[45] Moreover, a draft Convention concerning territorial asylum is at present being drafted on the initiative of the High Commissioner for Refugees. But it is the inter-American system which has sought, with the greatest perseverance, to ensure the protection of the right to asylum, as is borne out by the following Conventions: the Convention on Asylum of 20 February 1928, the Convention on Political Asylum of 26 December 1933, the Convention on Territorial Asylum of 28 March 1954 and the Convention on Diplomatic Asylum of 28 March 1954.[46]

Refugees, that is to say, persons who have been granted asylum—and, to a certain extent, also, those seeking asylum—are protected by the Convention Relating to the Status of Refugees of 28 July 1951, the scope of which, in time and space, was enlarged by the Protocol of 31 January 1967. Under the terms of its Statute of 14 December 1950, the United Nations High Commissioner for Refugees is responsible for assuming the function of providing international protection for refugees. In addition, it is to be noted that, owing to the deterioration of the refugee problem in Africa, the Organization of African Unity drew up the Convention Governing the Specific Aspects of Refugee Problems in Africa, dated 10 September 1969.

It is to be noted in conclusion that, by a fairly daring interpretation, the European Commission of Human Rights has judged that "the deportation or extradition of an alien to a particular country may in exceptional circumstances give rise to the question whether there would be 'inhuman treatment'..." (which is prohibited). "Such considerations might apply in cases where a person is extradited to a particular country where, due to the very nature of the regime of that country or to a particular situation in that country, basic human rights...might be either grossly violated or entirely suppressed." Thus, by means of the prohibition against inhuman treatment, protection is afforded, if not for the right to asylum, at least for the non-deportation principle in the context of Western Europe.[47] As this prohibition is also included in the universal instruments on human rights, and especially in the Covenant, the question may be raised as to whether this case-law does not also have a universal bearing.

(iii). THE RIGHT TO FREEDOM AND SAFETY

Everyone has the right to freedom and safety: to freedom which is a state enjoyed in the present, safety adds the certainty that that state will continue to be enjoyed in the future. The State must, however, be able to defend itself against those who interfere with the social order, for which it is responsible, by depriving them of their freedom.

Cases where it is authorized[48] to deprive the individual of his freedom

Article 9 of the Covenant stipulates that arrest and detention shall not be "arbitrary" and that no one shall be deprived of his liberty except "on such grounds and in accordance with such procedure as are established by law". It is thus the national legislature which has to specify those cases where a person can be deprived of his freedom and also to define the ground and procedure for so doing. The individual must then be deprived of his freedom in a manner which is not arbitrary,[49] i.e. neither *unlawful* because contrary to the law, nor *unjust* because unreasonable and contrary to the idea of justice.

The European Convention on Human Rights has availed itself in this connection of a method different from that of the Covenant in enumerating limitatively—actually defined in fairly general terms—the sole cases in which a person can be lawfully deprived of his freedom, namely: detention after conviction; arrest or detention for non-compliance with the lawful order of a court or in order to secure the fulfilment of any obligation prescribed by law; preventive detention; detention of a minor; arrest or detention with a view to deportation; expulsion; or extradition.[50]

Practically all of these cases have resulted in an abundance of case-law being formulated by the European Commission and Court of Human Rights, and mention may be made, by way of example, of the *Lawless v. Ireland*

and *Engel and others v. the Netherlands* cases as well as the *Vagrancy* cases.

Guarantees granted to persons deprived of their freedom[51]

A person deprived of his freedom shall benefit from certain guarantees so as to be able to defend himself against unjustified arrest or detention and to recover his freedom. These guarantees are: the right to be informed of the reasons for arrest; the right to be brought promptly before a judge and to be tried within a reasonable time or to be released—this raises the problem of the duration of remand in custody[52] and of preventive or provisional detention;[53] and the right to recourse before a court so that it can rule without delay upon the lawfulness of detention and the right to compensation in the event of unlawful arrest or detention.

Treatment of prisoners

All persons deprived of their liberty must be treated with humanity and with respect for the inherent dignity of the human person. Furthermore, a number of rules are aimed at the establishment of a liberal penitentiary system, the goal of which should be the reformation and social rehabilitation of prisoners. In particular, accused minors and young delinquents should be separated from adults; similarly, accused persons should be segregated from convicted persons.[54]

These few principles are developed and clarified in the "Standard Minimum Rules for the Treatment of Prisoners" which were adopted at Kyoto by the First United Nations Congress on the Prevention of Crime and the Treatment of Offenders in its resolution of 30 August 1955. Not binding on States, these "Rules" are aimed at setting out "what is generally accepted as being good principle and practice in the treatment of prisoners and the management of institutions" (Art. 1).[55] In addition, the UN Human Rights Sub-Commission has prepared a "draft body of principles for the protection of all persons under any form of detention or imprisonment" (See UN doc. A/35/401 (1980)).

(c). Protection of the right to justice

(i). THE GUARANTEED RIGHTS OF EVERYONE

The right to effective remedy

Anyone whose rights and freedoms are violated shall have an effective remedy before the competent judicial, administrative, legislative or other authority.[56] This remedy shall exist *notwithstanding* the fact that the violation has been committed by persons acting in an official capacity. It follows that by such remedy the person concerned shall be able to defend his human rights not only against the organs of the State, but also against other private persons ("notwithstanding that . . ."). We thus encounter the problem, debated by jurists, of the absolute character of human rights, that is to say, opposable both to the State and its organs and to mere individuals, and therefore applicable both in the relations between private persons and in the relations between the individual and the State: this is the problem known in the writings as that of the *Drittwirkung* of human rights.[57]

The right to a fair hearing

After establishing as a principle the equality of all before the tribunals and courts of justice—and in particular of nationals and aliens—the Covenant[58] enumerates in its Article 14.1 certain rights that all justice worthy of that name is in duty bound to respect: everyone has the right to a fair and public hearing by a competent, independent and impartial tribunal;[59] the hearing and the judgment shall be made public, although exceptions to this rule are authorized, particularly in the interest of minors and justice. These rights which are granted to all persons, natural or legal, accused, plaintiff or defendant, do not however seem to apply to *all* categories of litigation, but only to disputes relating to civil rights and obligations and to criminal charges. While, in general, it is relatively easy to define a criminal charge (although hesitations may arise in relation with disciplinary procedures),[60] it is far more difficult to pinpoint the notion of "civil rights and obligations". Is what is involved all "that is not covered by criminal law"? Is "civil" the equivalent of "private", in contrast with "public"? The question remains open.[61]

(ii). THE GUARANTEED RIGHTS OF ACCUSED PERSONS

A person charged with a criminal offence has additional and specific rights which are necessary for him to ensure his defense.[62] A person charged with a criminal offence shall, first of all, be presumed innocent until proven guilty according to law. This is a right which constitutes the very basis of all modern criminal law. But this right would be meaningless if it were not founded, as is the case in Article 15 of the Covenant, on the principle of the legality of offences and penalties, that is to say on the prohibitions of all retroactive penal legislation, it being understood that the general principles of law recognized by the community of nations are sufficient for an act or omission to be recognized as criminal.[63] This last interpretative provision clearly applies to "Nuremberg Law" and first of all to crimes against humanity.

In order to defend himself, an accused person shall be entitled to the following *minimum* guarantees, in full equality:

    (i) to be informed of the nature and cause of the charge against him;

    (ii) to have adequate time and facilities for the preparation of his defence and to communicate with counsel of his own choosing;

   (iii) to be tried without undue delay;[64]
   (iv) to be present at his trial and to defend himself in person or through
        legal assistance of his own choosing or, in certain conditions, to have
        legal assistance assigned to him without payment;
   (v) to examine the witnesses against him and to obtain the attendance
        and examination of witnesses on his behalf;
   (vi) to have the free assistance of an interpreter if he cannot understand
        the language used in court;
   (vii) not to be compelled to testify against himself or to confess guilt;
   (viii) to be able to appeal to a higher tribunal if convicted of a crime;
   (ix) to be compensated when there has been a miscarriage of justice;[65]
   (x) not to be tried or punished twice for the same offence.

(d). Protection of the family and of privacy

(i). PROTECTION OF THE FAMILY

The right to marry[66]

   Men and women of marriageable age have the right to marry and to found a
family. The marriage cannot be entered into without the free and full consent
of the intending spouses. These rules are developed and clarified in the
United Nations Convention on Consent to Marriage, Minimum Age for Marriage and Registration of Marriages of 10 December 1962, and in the Recommendation on the same subject, adopted by the General Assembly by its
Resolution 2018 (XX) of 1 December 1965.
   In addition, appropriate measures must be taken to ensure *equality* of
rights and responsibilities of spouses as to marriage, during marriage and at
its dissolution. This provision is one which is far from being applied in all
countries, as was shown by the work of the World Conference of the UN
Decade for Women, in 1980.[67]

The right to respect for one's family life

   Being the natural and fundamental group unit of society, the family is entitled to protection by society and the State.[68] This does not concern solely the
"lawful" family, for the natural family is just as entitled to protection. However, in order to be protected, family life must first of all exist, in the
sense that there must be bonds of kinship between those concerned, as well
as a community life or, at the very least, effective and regular relations.[69]
Although the conceptions of the "family" obviously vary from one society
to another, it is generally recognized that practically everywhere the natural family is less well treated than the lawful family and that such discrimination must end, particularly so far as the situation of the children is
concerned.

Respect for family life means first and foremost that the family shall be protected as a unit, both in respect of parents and in respect of parents and children. Thus, for instance, husband and wife are entitled to live together in the same country,[70] a very important requirement in the case of migrant workers, the son is entitled to join his father,[71] etc.

The rights of children

Every child is entitled, without any discrimination, to such measures of protection as are required by his status as a minor, on the part of his family, society and the State. He shall be registered immediately after his birth, have a name and be able to acquire a nationality.[72] These few rules are developed and considerably enlarged in the Declaration of the Rights of the Child, adopted by the General Assembly of 20 November 1959 by its Resolution 1386 (XIV), and are also the subject of many ILO Conventions.

In addition to the legislative and other achievements of the International Year of the Child in 1979, the UN Commission on Human Rights continued at its 1981 session its work on a draft convention on the rights of the child.[73]

(ii). THE PROTECTION OF PRIVACY

Honour, reputation and private life

No one shall be subjected to arbitrary or unlawful interference with his privacy, nor to unlawful attacks on his honour and reputation.[74] Private life, increasingly threatened by modern scientific and technological achievements in the form, for instance, of wiretapping devices and data banks, can scarcely be defined with precision. It signifies different things[75] according to the society involved and the environment in which the individual lives, and also takes on different meanings in the course of time. Since, in these circumstances, it is almost impossible to lay down hard-and-fast rules, the entire matter must be followed with constant vigilance, as recognized by the UN Commission on Human Rights.[76]

Home and correspondence[77]

The individual's home is inviolable. For interference to be permissible it must not be arbitrary, that is to say neither unreasonable nor capricious, and must be provided for by law. Freedom and secrecy of correspondence must be respected under the same conditions; by correspondence is to be understood, of course, all means of communication, such as the telephone, teleprinter, telegram, etc. Abuses in this field seem frequent, even though they are difficult to detect and to prove.[78]

(e). *Protection of intellectual activity*

(i). FREEDOM OF THOUGHT, CONSCIENCE AND RELIGION

Everyone shall have the right to freedom of thought, conscience and reli-gion,[79] which includes freedom to have or to adopt (and consequently to change) a religion or belief of his choice, and freedom, either individually or in community with others and in public or in private, to manifest his religion or belief in worship, observance, practice and teaching. Consequently, no one shall be subject to coercion which would impair his freedom to have or to adopt a religion or belief of his choice. For some years now, the United Nations has been striving to draw up a Convention or Declaration concerning religious intolerance which would develop, while enlarging them, the rules mentioned above. However, such a Convention or Declaration is a long way from being achieved.[80]

Freedom of conscience and religion is always invoked in support of the right to conscientious objection, of which it is alleged to constitute the legal basis: long limited to the refusal to bear arms on religious grounds, conscien-tious objection now tends to be justified also on moral or even political grounds. Furthermore, it is put forward to justify refusal to carry out other orders or actions, deemed to be unlawful or illegitimate, for instance, by a doctor refusing, on religious or moral grounds, to practise abortion. The problems arising here are always hard to resolve.[81]

In respecting freedom of conscience and religion, States also undertake to respect the freedom of parents to ensure the religious and moral education of their children in conformity with their own convictions.[82] Once again, giving effect to this freedom is not without some difficulty, as is shown by the experience of the European Convention on Human Rights.[83]

(ii). FREEDOM OF OPINION, EXPRESSION, INFORMATION AND COMMUNICATION

A pre-eminent human right, insofar as it allows everyone to have both an intellectual and political activity, freedom of expression[84] in the broad sense actually includes several specific rights, all linked together in a "continuum" made increasingly perceptible by modern technological advance. What is primarily involved is the classic notion of *freedom of opinion*, that is to say, the right to say what one thinks and not to be harassed for one's opinions. This is followed by *freedom of expression*, in the limited sense of the term, which includes the right to seek, receive and impart information and ideas, regardless of frontiers, either orally, in writing or in print, in the form of art, or through any other media of one's choice. When freedom of expression is put to use by the mass media, it acquires an additional dimension and be-comes *freedom of information*. A new freedom is being recognized which is such as to encompass the multiform requirements of these various elements, while incorporating their at once individual and collective character, their implications in terms of both "rights" and "responsibilities": this is the *right to communication*, in connection with which Unesco has recently undertaken considerable work with a view to its further elaboration and implementation.[85]

The political and social bearing of these freedoms is immense, and it is for this reason that all the international instruments on human rights, and first of all the Covenant, in Article 19, paragraph 3, rightly stress that the exercise of these freedoms carries with it "special duties and responsibilities",[86] justifying certain restrictions. These, however, expressly provided by law, must be necessary for respect of the rights or reputations of others or for the protection of national security or of public order, or of public health or morals. It is not always easy to decide on the cogency or lack of cogency of any particular restriction, as is shown by certain cases. Among the most important ones brought before the organs of the European Convention on Human Rights are the case *De Becker v. Belgium* (total deprivation of the freedom of expression of a "collaborator" with the occupying authorities during the war), the case *De Geillustreerde Pers. N.V. v. the Netherlands* (concerning the extent to which copyright may constitute a restriction of freedom of expression), the case *Handyside v. United Kingdom* (concerning publications considered obscene), the case *Sunday Times v. United Kingdom* (prohibition by the courts against the publication of an article, deemed to constitute interference in a case pending before the courts), the case *Sacchi v. Italy* (does the State monopoly over television broadcasts cover cable television broadcasts?), etc.

Certain abuses of freedom of expression are expressly stigmatized by the Covenant. Article 20[87] prohibits "any propaganda for war" and "any advocacy of national, racial or religious hatred that constitutes incitement to discrimination, hostility or violence".[88] Moreover, in order to guard against the danger to peace between peoples of the publication of inaccurate reports, the United Nations was led to draw up the Convention on the International Right of Correction of 16 December 1952. This Convention provides for a procedure whereby publication of a communiqué correcting an inaccurate report may be obtained. It is certain that the right to reply or make a correction is also of very great interest for private persons in the event of their honour and reputations being attacked. While the law of a fair number of States contains provisions establishing such a right or machinery for attaining the same objective (through the establishment of a Press Council, for instance),[89] only the American Convention on Human Rights includes as a human right the right to reply and to make a correction (Art. 14).

(f). Protection of political and trade union activity

Political activity which necessarily presupposes respect for intellectual freedoms, and first of all freedom of thought, opinion and expression, is bound to be manifested collectively through *meetings*. And the community of ideals, if not of interests, thus revealed is bound to give rise to freely constituted *associations* leading, thanks to specifically *political* rights, to the acquisition and defence of political power. In addition, freedom of association, in the form of the right to form trade unions, is aimed at allowing both workers and employers to organize themselves for the purpose of promoting and defending their social and economic interests.

(i). FREEDOM OF ASSEMBLY

The international human rights instruments, and first of all the Covenant,[90] recognize the right of peaceful assembly. The restrictions to which this right may be subject in conformity with the law are those which are necessary, in a democratic society, in the interests of national security or public safety, public order, the protection of public health or morals or the protection of the rights and freedoms of others. Freedom of assembly constitutes an "essential component" of the political and social life of a country, as pointed out by the European Commission of Human Rights in its report on the *Greek Case*.[91]

(ii). FREEDOM OF ASSOCIATION AND TRADE UNION FREEDOM

Everyone shall have the right to freedom of association with others, including the right to form and join trade unions for the protection of his interests.[92] This two-fold freedom may of course be subject to the usual restrictions which, provided by law, are necessary in a democratic society. But, in addition, the exercise of this right by members of the armed forces and the police[93] may be subject to specific legal restrictions.

Freedom of association, in regard to trade unions, is provided for not only in the Covenant on Civil and Political Rights (Art. 22), but also in the Covenant on Economic, Social and Cultural Rights (Art. 8), the latter being in this instance far more precise.[94] But trade union freedom is also—or rather *primarily*—protected by the International Labour Organisation pursuant to the provisions of its Constitution and of several ILO Conventions. Of these, the following are to be singled out, as was observed above:[95] Convention No. 87 on Freedom of Association and Protection of the Right to Organise of 9 July 1948, Convention No. 98 on the Right to Organise and Collective Bargaining of 1 July 1949 and Convention No. 135 on Workers' Representatives of 23 June 1971.

Many are the problems which have arisen concerning respect for freedom of association within the ILO (see chapter 12 *infra*)[96] and in the framework of the European Convention on Human Rights. Here mention may be made in particular of the cases brought before the European Court of Human Rights, namely the cases *National Union of Belgian Police v. Belgium*, *Swedish Union of Locomotive Conductors v. Sweden* and the *Schmidt and Dahlstrom v. Sweden* case.

(iii). POLITICAL RIGHTS

While civil rights allow the individual to enjoy his personal freedom and his *autonomy*, political rights are necessary for him to be able to organize his *participation* in the public affairs of the community to which he belongs. These are pre-eminently political rights in that they provide justification of the legitimacy and lawfulness of the power to be exercised in the community established as a State, which is the modern form of political authority. This is the perspective from which the following rights are provided for by the Covenant:[97] (1) the right to take part in the conduct of public affairs, directly or through freely chosen representatives; (2) the right to vote and to be elected at genuine periodic elections, which shall be by universal and equal suffrage and shall be held by secret ballot, guaranteeing the free expression of the will of the electors; (3) the right to have access, on general terms of equality, to public service in one's country.

These rights are to be implemented without any discrimination and "without unreasonable restrictions"; in other words, it will not be easy for them to be implemented and legislation relating to the exercise of these rights, both national and international, is absolutely indispensable. In this connection, neither the UN Convention on the Political Rights of Women of 20 December 1952, nor the OAS Convention on the Granting of Political Rights of Women of 2 May 1948 depart, on the whole, from the formulation of very general rules.

(g). Protection of economic activity

Linked up with the nature of the State's political and social system, the economic rights of man may be grouped together around two poles represented by the right to work, on the one hand, and the right to property, on the other. While the right to work has found its proper place—first place—in the Covenant on Economic, Cultural and Social Rights and in the legislative work of the International Labour Organisation, the status of the right to own property in international human rights law is uncertain, to say the least. Although it is included in the Universal Declaration of Human Rights (Art. 17),[98] it has been left out of the two Covenants of 1966. Nevertheless, it is contained in the International Convention on the Elimination of All Forms of Racial Discrimination of 1966 where it is mentioned as one of the civil rights and not as an economic, social or cultural right: "the right to own property alone as well as in association with others" (Art. 5). Admittedly, it was included, after a great deal of discussion, in the European Convention on Human Rights, not as the right to own property, but as a simple right to the "peaceful enjoyment of (one's) possessions" (Art. 1 of the First Protocol to the Convention). Likewise, it is included in the American Convention on Human Rights as the "right to property", although exercise of that right is subject to the fact that "usury and any other form of exploitation of man by man shall be prohibited by law" (Art. 21).

If one wishes to interpret this uncertainty which currently reigns in regard to the right to property as a human right, one may sum it up in two necessarily political attitudes. For some, the right to property is not an independent human right, for it is and must be an expression of the right to work for everyone and its exercise must be limited accordingly. It follows that it is not necessary to give the right to property a separate place since the right to work occupies its rightful—first place, as we have just seen—in the universal human rights instruments. For others, there can be no freedom and security of the human person without a certain amount of property, even if this is reduced to the basic elements of personal property. In this case, the right to property is not so much an economic right as a political right, and it is the implicit but indispensable basis of all the other civil and political rights in the international human rights instruments.

If there can be no expectation of this controversy being settled in the near future, it is partly because, in regard first of all to individuals, it is now tending to be superseded by the need to guarantee, protect and restore *first of all* the property of peoples and nations. The Covenant itself stresses this since its Article 47 states that nothing in it shall be interpreted as impairing the "inherent right of all peoples to enjoy and utilize fully and freely their natural wealth and resources". Such also is the purpose of Resolution 1803 (XVII) of the UN General Assembly of 14 December 1962 on "Permanent Sovereignty over Natural Resources",[99] and such, lastly, is the very object of the new international economic order, the implications of which for human rights are presently the subject of study within the UN.[100]

(h). Restrictions to civil and political rights

The exercise of civil and political rights may be subject to four series of restrictions. I shall not deal with those that are the consequence of measures of derogation justified by certain exceptional circumstances.[101] Nevertheless, mention must be made of the restrictions expressly provided by international instruments, reservations to those instruments and forfeiture of the right to exercise human rights in the case of abuse.

(i). PRESCRIBED RESTRICTIONS

The restrictions provided by the various international instruments on civil and political rights in fact constitute conditions governing their exercise. They are generally enumerated in paragraphs 2 or 3 of those Articles which, in their paragraph 1, guarantee various rights. The Covenant, like other international instruments, contains a general clause listing the different restrictions.[102] While the list of restrictions varies from one right to another, being adapted to their exercise, the following three requirements are practically always to be found:

(1) the restrictions must be provided by law;

(2) they must be deemed to be necessary in a democratic society;

(3) they must be applied in the interests of national security, public safety or public order, or for the protection of public health or morals or the protection of the rights and freedoms of others.[103]

The restrictions thus permitted to the guaranteed rights cannot be applied for any purpose other than that for which they have been prescribed. Although no provision of this kind is contained in the Covenant, in contrast with the regional Conventions,[104] there is no doubt that the prohibition against the misuse of power and procedure constitutes a general principle governing the implementation and interpretation of international treaties.

On the other hand, the Covenant expressly provides for what might be called the "most-favoured individual clause":[105] nothing in it, indeed, may be interpreted as limiting or derogating from any human rights which might be recognized or better protected under national law or international law.

(ii). RESERVATIONS

The Covenant contains no provision regarding reservations, contrary to the regional Conventions on human rights.[106] It is thus general international law, and in this particular case, the Vienna Convention on Treaties Law which applies. A reservation in respect of a provision in the Covenant is therefore possible provided that it is not incompatible with the object and goal of the Covenant. In practice, several States, have, by setting forth reservations, limited or altered the bearing of certain rights guaranteed by the Covenant.[107]

(iii). FORFEITURE OF THE RIGHT TO EXERCISE HUMAN RIGHTS

According to Article 5 of the Covenant—the equivalent of which is contained in the regional Conventions on human rights[108]—nothing in it "may be interpreted as implying for any State, group or person any right to engage in any activity or perform any act aimed at the destruction of any of the rights and freedoms recognized herein or at their limitation to a greater extent than is provided for in the present Covenant". This provision, which follows straight on from Article 30 of the Universal Declaration, provides not for the forfeiture of human rights but for the forfeiture of the right to exercise them for the purpose of destroying human rights or limiting them to a greater extent than is prescribed. Relating at once to the State, the individual and groups, it consequently makes it binding not only on the State but also on private persons to respect human rights: here again there arises the problem of the "Drittwirkung" of human rights referred to above.[109]

CONCLUSIONS by Frank C. Newman

What lessons might we learn from errors committed in the application of the human rights instruments promulgated by the United Nations over the first thirty years of its existence?

(a). The error of assuming that "the best words" are not operative

When an individual asks what the law says about his or her civil and political rights, he or she usually wants a reply that articulates the maximum protection. Thus, hypothetically, if the inquiry were to relate to abusive practices in mental hospitals in the United States, the reply should explain not only the "cruel and unusual punishment clause of the United States Constitution but also the "cruel, inhuman or degrading treatment or punishment" clauses of the International Bill of Human Rights.

For various reasons, sometimes explicable, jurists generally have not focused on the maximum protections. Illustratively, consider these excerpts:

"What must be avoided...(are) the conflicts which might arise between the instruments designed for the protection of our rights and freedoms. Conflicts of jurisdiction, or discrepancies in the definition, interpretation or application of the same right, could only bring confusion into a subject which ought to be clear and precise."[110]

"I think it is best to speak about the rights of men to live and to be free in the context of the European Convention on Human Rights, if only because the issues are so vast, seen on a world level, as to become unmanageable. But I shall of course want to say something about the United Nations Covenants. Another reason is that the issue of the "right to live and be free" which come our way and force themselves upon us are much better understood in the closer context with which we are familiar of Europe."[111]

In fact, "discrepancies in the definition, interpretation or application of the same right" do of course exist. We must identify them, as well as the confusion to which they give rise, in order to surmount them. On many occasions, especially when "the best words" seem inoperable, or unenforceable, or illusory, we may conclude that a lesser protection should be sought. That will come as no surprise to domestic lawyers, who often focus more on lesser (statutory) than on grander (constitutional) rights.[112] Nonetheless we must repudiate whatever tactics and strategies help perpetuate the myth that the grander rights are mere aspirations, not yet legitimately the business of lawyers.[113]

Related myopia are reflected in these comments:

"With the exception of the Western European area, human rights are still a political rather than a legal issue".[114]

"Of the many international documents containing the proclamation of procedural rights and guarantees, we will discuss here only the 1950 European Convention, whose provisions are not merely theoretical but are judicially enforceable."[115]

Many jurists who distinguish "legal" from "political" questions and "judicially enforceable" from "merely theoretical" provisions, tend to forget that when human rights law is violated the victims usually do not care whether their remedies are labeled "political", "legal", or "judicial". What must be considered pertinent are *all* the legal provisions and *all* the precedents that in fact help to void death sentences, stop torture, get innocent people out of prison, ensure fairer trials, strike at tyranny, starvation, related evils. It is of little concern whether those results are sometimes achieved by "political" rather than "legal" means or by an *ombudsman* and other investigators rather than by judges. The over-all insistence of the United Nations that individuals should always benefit from whatever rights are "best" is evidenced by these words in Art. 5.2 of Civil and Political Rights Covenant:

"There shall be no restriction upon or derogation from any of the fundamental human rights recognized or existing in any State Party to the present Covenant pursuant to law, conventions, regulations or custom on the pretext that the present Covenant does not recognize such rights or that it recognizes them to a lesser extent."

(b). The error of assuming that the less obviously applicable words are not operative

Does international law require a fair hearing? The answer is Yes, often. Three major documents contain these clauses:

Universal Declaration, Article 10

Everyone is entitled. . . to a fair and public hearing by an independent and impartial tribunal, in the determination of his rights and obligations and of any criminal charge against him.

Covenant on Civil and Political Rights, Article 14 (1)

. . . In the determination of any criminal charge against him, or of his rights and obligations in a suit at law, everyone shall be entitled to a fair and public hearing by a competent, independent and impartial tribunal established by law. . . .

European Convention on Human Rights, Article 6 (1)

(1) In the determination of his civil rights and obligations or of any criminal charge against him, everyone is entitled to a fair and public hearing within a reasonable time by an independent and impartial tribunal established by law.

—(Note that, in the lines above "civil" appears instead of "in a suit at law.") Interpreting all those words is tricky.[116] What must be stressed even more is that the requirement of a fair hearing is also articulated by countless other words, in each of those three documents and also in many other documents. Examples in the Covenant alone are Articles 2.3 (an effective remedy), 9 (detained persons), and 13 (aliens), plus wording as to what is "respect", "cruel inhuman or degrading treatment or punishment", "reasonable", "necessary", "arbitrary" or "unlawful." Each of those words, by itself, may imply rules that relate to due process, natural justice, equality of arms, *audi alteram partem*.[117]

Other illustrations of "less obviously applicable words" abound. The proscriptions of torture and of cruel, inhuman and degrading treatment that we quoted above, for instance, hardly justify ignoring this command of Art. 10.1 of the Covenant on Civil and Political Rights: "All persons deprived of their liberty shall be treated with humanity and with respect for the inherent dignity of the human person." That Art. 18 of the Covenant deals mostly with religion, whereas Art. 19 protects opinion and expression, by no means implies that Art. 18 therefore has no impact on the freedom to manifest one's non-religious beliefs. Art. 15.3 of the Covenant on Economic, Social and Cultural Rights requiring that governments respect "the freedom indispensable for scientific research and creative activity" clearly relates to the "freedom to seek, receive and impart information and ideas of all kinds, regardless of frontiers, either orally, in writing or in print, in the form of art, or through any other media" that Art. 19.2 of the Covenant on Civil and Political Rights purports to assure. Yet it may supplement those words, too.

Which protects civilians more, the doctrine of genocide or the doctrine of crimes against humanity? In recent years too little attention has been focused on that question.

In sum, ALL WORDS OF ALL RELEVANT DOCUMENTS MUST BE EXAMINED. If they are not, people will be ill-advised as to what truly are their human rights. The case law and practice that affect only the obviously applicable words may be misleading as to the full import of words less obviously applicable.[118]

(c). The error of assuming that precedents are persuasive merely because they exist

When the highest of courts deal with only a handful of the innumerable problems, to visualize or chart a hierarchy of precedents is complex. Thus, to contend that the human rights clauses of the UN Charter are binding because, in its *Namibia* opinion, the International Court of Justice said so, is one thing. It is quite different to construct borderlines for free speech, fair trial, political rights, etc. merely because the Supreme Court of Senegal, a district court in Oregon, a legal adviser in New Zealand, an *ad hoc* UN committee, or Afro-Asian or Latin American or Eastern or Western delegates said so.

In this chapter there is no room for examining theories on how rationally to apply precedents. We can note, though, that in the human rights field the matter rarely has been debated.[119]

I do not suggest that the compilers of precedents should ignore, gloss over, or censure any historical fact. We observed above, however, that the producers of case law and practice as to civil and political rights include judges, diplomats, investigators, censurers, etc. Obviously the persuasiveness of what all of them did and said is variegated. Users of their work will not promote human rights by arguing that, merely because all those people really did say and do certain things, future decisions as to comparable problems have thus been prescribed.

(d). The error of assuming that precedents do not exist when in fact they do

Case law and practice frequently are forgotten, not always unintentionally. Sometimes, though, the failure to mention precedents is so glaring that one tends to suspect conspiracies of silence.

In one UN document a country pronounced startlingly that "On the international level, the only crime that may be described as a 'crime against humanity' would seem to be *genocide*."[120] Another country criticized a UN text which confirmed that "the principles of the Geneva Conventions of 1949 must be strictly observed by all Governments whether or not they had signed them."[121] A third State reported that there was no racial discrimination in its country, apparently overlooking the many precedents that proscribe racial discrimination via laws that affect immigrants and indigenous populations.

Perhaps the boldest of all pretentions are those that involve Art. 2.7 of the UN Charter. Notwithstanding an immense jurisprudence that defines the terms "domestic jurisdiction" and "intervene", and notwithstanding their own governments' views and votes when some other government has been the recipient, the practice of nearly all delegates whose governments stand accused of civil and political rights violations is to invoke Art. 2.7. A study of summary records, to show how nations react to other nations' charges that civil and political rights have been violated would, I think expose this somewhat:

"What you allege is of course false. . . .

"What we are doing, though regrettable, is not illegal. . . .

"Several of you commit acts that are even more illegal and are worse violators of civil and political rights than we are. . . .

"Continued discussion by any of you will encroach on Art. 2.7 of the Charter".

In part, of course, precedents are not cited because they are not known, because truly they have been forgotten, because jurists who should be the world's teachers concerning them are often inefficient and ineffective publicists. Ready accessiblity to all documentation is what we most need to help cure the sin of assuming that precedents do not exist when in fact they do.

(e). The error of assuming that precedents from one's own nation are specially persuasive

We usually know more about our own national system than others, and that knowledge naturally influences us. Yet by no means are a nation's precedents always apt or correct or persuasive as to international standards on civil and political rights. To illustrate, for many years United States' delegates insisted strongly that, for the world, free speech should mean exactly what the United States Supreme Court has said it means for the United States of America; e.g. as to war propaganda and incitement of racial hatred. What, we might ask, makes that argument compelling?

Similarly, with commendable soul-searching, the British recently attempted to instruct us on exactly what is and is not "torture". Unfortunately, with rare exceptions they have not dealt with "cruel, inhuman and degrading treatment", which now of course is included in the international test regarding torture.

The list of examples seems endless. Many governments that generally treat their citizens well nonetheless exemplify blind spots. Nearly all governments simulate astonishment when they are reminded that their own practices regarding "public emergency", "ordre public", and analogous limitations are not in accordance with international law. Too many governments, for instance, would have us believe that certain economic development plans and certain economic crises justify all sorts of abuses.

(f). The error of assuming that foreign ministry pronouncements are consistent

A great bulk of the case law and practice that affect civil and political rights appears in documents pertaining to foreign ministry pronouncements. They may concern bilateral relations; often their focus is multilateral—concerning UN, Council of Europe, OAS, OAU and analogous matters.

Not surprisingly, diplomats and other representatives of nations often are more intent on declaring their substantive views than on developing, even within their own governments, consistent legal interpretations. Especially as to civil and political rights do they sometimes appear reckless concerning prior statements by their colleagues and predecessors.

It seems appropriate here to comment on a foreign ministry phenomenon that for too long has not been given enough attention. Demonstrably, I believe, foreign ministry officials who deal with civil and political rights problems throughout the world often are uninformed about the human rights laws that ought to affect those problems. Most delegates to the UN and other international fora are acceptably informed (compared, say, with legislators and administrators generally). Most of their colleagues back home, however, as well as colleagues posted at embassies, consulates, etc., all too often are inadequately trained, inadequately advised and inadequately motivated as to human rights.

(A notable exception was in Santiago during the Fall of 1973 and in 1974 when courageous ambassadors to Chile provided asylum and helped set up refugee centres. Even there, though, the concerns seemed more humanitarian than juridical.)

(g). The error of assuming that civil and political rights are "Western"

The trouble with assuming that civil and political rights are Western is that precedents from the West are then given more weight than those from other areas of the world.

Many of the great documents are Western (Magna Carta, the English and American Bills of Rights, the French Declaration of the Rights of Man, etc). But many of the great freedoms, e.g. fair trial, have roots that are traceable to Hammurabi, Cyrus, Eastern texts and innumerable non-Western jurists.

We must also keep in mind that non-Western contributions have been notable in recent times. Lawyers in Africa, for instance, defending dissidents in countries other than their own, have taught us a good deal about what the right-to-counsel really should mean. From India we have learned much as to imaginative and vigilant encouragement of the right-to-vote. Studies of tribal customs have influenced our education as to what Art. 14 of the Civil and Political Rights Covenant calls "a competent, independent and impartial tribunal established by law".

(h). The error of assuming that criminal laws concern criminal cases only

International criminal law is a vast and complex subject. Yet no one should deny its potential impact on civil and political rights. Here there is no room for a summary or *précis* of the case law and practice of international criminal law. There is room, however, for a warning that repeatedly seems to go unheeded.

This is the warning: *Human rights activists must remember that a main contribution of the relevant criminal law is its proscribing of illegal conduct.* What does that mean? It means that nearly all conduct proscribed in terms of criminal responsibility, criminal punishment, etc. is also proscribed in terms of civil responsibility, civil liability, etc.

Why is that important? For many reasons. A crucial fact is that too many people, once the word "Nuremberg" is mentioned for example, immediately begin discussing criminal intent, proof beyond a reasonable doubt and related concepts of penal law. Because those topics are labyrinthine, we tend to forget that governments and government officials may well have committed illegal acts whether or not the acts also were criminal.

That is exactly what happened, for example, in numerous discussions of "Nuremberg and Vietnam". The cost to human rights law was not that possibly guilty individuals escaped prosecution. The greater cost was that, too often, all the talk of criminality left undiscussed and unsettled the basic issues as to whether the new and brutal techniques of warfare that were used in Vietnam were illegal or not.

When issues as momentous as these are left undiscussed and unsettled (and there are many parallels to Vietnam), progress in civil and political rights is not encouraged.

NOTES

1. The International Bill of Human Rights means the Universal Declaration, the two UN Covenants and the Protocol to the Civil and Political Covenant. See F.C. Newman, "The International Bill of Human Rights: does it exist?" in A. Cassese (ed.), *Current Problems of International Law: Essays on UN Law and on the Law of Armed Conflict* (1975).

2. See Chapter 4, *supra*.

3. *The OAS and Human Rights* (1972), p. 109; *1968 Inter-American Yearbook on Human Rights* (1973), p. 191; see also A. Tankard, *The Human Family, Human Rights and Peace* (1973), p. 27. There appears to be no need juridically to distinguish civil from political rights. See the following excerpt from a speech made by Adlai Stevenson in 1964; "Civil rights—*the equality of and dignity of the individual human being*—is a universal issue, whatever form it may take within domestic jurisdiction. Indeed, after peace and war, it is the ultimate issue in almost all societies, the gut issue of the modern world. It is, I suppose, one of the things that makes the modern world modern." (Emphasis added.)

4. Illustratively, see P. Hassan, "The Word 'arbitrary' as used in the Universal Declaration of Human Rights: 'Illegal' or 'Unjust'?", 10 *Harv. Int. L .J.*, 225 (1969), and "The International Covenant on Civil and Political Rights: Background and Perspective on Article 9 (1)", 9 *Denver J. Int. L. and Pol.*, 153 (1973); *cf.* the tabular presentations on pp. 283, 291, 296-302 and 306-7 in F. C. Newman, "Natural Justice, Due Process and the New International Covenants on Human Rights: Prospectus", 1967 *Public Law* 274; and see J. Seeley, "Article 20 of the International Covenant on Civil and Political Rights: First Amendment Comment and Question", 10 *Va. J. Int. L.*, 333 (1970).

5. See E. Schwelb, "The International Court of Justice and the Human Rights Clauses of the Charter", 69 *AJIL*, 337 (1972); F.C. Newman, "Interpreting the Human Rights Clauses of the UN Charter", 5 *DH-HRJ*, 283 (1972). But see A. Nartowski, "Human Rights in the UN System (Development Trends)", 5 *Polis Yb. Int. L.*, 131, 141 (1972-1973).

6. Unfortunately, many lawyers who use the UN Standard Minimum Rules seem to neglect the terms of the opinion of the International Court of Justice in the Namibia Case and the commentary thereon by E. Schwelb (see *supra* note 5).

7. Some human rights are, of course, considered as being more fundamental than others. See, for example, Article 4, paragraph 2, of the Covenant on Civil and Political Rights ("No derogation...may be made") and doc. E/CN.4/Sub.2/354, 18 October 1974, p. 52 ("fundamental human rights").

8. See generally *United Nations Action in the Field of Human Rights*, 2nd ed., 1980 (UN Sales No. E.XIV.74.6). Before UN bodies, case law and practice tend to be given much more weight than that which Article 38(1)(d) of the Statute of the International Court of Justice refers to as "the teachings of the most highly qualified publicists".

9. See generally the authorities noted in the annex to this book entitled a select bibliography on international human rights law.

10. E. Rostow, "The Role of International Law in International Politics", 12 *Atl. Community Q.*, 500, 501 (1974-1975).

11. On the two senses of the term "self-executing", see K. Vasak, *La convention européenne des droits de l'homme*, Paris, 1964, p. 229. The question may also be raised in connection with at least some of the provisions of the Covenant on Economic, Social and Cultural Rights and the European Social Charter.

12. Cf. *Les droits de l'homme en droit interne et en droit international*, Brussels, 1968, 590 pages.

13. UN doc. A/CONF.32/5 (1968) para. 62.

14. See however John Carey, *UN Protection of Civil and Political Rights*, 1970, 205 pages; Louis B. Sohn and Thomas Buergenthal, *International Protection of Human Rights*, Bobbs-Merrill, New York, 1973, pp. 505-997.

168 Frank C. Newman and Karel Vasak

15. See the various volumes of the *Yearbook of the European Convention on Human Rights*.

16. See *supra*, Chapter 4.

17. Art. 3 of the Universal Declaration of Human Rights (UD), Art. 2 of the International Covenant on Civil and Political Rights (Covenant), Art. 2 of the European Convention on Human Rights (ECHR), Art. 1 of the American Declaration of the Rights and Duties of Man (AD), and Art. 4 of the American Convention on Human Rights (ACHR).

18. Unless otherwise indicated, all the treaties quoted in the present section are reproduced in the United Nations publication entitled *Human Rights—A Compilation of International Instruments of the United Nations* (1978 edition).

19. See for instance the judgment of the Federal Constitutional Court of the Federal Republic of Germany of 25 February 1975 and the judgment of the Constitutional Court of Austria of 11 October 1974, which reach opposite conclusions.

20. See Application *Bruggemann and Scheuter v. Federal Republic Germany* (No. 6959/75) declared admissible on 19 May 1976 by the European Commission of Human rights. As for the sources of the rulings of the commission and the European Court of Human Rights, the reader is referred to the list of applications declared admissible, applications dealt with and judgments rendered, which is given in the chapter on the Council of Europe, *infra*, Part II, Sub-Section 2, Chapter 16.

21. Art. 6 UD, Art. 6 Covenant, Art. 3 ACHR; no provision of this kind is included in the European Convention.

22. In the case of the American Convention, its scope seems to be limited, by Article 1, paragraph 2, to natural persons alone since it specifies: "For the purposes of this Convention, 'person' means every human being." See *Les droits de l'homme et les personnes morales*, Brussels, 1970, 166 pages.

23. The American Convention on Human Rights (Art. 20) not only protects everyone's right to a nationality but also adds to this the right to acquire the nationality of the country where one was born (*jus soli*).

24. Mention is also to be made in this context of the Convention of the Organization of African Unity governing the specific Aspects of the Problem of Refugees in Africa of 10 September 1969 (*RDH-HRJ*, Vol III (1970), No. 1).

25. Art. 5 UD, Art. 7 Covenant, Art. 3 ECHR, Art 5.1 ACHR.

26. Cf., for instance, Art. 4 of the Covenant. See *infra*, Part I, Chapter 5.

27. See *The Organization of American States and Human Rights, 1960-1967* (Washington, D.C., 1967) and *Inter-American Yearbook of Human Rights, 1968* (Washington, D.C., 1973) and the reports on situation regarding human rights in several countries by the Inter-American Commission on Human Rights and the Organization of American States. See also K. Vasak, *La Commission interaméricaine des droits de l'homme*, Paris, 1968, p. 124 *et seq.* and p. 155 *et seq.*

28. Established by the Nuremberg Tribunal in its judgment of 19 August 1947. Cf. Hanna Saba, "Les droits de l'homme et le problème de l'expérimentation médicale", *Mélanges Modinos*, Ed. Pedone, 1968, p. 260 *et seq* and *Protection of human rights in the light of scientific and technological progress in Biology and Medicine*, WHO/CIOMS, 1974, p. 181 *et seq.*

29. See "Patient's Bill of Rights" adopted in the U.S.A. by the American Hospital Association and Decree No. 74-22 of 14 January 1974 in France (*RDH-HRJ*, Vol. VII, 1974, p. 541 *et seq.*); and UN docs. A/34/273 (1979) and A/35/372 (1980).

30. Art. 4 UD, Art. 8 Covenant, Art. 4 ECHR, Art. 6 ACHR.

31. See the Preamble of the 1950 Convention which lists them.

32. Art. 8.3 Covenant, Art. 4.2 and 3 ECHR, Art. 6.2 and 3 ACHR.

33. See the report of the Commission set up under Art. 26 of the Constitution of the ILO: *Official Bulletin*, Vol. XLVI, No. 2, Supplement II, April 1963.

34. See the report of the commission set up in pursuant of Art. 26 of the Constitution of

the ILO: *Official Bulletin*, Vol. XLVI, No. 2, Supplement II, April 1963. See generally, Chapter 12 *infra*.

35. Art. 13 UD, Art. 12 Covenant, Art. 2, 3 and 4 Protocol No. 4 to the ECHR, Art. 22 ACHR.

36. *Ibid.*.

37. Cf. Art. 12.3 of the Covenant. The European and American Conventions include, in addition, the restrictions necessary in a democratic society for the protection of national security and the prevention of crime.

38. Art. 3.1 Protocol No. 4 to the ECHR, Art. 22.5 ACHR.

39. Consider, for example, the case of the Transkei and the other independent homelands established by South Africa.

40. Art. 12.4 Covenant.

41. This is precisely the problem of the Blacks in South Africa originating from Bantustans which have become "independent".

42. A similar provision is contained in the American Convention (Art. 22.6) but the European Convention contains nothing of the sort; an alien threatened by expulsion is nonetheless not without protection since Art. 3 of the European Convention, in prohibiting inhuman treatment, allows him, in accordance with the case-law of the national tribunals and that of the organs of the Convention, to claim the right not to be expelled in the event of his expulsion into a country exposing him, in that country, to the risk of being subjected to inhuman treatment, both physical and moral. See *infra*, Chapter 17.

43. Art. 4, Protocol No. 4 to the ECHR, Art. 22.9 ACHR.

44. The European Convention confines itself to prohibiting "the collective expulsion of aliens" (Art. 4 of Protocol No. 4 to the Convention).

45. Declaration on Territorial Asylum, adopted by Resolution 2312 (XXII) of the General Assembly. A Resolution concerning the right to asylum was also adopted by the Committee of Ministers of the Council of Europe on 29 June 1967 (Resoluton (67) 14: Asylum to persons in danger of persecution).

46. The International Court of Justice has had to concern itself with the various aspects of diplomatic asylum in the *Haya de la Torre* case.

47. See in particular *Baouya v. Federal Republic of Germany, Amekrane v. United Kingdom, Dolanyi v. Belgium, Becker v. Denmark*, etc.

48. In one case, it is expressly prohibited to deprive anyone of their freedom by Art. 11 of the Covenant: "No one shall be imprisoned merely on the ground of inability to fulfill a contractual obligation" (Cf. Art. 1 Protocol No. 4 to the ECHR and Art. 7.7 ACHR).

49. Cf. Art. 9 UD: "No one shall be subjected to arbitrary arrest, detention or exile."

50. Cf. Art. 7.2 and 3 ACHR, which, on the one hand, adopts the method of the Covenant.

51. Art. 9.2-5 Covenant, Art. 5.2-5 ECHR, Art. 7.4-6 ACHR.

52. Remand in custody is the period of time between the moment of arrest and that at which the person concerned is brought before a judge or other officer authorized by law to exercise judicial power. According to the Covenant, the accused should be tried "without undue delay"; under the European Convention, a period of four (and even five) days has been deemed acceptable (Application No. 2894/66).

53. Preventive or provisional detention is the period of time between the moment of arrest and that at which the person concerned has been tried. According to the European Convention, the period of time should be "reasonable". Obviously what is involved is a notion which should be interpreted according to the facts of each case (cf. in the framework of the European Convention on Human Rights the cases *Neumeister, Stögmüller, Matznetter, Ringeisen*, etc.).

54. Art. 10 Covenant, Art. 5.4-6 ACHR. No provision of this kind exists in the European Convention on Human Rights. However, problems concerning the treatment of prisoners are brought before the European Commission and Court of Human Rights on the

basis of prohibition against inhuman and degrading treatment (see, for instance, the *Simon-Herald v. Austria* and *Knechtl v. United Kingdom* cases, as well as the applications of the protagonists of the *"Red Army Fraction" v. Federal Republic of Germany: Meinhof, Baader, Meins, Grundmann, Berberich and Mahler*.

55. The United Nations "Standard Minimum rules" were revised in order for them to be adapted to the requirements of the current penal policy of the Member States of the Council of Europe by Resolution (73) 5 of the Committee of Ministers of 19 January 1973.

56. Art. 8 UD, Art. 2.3 Covenant, Art. 13 ECHR, Art. 25 ACHR.

57. This question is of interest in regard particularly to the right to respect for privacy which can be violated above all by private persons. See *Vie privée et droits de l'homme*, Brussels, 1973 and in particular the report of J. De Meyer, p. 363 *et seq.*, which refers the reader to other work on the *Drittwirkung* in the teachings.

58. Cf. Art. 10 UD, Art. 6.1 ECHR, Art. 8.1 ACHR.

59. It is consequently necessary first of all for the person concerned to have access to the tribunal: what is therefore involved is no less than a "right to the tribunal" (cf. the ruling delivered by the European Court of Human Rights in the *Golder v. United Kingdom* case).

60. The question arises for members of the national administration, the police, the armed forces, etc. With regard to the armed forces, see the judgment of the European Court of Human Rights in the case *Engels and others v. the Netherlands*.

61. Although this question was raised before the European Commission on Human Rights practically as early as 1955, it has not yet been settled once and for all. See, among the very large number of cases, the judgment of the European Court of Human Rights in the case *Ringeisen v. Austria* and the case *König v. Federal Republic of Germany* still pending.

62. Art. 11 UD; Art. 14.2-7 and Art. 15 Covenant; Art. 6.2-3 and Art. 7 ECHR; Art. 8.2-5 and Art. 9 and 10 ACHR.

63. See also Art. 7 ECHR and Art. 9 ACHR (the latter, however, does contain the interpretative provision concerning the "Nuremberg Law").

64. The qualifying expression "without undue delay" is obviously very vague and its interpretation depends on the facts of each case. Under the terms of the European Convention on Human Rights, the person concerned shall be tried within a "reasonable" time, a notion which is no more precise (see the cases *Soltikow, Huber*, etc.).

65. Cf. *Rebitzer v. Austria*, a friendly settlement of which was reached between the parties before the European Commission of Human Rights, where what was involved was an unjustified detention of more than nineteen years.

66. Art. 16 UD, Art. 23 Covenant, Art. 12 ECHR, Art. 17 ACHR.

67. See UN doc. A/CONF.94/35; and Chapter 10 *infra*.

68. Art. 12 UD, Art. 23 and Art. 17 Covenant, Art. ECHR, Art. 17 ACHR.

69. Such at all events is the jurisprudence of the European Commission of Human Rights: see H. Danelius, "A Survey of the Jurisprudence concerning the Right Protected by the European Convention on Human Rights", *RDH-HRJ*, Vol. VIII (1975), pp. 431-473, at p. 452.

70. Cf. *East African Asians v. United Kingdom*, examined by the Committee of Ministers of the Council of Europe in 1977.

71. Cf. *Allam and Khan v. United Kingdom*, a friendly settlement of which was reached by the European Commission of Human Rights.

72. Art. 24 Covenant, Art. 17.4 and 5, Art. 18 and 19 ACHR; no similar provision exists in the European Convention on Human Rights.

73. See UN docs. E/CN.4/1324 and Adds. (1980).

74. Art. 12 UD, Art. 17 Covenant, Art. 8 ECHR, Art. 11 ACHR.

75. In the *Eiriksson v. Iceland* case the question to be settled was whether the prohibition against having dogs in Reykjavik was not contrary to the right to respect for privacy: in its decision of 18 May 1976 the European Commission of Human Rights replied in the negative.

76. See the series of reports by the Secretary-General on human rights and scientific and technological developments, noted in the Bibliography *infra*.

77. Art. 12 UD, Art. 17 Covenant, Art. 8 ECHR, Art. 11 ACHR.

78. See the case *Klass and others v. Federal Republic of Germany*, pending before the European Commission of Human Rights, which concerns the conditions under which the German Law of 3 August 1968 organized the clandestine control of correspondence and telecommunications.

79. Art. 18 UD, Art. 18 Covenant, Art. 9 ECHR, Art. 12 ACHR. See also ILO Convention No. 111 on Discrimination (Employment and Occupation), 1958.

80. See Chapter 10 *infra*.

81. See for instance the *Grandath v. Federal Republic of Germany* case, concerning a Jehovah's witness, before the European Commission of Human Rights.

82. Art. 18.4 Covenant, Art. 2 Protocol No. 1 to the ECHR, Art. 12.4 ACHR.

83. In the case of the European Convention, the freedom of parents goes beyond the religious and moral education of their children in that it relates to "education" and "teaching" in general. See the *Linguistic cases against Belgium* (concerning the freedom of parents to give education to their children in the mother tongue), the cases *Karnell and Hardt v. Sweden* (concerning the religious education dispenses by the Lutheran Evangelical Church of Sweden), and the cases *Kjeldsen, Madsen and Pedersen v. Denmark* (concerning compulsory sex education in State schools).

84. Art. 19 UD, Art. 19 Covenant, Art. 10 ECHR, Art. 13 ACHR. See also ILO Convention No. 111 on Discrimination (Employment and Occupation), 1958.

85. See *Many Voices, One World: Communication and Society, Today and Tomorrow* (Report of the "MacBride Commission"), Paris/London/New York, Kagan Page/Unipub/ Unesco, 1980, pp. 172-174; and Final Report of a Colloquium on the New Human Rights: The 'Rights of Solidarity', Unesco doc. SS-80/CONF.806/12 (1980).

86. This is the only provision in the Covenant which includes a reference to the "duties" and "responsibilities" of those who exercise their human rights. But, as is stipulated in the Universal Declaration of Human Rights in its Article 29.1, "everyone has duties towards the community in which alone the free and full development of his personality is possible". The problem of "duties" and "responsibilities" in relation to freedom of the press is of particular concern to journalists. See the Report of the MacBride Commission, *supra* note 85, pp. 233-240.

87. A similar provision is contained in the American Convention (Art. 13.5) but *not* in the European Convention: moreover, several Contracting Parties to the European Convention, as well as other States, have expressed reservations concerning Art. 20 of the Covenant, considering its provision to be too broad and consequently to present dangers in respect of freedom of expression.

88. As regards racial hatred, the reader is also referred to Art. 4 of the International Convention on the Elimination of All Forms of Racial Discrimination which contains much more precise provisions and undertakings.

89. See K. Vasak, "Les conseils de presse", *RDH-HRJ*, Vol. VII (1974), p. 617 *et seq.*, and J. Clement-Jones, "Notes on Existing Press Councils", *RDH-HRJ*, Vol. VII (1974), p. 624.

90. Art. 20 UD, Art. 21 Covenant, Art. 11 ECHR, Art. 15 ACHR.

91. The *Greek Case*, report of the Commission, Vol. l, Part I, pp. 207-208.

92. Art. 20 UD, Art. 22 Covenant, Art. 11 ECHR, Art. 16 ACHR.

93. The American Convention on Human Rights goes further in the matter of restrictions in that exercise of the right of association by members of the armed forces and the police may be purely and simply forbidden to them. As for the European Convention, it confines itself to restrictions alone, but these may also be imposed on members of the administration of the State, as is provided for also by Art. 8.2 of the Covenant on Economic, Social and Cultural Rights. See also, in regard to members of the armed forces, the police

and the administration of the State, ILO Conventions Nos. 87 and 151, the European Social Charter (Art. 15) and the Covenant on Economic, Social and Cultural Rights. The least that can be said is that the solutions adopted are far from being the same.

94. The same duality is to be found in the European Convention on Human Rights (Art. 11) and in the European Social Charter (Art. 5).

95. See *supra*, Chapter 6.

96. See *Freedom of Association*, Digest of decisions of the Freedom of Association Committee of the Governing Body of the ILO, and the studies by N. Valticos listed in the bibliography, *infra*, Chapter 12.

97. Art. 21 UD, Art. 25 Covenant, Art. 23 ACHR. Article 3 of Protocol No. 1 to the ECHR contains a simple undertaking by States "to hold free elections at reasonable intervals by secret ballot, under conditions which will ensure the free expression of the opinion of the people in the choice of the legislature". However, the European Commission of Human Rights has recently interpreted this undertaking in such a way as to grant the individual the right to vote and to stand as candidate (Applications 6745/74 and 6746/74 v. Belgium).

98. The Universal Declaration of Human Rights *also* proclaims the right to "intellectual property" in its Art. 27.2: "Everyone has the right to the protection of the moral and material interests resulting from any scientific, literary or artistic production of which he is the author." It is in this sense that Conventions protecting copyright can be included in international human rights legislation.

99. See *Human Rights—UN Compilation*, (1978) p. 21.

100. A study on "The New International Economic Order and the Promotion of Human Rights" is being prepared by a Special Rapporteur of the Sub-Commission on Human Rights. See Sub-Commission res. 8 (XXXII) of 1979.

101. See *infra*, Chapter 8.

102. A general clause of this kind is included in the Universal Declaration of Human Rights: Article 29.2.

103. These are the grounds,; more or less numerous, on which restrictions may be allowed and which vary from one right to another.

104. Art. 18 ECHR, Art. 30 ACHR.

105. Art. 5.2 Covenant, Art. 60 ECHR, Art. 29b ACHR.

106. Art. 64 ECHR, Art. 75 ACHR.

107. See the list of reservations and declarations, registered by States Parties to the Covenant in UN doc. ST/LEG/SER. D/13 (1980) (Sales No. E.80.V.10) pp. 112-120.

108. Art. 17 ECHR, Art. 29a ACHR.

109. See *supra*, n.57.

110. P. Modinos, "Message to the Teheran Conference", B(68)28, 18 April 1968.

111. J. Fawcett, "The right to live and be free", in F. Vallat (Ed.), *An introduction to the study of human rights* (1970), p. 72.

112. L. Gostin, "Freedom of expression and the mentally disordered: philosophical and constitutional perspectives", 50 *Notre Dame Lawyer*, 419, 446 (1975) ("judicial attention has thus far focused on the statutory aspects"); see *Becker v. Denmark*, C(75)17, 23 May 1975 (United Nations Convention relating to Refugees or Art. 4 of the Protocol to the European Convention of Human Rights).

113. How do we identify legal instruments that may protect civilians in time of armed conflict? Too many military personnel and government officials consider that the basic document is the Fourth Geneva Convention. That is too narrow a view. Civilians are also protected by the UN Charter, the International Bill of Human Rights, the Nuremberg Doctrine of Crimes against Humanity, the Hague Conventions, the regional conventions, etc. See Annex I ("General Norms concerning respect for human rights in their applicability to armed conflicts"), A/8052, 18 September 1970; S. MacBride, "Human rights in armed conflicts: the inter-relationship between the humanitarian laws and the laws of

human rights", 9, *Revue de droit pénal militaire et de droit de la guerre*, 373 (1970; "Legal position under international penal law (of events in East Pakistan))", *ICJ Rev.*, no. 8 (June 1972). p. 26. Other references may be found in chapters 8 and 14 *infra*. "The international treaties on the protection of human rights in which the Member States have co-operated or to which they have adhered can also supply indications which may be taken into account within the framework of community law". See M. Zuleeg, "Fundamental rights and the law of European communities", S, *C.M.L.R.*, 446 (1971); J. Fawcett, "The Council of Europe and Integration", 1974, *Int. Affairs*, 242, 250 ("would there be overlaps between...(the Luxembourg) Court and the Commission, and Court of Human Rights in Strasbourg?"); G. Draper, *Civilians and the NATO Status of Forces Agreement* (1966) (relationship of Art. VII of the NATO Agreement to the European Convention of Human Rights).

114. K. Grzybowski, "Book Review", 68 *AJIL* 152 (1974).

115. M. Cappelletti, "Fundamental guarantees of the parties in civil proceedings (general report)", *Fundamental guarantees of the parties in civil litigation* (1973), p. 661, 685.

116. To sharpen the comparison, several words have been rearranged but not changed.

117. See F.C. Newman, "Natural Justice, Due Process and the New International Covenants on Human Rights: Prospectus", 1967 *Public Law*, 274, 279; cf. Fasla opinion (on review from UN Administrative Tribunal) 1973, ICJ Rep. 166, Summary in 68 *AJIL* 340, 348 (1974) ("official's right to a fair hearing").

118. Attitudes toward the UN Standard Minimum Rules for the Treatment of Prisoners illustrate the problem we have been examining. Officials often assume those rules are not "law" and, anyway, do not protect prisoners exempted from the rules' coverage. However, one of the main functions of the Rules is to specify the meaning of the words "cruel, inhuman or degrading treatment", which appear in the International Bill of Human Rights. For a jurist who works only with the Standard Minimum Rules the applicability of five Human Rights words would not be obvious. But often they carry more weight.

Some classifications are misleading. See, for example, *Legal Supp..* No. 11 (October 1974) and also *Forward in Europe*, Chapter II of which on penal law and criminology contains references which could well have been included in Chapter 1 on legal provisions relating to human rights.

119. Advisory opinion on the continued presence of South Africa in Namibia (Southwest Africa), *ICJ* Rep., 16 (1971).

120. E/CN.4/1010 (1969), p. 6; E/CN.4/Sub.2/L.583, 25 June 1973, p. 36 ("The relation between genocide and...crimes against humanity").

121. A/C.3/SR.1803, p. 10 ("States are bound only by those international instruments to which they are parties"); see also AC.3/SR.1799, p. 3; d'Amato, Gould and Woods, "War Crimes and Vietnam", 57 *Cal. L.R.* 1055, 1058, n. 15: "Whether the multilateral conventions generate rules of customary international law or whether they exist in parallel with customary rules to the same effect, the Nuremberg Tribunal held that provisions in the Hague Conventions of 1907 and the Geneva Conventions of 1929 were applicable to Germany not directly but because they were regarded as being declaratory of the laws and customs of war', *1 Trial Major War Crim.* 255 (International Military Tribunal, 1947), and held the Hague Conventions of 1907 applicable to World War II despite the formal exclusion in those conventions of wars which involved non-parties (Russia was not a party). See also *idem.*, p. 334 (applicable to Czechoslovakia though it was not a party). Even more remarkable was the extensive use of the 1929 Geneva Convention on Prisoners of War, to which Germany itself was not a party; see *United States v. von Leeb*, 11 *Trials of War Criminals before the Nuremberg Military Tribunals*, 462, 535-538 (1950); see also *Tanable Koshiro Case*, 11 L. *Rep. Trials War Crim.*, 1, 4 (UN War Crimes Comm'n., 1947) (applying the Convention to Japan, also a non-party)."

8 Principles and Norms of Human Rights Applicable in Emergency Situations: Underdevelopment, Catastrophes and Armed Conflicts

Stephen P. Marks

The notion of emergency situations and derogations from fundamental principles when public order so requires is common to all legal systems, including the system of the international protection of human rights.

This chapter concerns the problem of human rights in emergency situations with reference to three types of such situations, each different from the other but all sharing certain elements which reduce human rights to their most precarious level.

Since the situations to be examined are fundamentally different from each other, it is best to define beforehand what is meant by "emergency" situations. Let us first see what the dictionaries have to say.

According to one dictionary[1] an "emergency" may be defined as a "sudden unexpected happening; an unforeseen occurrence or condition; perplexing contingency or complication of circumstances; a sudden or unexpected occasion for action; exigency, pressing necessity." Emergency is an unforeseen combination of circumstances that calls for immediate action. From this definition two ideas emerge: the situations to be dealt with here are not "normal", "ordinary" situations, commonly to be met with in the implementation of human rights. They are consequently preceded or followed by situations regarded as normal, hence their *temporary* character. In addition, as the legal analysis of the consequences that are drawn from such situations shows, they do not call into question the *principles*, which remain valid.

Another dictionary[2] defines "emergency" as a "political term, to describe a condition approximating to that of war". This brings out even more clearly what is meant in this chapter by "exceptional circumstances": the extreme emergency situation is that of war and, the closer the emergency situation considered is to war, the more the difficulties encountered in respect of the protection of human rights are the same as those prevailing in time of war.

In short, an "emergency situation" will be understood here as one resulting from temporary conditions which place institutions of the State in a precarious position and which leads the authorities to feel justified in suspending the application of certain principles.

So long as the planet's resources are not distributed in accordance with each people's needs, the most deprived countries will have to contend with exceptional circumstances of "under-development".[3] The leaders of such countries often consider that the enjoyment of certain human rights is, in such circumstances, a luxury that their peoples cannot afford until a more or less long time has elapsed. Under-development thus constitutes the first emergency situation to be examined.

Earthquakes, famines, fires, floods and other "natural" catastrophes constitute other situations in which certain of the most fundamental rights (the right to life, the right to an adequate standard of living) may no longer be ensured by the authorities of a country, who feel it necessary to discontinue the application of other rights in order to protect the most essential rights. This is the second emergency situation which will be dealt with here.

Lastly, the third emergency situation is that of internal disturbances and armed conflicts, the body of law appertaining to which is, as we shall see, by far the most developed.

1. EMERGENCY ARISING FROM ECONOMIC AND SOCIAL CONDITIONS AS A WHOLE

> Many of our compatriots suffer from permanent malnutrition and from all the attendant mental and physical diseases; their poverty and their ignorance make all talk of human freedom derisory.
>
> Julius Nyerere

The economic and social conditions of those countries referred to as "developing countries" are characterized by poverty, disease, a runaway increase in population, inequalities and a whole series of factors which are measured statistically in relation to the so-called "developed countries". According to such criteria as *per capita* income, there are today over 800 million absolute poor in the world. The quantitative approach is open to criticism at two levels, the economic and the semantic: at the economic level because it does not take into account the differences in kind, and in particular the differences in structure, between the economically developed countries, the economy of which usually forms a whole in which all the elements interlock with each other, and the materially backward countries, the economy of which is disjointed, because it is formed of juxtaposed economies, and dominated, particularly through trade and as a result of movements in capital; and at the semantic level because development cannot be understood solely in terms of economic growth, an increase in productivity, national income, availability of consumer goods, etc., but must be viewed in the specific context of each society, of each national situation, and encompass the most varied aspects of social and cultural life[4]. Thus the economically "developed" countries are often "under-developed" from the point of view of quality of life, measured in terms of participation by all social groups in the active life of the nation and the effort to bring about full development of each human being, and the equilibrium between man and his natural environment. Thus understood, "development" calls for changes, both in the materially backward countries and in the economically advanced countries. The Executive Board of Unesco, in 1969, clearly and eloquently expressed man's role in development and the link the latter has with human rights in the following terms:

"Development is meaningful only if man, who is both its instrument and beneficiary, is also its justification and end. It must be integrated and harmonized: in other words it must permit the full development of the human being on the spiritual, moral and material level, thus ensuring the rights of man in society, through respect for the Universal Declaration of Human Rights".[5]

More recently, Unesco, in the introduction to the chapter in its Medium-Term Plan devoted to "Man as the Centre of Development", explained the links between peace, human rights and development in the following way:

"Conditions will be favourable to development only if there is a general climate of peace conducive to the mobilization of all available resources for the achievement of economic growth and social well-being, and if the dignity of the individual and his place and role within the community are given due recognition by the full observance of human rights. But the converse is equally true: the promotion of human rights and the reinforcement of peace are inconceivable without an improvement in the material living conditions of the population at large, which can only be achieved by development. The necessary implication is, not perhaps that all men must immediately be able to enjoy the fruits of development and of effective equality of circumstances and of opportunity, but at least that a movement to improve the lot of all must be launched, that the most obvious ills must be remedied, that efforts must be made to improve living conditions in accordance with the requirements of justice, that peoples must have a share in decisions concerning the paths to be followed in their development and must themselves work for it, and that new horizons with tangible prospects of improvement must be opened up for them".[6]

It is important to reflect seriously on the meaning of development which is more than a question of economic parameters—in order to understand the problems of human rights in the developing countries. Under-development, understood holistically, is of course the result of the internal structures of the countries concerned, but also and above all of the structural relations between the developed countries of the "centre" (North) and the under-developed countries of the "periphery" (South). Under-development consequently has historical and structural causes which must be understood before a judgment can be made of the state of human rights in those countries. The state of these rights is necessarily bound up with the structures and mechanisms involved in the exploitation of resources, the domestic and international market, and political and military alliances at the world level. In any case, most developing countries and particularly the poorest among them do not exercise full sovereignty over their resources, do not control the price of the raw materials that they sell to the industrial countries and even less the price of the manufactured goods that they have to buy, and their economic infrastructure has been developed as a result of either direct foreign domination (through colonialism or occupation) or indirect foreign domination by way, for instance, of foreign landowners.[7] The form of this domination varies in time and in space but it is always present when one takes a close look at the position of the developing countries and it is inseparable from the problem of human rights.

This being so, it is understandable that the self-determination of countries and peoples and sovereignty over their natural resources should be regarded as fundamental principles of human rights, set forth in Article 1 of the two United Nations Covenants and analyzed elsewhere in the present work.[8] It can be said that the elimination of the fundamental causes of under-development is itself a human right. However, it is not only the elimination of colonialism and neo-colonialism which constitutes the link between human rights and development: the right to development has itself been considered as a human right.[9] Indeed the existence of this right has been affirmed by the Commission on Human Rights of the UN, particularly in Resolution 4 (XXXIII), 4 and 5 (XXXV) and 6 (XXXVI), and by the General Conference of Unesco, particularly in Article 3 of the Declaration on Race and Racial Prejudice. The General Assembly adopted the Commission's position on the existence of this right in Resolution 34/46 of 7 December 1979.

It is not the purpose of this chapter to analyze the interrelations between development and human rights,[10] nor the right to development as a human right; but far more modestly to raise the question as to whether and to what extent under-development, in international human rights law, constitutes an emergency situation giving rise to the application of special rules relating to the implementation of human rights?

The basic texts

In Chapter IX of the Charter of the United Nations on international economic and social co-operation, the goals of (a) higher standards of living, full employment and (b) conditions of economic and social progress and development are placed before (c) universal respect for, and observance of human rights and fundamental freedoms among the objectives to be promoted by the United Nations "with a view to the creation of conditions of stability and well-being which are necessary for peaceful and friendly relations among nations". Admittedly, Article 55 does not establish a hierarchy between the three paragraphs (economic and social development, cultural and education co-operation and respect for human rights), but it seems clear that the first is at least as important as the other two.

It was indeed on account of Article 55(a) that the drafters of the Universal Declaration of Human Rights added to the draft Preamble a clause according to which the peoples of the United Nations "have determined to promote social progress and better standards of life in larger freedom".[11] The view was not taken, however, that for the purposes of human rights, a distinction between States according to their level of development belonged in a declaration proclaimed to be "a common standard of achievement for all peoples and all nations" and which was to be implemented by "progressive measures, national and international".

Moreover, the Declaration contains, in Article 29 (7), a clause on the limitation to which human rights shall be subject and which must be determined by law for the purpose of meeting, *inter alia*, the just requirements of "morality...and the general welfare in a democratic society".[12] During the discussion on this paragraph, Commission III of the General Assembly seems to have interpreted the words "the general welfare" as signifying economic and social requirements.[13] Although the idea of an emergency situation arising from social and economic conditions may be considered to originate with article 29 of the Universal Declaration, the developing countries were not being referred to specifically.

It was necessary to wait for the International Covenant on Economic, Social and Cultural Rights of 1966[14] for this idea to be clarified, but only as regards the status of aliens. Thus, Article 2, paragraph 3, of the Covenant reads: "Developing countries, with due regard to human rights and their national economy, may determine to what extent they would guarantee the economic rights recognized in the present Covenant to non-nationals".

The place given to this idea, and to the rights to self-determination and to sovereignty over natural resources in the Covenant, reflects the shift in the power base of the countries involved between 1948 (the Declaration) and 1966 (the Covenants). This evolution was subsequently to become far more rapid and the notion of an emergency situation in the sense understood in this chapter was quickly to emerge.

On the occasion of the International Conference on Human Rights, convened by the General Assembly to mark the twentieth anniversary of the Universal Declaration of Human Rights[15] and held in Teheran from 22 April to 13 May 1968, a special study on "Some Economic Foundations of Human Rights" was prepared by Mr. José Figueres.[16] On the basis of this study, the Conference adopted Resolution XVII entitled "Economic development and human rights" which includes the following paragraphs:

"*The International Conference on Human Rights,*
Believing that the enjoyment of economic and social rights is inherently linked with any meaningful enjoyment of civil and political rights and that there is a profound inter-connection between the realization of human rights and economic development,
Noting that the vast majority of mankind continues to live in poverty, suffer from squalor,

disease and illiteracy and thus leads a sub-human existence, constituting in itself a denial of human dignity,
Noting with deep concern the ever-widening gap between the standards of living in the economically developed and developing countries,
Recognizing that universal enjoyment of human rights and fundamental freedoms would remain a pious hope unless the international community succeeds in narrowing this gap,
Considering the close relationship between the terms of international trade and other economic, fiscal and monetary measures, national or international, on the one hand, and the possibility of narrowing this gap by rapid economic development, on the other,"

The central idea of this resolution is taken up again in the "Proclamation of Teheran", adopted at the closure of the Conference, which stipulates in operative paragraphs 12 and 13:

"12. The widening gap between the economically developed and developing countries impedes the realization of human rights in the international community.

. . .

13. Since human rights and fundamental freedoms are indivisible, the full realization of civil and political rights without the enjoyment of economic, social and cultural rights, is impossible. The achievement of lasting progress in the implementation of human rights is dependent upon sound and effective national and international policies of economic and social development".

The "inherent correlation between the enjoyment of human rights and economic development" referred to in Resolution XVII and the obstacle constituted by the gap between economically developed and under-developed countries is now at the centre of the reflections on the implementation of human rights at the United Nations and elsewhere.[17] The implications of the argument that under-development constitutes an emergency situation concern not only civil and political rights—but also economic, social and cultural rights—for the enjoyment of the former are not possible without that of the latter. Indeed, after considering a study on economic and social rights,[18] the Economic and Social Council affirmed "its conviction that early realization of economic, social and cultural rights can be achieved only if all countries and peoples are able to attain an adequate level of economic growth and social development and if all countries institute all necessary measures with a view to eliminating inequality in income distribution and social services in accordance with the International Development Strategy for the Second United Nations Development Decade".[19]

Although the text relating to the International Development Strategy[20] indicates with a certain precision the goals and objectives pursued together with measures calculated "to create in the world a more just and more rational economic and social order", it was soon superseded by decisions which go a great deal further in attempting to identify the causes of, and solutions to, under-development in the world and which tell us more about the links between development and the protection of human rights.

The most far reaching event in this regard was the Sixth Special Session of the United Nations General Assembly, which adopted the Declaration and Programme of Action on the *establishment of a new international economic order* (3202 (S-VI)). As regards the causes of under-development, the Declaration unhesitatingly states that "the remaining vestiges of alien and colonial domination, foreign occupation, racial discrimination, *apartheid* and neo-colonialism in all its forms continue to be among the greatest obstacles to the full emancipation and progress of the developing countries and all the peoples involved". It recalls that the present system "was established at a time when most of the developing countries did not even exist as independent States" and is therefore "in direct conflict with the current developments in international political and economic relations". From the relation of interdependence existing among all the members of the world community, it draws the conclusion that the prosperity of all depends on that of the constituent elements and that it is consequently necessary to put an end to the imbalance existing between developed countries and under-developed countries. Further to these decisions, and in conformity with Section VI of the Programme of Action, the General Assembly adopted, at is 29th session, the *"Charter of the Economic Rights and Duties of States"*[21] as the "first step in the codification and developments of the matter". The Charter begins by reaffirming the "fundamentals of international economic relations" which consists of fifteen principles including "respect for human rights and fundamental freedoms". However, there is no mention of human rights as such either in the Declaration, or in the Programme of Action, or elsewhere in the Charter. Be that as it may, from the standpoint of the implementation of human rights, the provisions of these texts do identify some of the structural changes to be made before the Third World countries and the developed countries can be considered equals. It is indicative of the increasing tendency to link respect for human rights to the establishment of a new international economic order that the Commission on Human Rights decided to expand its traditional agenda item on realization of economic, social and cultural rights and special problems of developing countries to include:

"the effects of the existing unjust international economic order on the economies of the developing countries, and the obstacle that this represents for the implementation of human rights and fundamental freedoms".[22]

Two other post-1974 statements of the development-human rights *problématique* deserve mention: in defining the concepts which should guide future human rights work in the UN system, the General Assembly, in 1977, affirmed, *inter alia*:

"1 (b)The full realization of civil and political rights without the enjoyment of economic, social and cultural rights is impossible; the achievement of lasting progress in the implementation of human rights is dependent upon sound and effective national and international policies of economic and social development".[23]

Whatever view one may have on the claims put forward by Third World countries—and they have been criticized either for going too far and endangering development prospects for all or for being oriented towards the élites and neglecting the real development problems of the dominated masses—the fact remains that, for these countries, until a new international economic order is achieved, the economic and social conditions of under-development will constitute an emergency situation making the implementation of at least some human rights difficult, if not impossible.

Even in this case, however, the *principle* of the *enjoyment* of all human rights remains unchallenged;[24] only the *exercise* of certain rights may not be fully ensured, or may even be discontinued so long as the emergency situation lasts.

The reality of under-development and the implementation of certain human rights

While *slavery* has been practically eliminated since the anti-slavery movement of the 19th century and is prohibited by legislative provisions established in the 20th century, cases of its persistence have been pointed out, particularly in the developing countries. The practice of slavery in its classic form has been attributed to the consequences of economic and social conditions, such as nomadism and a very low level of national income which does not make it possible to pay for the services provided by the slave.[25] Considering the large number of developing countries which have ratified the Slavery Convention and the Supplementary Convention on the Abolition of Slavery,[26] it can be said that the developing countries recognize the absolute character of the prohibition against slavery, for, despite the difficulties encountered in the attempt to eliminate it completely in the world, under-development cannot be considered to be a justification or an excuse for the condition of slavery.

The same is true for *torture and cruel, inhuman or degrading treatment.* Even though one of the explanations given for the persistence of torture is that the developing countries do not have the means to provide adequate training for the police and to obtain the desired information in any other way, the obligation to abolish torture and similar practices is incumbent on all States, regardless of their level of development.[27]

The prohibition of *genocide* is a third example of a human right which no country feels justified in violating.[28] The most recent cases of this crime have, however, occurred in developing countries.[29]

As regards the right to a *fair trial*, the independence of the judiciary, the rights to defence, the adversary character of the procedure, and the making public of the proceedings, all these elements seem to be regarded as fundamental guarantees which do not depend on the state of development.[30] Improving the administration of justice and the use of legal aid on a large scale, however, require means which are not available to many countries, but the most elementary principles of justice are recognized to be binding upon all countries without exception.

The right to *free choice of employment*, recognized by Article 23 of the Universal Declaration offers a more difficult example. The participants in the United Nations seminar held in Dakar in 1966 held the view that the economic and social situation of Africa did not make it possible, for the time being, to implement that right, for the need to protect the population against unemployment sometimes made it necessary for a certain amount of control to be exercised in respect of choice of employment.[31] Constraint in this regard may take several forms: compulsory civilian service for the unemployed, the obligation to perform work useful to the community, the obligation to work land in conformity with a development plan, guidance at the level of training, etc. Sometimes it will be difficult to distinguish between restrictions on free choice of employment in order to meet the needs of development, and forced labour, prohibited by the ILO Conventions.[32] Like all exceptions in the matter of human rights, this particular one may be compatible with human rights only insofar as it is in the general interest, effectively required by the situation and proportionate to the needs involved.

It has often been observed that the *right to private property* has undergone a negative evolution since the Universal Declaration. Its very existence was challenged at the time that Article 17 of the Declaration was being drawn up.[33] While the restrictions on this right may be related to under-development, the right itself has been called into question by the developing countries,[34] some of which pointed out that this right may impede development.[35] In any case, the right to property is not included in the 1966 Covenants and is subject to an important limitation founded on the general interest in the European[36] and American[37] regional conventions.

Far more difficult is the question of *freedom of expression and of the press*. While the right to seek, receive and impart information has given rise to complex problems in the developed countries, its implementation meets with different and more considerable problems in the developing countries. The consequences of unlimited freedom in this field can indeed be easily imagined for a country that has very small resources at its disposal for a national press, for television and radio programmes, for the training of journalists and media technicians, etc. Such a State is at the mercy of those who possess such resources, that is to say, of a class of society which does not represent the mases, or of foreign interests. It is then generally recognized that a balance must be established between the maintenance of national solidarity and unity, on the one hand, and the right of everyone to express himself or herself freely and to receive information, on the other.[38] Considering the precarious situation of certain newly independent States, it is not surprising that they restrict freedom of information more than in the developed countries. Moreover, information plays an essential role in the education and mobilization of the

people and consequently in the development process. It may then seem a
necessity for the State to hold a monopoly. But such a situation may also lead
to arbitrariness or may prevent the masses from learning the truth about
facts which concern them.

In contrast with the developed countries, the problem of information arises
in the developing countries both at the level of the technical facilities (print-
ing presses, radio and television broadcasting stations, film studios and cin-
emas, press agencies, etc.) and at the level of political structures and attitudes
(existence or not of an opposition party, level of political awareness of the
masses, etc.). In most cases, no private group commands the necessary capital, unless it is foreign or financed from abroad, to found information enterprises. A certain degree of government intervention to make the media more
independent of such foreign interests may, in the view of the countries concerned, be necessary. As a communication network becomes established, and
as political stability becomes assured, the restrictions to which the exercise
of freedom of information is subject lose their justification and greater freedom is required.

The last example to be examined is that of *freedom of association*. The
political reasons invoked in regard to freedom of information also hold for
political association, insofar as the existence of a single party is considered by
several newly independent countries to be essential for development. Thus,
for instance, the African countries need to be able to rely on national unity in
order to reap the fruits of development in the face of colonial concupiscence
and the special interests of tribes or other groups.[39]

Any exception to the principle of freedom of political association, justified
by the specific conditions of the developing countries, must however be compatible with *each person's right to take part in the conduct of public affairs in
his or her country*, to choose his or her representatives or be elected in
genuine periodic elections by universal suffrage and by secret ballot. The
right to take part in political life must be the object of special attention in a
single-party system in order for the party to become and to remain the
expression of the will of the governed.[40] If the party becomes the tool of a
dominant minority which seeks to stay in power by means of bogus elections,
then the development of the entire country suffers.[41] In such cases, the only
remedy seems to lie in clandestine action and in the use of violence by the
opposition. Here as elsewhere in this chapter, the dialectic expressed by the
third preambular paragraph of the Universal Declaration comes into play:
"...it is essential, if man is not to be compelled to have recourse, as a last
resort, to rebellion against tyranny and oppression, that human rights should
be protected by the rule of law".

*Misuse of under-development as a pretext for abusive limitations on human
rights*

For one of the most outstanding African jurists and former President of
the UN Commission on Human Rights, "all these developing States, con-

stantly threatened by disorder and economic difficulties, consider themselves to be permanently in an emergency situation".[42] In his view, what is involved is not so much justifying exceptions to the exercise of certain human rights on account of the conditions of under-development, but rather issuing a warning against the abuses which may result from using a limited emergency situation as an excuse which is perpetually invoked. "One must not wait for under-development to be throttled once and for all (if ever it can be) in order subsequently to attempt to observe the rules governing human rights and freedoms".[43]

In requesting the study on the question of the duties of the individual and the limitations to the exercise of human rights, the Sub-Commission on Prevention of Discrimination and Protection of Minorities stated that "limitations imposed on the exercise of human rights should not serve to justify an abuse which would lead to violations of human rights".[44] The rules of interpretation generally applied to clauses of exception[45] should, moreover, prevent certain abuses of the notion of emergency arising from the state of under-development. First of all, certain rights are to be respected at all times and in all places. Secondly, the restrictions must be provided by law[46] and applied solely for the purpose for which they have been provided and, above all, should not serve as a pretext for political repression. Lastly, they should not give rise to any discrimination on grounds of race, sex, colour, language, religion or social condition. The specific character of the emergency situation arising from under-development makes it possible to consider as inadmissible in international human rights law any emergency measure taken to protect the privileges of an élite or a dominant minority and which does not contribute to the economic liberation of the entire population.

The full exercise of all human rights must of course be guaranteed as soon as social and economic conditions permit. But how, in the absence of reliable indicators and competent bodies, can one judge whether these conditions have been met or the emergency situation ended? What steps can be taken to prevent those practices which have become customary during the "emergency situation" from continuing indefinitely, without even the rulers and the governed realizing it? The application of the notion of emergency to conditions of under-development must therefore be handled with utmost care. The struggle for liberation against colonialism and neo-colonialism and for development in the interest of the populations of the under-developed countries is also the struggle for human rights. If the exercise of certain rights is discontinued on account of that struggle, considered as an emergency situation, which, by definition, is temporary, then the measures must also be temporary and they do not in any case derogate from the principle, which remains valid, of universal respect for, and observance of, human rights, based on the UN Charter.

This difficulty of determining the duration of the emergency situation in the case of under-development does not arise in the situation arising from *force majeure*.

2. EMERGENCY ARISING FROM *FORCE MAJEURE*: NATURAL CATASTROPHES

> When something is described as a "nat-
> ural" disaster, it is in most cases merely
> because its causes or workings cannot
> be discerned nor a remedy found.
>
> Amadou-Mahtar M'Bow

Impact of catastrophes on human rights in general

The emergency situation which arises on the occasion of natural catastrophes[47] generally, but not necessarily, begins the moment that the event takes
place. Insofar as the catastrophe has been foreseen—and it is the role of the
Red Cross and of the United Nations Disaster Relief Co-ordinator to assist
States in anticipating and planning relief[48]—it is for the government of the
country affected to take the necessary measures to reduce in advance the
effects of the event in the interests of the entire population.

Over and above the measures relating to the planning of relief which do not
affect the exercise of human rights (appointment of a single co-ordinator,
training of administrative and medical personnel, storage of tents, blankets,
foodstuffs, etc.), it may conceivably be necessary to impose, prior to the
disaster, certain restrictions on freedom of movement and residence (forced
evacuations from areas in danger of being affected), the freedom of the press
and other information media (the need to inform the population of what
should be done and to avoid panic)[49], freedom of employment (use of the
labour force to build shelters, dykes, etc.), the right to property (requisi-
tions) and other rights which may be subject to the strictly necessary limitations for the purpose, under the terms of the international instruments, of
meeting the just requirements of the general welfare (Art. 29 of the Universal Declaration) or for the protection of national security, public order or
public health (*inter alia*, Arts. 19 and 21 of the Covenant on Civil and Political Rights).

In the few texts currently in force which expressly provide for exceptions
in cases of *force majeure*, in particular certain ILO Conventions, the period
of emergency includes the "threat" of danger, that is to say, the period before
the event. A provision concerning exceptions in cases of war or emergency is
included in at least eight international labour conventions.[50] Taking the Convention (No. 29) on Forced Labour, 1930, as an example, the obligations it
contains do not apply to "any work or service exacted in cases of emergency,
that is to say, in the event of war or of a calamity or *threatened* calamity, such
as fire, flood, famine, earthquake, violent epidemic or epizootic diseases,
invasion by animal, insect or vegetable pests, and in general, any circumstances that would endanger the existence or the well-being of the whole or

part of the population".[51] In addition to containing an excellent definition of emergency situations this paragraph illustrates the possibility of taking into account, in a legal text, the period which precedes the calamity ("threatened calamity", "any circumstance that would endanger"). The ILO Committee of Experts on the Application of Conventions and Recommendations specifies in this connection that "the length and extent of compulsory service, as well as the purposes for which it is used, should be strictly limited in accordance with the requirements of the situation" and it compares this stipulation with that of Article 4 of the International Covenant on Civil and Political Rights.[52]

This being said for the period before the natural catastrophe, we shall now analyse the derogation clauses of human rights instruments which may apply after the outbreak of such catastrophes to other emergency situations.

Derogation clauses

The derogation clause is contained essentially in Article 4 of the Covenant on Civil and Political Rights, Article 15 of the European Convention and Article 27 of the American Convention.[53] These three texts do not, however, allow derogations to be made from the right to life, from the prohibition against torture and inhuman or degrading treatment or punishment, from the prohibition against slavery and from the principle of the lawfulness and non-retroactivity of penal laws. The list of these rights is reproduced in Table I. In addition, the authorized derogations must not be inconsistent with other obligations under international law, must be strictly required by the exigencies of the situation and be notified to the competent body.

It will be the competent body's task to assess whether the public emergency invoked following the natural catastrophe justifies the application of the derogation clause. Case-law in this field, in particular that of the European Commission and Court of Human Rights, relates to situations of conflict, and the case of a natural catastrophe has not yet arisen. The ILO Committee of Experts on the Application of Conventions and Recommendations has had occasion to express its opinion concerning a situation involving a natural catastrophe, namely the Nicaragua earthquake:

"The Committee has taken cognizance, with deep regret, of the earthquake suffered by the city of Managua and of the magnitude of this national catastrophe. In extending to the government of Nicaragua its profound sympathy and expressing its sincerest wishes for a rapid return to normalcy, the Committee, fully conscious of the seriousness of the situation in the country and the difficulties arising for the normal fulfilment of its international obligations, has considered it necessary to suspend the examination of the questions relating to the application of ratified Conventions by this country. The Committee hopes that the Government will be in a position in due course and with the help of the ILO to give full effect to its obligations under the conventions ratified by Nicaragua".[54]

In this instance what was involved was a town and consequently only part of the population. The text of the Convention Concerning Force or Compul-

Table 8.1
Human Rights Norms Applicable in Cases of Non-International Armed Conflicts of Public Emergency Threatening the Life of the Nation

Norm	Article establishing the norm which remains applicable at all times and in all places				
	ECHR[1] (see Art.15)	COV. C and P[2] (see Art.4)	ACHR[3] (see Art.27)	Geneva Conventions	Protocol II[4]
Right to life	Art.2[5]	Art.6[5]	Art.4	Art.3a	Art.4.2.a.e
Prohibition against torture, degrading treatment or punishment	Art.3	Art.7	Art.5 (1)	Arts.3 & 6	Art.4.2.a.e
Prohibition against slavery and servitude	Art.4 (1)	Art.8(1 & 2)	Art.6	Art.3b[7]	Art.4.2.c.f[7]
Principle of lawfulness and retroactivity	Art.7(1)[6]	Art.15(1)[6]	Art.9	Art.3d[8]	Art.6.2.
Prohibition against medical experiments		Art.7			Art.5.2.e
Non-imprisonment for debts		Art.11			
Recognition of legal personality		Art.16	Art.3		Art.5.1.d.
Freedom of thought, conscience and religion		Art.18	Art.12		
Political rights			Art.23		
Protection of the family			Art.17[9]		Art.4.2.e,5.2.a
Right to a name			Art.18		
Rights of the child			Art.19		Art.4.3
Right to a nationality			Art.20		

NOTES:

1. ECHR—European Convention on Human Rights.
2. COV. C and P—International Convention on Civil and Political Rights.
3. ACHR—American Convention on Human Rights.
4. Protocol—Protocol Additional to the Geneva Conventions of 12 August 1949, and Relating to the Protection of Victims of Non-International Armed Conflicts.
5. Except for death resulting from "the use of force which is no more than absolutely necessary" (Art.2) or "lawful acts of war" (Art.15).
6. Except for crimes according to the general principles of law (7(2) and 15(2)).
7. Prohibition against the taking of hostages.
8. Indispensable judicial guarantees, prohibition of summary convictions.
9. This relates to the right to marry and protection of the rights of spouses in the ACHR, whereas Art.4.2.e of Protocol II concerns the protection of women against indecent assault, and Art.5.2.a concerns the detention of men and women belonging to the same family.

sory Labour, quoted above, specified, moreover, that the danger may concern "the whole or part of the population", which appears normal where natural catastrophes are concerned. The precedents of the organs of the European Convention, on the other hand, seems more restrictive, for in the case *Gerard Lawless v. Republic of Ireland*,[55] the Court defined a "public emergency threatening the life of the nation" as "an exceptional situation of crisis or emergency which affects *the whole population* and constitutes a threat to the organized life of the community of which the States is composed".[56] True, this precedent relates to situations of conflict and not cases of natural catastrophes, and the question consequently arises whether the interpretation given of Article 15 by the Commission would be the same in the event of a natural catastrophe affecting only part of a State's territory.

In addition to derogation clauses, the international texts provide for a number of restrictions, either in the formulation of certain rights or in specific clauses of exception. The remainder of this section concerns the possible use of these restrictions in cases of natural catastrophe, but applies, *mutatis mutandis*, to situations of conflict which are examined further on.

The articles relating to the right to life (Art. 6 of the Covenant on Civil and Political Rights, Art. 2 of the European Convention, Art. 4 of the American Convention) make an exception for the death penalty (and in the sole case of the European Convention, for death when it results "from the use of force which is no more than absolutely necessary"): a) in defence of any person from unlawful violence; b) in order to effect a lawful arrest or to prevent the escape of person lawfully detained; c) in action lawfully taken for the purpose of quelling a riot or insurrection. All these cases justifying deprivation of life could occur during natural catastrophes.

The prohibition against forced labour (Art. 8 of the Covenant, Art. 4 of the European Convention, Art. 6 of the American Convention, ILO Conventions No. 29 and No. 105) does not cover work required of a person under detention or "any service exacted in cases of emergency or calamity threatening the life or well-being of the community" or "any work or service which forms part of normal civil obligations".[57] The attitude of the ILO Committee of Experts in regard to the question of forced labour in cases of catastrophe has already been mentioned. As for the European Commission, it examined this provision in particular in the *Iversen v. Norway* case[58]: this case concerned a Norwegian dentist assigned against his will to a remote region in the north of the country, in accordance with a provisional law of 1956. While four of the six members of the majority of the Commission (which concluded that the application was not admissible) considered that the work demanded of Iversen was neither unjust nor oppressive and that the Commission consequently did not need to judge of the applicability of Art. 4 (3), the two others were however of the opinion that the service in question constituted a reasonable service in the case of an emergency threatening the well-being of the community within the meaning of that Article.

As regards the right to liberty, the limitations prescribed in the texts (Art. 5 of the European Convention, Art. 7 of the American Convention, Arts. 9 and 10 of the Covenant on Civil and Political Rights) authorize lawful arrests and detentions in normal circumstances. It is also permitted to detain a person likely to spread an infectious disease (Art. 5 (1) (e) of the European Convention), which may prove to be necessary during a natural catastrophe, particularly during an epidemic.

In general the articles of international human rights treaties which reaffirm or proclaim a right contain a second paragraph setting out the limitations which may be invoked and applied in cases of natural catastrophe as well as other emergency situations.

Like emergencies arising from social and economic conditions as a whole, those founded on *force majeure* resulting from a natural catastrophe must be handled with care. The temptation is great to plead the need to waive international human rights norms in order to cope with the consequences of a natural catastrophe. Natural catastrophe, provided that it constitutes a public emergency threatening the life of the nation, may be invoked under the conditions laid down by the international human rights law in order to take measures derogating from certain human rights but not from all of them. Similarly, when a natural catastrophe makes it necessary for human rights to be subjected to certain restrictions, these are limited by the provisions mentioned above. In practice, in contrast with the emergency situation founded on under-development, emergencies arising from natural disasters have not been the subject of many discussions from a human rights perspective. The reason for this may be that such emergencies correspond more closely to the situations provided for in the international instruments and have, for that reason, greater chance of being controlled by the competent organs.

3. EMERGENCY ARISING FROM THE EXISTENCE OF INTERNAL DISTURBANCES AND ARMED CONFLICTS

> ...between the oppressors and the oppressed everything is settled by force.
>
> Franz Fanon

The relationship between violence and human rights

While under-development is often regarded as a form of *structural violence*, while natural catastrophes are essentially the result of the *violence of nature* often aggravated by conditions of under-development, the emergency situation which is the subject of the third part of this chapter concerns the *direct and open violence of individuals and groups*.

Municipal law regulates human conduct under the control of the State which has a monopoly over the use of force. It is in the logic of this system that the use of force which is not authorized by the State is regarded as an aberration in relation to the legal system considered. But the internal legal system may itself be founded on violations of human rights. Is violence carried out against the authority of the State for the purpose of protecting human rights recognized in international human rights law? Do limits exist to the use of violence by the State, limits imposed by international human rights law? Such are the questions which arise when one examines the relationship between violence and human rights.

The dialectic between human rights and violence did not escape the drafters of the Universal Declaration. The third preambular paragraph stipulates that: "it is essential, if man is not to be compelled to have recourse, as a last resort, to rebellion against tyranny and oppression, that human rights should be protected by the rule of law".

The idea, of course, is not new. Without going all the way back to Socrates' *Apology*[59] the following passage from Vattel, writing in the middle of the 18th century, illustrates the tradition of the right of resistance: "...as for those monsters who, bearing the title of sovereigns, make themselves the bane and horror of mankind, they are wild beasts that all men of feeling justly want to eliminate from the earth".[60]

While the French Declaration of 1789 and especially that of 1793 as well as the United States Declaration of Independence establish the right to revolt in a revolutionary context, the 1948 Universal Declaration is primarily the expression of a movement to preserve peace for all time. But in an international "order" where law is the result of power relations,[61] peace founded in injustice and violation of human rights cannot last and inevitably leads to violence.[62]

As defined by international human rights law, human rights include two dimensions which make it easier to understand their relationship to violence: *oppression* is negation, through direct or structural violence, of civil and political rights; *misery* is the negation, essentially through structural violence, of economic, social and cultural rights which results from inequalities between individuals, groups and States. The institutions for the protection of human rights which operate in conformity with the provisions of international conventions may alleviate certain effects of those structures, but they are incapable of bringing about by themselves the political changes necessary for oppression and hardship to disappear. Such changes are very often achieved by violence, and it is here that lies the central aspect of the relationship between violence and human rights.[63]

The social sciences, and in particular political science and peace and conflict research, have developed typologies, models and indicators which distinguish between the different manifestations of violence.[64] To understand violence from the point of view of the international dimensions of human rights, four types of situations should be distinguished, namely, international disturbances and tensions, internal armed conflict, wars of national liberation and international wars.

Internal disturbances and tensions

Public order is threatened when individuals or groups commit acts of non-organized violence, that is to say, violent acts which do not constitute military operations conducted in accordance with a concerted plan. Such acts are usually repressed in accordance with a national penal law; from the point of view of international human rights law, there are no *a priori* grounds for considering such a situation as justifying a derogation from the applicable rules. Likewise, internal tensions, caused by opposing political forces and not entailing military operations, do not necessitate the application of emergency measures.

It is only when internal disturbances constitute a real threat to the life of the nation that the international instruments provide for the possibility of derogating from the rules normally applicable. In fact, the problem here is one of assessment of the solution which depends primarily on the national authorities and where appropriate, on the case-law of the controlling organ under international instruments.

In cases of internal disturbances which do not constitute an emergency situation, certain problems may arise, particularly with respect to mass arrests of persons charged with political offenses. Special international standards have been drawn up to improve the protection of prisoners, namely, the "Standard Minimum Rules for the Treatment of Prisoners" adopted by the First United Nations Congress on the Prevention of Crime and the Treatment of Offenders in its Resolution of 30 August 1955. The purpose of these rules is to set out "what is generally accepted as being good principle and practice in the treatment of prisoners and the management of institutions", without however precluding new methods and practices, provided that they are consonant with the principles governing the protection of human dignity. Of these rules, mention should be made of non-discrimination, freedom of belief, respect for human dignity and a whole series of standards concerning the distribution of prisoners, accommodation, hygiene, discipline, etc.; the right to make requests or complaints to the prison administration is also recognized; lastly, special rules are prescribed for certain categories of prisoners and persons under detention. The implementation of these rules was on the agenda of the Fifth and Sixth United Nations Congresses held respectively in Geneva in September 1975 and in Caracas in September 1980[65] and additional standard-setting activities have supplemented them considerably. Among the draft instruments which hopefully will soon be widely accepted are a Convention on torture and other cruel, inhuman and degrading treatment or punishment,[66] a body of principles for the protection of all persons under any form of detention of imprisonment[67] and a set of principles of medical ethics relevant to the role of health personnel in the protection of persons against torture and other cruel, inhuman or degrading treatment or punishment.[68]

Certain provisions of the general human rights instruments assume particular importance during periods of internal disturbances. These are primarily the protection of individual freedom against arbitrary arrest and detention, guarantees of a fair hearing, including the non-retroactivity of criminal laws, the right to be defended, the prohibition of torture and inhuman or degrading treatment and punishment, and freedom of association.

Every day cases arise, in every region of the world, illustrating the lack of respect for these rights in periods of internal disturbances. International human rights law is now sufficiently developed for it to be possible to consider that the State which fails to respect the human rights provisions applicable to such situations does not fulfil its obligation, assumed under the Charter of the United Nations, to promote respect for, and observance of, human rights.

Armed conflicts not of an international character

When a conflict assumes the dimensions of an armed confrontation, the life of the nation is immediately considered to be threatened, with the result that the derogation clauses are able to be invoked. In such cases, all those human rights norms from which no derogation is allowed remain applicable.

These norms are confirmed or supplemented by the specific law of non-international armed conflicts which forms part of humanitarian law, outlined elsewhere.[69] Although the Universal Declaration did influence the drafters of the Geneva Conventions,[70] the systems of international human rights law and that of humanitarian law tackle the problem of internal armed conflicts in different ways. The first falls in the framework of *jus ad bellum* as envisaged by the Charter of the United Nations, according to which recourse to force is prohibited and which is consequently aimed at the preservation of peace. The second, on the other hand, forms part of *jus in bello*: it establishes rules governing the use of force without examining the causes of the conflict in accordance with the principles of the Red Cross and in particular the principles of humanity.[71]

Present-day humanitarian law is not confined to conventional situations of war; it also provides, in Article 3 common to the four Geneva Conventions of 12 August 1949, for norms applicable to "armed conflict not of an international character occurring in the territory of one of the High Contracting Parties".[72] According to the commentary on the Geneva Conventions, Article 3 "ensures at least the application of humanitarian rules recognized as being essential by civilized peoples".[73] Briefly summarized these are the rules of *non-discrimination corporal well-being* (prohibition of murder, mutilation, cruel or humiliating treatment and torture), *personal freedom* (prohibition of the taking of hostages and of summary executions) and *elementary due process*.

These rules may have a lesser or greater scope according to whether they are interpreted, as is recommended in the commentary,[74] in the light of other articles in Conventions concerning "human treatment". It is stipulated, in addition, that "the Parties to the conflict should...endeavour to bring into force, by means of special agreements, all or part of the other provisions of the present Convention".

Aware both of the difficulties involved in having a common article 3 applied by the parties to an internal conflict and of the need to extend the list of the recognized rights, the ICRC examined this problem at meetings of experts (1953, 1955, 1962 and 1969), International Conferences of the Red Cross (Istanbul, 1969; Teheran, 1972), a consultation of experts (1970) and conferences of government experts (1971, 1972). The United Nations Conference on Human Rights of 1968 marked a turning point in this connection in that it recognized "the need for additional international humanitarian conventions or for possible revision of existing Conventions to ensure the better protection of civilians, prisoners and combatants in all armed conflicts..." It also requested the Secretary-General, after consultation with the ICRC, to draw the attention of Member States to the rules existing on the subject.[75]

It was in this context that the Swiss Federal Government convened the Diplomatic Conference on "the reaffirmation and development of international humanitarian law applicable in armed conflicts" which met in 1974, 1975, 1976 and 1977. Considerable preparatory work was carried out by the ICRC on the question of non-international conflicts[76]. This work culminated in the drafting of one of the two additional Protocols to the Geneva Conventions dealing specifically with the protection of victims of non-international armed conflicts.[77] The "fundamental guarantees" are defined in Article 4 of the Protocol II as follows:

"Article 4 (Fundamental guarantees)
1. All persons who do not take a direct part or who have ceased to take part in hostilities, whether or not their liberty has been restricted, are entitled to respect for their person, honour and convictions and religious practices. They shall in all circumstances be treated humanely, without any adverse distinction. It is prohibited to order that there shall be no survivors.
2. Without prejudice to the generality of the foregoing, the following acts against the persons referred to in paragraph 1 are and shall remain prohibited at any time and in any place whatsoever:
  (a) violence to the life, health and physical or mental well-being of persons, in particular murder as well as cruel treatment such as torture, mutilation or any form of corporal punishment;
  (b) collective punishment;
  (c) taking of hostages;
  (d) acts of terrorism;
  (e) outrages upon personal dignity, in particular humiliating and degrading treatment, rape, enforced prostitution and any form of indecent assault;
  (f) slavery and the slave trade in all their forms;

(g) pillage;

(h) threats to commit any of the foregoing acts".

Furthermore, special rules are provided in Article 5 of the Protocol for persons deprived of liberty, and principles of penal law, in particular the prohibition of retroactive laws and punishments, the presumption of innocence, the protection against self-incrimination, and the right to be present at trial with all necessary rights and means of defence are reaffirmed.

Wars of liberation

Although the drafters of the 1949 Geneva Conventions did not lay down special rules for armed conflicts in which one of the parties claims to be availing itself of its right to self-determination[78] the delegates to the 1974-1977 Diplomatic Conference and the ICRC attached particular importance to this question, no doubt because the States participating in the Conference were more numerous and less European in 1974 than in 1949 and several of them had acquired their independence through wars of liberation. The importance of this matter was further illustrated by the presence of observers from liberation movements engaged in combat and the disagreement which arose in connection with some of these movements.

Closely bound up with the international dimensions of human rights, the right of peoples to self-determination is in fact enshrined among the purposes and principles of the United Nations (Articles 1 and 2 of the Charter) and has been reaffirmed many times in the context of human rights. The first operative paragraph of the Declaration on the Granting of Independence to Colonial Countries and Peoples stipulates: "The subjection of peoples to alien subjugation, domination and exploitation constitutes a denial of fundamental human rights...". This right is again reaffirmed in Article 1 of the two 1966 Covenants; it is dealt with in detail in another chapter.[79]

The United Nations General Assembly has insisted for several years that the rules of humanitarian law should apply to combatants in movements engaged in the struggle of peoples labouring under the yoke of colonial and foreign domination to secure their liberation and self-determination.[80]

Thus the first phase consisted in granting to combatants in liberation movements the protection provided for war prisoners according to the 3rd Geneva Convention. The ICRC attempted to do this by proposing to the Diplomatic Conference that a paragraph worded as follows to Article 42—"new category of prisoners of war"—of Draft Protocol I (international armed conflicts) be added:

"3. In cases of armed struggle where peoples exercise their right to self-determination as guaranteed by the United Nations Charter and the "Declaration on Principles of International Law concerning Friendly Relations and Co-operation among States in accordance with the Charter of the United Nations", members of organized liberation movements who comply with the aforementioned conditions shall be treated as prisoners of war as long as they are detained".[81]

Doctrine is divided on the question[82] especially since what is involved is granting a legal status to wars of liberation by equating them, for the purposes of the application of the Geneva Conventions, with international armed conflicts. Aware of these divergencies of opinion the ICRC took the view that draft paragraph 3 of Article 42 of Draft Protocol I quoted above was sufficient and that it was not fitting to include a reference to wars of liberation in the article devoted to the scope of the Protocol. The Committee responsible for Article 1 (general principles) of Protocol I considered, however, that it was not sufficient and it adopted the following paragraph:

"The situations referred to in the preceding paragraph include armed conflicts in which peoples are fighting against colonial domination and alien occupation and against racist regimes in the exercise of their right of self-determination, as enshrined in the Charter of the United Nations and the Declaration on Principles of International Law concerning Friendly Relations and Co-operation among States in accordance with the Charter of the United Nations".[83]

If the Protocol containing this provision in its Article 1, paragraph 4, is ratified by a large number of States, there will no longer be any doubt as to the applicability to wars of liberation of the norms of international law relating to the protection of victims of international armed conflicts.

International warfare

According to article 2 common to the four Geneva Conventions, all the provisions of those Conventions shall apply when two or more Contracting Parties are engaged in an armed conflict, "even if the state of war is not recognized by one of them". They shall also apply "to all cases of partial or total occupation of the territory of a High Contracting Party, even if the said occupation meets with no armed resistance".

A summary of these norms is given in another chapter[84] and, for a more thorough examination, reference must be made to the *travaux préparatoires* and the actual texts of the Conventions[85] and of the Additional Protocols[86] as well as to the Commentary of the ICRC[87] and to the standard manuals on the law of war and humanitarian law.[88]

It is worth recalling, however, for the purposes of the present chapter, some of the norms of humanitarian law applicable in international conflicts, in order to bring out the nature and specificity of this branch of international law. Generally speaking, the purpose of these norms is to ensure that "the belligerents shall not inflict on their adversaries harm out of proportion to the object of warfare which is to destroy or weaken the military strength of the enemy".[89] Some of these norms come under the so-called law of the Hague (by virtue mainly of Convention No. IV of 1907 signed at the Hague and of the Regulations annexed to that Convention), the fundamental principle of which is that "the belligerents do not have an unlimited choice of the means of inflicting damage on the enemy";[90] others form part of what is known as law of Geneva (by virtue of the Conventions of 1949 signed at Geneva) according to which "persons placed *hors de combat* and those not participating directly in the hostilities shall be respected, protected and treated humanely".[91]

It may seem naïve to affirm such principles when those in charge of military operations seek but one thing: to win the conflict at the least cost for their side, and may even seek the total destruction of the enemy regardless of any strategic consideration. The temptation is to conclude cynically that military exigencies will always prevail in their minds over humanitarian principles. Experience shows however that it is not impossible to reconcile humanitarian considerations with military exigencies and to involve the military, who, better than anyone, are acquainted with the horror of war, in this task. The ratifications of the Geneva Conventions (more than 150) and the entry into force on 7 December 1978 of the additional Protocols prove that, at least at the level of legal commitment, the military and diplomatic authorities of practically all countries wish to see military exigencies reconciled with humanitarian principles. So long as the causes of armed conflicts have not been eliminated, these norms of humanitarian law constitute a hope for the victims of such conflicts; the effective application depends on their dissemination and on the political will of the parties to the conflict to respect them.

From the very general principles mentioned above a number of more specific principles derive which are common to the different categories of victims of war, as well as principles pertaining to the protection of wounded, sick and shipwrecked persons (Conventions I and II), principles pertaining to the treatment of prisoners of war (Convention III) and principles pertaining to the protection of civilians (Convention IV).

A soldier who has been placed *hors de combat* is to be given shelter and to be treated humanely. Medical care is to be given without discrimination, except for reasons of medical urgency. Medical and religious personnel must not be prevented from performing their functions, but they must observe strict military neutrality. Should they fall into the hands of the enemy, the latter can retain them only if the medical and religious needs of prisoners of war so require; otherwise, repatriation is the rule. Even under detention, such personnel enjoy certain facilities for the performance of their functions. Other provisions of Conventions I and II concern the medical care dispensed by the civilian population and relief societies, the immunity of medical buildings and establishments, the assignment of medical material, the means of transport and the distinctive emblem.

As for prisoners of war (POWs), their treatment is governed by the 143 articles of Convention III. The detaining Power must treat them humanely, respect their persons and their honour, and cannot transfer them to the territory of a country which is not a party to the Convention. The sole information that a POW is required to provide concerns his surname, first names, age, rank and regimental number. The places of internment must be salubrious and life must be organized in them in such a way as to maintain the physical and mental health of POWs, including, adequate food and medical care and the possibility of practising one's religion and of having intellectual and sports activities. Detailed provisions govern work, financial resources, relations with the outside and with the authorities, discipline and repatriation. In order for POWs to be acquainted with these provisions, the Convention must be posted.

Lastly, norms pertaining to the protection of the civilian population are contained in the 159 articles of Convention IV. While "safety zones", intended for wounded, sick, and disabled persons, expectant mothers, women with young children and aged persons, have not been established as the Convention provides (but without making it an obligation), it may sometimes be possible to establish a "neutralized zone" in the region where fighting is taking place for the protection of the local population and the wounded and sick. Apart from these provisions, wounded and sick non-combatants, the infirm, and expectant mothers are entitled to particular protection and respect. Civilian hospitals and their personnel are protected and all civilians are entitled to give news to their families and to receive news from them. The most important norm concerning the civilian population is contained in article 27 of Convention IV which stipulates:

"Protected persons are entitled, in all circumstances, to respect for their persons, their honour, their family rights, their religious convictions and practices, and their manners and customs. They shall at all times be humanely treated, and shall be protected especially against all acts of violence of threats thereof and against insults and public curiosity".

Furthermore, protected persons must not be compelled to provide information, and it is specifically forbidden to cause them physical suffering ("not only...murder, torture, corporal punishments, mutilation and medical and scientific experiments not necessitated by the medical treatment of a protected person, but also...any other measures of brutality whether applied by civilian or military agents"), to subject them to collective penalties, measures of intimidation or of terrorism, or reprisals. Pillage and the taking of hostages are also prohibited. These are but a few examples of the rules concerning the general protection of populations against certain effects of war and the status and treatment of protected persons. Other provisions of the Convention deal more particularly with aliens on the territory of a party to the conflict, occupied territories and the treatment of internees.

The ICRC and the Diplomatic Conference have endeavoured to develop measures for the protection of victims of international armed conflicts. This subject is dealt with by Protocol I, which supplements the Geneva Conventions, particularly with regard to wounded, sick and shipwrecked persons, methods and means of combat, prisoner-of-war status and the civilian population.

Some of the norms of protection provided for by the Protocol are particularly relevant to human rights. For instance, Article 11 protects the physical and mental well-being of protected persons and prohibits, in particular, mutilations or medical or scientific experiments not justified by medical treatment. Persons carrying out medical activities compatible with professional ethics cannot be punished for those activities nor be compelled to act in a manner contrary to the rules of professional ethics or to reveal information concerning the adverse party (Article 16). In addition, reprisals against the wounded, the sick and medical personnel are prohibited (Article 20). As regards methods and means of combat, the following basic rules are reaffirmed in Article 35:

"Article 35 (Basic rules)
1. In any armed conflict, the right of Parties to the conflict to choose methods or means of warfare is not unlimited.
2. It is forbidden to employ weapons, projectiles, and material and methods of warfare of a nature to cause superfluous injury or unnecessary suffering.
3. It is prohibited to employ methods or means of warfare which are intended or may be expected to cause widespread, long-term, and severe damage to the natural environment".

Perfidy (Article 37), the refusal to give quarter (Article 40), and attacks on an enemy *hors de combat* (Article 41) are also prohibited.

The basic rule concerning respect for the civilian population specifies that "the Parties to the conflict shall at all times distinguish between the civilian population and combatants and between civilian objects and military objectives and accordingly shall direct their operations only against military objectives" (Article 48). In addition, "acts or threats of violence the primary purpose of which is to spread terror among the civilian population", "indiscriminate attacks" and "reprisals" against civilians are prohibited (Article 51).

Article 75 lists the fundamental guarantees enjoyed by civilians in the power of a Party to the conflict and not protected by the Geneva Conventions, namely, nationals of the interested Party to the conflict and combatants who do not fulfil the conditions necessary for them to be considered as prisoners of war.[92] The norms applied to them are those of humane treatment covered by Articles 27, 31, 32, 33 and 34 of the 4th convention and reiterated in Article 4 of Protocol II,[93] together with the judicial guarantees affirmed in Articles 64 to 75 of the 4th Convention, including the principle of the personal character of penal responsibility, the principle *non bis in idem*, presumption of innocence, and the non-retroactivity of penal law. Lastly, special measures are prescribed for women and children (articles 76-78).

The means employed to supervise the implementation of the Geneva Conventions are examined in another chapter.[94]

4. COMPARISON BETWEEN THE DIFFERENT TYPES OF CONFLICT SITUATIONS IN TERMS OF THE APPLICABLE NORMS AND THE NOTION OF *JUS COGENS*

It has become clear that the different situations of violence considered here give rise to the application of norms pertaining either to international human rights law (IHRL) or to the international law of armed conflicts (ILAC),[95] or to both at the same time. The level of protection afforded by IHRL is highest in time of peace and diminishes as a situation approaches war, as when, for instance, attacks on life due to "lawful acts of war" are permitted. Conversely, the level of protection afforded by ILAC is relatively limited in peacetime (obligation to disseminate the Conventions, to modify legislation, etc.), but is very developed when there is a situation of international war. The relationship between the two systems is illustrated diagramatically in Table II. The two curves cross roughly at the moment of civil war. For IHRL this means a public emergency threatening the life of the nation, during which the applicable norms may be restricted to those considered as non-derogatable. For ILAC, the situation is one in which common article 3 of the Geneva Conventions and article 4 of Protocol II apply. In other words at the intersection of the two curves the minimum norms of the two systems apply.

Table II also shows that the level of protection afforded both by IHRL and ILAC never descends below respect for norms having the character of *jus cogens*. What is meant by this? As it appears in articles 44, 53, 60, and 64 of the Vienna Convention on the Law of Treaties and in the deliberations of the International Law Commission, the conception of *jus cogens* is founded on the legal effects of a norm having the character of *jus cogens*. What is involved, according to article 53 of the Vienna Convention, is a norm accepted and recognized by the international community of States as one from which no derogation is permitted and which can only be modified by a subsequent norm of the same character. Such was the conception of several delegates to the 1949 Diplomatic Conference in regard to the nature of the norms of the Geneva Conventions.[96] Moreover, several articles can be interpreted along these lines on account of their objective nature, since they establish obligations which are not of a contractual character.[97] Common article 3 defines rules which are applicable "at any time and in any place" and lays down, according to the Commentary, imperative rules.[98] Similarly the provisions of IHRL relating to emergency situations have the effect of limiting the power of the contracting States to discontinue the application of certain articles.[99]

Another approach to the notion of *jus cogens* consists in examining the content of the norms. Professor Verdross includes, for instance, "all norms of general international law created for humanitarian purpose" among the norms of *jus cogens*.[100] The International Law Association has identified as deserving urgent solution the question of the "imperative character in respect of the norms of international law (*jus cogens*) of the principles relating to the pro-

Table 8.2
Comparison of Level of Protection as a Function of the Type of Conflict Under International Human Rights Law and International Humanitarian Law

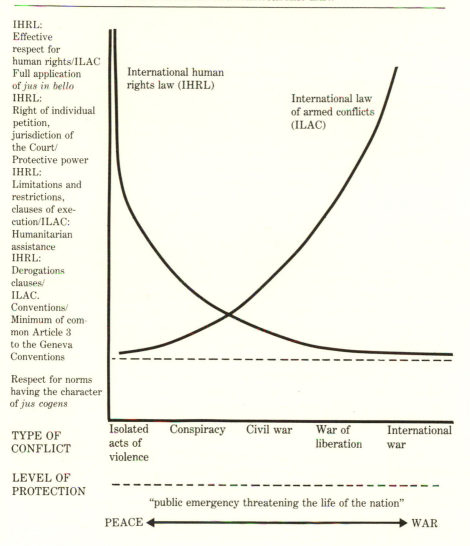

IHRL:
Effective
respect for
human rights/ILAC
Full application
of *jus in bello*
IHRL:
Right of individual
petition,
jurisdiction of
the Court/
Protective power
IHRL:
Limitations and
restrictions,
clauses of exe-
cution/ILAC:
Humanitarian
assistance
IHRL:
Derogations
clauses/
ILAC.
Conventions/
Minimum of com-
mon Article 3
to the Geneva
Conventions

Respect for norms
having the character
of *jus cogens*

International human
rights law (IHRL)

International law
of armed conflicts
(ILAC)

TYPE OF
CONFLICT

| Isolated acts of violence | Conspiracy | Civil war | War of liberation | International war |

LEVEL OF
PROTECTION

"public emergency threatening the life of the nation"

PEACE ◄——————————————————► WAR

tection of the human person contained in the Geneva Conventions".[101] It would no doubt be false to claim that all the norms of ILAC and all the rights of IHRL from which there can be no derogation have the character of *jus cogens*. Rosalyn Higgins considers that "neither the wording of the various human rights instruments nor the practice thereunder lead to the view that all human rights are *jus cogens*," although she does recognize that "there certainly exists a consensus that certain rights—the right to life, to freedom from slavery or torture—are so fundamental that no derogation may be made".[102] Indeed, not to consider some norms of IHRL and ILAC as imperative norms having the character of *jus cogens* would disregard the obvious legal effects of certain instruments and the fundamental character, unchallenged by the international community, of several principles.

Table III below shows the interface of these norms and points out in particular that certain norms considered to be fundamental in IHRL are not so considered in ILAC and vice-versa, while other are common to IHRL and ILAC and, more often than not, are also norms having the character of *jus cogens* (JC).

Conclusion

The three types of emergency situations examined in this chapter differ from each other in many respects, but they also have many features in common. For countries which have not known affluence for centuries, if ever they did, under-development is the rule rather than the exception. On the other hand, a natural catastrophe places before the national authorities a new situation with which they may not be able to cope. Armed conflicts, produce situations in which the authorities are challenged either from within or outside the country by a military force which, by definition, does not wish to comply with the laws of the State in question. The three situations differ as to their duration, the appropriate means of contending with them, the relationship between the national authorities and the population, and the sources of the applicable rules.

They nevertheless have enough in common for it to be possible to put forward a few general ideas concerning human rights in emergency situations. First of all, all three types of situations relate to major concerns of the international community. The establishment of a new international economic order provides, for the whole of the United Nations system, fresh impetus for the fight against under-development; the establishment and development of the office of the United Nations Disaster Relief Co-ordinator and the magnitude of recent catastrophes illustrate the growing importance of this question; the Geneva Diplomatic Conference, in which more than 130 delegations participated, and the deadly internal as well as inter-State conflicts which have arisen in many parts of the world, emphasize the need to adapt the relevant laws to current realities.

Table 8.3
Interface Between International Law of Armed Conflicts and International Human Rights Law Showing the Place of Norms Having the Character of *Jus Cogens*

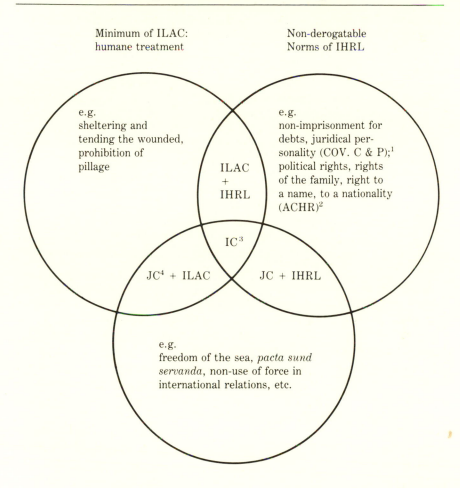

Minimum of ILAC: humane treatment

Non-derogatable Norms of IHRL

e.g. sheltering and tending the wounded, prohibition of pillage

ILAC + IHRL

e.g. non-imprisonment for debts, juridical personality (COV. C & P);[1] political rights, rights of the family, right to a name, to a nationality (ACHR)[2]

IC[3]

JC[4] + ILAC

JC + IHRL

e.g. freedom of the sea, *pacta sund servanda*, non-use of force in international relations, etc.

NOTES:
1. COV. C & P—International Convention on Civil and Political Rights.
2. ACHR—American Convention of Human Rights.
3. IC—The "indestructible core" of human dignity (prohibition of torture, slavery, degrading or humiliating treatment or punishment, the arbitrary deprivation of life, adverse discrimination and judicial guarantees recognized as indispensable).
4. JC—Norms having the character of *jus cogens*.

More important than the topicality of these questions are the links which exist between them. Speaking of the drought in Africa, the Director-General of Unesco said:

"We must learn fast, very fast, from this terrible experience in view of the imminence, if not already the actual presence, of other calamities, caused in this case by an economic crisis and a recession, the effects of which, by their unequal impact on nations and social groups, bring starkly into the open the inequalities which were previously concealed from many people by affluence and its attendant sense of well-being in the wealthier countries. . . . Yet these dire events are not the result of fate, to be received with resignation. When something is described as a "natural" disaster, it is in most cases merely because its causes or workings cannot be discerned nor a remedy found".[103]

"Natural" disasters, indeed have a much more devastating effect upon the developing countries than upon the rich countries, precisely because the state of under-development makes them more vulnerable. And these same under-developed countries are the theatre of armed conflicts, which the major industrial powers have been able to eliminate from their mutual relations by shifting them towards the under-developed periphery.

These three situations relate to moments in the life of a State entity when that entity is least inclined to burden itself with human rights. Concerned by the need to assure the survival of the nation, the national authorities wish to be bound by as few constraints as possible.

In these circumstances, it is essential and urgent to define clearly the human rights obligations that States must respect whatever the situation prevailing on their territories. Considering themselves to be engaged in the struggle for human rights when they take measures in favour of development, to assist victims of disasters, to liberate themselves or to repulse the aggressor, States will reveal the full measure of their attachment to human rights by respecting the human rights applicable in such exceptional circumstances which, it is to be hoped, will be more and more "exceptional" in fact. As long as these conditions exist, they will reduce human rights to their most precarious level and it is at that level that we can see the extent to which human rights are reality or mere illusion.

NOTES

1. H.C. Black, *Black's Law Dictionary* (5th Edition), West Publishing Co., Minnesota, 1979, p. 469.

2. *A Supplement to the Oxford English Dictionary*, Vol. 1, A-G, p. 934, Oxford, 1972.

3. The significance of the notion of under-development, a term covering a highly complex reality, is briefly discussed below.

4. One of the best descriptions of the terminological and methodological problems of the notions of "development" and "under-development" is to be found in Gunnar Myrdal, *Asian Drama: An Inquiry into the Poverty of Nations*, the Twentieth Century Fund, New York, 1968, Vol. III, Annex 1, pp. 1839-1878. More recently, among the hundreds of outstanding contributions to the understanding of the problems of development, Willy Brandt, in his introduction to the report of the commission he chaired, wrote: "One must

avoid the persistent confusion of growth with development. . ." *North-South, a Program for Survival. The Report of the Independent Commission under the Chairmanship of Willy Brandt*, the MIT Press, Cambridge, Massachusetts, 1980, p. 23. (Hereinafter referred to as "Brandt Commission Report").

5. See Malcolm S. Adiseshiah: *It is time to begin: the human role in development: some further reflections for the seventies*, Unesco, Paris, 1972.

6. General Conference, Nineteenth Session, Medium-Term Plan (1977-1982), Unesco, 1977, para. 323. Concerning the interrelationship between human rights, peace and development, see the report of a UN seminar on the subject held in New York on 3-14 August 1981, Doc. ST/HR/SER.A/10; and Stephen Marks, "The Peace—Human Rights—Development Dialectic", *Bulletin of Peace Proposals*, Vol. 11, No. 4, 1980, pp. 339-347.

7. Among the vast literature on this subject, see, for example, the Brandt Commission Report, Chapters 1, 2, 3, 4, 9, 12, 13; Dieter Ernst (ed.) *"The New International Division of Labour, Technology, and Under-Development, Consequences for the Third World"*—Campus Verlag, Frankfurt/New York, 1980; Mohammed Bedjaoui *"Towards a New International Economic Order"*, Unesco, Paris, Holmes and Meier Pub., New York-London, 1979.

8. See *supra*, Chapter 1. See also, Héctor Gros Espiell, "The Implementation of United Nations Resolutions Relating to the Right of Peoples under Colonial and Alien Domination to Self-Determination", report for the UN Sub-Commission on Prevention of Discrimination and Protection of Minorities, UN Doc. E/CN4/Sub.2/390, in particular the analysis of the definition, scope and legal nature of self-determination.

9. Although earlier formulations have been made, the first systematic attempt to define this right was made by Kéba M'Baye. See "Le droit au développement comme un droit de l'homme", *RDJ/HRJ*, Vol. V, No. 2-3, pp. 503-534 (1972), "The Emergence of the 'Right to Development' as a Human Right in the Context of a New International Economic Order", Unesco, Doc. SS-78/CONF.630/8, and "Le développement et les droits de l'homme", Rapport introductif, Colloque de Dakar sur le développement et les droits de l'homme (Septembre 1978), *Revue sénégalaise de Droit*, December 1977, No. 22, pp. 19-51, esp. 33-51. A considerable amount of background material on the subject may be found in the report of Unesco's expert meeting of 1978 on "Human Rights, Human Needs and the Establishment of a New International Economic Order", which was submitted to the Commission on Human Rights for its consideration of the right to development, along with the Secretary-General's report (E/CN.4/1334). See also Stephen Marks, "Emerging Human Rights: A New Generation for the 1980s?" *Rutgers Law Review*, Vol. 33, No. 2, 1981, pp. 444-445.

10. One of the first articles to tackle this problem clearly is that of Karel Vasak, "Droit de l'homme et sous-développement", *Comprendre*, No. 31-32, Société européenne de culture, Venice, 1968, pp. 1-6. See also, Stephen Marks, "Human Rights and Development: Some reflections on the study of development, human rights and peace", *Bulletin of Peace Proposals*, Vol. 8, No. 3, 1977, pp. 236-246; Philip Alston, "Human Rights and the New International Development Strategy", *Bulletin of Peace Proposals*, Vol. 10, No. 3, 1979, pp. 281-290; Osita C. Eze, "Les droits de l'homme et le sous-développement", *RDJ/HRJ*, Vol. XII, Nos. 1-2, pp. 5-18; see also "Study on the New International Economic Order and the Promotion of Human Rights", Progress Report by Raúl Ferrero, Special Rapporteur, Sub-Commission on Prevention of Discrimination and Protection of Minorities (UN Doc.E/CN.4/Sub.2/477, 18 August 1981).

11. See, concerning the origin of this clause, Albert Verdoodt, *Naissance et signification de la Déclaration universelle des droits de l'homme*, Louvain-Paris, 1964, pp. 308-309.

12. Pursuant to Resolution 9 (XXVII) of the Sub-Commission on Prevention of Discrimination and Protection of Minorities, a Special Rapporteur prepared a "Study of the Individual's Duties to the Community and the Limitation on Human Rights and Freedoms under Article 29 of the Universal Declaration of Human Rights" (UN doc.E/CN.4/Sub.2/432/Rev.1, and Adds.1-7). The special Rapporteur mentions, in connexion with this clause, that "in certain regions of the world community. . .the pressing necessity is the satisfaction of basic

social needs, the promotion of the well-being and economic security of the great masses."
(UN Doc. E/CN.4/Sub.2/432, (Rev.1), para. 584).

13. Verdoodt, *op. cit.*, pp. 269 and 271.

14. For a more detailed account of this Covenant, see *supra*, Chapter 5 and *infra* Chapter 11.

15. Resolution 2081 (XX) of 20 December 1965, Resolution 2217 (XXI) of 19 December 1966 and Resolution 2339 (XXII) of 18 December 1967.

16. Document A/CONF.32/L.2.

17. The value of the affirmations of the Proclamation is in this respect challenged by some, e.g. Moskowitz, *International Concern with Human Rights*, Sijthoff, Leyden; Oceana Publications Inc., Dobbs Ferry, N.Y., 1974, pp. 18-20.

18. Requested by the Commission in its Resolution 14 (XXV) of 13 March 1969, the study was published in 1973 under the reference number E/CN.4/1108 and Add. 1 to 10; supplemented by observations, conclusions and recommendations, it was revised in 1974 (E/CN.4/1131 and Corr. 1).

19. Operative paragraph 2 of Resolution 1867 (LVI) adopted on 17 May 1974. For more recent developments in relation to the International Development Strategy, see Alston, *loc. cit.*

20. See Resolution 2626 (XXV) of 24 October 1970.

21. See document A/9946 of December 1974.

22. Commission Resolution 6 (XXXVI). Pursuant to the same resolution, the United Nations organized a seminar on this subject in Geneva on 30 June-11 July 1980. See Report ST/HR/SER.A/8).

23. General Assembly Resolution 32/130 of 16 December 1977, para. (b).

24. It is worth quoting in this regard para. 1 (a) of Resolution 32/130, which has already been mentioned: "All human rights and fundamental freedoms are indivisible and interdependent".

25. United Nations Division of Human Rights, *Seminar on Human Rights in Developing Countries*, Dakar, 8-22 February 1966, Report under reference number ST/TAO/HR/25, para. 20. See also report of the Working Group on Slavery of the Sub-Commission on Prevention of Discrimination and Protection of Minorities at its fifth session (E/CN.4/Sub.2/434.) According to information submitted to the Sub-Committee there are still 250,000 slaves in the world. To take the example of Mauritania, the information minister, Dahane Ould Ahmed Mahmoud, declared in July 1980 that "Slavery is the most primitive, hateful form of exploitation of man by man. We know it still exists in our country. The previous colonial and neo-colonial regimes tried to cover up the practice. It will take a long process before we are finally rid of this hateful practice." (*International Herald Tribune*, 12 September 1980.)

26. Nearly one hundred developing countries have ratified one or both instruments.

27. ST/TAO/HR/25/, paras. 36-43.

28. The Convention on the Prevention and Punishment of the Crime of Genocide has been ratified by over 50 developing countries.

29. See "Study of the Question of the Prevention and Punishment of the Crime of Genocide", prepared for the Sub-Commission on Prevention of Discrimination and Protection of Minorities. UN Doc. E/CN.4/Sub.2/416.

30. See, for instance, United Nations Division of Human Rights, *Seminar on Special Problems relating to Human Rights in Developing Countries*, Nicosia, Cyprus, 26 June to 9 July 1969, report published in 1970, reference number ST/TAO/HR/36, paras. 87-100 and 151. The magistrates, lawyers and professors of law participating in the Conferences of Jurists organized by the International Commission of Jurists in Athens (1951), Delhi (1959), Lagos (1961), Bangkok (1965), Barbados (1971), and Dakar (1978) did not fail to emphasize the fundamental need for independent and impartial tribunals in the developing countries. As regards the Arab States, the Symposium of Human Rights and Fundamental Freedoms in the Arab Homeland, organized by the Union of Arab Lawyers in Baghdad on 18-20 May

1979, called on Arab States to abolish tribunals of exception, apply due process of law and guarantee the independence of the judiciary. Similarly, the African Charter of Human and Peoples' Rights, which was adopted in June 1981, includes substantial provisions concerning the administration of justice. At the colloquium on Human Rights and Economic Development in Francophone Africa, held in Butare, Rwanda, the participants agreed that "the autonomy and independence of the judiciary must be strengthened in order to ensure the proper and impartial administration of justice". See Hurst Hannum, "The Butare Colloquium on Human Rights and Economic Development in Francophone Africa: A Summary and Analysis", *Universal Human Rights*, Vol. 1, No. 2 (April-June 1979), pp. 63-87, at p. 84.

31. ST/TAO/HR/25, paras. 60-87.

32. See *supra*, Chapter 6 and *infra*, Chapter 12.

33. Verdoodt, *op. cit.*, pp. 170-175.

34. ST/TAO/HR/25, paras. 88-105.

35. *Ibid.*, para. 92.

36. Additional Protocol to the European Convention on Human Rights, of 20 March 1952, Article 1.

37. American Convention on Human Rights of 22 November 1969, Article 21.

38. ST/TAO/HR/25, paras. 128-149. See more generally International Commission for the Study of Communication Problems, *Many Voices, One World*, Kogan Page, London/Unipub, New York/Unesco, Paris, 1980.

39. Cf. ST/TAO/HR/25, paras. 150-179.

40. An International Seminar on Human Rights, Their Protection and the Rule of Law in a One-Party State convened by the International Commission of Jurists in Dar-es-Salaam in September 1976 concluded "that the one-party system was fully consistent with the preservation of fundamental human rights and the maintenance of the rule of law, *provided that its political form was a truly democratic one* (emphasis added), *Human Rights in a One-Party State*, Search Press, London, 1978, p. 110.

41. The Unesco text quoted earlier continues as follows: "Development imposed from above may well remedy certain injustices and reduce potential sources of conflict, but it cannot contribute to the promotion of human rights and the strengthening of peace as decisively as development centered on man, and that alone, can do".

42. Kéba M'Baye, "Les réalités du monde noir et les droits de l'homme", *RDH/HRJ*, Vol. II, No. 3, 1969, p. 389.

43. *Ibid.*, p. 383.

44. Resolution 9 (XXXVII) adopted on 21 August 1974 by 13 votes to 0, with 10 abstentions. The work plan of the study requested by this resolution includes examination of the question whether the "general welfare" can be regarded as a justification for temporary limitations to certain rights and freedoms with a view to the acceleration of economic and social development in the developing countries or to ensure environmental protection or public health. E/CN.4/Sub.2/L.627, annex, paras. 18, 19.

45. The legal analysis of these rules, based on the principal human rights instruments, will be provided in the next section. See also Rosalyn Higgins, "Derogations from Human Rights Treaties", *The British Yearbook of International Law, 1967-1977*, pp. 281-320.

46. See Oscar M. Garibaldi, "General Limitations on Human Rights: The Principle of Legality", *Harvard International Law Journal*, Vol. 17 (1976), pp. 503-557.

47. By natural catastrophe is meant, in particular, epidemics, famines, earthquakes, floods, tornadoes, typhoons, cyclones, avalanches, hurricanes, volcanic eruptions, drought and fire. The definition given by the Red Cross is as follows: "A disaster is a catastrophic situation in which the day-to-day patterns of life are—in many instances—suddenly disrupted and people are plunged into helplessness and suffering and, as a result, need protection, clothing, shelter, medical and social care, and other necessities of life". League of Red Cross Societies, *Red Cross Disaster Relief. Handbook*, 1976, Chapter II, p. 13.

48. By Resolution 2816 (XXVI) of 14 December 1971, the General Assembly invited the Secretary-General to appoint a relief co-ordinator, whose office (UNDRO) entered into service on 1 March 1972. The Red Cross has developed principles of action and planning in cases of disaster. See League of Red Cross Societies, *Red Cross Disaster Relief. Handbook*, 1976.

49. On the problems of control by the State of public information in time of natural disaster, see *Disaster Prevention and Mitigation, A Compendium of Current Knowledge*, Vol. 10, "Public Information Aspects", Office of the United Nations Disaster Relief Co-ordinator, United Nations, New York, 1979.

50. Hours of Work (Industry), 1919 (No. 1), Art. 14; The Night Work of Young Persons (Industry), 1919 (No. 6), Art. 4; Forced Labour, 1930 (No. 29), Art. 2(2) (d); Hours of Work (Commerce and Offices), 1930 (No. 30), Art. 9; Hours of Work (Mines and Coal) (revised), 1935 (No. 46), Art. 16; The Night Work of Young Persons (Industry) (revised), 1948 (No. 90), Art. 5; Work Clauses (Public Contracts), 1949 (No. 94), Art. 8; and Weekly Rest (Commerce and Offices), 1957 (No. 106), Art. 13.

51. Art. 2, para. 2 (d). Emphasis added.

52. *Forced labour*, extract from the report of the thirty-eighth session (1968) of the Committee of Experts on the Application of Conventions and Recommendations, ILO, Geneva, 1968, p. 201.

53. To this list may be added the derogation clauses of exception contained in the International Labour Conventions mentioned above and Article 30 of the European Social Charter. This last article authorizes derogations from the obligations of the Charter without identifying the obligations which have to be respected even in emergency situations.

54. International Labour Conference, 58th session, 1973, Report III (Part 4A).

55. Petition No. 332/57, *Yearbook 2*, pp. 309-341.

56. *Publications of the European Court*, Series A, 1961 p. 56 *et seq.* (emphasis added). In its definition given in the same case, the Commission states that the emergency "affects not certain individual groups, but the whole population". *Publications of the European Court*, Series B, 1960-1961.

57. The passages quoted are from Art. 8 of the Covenant; the other texts are almost identical, except for that of the International Labour Conventions, already quoted.

58. Application No. 1468/62, *Yearbook 6*, p. 279.

59. For the history and theory of the right and duty of resistance, see Haim A. Cohn, "The Right and Duty of Resistance", *RDH/HRJ*, Vol. I, No. 4, 1968, pp. 491-516.

60. E. de Vattel, *Le droit des gens ou principes de la loi naturelle appliqués à la conduite et aux affaires des nations et des souverains*, 1758, new edition, Paris, 1830, Book II, Chapter IV. para. 56.

61. This generally recognized principle is expressed by numerous authors, including, in particular, B.V.A. Roling, *International Law in an Expanding World*, Pjanbatan, 1980.

62. This idea was reaffirmed by the General Conference of Unesco at its 18th session in Resolution 11, preambular para. 17: "Considering that peace cannot consist solely in the absence of armed conflict but implies principally a process of progress, justice and mutual respect among the peoples designed to secure the building of an international society in which everyone can find his true place and enjoy his share of the world's intellectual and material resources, and that *a peace founded in injustice and violation of human rights cannot last and leads inevitably to violence*" (underlining added).

63. On the necessity to have recourse to armed struggle to achieve respect for human rights, see P. Pierson-Mathy, *La création de L'Etat par la lutte de libération nationale; le cas de Guinée Bissau*, Collection "New Challenges to International Law", Paris, Unesco, 1980.

64. See Johan Galtung, "The Specific Contribution of Peace Research to the Study of the Causes of Violence: Typologies", in A. Joxe (ed.), *Violence and its Causes*, Paris, Unesco, 1980, pages 83-96.

65. See Fifth United Nations Congress on the Prevention of Crime and the Treatment of Offenders (Geneva, 1-12 September 1975), "The Treatment of Offenders, in Custody or in the Community, with Special Reference to the Implementation of the Standard Minimum Rules for the Treatment of Prisoners Adopted by the United Nations", Working Paper prepared by the Secretariat, Document A/CONF56/6; and Sixth United Nations Congress on the Prevention of Crime and the Treatment of Offenders (Caracas, Venezuela, 25 August to 5 September 1980), "The Implementation of the United Nations Standard Minimum Rules for the Treatment of Prisoners", Working paper prepared by the Secretariat, Document A/CONF.87/11.

66. This draft convention was prepared further to a proposal of the Fifth United Nations Congress, endorsed by the General Assembly in Resolution 3452 (XXX) of 9 December 1975. By resolutions 32/62, 33/178, 34/167, 35/178 and 36/60 the General Assembly requested the Commission on Human Rights to draw up the Convention.

67. The General Assembly requested the Commission on Human Rights to study this question in its resolution 3453 (XXX) of 9 December 1975. The Commission asked the Sub-Commission on the Prevention of Discrimination and Protection of Minorities to draw up a body of principles. The draft was adopted by the Sub-Commission in 1978 (resolution 5 C (XXXI). By its resolution 34/169 of 17 December 1979, the General Assembly adopted the Code of Conduct for Law Enforcement Officials, but decided, by resolution 35/177 of 15 December 1980 to defer to its thirty-sixth session the draft Body of Principles for the Protection of All Persons under any Form of Detention or Imprisonment. In relation to this subject, Daniel O'Donnel of the staff of the International Commission of Jurists (ICJ) prepared a study on "States of Siege or Emergency and Their Effects on Human Rights" with recommendations by the ICJ which was submitted to the Sub-Commission (Doc. E/CN.4/Sub.2/NGO/93, 26 August 1981).

68. By its resolution 3453 (XXX) of 1975, the General Assembly invited the World Health Organization to give further attention to the study and elaboration of principles of medical ethics relevant to the protection of persons subjected to any form of detention or imprisonment against torture and other cruel, inhuman or degrading treatment or punishment. The invitation was conveyed to the WHO by resolution 31/85 of 13 December 1976. In January 1979, the Executive Board of WHO decided to endorse the principles set forth in a report of the Director General on "Development of codes of medical ethics" containing, in an annex, a draft body of principles prepared by the Council for International Organizations of Medical Sciences. The draft principles were brought to the attention of the General Assembly at its 34th session (document A/34/273), which requested the Secretary General to circulate the draft Code of Medical Ethics to Member States, Specialized Agencies concerned and NGO's and to report to the 35th session (resolution 34/168). Comments were communicated to the General Assembly (Docs. A/35/37 and Add. 1 and 2, A/36/140 and Add. 1-4), who continued considering the matter in 1982 (resolution 36/61).

69. See *supra*, Chapter 5 and further on in this chapter.

70. Several draft Preambles to the Conventions contained a direct reference to the Declaration but were not adopted by the Diplomatic Conference. See Records of the Diplomatic Conference of Geneva, Vol. III (Annexes), pp. 96-100 and the proceedings, Vol. II-A, pp. 761-766.

71. This is the principle of endeavouring "to prevent and alleviate human suffering wherever it may be found" which was affirmed, *inter alia*, by the 20th International Conference of the Red Cross, Vienna, 1965.

72. These terms were first employed at the 17th International Conference of the Red Cross at Stockholm in 1948. The more conventional terms of "civil war" still appeared in the resolutions of the 10th and 16th International Conferences of the Red Cross.

73. ICRC, *The Geneva Conventions of August 12, 1949, Commentary*, Vol. IV, Geneva 1956, p. 39.

74. *Ibid.*, pp. 44-46.

75. Resolution XXIII. See also General Assembly Resolution 2677 (XXV) of 9 December 1970.

76. See, *inter alia*, "Protection of victims of non-international conflicts", report submitted by the ICRC to the 21st International Conference of the Red Cross, Istanbul, September 1969, published in Geneva, May 1969; and volume V of the documentation submitted by the ICRC under the same title to the Conference of Government Experts, Geneva, May-June 1971, published in Geneva, January 1971.

77. The material field of application of Protocol II expressly excludes "situations of internal disturbances and tensions, such as riots, isolated and sporadic acts of violence and other acts of a similar nature, as not being armed conflicts". This Protocol shall apply to all conflicts which are not covered by Protocol I (i.e. conflicts between two or more Contracting Parties or wars of national liberation) "which take place in the territory of a High Contracting Party between its armed forces or other organized armed groups which, under responsible command, exercise such control over a part of its territory so as to enable them to carry out sustained and concerted military operations and to implement this Protocol". (Article I of Protocol II). These two Protocols were adopted by the Diplomatic Conference on 10 June 1977 and entered into force on 7 December 1978 in accordance with Article 25 of Protocol I and Article 23 of Protocol II.

78. The draft submitted by the ICRC to the Stockholm Conference of 1948 quoted as examples of non-international armed conflicts "civil war, colonial conflicts, or wars of religion". The Conference decided not to include examples.

79. See K.J. Partsch, *supra*, Chapter 4.

80. Among the many resolutions the following may be quoted for reference: 2767 (XXVI), 2795 (XXVI), 2796 (XXVI), 2871 (XXVI), 2874 (XXVI), 2908 (XXVII), 2918 (XXVII), 2945 (XXVII), 2946 (XXVII), 2955 (XXVII), 2979 (XXVII) and 2980 (XXVII).

81. The conditions are those required of "organized resistance movements", namely: "(a) that they are under a command responsible to a Party to the conflict for its subordinates; (b) that they distinguish themselves from the civilian population in military operations; (c) that they conduct their military operations in accordance with the Conventions and the present Protocol". See ICRC, *Draft Additional Protocols to the Geneva Conventions of August 12, 1949. Commentaries*, Geneva, 1973, pp. 48-54.

82. See the favourable interpretation of Georges Abi-Saab, "Wars of National Liberation and the Laws of War", *Annales d'études internationales*, Vol. 3, Geneva, 1972, pp. 93-117; and the unfavourable interpretation of Henri Meyrowitz, "Les guerres de libération et les Conventions de Genève", *Politique Étrangère*, 39th year, No. 6, 1974, pp. 607-727. See also, Michel Veuthey, *Guérilla et droit humanitaire* Institut Henry-Dunant, Geneva, 1976, La guérilla: le problème du traitement des prisonniers", *Annales d'études internationales*, Vol. 3, Geneva, 1972, and "Guerres de libération et droit humanitaire", *RDH/HRJ*, Vol. VII, No. 1, pp. 99-107, and Charles Chaumont, "La recherche d'un critère pour l'intégration de la guérilla au droit international humanitaire comtemporain", *Mélanges offerts à Charles Rousseau, La Communauté internationale*, Editions A. Pédone, Paris, 1974, pp. 43-61; Bert V.A. Röling, "The Legal Status of Rebels and Rebellion", *Journal of Peace Research*, Vol. XIII, 1976, pp. 149-163, and Natalino Ronzitti, "Wars of National Liberation—A Legal Definition", *The Italian Yearbook of International Law*, Vol. I, 1975, pp. 192-205. Meyrowitz has proposed that this category of conflicts be considered as a distinctive category of international but not inter-State armed conflict. Henri Meyrowitz, "La guérilla et le droit de la guerre: problèmes principaux", *Revue belge de droit international*, Vol. VII, 1971-1, pp. 56-72, p. 64.

83. The amendments proposed at the First Diplomatic Conference with a view to extending the application of the Conventions and the Protocols to wars of liberation are to be found under reference CDDH/1/5, 11, 13, 41, and 42. The text just quoted, CDDH/1/71, was submitted by Argentina, Honduras, Mexico, Panama and Peru and adopted by 70 votes to 21 with 13 abstentions.

84. See *supra*, Chapter 5.

85. *Final Record of the Diplomatic Conference of Geneva of 1949*, 4 vols., Bern, Federal Political Department, 1949.

86. *Final Record of the Diplomatic Conference on the Reaffirmation and Development of International Humanitarian Law Applicable in Armed Conflicts* (1974-1977), 17 vols., Bern, Federal Political Department, 1978.

87. ICRC, *The Geneva Conventions of August 12, 1949, Commentary*, published under the direction of Jean S. Pictet, Vol. I to IV, Geneva, 1952-1960.

88. Delio Jaramillo Arbelaez, *Derecho internacional humanitario (Convenios de Ginebra)*; Bogota, Colombia, Universidad Santo Thomas de Aquino, 1975; G. Balladone-Pallieri, *Diritto Bellico*, 2nd édition, Padova, CEDAM, 1954; S.D. Bailey, *Prohibitions and Restraints in War*, London, Oxford University Press, 1972; G. Cansacchi, *Nozioni di Diritto Internazionale Bellico*, 4th éd. Torino, Giappichelli, 1963; E. Castren, *The Present Law of War and Neutrality*, Helsinki, Suomalaisen k.s.k.o., 1954; G. L. Dorsey (ed.) *The Law of Conflict*, Saint Louis, 1973; G.I.A.D. Draper "The Geneva Conventions of 1949"; *Collected Courses of the Hague, Academy of International Law*, Vol. 114, 1965; R.A. Falk, *Law Morality and War in the Contemporary World*, New York, Praeger, 1963; L. Friedman, *The Law of War: A Documentary History*, New York, Random House, 1972, 2 vols; M. Greenspan, *The Modern Law of Land Warfare*, Berkeley, University of California Press, 1959; A. Guerrero Burgos, *Nociones de Derecho de Guerra*, Madrid, Jura, 1955; J. Hinz, *Kriegsvölkerrecht*, Cologne, Heymanns, 1957; F. Kalshoven, *The Law of Warfare: A Summary of its Recent History and Trends in Development*, Leyden, Sijthoff and Geneva, Henry Dunant Institute, 1973; R.J. Miller, *The Law of War*, Lexington Books, Massachusetts, 1975; M.S. McDougal et F.P. Feliciano, *Law and Minimum World Public Order: The Legal Regulation of International Coercion*, New Haven, Yale University Press, 1961; L. Oppenheim (H. Lauterpacht, ed.) *International Law: A Treatise*, Vol. II: *Disputes, War and Neutrality*, 7th éd., London, 1963; J.S. Pictet, *Les principes du droit international humanitaire*, Geneva, 1966; J.S. Pictet, *Humanitarian Law and the Protection of War Victims* (series of lectures given at the International Institute of Human Rights, Strasbourg, 1972), Henry Dunant Institute, 1975; A.I. Poltorak & L.I. Savinskij, *Vooruzhennye Konflikty imezhdunarodnoe pravo osnovnye problemy* (Armed Conflicts and International Law, Basic Problems), Moskva, Nauka, 1976; G. Schwarzenberger, *International Law as Applied by International Courts and Tribunals*, Vol. 2: *The Law of Armed Conflict*, Westview Press, Boulder, Colo. and London, 1968; J. Stone, *Legal Controls of International Conflict: A Treatise on the Dynamics of Disputes and War—Law*, 2nd éd., Revised, New York, Rinehart and Company, 1959; D.W. Ziegler, *War, Peace and International Politics*, Boston. See also J. Toman & Huynh Thi Huong, *International Humanitarian Law. Basic Bibliography*, Geneva, Henry Dunant Institute, 1979 for extensive additional references.

89. The terms chosen to express this principle, as well as several others referred to further on, are taken from J. Pictet, *Humanitarian Law and the Protection of War Victims* (series of lectures given at the International Institute of Human Rights, Strasbourg, 1972), Henry Dunant Institute, 1975, p. 31.

90. *Ibid.*, p. 33.

91. *Ibid.*

92. These conditions are set out in article 44 of Protocol I.

93. The text of this article is reproduced above.

94. See *infra*, C. Dominicé, Chapter 14.

95. It is possible to conceive of humanitarian law as a branch of IHRL since what is involved is "respect for human rights in periods of armed conflict" to adopt the terms used by the United Nations since the Teheran Conference (see Resolutions 2444 (XXIII), 2852 (XXVI) and 3032 (XXVII)). For the sake of clarity, IHRL and ILAC are considered here to be two separate systems of legal protection. The two systems are also systematically compared in Aristidis S. Calogeropoulos-Stratis, *Droit humanitaire et droit de l'homme. La*

protection de la personne en période de conflit armé, Graduate Institute of International Studies, Geneva, 1980.

96. See for instance, *Records of the Diplomatic Conference of Geneva*, Vol. III (Annexes), No. 187, 188, 189, pp. 97-98.

97. It is possible to analyze in this way common articles 1 and 2 of the four Conventions, article 7/7/7/8 respectively and 51/52/131/148 respectively. See also article 60, para. 5, of the Vienna Convention.

98. *Commentary*, vol. IV, p. 40.

99. See Table 8.1.

100. *"Jus dispositivum* and *jus cogens* in International Law", *American Journal of International Law*, 1966, Vol. 60, p. 59. See also *The Concept of Jus Cogens in International Law, Papers and Proceedings* (report of the Conference organized by the Carnegie Foundation at Lagonissi, Greece, April 1966, Geneva, 1967, pp. 13, 99, 106 and 107.

101. Resolution adopted at the 54th Conference, The Hague, 1970.

102. Rosalyn Higgins, "Derogations under Human Rights Treaties", *The British Yearbook of International Law 1976-1977*, Oxford, Clarendon Press, 1978, p. 282.

103. Address by Mr. Amadou-Mahtar M'Bow at the opening of the 12th Summit Conference of the Organization of African Unity, Kampala, 29 July 1975.

Part II
International Institutions
for the Protection and
Promotion of Human Rights

9 The Distinguishing Criteria of Institutions

Karel Vasak

The growing importance of human rights in contemporary society is shown not only by the increasing number of relevant texts of varying legal value, but also by the great diversity of institutions competent in the matter. It has become apparent that a halt should be called in the "output" of legal texts: if, nevertheless, the international community as a whole, through the intermediary of the United Nations or its specialized agencies, or a group of States forming together a regional organization feel a pressing need to draft new instruments, it is to be hoped that these instruments will not take the form of independent Conventions but will become genuine regulations governing the application and interpretation of the major general Conventions of human rights (Covenants, European and American Conventions). It can indeed be asserted that the "new" human rights can practically all be attached, by way of interpretation, to one of the rights already included in the general Conventions. Thus, the unity of the field of human rights would be better protected, and at the same time the so-to-speak constitutional character of the major general Conventions on human rights would be emphasized.

Does a halt also need to be called in the case of human rights institutions? Here, too, it is essential that "the variety of the machinery should be neither a symbol nor a cause of anarchy".[1] It is necessary, therefore, to take stock of the situation, and I wish to indicate a few signposts towards that end. The approach here will not be to describe the existing institutions, but to make a comparative analysis of them based on five criteria: the task of the institution; the functions carried out by the institution; the scope of the activity of the institution; the technique used by the institution; the legal nature of the institution.

1. THE TASK OF HUMAN RIGHTS INSTITUTIONS

Institutions responsible for implementing human rights are usually entrusted with one of two tasks, very seldom with both at the same time: the promotion of human rights or the protection of human rights. This distinction is so

well-known at the international level that the reasons behind it tend to become blurred; it must therefore be clarified before it can be used for a review
of existing institutions.

(a). Promotion and protection of human rights

In States where the legal system is based on Roman law, the notion of
"promotion" has only recently gained a foothold, to describe an aspect of
business life in the United States—sales promotion. Admittedly these States
were already familiar with "social promotion": the effort to disprove, through
legislative reforms, the Marxist analysis of a society composed of permanently antagonistic classes. The notion of promotion as applied to human
rights has kept a certain Anglo-Saxon, above all American, overtone. For a
long time it set a problem for the drafters of international texts on human
rights, who translated it into French as *progrès* or *développement*,[2] until it
was finally decided not to attempt a translation at all but to use the same
word which, after all, is perfectly good French.

The promotion of human rights[3] implies action resolutely directed toward
the future: the question of human rights is seen as containing a lacuna,
because they are not all, or are only incompletely, guaranteed under national
legislation or international law, or because they are not sufficiently understood by the persons entitled to them or by the States and their subsidiary
bodies which are bound to respect them. In these circumstances, a body for
the promotion of human rights will attempt to determine inadequacies and
even violations, not so much in order that they may be punished but rather
that similar situations may be prevented from recurring in the future.

The "protection" of human rights appears to have, in many respects, a
diametrically opposed aim. Intended to ensure the observance of human
rights as established under existing law, the institution for protection leads,
by the sanctions to which protection necessarily gives rise, towards a future
that perpetuates the past. It relies mainly on court process, whereas the
institution for promotion will make use of every available legislative technique, including studies, research, reports, and the drafting of texts.

It is not surprising that the socialist countries, which consider contemporary law and society to be doomed, have always shown, at the international
level, a clear preference for institutions designed to promote human rights.[4]
Similarly, in developing countries, to protect human rights in the social conditions now existing would mean accepting that man should live there as he
does now, whereas it is first necessary, if not to create him, at least to
transform him.

The contradiction described above between promotion and protection, however, is not so insoluble as it may appear from our analysis. First of all, it is
clear that promotion is the first, and the necessary, stage leading to protection: if this were not so, the only result of promotion would be the "blue-sky
laws", well known in Latin America, in which case it could hardly be called

promotion at all. Furthermore, there are many examples to show that the international promotion of human rights leads to national protection. Nor does the protection of human rights tend to preserve outdated social structures to the extent that one might think since, sooner or later, it shows up the gaps and injustices and thus compels the legislature to intervene.

Should the distinction between the promotion and the protection of human rights be abandoned? The answer seems to be no, at least at the international level; for it is a realistic distinction which requires progress to be achieved by stages, in line with the political, social and legal development of the States belonging to the international community; it makes it possible to do justice to certain bodies for the promotion of human rights, such as the United Nations Commission on Human Rights, which are often—too often—judged by standards applicable to bodies for protection; and in any event it inevitably raises the question whether there should not be two bodies corresponding to the two tasks—promotion and protection—or whether it would be preferable for the present, when international law is insufficiently developed, to have one single body instead of the confusion of having two.

(b). Institutions for the promotion and institutions for the protection of human rights

The criteria for promoting and protecting human rights, as applied to existing institutions, give rise to several observations.

i) National human rights institutions are usually institutions for protection: they are seldom institutions for the promotion of human rights. The question therefore arises whether each state should not set up a competent body for this purpose, responsible for preparing the reforms made necessary in the field of human rights by social developments. Several countries have already set up such a body for a major branch of law or for law in general (e.g. the Law Reform Commission in the United Kingdom). National Commissions on human rights, the establishment of which has often been called for, both at the United Nations and within the OAS, and which could operate along lines similar to the National Commissions for Unesco, could thus assume a role of which they are worthy.

ii) Bodies for promoting and protecting human rights are just as necessary at the international level; indeed, although the European Commission and Court of Human Rights are bodies of protection *par excellence*, their action had very rapidly to be supplemented by that of a body for promotion, the Committee of Experts on Human Rights which, beginning as an *ad hoc* body, has gradually become a permanent one.

iii) If an international body for the promotion of human rights is successful, it cannot help but assume the task of protection. This development has been particularly spectacular in the case of the Inter-American Commission on Human Rights which, though set up in 1960 merely to promote human rights, now performs almost exclusively the tasks of protection—to the point that there is nothing, apart from the legal basis of its powers, to distinguish it now from its European counterpart.[5] The same development, however, is taking place within the United Nations Commission on Human Rights, especially since its 23rd session in 1967. It is not by chance that this development coincided with the Commission's enlargement and the admission of representatives of several States which had only recently become independent.[6]

iv) At the outset, that is, immediately after the Second World War, the feature which distinguished a body for the promotion of human rights from a body for their protection was the action that the latter took on individual petitions; this presupposed that the procedure for such petitions was the only one whereby human rights could be protected. The equation of a body for the protection of human rights with a body competent to examine, as a court, individual petitions was for a long time a vicious circle, in which those concerned had almost voluntarily imprisoned themselves, and which they succeeded in breaking out of only in the late 1960s. It is now recognized that, in order to protect human rights, it is not always necessary to put a State on trial and then condemn it: the right of individual petition may become a right to ordinary petition, or a mere source of information, without thereby lessening the effectiveness of the protection. The experience of various United Nations bodies on petitions and that of the Inter-American Commission on Human Rights tend to bear this out.[7]

2. THE FUNCTIONS CARRIED OUT BY HUMAN RIGHTS INSTITUTIONS

Human rights institutions may perform one or more of the following five functions which constitute as many component parts of a complete system for the control of the observance of human rights: information, investigation, conciliation, decision, and sanction. Indeed, human rights will be effectively protected only when all these five functions are fully exercised at the international level. An analysis of existing institutions for the protection of human rights, based on these functional standards, shows up many gaps and also a deplorable duplication of work.

(a). Information

There are many international organisations which compile information on the position of human rights in various countries. The United Nations, for example, publishes a Human Rights Yearbook based on such information.

Mention should also be made here of the *periodic reports* procedure, intended to represent a common law generally applicable in the international supervision of the execution of undertakings given by States in the field of human rights. Moreover, this procedure, by reason of the consequences which it might have, occupies a place halfway between the functions of information and investigation. While the International Labour Organisation was the forerunner in the procedure, it was not until the late 1960s, that the UN succeeded in perfecting the system created by Resolution 624 B (XXII) of the Economic and Social Council, whereas Unesco bases its approach on a specific provision of its constitution. Regional organizations such as the Council of Europe (Article 57 of the European Convention on Human Rights) and the Organization of American States (Resolution XXII of the Second Extraordinary Inter-American Conference at Rio de Janeiro) have instituted similar machinery. The danger of duplication is, however, particularly marked here.

(b). Investigation

There are fewer human rights institutions responsible for making investigations. These may be *ad hoc* bodies set up in specific circumstances (e.g. the fact-finding mission of the United Nations General Assembly in Vietnam to examine the situation of the Buddhists, the *ad hoc* group of the United Nations Commision on Human Rights responsible for examining the situation of prisoners and detainees in South Africa) or permanent bodies set up under a convention or analogous instrument. The second type, which in the past was exceptional, will now be able to become current practice within the United Nations (the Committee on the Elimination of Racial Discrimination set up under the Convention of the same name and the Human Rights Committee set up under the Covenant on Civil and Political Rights). There are many such bodies in the International Labour Organisation (the Commission of Inquiry set up under Article 28 of the ILO Constitution, the Committee on Freedom of Association of the Governing Body, the Fact-Finding and Conciliation Commission on Freedom of Association) and in two regional organizations (the Council of Europe and the Organization of American States, with their Commissions of Human Rights).

The crucial point here of course is who can initiate the procedure. It is never the investigating body itself (although in some cases it would be useful if it were, if only to make the principle of the Rule of Law prevail in the field of human rights) and seldom an individual, but usually Government. The procedures employed by the various bodies of inquiry vary widely. Even though the rulings of international human rights bodies are reached on the basis of deep-seated conviction, these rulings nevertheless come at the end of procedures which often leave much to be desired for their outcome to be generally convincing. While it is not possible to unify the rules (generally deduced from practice) relating to the admission of evidence, those rules could at least be examined with regard, in particular, to the following aspects: the privileges and immunities enjoyed by witnesses (cf. the incidents following the ILO investigation in Chile);[8] the hearing of all parties concerned in the investigation; the intervention of third parties in the procedure, etc.

(c). Conciliation

Wary of the system of decisions as encroaching upon their sovereignty, States are inclined to take refuge in the field of conciliation: all the institutions responsible for making investigations are simultaneously offered the possibility of concluding their work by an attempt at conciliation. The intention is praiseworthy insofar as it thus becomes possible to avoid judgments which damage the prestige of a State in a field where the political element has not lost all its prerogatives. The fact remains, however, that conciliation applied to human rights is somewhat self-contradictory in that it suggests that, despite their sacred and inviolable nature, human rights can be "negotiated". It would therefore be worthwhile to stress exactly what limits of conciliation are consistent with respect for human rights, limits which the European Commission of Human Rights, in particular, has been led to lay down each time that it has approved the friendly settlement of a case brought before it.[9]

(d). Decision

There are very few human rights institutions which at present have the power to make decisions and, above all, judicial decisions. Only the European Court of Human Rights and the Inter-American Court of Human Rights can be mentioned in this respect, and even their jurisdiction is optional in the sense that they require express acceptance by the States. Whenever the Committee of Ministers of the Council of Europe rather than the Court has been required to make a decision on the merits of a case in accordance with Article 32 of the Rome Convention, it has not sought to divest itself of its political character but has done just the opposite. Although formally a decision, the act by which it concludes the procedure (by a "resolution" and not a "decision") more often than not resembles a political settlement, far removed from the judgment that the Court might have given in the same case.[10]

It would be a mistake, however, to take a narrow legalistic view of this and to under-estimate the value of institutions which do not make decisions but limit themselves to mere "recommendations". Depending on the action taken to put it into effect, a recommendation may prove to be as important as a decision, while being more acceptable to the State to which it is addressed.

(e). Sanctions

There are no human rights institutions empowered to impose sanctions. Even the European Court of Human Rights can only award, under Article 50 of the Convention, just satisfaction, i.e. generally compensation, to the victim of a violation, and only subject to certain well-defined conditions. It is, therefore, only within the *political* framework that violations of human rights can be the subject of sanctions.[11] There is no better proof that this situation is unsatisfactory than the fruitless efforts to oblige South Africa to put an end to policies that obviously run counter to every notion of human rights. In the face of this, the jurist can only redouble his efforts to wield the only weapon at his disposal: *public opinion*. For, in the last analysis, it is public opinion that is able to impose the most serious sanctions on the recalcitrant State by banishing it from the world community.

3. THE SCOPE OF ACTIVITY OF HUMAN RIGHTS INSTITUTIONS

Action to promote and protect human rights is carried out on three levels—national, regional and universal—by institutions whose competence is thus geographically delimited.

i) The heaviest burden falls, and should fall, on the *national institutions*, which are of course the most numerous. Although obviously not all can be mentioned here, a few, because of their value as examples, are especially noteworthy, as has been recognized by the United Nations: the French *Conseil d'Etat*, the Soviet *Procuratura*, the Scandinavian *Ombudsman*, and the Japanese Bureau of Civil Liberties. Similarly, certain procedures have become widespread because of their reputation as effective safeguards: the English *habeas corpus*, the Mexican *amparo*, and the Brazilian *mandato de seguranza*.

ii) Formerly regarded as an interference in the relations between the United Nations and its Member States, the *regional institutions* now enjoy the status which their character deserves, though it is unlikely that they will be integrated into a universal system in the near future. Mention may be made here of the bodies of the European Convention on Human Rights, those of the European Social Charter, and the Inter-American Commission on Human Rights. In this context, it would be advisable to re-examine favourably the frequently repeated proposals for the establishment of regional commissions on human rights where they do not yet exist.

iii) There are already a number of *universal institutions* within the United Nations (Commission on Human Rights, with its Sub-Commission on Prevention of Discrimination and Protection of Minorities, Commission on the Status of Women, the Committee on the Elimination of Racial Discrimination set up under the terms of the 1965 Convention, Human Rights Committee etc.), within the International Labour Organisation (bodies responsible for keeping under review the application of International Labour Conventions and Recommendations, and those for examining complaints and claims referring to ratified conventions or to freedom of association), and within Unesco (Conciliation and Good Offices Commission set up under the Convention against Discrimination in Education and the Committee on Conventions and Recommendations).

Because of this proliferation of institutions, it is all the more essential to set up a body capable of dealing with human rights on a world-wide scale, without reference to the level—national, regional or universal—at which these rights operate. One may sense that this is the constructive role to be played by a United Nations High Commissioner for Human Rights, the creation of which office has been proposed following the precedent relating to the protection of refugees. The idea of a United Nations High Commissioner for Human Rights[12] has been the subject of frequently impassioned discussions. Insofar as the office of the United Nations High Commissioner was to be a body for the protection of human rights and consequently a means of combating violations of human rights, the project seems to have fallen through, at least for the time being. Moreover, it must be recognized that the application of the Convention on Elimination of Racial Discrimination, the development of procedures in accordance with ECOSOC Resolutions 1235 and 1503 and the entry into force of the Covenants on Human Rights, as imperfect as all these factors may be in certain regards, remove a great deal of substance from the project to appoint a High Commissioner for Human Rights.

At the same time, however, the development of the world-wide character of human rights (especially as regards human rights norms), accompanied by tendencies towards dispersion (especially as regards the implementation of those norms), provides a new, albeit different, justification for the project to appoint a High Commissioner. What is now needed is probably not so much a man as an institution (a Commissioner's Office rather than a Commissioner), the dual function of which should be: a) to co-ordinate all human rights machinery, bodies and procedures operating both at the world level (United Nations, on the one hand, specialized agencies on the other) and at the regional level, to increase this effectiveness and avoid the duplication of work and procedures; b) to give thought to the reforms to be proposed, at national and world levels, and thereby to give a real object and hence new impetus to the human rights consultative services existing at the United Nations and elsewhere.

4. THE TECHNIQUES USED BY INSTITUTIONS FOR THE PROTECTION OF HUMAN RIGHTS

When their task is to protect human rights, international human rights institutions use various techniques, some of which emphasize the specificity of international human rights law. These are: techniques for the political supervision of the observance of human rights; techniques of supervision by means of reports; and, lastly, techniques of supervision by means of complaints, petitions or communications, brought by States or individuals.

(a). Political supervision

What is involved here is machinery which, not having been specifically set up for the purpose of supervising the observance of human rights by Member States of the international community, may nevertheless be used to that end, especially when it forms part of the machinery of organizations whose principle objectives include the protection of human rights. Most of the competent bodies then base their "judgments" on the constitution of the organization or sometimes even on texts whose binding character is not universally recognized, such as the Universal Declaration or the American Declaration of Human Rights.

At the United Nations the General Assembly may take action in the form of recommendations to "facilitate the enjoyment of human rights and fundamental freedoms", and it has not failed to do so on several occasions, particularly in relation to the human rights situation in southern Africa. In matters of colonialism, the General Assembly has used human rights as a means of fighting for the right to self-determination, recognized as the first and most indispensable of human rights. Thus the Committee of Twenty-Five, set up on 27 November 1961, has the task of examining the application of the Declaration on the Granting of Independence to Colonial Countries and Peoples, adopted on 14 December 1960.

Generally speaking, the regional organizations provide for the observance of human rights in their constitutions, as a result of which any State that violates those rights can be expelled. This possibility is expressly provided for by Article 8, combined with Article 3, of the Statute of the Council of Europe. When the Greek Government that came into power after the 1967 *coup d'état* withdrew, legally speaking, from the Council of Europe in December 1969, what it was in fact doing was forestalling the inevitable outcome of the procedure aimed at expelling it from the Organization.

Similarly, the Organization of American States includes human rights among its principles (Article 5 (j)) and it is in the Bogotá Charter, which forms the constitution of the OAS, that the relations between democracy and human rights are emphasized with particular clarity (Preamble, Article 5 d). However, no sanction is expressly provided for in the event of human rights being violated, since provision for the expulsion of a State in such circumstances was not included in the Bogotá Charter. Difficulties consequently arose in 1962 in connection with Cuba which was not legally expelled from the OAS but which was considered to have "voluntarily set itself outside the inter-American system" (Resolution VI of the 8th meeting of consultation of Ministers of Foreign Affairs at Punta-del-Este, January 1962). The Inter-American Commission on Human Rights nevertheless continued to investigate the position of human rights in Cuba, considering that the expulsion measure had been directed against "the present government of Cuba, but not the Cuban State".[13]

The Organization of African Unity also reaffirmed in its constitutional Charter of Addis Ababa the acceptance by its Member States of the Universal Declaration of Human Rights (Preamble), for which there was to be "due" regard in "intentional co-operation" (Article II). Although human rights are included among the objectives of the Organization (Article II), they are not listed among its principles (Article III). Moreover, it is to be noted that, insofar as human rights come under the domestic jurisdiction of states, it could even be maintained that the principle of non-interference in the domestic affairs of States contained in Article III of the Addis Ababa Charter very seriously limits the implementation of the "human rights" objective mentioned in Article II. The Addis Ababa Charter is thus not a model of clarity nor does it reveal any marked determination with regard at least to the use of the political machinery of the OAU for the purpose of ensuring respect for human rights by Member States. However, in recent years the subsidiary bodies of the OAU have taken measures in certain cases involving violations of human rights. Moreover, in 1979 the process of drafting an "African Charter of Human and Peoples' Rights" was begun within the OAU framework.

In the case of the League of Arab States, the relevant constitutional texts contain no mention of human rights. However, the Council of the League of Arab States set up, on 3 September 1968, by its Resolution 24/43, a Permanent Arab Commission on Human Rights which, as a mere body for the promotion of human rights, has, *inter alia*, drawn up a Declaration of the Rights of Arab Citizens.

(b). Supervision by means of reports

It could be said that what is involved here is a common law technique employed by international human rights institutions to supervise the observance of human rights by Member States of international organizations or parties to the conventions on human rights. There are a large number of texts providing for a procedure consisting in the submission of reports, which are either optional (system of periodic reports to the United Nations, for instance) or compulsory (when prescribed by conventions on human rights). The outstanding example here is provided by the International Labour Organisation which has so developed this technique that it is now of unquestionable effectiveness.[14]

The most important problem arising here is that of the action taken on the reports submitted by States. In some cases, as for instance in that of the European Convention on Human Rights (Article 57), the basic text may contain no mention of the action to be taken on reports. But, as a general rule, the reports are examined by specialized bodies composed of independent experts (for instance, by the ILO Committee of Experts on the Application of Conventions and Recommendations). The examination procedure, often highly complex and involving several bodies, results in the formulation of observations or recommendations which are addressed to all Member States or to a particular State designated by name.

Comparison of the different methods involving the technique of supervision by means of reports reveals that this technique is particularly effective when:

-the reports are submitted at relatively frequent intervals;
-they are submitted in accordance with a plan which takes the form of a detailed questionnaire;
-such reports are examined by an independent and impartial body, the members of which are appointed for a sufficiently long period;
-that body is not obliged to confine itself solely to reports and may seek to clarify the information they contain by reference to appropriate publications;
-such reports are transmitted, for comments, to private, national or international organizations;

-they may lead to the adoption of recommendations the effectiveness of which will depend on the extent to which they are able to be of a specific rather than a general character;

-the entire procedure, or at least the final part of the procedure (final report accompanied by recommendations), is made public.

(c). Supervision by means of petitions or complaints[15]

This technique, far more developed than the previous one, takes various forms according to whether the petition is able to be brought solely by States or also by private individuals, whether or not they are victims of an alleged violation of human rights.

The body with responsibility for the procedure instituted by the lodging of the complaint may be of an administrative character (as was the case for the petitions of members of minorities, considered first of all by the minorities section of the Secretariat of the League of Nations), political (as is the case for all the United Nations bodies which have to deal with petitions relating to trust or non-autonomous territories), quasi-judicial (for instance, the Inter-American Commission on Human Rights, perhaps so under its "regular" procedure, but certainly so during the "special" procedure for examining the individual complaints regarding the violation of human rights) or judicial (for instance, the European Commission of Human Rights when considering the admissibility of petitions). Several bodies of different kinds may be involved or even a single body, in which case it will change in nature as the procedure develops (the European Commission of Human Rights). The procedure may *result* in the drawing up of a report (as by the Human Rights Committee of the Covenant on Civil and Political Rights in the case of a communication by one State against another State, under Article 41), the adoption of a recommendation (as by the Committee of Ministers of the Council of Europe in accordance with the provisions of the European Social Charter) or the delivering of a decision (as by the Committee of Ministers under Article 32 of the European Convention on Human Rights) or a judgment (by the European Court of Human Rights).

There is scarcely any doubt that this technique, particularly insofar as it involves the right of individual appeal, constitutes the corner-stone of the entire machinery for the implementation of human rights. It has been effectively used at the United Nations by the competent institutions for colonial and non-autonomous territories to attain political objectives (and primarily respect for the right to self-determination). Within the Organization of American States, while the procedure is instituted by individuals, it has a collective bearing: the complaint addressed to the Inter-American Commission on Human Rights changes nature in the course of the procedure and becomes a source of information as to the state of human rights in the country concerned. At the United Nations the procedure for the examination of individual communications in pursuance of Resolution 1503 of the Economic and Social Council is developing largely along the same lines.

It is, however, primarily in the context of the Council of Europe that this technique constitutes an essential feature of a true European human rights law; although limited to one region, this technique, as provided for by the European Convention on Human Rights, is an asset to the entire international community.

5. THE LEGAL NATURE OF THE INSTITUTION

Human rights institutions may be either governmental, and consequently governed by international law, or non-governmental, in which case they are legal entities, subject to the laws of a Member State of the international community.

Governmental human rights institutions are the fundamental subject of this treatise. Established either by an existing international organization, or under a specific human rights treaty, such governmental institutions differ from each other in respect, particularly, of the independent or non-independent character of their members. Some of them are, by virtue of their statutes, composed of governments, in which case the representatives of those governments are provided with instructions which it is impossible to divest of all political considerations (United Nations Commission on Human Rights, etc.). Others are composed of members appointed in an individual capacity, as experts (e.g. the United Nations Sub-Commission on Prevention of Discrimination and Protection of Minorities, the Committee on the Elimination of Racial Discrimination) or as persons qualified to exercise judicial or quasi-judicial functions (European Commission and Court of Human Rights, ILO Committee of Experts on the Application of Conventions and Recommendations, and the ILO Commission of Inquiry set up to deal with complaints submitted under the Constitution of the ILO, etc.). Intermediate situations may even arise, as in the case of the *ad hoc* committees of the United Nations Commission on Human Rights whose members are chosen, in an individual capacity, among the representatives of Governments on the Commission.

Non-governmental institutions are private, "voluntary" organizations which, by definition, purport to be independent of governments. Composed of individuals or associations of individuals, they have played and continue to play a considerable role in the field of human rights. It was essentially their action which resulted in the establishment, under the terms of the Charter of the United Nations, of a specific human rights body, the Commission on Human Rights; and it is to their permanent credit that the Universal Declaration of Human Rights originated with them. Acting above all as bodies for the promotion of human rights, they also contribute to their protection by identifying, through using their own methods (on-the-spot investigations, the sending of observers selected from the judiciary to political trials, etc.), violations of human rights, by notifying international bodies for the protection of human rights of such violations (availing themselves, for instance, of the right of petition recognized in Article 25 of the European Convention on Human Rights or similar provisions in other human rights treaties) or by assistance, either materially or in the form of legal assistance, to individuals who are victims of violations of human rights.

The international organizations, and particularly those with specific responsibilities in the matter of human rights, have defined, in more or less precise terms, their relations with non-governmental institutions. Thus, under Article 71 of the San Francisco Charter, legal provision for "consultation" with non-governmental organizations (NGOs) has been established by the United Nations. Other international organizations have to a large extent taken their cue from this.

There are many NGOs concerned with human rights: a systematic study of such organizations from the political, sociological and legal points of view still needs to be carried out.[16] Among the most active, the following deserve to be mentioned: the International Association of Democratic Lawyers, the International Commission of Jurists, Amnesty International, the International League of Human Rights and the International Federation of Human Rights, etc. One NGO deserves to be mentioned separately, the International Committee of the Red Cross.[17] This is a Swiss private law organization, composed exclusively of Swiss citizens, but which has been invested, by custom and by express provisions of the 1949 Geneva Conventions and the 1977 Protocols thereto, with important humanitarian functions.

NOTES

1. See René Cassin, Preface to *La Commission interaméricaine des droits de l'homme*, Karel Vasak, Libraire générale de droit et de jurisprudence, 1968.

2. See for instance Art. 1, para. 3, of the Charter of the United Nations: "The purposes of the United Nations are:...3. To achieve international co-operation...in *promoting* and *encouraging* respect for human rights and for fundamental freedoms for all...". (Emphasis added.) The efforts made, when the Charter was being prepared, to pass from the stage of the promotion to that of the protection of human rights were unsuccessful.

3. The two tasks of "promoting" and "protecting" human rights were the focus of discussions in 1960 when the status of the Inter-American Commission on Human Rights, set up in August 1959, was to be determined. It seems to have been at that time that, within the Council of the OAS, the grounds for, and the consequences of, the distinction were most clearly set forth.

4. Cf. F. Przetacznik: "L'attitude des Etats socialistes à l'égard de la protection internationale des droits de l'homme", *RDH/HRJ*, Vol. VII, No. 1 (1974), p. 175.

5. See Karel Vasak, *La Commission interaméricaine des droits de l'homme*, op. cit., in particular p. 139 *et seq.*

6. See J.B. Marie, *La Commission des droits de l'homme des Nations Unies*, Paris, Pédone, 1975, p. 233 *et seq.*

7. It is highly profitable to consult in this connection Glenda da Fonseca, *How to File*

Complaints of Human Rights Violations—A Practical Guide to Intergovernmental Procedures, Geneva, The World Council of Churches, 152 pages.

8. See the report of the Fact-Finding and Conciliation Commission on Freedom of Association: *The Trade Union Situation in Chile*, Geneva, ILO, 1975.

9. It appears that, in addition to the necessary respect for human rights as provided for by the European Convention, the Commission, when it has to close the procedure by reporting a friendly settlement, seeks above all to ascertain that the alleged victim, i.e. generally the petitioner himself, has been completely free to accept or refuse the settlement.

10. In the American Convention on Human Rights the Commission expresses its opinion if the case has not been submitted to the Court. But the powers thus attributed to the Commission are very different from the powers of a genuine court, as emerges from Article 51 of the Convention:

" 1. If, within a period of three months from the date of the transmittal of the report of the Commission to the States concerned, the matter has not been either settled or submitted by the Commission or by the State concerned to the Court and its jurisdiction accepted, the Commission may, by the vote of an absolute majority of its members, set forth its opinion and conclusions concerning the question submitted for its consideration.

2. Where appropriate, the Commission shall make pertinent recommendations and shall prescribe a period within which the State is to take measures that are incumbent upon it to remedy the situation examined.

3. When the prescribed period has expired, the Commission shall decide by the vote of an absolute majority of its members whether the State has taken adequate measures and whether to publish its report."

The pressure that the Commission is thus brought gradually to exercise upon the State concerned by the series of decisions that it makes, and which scarcely resemble judicial decisions, seems typical of a political body. If this Article 51 is compared with Article 52 of the European Convention, the similarity of the solutions adopted will be seen, despite the difference in respect of the bodies required to act.

11. It was the suspension of the Treaty of Association between Greece and the European Commission (and hence the suppression of a number of economic advantages), decided by the Council of Ministers of the European Communities, which constituted the true sanction to emerge from the decision of the Committee of Ministers of the Council of Europe noting that the Greece of the Colonels had violated numerous provisions of the European Convention on Human Rights, although these two decisions: a) were each taken in a different legal framework; b) were not based on the same human rights provisions; c) apparently did not follow on from each other in time.

12. See for instance, G. Mansuy, "Un médiateur des Nations Unies pour les droits de l'homme", *RDH/HRJ*, Vol. VI, No. 2, 1973, p. 235.

13. The entire legal interpretation may seem questionable, from the "expulsion" (which is claimed not to be such, whereas the Inter-American Commission holds the opposite view), up to the decision of the Commission to continue to exercise its powers with regard to Cuba (for the entire Cuban question, see K. Vasak, *La Commission interaméricaine des droits de l'homme, op. cit.*, p. 130 *et seq.*).

14. In this connection, see especially the work of N. Valticos (e.g. *Droit international du travail*, Paris, Dalloz, 1970 and Supplement, 1973) and that of E.A. Landy, *The Effectiveness of International Supervision—Thirty Years of ILO Experience*, Dobbs Ferry, N.Y., Oceana, 1966.

15. The terminology is uncertain since the same individual act can be described as a "petition", "application", "denunciation" or "communication" (see below, where the various categories of individual petitions are analyzed).

16. See L.S. Wiseberg and H.M. Scoble, "Human Rights NGOs: Notes towards Comparative Analysis", in *RDH/HRJ*, Vol. IX, No. 4, 1976, and other references in the Bibliography of this book.

17. See H. Knitel, *Les délégations du Comité international de la Croix-Rouge*, Geneva, 1967, 134 pages.

Sub-Part I:
Universal Institutions

10 The Principal Institutions and Other Bodies Founded Under the Charter

Egon Schwelb and Philip Alston

Among the purposes of the United Nations according to its Charter is the achievement of international co-operation "in promoting and encouraging respect for human rights and for fundamental freedoms for all without distinction as to race, sex, language or religion" (Article 1(3)). All of the principal and many of the subsidiary organs of the United Nations have the task of acting on human rights matters (Article (1) and (2)). The first part of the present chapter focuses on the role played by each of these organs and the second part on the procedures and practices which they have adopted in human rights matters. The following chapter, 11, is directly complementary and deals with the institutions and procedures which have been established under specific United Nations human rights conventions, such as the International Covenants on Human Rights.

The present survey of thirty-five years of United Nations action, between 1945 and 1980, is inevitably incomplete and wherever possible relevant documentary references or key resolutions have been noted either in the text or in the footnotes to enable the reader to pursue the matter further. Before commencing our survey of the major United Nations human rights organs it is appropriate to note the allocation of functions provided for by the Charter.

The main responsibility for the discharge of the functions of the Organization in the promotion of respect for and observance of human rights is vested in the *General Assembly* and, under its authority, in the Economic and Social Council (Article 60). The *Security Council* was repeatedly called upon to investigate disputes or situations arising out of claimed human rights violations which might lead to international friction (Article 34). To encourage respect for human rights and fundamental freedoms is one of the basic objectives of the trusteeship system. It follows that action on human rights comes also within the functions and powers of the *Trusteeship Council* (Articles 76 (c) and 87). The *International Court of Justice* has had occasion to make important pronouncements on questions of human rights, both when acting in contentious cases and when rendering advisory opinions. The Secretary-General acts in that capacity in all meetings of the principal organs (with the exception of the Court) and, as a consequence, the *Secretariat* has had to perform important functions in the human rights field (Articles 97 to 99 of the Charter).

1. THE PRINCIPAL ORGANS OF THE UNITED NATIONS AND THE SUBSIDIARY ORGANS ACTIVE IN HUMAN RIGHTS MATTERS ESTABLISHED UNDER THE CHARTER

(a). General Assembly

The General Assembly consists of all the Member States of the UN (Art. 9), each of which has one vote (Art. 9). In December 1979, UN membership was 151 States. The General Assembly meets in regular annual sessions and in special sessions as required (Art. 20). By December 1980, eleven "special" sessions and seven "emergency special" sessions had been held. The Assembly adopts its own rules of procedure (Art. 21) which, since their enactment in 1947 (G.A. res. 173(II)), have frequently been amended.[1]

(i) THE MAIN COMMITTEES OF THE GENERAL ASSEMBLY

Questions before the General Assembly are either considered directly by the Assembly in plenary meetings or are considered by the plenary on the basis of a report from one of the Assembly's committees. All Member States are represented on the seven "Main Committees." These deal with: disarmament and related matters (First Committee); economic and financial matters (Second Committee); social, humanitarian and cultural matters (Third Committee); decolonization matters (Fourth Committee); administrative and budgetary matters (Fifth Committee); and legal matters (Sixth Committee). There is also a Special Political Committee. Questions concerning human rights are usually referred to the Third Committee. However, other Main Committees, notably the Special Political Committee and the First, Fourth and Sixth Committees also deal with subjects where human right issues play an important role.

(ii) VOTING IN THE GENERAL ASSEMBLY

The Charter (Art. 18) provides that decisions of the Assembly on "important questions" shall be made by a two-thirds majority of the members present and voting and that decisions on other questions shall be made by a (simple) majority of those present and voting. The list of "important questions" contained in the Charter includes those concerning the maintenance of international peace and security, admission of new Members, expulsion of Members etc., but it does not include human rights questions as such. However, by a simple majority, the Assembly may determine additional categories of questions to be decided by a two-thirds majority (Art. 18(3)). No general decision to add the category of human rights questions to the list of "important questions" has ever been made. But since Article 18(2) does not appear to contain an exhaustive list of such questions, there are cases on record in which the General Assembly decided to require a two-thirds majority for the adoption of certain decisions on human rights matters. Thus, when the draft Convention on the Political Rights of Women, recommended for adoption by the Third Committee, was being considered in a plenary meeting in 1952, a representative claimed that the territorial application clause (the "colonial clause") of the draft required a two-thirds majority for adoption. The President ruled that the draft resolution and the draft convention attached to it constituted a question of importance and therefore required a two-thirds majority. There was no objection to this ruling and, in the event, the clause, which received a simple majority only, was held not to have been adopted. The draft convention was adopted without the "colonial clause."[2] By contrast, in January 1957, the Assembly approved by simple majority the inclusion of such a clause in another human rights convention, the draft Convention on the Nationality of Married Women. The question whether the clause, or the draft convention as a whole, might require a two-thirds majority for adoption, was not raised at all.[3]

In United Nations jurisprudence the right of peoples and nations to permanent sovereignty over their natural wealth and resources is a question which comes within the overall field of human rights. This follows from a series of resolutions and from Article 1 of both International Covenants on Human Rights. When the General Assembly considered and eventually adopted the Declaration on Permanent Sovereignty over Natural Resources in 1962, it decided that the draft declaration was an important question within the meaning of Article 18(2) of the Charter.[4]

Questions relating to the operation of the trusteeship system are expressly listed in Article 18(2) among the "important questions." Questions relating to non-self-governing territories do not appear in that list. It has therefore been argued that matters of anti-colonialism and self-determination, while undoubtedly important, are not "important questions" in the technical sense of the purposes of Article 18(2). In several instances the General Assembly acted on this interpretation, while in others it decided that the concrete question which it had before it of the non-self-governing territory was an "important question." Usually the decision for the one or the other interpretation has been made by a very narrow majority.[5]

It should be added that the rules about voting, described above, apply only to proceedings of plenary meetings of the General Assembly. Decisions of committees, including the Main Committees, are made by a (simple) majority of the members present and voting. In both the plenary and the Main Committees the rule applies that when a proposal has been adopted or rejected, it may not be reconsidered at the same session unless the Assembly (or the Committee respectively) so decides by a two-thirds majority.

The experience of past sessions of the General Assembly shows that, in matters of human rights, decisions have usually been taken by votes in which

a two-thirds majority was actually obtained, and in most cases considerably
exceeded, without the question of the "importance" of the item and the
majority required being raised. Many decisions in matters of human rights
have been taken without dissenting votes.

(iii) THE FUNCTIONS AND POWERS OF THE GENERAL ASSEMBLY IN HUMAN
RIGHTS MATTERS

Under Article 13(1)(b) of the Charter, the General Assembly has two principal obligations in matters of human rights: to *initiate studies*; and to *make
recommendations* for the purpose of "assisting in the realization of human
rights and fundamental freedoms for all without distinction as to race, sex,
language or religion." In the initiation of studies the Assembly has requested
studies from: the Economic and Social Council and its subsidiary organs; the
Secretary-General; specialized agencies; other bodies, including its own subsidiary organs; several bodies jointly; and Member States. The Assembly
also receives and considers reports from the Security Council and from other
organs of the UN. In particular, the annual report of the Economic and Social
Council is the occasion for the Assembly's initiation of additional investigations and studies, and for taking action of various kinds.

The *recommendations* which the General Assembly makes on matters of
human rights are technically not legally binding on States. However, in
evaluating the authority of recommendations of the Assembly one has to bear
in mind that, in Articles 55 and 56 of the Charter, all Members have pledged
themselves to take joint and separate action in co-operation with the Organization, to promote universal respect for, and observance of, human rights and
fundamental freedoms.

Anticipating what will be said below about the functions and powers of the
Economic and Social Council, it should be mentioned here that, under Article 62(3) of the Charter, the Council may prepare draft conventions for
submission to the General Assembly with respect to matters falling within
its competence. Over the years, the Assembly has, both on its own initiative
and on the recommendation of the Council and other organs, adopted and
opened for signature and ratification an impressive number of international
treaties (conventions) dealing with human rights questions. These include
both instruments of a comprehensive character, such as the International
Convenants on Human Rights, and instruments limited to specific problems, such as genocide, various questions of the status of women, the elimination of racial discrimination, and others. An original contribution of the
UN General Assembly has been the proclamation of solemn, standard-setting
Declarations in matters of human rights, adopted by Assembly resolution
and not given the form of an international treaty. These include the Universal Declaration of Human Rights of 1948 and a variety of others which are
considered below.

(b). Subsidiary Organs of the General Assembly

(i) GENERAL SURVEY

The General Assembly may establish such subsidiary organs as it deems necessary for the performance of its functions (Art. 22). Many of the innumerable subsidiary organs which the Assembly has created under this provision have been, or are, either largely or exclusively concerned with human rights issues. However, they vary considerably in type and importance. Some are of an *ad hoc* character, others are more permanent.

By way of example, mention may briefly be made of some of these organs. Among the institutions which have been established are the International Children's Emergency Fund (UNICEF) created in 1947, the Relief and Works Agency for Palestine Refugees in the Near East (UNRWA) created in 1949, and the Office of the High Commissioner for Refugees (UNHCR) which was established in 1951. The Assembly has also appointed commissions to deal with a wide range of issues. They include for example: an *Ad Hoc* Commission to deal with the question of prisoners of war from the Second World War (1950); a Commission to investigate whether conditions in the Federal Republic of Germany, in Berlin and in what was then called the Soviet Zone of Germany were such that genuinely free and secret elections could be held (1950); a Good Offices Commission to deal with the question of the treatment of people of Indian origin in South Africa (1952); a Commission to study the racial question in South Africa (1952); and a commission of inquiry to investigate reported atrocities in Mozambique (1973).

In the following pages several of the more important subsidiary organs established by the General Assembly in the field of human rights will be considered in depth.

(ii) THE SPECIAL COMMITTEE AGAINST APARTHEID

The procedures adopted and the measures applied by the UN in the struggle against *apartheid* are examined in a subsequent part of this Chapter[6]. In the present context it is sufficient to note the background which led the General Assembly to establish the Special Committee Against *Apartheid*.

The problem of human rights and discrimination in South Africa has occupied the UN since the very first session of the General Assembly, in 1946 (G.A. res. 44(I)). The Organization's concern was initially limited to the question of the treatment of Indians (or people of Indian and Pakistani origin) in South Africa, but in 1952 was extended to cover the whole question of race conflict resulting from the policies of *apartheid* (G.A. res. 616A and B(VII)). In that year the General Assembly established a Commission "to study the racial situation in the Union of South Africa in the light of the Purposes and Principles of the Charter, with due regard to the provision of Article 2, paragraph 7 [the 'domestic jurisdiction clause'] as well as the" human rights provisions of the Charter (G.A. res. 616A(VII)). For each of the next three years the Commission reported to the Assembly.[7] The Assembly found that the racial policies of the Government of South Africa and their consequences were contrary to the Charter, a finding that was to be repeated on many later occasions with increasing emphasis.

In 1962, the General Assembly established a permanent organ, the Special Committee on the policies of *apartheid* of the Government of South Africa with the mandate to keep the racial policies of that Government under review and to report to the Assembly or to the Security Council or to both from time to time (G.A. res. 1761(XVII) of 1962). In 1970, the Committee was renamed the Special Committee on Apartheid and in 1974 it became the Special Committee Against Apartheid (G.A. res. 3324(XXIX)). In 1965 the General Assembly decided to enlarge the eleven-member Special Committee to include six States from amongst those of major importance in world trade and having primary responsibility under the Charter for the maintenance of international security, i.e. permanent members of the Security Council. But of those eligible, only the USSR indicated its willingness to serve on the Committee. In 1966, the Assembly deplored the refusal of South Africa's main trading partners, including three permanent members of the Security Council, to join the Committee (G.A. res. 2202A (XXI)). Of the 18 members of the Committee in 1980 none was a permanent member of the Security Council.

The mandate of the Special Committee, its work and the response of the General Assembly to its reports and recommendations are described later in this Chapter.

(iii) THE SPECIAL COMMITTEE ON THE SITUATION WITH REGARD TO THE
     IMPLEMENTATION OF THE DECLARATION ON THE GRANTING OF
     INDEPENDENCE TO COLONIAL COUNTRIES AND PEOPLES

On 14 December 1960 the General Assembly adopted a historic resolution (1514(XV)) by which it solemnly proclaimed "the necessity of bringing to a speedy and unconditional end colonialism in all its forms and manifestations". In the preamble to the Declaration on the Granting of Independence to Colonial Peoples and Countries the Assembly emphasized the importance of human rights and expressed the belief that "the process of liberation is irresistible and irreversible and that, in order to avoid serious crises, an end must be put to colonialism and all practices of segregation and discrimination associated therewith". The Declaration declared that "all peoples have the right to self-determination; by virtue of that right they freely determine their political status and freely pursue their economic, social and cultural development". It further rebutted traditional colonialist arguments by stating that inadequacy of political, economic, social or educational preparedness should never serve as a pretext for delaying independence.

In 1961, the Assembly established international machinery to implement the Declaration in the form of a Special Committee on the Situation with regard to the Implementation of the Declaration of Granting the Independence to Colonial Countries and Peoples (G.A. res. 1654 (XVI). The Special Committee's membership has been enlarged from 17 in 1961 to 24 in 1962 and to 25 in 1980 (G.A. decision 34/310).

The mandate of the Special Committee has been revised from time to time by the Assembly. Thus in 1979 the Special Committee was requested: to formulate specific proposals for the elimination of the remaining manifestations of colonialism; to make concrete suggestions which could assist the Security Council in considering appropriate measures under the Charter with regard to developments in colonial Territories that are likely to threaten international peace and security; to continue to examine the compliance of Member States with the Declaration and with other relevant resolutions on decolonization; to continue to pay particular attention to the small Territories; and to take all necessary steps to enlist world-wide support in the achievement of the Declaration's objectives (G.A. res. 34/94).

Procedures followed by the Special Committee include the collection of relevant information, the preparation of reports, the receipt of petitions and the hearing of petitioners, and undertaking visiting missions to specific Territories. To assist in these tasks the Special Committee has established a comprehensive machinery of subordinate organs. In keeping with decisions of the General Assembly, representatives of those national liberation movements which are recognized by the Organization of African Unity participate as observers, i.e. without a vote, in the relevant proceedings of the Assembly's Fourth Committee.

There has been and continues to be an intensive relationship between the Special Committee and other UN organs. Thus, in the resolution establishing the Special Committee, the Assembly requested one of the *principal* organs of the UN, the Trusteeship Council, to *assist* the Special Committee in its work. In accordance with the Assembly's request the Special Committee has apprised the Security Council of a number of developments which may threaten international peace and security, including the situations in Southern Rhodesia (Zimbabwe), South West Africa (Namibia), Aden and the Territories formerly under Portuguese control.

Although the Commission on Human Rights and the Special Committee have not worked closely together, the latter was instrumental in the Commission's adoption in 1970 of a new procedure for the consideration of communications relating to gross violations.[8]

The extent of co-operation by the specialized agencies with the work of the Special Committee has varied from agency to agency. In 1967 the Assembly emphasized the importance of all UN-related international organizations extending such co-operation (G.A. res. 2311(XXII)). However, in subsequent years certain difficulties arose between the General Assembly and the Special Committee on the one side and the International Bank for Reconstruction and Development (World Bank) and the International Monetary Fund on the other.[9] Despite extensive discussions the issue has not been resolved to the Assembly's satisfaction. Its 1979 resolution, in which it expressed regret that the IBRD and the IMF had not taken the necessary steps to help implement the Declaration and related resolutions and deplored the practices of those agencies which continued co-operation with the colonialist, racist minority régime in South Africa, is typical of many earlier ones (G.A. res. 34/42).

Another focus of particular concern for the Committee has been the activities of foreign economic interests operating in Namibia, former Southern Rhodesia, and South Africa. The Assembly has declared that the collaboration of these interests with the relevant régimes is detrimental to the interests of the oppressed peoples and impedes the implementation of the Declaration. It has also condemned all those countries, some of which have been specifically named, which continue to maintain political, diplomatic, economic, trade, military, nuclear, and other relations with the racist régimes (G.A. res. 34/41 of 1979).

The Special Committee has submitted a report to the General Assembly each year since 1963.[10] Examples of decolonization issues which have recently been considered by the Assembly include the situations in Western Sahara, Belize, and East Timor and in Territories administered by Australia, New Zealand, the United Kingdom and the United States. Among the Territories administered by the latter are Guam, American Samoa and the US Virgin Islands.

Thus, in institutional terms, the Special Committee has established the most elaborate machinery of all the Assembly's subsidiary organs and has conducted activities of unparalleled scope and comprehensiveness. Some notable characteristics of the approach adopted by the Special Committee are: its emphasis on the economic aspects of its task; the extent to which it investigates the situation in specific countries; and the degree of sophistication of its petition procedures.[11] The large number of former dependent territories which have become independent in recent years is one testimony to the important and wide-ranging impact of the 1960 Declaration.

(iv) UNITED NATIONS COUNCIL FOR NAMIBIA

In 1967 the UN Council for South West Africa was established by the General Assembly (res. 2248(S-V)). The following year it was renamed the UN Council for Namibia. Its primary function is to administer Namibia until independence, with the maximum possible participation of the Territory's people. The Council consists of 25 Member States and its executive and administrative tasks are performed by the UN Commissioner for Namibia. The Council works through a Steering Committee and three Standing Committees.

In 1979 the General Assembly called upon the Council, in discharging its responsibilities, to denounce all fraudulent constitutional schemes through which South Africa might attempt to perpetuate its oppression and exploita-

tion; to endeavour to ensure non-recognition of any administration not issuing from free elections in Namibia under UN supervision; to secure the
territorial integrity of Namibia; and to continue to mobilize international
support for the withdrawal of the illegal administration of South Africa from
Namibia (G.A. res. 34/92 A).

(v) THE UNITED NATIONS HIGH COMMISSIONER FOR REFUGEES (UNHCR)

The Office of the UNHCR was established as of 1 January 1951 by the
General Assembly[12] as a successor to the short-lived International Refugee
Organization. The High Commissioner is not, as is often erroneously assumed,
a part of the UN Secretariat. Rather, he is a subsidiary organ of the Assem-
bly, elected by it and reporting to it annually through the Economic and
Social Council.

The High Commissioner's function is to provide international protection to
refugees who fall within the scope of his Statute by (a) promoting the conclusion and ratification of international conventions for the protection of refugees, supervising their application, and proposing amendments thereto; (b)
promoting, through special agreements with Governments, the execution of
any measures calculated to improve the situation of refugees and to reduce
the number requiring protection; (c) assisting governmental and private efforts to promote voluntary repatriation or assimilation within new national
communities; (d) promoting the admission of refugees to the territories of
States; (e) endeavouring to obtain permission for refugees to transfer their
assets and especially those necessary for their resettlement; (f) obtaining
from Governments information concerning the number and conditions of refugees in their territories and the laws and regulations concerning them; (g)
keeping in close touch with the Governments and intergovernmental organizations concerned; (h) establishing contact with private organizations dealing
with refugee questions; and (i) facilitating the co-ordination of the efforts of
private organizations concerned with the welfare of refugees.

Under the terms of the Statute a "refugee" is any person "who is outside the
country of his nationality or, if he has no nationality, the country of his former
habitual residence, because he has or had well-founded fear of persecution by
reason of his race, religion, nationality, or political opinion and is unable or,
because of such fear, is unwilling to avail himself of the protection of the
government of the country of his nationality, or, if he has no nationality, to
return to the country of his former habitual residence" (Statute, para. 6B).

"Protection" of refugees is interpreted to mean legal and "quasi-consular"
protection and does not include the provision of material assistance. Thus
while the administrative expenses of the Office of the UNHCR are part of the
regular UN budget all other expenditures are financed by voluntary contributions (Statute, para. 20).

In practice, the competence of the High Commissioner, both as to the
persons on whose behalf he acts and as to the procurement of financial and

other means, has been interpreted liberally from the outset. Thus the High Commissioner has consistently been requested by the General Assembly to extend his good offices whenever appropriate and to assist persons who do not, strictly speaking, come within his mandate. In recent years, as the size and complexity of the refugee problem in many parts of the world has grown dramatically, the High Commissioner's responsibilities have increased accordingly. His main efforts have been directed towards: the prevention of *refoulement* (the return of a person to a country where he has reason to fear persecution); the granting of asylum, at least on a temporary basis; and the observance of the traditional obligations to rescue those in distress at sea. In his 1979 report the High Commissioner notes serious difficulties encountered in these areas and "instances where lack of respect for the fundamental human rights of refugees have led to tragic consequences."[13]

The main aim of UNHCR assistance programmes financed from voluntary funds is to help Governments in the search for durable solutions for refugees and displaced persons of concern to the High Commissioner and in the promotion of self-sufficiency within the shortest period of time. Where appropriate, UNHCR actively supports all efforts in favour of the return of refugees to their country of origin or former habitual residence by means of voluntary repatriation. However, in many cases of continued asylum, local integration forms the bulk of UNHCR assistance; such integration is possible in both urban and rural areas, depending on the nature of the case. In cases where durable solutions are not possible in countries of first asylum, resettlement in third countries becomes necessary.

The magnitude of recent problems dealt with by UNHCR is illustrated by the fact that the number of refugees and displaced persons increased by an average of 2000 per day for the whole of 1978. The tragic events in South-East Asia, which reached their height in 1979, greatly enlarged this average. Thus, between 1975 and July 1979 over a million persons left their countries from the three States of the Indo-China peninsula alone. Of those, over 550,000 sought asylum in South-East Asia.[14] In addition, other major refugee problem areas include Bangladesh, the horn of Africa, Zaire, Nicaragua, Cuba, and Southern Africa, to mention only a few.

In conclusion, it should be noted that Palestine refugees do not come within the competence of the High Commissioner. The Statute provides that his competence does not extend to persons who receive protection and assistance from other UN organs. Thus, the relevant agency in Palestine is the UN Relief and Works Agency for Palestine Refugees in the Near East (1980 report in UN doc. A/35/13).

(c). Economic and Social Council

(i) COMPOSITION, FUNCTIONS AND PROCEDURES

The Economic and Social Council (ECOSOC) is, under the authority of the General Assembly, the principal organ of the UN with responsibility in matters of international economic and social co-operation, and the promotion of universal respect for, and observance of, human rights. Originally composed of 18 members it now has 54 members who are elected by the Assembly on the basis of an equitable geographical distribution. While this basis is not specified in the Charter it is considered legally binding. Each member of ECOSOC has one vote and all of its decisions are taken by a majority of the members present and voting.

ECOSOC adopts its own rules of procedure which it has amended on a number of occasions.[15] The Council normally holds one organizational session and two regular sessions each year. Special sessions may also be held. Human rights matters are generally dealt with at the first regular session of the year. The Council has three "sessional" committees—the Economic, Social and Coordination Committees. Human rights items are generally referred to the Social Committee on which all Council members are represented, although some are dealt with directly in plenary meetings. In 1948, the Council established a separate Human Rights Committee to consider the draft of the Universal Declaration of Human Rights and the Final Act of the Freedom of Information Conference (Doc. E/CONF. 6/79). However, this Committee was not continued. The reports of the Social Committee, which contain draft resolutions and draft decisions, are submitted to the Council for final action in plenary meetings.

In addition to its sessional committees the Council has also established, in 1976, a sessional Working Group to assist it in the examination of reports under the International Covenant on Economic, Social and Cultural Rights. The work of this group is considered below.

(ii) THE FUNCTIONS AND POWERS OF ECOSOC IN HUMAN RIGHTS MATTERS

The Charter (Article 62 (2)) vests in ECOSOC the power to make recommendations for the purpose of promoting respect for, and observance of, human rights and fundamental freedoms for all. The Council may prepare draft conventions for submission to the General Assembly, with respect to matters falling within its competence and it may call international conferences on such matters (Art. 52). ECOSOC is the organ which is responsible for agreements with the specialized agencies, a matter which is of great importance for human rights questions, particularly in regard to those agencies (ILO, Unesco and WHO) which engage in essential activities in the human rights field. ECOSOC may co-ordinate the activities of the agencies through consultation and recommendation (Art. 63). However, the Council's effectiveness in this regard has been limited[16] and in 1979 it decided to extend the terms of reference of the Commission on Human Rights to provide that the Commission will assist the Council in its human rights co-ordination role (E/RES/1979/36).

The Charter also empowers the Council to obtain regular reports from the specialized agencies and to arrange with the Members of the UN and with the agencies to obtain reports on the steps taken to give effect to its own recommendations and to relevant General Assembly recommendations (Art. 64

(1)). The system of periodic reports in the field of human rights which was introduced by the Council in 1956 is considered below.

ECOSOC is also called upon to make suitable arrangements for consultation with non-governmental organizations which are concerned with matters within its competence (Art. 71). In 1950, the Council enacted detailed arrangements for consultation with non-governmental organizations. These were replaced in 1968 by new arrangements contained in Council resolution 1296 (XLIV). In establishing consultative relations with organizations, ECOSOC distinguishes between organizations in general consultative status (category I); organizations in special consultative status (category II); and organizations which can make occasional and useful contributions and are included in a list known as the Roster. Organizations in category I may propose to a committee of the Council that it request the Secretary-General to place items of special interest to them on the provisional agenda of the Council. Organizations in categories I and II may designate authorized representatives to sit as observers at public meetings of the Council and its subsidiary bodies. Subject to certain conditions as to size and substance, they may submit written statements for circulation and may be given hearings. Similar provisions apply to consultation of non-governmental organizations with Commissions, *Ad Hoc* Committees and other subsidiary organs of the Council.

The responsibilities of ECOSOC were re-defined by the General Assembly in 1977 in the context of an overall restructuring of the economic and social sectors of the UN system. They include:

(a) To serve as the central forum for the discussion of international economic and social issues of a global or interdisciplinary nature and the formulation of policy recommendations thereon addressed to Member States and to the UN system as a whole;

(b) To monitor and evaluate the implementation of overall strategies, policies and priorities established by the General Assembly;

(c) To ensure the overall co-ordination of the activities of the UN system in the economic, social and related fields;

(d) To carry out comprehensive policy reviews of operational activities throughout the UN system.

(GA res 32/197 (1977) Annex)

(d). Subsidiary Organs of ECOSOC Other than the Functional Commissions

As a general rule ECOSOC does its substantive work through subsidiary organs and on the basis of reports submitted to it by these organs. Article 68 of the Charter provides that the Council shall set up commissions in economic and social fields *and for the promotion of human rights*, and such other commissions as may be required for the performance of its functions.

In the human rights field two commissions have been established: the Commission on Human Rights and the Commission on the Status of Women. Their central role and that of their subsidiary organs and bodies in UN human rights endeavours is described below.

   In addition to these two functional commissions of general competence, the
Council has entrusted important human rights assignments to other subsidiary organs. Some of these, by way of example, are:

- The *ad hoc* Committee on the Drafting of the Genocide Convention which was appointed
  in 1948, prepared a draft which was approved by the Assembly in the same year;
- The *ad hoc* Committee on Statelessness and related problems which was established in
  1949 and whose work resulted in the adoption of the 1951 Convention on the Status of
  Refugees;
- Subsidiary organs established to deal with the question of slavery and related practices;[17]
- The *ad hoc* Committee on Forced Labour consisting of five independent members appointed jointly by the UN Secretary-General and the ILO Director-General pursuant to a
  1951 resolution of ECOSOC (res. 350 (XII)). Its task was to study the nature and extent of
  the problem raised by the existence in the world of systems of forced or "corrective"
  labour, which were employed as a means of political coercion or punishment for holding or
  expressing political views, and which were on such scale as to constitute an important
  element in the economy of a given country. The Committee's report (doc. E/2431 (1953))
  had a major impact both on international legislation on the subject and on the actual
  situation in some of the countries concerned.
- The Sessional Working Group on the Implementation of the International Covenant on
  Economic, Social and Cultural Rights established by ECOSOC decision 1978/10 in accordance with its earlier resolution 1988 (LX) (1976). The Group's role is discussed in Chapter
  11 below.

(e). Commission on Human Rights

(i) GENERAL QUESTIONS

UN commissions such as those on Human Rights, Social Development, Population and Narcotic Drugs are referred to as "functional" commissions to
distinguish them from "regional" commissions such as the Economic Commission for Latin America.

   The establishment of the Commission on Human Rights was recommended
in the report of the Preparatory Commission of the United Nations[18] in 1945
and decided upon by ECOSOC at its first session, in February 1946 (res.
5(I)). Initially, the Commission was to consist of a nucleus of nine members
appointed in their individual capacity, hence the designation as a "nuclear
Commission." In its report to the Council (E/38/Rev.1) the nuclear Commission recommended that "all members of the Commission on Human Rights
should serve as non-governmental representatives." The Council did not agree
and decided at its second session, in June 1946, that the Commission should
consist of one representative from each of eighteen members of the UN
selected by the Council (res.9(II)). To those who wanted the Commission to
consist of persons serving as individuals and not as representatives of governments, a small concession was made by providing that "with a view to
securing a balanced representation in the various fields covered by the Commission, the Secretary-General shall consult with the governments so selected before the representatives are finally nominated by these governments
and confirmed by the Council." In the 34 years following the enactment of

this provision no case of the Secretary-General objecting to the qualification of a representative, or of the Council refusing to confirm him, has become known.

The membership of the Commission was increased to 22 in 1961, to 32 in 1966 and to 43 in 1979 (Council res. E/1979/36). The 43 members are elected for three-year terms by the Council on the basis of an equitable geographic distribution. In 1980, there were 11 members from African States, 9 from Asian States, 8 from Latin American States, 10 from Western European and other States (including the United States of America) and 5 from socialist States of Eastern Europe. The Commission operates under the rules of procedure of the functional commissions of ECOSOC.[19] Although the Commission presently meets annually for a single period of six weeks, with an extra week for meetings of working groups, it has decided to consider: (i) the possibility of creating an inter-sessional role for the Commission's Bureau (Chairman, Vice-Chairman and Rapporteur); and (ii) the possible need to convene emergency sessions of the Commission in order "to consider responding to reports of mass and flagrant violations of human rights of an urgent nature" (CHR res. 28 (XXXVI) of 1980).

(ii) THE COMMISSION'S TERMS OF REFERENCE

ECOSOC resolved in 1946[20] that the work of the Commission on Human Rights shall be directed towards submitting proposals, recommendations and reports to the Council regarding:

"(a) An international bill of rights;
 (b) International declarations or conventions on civil liberties, the status of women, freedom of information and similar matters;
 (c) The protection of minorities;
 (d) The prevention of discrimination on grounds of race, sex, language or religion;
 (e) Any other matter concerning human rights not covered by items (a), (b), (c) and (d)."

In 1979 the Council (res. E/1979/36) added the following provision to these terms of reference:

"The Commission shall assist the Economic and Social Council in the co-ordination of activities concerning human rights in the United Nations system."

Under the Council resolutions of 1946, the Commission "shall make studies and recommendations and provide information and other services at the request of the Economic and Social Council." It shall also "submit at an early date suggestions regarding the ways and means for the effective implementation of human rights and fundamental freedoms."

In its 1979 resolution the Council also reaffirmed that the Commission will be guided by the standards in the field of human rights as laid down in the various international instruments in that field. It further noted that, in conformity with the Charter, the Universal Declaration and the relevant international instruments, the Commission, in fulfilling its tasks, should take into account the concepts contained in General Assembly resolution 32/130 of 1977.

(iii) SURVEY OF THE COMMISSION'S APPLICATION OF ITS TERMS OF REFERENCE

1. *The International Bill of Rights*

From the outset the Commission devoted its major energies to preparing an "International Bill of Human Rights." At its second session in 1947 the Commission decided to use this term to refer to: a) the proposed declaration, b) the then contemplated single Covenant on Human Rights, and c) the measures of implementation. The history of the adoption of the Universal Declaration of Human Rights by the General Assembly on 10 December 1948 has been traced in Part I of this book. In 1952, the Assembly decided to prepare two Covenants, one on civil and political rights and the other on economic and social rights (G.A. res. 543 (VI)). The Commission completed its contribution to the drafting of the Covenants in 1954 but they were not finally adopted by the General Assembly until 16 December 1966. Both the International Covenant on Economic, Social and Cultural Rights and the International Covenant on Civil and Political Rights, as well as the Optional Protocol to the latter entered into force in 1976. On 1 January 1982 these instruments had received 68, 69 and 26 ratifications respectively. The Covenants' substantive provisions were dealt with in Part I of this Manual and their procedural aspects are considered in Chapter 11.

While the Covenants are clearly binding as treaties in international law for those States which have ratified them, the status of the Universal Declaration is less certain. Much has been written on the subject and it is generally agreed that the Universal Declaration possesses high moral and political authority. In addition, it: has become an international standard by which the conduct of governments is judged both within and outside the UN; has inspired a great number of international and regional treaties; is cited as the basis and justification for many important decisions taken by UN bodies; is reflected in many national constitutions, in national legislation and in the decisions of both national and international courts; and has been claimed by many scholars to have acquired the force of law as part of the customary law of nations.[21]

2. *Other instruments in the drafting of which the Commission has played a significant role*

A comprehensive list of conventions and declarations adopted by the UN in the human rights field is contained in Annex 1 of this book. In the present section only some of these are noted.

Declaration of the Rights of the Child (1959). It was originally prepared in 1950 by the UN's Social Commission and was referred to the Commission for its consideration. After work at its 1957 and 1959 sessions the Commission presented a draft Declaration to ECOSOC and this was subsequently adopted by the General Assembly in 1959 (res. 1386 (XIV)). In addition, the Commission is currently drafting a convention on the rights of the child and expects to submit a complete draft to the General Assembly in 1982.[22]

United Nations Declaration on the Elimination of All Forms of Racial Discrimination (1963). This Declaration (and its companion Convention) is one of the results of a chain of events which started as a reaction to an epidemic of swastika-painting and other "manifestations of anti-Semitism and other forms of racial and national hatred and religious and racial prejudices of a similar nature," which occurred in many countries in the winter of 1959/1960. The Sub-Commission on Prevention of Discrimination and Protection of Minorities, which happened to be in session at that time (January 1960), adopted a resolution condemning the events and recommending action to its superior bodies (E/CN.4/800). Subsequently, the General Assembly decided that four instruments were to be prepared, *viz.* a draft declaration and a draft convention on the elimination of all forms of racial discrimination and a draft declaration and a draft convention on the elimination of all forms of religious intolerance (G.A. res. 1780 and 1781 (XVII) of 1962). All four instruments were to be prepared by the Commission bearing in mind the views of the Sub-Commission and of governments. The Racial Discrimination Declaration was adopted by the Assembly in 1963 (res. 1904 (XVIII)) and the Convention in 1965 (res. 2106 (XX)).

Declaration on the Elimination of Religious Intolerance. Although the Sub-Commission prepared a preliminary draft on this subject in 1963 (E/CN.4/873), which was considered by the Commission and submitted to the General Assembly in 1964, serious disagreements delayed the adoption of an international instrument. At its 36th session in 1981 the General Assembly finally adopted the Declaration on the Elimination of All Forms of Intolerance and of Discrimination Based on Religion or Belief.[23]

Declaration on Territorial Asylum (1967). Article 14 of the Universal Declaration provides that everyone has the right to seek and to enjoy in other countries asylum from persecution. This provision was criticized because it set forth the right "to seek" asylum without an indication that the asylum should be granted. Thus between 1957 and 1960 the Commission prepared a draft Declaration on Territorial Asylum which was formally adopted by the General Assembly in 1967 (res. 2312 (XXII)).[24] The Declaration on Territorial Asylum, while not proclaiming a right to be granted asylum, goes beyond the provisions of the Universal Declaration in stating that the situation of persons entitled to invoke Article 14 of the Universal Declaration is, without prejudice to the sovereignty of States, of concern to the international community. The Declaration also provides that a person coming under Article 14 of the Universal Declaration shall not be subjected to measures such as rejection at the frontier or expulsion or compulsory return to any State where he may be subjected to persecution.

Declaration on the Protection of All Persons from Being Subjected to Torture and Other Cruel, Inhuman or Degrading Treatment or Punishment. In 1975, the General Assembly, on the recommendation of the Fifth UN Congress on the Prevention of Crime and the Treatment of Offenders, adopted this Declaration (G.A. res. 3452 (XXX)). In 1977 the Assembly requested the Commission to draft a convention on the same subject and this work continued at the 1982 session of the Commission.

Convention on the International Right of Correction (1952). The origins of the Convention are noted below in connection with the Sub-Commission on Freedom of Information and of the Press. The Convention was adopted in 1952 (G.A. res. 630 (VII)), but had only received 11 ratifications by 1 January 1982. Its objective is to ensure that a person referred to in a printed report should have the right to convey his side of the question to readers.

International Convention on the Elimination of All Forms of Racial Discrimination (1965). This Convention is examined in the following chapter.

Convention on the Non-Applicability of Statutory Limitation to War Crimes and Crimes Against Humanity (1968). In 1965 the question of the punishment of war criminals and persons who have committed crimes against humanity was brought before the UN organs. The issue was the problem of the application of statutory limitation to these crimes. It has aroused interest because of legislation extending the period of statutory limitation which was then being enacted by the Federal Republic of Germany. Under the Convention subsequently adopted by the Assembly (res. 2391 (XXIII)) no statutory limitation shall apply to war crimes and crimes against humanity, as re-defined in it, irrespective of the date of their commission.

International Convention on the Suppression and Punishment of the Crime of Apartheid (1973) (G.A. res. 3068 (XXVIII)). While this is examined in the following chapter it is of note in the present context because some of the functions set out in the Convention are performed by the Commission on Human Rights.

3. *Other International Instruments of Major Importance in the Human Rights Field*

Once again, only a selection of relevant instruments can be noted in the present Chapter. Those relating to the status of women are considered in a later section of this Chapter.

Declaration on the Granting of Independence to Colonial Countries and Peoples (1960)(G.A. res. 1514 (XV)).

Declaration on Social Progress and Development (1969)(G.A. res. 2542 (XXIV)). The Declaration is unique in the domain of instruments relating to general development questions since it contains a great number of provisions which deal with human rights in the most technical sense.

Declaration on the Rights of Mentally Retarded Persons (1971) (G.A. res. 2856 (XXVI)). It defines a series of rights for the dignity, well-being and interests of the mentally retarded person.

Standard Minimum Rules for the Treatment of Prisoners (1957). These were approved by ECOSOC in resolution 663 C (XXIV) and 2076 (LXII).

Principles of international co-operation in the detection, arrest, extradition and punishment of persons guilty of war crimes and crimes against humanity (1973)(G.A. res. 3074 (XXVIII)).

Universal Declaration on the Eradication of Hunger and Malnutrition (1974). Adopted by the 1974 World Food Conference and endorsed by the General Assembly (res. 3348 (XXIX)).

Declaration on the Protection of Women and Children in Emergency and Armed Conflict (1974)(G.A. res. 3318 (XXIX)).

Declaration on the Rights of Disabled Persons (1975)(G.A. res. 3447(XXX)).

Declaration on the Use of Scientific and Technological Progress in the Interests of Peace and for the Benefit of Mankind (1975) (G.A. res. 3384 (XXX)).

International Declaration against Apartheid in Sports (G.A. res. 32/105 M(1977)).

Declaration on the Preparation of Societies for Life in Peace (1979) (G.A. res. 33/73).

International Convention Against the Taking of Hostages (1979) (G.A. res. 34/146).

Code of Conduct for Law Enforcement Officials (1979) (G.A. res. 34/169).

4. *Human Rights-Related Instruments Being Considered by UN Organs as of 1982*

Some of these instruments, such as those relating to the rights of the child, to torture, and to the elimination of religious intolerance, have already been noted before. In addition, various UN organs are presently at different stages in the preparation of important new instruments. These include the following:

Draft general principles on equality and non-discrimination in respect of persons born out of wedlock. (E/1978/14 and Add. 1-8)

Body of principles for the protection of all persons under any form of detention and imprisonment. (E/CN.4/1296(1978) para. 109)

Draft declaration on the human rights of individuals who are not citizens of the country in which they live (E/CN.4/1336 and E/CN.4/1354 and Adds. (1979)).

Draft declaration on the rights of members of national, ethnic, religious and linguistic minorities. (E/CN.4/NGO/231 (1979) and E/CN.4/L.1367/Rev.1 (1980))

Draft code of medical ethics (A/34/273(1979)).

Draft international convention on the protection of the rights of all migrant workers and their families (A/34/535 and Add. 1 and G.A. res. 34/172 (1979)).

Draft international convention against *apartheid* in sports (A/34/36 (1979)).

The drafting of an international convention to outlaw mercenarism in all its manifestations is also under consideration by the General Assembly (res. 34/140 (1979)).

The elaboration of a draft declaration confirming common United Nations principles and standards defining limitations and restrictions on the exercise of certain human rights was proposed by the Sub-Commission in 1980 (res.7(XXXIII)).

The Sub-Commission has entrusted one of its members (Mrs. Erica-Irene A. Daes) with the task of submitting to it in 1981: (a) guidelines related to procedures for determining whether adequate grounds exist for detaining persons on the grounds of mental ill-health, and (b) principles for the protection, in general, of persons suffering from mental disorders (res.11 (XXXIII)(1980)).

5. *Ratification of human rights instruments*

While the drafting of international human rights instruments continues apace, it is only very recently that attention has been focused institutionally

on the need to promote widespread ratification of such instruments. The
encouragement of ratification by States has long been an important characteristic of the system of international labour standards developed by the ILO
(see Chapter 12, *infra*) and has also been emphasized by the United Nations
High Commissioner for Refugees (A/CONF.32/15 (1967)). The chart presented
at the end of this book demonstrates that, while many ratifications have been
achieved, there is considerable unevenness in the number of ratifications by
different States and in the extent to which different instruments have been
ratified.

In 1979 the Sub-Commission, at the suggestion of a non-governmental
organization (E/CN.4/Sub.2/NGO.80 and Add.1 and NGO.82) formally acknowledged the importance of actively promoting ratification by establishing a
sessional working group to meet each year during the sessions of the Sub-
Commission in order to consider ways and means of encouraging Governments which have not yet done so to ratify or adhere to the major international
human rights instruments (Sub-Commission resolution 1 B (XXXIII) (1979)).
In the same resolution the Sub-Commission requested Governments to inform it, through the Secretary-General, of the circumstances which so far
have not enabled them to ratify or adhere to particular instruments and to
explain any particular difficulties which they may face, in respect of which
the United Nations could offer any assistance. The task of the working group
is to examine the replies received from Governments and, where appropriate, to consider what forms of assistance might be provided by the United
Nations to facilitate ratification. At the first session of the Group, in 1980,
considerable discussion was devoted to the questions of whether the Sub-
Commission was competent: (a) to request such information from Governments; and (b) to invite Government representatives "for discussion with
members of the Working Group with a view to providing further clarification." The Group eventually concluded that representatives of States could
be invited for clarification and discussions but that their appearance could not
be demanded. It also noted that its task was not inquisitorial or adjudicatory
but was to encourage and facilitate universal acceptance of human rights
instruments (E/CN.4/Sub.2/453). Nevertheless, the establishment of the group
and its implicit acceptance by the Commission constitute a significant development in terms of the international community's endeavours to encourage
States to undertake formal legal obligations in the field of human rights.

6. *Other Activities of the Commission on Human Rights*

While the Commission has devoted a considerable amount of time to the
preparation of international standard-setting instruments in the human rights
field, its work has also developed in a variety of other directions.[25] Writing in
1975 one scholar distinguished three major stages in UN human rights activities.[26] The first stage (1945-55) was devoted mainly to *standard-setting* and

included the adoption of the Universal Declaration of Human Rights and the preparation of the two International Covenants. During the second stage (1955-65) the UN focused mainly on the *promotion* of respect for human rights. Its endeavours included the institution of a system of periodic reporting on human rights, the establishment of a programme of advisory services and the preparation of studies on a variety of topics. The third stage (1965-present) has been increasing emphasis on international *protection* of human rights and has involved the development of a more effective communications (i.e. complaints) procedure, efforts to deal with specific situations involving gross violations of human rights, and the undertaking of a series of operational fact-finding activities. Since 1977, a fourth stage has also emerged, which emphasizes the *structural* and economic aspects of human rights issues. The first of these stages has been considered above and the other three are considered in the second part of this Chapter.

One further matter which warrants mention at this point is the tendency of the Commission in recent years to take action without prior reference to ECOSOC. Council resolutions 5(I) and 9(II) of 1946 provide that the work of the Commission shall be directed towards submitting proposals, recommendations and reports to the Council. They do not provide for direct and independent action by the Commission. Nevertheless, in recent years the Commission has taken action in response to a number of violations situations without having obtained the prior consent of the Council.[27]

(f). Sub-Commission on Prevention of Discrimination and Protection of Minorities

Originally, four Sub-Commissions, in addition to the Commission on Human Rights, were to have been established by ECOSOC. One of these, the Sub-Commission on the Status of Women became a full commission in 1946 (Council res. 11 (II)), and another, the Sub-Commission on Freedom of Information and the Press, was established in 1947. The work of these two organs is considered below. In 1947, the Commission decided to establish a single Sub-Commission, rather than two separate ones, to deal with both the prevention of discrimination and the protection of minorities.

The main distinguishing feature of the Sub-Commission is that its members are independent experts, acting in their individual capacities. They are elected for three years by the Commission from nominations made by States. In addition to the role of governments in electing the Sub-Commission members, governments also have the right to withhold their consent to one of their nations serving on the Sub-Commission. Membership of the Sub-Commission has increased from 12 in 1947 to 14 in 1959, 18 in 1965 and 26 since 1969. In geographical terms 12 are elected from the Afro-Asian States, 6 from Western European and other States, 5 from Latin American States and 3 from Eastern-European States. As of 1980, sessions of the Sub-Commission last for four weeks (Council res. E/1979/36). A proposal by the Sub-Commission that its name be changed to the "Sub-Commission of Experts on Human Rights" was not endorsed by the Commission in 1980.

The Sub-Commission has frequently been criticized by its superior bodies, generally on the grounds that its approach was too radical. In 1951 an unsuccessful attempt was made to abolish the Sub-Commission. This followed a decision by the Commission in 1950 not to forward various proposals submitted by the Sub-Commission to the Council and to take no action at all on others. In 1951 the Council decided to discontinue the Sub-Commission after a final session in October 1951 (Council res. 414 (XIII)). However, when the General Assembly considered this decision, it noted that the full application and implementation of the principle of non-discrimination are matters of supreme importance and should constitute the primary objectives of UN work. It therefore invited the Council to authorize the Sub-Commission to continue its work and, especially, to convene a session in 1952 (G.A. res. 532 B (VI) of 1952). The Council subsequently reversed itself and complied with the decision of the Assembly (Council res. 443 (XIV) of 1952).

(i) THE TERMS OF REFERENCE OF THE SUB-COMMISSION, THEIR INTERPRETATION
    AND APPLICATION

When establishing the Sub-Commission in 1947, the Commission described the task of the Sub-Commission in general terms as being: "to examine what provisions should be adopted in defining the principles to be applied in the field of the prevention of discrimination on grounds of race, sex, language or religion, and in the field of the protection of minorities, and to make recommendations to the Commission on urgent problems in these fields" (E/259, para. 19). In 1949, the terms of reference were "clarified and extended in scope" to read as follows:

"(a) to undertake studies, particularly in the light of the Universal Declaration of Human Rights and to make recommendations to the Commission on Human Rights concerning the prevention of discrimination of any kind relating to human rights and fundamental freedoms and the protection of racial, national, religious and linguistic minorities; and
(b) to perform any other functions which may be entrusted to it by the Economic and Social Council or the Commission on Human Rights."

No definite interpretation of "prevention of discrimination" as distinct from "protection of minorities" has been agreed upon in treaty form or by a prinicipal organ. For the purpose of interpreting the terms of reference of the Sub-Commission it is, however, appropriate to quote from a statement on terminology which the Sub-Commission adopted at its first session in 1947 and which has never been challenged by a higher organ. "Prevention of discrimination," the Sub-Commission said, "is the prevention of any action which denies to individuals or groups of peoples equality of treatment which they may wish." "Protection of minorities" on the other hand, is "the protection of non-dominant groups which, while wishing in general for equality of treatment with the majority, wish for a measure of different treatment in order to preserve basic characteristics which they possess and which distinguish them from the majority of the population... The characteristics meriting such protection are race, religion and language" (E/CN.4/52, chap. V).

In its first years the Sub-Commission devoted a great part of its efforts to the question of the protection of minorities. Due to the reluctance of Governments to commit themselves in regard to this "complex and delicate question," the General Assembly decided not to deal with it in the text of the Universal Declaration of Human Rights, but requested a further study of the problem by the Commission and the Sub-Commission (G.A. res. 217 C (III) of 1948). The result, *inter alia*, of these studies is Article 27 of the International Covenant on Civil and Political Rights, the only general norm dealing with the problem of minorities to be produced by the United Nations. It provides that, in those States in which ethnic, religious or linguistic minorities exist, persons belonging to such minorities shall not be denied the right, in community with the other members of their group, to enjoy their own culture, to profess and practice their own religion, or to use their own language. Following the adoption of the Covenant, in 1966, the Sub-Commission initiated a study of the principles contained in it. The outcome of the study is noted below.

In addition to making an important contribution to the drafting of a number of international standards, some of which were noted earlier, the Sub-Commission has undertaken studies on a wide range of topics. Some of these are considered below. Moreover, it has played an important role in prompting studies and other activities to be undertaken by specialized agencies such as Unesco and ILO. The part played by various working groups of the Sub-Commission has also been very significant and the work of some of these, such as those dealing with communications and with the ratification of international human rights instruments, is noted below.

In the present context it is proposed only to consider the Working Group on Slavery which was established in 1974 (Sub-Commission res. 11 (XXVIII)). The question of slavery has long occupied the attention of the UN and, before it, of the League of Nations.[28] It should be noted, however, that the current UN usage of the term 'slavery' covers a variety of slavery-like practices. This interpretation has enabled the Slavery Working Group to perform very useful work relating to fields as diverse as prostitution, child labour, debt bondage, *apartheid*, migrant workers and, of course, slavery, the slave trade and the traffic in persons.[29]

(g). Sub-Commission on Freedom of Information and of the Press

This Sub-Commission was also established by the Commission in 1947 and was composed of 12 persons serving in their individual capacities. Its function was, "in the first instance, to examine what rights, obligations and practices should be included in the concept of freedom of information," to report on any issues that might arise from such examination and to perform any other functions which might be entrusted to it by the Council or by the Commission (E/259 (1947), Chap. III). It held only five sessions, between 1947 and 1952, and its mandate was terminated by ECOSOC (res. 414 (XIII) of 1951). The first session of the Sub-Commission was mainly devoted to preparations for the UN Conference on Freedom of Information which met in 1948.[30] At its second session it drafted provisions of freedom of expression and information for inclusion in the Universal Declaration and the Covenants. At its fourth and fifth sessions the Sub-Commission completed the drafting of an International Code of Ethics for Journalists. At its final session it condemned as an infraction of freedom of information and of the press, the action of the Argentine police in closing the newspaper *La Prensa*.[31]

(h). Commission on the Status of Women

(i) GENERAL

The central importance of the UN's commitment to the principle of equality between men and women, meaning equality in their dignity and worth as human beings as well as equality in their rights, opportunities and responsibilities has already been noted in Chapter 4 of this book. The principle of non-discrimination is affirmed not only in the Charter (Preamble and Articles 1, 8, 13, 55, 56 and 75) but in a large range of instruments adopted by the UN and by the specialized agencies.

At its first session ECOSOC resolved to establish a Sub-Commission on the Status of Women which would submit proposals, recommendations and reports to the Commission on Human Rights (Council res. 5 (I) of 1946). However, at its second session the Council conferred upon the Sub-Commission the status of a full Commission reporting directly to ECOSOC (res. 11 (II) of 1946). Its constitutional and legal status and its rules of procedure are thus the same as for the Commission on Human Rights. Membership of the Commission on the Status of Women has increased from 15 in 1947 to 18 in 1951, 21 in 1961 and 32 since 1966. States are elected to membership of the Commission for four-year terms and on the basis of an equitable geographical distribution. There are currently 8 members from African States, 6 from Asian States, 6 from Latin American States, 8 from Western European and other states and 4 from the Socialist States of Eastern Europe.

In 1978, the Commission adopted a resolution stating its conviction that it discharges important and essential functions with a view to the advancement of women and urging its continuation as a separate Commission (res. 9 (XXVII)). Nevertheless, proposals to abolish the Commission, in the context of an overall restructuring of the economic and social sectors of the UN system, are to be considered again by the General Assembly in 1980 (G.A. decision 34/453).

(ii) THE TERMS OF REFERENCE OF THE COMMISSION ON THE STATUS OF WOMEN

The functions of the Commission are (a) to prepare recommendations and reports to the Economic and Social Council on promoting women's rights in political, economic, civil, social and educational fields, and (b) to make recommendations to the Council on urgent problems requiring immediate attention in the field of women's rights with the object of implementing the principle that men and women shall have equal rights, and to develop proposals to give effect to such recommendations. (Council res. 11 (II)(1946) and 48 (IV)(1947). It may be noted that while matters relating to discrimination on the ground of sex also continue to be within the competence of the Commission on Human Rights, the Commission on the Status of Women has been the dominant organ dealing with these issues.

(iii) APPLICATION OF THE COMMISSION'S TERMS OF REFERENCE

In order to avoid duplication of the survey in Chapter 4, it is proposed, in the present context, only to consider the principal international instruments which have been initiated by the Commission on the Status of Women or in the preparation of which it has played a major role.[32]

Declaration and Convention on the Elimination of All Forms of Discrimination against Women.
The Declaration was drafted by the Commission on the Status of Women between 1965 and 1967 and adopted by the General Assembly in 1967 (res. 2263 (XXII)). The Declaration contains many international standards and deals with issues such as political rights, nationality, rights under civil law, discriminatory provisions of penal law, traffic in women, educational rights and economic rights. It also provides for regular reports on relevant action by States. Since 1970, these reports have been considered by the Commission.
In 1972, the Commission declared that existing international instruments relating to the status of women were inadequate and that a new instrument was required (Commission res. 5 (XXIV)). The first draft of a convention was prepared by a working group of the Commission in 1974 (E/5451). The revised draft was adopted by the Commission in 1976 and forwarded to the General Assembly which adopted it on 18 December 1979 (G.A. res. 34/180).
The Convention on the Elimination of All Forms of Discrimination against Women is comprehensive in scope and requires the adoption by States of a broad range of policy measures. In its preamble the Convention recalls "that discrimination against women violates the principles of equality of rights and respect for human dignity, is an obstacle to the participation of women, on equal terms with men, in the political, social, economic and cultural life of their countries, hampers the growth of the prosperity of society and the family, and makes more difficult the full development of the potentialities of women in the service of their countries and of humanity." It also notes that a

change in the traditional role of men as well as the role of women in society
and in the family is needed to achieve full equality between men and women.

The term "discrimination against women" is defined in Article 1 of the
Convention to mean "any distinction, exclusion or restriction made on the
basis of sex which has the effect or purpose of impairing or nullifying the
recognition, enjoyment or exercise by women, irrespective of their marital
status, on a basis of equality of men and women, of human rights and fundamental freedoms in the political, economic, social, cultural, civil or any other
field".

In accordance with a policy of eliminating discrimination against women,
States Parties to the Convention undertake: (a) To embody the principle of
equality of men and women in their national Constitutions or other appropriate legislation if not yet incorporated therein, and to ensure, through law and
other appropriate means, the practical realization of this principle; (b) To
adopt appropriate legislative and other measures, including sanctions where
appropriate, prohibiting all discrimination against women; (c) To establish
legal protection of the rights of women on an equal basis with men and to
ensure through competent national tribunals and other public institutions the
effective protection of women against any act of discrimination; (d) To refrain
from engaging in any act or practice of discrimination against women and to
ensure that public authorities and institutions shall act in conformity with
this obligation; (e) To take all appropriate measures to eliminate discrimination against women by any person, organization or enterprise; (f) To take all
appropriate measures, including legislation, to modify or abolish existing
laws, regulations, customs and practices which constitute discrimination against
women; and (g) To repeal all national penal provisions which constitute discrimination against women (Art. 2).

In the broadest terms Part I of the Convention provides that:

"States Parties shall take in all fields, in particular in the political, social, economic and
cultural fields, all appropriate measures, including legislation, to ensure the full development and advancement of women, for the purpose of guaranteeing them the exercise and
enjoyment of human rights and fundamental freedoms on a basis of equality with men."

The Convention also recognizes the need for reverse discrimination in
appropriate circumstances (Art. 4) and for measures to modify social and
cultural patterns of conduct which are based on ideas of inferiority or on role
stereotypes (Art 5).

The second and fourth parts of the Convention deal with civil and political
rights and contain provisions relating to equality: in political and public life
(Art 7); of representation at the international level (Art. 8); in questions of
nationality (Art. 9); before the law (Art. 15); and in matters relating to
marriage and family relations (Art. 16).

In some respects, however, Part II which relates to economic, social and cultural rights, represents the greatest progress when compared to the earlier Declaration. Article 10, concerning education, provides not only for equality of access to all levels of schooling and of access to the same curricula, the same examinations, teaching staff with qualifications of the same standard and school premises and equipment of the same quality, but also for "the elimination of any stereotyped concept of the roles of men and women at all levels and in all forms of education." The same article also requires that appropriate measures be taken to ensure: the same opportunities for access to programmes of continuing education, including adult and functional literacy programmes; the reduction of female student drop-out rates and the organization of programmes for girls and women who have left school prematurely; the same opportunities to participate actively in sports and physical education; and access to specific educational information to help to ensure the health and well-being of families, including information and advice on family planning.

The right to work and to equal opportunities for and conditions of employment are also specifically included in the Convention (Art. 11). Paragraph 2 of the same article specifies measures which should be taken by States in order to prevent discrimination against women on the grounds of marriage or maternity and to ensure their effective right to work. They include, for example, measures to prohibit dismissal on the grounds of pregnancy or of maternity leave and discrimination in dismissals on the basis of marital status.

The Convention also deals with the elimination of discrimination against women in the field of health care (Art 12) and in other areas of economic and social life including all aspects of cultural life (Art 13). States Parties are required to take account of the particular problems faced by rural women and to take all appropriate measures to eliminate discrimination against them "in order to ensure, on a basis of equality of men and women, that they participate in and benefit from rural development" (Art. 14). The Convention's implementation procedures are dealt with in the following chapter.

The Convention thus contains not only anti-discrimination measures, but provisions requiring States to take a wide range of positive and constructive actions designed to advance the status of women in different fields.

Convention on the Political Rights of Women.
The Convention was drafted by the Commission on the Status of Women on its own initiative (E/1316 (194) para. 18) and was adopted by the General Assembly in 1952 (res. 640 (VII)). By January 1982 it had been ratified by 86 States. Under the Convention, women are: entitled to vote in all elections; eligible for election to all publicly elected bodies established by national law; and entitled to hold public office and exercise all public functions on equal terms with men.

Convention on the Nationality of Married Women.

This subject had first been dealt with at the international level by the Hague Convention of 1930.[33] The Commission on the Status of Women first proposed such a convention in 1949 (E/1316, para. 31). ECOSOC proposed that the drafting of the Convention be undertaken by the International Law Commission (res. 304 D (XI) of 1950) on the grounds that, if it was to do the job, it would be necessary to examine the whole subject of nationality, including statelessness (A/2163, para. 30). As a consequence, the responsibility for drafting reverted back to the Commission on the Status of Women. The Convention was adopted by the Assembly in 1957 (res. 1040 (XI)) but by January 1982 had received only 54 ratifications. Under the Convention each State Party agrees, *inter alia*, that neither the celebration nor the dissolution of a marriage between one of its nationals and an alien, nor the change of nationality by the husband during marriage, shall automatically affect the nationality of the wife. Neither the voluntary acquisition of the nationality of another State, nor the renunciation of his nationality by a husband shall prevent the retention of her nationality by the wife.

Recommendation and Convention on Consent to Marriage, Minimum Age for Marriage, and Registration of Marriages.

These matters were taken up by the Commission in 1957 (res. 8 (XI)). The Convention was adopted by the General Assembly in 1962 (res. 1763 A (XVII)) and the Recommendation in 1965 (G.A. res. 2018 (XX).[34] The substantive provisions of the two differ only in so far as the Recommendation expressly provides that the minimum age for marriage should be not less than 15 years, while the Convention leaves the specification of the minimum age to each State party.

Declaration on the Protection of Women and Children in Emergency and Armed Conflict.

Concern for the plight of women and children in emergency situations was expressed by the Commission on the Status of Women in 1970 (res. 4 (XXII)). Following a series of consultations involving the Commission and a number of other bodies the General Assembly adopted the Declaration in 1974 (res. 3318 (XXIX)).

(iv) OTHER DEVELOPMENTS IN THE FIELD OF WOMEN'S RIGHTS

In 1972 the General Assembly endorsed a recommendation by the Commission on the Status of Women and proclaimed 1975 International Women's Year (G.A. res. 3010 (XXVII)). The principal objectives of the Year were to promote equality between men and women, to ensure the integration of women in all development activities, and to increase the contribution of women to the strengthening of world peace. The World Conference of the International Women's Year was held in Mexico City in 1975 and produced several documents of considerable importance: the Declaration of Mexico on the Equality of Women and their Contribution to Development and Peace, 1975; and the World Plan of Action for the Implementation of the Objectives of the International Women's Year.[35] It also endorsed relevant plans of action for the various UN regional economic and social commissions. These documents constituted a blueprint for national action, supported by action at the regional and global levels, to achieve the goals of International Women's Year over a period of ten years and beyond, if necessary.

In accepting these proposals, the General Assembly (res. 3520 (XXX) of 1975) proclaimed the period 1976-1985 to be the "United Nations Decade for Women: Equality, Development and Peace." It also decided to convene a Conference at the mid-term of the Decade in order to review and evaluate the progress made in implementing these objectives. At the Conference, held in Copenhagen in July 1980, a Programme of Action for the second half of the Decade was adopted along with 48 resolutions on a wide variety of subjects—including political, social, economic and cultural issues affecting all areas of the world.[36] Among the texts approved were subjects ranging from the situation of women in southern Africa and Namibia, El Salvador, Chile, Lebanon, Bolivia, Sahrawi women and women of the Pacific; to payment of alimony, assistance to disabled women, problems of rural women, migrant women, and women refugees and displaced women. Recommendations were also set forth in resolutions with regard to family planning, elderly women, battered women and violence in the family, women living in conditions of extreme poverty, and the education of young women. The Conference, by consensus, recommended that the General Assembly in 1980 should consider the convening in 1985 of another world conference on women to review and appraise the achievements of the Decade.

The Programme of Action was based on a review and appraisal of progress made and obstacles encountered in implementing the 1975 World Plan of Action. It begins with an introduction, a historical perspective and a conceptual framework and its stated purpose is to refine and strengthen practical measures for advancing the status of women, and to ensure that women's concerns were taken into account in the formulation and implementation of the international development strategy for the Third United Nations Development Decade.

On the basis of a review of past experience the Programme draws three lessons for the future: First, measures for women which are isolated from the major priorities, strategies and sectors of development cannot result in any substantial improvement in attaining the goals of the Decade. Second, legislative and developmental action, unless accompanied by positive and concerted action to change attitudes and prejudices, cannot be fully effective. Third, "mere provision of equal rights, development services and opportunities will not, by themselves, help women to avail of them, without simultaneous special supportive measures," for example, legal aid, earmarking of benefits, information and knowledge and institutional innovation.

In its *conceptual framework*, the Programme deals with four main areas: (a) the interrelation of the situation of women and the objectives of the Decade; the relation between the existing world economic situation and world peace and security; (b) the impact of the unjust world economic relations on the role of women in development: the need for a new international economic order to reduce the gap between the labour input of women and their socio-economic returns; (c) the need to include new data and strategies concerning the participation of women in development in the Third United Nations Development Decade; and (d) the interrelation of the objectives of the Decade and the sub-theme of the World Conference—employment, health and education.

The Programme also contains sets of objectives and priority areas for the final five years of the Decade at the national, regional and international levels, as well as special sections devoted to measures of assistance for particular groups of women.

Several reporting systems have been established by the UN to monitor progress in the implementation of international instruments relating in full or in part to the status of women.[37] Since 1979 these systems have been integrated into a single system and the relevant procedures simplified in order to encourage the submission of more and better reports (G.A. res. 33/186 of 1979).

While much of the work of the UN in this field has been devoted to stimulating appropriate action at the national and regional levels, a large variety of programmes has also been established by the specialized agencies. Some of these have resulted from the emphasis attached to women's issues at international conferences held since 1975. These include the World Employment Conference (1976), the World Conference on Agrarian Reform and Rural Development (1979), and the UN Conference on Science and Technology for Development (1979). The recommendations relating to women and development which emerged from these and a number of other UN conferences held between 1975 and 1980 have been compiled in a single document (A/CONF.94/19 (1980)).

(i). Security Council

Under the original text of Article 23 of the Charter the Security Council consisted of five permanent members (China, France, the USSR, the United Kingdom and the United States) and six non-permanent members, elected by the General Assembly. By an amendment to Article 23, adopted in December 1963, and which came into force on 31 August 1965, the number of non-permanent members was increased from six to ten and the membership of the Council from eleven to fifteen. Each member of the Security Council has one vote. Decisions of the Security Council on procedural matters shall be made by an affirmative vote of nine members.

Decisions on all other matters, i.e. on matters which are not merely procedural, shall be made by an affirmative vote of nine members including the concurring votes of the permanent members (Article 27 as amended in 1963/1965). The Charter also provides that, in the matter of the settlement of disputes and in decisions concerning the reference of local disputes to regional agencies, a party to a dispute shall abstain from voting. This rule does not apply to Security Council action with respect to threats to the peace, breaches of the peace, and acts of aggression (Chapter VII of the Charter). In such matters a party to the dispute has the right to vote. In regard to the provision of Article 27 (3) that a decision on a non-procedural matter "shall be made by an affirmative vote of nine members including the concurring votes of the permanent members" it should be added that the voluntary abstention of a permanent member of the Security Council is not to be considered as having the effect of defeating the decision. The International Court of Justice stated in its Advisory Opinion on Namibia of 1971 that "the proceedings of the Security Council extending over a long period supply abundant evidence that presidential rulings and the positions taken by members of the Council, in particular its permanent members, have consistently and uniformly interpreted the practice of voluntary abstention by a permanent member as not constituting a bar to the adoption of resolutions."[38]

The Security Council, when dealing with disputes or situations likely to endanger the maintenance of international peace and security (Chapter VI), and when taking action under Chapter VII of the Charter, has repeatedly made pronouncements on questions of human rights. Some examples will be given in the paragraphs that follow.

In 1960, the Security Council had before it, for the first time, the question of race conflict in South Africa, when it considered the complaint of a number of Member States concerning "the situation arising out of the large-scale killings of unarmed and peaceful demonstrators against racial discrimination and segregation" in that country. The Council called upon South Africa to abandon its policies of *apartheid* and racial discrimination and called for arrangements that would help in upholding the purposes and principles of the Charter (Security Council res. 134 (1960)). In a resolution adopted on 7 August 1963 the Council strongly denounced the policies of South Africa in its perpetuation of racial discrimination as being inconsistent with the principles contained in the Charter and contrary to South Africa's obligations as a Member of the United Nations. It called upon the Government of South Africa to liberate all persons imprisoned, interned or subjected to other restrictions for having opposed the policy of *Apartheid* (res. 181 (1963)). In a resolution of 4 December 1963 the Council repeated its criticism and its appeal and, in addition, stressed that the discriminatory and repressive measures are in violation of the Universal Declaration of Human Rights. The Security Council also requested the Secretary-General to establish a small group of recognized experts to examine methods of resolving the situation in

South Africa through full, peaceful and orderly application of human rights and fundamental freedoms of all inhabitants regardless of race, colour and creed. (Council res. 182 (1963)). On 18 June 1964, in a resolution in which it again invoked, *inter alia*, the Universal Declaration, the Security Council endorsed the main conclusion of the Group of Experts appointed by resolution 182 (1963) that "all the people of South Africa should be brought into consultation and thus be enabled to decide the future of their country at the national level" (res. 191 (1964)). Thus the Security Council endorsed a programme for the fundamental restructuring of a Member State in order to bring its public institutions in line with the human rights provisions of the Charter. In a number of resolutions adopted throughout the 1970s, the Council reaffirmed its earlier resolutions and recognized the pursuance of their human and political rights as set forth in the Charter and in the Universal Declaration.

While the major concern of Security Council decisions on the question of *apartheid* has been human rights, its primary concern in dealing with the question of Namibia (South West Africa) has been the international status of that country. However, the Council's decisions on Namibia also contain strong human rights elements. In 1968, in noting the General Assembly's termination of South Africa's Mandate over Namibia (G.A. res. 2145 (XXI) of 1966), the Council addressed itself to a human rights matter by calling upon South Africa to discontinue an illegal trial of Namibians in a South African court and to release and repatriate the persons concerned (Council res. 245). In a 1972 resolution it strongly condemned repressive measures against African labourers in Namibia and called upon the South African government to abolish any system of labour which did not respect the provisions of the Universal Declaration of Human Rights (res. 310). It also called upon all States whose nationals and corporations are operating in Namibia to use all available means to ensure that such nationals and corporations conform in their hiring policies to the basic provisions of the Universal Declaration of Human Rights. This may be considered an instance of enforcement of the Universal Declaration by the Security Council, which treated respect for the basic provisions of the Declaration as a legal obligation of States as well as of their nationals.

In 1976, the Security Council condemned "the continued illegal occupation" of Namibia by South Africa and the latter's illegal and arbitrary application of "racially discriminatory and repressive laws and practices in Namibia" (res. 385). The Council also demanded that, pending the transfer of power to the UN so that free elections can be held, South Africa should "comply fully in spirit and in practice with the provisions of the Universal Declaration."

In 1977, the Council determined that the acquisition by South Africa of arms and related material constitutes a threat to the maintenance of international peace and security and decided that all States should cease any arms-related trade and co-operation with South Africa (res. 418). In 1979, the General Assembly repeated its previous call for the Council to impose comprehensive and mandatory sanctions against South Africa in order to ensure its compliance with UN resolutions (G.A. res. 34/92 G).

An example of strong action by the Security Council in a human rights related matter is its imposition of mandatory sanctions against the illegal minority régime in Southern Rhodesia (Zimbabwe) (Council res. 232 of 1966 and 253 of 1968). It was the first time in UN history that such sanctions had been imposed. Following the 1979 Lancaster House agreement on the resolution of the Zimbabwe issue, the Security Council called upon Member States to lift their sanctions (res. 460 of 1979).

A recent instance of Security Council action in a situation partly involving human rights questions was the adoption of a resolution calling upon Iran to immediately release the personnel of the United States Embassy who were being held in Teheran, to provide them protection and to allow them to leave the country (res. 457 of 1979).

(j). Trusteeship Council

The Trusteeship Council is a principal UN organ, set up to assist the General Assembly, under whose authority it operates, in carrying out its functions relating to the International Trusteeship System provided for in Chapter XII of the Charter. One of the basic objectives of the system is "to encourage respect for human rights and fundamental freedoms for all without distinction as to race, sex, language or religion."

Eleven Trust Territories have been administered under the system but by 1980 only one remained—that of the Trust Territory of the Pacific Islands, administered by the United States. This is administered by the Trusteeship Council, under the authority of the Security Council rather than the General Assembly, because it has been designated a strategic area in accordance with the relevant provisions of the Charter. Since termination of the final trusteeship is expected soon, the provisions of the Charter relating to the Trusteeship Council do not warrant lengthy consideration. They are now principally of historical interest.

Article 87 of the Charter provides that the General Assembly and, under its authority, the Trusteeship Council, in carrying out their functions, may: consider reports submitted by the administering authority; accept petitions and examine them in consultation with the administering authority; provide for periodic visits to the respective Trust Territories; and take these and other actions in conformity with the terms of the trusteeship agreements. The administering authority for each Trust Territory within the competence of the General Assembly is required to make an annual report to the Assembly (Art. 86). Among the basic objectives of the system, in addition to the promotion of human rights, are: the promotion of the political, economic, social, and educational advancement of the inhabitants; and the progressive development of the Trust Territories towards self-government or independence (Art. 76).

(k). Secretariat

The Secretariat is one of the principal organs of the UN and comprises the Secretary-General and such staff as the Organization requires. The Secretary-General is the UN's chief administrative officer and acts in that capacity in meetings of all UN organs. He is also required to perform whatever other functions are entrusted to him by those organs (Articles 97-101 of the Charter). Thus the human rights organs of the UN are "serviced" by the Secretariat. The primary organizational unit in this field within the Secretariat is the Division of Human Rights which, in 1974, was transferred from New York to Geneva. The Division provides secretarial services to such bodies as the Third Committee of the General Assembly, the Economic and Social Council and its Social Committee, the Commission on Human Rights and its Sub-Commission, the Committee on the Elimination of Racial Discrimination, the Human Rights Committee, and a variety of subsidiary bodies. It also: carries out research at the request of these organs; handles materials and prepares reports under procedures for monitoring the implementation of human rights established by various UN organs or included in international instruments; collects and disseminates information and prepares publications on human rights; and administers the programme of advisory services.

In the early years of the UN, the Division of Human Rights was part of the Department of Social Affairs. This was changed in 1958 and again in 1972. The Division presently reports to the UN Under Secretary-General for Political and General Assembly Affairs. The General Assembly in 1979 (res. 34/47) and the Commission on Human Rights in 1980 (res. 22 (XXXVI)) has requested the Secretary-General to consider redesignating the Division as a "Centre for Human Rights." The effect of such a change would be increased status within the Secretariat.

The Commission on the Status of Women was, until 1972, serviced by a Section within the Division of Human Rights. Since that time these duties have been performed by the Advancement of Women Branch of the Centre for Social Development and Humanitarian Affairs in the Department of Economic and Social Affairs. This branch was transferred from New York to Vienna in 1979.

Other parts of the Secretariat also contribute to the human rights work of the organization. Thus the Office of Legal Affairs is responsible for advising the Secretariat and other organs on legal questions and the Department of Political and Security Council Affairs, the Department of Political Affairs, Trusteeship and Decolonization and the Office of Public Information also perform important functions in matters which relate to human rights.

(i) THE GOOD OFFICES ROLE OF THE SECRETARY-GENERAL

It is established diplomatic practice that Heads of State and executive heads of intergovernmental organizations are entitled to intercede on humanitarian grounds with their counterparts involved in particular situations. Such inter-cession may be aimed at drawing attention to the plight of a particular indi-vidual or group and is undertaken in a spirit of mutual respect and confidentiality. It is thus to be distinguished from interference in the internal affairs of States, a practice which is prohibited under Article 2 (7) of the UN Charter. The nature of the humanitarian intercession and the extent to which a matter is pursued vary according to the circumstances of each particular case. While it is common knowledge that the UN Secretary-General uses his "good of-fices" in efforts to achieve humanitarian objectives in line with the principles of the UN Charter, reference to specific action of this nature has, until recently, been included only infrequently in resolutions or other public ac-tions of UN organs. However, in recent years, the Secretary-General has been called upon on a number of occasions to continue and intensify the good offices envisaged in the Charter of the United Nations in the field of human rights.[39] In 1979, the General Assembly also stressed the important role that the Secretary-General can play in situations of mass and flagrant violations of human rights (res. 34/175). The Commission on Human Rights has also re-quested the Secretary-General to use his good offices to ensure the full en-joyment of human rights by UN staff members (res. 31 (XXXVI)(1980)). In his report to the UN, Secretary-General Waldheim noted that, because of the nature of the problem, little or nothing can be said publicly about the efforts made in the exercise of his good offices function. "Past experience has dem-onstrated that it is best to proceed on purely humanitarian grounds, and usually with the utmost confidentiality. Not only does this approach work to the advantage of the victims, but it also avoids the political sensitivity often associated with such cases,"[40] However, as the Secretary-General observed in 1979, a cautious approach should not be allowed to degenerate into expedi-ency on so vital a matter of principle (A/34/1Add.1).

(ii) ANNUAL REPORTS OF THE SECRETARY-GENERAL ON THE WORK OF THE
	ORGANIZATION

These annual reports review developments in the various fields of UN activi-ties and regularly include a section devoted to human rights questions. In addition, an Introduction to the Report is issued, in which the Secretary-General has often expressed his views on human rights issues.

Thus in 1970, U Thant drew attention to the growing problem of torture and noted that "it is imperative for all States and groups to denounce such despicable practices" (A/8001/Add.1). The following year the Secretary-General focussed on the problem of human rights violations within the frontier of a State. He observed that "theoretically the United Nations has little standing in such situations—and they are all too common. Legally the membership of the United Nations has done an admirable job on human rights. The neces-sary texts exist. But practically where does an individual or a group of individuals find recourse against oppression within their own country?" In response he noted the importance of world public opinion and called for a determined effort to give justice a world-wide dimension (A/8441/Add.1).

Secretary-General Waldheim has drawn attention on several occasions to the problem of reconciling the principle of national sovereignty with the ideals expressed in the Universal Declaration.[41] In 1977 he stated that "the fundamental principle is that the respect for individual human dignity is based on universally accepted values and therefore abuses of human rights, wherever they may occur, are a legitimate subject for international concern." (A/32/1/Add.1).

(l). International Court of Justice

The ICJ is the principal judicial organ of the UN and its Statute forms an integral part of the UN Charter. In the present manual it is not proposed to undertake a comprehensive survey of the role and practice of the Court. In brief, only States may be parties in contentious cases before the Court but the Court may be requested by the General Assembly, the Security Council, and by other organs authorized by the Assembly, to give an advisory opinion on legal questions. Thus individuals and non-governmental organizations do not have access to the Court.

The Court has frequently been called upon to examine human rights questions, both in contentious and in advisory proceedings. In some cases the Court has had to address itself directly to the interpretation of a human rights treaty. In other cases human rights questions have arisen indirectly.

An example of the former group are the Colombian-Peruvian asylum case in 1950[42] and its sequel, the Haya de la Torre case of 1951,[43] in which the Court had to decide a dispute concerning diplomatic asylum and to interpret the Convention on the Right of Asylum signed at Havana in 1928.[44]

Between 1950 and 1971 the Court rendered four advisory opinions relating to the international status of South-West Africa (Namibia). It was also presented with a dispute relating to the same subject in contentious proceedings instituted by Ethiopia and Liberia against South Africa, in which a judgment on preliminary objections (1962) and a judgment (Second Phase 1966) were rendered. These advisory opinions and judgments contained strong human rights elements, while the actual holdings related primarily to other questions such as whether South-West Africa had remained a territory under Mandate after the dissolution of the League of Nations and whether South Africa remained bound by the obligations of a Mandatory: whether the United Nations was the successor to the League as supervising authority; whether Ethiopia and Liberia as former Members of the League of Nations had *locus standi* in regard to the fulfilment by the Mandatory of its obligations under the Mandate; and whether South Africa's Mandate had been legally and validly terminated by the General Assembly in 1966.[45] In the last of the advisory opinions, which was rendered at the request of the Security Council in 1971, the Court found that the General Assembly's conclusion that South

Africa had failed to fulfil its obligations in respect of the administration of the Mandated Territory and the termination of the Mandate were justified because, *inter alia*, through its policy of *apartheid* South Africa had committed flagrant violation of the purposes and principles of the Charter.

The advisory opinions on the Interpretation of Peace Treaties of March 1950 and (Second Phase) of July 1950[46] were requested by the General Assembly because of its continuing interest and its increased concern at the grave accusations made against Bulgaria, Hungary and Romania with regard to the observance of human rights and fundamental freedoms in these countries. (G.A.res. 294 (IV) of 22 October 1949). The questions put to the Court did not concern the substance of the human rights situation in the three countries, but primarily their obligation to appoint representatives to Commissions which, under the three Peace Treaties, were competent to decide the disputes.

The request for the advisory opinion on reservations to the Genocide Convention (1951) was directed towards receiving advice on the admissibility of certain reservations to that Convention.[47] In its opinion the Court proceeded from its finding that the principles underlying the Convention are principles which are recognized by civilized nations as binding on States even without any conventional obligation. In 1970, the Court had the opportunity to affirm, and to elaborate upon, this statement. In its judgment in the Barcelona Traction Case[48] between Belgium and Spain (Second Phase), the Court distinguished between obligations which States have *erga omnes* and obligations the performance of which is the subject of diplomatic protection. Obligations *erga omnes* derive, for example, in contemporary international law, from the outlawing of acts of aggression and of genocide, as also from the principles and rules concerning the basic rights of the human person, including protection from slavery and racial discrimination. Some of the corresponding rights of protection have entered into the body of general international law; others are conferred by international instruments of a universal or quasi-universal character.

In the advisory opinion on the effect of awards of compensation made by the UN Administrative Tribunal of 1954,[49] the International Court of Justice stated that the General Assembly had not, under the law as it then stood, the right on any grounds to refuse to give effect to an award of compensation made by the Administrative Tribunal in favour of a staff member of the United Nations whose contract of service has been terminated without his assent. The Court replied to the General Assembly's request for an opinion notwithstanding the fact that the questions submitted to it closely concerned the rights of individuals. The mere fact that it is not the rights of States which are at issue does not deprive the Court of a competence expressly conferred on it by its Statute.

In the opinion concerning judgments of the Administrative Tribunal of the ILO upon complaints made against Unesco[50] (1956), the Court upheld its

competence to entertain a request for an advisory opinion for the purpose of
reviewing judicial proceedings involving individuals.

In 1955, by resolution 957 (X) the General Assembly amended the Statute
of the United Nations Administrative Tribunal by providing that a Member
State, the Secretary-General or a person in respect of whom a judgment has
been rendered by the Tribunal, may object to the judgment on certain specified grounds by a written application addressed to a Committee of the General Assembly asking it to request an advisory opinion of the International
Court of Justice on the matter. The grounds for applying to the Committee
are that the Tribunal: has exceeded its jurisdiction or competence; has failed
to exercise jurisdiction vested in it; has erred on a question of law relating to
the provisions of the Charter; or has committed a fundamental error in procedure which has occasioned a failure of justice. The Committee is composed
of the Member States the representatives of which have served on the General Committee of the most recent regular session of the General Assembly.
If the Committee decides that there is a substantial basis for the application
it shall request an advisory opinion of the Court. When such a request has
been made, the Secretary-General shall either give effect to the opinion of
the Court, or request the Administrative Tribunal to confirm its original
judgment or give a new judgment, in conformity with the opinion of the
Court. By 1973, sixteen applications had been made to the Committee for the
review of judgments of the Tribunal, but only in regard to one had the
Committee decided that there was a substantial basis for the application and
only that one reached the Court. The Court held that it was competent to
give the opinion and that there was nothing in the system of judicial review
established by General Assembly resolution 957 (X) which is incompatible
with the general principles governing the judicial process. The Court also
decided, as in the earlier case of Unesco in 1956, not to hold a public hearing
for the purpose of receiving oral statements in order to safeguard the equality of the parties. In its Advisory Opinion of 12 July 1973,[51] the Court found
that the Administrative Tribunal had not failed to exercise the jurisdiction
vested in it and that it had not committed a fundamental error in procedure
which had occasioned a failure of justice.

In the two nuclear test cases, both involving France,[52] the International
Court of Justice held that the claims of Australia and New Zealand no longer
had any object and that the Court was therefore not called upon to give a
decision thereon. In his Separate Opinions in both cases Judge Petrén recalled, in connection with the *locus standi* of the Applicant States, previous
developments in the domain of human rights and referred, albeit with a
certain reservation, to the statement of the Court in the *Barcelona Traction
Case*, which listed violations of basic rights of the human person as creating
obligations *erga omnes* of the States concerned. Judge *ad hoc* Sir Garfield
Barwick also referred in his Dissenting Opinions to what he described as the
obiter dictum in the Barcelona Traction Case.

In December 1979, in the case concerning United States Diplomatic and Consular Staff in Teheran, the Court made an Order in which it indicated provisional measures which should be taken by the government of the Islamic Republic of Iran pending the Court's final decision in the case. The Court decided that the government of Iran had violated a number of its international legal obligations and that, *inter alia*, it should immediately secure the release of the hostages.[53]

Jurisdiction of the International Court of Justice in disputes concerning the interpretation and application of human rights conventions of the UN system.
Most but not all human rights conventions which have come into being under the auspices of the United Nations and the specialized agencies contain provisions—the specific wording differs from instrument to instrument—to the effect that any dispute between States Parties to the Convention which relates to its interpretation or application and which cannot be settled by other means shall be referred to the International Court of Justice at the request of any one of the parties to the dispute.

However, the International Covenants on Human Rights do not specifically provide for adjudication by the Court. The draft of the International Covenant on Civil and Political Rights prepared by the Commission on Human Rights in 1954 provided that the Covenant's implementing body, the Human Rights Committee should recommend to the Economic and Social Council that the Council request the Court to give an "advisory opinion on any legal questions connected with a matter of which the Committee is seized" (E/2573). This provision was deleted by the Third Committee of the General Assembly in 1966 (A/6546).

2. PROCEDURES USED AND ACTION TAKEN BY UNITED NATIONS ORGANS IN HUMAN RIGHTS MATTERS

(a). Consideration of violations and communications relating thereto
The United Nations is variously estimated to receive annually between 30,000 and 40,000 communications or complaints alleging human rights violations. In order to deal with these complaints a number of different procedures has been established. For analytical purposes a distinction may be drawn between "petition-recourse" and "petition-information" procedures both of which are briefly discussed below.[54] Petition-recourse procedures are those which require the consideration and disposal of complaints on a case by case basis. The primary objective of petition-information procedures is to facilitate the accumulation of information relating to a general situation concerning a class of persons such as "missing" persons or those living under the system of *apartheid*. But, as Tardu notes, the distinction is not at all sharp since each system may bring relief to both individuals and classes.

The following analysis does not deal with the very important communications procedures established under (a) the Optional Protocol to the International Covenant on Civil and Political Rights or (2) the Convention on the Elimination of All Forms of Racial Discrimination. Both of these are analysed in Chapter 11.

(i) EVOLUTION OF THE PROCEDURES UNDER ECOSOC RESOLUTIONS 1235 (XLII) AND 1503 (XLVIII)

When the Commission on Human Rights convened for its first regular session in January 1947, a great number of letters addressed to the United Nations or any of its organs had already been received, many of which contained complaints about the violation of human rights. On the recommendation of a Sub-Committee which it had appointed to look into the question of what to do with, or in regard to, these communications, the Commission decided upon a procedure which, as later modified in technical details, involved the compilation and distribution to members of the Commission of two lists of communications: (i) a *non-confidential* list containing a brief indication of the substance of each communication which deals with the *principles* involved in promotion of respect for and observance of human rights, and (ii) a *confidential* list containing a brief indication of the substance of *other* communications concerning human rights and furnish this list to members of the Commission in *private* meeting. The "other communications" include, of course, communications alleging that human rights have been violated. The report of the first session contained, in this context, the statement that "The Commission recognizes that it has no power to take any action in regard to any complaints concerning human rights."[55] This statement was approved by the Economic and Social Council in its resolution 75(V) of 5 August 1947 and the approval was repeated in a consolidated resolution on communications concerning human rights which the Council adopted in 1959 (Council resolution 728 F (XXVIII) of 30 July 1959).

The Commission on the Status of Women, whose constitutional status is, as shown above, the same as that of the Commission on Human Rights, refused to adopt an analogous self-denying ordinance. On the contrary, it asked that its right to make recommendations to the Council on urgent problems requiring immediate attention in defence of women's rights be strengthened and it also asked for an improvement of the rules governing communications.[56] ECOSOC decided, however, contrary to the wish of the Commission on the Status of Women that it, the Council, "recognizes that, as in the case of the Commission on Human Rights, the Commission on the Status of Women has no power to take action in regard to any complaints concerning the status of women" (res. 76 (V) of 5 August 1947). Resolution 76 (V) was later amended, as was resolution 75 (V), to provide for separate non-confidential and confidential lists (Council res. 3041 (XI) of 1950).

Criticism and attempts at reform.

The decisions taken by the Commission on Human Rights and by the Council met with widespread criticism. The two Sub-Commissions, whose members were persons serving in their individual capacity and not as government representatives, recommended amendments of Council resolution 75 (V), which would make it possible to take action in certain cases.[57] In regard to the recommendations of the Sub-Commission on Discrimination and Minorities, the Commission on Human Rights decided not to sanction any change in the procedure.[58] As far as the recommendations of the Freedom of Information Sub-Commission were concerned, the Economic and Social Council approved the proposal for the compilation twice a year of a list of communications on freedom of information, but expressly decided that this was not to apply to communications which contained criticism or complaints against Governments in the field of freedom of information (Council resolution 240 C (IX) of 28 July 1949).

Even before the two Sub-Commissions had made their unsuccessful attempts, the Secretary-General took the matter up with a view to contributing to an improvement of the arrangements. He submitted to the Commission on Human Rights a report "on the present situation with regard to communications concerning human rights" (Doc. E/CN.4/165, 2 May 1949) the principal recommendation of which was that the Commission should propose to the Council to amend its resolution 75 (V) of 1947 to the effect that, in particular cases affecting very great numbers of persons or having international repercussions, the Commission should be requested to examine the communication and the reply which might be given by the Government concerned and bring to the attention of the Council cases which, in the opinion of the Commission, merit the attention of the Council. The Commission on Human Rights took no action on these lines at the time. Arrangements of a similar character were, however, planned and enacted two decades later, as will be seen below when the procedures for the consideration of allegations of a consistent pattern of gross violations of human rights will be examined.

The "no power to take action" doctrine proclaimed by the Commission and ECOSOC was also the object of very severe scholarly criticism, particularly by Professor Hersch Lauterpacht. In his report (para. 12) the Secretary-General drew the Commission's attention to Lauterpacht's writings which had appeared by then.[59]

Between 1949 and 1959, individual Governments and groups of Governments made repeated attempts to bring about a change in the ruling that the Commission on Human Rights had no power to act on complaints of the violation of human rights. Thus, for example, at the 6th session in 1951/1952, the General Assembly invited the Council to give the Commission on Human Rights instructions with regard to communications and to request the Commission to formulate its recommendations on them (G.A. res. 542 (VI) of

1952), thus clearly indicating that it considered the then existing situation
unsatisfactory. The Council refused to pursue this directive and decided to
take no action (Council res. 441 (XIV) of 1952). The General Assembly action
had been sponsored by Egypt. On later occasions, Argentina, Belgium, Greece,
India, Israel and the Philippines, in addition to Egypt, made equally unsuccessful attempts.[60]

Repeal or modification of the "no power to act" doctrine.
The "no power to act" doctrine was bound to collapse under the impact of
the increasing force of the struggle against racial discrimination in colonial
territories and in southern Africa. It was the Special Committee on the
Situation with regard to the Implementation of the Declaration on the Granting of Independence to Colonial Countries and Peoples (the Committee of
Twenty-Four) which, in 1965, set in motion the events which led to the
breach in the "no power to act" doctrine and eventually to the new procedures set forth in Council resolution 1235 (XLII) of 1967 and 1503 (XLVIII)
of 1970 which will be described presently. The Committee of Twenty-Four
drew attention to the evidence submitted by petitioners concerning violations of human rights in certain territories in southern Africa, whereupon the
same Economic and Social Council which had consistently ruled that the
Commission on Human Rights has no power to act on violations of human
rights, invited the Commission to consider as a matter of importance and
urgency the question of the violation of human rights, including policies of
racial discrimination and segregation and of *apartheid* in all countries, with
particular reference to colonial and other dependent countries and territories, and to submit its recommendations on measures to halt those violations
(Council res 1102 (XL) of 1966). The task of devising the principles and
procedures which were to apply in the performance of this new assignment
occupied the Sub-Commission, the Commission on Human Rights, ECOSOC
and the General Assembly for the following five years (1966 to 1971). It is not
proposed to present here a complete legislative history of the texts which
were eventually adopted. Only several important stages will be mentioned.

(1) The General Assembly invited the Council and the Commission to give
urgent consideration to ways and means of improving the capacity of the
United Nations to put a stop to violations of human rights *wherever they may
occur* (G.A. res. 2144 A (XXI), para 12, of 1966), thus confirming that the
new activities should not be restricted to dependent territories and to questions of racial discrimination.

(2) The Commission decided by resolution 8 (XXIII) adopted in March
1967, to give annual consideration to the question of violations of human
rights and fundamental freedoms, including policies of racial discrimination
and segregation and of apartheid, in all countries, with particular reference
to colonial and other dependent countries and territories. It requested the
Sub-Commission to prepare, for the use of the Commission in its examination

of this question, a report containing information on violations of human rights from all available sources and to bring to the attention of the Commission any situation which it has reasonable cause to believe reveals a consistent pattern of violations of human rights and fundamental freedoms. (E/4322 (1967) para. 394).

(3) In resolution 1235 (XLII) of 6 June 1967 ECOSOC noted resolution 8 (XXIII) of the Commission on Human Rights and welcomed its decision. It proceeded to make a final break with the "no power to act" doctrine of resolution 75 (V) of 1947. It, *inter alia*, authorized the Commission and the Sub-Commission "to examine information relevant to *gross violations* of human rights and fundamental freedoms, *as exemplified* by the policy of *apartheid* as practised in...South Africa and in...South West Africa..., and to racial discrimination as practised *notably* in Southern Rhodesia, *contained in communications listed by the Secretary-General pursuant to Economic and Social Council resolution 728 F (XXVIII)...*" (emphasis added). In the same resolution, the Council decided that the Commission may, in appropriate cases, make a thorough study of situations which reveal a consistent pattern of violations of human rights as exemplified by the policies of *apartheid* and racial discrimination in Southern Africa.

(4) These decisions having been taken, the organs addressed themselves to prescribing procedures through which the Commission on Human Rights would perform the new task, particularly how and by whom the very great number of allegations constantly coming in should be screened, how and by whom those worthy of being examined should be selected, how and by whom controversial facts should be established and what the role of Governments in this enterprise should be. On the basis of a draft prepared by the Sub-Commission and the Commission and after, in 1969, the draft had been referred back to the Commission by the Council and transmitted to States Members for consideration and comment, the Council adopted resolution 1503 (XLVIII) of 27 May 1970 on the "Procedure for dealing with communications relating to violations of human rights and fundamental freedoms."

(5) In paragraph 2 of resolution 1503 the Council delegated to the Sub-Commission the task of devising appropriate procedures for dealing with the question of admissibility of communications received under Council resolution 728 F (XXVIII) and in accordance with Council resolution 1235 (XLII). In 1971, the Sub-Commission in its resolution 1 (XXIV) adopted provisional rules for dealing with the question of admissibility.

(6) Thus, the United Nations procedures for dealing with communications relating to the violation of human rights are laid down in a body of provisions which consists of resolutions 1235 (XLII) and 1503 (XLVIII) of the Economic and Social Council and of the provisional rules adopted by the Sub-Commission in resolution 1 (XXIV). Resolution 728 F (XXVIII), i.e. the revised version of resolution 75 (V), has remained in force, apart from those of its provisions which have *pro tanto* been repealed by resolutions 1235 and 1503.

(ii) STAGES OF THE PROCEDURE UNDER RESOLUTIONS 728 F, 1235 AND 1503[61]

(1) Provided that a communication is intended for the UN ("however addressed," in the words of Council res. 728 F (XXVIII)), it is eligible for consideration, irrespective of its form. Those communications which are clearly intended for submission to the Human Rights Committee under the Optional Protocol and which appear to fulfill the conditions for receivability laid down in the Protocol are not channeled into the 1503 procedure.

(2) The remaining communications are screened by a five-member Working Group on communications of the Sub-Commission on Prevention of Discrimination and Protection of Minorities. It refers to the Sub-Commission those communications which appear to reveal a consistent pattern of gross and reliably attested violations of human rights. The Sub-Commission considers these along with the replies, if any, of governments, and determines, on the basis also of all "other relevant information," which particular situations (as opposed to individual communications) it will refer to the Commission. Since 1974 the Sub-Commission has annually communicated its findings to the Commission in confidential reports containing all relevant materials.

(3) Since 1974 the practice of the Commission has been to establish its own working group to examine the materials submitted by the Sub-Commission. In 1978 it formally decided to invite the States directly concerned to address the Commission and to reply to questions put by members (Commission decision 5 (XXXIV)).

(4) Under resolution 1503 the Commission can, in relation to any situation referred to it by the Sub-Commission:

(a) decide not to act;

(b) decide to discontinue consideration under 1503 and to consider the situation under another procedure;

(c) decide to undertake a thorough study of the situation in accordance with resolution 1235 (XLII) of 1967. The making of such a study is not conditional upon the consent of the government(s) concerned or of any higher UN organ. This was done in 1979 in the case of Equatorial Guinea (res. 15 (XXXV)); or

(d) decide on an investigation by an *ad hoc* committee. This alternative is dependent on the express consent of the State concerned, requires the prior exhaustion of all domestic remedies and must not relate to a matter already being dealt with under other UN or regional procedures. The *ad hoc* committee's procedure and all actions envisaged in the implementation of the resolution in general shall be confidential. The *ad hoc* committee shall report to the Commission with its observations and suggestions and on the basis of this report the Commission may decide to make recommendations to the Council.

(5) It should be noted that resolution 1503 provides that "all actions" envisaged in its implementation "shall remain confidential until such time as the Commission may decide to make recommendations to the Economic and So-

cial Council." Thus the meetings of all relevant bodies are held in private and their records and all other documents relating thereto are confidential. A major development facilitating better public knowledge of how the procedure works occurred in 1979 when the Commission decided, in the case of Equatorial Guinea, to discontinue confidential consideration under the 1503 procedure and to make public all the relevant, previously confidential, materials.[62]

(6) Resolution 1503 is silent about the action which the Economic and Social Council might take when it receives a recommendation from the Commission on Human Rights. This question is regulated in Article 62 (1) and (2) of the United Nations Charter. Since 1948, it has been well established that the Council's authority to make recommendations under Article 62 is by no means restricted to making "general" recommendations. The Council has the power, and has repeatedly made use of it, to address recommendations to individual Members of the United Nations.[63]

(iii) RELATIONSHIP BETWEEN THIS PROCEDURE AND OTHER RESPONSES TO HUMAN
RIGHTS VIOLATIONS

Considerable debate has taken place in the Commission on the question of the relationship between the procedure under resolutions 728 F, 1235 and 1503 and the Commission's consideration of other human rights situations. While certain procedural problems have arisen[64] it is clear both from the resolutions of the General Assembly (res. 2144 (XXI) (1966)) and ECOSOC and on the basis of the consistent practice of the Commission that it has a general competence to examine questions of human rights violations. Thus, later in this chapter, consideration is given to a variety of measures which have been taken in the field of fact-finding, the preparation of studies and other areas in response to violations. The Commission determines for itself whether to consider particular situations publicly or confidentially. As long as "all action envisaged in the implementation" of the 1503 procedure remains confidential, there would seem to be no restriction on the Commission's competence to consider publicly the human rights situation in any country. To facilitate this confidentiality, the Chairman of the Commission has, in each year since 1978, prior to the Commission's public debate on violations, publicly announced the names of the countries in respect of which the Commission has taken confidential decisions. However, neither the nature of the decisions nor the information on which they are based have been disclosed. Nevertheless, it would appear that a situation in a particular country which has been dealt with under the 1503 procedure could be publicly discussed by the Commission.

One further matter which warrants consideration is the competence of the Commission to intervene on behalf of individuals. While the Commission has taken such action in regard to imprisoned Black leaders in South Africa (decision 2 (XXXIII) (1977)) and politicians detained in Chile (decision 1 (XXXII) (1976)) this has occurred in the context of situations already identified as constituting consistent patterns of gross violations of human rights. In

1980 the question was considered at length by the Commission in connection with a proposal to send a telegram to the Government of the USSR concerning the case of Mr. Andrei Sakharov who was alleged to have been "removed from his home in Moscow and confined in Gorki."[65] The Commission eventually adopted a compromise decision to defer consideration of the matter to its following session (decision 11 (XXXVI)(1980)). At the same session, the Commission adopted one resolution appealing to all Governments to encourage and support individuals to promote the effective observance of human rights (resolution 23 (XXXVI)) and another calling upon Governments to ensure the strict application of principles governing the fundamental safeguards of the individual so that no one can be prosecuted or persecuted merely because of his family or other connection with a suspected, accused or convicted person (resolution 26 (XXXVI)).

(iv) SHORTCOMINGS OF THE UNITED NATIONS PROCEDURES

Despite the complexity of these various procedures and the amount of effort and debate expended on their inevitably flawed design, a large number of criticisms may be levelled against the results they have achieved. Some indication of these was provided by the Director of the UN Division of Human Rights in his opening statement to the Commission in 1980:

"Our experience so far leads me to ask... whether some of the assumptions under which we have been working are still valid. Is it satisfactory to place so much emphasis on the consideration of situations in confidential procedures thereby shutting out the international community and oppressed peoples? Are certain procedures in danger of becoming, in effect, screens of confidentiality to prevent cases discussed thereunder from being aired in public?

While there is probably no alternative to trying to co-operate with the Governments concerned, should we allow this to result in the passage of several years while the victims continue to suffer and nothing meaningful is really done? How can we deal with governments which do not act in good faith or abuse the procedures of the Commission by pretending to co-operate while in fact violations of human rights continue to take place?

Aside from these questions relating to what we have been doing, there are questions as to what we have probably not been doing at all. How, for example, do we handle urgent situations, particularly between sessions of the Commission? The Commission plans to consider in the future the role which its Bureau could play in this area. Perhaps something meaningful may arise out of this.

How do we identify situations of violations for the attention of the Commission? Is this left too much to political convenience? Is there a case for the Commission to request annually, probably from one of its members acting as special rapporteur, a World Report on Human Rights to form the basis of its consideration of the item on violations of human rights?...

Furthermore, after the Commission has identified a situation as being one about which it should act, to what extent does it apply measured or balanced criteria in deciding upon the response to the situation? Is the decision to be taken left too much to individual governmental initiative, or is there a role for the Bureau of the Commission in weighing and measuring the response to be made?"[66]

Many of the problems thus identified have not arisen accidentally. The 1503 procedure has met and will continue to meet with opposition on the part of powerful and influential governments. Only when this opposition is countered by a preponderance of world public opinion and a determined stand by concerned governments will the ability of the UN to respond promptly, effectively and objectively to human rights violations be ensured.

(v) COMMUNICATIONS CONCERNING THE STATUS OF WOMEN

It will be recalled that the Economic and Social Council, by resolution 76 (V) of 1947, amended by resolution 304 (XI) of 1950, adopted rules for the handling of communications concerning human rights as laid down in resolution 75 (V) of 1947. When, in 1959, resolution 75 (V) was replaced by a consolidated text in resolution 728 F (XXVIII), no corresponding adjustments were made in resolution 76 (V), but the substance of the regulations applicable to the two Commissions remained the same. However, when by resolutions 1235 (XLII) and 1503 (XLVIII) fundamental changes were introduced in regard to human rights communications which appear to reveal a consistent pattern of gross and reliably attested violations of human rights and fundamental freedoms, no provision was made for the Commission on the Status of Women to be involved in the procedures. Nevertheless, as far as substance is concerned, gross violations consisting of discrimination on the grounds of sex are not outside the competence of the organs actually charged with the implementation of the procedures.[67]

Under resolution 76 (V) the Commission on the Status of Women dealt with the item "communications concerning the status of women" in a routine way: it appointed a Committee on Communications, decided that the originals of the communications in the non-confidential list should be made available to all members at their request, and received and took note of the confidential list at a closed meeting. However, in 1970 and 1972, the communications item did not appear on the Commission's agenda at all. In 1974, the Commission decided by majority vote after lengthy debate no longer to consider communications (E/5451) in view of the establishment of the 1503 procedure. However, ECOSOC withheld its endorsement of this decision and, in 1975, invited the Commission to reconsider (res. 86 (LVIII)). The latter effectively reversed its decision in 1976 (E/5909, chap. 1, draft res. X) but ECOSOC took no further action until 1980 when it requested both the Commission on Human Rights and the Commission on the Status of Women to submit their respective views on the matter to the Council in 1982 (Council res. 1980/39).

In the meantime, the Secretariat, in 1980, issued, for the first time, a comprehensive non-confidential list of all communications dealing with the status of women received by the UN as a whole (E/CN.6/CR.25). It may also be noted that the Convention on the Elimination of All Forms of Discrimination against Women, adopted by the General Assembly in 1979, contains no provisions relating to the receipt or consideration of relevant communications.

(vi) OTHER UNITED NATIONS HUMAN RIGHTS PETITION PROCEDURES

In addition to the mechanisms for the consideration of communications which have been discussed above, a wide range of UN bodies receives petitions or communications relating to specific matters. In the present context, it is proposed only to list the relevant bodies since all are considered elsewhere either in the present or the following chapter. Although the mode of response varies considerably from one to another, the mandate of each of the following bodies enables it, *inter alia*, to receive and consider relevant petitions: (1) the *Ad Hoc* Working Group of Experts on Human Rights in southern Africa; (2) the Special Committee to Investigate Israeli Practices Affecting the Human Rights of the Population of the Occupied Territories; (3) the *Ad Hoc* Working Group to inquire into the situation of human rights in Chile (terminated in 1979); (4) the Working Group on Enforced or Involuntary Disappearances; (5) the Special Committee on the Situation with regard to the Implementation of the Declaration on the Granting of Independence to Colonial Countries and Peoples; (6) the Special Committee against *Apartheid;* (7) the United Nations Council for Namibia; (8) the Security Council; and (9) the Trusteeship Council.

Two other procedures, established under ECOSOC resolutions may also be mentioned. In accordance with Council resolutions 277 (X) and 474 A (XV) communications alleging infringements of trade union rights received from Governments or trade union or employers' organizations against ILO Member States are sent to the ILO's Governing Body which in turn considers whether to refer the communication to the ILO Fact-Finding and Conciliation Commission. The second procedure, by which the UN Secretary-General transmits any information received on forced labour to the ILO Director-General, was established by Council resolution 607 (XXI) of 1956.

(b). System of periodic reports on human rights

In resolutions adopted in 1949 and 1950 (210 (VIII) and 283 (X)) the Economic and Social Council made arrangements for general reporting by States Members on the implementation of recommendations on economic and social matters (the term "social" including "human rights") but, considering the great burden this scheme placed on both Governments and the Secretariat, it was discontinued in 1952 (Council res. 450 (XIV)).

In 1950, the Commission on Human Rights requested that a system of annual human rights reports by States be established (E/1681 para. 47) but ECOSOC returned the proposal to the Commission for further study (res.303 E (XI) (1950)). In 1953 the idea, which had been proposed by France three years earlier, received the strong support of the United States delegation in the following circumstances: the Administration of President Eisenhower declared in early 1953, in a statement by Secretary of State Dulles, radically changing the policy of its predecessor, that it did not favour "formal undertakings" as the proper way to achieve throughout the world the goals of human liberty, and that it did not believe in "treaty coercion" and would therefore not become a party to any covenant on human rights or sign human rights conventions of a more limited scope.[68] As a substitute the United States delegation proposed what it called a new "programme of practical action" consisting of three series of activities: (a) periodic reporting by States; (b) studies of specific rights or groups of rights; (3) advisory services in the field of human rights. The United States representative on the Commission on Human Rights proposed therefore at the 1953 session of the Commission three draft resolutions relating to those three branches of its proposed "programme of practical action," including one on "annual reports on human rights" (E/2447 paras. 263-68).

Later in 1953 the General Assembly (res. 739 (VIII)), in asking the Commission to prepare recommendations on the subjects of the three draft resolutions, made clear that they would "supplement" and not replace the provisions of the Covenants. This was reiterated in 1956 in Commission resolution I which made it clear that a system of annual reports was a step proposed "without prejudice to the adoption and ratification of the Covenants on human rights, including the measures of implementation provided therein."

On the basis of this recommendation of the Commission, the Council established a system of period reports on human rights by its resolution 624 B (XXII) of 1 August 1956.

Considering that the purpose of the resolution would best be served by consolidating and reducing the frequency of the envisaged reports, it requested States Members of the United Nations and of the specialized agencies to transmit reports every three years. Each report was to describe developments and the progress achieved during the preceding three years in the field of human rights, and measures taken to safeguard human rights in the metropolitan area of the reporting State and in its Non-Self-Governing and Trust Territories; the report to deal with the rights enumerated in the Universal Declaration of Human Rights and with the right of peoples to self-determination.

In 1965 important changes in the reporting system as defined in 1956 were introduced. By Resolution 1074 C (XXXIX) of 28 July 1965, the Council called for submission of information within a continuing three-year cycle, scheduled as follows: (a) in the first year, on civil and political rights; (b) in the second year, on economic, social and cultural rights; and (c) in the third year, on freedom of information.

Resolution 1074 C provided for the Sub-Commission on Prevention of Discrimination and Protection of Minorities to study the materials received under the reporting procedure and to report thereon with comments and recommendations to the Commission. On the only occasion when the Sub-Commission was called upon to act in performing this new assignment, in 1967, considerable difficulties arose. A Special Rapporteur of the Sub-Commission had been requested to prepare a short study covering salient developments in human rights during the period under review. In an annex to the study he presented a restricted document, consisting of a summary of information contained in observations received from non-governmental organizations and of comments by Governments concerned. A member moved that the Annex should be destroyed and the Sub-Commission decided by 8 votes to 6, with 4 abstentions, to withdraw it.[69] The subsequent re-scheduling of the sessions of the Sub-Commission was then used to relieve it of further responsibility for reviewing the reports (Council res. 1230(XLII)(1967)).

In resolution 1074 C the Commission was also requested to establish an *ad hoc* committee having as its mandate the study and evaluation of the periodic reports and other information received under the terms of the resolution and to submit to the Commission comments, conclusions and recommendations of an objective character.

At the subsequent sessions of the Commission the *ad hoc* committee played a most important role. It usually prepared the drafts of the resolutions evaluating the reports and these were regularly adopted by the Commission. However, such evaluations have always been general in character. The *ad hoc* committee and the Commission have never dealt with concrete situations and specific problems, the measures taken to deal with them and the results obtained. However, the Commission has made some attempts to make the procedure more meaningful. Thus, for example, in 1973, (res. 24 (XXIX)) it requested Governments to indicate the limitations that they have imposed on the exercise of civil and political rights and freedoms and, in cases of emergency measures, to specify the extent to which individual freedoms can still be enjoyed, the constitutional and other safeguards which remain valid, and the legal process by which civil and political rights and freedoms will be fully restored. In the same resolution, the Commission urged Governments to place greater emphasis on difficulties encountered, for example, difficulties confronting a federal government in obtaining agreement to new legislation from federal units; difficulties arising from particular situations such as the presence within a country of ethnic, racial or religious minorities; difficulties brought about by an insurrection or threat to national security; technical legal difficulties; and difficulties encountered in the implementation or acceptance by the people of laws which have been recently enacted. In the same resolution and in another in 1974 (res. 12 (XXX)) the Commission, in evaluating the reports, drew attention to a series of favourable developments but also noted a number of areas in which problems had arisen.

In 1971 a proposal was made in the Commission to extend the reporting cycle to nine years (E/4949 paras. 291-95). Later that year ECOSOC introduced a six-year cycle (res. 1596 (L) (1971)). The consequences of this decision are that an event occurring in 1981 might conceivably not be reported upon until 1987 or even later. In practice, the system appears to have achieved very little, in part because the *ad hoc* committee has never sought to achieve a dialogue with Governments. Moreover, although the Committee met in 1977 (E/CN.4/1226) and in 1979 (E/CN.4/1304), the Commission has postponed consideration of the periodic reports at every session since 1978.[70]

The possibility exists for non-governmental organizations to participate in the reporting procedure through the submission of comments and observations of an objective character on the human rights situation designed to assist the Commission in its consideration of the reports (Council res. 888 B (XXXIV) (1962) and 1074 C (XXXIX) (1965). In the latter resolution, the Secretary-General was requested to forward for comments to the State concerned any relevant material received from NGOs. The importance of NGOs' reports was again noted in Council resolution 1596 (L) of 1971. Nevertheless very limited use would appear to have been made of this mechanism.

(c). United Nations studies in the field of human rights

(i) GENERAL

The UN Charter expressly provides for studies to be undertaken in human rights matters [articles 13 (1) (b) and 62 (1) and (2)]. Studies may be undertaken in order to obtain detailed information before taking action, to educate world opinion or, as stated by the Commission on Human Rights in 1956 when it initiated a programme of study of specific rights, to ascertain the existing conditions and the difficulties encountered in the work for the wider observance of human rights. In a number of cases studies have been specifically undertaken with a view to elaborating an international instrument such as a Declaration or Convention.

In general terms, studies have been prepared by: (1) specially appointed groups, as when a Committee of Experts serving in their personal capacities prepared a report on slavery (E/1988): (2) Special Rapporteurs of the Commission: (3) Special Rapporteurs of the Sub-Commission;[71] (4) the specialized agencies at the request of ECOSOC; and (5) the Secretary-General. In the latter case, the study is prepared within the Secretariat and issued, as requested by the organ concerned, as a report of the Secretary-General. In the case of studies by Special Rapporteurs the degree and nature of the assistance provided by the Secretariat in the preparation of the study vary considerably from one to another. In all cases, however, responsibility for the approach and contents of the report remains with the Special Rapporteur.

The sources of information used in the preparation of studies generally include: (1) Governments; (2) the Secretary-General (i.e. published UN documents and unpublished UN information); (3) the specialized agencies; (4) non-governmental organizations; and (5) writings of recognized scholars and scientists.[72]

Before taking note of some of the main studies which are currently being prepared, it is useful to trace the development of one particular study in order to obtain some indication of the approach adopted in the preparation of a major study. It illustrates the thoroughness of the process, the extent to which the commissioning body and Governments are consulted, and the delays which are often involved. Other reports may be prepared far more rapidly and with a minimum of prior consultation.

Subject to the approval of the Economic and Social Council the Commission selected, as its first subject for study, the right of everyone to be free from arbitrary arrest, detention and exile. The Economic and Social Council approved this selection by resolution 624 B (XXII), section II, of 1 August 1956. The Commission appointed a committee of 4 of its own members to prepare the study. It submitted a preliminary report to the Commission's thirteenth session (1957) and progress reports to the 14th to 16th sessions (1958, 1959, 1960). It presented a substantive report to the 19th session (1961), when the Commission decided to transmit it to Governments for comments and asked the four-member committee to revise it in the light of comments and also to include in its revised report draft principles on the right of everyone to be free from arbitrary arrest, detention and exile.[73] The revised report was submitted in 1962. It was published in printed form in 1964.[74] In preparing the report the Committee prepared a monograph on each country. It forwarded the drafts of the country monographs to the Governments concerned for checking, verification and comment and revised them in the light of the observations received. Where no observations were received this was indicated. Part I of the study deals with fundamental principles; part II with arrest and detention of persons suspected or accused of a criminal offence; part III with detention on grounds unconnected with criminal law, e.g. detention of narcotic addicts and alcoholics; part IV with arrest and detention in emergency and exceptional situations; and part V with exile. Part VI contains the draft principles on freedom from arbitrary arrest.

The most immediate result of the study was a decision in 1961 by the Commission to request the Committee to prepare a separate study of the right of arrested persons to communicate with those whom it is necessary to consult in order to assure their defence or to protect their essential interests. The study was completed in 1969 (E/CN.4/996). Although the draft principles attached to the first study were circulated to Governments for comments and the subject placed on the agenda for most of the intervening years, it was not until 1977 (Commission resolution 8 (XXXIII)) that the Sub-Commission was requested to prepare a Draft Body of Principles for the Protection of all Persons under Any Form of Detention or Imprisonment. These were adopted by it in 1978 and circulated to Governments for comments in 1979 (A/34/146).

(ii) STUDIES IN PROGRESS AT PRESENT

All of the major studies which had been completed as of January 1981 are listed in the Bibliography of this book (see section 1 (B) (1)). At that time the following studies of the Sub-Commission were in progress:

(1) Study of the problem of discrimination against indigenous populations, by Mr. José R. Martinez Cobo (Ecuador), ECOSOC resolution 1589 (L) (1971).
(2) Study on the implication for human rights of states of siege and emergency, by Mrs. Nicole Questiaux (France), Sub-Commission resolution 10 (XXX) (1977) and 5 D (1978) and ECOSOC resolution 1979/34.
(3) Extension and updating of the Report on Slavery (UN Sales No. 67.XIV.2), by Mr. Benjamin Whitaker (UK), ECOSOC decision 1980/123.
(4) Study of the independence and impartiality of judiciary, jurors and assessors and the independence of lawyers to the end that there shall be no discrimination in the administration of justice and that human rights and fundamental freedoms may be maintained and safeguarded, by Mr. L.M. Singhvi (India), ECOSOC decision 1980/24.
(5) Study of the exploitation of child labour, taking into account all the economic, social, cultural and psychological dimensions of the problem, by Mr. Abdelwahab Bouhdiba (Tunisia), ECOSOC decision 1980/125.
(6) Study of the new international economic order and the promotion of human rights, by Mr. Raúl Ferrero (Peru), ECOSOC decision 1980/126.
(7) Study of the discriminatory treatment of members of racial, ethnic, religious or linguistic groups at the various levels in the administration of criminal justice proceedings, such as police, military, administrative and judicial investigations, arrest, detention, trial and execution of sentences, including the ideologies or beliefs which contribute or lead to racism, by Mr. Abu Sayeed Chowdhury (Bangladesh), ECOSOC resolution 1980/28.
(8) Study of relevant guidelines on the uses of electronics which may affect the rights of the person and the limits which should be placed on such uses in a democratic society, by a member of the Sub-Commission to be designated by the Sub-Commission's chairman, Sub-Commission resolution 12 (XXXIII) (1980)).

Note should also be taken of the following proposed studies:
(1) The Sub-Commission has requested the Secretary-General to undertake, together with the ILO, an in-depth world-wide study of debt bondage, taking into account all the relevant economic, social and legal aspects and the interconnections with other slavery-like practices (resolution 6 B (XXXI) (1978)).
(2) In 1980 ECOSOC authorized the Sub-Commission to designate a special rapporteur from among its members to carry out a study on political, economic, cultural and other factors underlying situations leading to racism, including a survey of the increase or decline of all forms of racism and racial discrimination (res. 1980/28). The question was considered by the Sub-Commission in 1981.
(3) The Commission has requested the Sub-Commission to prepare a study on ways and means of ensuring the implementation of the United Nations resolutions on *apartheid*, racism and racial discrimination and submit it to the Commission in 1982 (Commission res. 14 D (XXXVI)).

The above list of studies presently in the Sub-Commission's 'pipeline' indicates that there has been a proliferation of requests for studies and that the subjects considered range over a broad spectrum of human rights concern. It is of interest to note that the Director of the UN Division of Human Rights, in his opening address to the 1980 session of the Sub-Commission, queried "whether the Sub-Commission is deriving full benefits from the multiplicity of studies which it has undertaken." He emphasized the need to seek ways and means of drawing the attention of the international community to studies, to consider appropriate follow-up action and to make cross-sectoral analysis of the findings of studies.[75]

(iii) STUDIES OF THE COMMISSION ON THE STATUS OF WOMEN

Since its establishment the Commission on the Status of Women has been engaged in the collection of information of a legal, economic and social character as a basis for its recommendations and for the preparation and drafting of international instruments. In the present context it is not proposed to undertake a comprehensive review of all the studies prepared for the Commission. Rather, note will be taken of some of the more significant studies prepared in recent years, with particular emphasis on those which were presented to the World Conference of the United Nations Decade for Women: Equality, Development and Peace held in 1980. While some of these studies emanated from the Commission on the Status of Women, others did not.

- Study of the interrelationship of the status of women and family planning, by Mrs. H. Sipila (E/CN.6/575 and Add.1-3 (1974)):
- Report on the status of the unmarried mother: law and practice (E/CN.6/540 (1970)):
- Review and evaluation of progress made and obstacles encountered at the national level in attaining the objectives of the World Plan of Action (A/CONF.94/30); cf. also (A/CONF.94/8-13);
- Women in rural areas (A/CONF.94/28);
- Technological change and women workers: the development of microelectronics (A/CONF.94/26);
- Information and communication as a development resource for the advancement of women (A/CONF.94/27);
- The effects of science and technology on the employment of women (A/CONF.94/29);
- Report of a seminar on women and the media (A/CONF.94/BP.10);
- Report of the Special Rapporteur on the influence of the mass communications media on attitudes towards the roles of women and men in present-day society (E/CN.6/627 (1980));
- Seminar on traditional practices affecting the health of women and children (A/CONF.94/BP.9);
- Status and role of women in education and in the economic and social fields (A/34/577 and Add.1);

- Review and evaluation of global and regional programmes of the United Nations system, 1975-1980 (A/CONF.94/31);
- Effective mobilization of women in development (A/35/82).

(d). Advisory services in human rights

The programme of advisory services in human rights was the third component of the "programme of practical action" initiated by the Commission on Human Rights in 1953. In that year the General Assembly authorized the Secretary-General to provide advisory services in promoting and safeguarding the rights of women (res. 729 (VIII)) and in the eradication of discrimination and the protection of minorities (res. 730 (VIII)). In 1954, the promotion of freedom of information was added to this list (res. 839 (IX)). In response to a resolution by the Commission on "Human Rights Technical Assistance" (res. VII (XI) (1955)) and a recommendation by ECOSOC (res. 586 E (XX) (1955), the General Assembly decided in 1955 (res. 926 (X)) to consolidate these existing programmes, along with the measures proposed by the Commission, into a programme of "advisory services in the field of human rights." The latter term was adopted on the grounds that use of the term "technical assistance" might have deterred Governments from making use of the programme. Governments were unlikely to seek outside assistance in a matter like human rights because to do so might be interpreted as an admission of weakness. The term "advisory services," on the other hand, would suggest to Governments that when they invited a seminar to be held on their territory this was a sign of strength rather than of weakness, an invitation to learn from their successes in regard to the problem to which the seminar was to be devoted.

Under the advisory services programme the Secretary-General is authorized, subject to the directions of ECOSOC, to make provision, at the request of Governments, for the following forms of assistance: (a) advisory services of experts; (b) fellowships and scholarships; (c) seminars.

(i) HUMAN RIGHTS SEMINARS

The seminars provided for in the programme of advisory services in human rights are by far the most important part of it. The participants, who are nominated by Governments and confirmed by the Secretary-General, attend in their personal capacity. It is required that they are well-qualified in their respective fields. They have included cabinet ministers, attorneys-general, solicitors-general, judges of high courts, senior government officials, newspapers publishers, editors and writers, and many others. There would seem, however, to have been an increase in recent years in the proportion of participants holding diplomatic or other government posts and a concomitant reduction in the number of independent expert participants. The seminar discussions are documented by background papers prepared by expert consultants and documentation prepared by the Secretariat. Each participant is expected to submit a paper outlining the relevant situation and developments in his own country, so that the seminar can proceed to discuss and compare experiences. The seminar reports, which appear in the series ST/TAO/HR/—, and beginning in 1978 in the series ST/HR/SER.A/—, summarize the discussions and any conclusions which may have been reached by consensus. In general, it can be said that the "seminars" are, in fact, international or regional conferences of persons nominated by their Governments, though not formally representing them. As of January 1982, 60 such seminars have been held; some of them have been "regional" seminars, others "interregional" or "international" seminars. Seminars have been held in all parts of the world; none have been held at UN Headquarters in New York.

(ii) SERVICES OF EXPERTS

Only a few Governments have availed themselves of the expert services provided for under the programme. Two Governments received advice concerning elections, electoral laws, procedures and techniques. Others asked for assistance in questions relating to the status of women. In 1980 the Secretary-General informed the Commission that a further inquiry had recently been received from an unspecified Government concerning the availability of expert services.

Although apparently not envisaged as a part of the advisory services programme, it is relevant to note in the present context that at its 1980 session the Sub-Commission (Resolution 3 (XXXIII)) recommended to the Commission on Human Rights that it make recommendations to the Economic and Social Council: (i) to consider the proposal for setting up a Human Rights Assistance Fund to help countries to achieve at least minimum standards of human rights laid down in the international instruments on human rights in a practical and purposeful manner on an urgent basis (ii) to assist in the introduction of human rights education and, if practicable, of Human Rights Centres in all schools, colleges and universities in all the countries of the world; and (iii) to request all Member States of the United Nations to translate important United Nations Conventions, Declarations and Principles relating to Human Rights in their respective languages spoken and used by minorities and other ethnic, cultural and linguistic groups in so far as it may be practicable. Such a fund would, if established, be a major breakthrough in the context of positive, practical measures taken by the United Nations for the promotion of human rights.

(iii) FELLOWSHIPS

Under the terms of General Assembly resolution 926 (X), human rights fellowships are available to qualified candidates nominated by Member States who are planning to study any subject in the field of human rights which is of concern to the United Nations (as defined in relevant United Nations Covenants, Declarations and Resolutions) provided that the subject is not one that falls within the scope of other existing technical assistance programmes or one for which adequate advisory assistance is available through a specialized agency. In the selection of candidates, preference is given to persons having direct responsibilities in the field of the implementation of human rights in their respective countries.

The number of fellowships granted each year depends on the financial resources available, which, in most years, have not been great. The number was 21 in 1962 but reached a high of 63 in the 1960s. By 1979, the number had fallen to 25. Of these, recipients included government officials with responsibility for the administration of justice and for drafting legislation as well as officials of ministries of justice, education, foreign affairs and interior and of the police departments (E/CN.4/1377 (1980)).

Mention should also be made of pilot projects in which fellowships have been used for groups rather than individual training. Some regional training courses have also been held and another is planned for 1981 (ECOSOC resolution 1978/14).

(e). Public information activities

Action taken by the Commission in recent years has reflected a growing awareness of the central role of grass-roots efforts to promote and protect human rights. Thus in addition to emphasizing the importance of establishing national and local human rights institutions,[76] the Commission has sought to foster greater knowledge and awareness by the peoples of the world of their human rights. Thus in 1979 and 1980 it urged all Governments to consider action to facilitate publicity regarding United Nations human rights activities and it requested the Secretary-General, in co-operation with Unesco and ILO, to draw up and implement a world-wide programme for the dissemination of international human rights instruments in as many languages as possible.[77]

(f). The struggle against racial discrimination and apartheid

The preceding survey of the activities of United Nations organs has shown that very many of them have been engaged and continue to be engaged in action aimed at the elimination of racial discrimination and *apartheid*. We have seen that the General Assembly, in plenary meetings and in its relevant Main Committees, has for many years devoted a large part of its work, energy and time to this task. One of its permanent subsidiary organs, the Special Committee against *Apartheid*, deals exclusively with this problem and another, the Committee of Twenty-five, has constantly taken action on racial discrimination in dependent territories. Energetic action in this field by the Security Council in regard to South Africa, Namibia and the former Portuguese-dominated Territories in Africa has been taken. Prior to its independence in 1980, the question of Zimbabwe (Southern Rhodesia) had been on the agenda of the Security Council since 1975 and action under Chapter

VII of the Charter was taken. The Economic and Social Council and the Commission on Human Rights have been active on the anti-*apartheid* front for many years. The Sub-Commission on Prevention of Discrimination and Protection of Minorities is by definition an organ called upon to aim at the elimination of apartheid and racial discrimination. Also other functional commissions, the Commission on the Status of Women and the Commission for Social Development, have partaken of this work within their respective fields. While the task of the Trusteeship Council is almost completed because most of the Trust Territories are now independent or parts of independent States, it remains interested in action against racial discrimination.

The present section will be restricted to describing briefly some of the specific arrangements which have been made by some of these organs in this field. Such a review is particularly useful in that it provides an overview of the type of activities undertaken by the UN in response to a particularly pressing problem. Moreover, many of the techniques which have been thus developed have subsequently been applied in other situations of human rights violations not involving racial discrimination. Thus in some respects the struggle against racial discrimination and *apartheid* has acted as a testing ground on which to experiment with measures designed both to promote and protect human rights and which might later be adapted for use in other situations. The review focuses both on bodies which have been established and on the techniques which have been applied. It does not, however, go over the ground covered earlier relating to the drafting and adoption of international instruments, which has also been a technique of major importance. Some indication of the scope, number and variety of resolutions adopted by organs of the UN may be gained from the list of resolutions adopted by the General Assembly in 1979 relating to the policies of *apartheid* which is contained in the following section dealing with the Special Committee against *Apartheid*.

(i) THE SPECIAL COMMITTEE AGAINST APARTHEID

The background to the establishment of the Special Committee in 1962 has been described earlier. Its mandate has been expanded and elaborated upon by later decisions of the General Assembly, most of which were adopted on the recommendation of the Committee. Thus the Special Committee has been authorized to receive and consider petitions; to consult specialized agencies, regional organizations, States and non-governmental organizations; to take additional steps to promote assistance to the national movement of the oppressed people of South Africa against the policies of *apartheid*, in consultation with the Organization of African Unity; constantly to review all aspects of the policies of *apartheid*, including legislative, administrative and other racially discriminatory measures and efforts of South Africa to extend its inhuman policies of *apartheid* beyond the borders of South Africa; to promote maximum participation by trade unions at the national and international level in action against *apartheid* in South Africa; to undertake studies concerning the economic and other interests impeding decolonization and the eradication of *apartheid* in southern Africa; to organize seminars, etc. from Headquarters, including a special session in various European capitals in 1974, and to organize a seminar to consider the present situation in South Africa and the means for promoting public action against *apartheid*.[78]

The substance of the work done by the Special Committee on *Apartheid* is best described in its annual reports to the General Assembly (A/35/22 (1980)). In the present context it is sufficient to say that the General Assembly has condemned the policies of *apartheid* as a crime against humanity and as a crime against the conscience and dignity of mankind; and that it has recommended various forms of sanctions against South Africa and repeatedly appealed to the Security Council to apply Chapter VII of the Charter against South Africa.

Thus for example in 1979 the General Assembly adopted resolutions 34/93 A-R dealing with: A. Situation in South Africa; B. United Nations Trust Fund for South Africa; C. International Conference on Sanctions against South Africa; D. Arms embargo against South Africa; E. Nuclear collaboration with South Africa; F. Oil embargo against South Africa; G. Bantustans; H. Political prisoners in South Africa; I. Assistance to the oppressed people of South Africa and their national liberation movement; J. Dissemination of information on *apartheid*; K. Women and children under *apartheid*; L. Role of the mass media in international action against *apartheid*; M. Role of non-governmental organizations in international action against *apartheid*; N. *Apartheid* in sports; O. Declaration on South Africa; P. Relations between Israel and South Africa; Q. Investments in South Africa; R. Programme of work of the Special Committee against *Apartheid*.

(ii) THE AD HOC WORKING GROUP OF EXPERTS

In 1967, the Commission on Human Rights considered a letter from the Acting Chairman of the Special Committee on Apartheid stating that evidence of the continuing ill-treatment of prisoners, detainees and persons in police custody in South Africa was (still) being received, and expressing the Special Committee's hope that the Commission will take steps to secure an international investigation with a view to ameliorating the conditions of the victims. In response the Commission decided to establish, in accordance with ECOSOC res. 9(II)(1946), an *Ad Hoc* Working Group of Experts composed of eminent jurists and prison officials to investigate the charges of torture and ill-treatment of prisoners, detainees or persons in police custody in South Africa.[79] Council resolution 9 (II), on which the Commission based its action, is the second of the two resolutions of 1946 establishing the Commission on Human Rights and defining its functions. One of its provisions is to the effect that the Commission is authorized to call in *ad hoc* working groups of non-governmental experts in specialized fields or individual experts, without further reference to the Council, but with the approval of the President of the

Council and the Secretary-General. The proposition that council resolution 9 (II) was a sound legal basis for the establishment of the *Ad Hoc* Working Group of Experts was doubted by some, particularly as the "non-governmental experts" appointed to constitute the group were members of the Commission, i.e. government representatives. The question became moot very soon after the 1967 session of the Commission, when the Economic and Social Council welcomed the decisions of the Commission set out in its resolution 2 (XXIII) and condemned the Government of South Africa for refusing to co-operate with the United Nations in expediting the work of the *Ad Hoc* Working Group (Council resolution 1236 (XLII) of 6 June 1967). The Council also referred to the *Ad Hoc* Working Group allegations of the infringement of trade union rights in South Africa made by the World Federation of Trade Unions and transmitted to the United Nations by the International Labour Office, because South Africa had ceased to be a Member of the ILO. (Council res. 1216 (XLII)(1967). The Ad Hoc Working Group was requested to report to the Council on its findings on the trade union rights complaint.

Since then the Ad Hoc Working Group has been very active in both lines of its work, and has submitted comprehensive reports on its findings which have led to action by the higher bodies, including the General Assembly. In 1968, the Commission (res.2 (XXIV)) enlarged the mandate of the group to cover South West Africa, Southern Rhodesia, Mozambique, Angola and other Portuguese territories in Africa. Resolution 5 (XXIV) of the Commission led to the adoption of General Assembly resolution 2440 (XXIII)(1968) which condemned the practice of torture, inhuman and degrading treatment of detainees and prisoners and called upon the Government of South Africa to take certain defined steps to remedy the situation. In 1969, the mandate of the Working Group was further enlarged. It was requested, *inter alia*, to make an inquiry into the question of capital punishment in southern Africa (Commission res. 21 (XXV)). In 1969, on the basis of the group's report, the General Assembly (res. 2547 A (XXIV)) requested the Secretary-General to establish, maintain and publicize an up-to-date register of persons subjected to imprisonment, detention, banishment and other restrictions, and of persons who have been victims of brutality for their opposition to *apartheid* and racial discrimination.

In 1972, the Working Group submitted a study to the Commission on the question of *apartheid* from the point of view of international penal law (E/CN.4/1075). Since that time the Working Group has submitted a variety of reports to the Commission on different aspects of the situation in southern Africa. Thus in 1980 the Commission considered a special report of the Group on certain cases of torture and murder of detainees in South Africa (E/CN.4/1366) and a progress report on a study on the action taken to implement the recommendation made by the Working Group since its establishment (E/CN.4/1365). In accordance with a resolution of the General Assembly (34/24 of 1979) one of the Group's activities in 1980 was the preparation of a study on ways and means of implementing international instruments such as the International Convention on the Suppression and Punishment of the Crime of *Apartheid*. Its other activities in 1980 included: the continuation of its inquiries relating to persons suspected of having been guilty in Namibia of the crime of *apartheid* or of a serious violation of human rights; and the continuation of its study of the policies and practices which violate human rights in southern Africa (Commission res. 9 (XXXVI) (1980)). In the latter connection the Group was requested to bring immediately to the attention of the Commission's Chairman any particularly serious violations of which it learns during its study, "so that he may take whatever action he deems appropriate."[80] It is also of interest to note, in relation to the methods used by the UN to fight against *apartheid*, that in 1980 the Commission requested the Secretary-General to prepare a one-page summary of the findings of the Group and to publish it in the world's leading newspapers, together with the Commission's condemnation of the violations of human rights in South Africa (res. 9 (XXXVI)).

(iii) SPECIAL RAPPORTEURS

Both the Commission and the Sub-Commission have made use of the technique of appointing Special Rapporteurs to study particular issues relating to the struggle against racial discrimination and *apartheid*. Thus in 1967 the Commission appointed Mr. M. Ganji (Iran) to survey past UN action in its efforts to eliminate the policies and practices of *apartheid*, to study the relevant legislation and practice and to report and make recommendations on measures which might be taken by the General Assembly (res. 7 (XXIII)). In 1968, the Assembly (res. 2439 (XXIII)) endorsed the Special Rapporteur's recommendations (contained in E/CN.4/949 and Add.) that the Government of South Africa, in order to conform with its obligations under the UN Charter should undertake to repeal, amend and replace certain specified discriminatory laws. Recommendations contained in the Special Rapporteur's second report (E/CN.4/979 and Add. (1969)) were also endorsed by the Assembly (res. 2547 B (XXIV) (1969)). The mandate of the Special Rapporteur was terminated by the Commission in 1970.

In 1974 the Sub-Commission (res. 2 (XXVII)) with the prior authorization of ECOSOC (res. 1864 (LVI)) appointed Mr. A. Khalifa (Egypt) as Special Rapporteur to study the adverse consequences for the enjoyment of human rights of political, military, economic and other forms of assistance given to colonial and racist régimes in southern Africa. The resulting report[81] thoroughly documents the extent of foreign trade and assistance with the countries concerned and notes the network of repression by which the policy of *apartheid* is enforced. The report notes that "far from exerting leverage for changed policies, foreign funds are building up South Africa's economy so that it will be better able to resist any challenges to *apartheid* from the international community" and concludes that "a mandatory arms embargo, a complete withdrawal of economic interests and the severing of economic relationships are the minimum pressures required to bring about drastic change."

Other studies by Special Rapporteurs currently in progress, and which have been listed above, are also relevant in the present context.

(iv) THE GROUP OF THREE

The International Convention on the Suppression and Punishment of the Crime of Apartheid provides for the appointment by the Chairman of the Commission on Human Rights of a group of three members of the Commission, who are also representatives of States Parties to the Convention, to consider the reports of states under the Convention. The work of this group is analyzed in Chapter 11.

(v) SPECIAL YEARS AND THE DECADE FOR ACTION TO COMBAT RACISM
    AND RACIAL DISCRIMINATION

At the suggestion of the International Conference on Human Rights in 1968[82] the General Assembly (res. 2544 (XXIV) (1969)) designated 1971 as International Year for Action to Combat Racism and Racial Discrimination.[83] In 1972, (res. 2919 (XXVII)) the Assembly launched a Decade under the same title to begin in 1973, on the 25th anniversary of the Universal Declaration of Human Rights. The goals of the programme for the Decade (contained in GA res. 3057 (XXVIII) (1973)) are: to promote human rights and fundamental freedoms for all; to arrest any expansion of racist policies, to counteract the emergence of alliances based on mutual espousal of racism and racial discrimination; to resist any policy and practices which lead to the strengthening of the racist regimes and contribute to the sustainment of racism and racial discrimination; to identify, isolate and dispel the fallacious and mythical beliefs, policies and practices that contribute to racism and racial discrimination and to put an end to racist regimes.

The Programme adopted in 1973 also recommended a range of measures to be taken at both the national and international levels and provided for the holding, in 1978, of a World Conference to Combat Racism and Racial Discrimination. In addition to a Declaration and Programme of Action the Conference also adopted a number of resolutions.[84] The Declaration states that "any doctrine of racial superiority is scientifically false, morally condemnable, socially unjust and dangerous, and has no justification whatsoever" and declares that the elimination of racial discrimination is "an imperative norm of the international community." The Declaration deals not only with southern Africa but also with: the question of Palestine; the role of national, ethnic and other minorities; the rights of indigenous peoples, immigrants and migrant workers; and the special problems for women and children which flow from discriminatory practices. In the Programme of Action the Conference dealt with measures to be taken at the national, regional and international levels and measures for support to victims of racism, racial discrimination and *apartheid*. At the national level the Conference called upon all Governments to ensure that legislative, judicial, administrative and other measures are adopted to prohibit in their respective countries any manifestations of racism and racial discrimination, regardless of whether or not discriminatory practices prevail. The Declaration and the Programme of Action were subsequently approved by the General Assembly (res. 33/99 (1978)).

In 1979, the Assembly adopted a four year programme of activities for the latter part of the Decade (res. 34/24). These activities include, for example, the holding of a seminar in 1981 to study the formulation of effective measures to prevent transnational corporations and other established interests from collaborating with the racist régimes in southern Africa, and the preparation by the Sub-Commission of a study on ways and means of ensuring the implementation of the UN resolutions on *apartheid*, racism and racial discrimination (see Commission res. 14 (XXXVI)). It has been suggested that a second world conference be held in 1983.

It should also be noted that in 1977 the General Assembly proclaimed the year beginning on March 21, 1978 to be International Anti-*Apartheid* Year and endorsed a programme of activities for the year (res. 32/105 B).

(vi) PREPARATION OF LISTS OF ENTITIES

As a follow-up to the Khalifa study referred to above, the Sub-Commission invited the Special Rapporteur to prepare the necessary material for a provisional general list identifying those individuals, institutions including banks and other organizations or groups, as well as representatives of States, whose activities constituted political, military, economic or other forms of assistance to the colonial and racist régimes in southern Africa (Commission res. 7 (XXXIII) and Sub-Commission res. 1 (XXX) (1977)). The revised list was submitted to the General Assembly in 1980 and the Special Rapporteur was requested to continue to update the list each year.[85]

(vii) SEMINARS

As noted above, and in the bibliography, a number of seminars has been held on subjects relating to racism, racial discrimination and *apartheid*. These include: a symposium on the exploitation of Blacks in South Africa and Namibia and on prison conditions in South African jails; a European regional seminar on recourse procedures available to victims of racial discrimination; a round-table on the teaching of problems of racial discrimination; and a seminar on political, economic, cultural and other factors underlying situations leading to racism. In addition to these seminars, which were organized by the UN Division of Human Rights, a variety of other meetings have taken place within the UN system on issues such as women under *apartheid*[86] and South Africa after *apartheid*: dismantling the structure and heritage of racism.[87]

(viii) STUDIES

Many of the studies undertaken in this area have been referred to earlier in this chapter. In the present context only two will be noted. The proposal to undertake the first of these has not yet been endorsed by the General Assembly. It involved a recommendation by ECOSOC that the Assembly should arrange for a study to be made of the South African Government's legitimacy, in view of its policy of *apartheid* and in particular its systematic refusal to apply the principles of the Charter of the United Nations, of international law and of the Declaration on Principles of International Law concerning Friendly Relations and Co-operation among States in accordance with the Charter of the United Nations, and then to draw from that study all appropriate conclusions of law and of fact (ECOSOC decision 1979/33). Such a study would be a path-breaking exercise with considerable potential significance for the international law of human rights.

The second study which may be noted is one prepared by the Secretary-General on "*apartheid* and colonialism as collective forms of slavery" (E/CN.4/Sub.2/449 (1980)). The study concludes, on the basis of relevant international instruments and decisions, that the international community has recognized that the *apartheid* system in South Africa is not simply a racial discrimination problem to be solved through education and political and social reforms. "Rather, it has been increasingly understood that the essence of *apartheid* lies in the dispossession of the black population through the imposition of quasi-colonial rule, and in the harnessing of the labour of the vanquished indigenous people through a variety of coercive measures for the profit of white investors, both South African and foreign. The international community has therefore described the *apartheid* system as a slavery-like practice imposed on an entire collectivity, which can be eradicated only through a complete restructuring of the existing political and economic relationships."

(ix) SPECIAL FUNDS

In addition to the funds provided by the specialized agencies such as Unesco, ILO, WHO and FAO and by UN organs such as UNICEF and UNDP, the UN has established two trust funds to provide relief and assistance to victims of *apartheid* and racial discrimination in southern Africa: the UN Trust Fund for South Africa (A/34/661) and the UN Trust Fund for Namibia (A/35/24).

(g). United Nations practice in fact-finding in human rights matters

The term "fact-finding" is a technical one used to describe efforts undertaken to ascertain the situation of human rights either in regard to a particular country (as in the reports on South Africa discussed above) or in regard to a particular problem (as in the case of "disappeared" persons). The objective of the process is not primarily to document the extent and nature of human rights violations which have occurred but to encourage and facilitate the restoration of respect for human rights. While the number of United Nations fact-finding exercises has grown considerably in recent years it must be emphasized that the practice adopted in each case is generally carefully tailored to the particular circumstances. As a result only a limited number of useful generalizations can be made as to the practice which has been adopted.[88]

In addition to fact-finding exercises which have been conducted within the framework of the confidential 1503 procedures described above (most of the details of which are not publicly known), United Nations fact-finding missions have visited South Vietnam, in 1973 (A/5630); Quinetra in 1976 and 1977; Chile in 1978 (A/ 33/331); Equatorial Guinea in 1979 and 1980 (E/CN.4/1371) and the Islamic Republic of Iran (1980). Other exercises which have been undertaken have concerned the occupied territories in the Middle East,[89] Chile,[90] Democratic Kampuchea,[91] Guatemala,[92] Nicaragua,[93] Portuguese Mozambique, South Africa and Bolivia,[94] and the general question of missing or disappeared persons. The practice of the various United Nations organs indicates that a fact-finding exercise may be initiated with respect to any situation involving a consistent pattern of gross violations of human rights. This formula which uses the wording of ECOSOC resolution 1503 (XLVIII) is not susceptible to precise definition and in practice has been interpreted increasingly liberally.

As well as gathering information over a period of time United Nations fact-finding bodies have in different cases been empowered to take urgent measures for the protection of victims. These include: the use of the good offices role of the Secretary-General or the Chairman of the Commission on Human Rights (for example, Commission resolution 9 (XXXVI) (1980)); the making of direct representations to the Government concerned; the establishment of direct contacts by the Secretary-General (e.g. Commission resolution 30 (XXXVI) (1980)); the despatch of telegrams to relevant Governments (Commission decision 12 (XXXV) (1979)). A fact-finding body may also receive a broader mandate, as in the case of the Working Group on missing and disappeared persons established by the Commission in 1980 (resolution 20 (XXXVI)) which was invited "in establishing its working methods, to bear in mind the need to be able to respond effectively to information that comes before it and to carry out its work with discretion." Accordingly, during 1980 the Group took action in response to urgent reports of enforced or involuntary disappearances "in cases where immediate action was warranted to save lives."[95]

At its 1980 session, the Sub-Commission adopted several important resolutions relating to fact-finding. The most significant of them would, if approved by the Commission, enable the Sub-Commission's Chairman, in consultation with its Vice-Chairmen and Rapporteur and the Secretary-General, and with the consent of the governmental authorities concerned, to arrange for one or more Sub-Commission members "to visit, with a view to examining first-hand, and reporting to the Sub-Commission at its thirty-fourth (1981) session, upon the human rights problems in any countries which were the subject of discussions at the Sub-Commission's thirty-third session, together with any other human rights problems of comparable magnitude which may come to the attention of such member or members during their examination" (resolution 22 (XXXIII)). In another resolution the Sub-Commission recognized the need to have at its disposal adequate information reflecting the situation in different countries and systems and recommends the creation of an information gathering service within the United Nations Division of Human Rights (resolution 19 (XXXIII) (1980)). At present no such general service is available anywhere within the United Nations system.

In general terms then it can be seen that as the use of fact-finding procedures has expanded in recent years so too has the diversity of approaches adopted by United Nations organs. Proposals to create an intersessional role for the Bureau of the Commission would, if adopted, add significantly to the flexibility, timeliness and perhaps effectiveness of procedures in this area.[96]

Conclusion

The foregoing survey has focused primarily on the organs established and the procedures adopted by the United Nations in the field of human rights. Policy approaches have not been directly surveyed, although they are in fact the prime determinants of both procedures and practice. Nevertheless, it would be remiss to neglect to note the fundamental change in direction which is discernible in United Nations human rights policies at least since 1977. In adopting a structural approach to human rights issues, the United Nations has attached much greater weight than before to the various forms of structural interdependence which determine the extent to which human rights are respected and enjoyed. Thus, for example: (1) the relationship between internal and external factors has been acknowledged in the context of the link between the establishment of a new international economic order and the promotion of human rights; (2) the interdependence of efforts to achieve development, peace and respect for human rights has been emphasized; (3) the importance of social, cultural and, in particular, economic factors underlying large scale violations of human rights has been analyzed not only in general terms but also in relation to specific situations; (4) recognition of the dynamism of the human rights tradition has been achieved through exploration of concepts such as the right to development and the right to peace and (5) the fundamental importance of regional, national and local self-reliance in terms of the struggle to win respect for human rights has been recognized through a renewed emphasis on the need to establish human rights mechanisms at all these levels.

The broad outline of this structural approach was traced by the General Assembly in a landmark resolution in 1977 (resolution 32/130). It is appropriate to conclude this review by quoting paragraph 1 of that resolution by which the Assembly decided that the approach to the future work within the United Nations system with respect to human rights questions should take into account the following concepts:

(a) All human rights and fundamental freedoms are indivisible and interdependent; equal attention and urgent consideration should be given to the implementation, promotion and protection of both civil and political, and economic, social and cultural rights;

(b) "The full realization of civil and political rights without the enjoyment of economic, social and cultural rights is impossible; the achievement of lasting progress in the implementation of human rights is dependent upon sound and effective national and international policies of economic and social development," as recognized by the Proclamation of Teheran of 1968;

(c) All human rights and fundamental freedoms of the human person and of peoples are inalienable;

(d) Consequently, human rights questions should be examined globally, taking into account both the overall context of the various societies in which they present themselves, as well as the need for the promotion of the full dignity of the human person and the development and well-being of the society;

(e) In approaching human rights questions within the United Nations system, the international community should accord, or continue to accord, priority to the search for solutions to the mass and flagrant violations of human rights of peoples and persons affected by situations such as those resulting from *apartheid*, from all forms of racial discrimination, from colonialism, from foreign domination and occupation, from aggression and threats against national sovereignty, national unity and territorial integrity, as well as from the refusal to recognize the fundamental rights of peoples to self-determination and of every nation to the exercise of full sovereignty over its wealth and natural resources;

(f) The realization of the new international economic order is an essential element for the effective promotion of human rights and fundamental freedoms and should also be accorded priority;

(g) It is of paramount importance for the promotion of human rights and fundamental freedoms that Member States undertake specific obligations through accession to or ratification of international instruments in this field; consequently, the standard-setting work within the United Nations system in the field of human rights and the universal acceptance and the implementation of the relevant international instruments should be encouraged;

(h) The experience and contribution of both developed and developing countries should be taken into account by all organs of the United Nations system in their work related to human rights and fundamental freedoms.

NOTES

1. The latest version is contained in Doc. A/520/Rev.13 (Sales No. E. 79. I. 11).

2. Verbatim record of the 409th plenary meeting, 20 December 1952; G.A. res. 640 (VII).

3. Verbatim record of the 647th plenary meeting, 29 January 1957; G.A. res. 1040 (XX).

4. Verbatim record of the 1193rd and 1194th plenary meetings, 14 December 1962; G.A. res. 1803 (XVII).

5. See, e.g, the verbatim records of the 656th and 657th meetings, 20 February 1957.

6. See section 2 (f) *infra.*

7. See A/2505 (1953), A/2719 (1954), and A/2953 (1955).

8. See the report of the Special Committee in A/6000/Rev. 1 (1965) para. 463. The procedure adopted is considered below.

9. See A/6825. For analysis see Samuel Bleicher, "UN v. IBRD: A Dilemma of Functionalism," *International Organization*, Vol. 24, 1970, pp. 31-47.

10. The most recent report is contained in A/35/23 (1980).

11. Reservations as to the petitions and communications procedures have been expressed by certain members of the Special Committee. See A/5238, paras. 16-111.

12. G.A. res. 319 (IV) of 1949, supplemented by res. 428 (V) of 1950 to which the Statute of the Office is annexed.

13. A/34/12, para. 2.

14. For details of the UN role in South East Asia see A/34/627 (1979) and for a report on UNHCR assistance activities in 1979-1980 see A/35/12 (1980).

15. See doc. E/5715 (Sales No. E. 75. I.15).

16. See Robert McLaren, "The UN System and its Quixotic Quest for Co-ordination", *International Organization*, Vol. 34, 1980, pp. 139-48.

17. As these matters are now dealt with by the Sub-Commission on Prevention of Discrimination and Protection of Minorities they are treated below in that context.

18. Report of the Preparatory Commission of the United Nations, Doc. PC/20, 23 December 1945, Chap. III, sec. 4, paras. 15-16.

19. See doc. E/5975 (Sales No. E. 77. I. 10).

20. Council res. 5 (I) of 16 February 1946 and (II) of 21 June 1946.

21. For an opinion prepared by the UN Office of Legal Affairs in 1962 on the status of "declaration in general," see Official Records of the Economic and Social Council, Thirty-fourth Session, Supp. No. 8, para. 105.

22. G.A. res. 36/57.

23. G.A. res. 36/55.

24. See A. Grahl-Madsen, *Territorial Asylum*, Stockholm, 1980.

25. For an incisive and constructively critical analysis see Theo C. van Boven, "The United Nations and Human Rights: A Critical Appraisal," *Bulletin of Peace Proposals* (Oslo), Vol. 8, 1977, pp. 198-208.

26. Jean-Bernard Marie, *La Commission des droits de l'homme de l'ONU*, Paris, Pédone, 1975.

27. See, for example, E/5464, Chap. XIX B (I); and Commission decisions 2 (XXXV) and 12 (XXXV) (1979).

28. This work is recorded in a number of UN reports, including E/2673 and Add. (1955), E/2824 (1956), E/4168/Rev.1 (UN Sales No. E.67.XIV.2 (1967) and E/CN.4/Sub.2/322 (1971).

29. The reports of the Group are contained in E/CN.4/Sub./AC.2/3 (1975); E/CN.4/Sub.2/373 (1976); E/CN.4/Sub.2/389 (1977); E/CN.4/Sub.2/410 (1978); E/CN.4/Sub.2/434 (1979) and E/CN.4/Sub.2/447 (1980).

30. The Conference's Final Act is contained in E/CONF.6/79 (1948).

31. The reports of the Sub-Commission are contained in: E/441 (1947); E/CN.4/80 (1948); E/1369 and Add. 1 (1949); E/1672 (1950); and E/2190 (1952). See also Eek, *Freedom of Information as a Project of International Legislation*, Uppsala, 1953.

32. See generally *United Nations Action in the Field of Human Rights*, 1980, Chap. VI; and Bruce, "Work of the United Nations relating to the Status of Women," *Revue des droits de l'homme*, Vol. IV, Nos. 1 & 2, 1971, pp. 365-412; and Galey, "Promoting Nondiscrimination Against Women: The UN Commission on the Status of Women," *International Studies Quarterly*, Vol. 23, 1979, pp. 273-302.

33. League of Nations, Treaty Series, Vol. 179, No. 4137.

34. See Schwelb, "Marriage and Human Rights," *American Journal of Comparative Law*, Vol. 12, 1963, p. 337.

35. See *Report of the World Conference of the International Women's Year*, Mexico, 1975, UN Sales No. E.76.IV.1 (E/CONF.66/34).

36. The conference generated a number of important reports which were issued as docu-

ments A/CONF.94/1-20 (1980). See also E/CN.6/622 (1980) and A.35/82 (1980). The report of the conference is contained in A/CONF.94/35.

37. The relevant instruments are: (i) the Declaration on the Elimination of Discrimination against Women (ECOSOC res. 1325 (XLIV) (1968) and 1677 (LII) (1972); (ii) the 1975 World Plan for Action (G.A. res. 3490 (XXX)(1975); and (iii)) the International Development Strategy for the Second UN Development Decade (G.A. res. 2626 (XXV)(1970)).

38. Legal consequences for States of the continued presence of South Africa in Namibia (South West Africa) notwithstanding Security Council resolution 276 1970, Advisory Opinion, *I.C.J. Reports* 1971, p. 16 and p. 22.

39. Commission on Human Rights res. 31 (XXXVI) and 27 (XXXVI)(1980); General Assembly res. 3/173 (1978) and 34/175 (1979).

40. A/33/1/Add. 1 (1978); see also A/9601/Add. 1 (1974).

41. See the address by the Secretary-General to the World Conference to Combat Racism and Racial Discrimination, 1978, UN Sales No. E.79.XIV.2 (A/CONF.92/40) pp. 29-33.

42. Colombian-Peruvian asylum case, Judgment of November 20, 1950, *I.C.J. Reports* 1950, p. 266.

43. Haya de la Torre case (Colombia/Peru), Judgment of June 13, 1951, *I.C.J. Reports* 1951, p. 71.

44. 132 League of Nations Treaty Series 323; *American Journal of International Law*, Vol. 22 (1928), p. 158.

45. International Status of South West Africa, Advisory Opinion: *I.C.J. Reports* 1950, p. 128; South West Africa - Voting procedure, Advisory Opinion of 7 June 1955: *I.C.J. Reports* 1955, p. 67; Admissibility of hearings of petitioners by the Committee on South West Africa, Advisory Opinion of June 1st, 1956; *I.C.J. Reports* 1956, p. 23; South West Africa Cases (Ethiopia v. South Africa; Liberia v. South Africa, Preliminary Objections, Judgment of 21 December 1962; *I.C.J. Reports* 1962, p. 319; South West Africa, Second Phase, Judgment, *I.C.J. Reports* 1966, p. 6; Legal consequences for States of the continued presence of South Africa in Namibia (South West Africa), Advisory Opinion, *I.C.J. Reports* 1971, p. 16.

46. Interpretation of Peace Treaties, Advisory Opinion: *I.C.J. Reports* 1950, p. 65 and Second Phase *ibid.*, p. 221.

47. Reservations to the Convention on Genocide, Advisory Opinion: *I.C.J. Reports* 1951, p. 15 and p. 23.

48. Barcelona Traction, Light and Power Company, Ltd., Judgment of 6 February 1970, *I.C.J. Reports* 1970, p. 3, paragraph 34 on p. 32.

49. Effect of awards of compensation made by the U.N. Administrative Tribunal, Advisory Opinion of 13 July 1954, *I.C.J. Reports* 1954, p.47.

50. Judgments of the Administrative Tribunal of the International Labour Organisation upon complaints made against the United Nations Educational, Scientific and Cultural Organization, Advisory Opinion of 23 October 1956, *I.C.J. Reports* 1956, p. 77.

51. Application for Review of Judgment No. 158 of the United Nations Administrative Tribunal, Advisory Opinion, I.C.J. Reports 1973, p. 166.

52. Australia v. France, and New Zealand v. France, Judgments of 20 December 1974, *I.C.J. Reports* 1974, p. 253 and p. 457.

53. United States of America v. Iran, Order of 15 December 1979, contained in Security Council Doc. S/13697 (1979).

54. See M.E. Tardu, *Human Rights: The International Petition System* (1979-80) Vol. I and General Introduction to Vol. 2.

55. E/259 (1947) paras. 21 and 22.

56. E/281/Rev. 1 (1947).

57. Reports of the second session of the Sub-Commission on Prevention of Discrimination and Protection of Minorities (1949), E/CN.4/351, paragraphs 28-30, resolution G, and draft resolution VI; and of the 3rd session (1950), E/CN.4/358, paragraphs 19-21 and draft resolu-

tion VI; Report of the 3rd session of the Sub-Commission on Freedom of Information and of the Press (1949), E.S.C.O.R. 9th session (1949), Supplement No. 10 A, E/1369, Chapter V, paragraphs 22-27, draft resolution B.

58. E/1681 (1950).

59. For a comprehensive restatement of Lauterpacht's views, see his *International Law and Human Rights*, New York, Praeger, 1950 (reprinted 1968), pp. 223-262.

60. Many of the documents relating to the question of communications concerning human rights are reproduced in full or in summary form in Sohn and Buergenthal, *International Protection of Human Rights*, Indianapolis, Bobbs-Merrill, 1973, pp. 748-856. See also Cassesse, "The Admissibility of Communications on Human Rights Violations," 5 *RDH/HRJ*, 1972, pp. 375-393; Carey, *UN Protection of Civil and Political Rights* 1970, Chapter IX; *idem*, "Progress on Human Rights at the United Nations," 66 *AJIL*, 1973, pp. 107 *et seq.*; Humphrey, "The Right of Petition in the United Nations," 4 *RDH/HRJ*, pp. 463 *et seq.*; Newman, "The United Nations Procedures for Human Rights Complaints," 34 *Annales de droit*, 1974, pp. 129 *et seq.*; Ruzié, "Du droit de pétition individuelle en maitière de droits de l'homme," *ibid.*, pp. 89 *et seq.*; Schwelb, *Complaints by Individuals to the Commission on Human Rights: 25 Years of an Uphill Struggle (1947-1971) in the Changing International Community*, Mouton, The Hague, 1973; and J. Möller, "Petitioning the United Nations," *Universal Human Rights*, Vol.1,No.4, pp 57-72.

61. See generally E/CN.4/1317 (1979) for the Secretary-General's analysis of some relevant UN procedures.

62. Commission resolution 15 (XXXV); for information see the report of the Special Rapporteur in E/CN.4/1371 (1980).

63. Repertory of United Nations Practice, Vol. III, Article 62 (1), par. 73 *et seq.*

64. See E/CN.4/1273 and Add. 1-5 (1978).

65. E/CN.4/L.1483. The debate on this issue is recorded in E/1980/13, Annex V.

66. Reprinted in UN *Bulletin of Human Rights*, No. 27, Jan-March 1980, pp. 10-13.

67. E/CN.6/552(1972) Paras. 227-28.

68. Statement by Secretary of State Dulles before the United States Senate Judiciary Committee, 6 April 1953, reproduced in "Review of the United Nations Charter, A Collection of Documents, 83rd Congress, 2nd Session," Senate Document No. 87, 1954, pp. 295-296.

69. See Philip Alston, "The United Nations Specialized Agencies and Implementation of the International Covenant on Economic, Social and Cultural Rights," *Columbia Journal of Transnational Law*, Vol. 18, 1979, pp. 79-118.

70. Recent materials relating to the periodic reporting procedure are contained in: E/CN.4/1214 and Add. 1-20; E/CN.4/1215 and Add.1-3; E/CN.4/1224; E/CN.4/1225; and E/CN. 4/1300-1303. Cf. Also the reporting procedure under the International Covenant on Economic, Social and Cultural Rights, described in Chapter 11, *infra*.

71. Standard directives relating to the preparation of studies by special rapporteurs are contained in Sub-Commission resolution B of 1954 (E/CN.4/703, para. 97) as amended by Commission resolution III of 1954 (E/2573, para. 418).

72. In a 1980 resolution 19 (XXXIII) the Sub-Commission recalled Commission res. 8 (XXIII) and recognized: (1) "that the sources of information available to the Sub-Commission are limited and dependent mostly on non-governmental organizations" and (2) "that the Sub-Commission in order to carry out the mandate given to it requires adequate information reflecting the situation in different countries and systems." It thus recommended the creation of an information gathering service within the UN Division of Human Rights.

73. E/3456 (1961) paras. 34-49, Commission res.2(XVII)(1961).

74. E/CN.4/826/Rev.1, UN Sales No. 65 XIV.2.

75. UN Geneva, Press Release No. HR/928, 18 August 1980.

76. See Commission resolutions 23 (XXXIV) (1978) and 24 (XXXV) (1979); and ST/HR/SER.A/2 (1978).

77. Commission resolution 24 (XXXVI) (1980); and ECOSOC resolution 1980/30.

78. G.A. resolutions 1881 (XVIII) of 1963; 2054 (XX) of 1965; 2202 A (XXI) of 1966; 2307 (XXII) of 1967; 2396 (XXIII) of 1968; 2506 (XXIV) of 1969; 2671 (XXV) of 1970; 2775 (XXVI) of 1971; 2923 (XXVII) of 1972 and 3151 A B and D (XXVIII) of 1973; 3324 D (XXIX) of 1974; 31/6 G and J of 1976; 32/105 I of 1977; 33/183 J of 1979; and 34/93 R of 1979.

79. See Commission res.2(XXIII)(1967); E/4322 paras.186-270; Ermacora in *HRJ/RDH*, Vol. I, No. 2, 1968, p.160; Carey, *ibid.*, p. 531; and Carey, *UN Protection of Civil and Political Rights*, New York, Syracuse Press (1970), p. 95.

80. In fact, the Chairman of the Commission sent a message to the Foreign Minister of South Africa on 25 August 1980 calling on that Government to cease certain activities of which the Group learned during a field mission of enquiry in London, Tanzania, Angola and Geneva. See *United Nations Chronicle*, September-October 1980, p. 67.

81. E/CN.4/Sub.2/383/Rev.2. UN. Sales No. E.79.XIV.3 (1979).

82. A/CONF.32/41, UN Sales No. E.68.XIV.2. (1968), res. XXIV.

83. See A/7649, E/4818 paras. 16-21 and General Assembly resolution 2646 and 2647 (XXV) (1970) and 2784 and 2785 (XXVI) (1971).

84. A/CONF.92/40,UN Sales No. E.79.XIV.2. (1979).

85. The list was contained in E/CN.4/Sub.2/425 and Corr.1-2 and Add.1-6 (1979). See Commission res. 11 (XXXVI) (1980), ECOSOC decision 1980/131 and Sub-Commission res. 2 (XXXIII) (1980).

86. See A/CONF.94/BP.16 and 17; and A/CONF.94/7/Rev.1 (1980).

87. United Nations Institute for Training and Research Seminar, Geneva, October 1980, report submitted to General Assembly in 1980.

88. See generally B.G. Ramcharan, "United Nations Practice in Fact-Finding and on-the-spot investigations in the field of human rights," International Institute of Human Rights, Summary of Lectures, Eleventh Study Session, 1980, Strasbourg, 47 p.

89. Of particular importance in this regard are the reports prepared by the Special Committee to Investigate Israeli Practices Affecting the Human Rights of the Population of the Occupied Territories which was established by General Assembly resolution 2443 (XXIII) (1968). The Committee has submitted the following reports A/8089 (1970); A/8389 and Add.1 (1971); A/8828 (1972); A/9148 and Add.1 (1973); A/9817 (1974); A/10272 (1975); A/31/218 (1976); A/32/284 (1977); A/33/356 (1978); A/34/631 (1979). Other studies relating to this issue are listed in E/CN.4/Sub.2/454 (1980). See also Sub-Commission res. 14 (XXXIII) (1980).

90. The most recent reports are contained in A/34/583 and Add.1; E/CN.4/1362; E/CN.4/1363 and E/CN.4/1381.

91. See E/CN.4/Sub.2/414 and Add.1-8; and E/CN.4/1335.

92. See Commission res. 32 (XXXVI) (1980).

93. E/CN.4/Sub.2/426 and E/CN.4/1372.

94. See Sub-Commission res. 23 (XXXIII) (1980).

95. United Nations Geneva Press Release HR/967, 19 September 1980.

96. These were considered by the Commission in 1981. See Commission resolution 28 (XXXVI) (1980) and Sub-Commission resolution 25 (XXXIII) (1980). The Bureau, which is elected at each session, is composed of the Chairman, three Vice-Chairmen and the Rapporteur, each of whom is from a different one of the five geo-political groups.

11 United Nations Institutions and Procedures Founded on Conventions on Human Rights and Fundamental Freedoms

Kamleshwar Das

GENERAL INTRODUCTION*

The United Nations has adopted conventions relating to human rights and fundamental freedoms either in the General Assembly or by conferences called by it or by the Economic and Social Council. It is not proposed here to ascribe to the conventions their place or hierarchical position in relation to other forms of action taken by the United Nations to achieve the goals of the Charter relating to human rights.[1]

Conventions on human rights have been adopted under normal rules of procedure of the General Assembly (usually its Third Committee and, in some instances, its Sixth Committee have been involved) or under those adopted by conferences. They may or may not have been adopted by special majority votes. While all Member States participate in the General Assembly, the conferences have been open also to such non-Member States as have been invited to participate. All such States have not actually taken part in the deliberations or voted upon the conventions, but they were at all times free to do so. The actual number of States attending conferences has differed but has rarely been very high: 51 States participated in one and 26 in another.[2]

No general rules for the preparation of conventions on human rights have been established as, for example, for the conventions to be drawn up by the International Law Commission or by the International Labour Organisation. It will suffice to note that most of them have gone through various stages in their drafting. There has generally been enquiry as to the views of Governments (sometimes those of non-Member States) on draft conventions and numerous bodies have been associated in the preparatory work.[3]

There have been, in appropriate instances, consultations and participation of United Nations offices, like that of the Office of the High Commissioner for

*The original version of this chapter was written by Kamleshwar Das and appeared in the French edition of this book. This revised English version was prepared by Philip Alston independently of the original author. However, a draft was sent to him for comments and many of his suggestions were subsequently incorporated.

Refugees, and of specialized agencies, sometimes also of certain regional inter-governmental organizations. At some stage or another in the preparation of conventions, non-governmental organizations in consultative status with the Economic and Social Council have had opportunities to submit written or oral observations to them. On occasion, proposals submitted, for example, by a specialized agency, have been discussed and even espoused by a member of a body and voted upon. Accordingly, it cannot be assumed unequivocally that all United Nations conventions on human rights contain texts emanating from governments only and that they have no non-governmental contents.[4]

As noted in previous chapters, an undertaking to draft an international bill of human rights was given at the San Francisco Conference in 1945.[5] The relationship between the Universal Declaration of Human Rights and the International Covenants has been noted in Chapter 10. The present Chapter, in addition to dealing with the Covenants and the Optional Protocol, also deals with other conventions on human rights and fundamental freedoms adopted by the United Nations or conferences called by it (see annex I of this textbook). All of them are now in force.

Whatever the position of States when participating or not in the adoption of the conventions on human rights, all the conventions provide for ratification or accession by States eligible to do so before they become binding on them. Usually the States Members of the United Nations or members of the specialized agencies, or parties to the Statute of the International Court of Justice, or members of the International Atomic Energy Agency have been eligible to ratify or accede to the conventions, with the exception of the International Convention on the Suppression and Punishment of the Crime of Apartheid, which is open to all States for ratification or accession. The number of ratifications or accessions required to bring a convention into force varies from two to thirty-five.[6]

The principle of *pacta sunt servanda* is of general application to all obligations internationally binding on a State under these conventions.[7] The principle is of particular relevance in human rights conventions where obligations are not only concerned with the external relations of States, but equally, if not predominantly, with recognizing, reinforcing, improving, altering and generally affecting national rights and status of the individual.

It would be unrealistic to disregard the question of reservations since they affect the relationship between States parties to a convention, the scope and contents of its provisions, and procedures and institutions established by it particularly for its international implementation. It may be regretted, therefore, that the injunction of the General Assembly in resolution 598 (VI) of 12 January 1952 endorsing the International Law Commission's recommendation that clauses or reservations should be inserted in future conventions has often been ignored and nowhere more conspicuously than in the International Covenants on Human Rights.[8]

That international institutions of implementation face problems in the area of reservations has already arisen in the Committee on the Elimination of Racial Discrimination, established under the International Convention on the Elimination of All Forms of Racial Discrimination which contains an article on reservations.

In 1978, the Committee, after lengthy discussion on the subject of reservations, received replies to a number of questions which it had posed to the UN Office of Legal Affairs. It then noted its agreement with the following clarifications made in the Office's document:

"(a) The Committee must take the reservations made by States parties at the time of ratification or accession into account: it has no authority to do otherwise. A decision—even a unanimous decision—by the Committee that a reservation is unacceptable could not have any legal effect;

(b) A reservation made at the time of signature has to be confirmed at the time of ratification, otherwise it is considered as not having been maintained; and

(c) Declarations other than reservations have no legal effect at all on the obligations of the declaring State under the Convention—precisely because if this were not the case such declarations would have to be considered as reservations."[9]

National measures required to bring the provisions of a convention into effect within States parties are of the utmost importance and they are the primary means of implementing the provisions of human rights conventions.[10] These conventions frequently contain provisions requiring States parties to take the necessary steps under their constitutional processes to adopt such legislative or other methods as may be necessary to give effect, progressively or otherwise, as the case may be, to the rights recognized in the conventions. Substantive obligations, in many of these conventions are also stated in terms of an obligation to enact legislation or to take other domestic action to achieve specifically stated purposes.

The purposes of the international institutions and procedures described hereafter, particularly those of the International Convention on the Elimination of All Forms of Racial Discrimination and the International Covenants on Human Rights and the Optional Protocol to the Covenant on Civil and Political Rights are: to offer aid, assistance, advice and co-operation; to guide, persuade and stimulate self-help, especially under the reporting systems; and to provide preventive and curative remedies through negotiations, fact-finding, good offices, conciliation, expression of views and, in certain instances, suggestions and recommendations, general or otherwise, some of which are placed on an optional basis requiring separate declarations by States parties.[11]

It is not the aim to use coercion, to utilize punitive measures or to impose specific sanctions. It may well be that further insight into the purpose of these institutions and procedures will be forthcoming when the United Nations completes its consideration of the subject of "State Responsibility" which is being pursued currently by the International Law Commission.

The other conventions, besides the one adopted in 1973 on the question of
apartheid and the 1979 Convention on discrimination against women do not
have specific systems of international implementation, though some provide
for reports and information on giving effect to provisions of the Convention,
and, for the Convention relating to the Status of Refugees and the Protocol to
it, the Office of the United Nations High Commissioner for Refugees plays a
significant role in their implementation. Possibilities of an international criminal jurisdiction have been brought up in the case of some Conventions.

United Nations organs and bodies have by resolutions provided for reporting and other means of ascertaining the application of the provisions of certain conventions, not always confining such actions to States parties.

Even in the case of the Covenants, the Protocol and the Convention on the
Elimination of All Forms of Racial Discrimination, UN organs like the Economic and Social Council and the General Assembly are brought into the
machinery of implementation. Thus, there is a large uncharted area of concern by the UN system which often seems to dissolve into the machineries of
implementation, and it would be a bold assertion to say that the machinery of
any convention will always remain isolated and self-contained. This is, however, not peculiar to the UN conventions on human rights, it may be and
often is true of the conventions on human rights of the specialized agencies
and other inter-governmental organizations.[12]

Nor can the existence of this situation or its development be criticized on
narrow legal grounds. For it is well-nigh impossible to imagine the implementation of the Covenants without the co-operation of the individual, the
community, the States and all those who form parts of the international
order. It would be unrealistic, for instance, to consider human rights conventions in isolation from international society, the existence of peace and disarmament; from political, economic and social conditions, relations and
development; from policies and programmes on population, environment,
natural resources, agriculture and land reform, science and technology, health
and education; from the problems arising out of foreign trade and investments and multinational corporations; from colonialism, racism, *apartheid*,
discrimination against women, and discrimination of other kinds; and from
the existence of rampant poverty among two-thirds of humanity; or not to
give special regard to the children, young people, the elderly and the aged,
the handicapped and the displaced.

It should be remembered that discussion and provisions of international
machinery for the implementation of conventions and agreements on human
rights matters, as well as some working experience of them, goes back a long
way, though it has received greater attention since the San Francisco Conference and the preparation of the International Bill of Human Rights. Its
importance was reiterated by the Economic and Social Council in Resolution
1101 (XL) of 2 March 1966, in which the Council recommended that future
conventions in the field of human rights should contain appropriate provisions

for their implementation and urged that the organizational and procedural arrangements for the implementation of existing conventions in the field be fully utilized.

It is to the future that the institutions and procedures of implementation of human rights of the Covenants and of the other conventions are directed. That is reason enough to consider them in a way which, while not being comprehensive, contains the required material to understand them and provides for those concerned with the place of United Nations conventions in the promotion and protection of human rights. It is not their past history or doubtful adequacy, or even comparability to other international and regional systems, which is going to determine their potentialities. They will become a living force in promoting and protecting the dignity and worth of the human person and in the pursuit of his or her development, happiness and equality in larger freedom only through a multi-disciplinary approach, which avoids long-term disunity and helps to resolve deep-rooted problems and tensions, however intractable they may appear to be. Accordingly, there is need for knowledge and comprehensive treatment of the subject with vision and understanding on the part of governments and others, particularly non-governmental organizations, various institutions and universities and academicians, as well as writers in law, politics, economic, social and cultural matters. There must of course be recourse to the voluminous documentation of the United Nations which has much to offer in the way of understanding the fengs and aspirations of the governments and the peoples they represent. Much more needs to be known about national institutions and systems, both in theory and in practice to gain a better perspective of the issues and problems which will face the international institutions and procedures. There is need, further, for greater public awareness and popular participation, and deliberations within countries, between governments, non-governmental bodies, the community and individuals, as well as for codes and measures of self-discipline and self-regulation in crucial areas of public and private life, especially in many professions, occupations and organizations.[13]

(a). The International Convention on the Elimination of All Forms of Racial Discrimination

The Convention, which had 108 States parties as of January 1, 1982, provides for a Committee on the Elimination of All Forms of Racial Discrimination of eighteen experts of certain qualifications, nationals of States parties nominated and elected by them. The Committee receives reports and information from States parties to the Convention on measures which they have taken to give effect to the provisions of the Convention, on the basis of which the Committee may make suggestions and general recommendations. The Committee lends its good offices to the States parties concerned who submit a matter to it concerning the failure to give effect to the provisions of the Convention after an initial exchange between them of inter-States communications and on failure of adjustment of the matter to their satisfaction by any means open to them. The functions of the Committee are to ascertain the requirements relating to the exhaustion of domestic remedies and to obtain and collate all the information it deems necessary. After this an *ad hoc* conciliation commission is appointed, normally consisting of members agreed to by parties to a dispute, to consider the matter. The Commission, after fully considering the matter submits a report which may contain such recommendations as it may think proper for the amicable solution of the dispute. The Committee may also receive and consider communications from individuals or groups of individuals claiming to be victims of violations of any of the rights of the Convention, provided the States parties have agreed by special declarations to such consideration and at least ten States parties have made the declarations. The Committee has been assigned advisory functions in relation to copies of petitions and reports which it may receive from the competent bodies of the United Nations relating to all Trust, Non-Self-Governing Territories and other territories to which the Declaration on the Granting of Independence to Colonial Countries and Peoples contained in General Assembly Resolution 1514 (XV) applies. It is also to report annually to the General Assembly on its activities. The Convention contains provisions concerning the relationship of its implementation machinery to others of the United Nations and specialized agencies, including other provisions of general or special international agreements in force between States parties to the Convention. There is, further, a settlement of disputes clause involving the International Court of Justice.

i) THE COMMITTEE ON THE ELIMINATION OF RACIAL DISCRIMINATION (CERD) (ARTICLES 8 AND 10)

Nature and composition

Article 8 relating to the establishment of a Committee on the Elimination of All Forms of Racial Discrimination was based on a compromise between those who wished it to be composed of representatives of States parties (a Committee of eighteen members elected by and from among States parties) and those who desired to have persons with certain qualifications nominated by States parties and elected by the General Assembly. According to Article 8, the Committee consists of eighteen "experts of high moral standing and acknowledged impartiality", who "serve in their personal capacity". Each State party may nominate one person from among its own nationals. Elections are held by secret ballot at a meeting of the States parties, where the presence of two-thirds of the States parties constitutes a quorum, and those nominees who obtain the largest number of votes and an absolute majority vote of those present and voting are elected. In the election, consideration is given to "equitable geographical distribution and to the representation of the different forms of civilization as well as of the principal legal systems". Members serve for four years with elections for half of the membership every two years.

Seven elections have been held as of January 1982. The membership of the Committee has reflected the changing pattern of geographical representation among the States parties, which seems to have lately provided for election of four experts each from Africa, Asia, Western Europe and other States and three each from Latin American and Eastern Europe.

Rules of procedure, officers, secretariat and place of meeting

Under Article 10 of the Convention the Committee adopts its own rules of procedure. So far it has adopted rules of a general nature based upon those of United Nations organs as well as certain rules pertaining to Articles 9 and 11 to 13 of the Convention, which it has decided to consider as provisional rules of procedure.[14]

A significant rule adopted by the Committee is Rule 14 whereby each member on assuming his duties makes the following solemn declaration in open Committee: "I solemnly declare that I will perform my duties and exercise my powers as a member of the Committee on the Elimination of Racial Discrimination honourably, faithfully, impartially and conscientiously". This declaration is the same as that made by members of the International Court of Justice under Article 5 of the rules of the Court.

The rules provide for two regular sessions annually, each of three weeks duration. Special sessions are to be convened by the Committee's decision and, when not in session, by the Chairman in consultation with the officers of the Committee or at the request of the majority of its members or a State party. A majority of the members of the Committee constitute a quorum for a meeting, but the presence of two-thirds of the members is required for a decision to be taken. Subsidiary bodies may be set up as the Committee deems necessary. The Committee defines their composition and mandates, but leaves them free to elect their officers and adopt their own rules of procedures, subject to the provisions of the Convention and the financial implications involved. The meetings of the Committee and its subsidiary bodies are held in public, unless the Committee decides otherwise, or it appears from the relevant provisions of the Convention that the meeting should be held in private.

The annual reports of the Committee to the General Assembly show that actions are often taken in the Committee without a formal vote. As the rules stand, decisions in the Committee are to be made by a majority vote, except where otherwise provided for by the Convention. In a meeting, for which a quorum of two-thirds of the members of the Committee is required for decisions, such decisions may be adopted by the affirmative vote of seven members or less since, following United Nations practice, "members present and voting" are regarded as those casting an affirmative or negative vote. In contrast, Article 39.2(b) of the Covenant on Civil and Political Rights stipulates that decisions of the Human Rights Committee "shall be made by a majority vote of the members present".

As the reports to the General Assembly often set out various views expressed in the Committee, sometimes even identifying the members who made them, the Committee has never formally discussed the question of whether dissenting views or reservations made by individual members should be specifically set out in its reports but, where so requested by a member, this has usually been done.

In accordance with Article 10.2 of the Convention, the Committee elects its officers for a term of two years. So far it has elected a Chairman, three Vice-Chairmen and one Rapporteur, usually following the principle of regional geographical distribution.

Although the expenses of the Committee members for their travel and daily subsistence allowances are borne by States parties, the Committee's main expenses fall upon the regular budget of the United Nations. The Committee's secretariat is to be provided by the United Nations, which means making available personnel for its substantive work as well as all conference and documentation services and facilities.

While Article 10 states that the meetings of the Committee are normally to be held at Headquarters, any meetings which the committee may hold away from Headquarters which involve extra expense by the United Nations have to be approved by the General Assembly.

Documents and their availability

Until 1974, distribution of the Committee's documents, with the exception of the annual report to the General Assembly, was restricted to members, States parties, and others directly concerned. Thereafter States reports were made generally available if so requested by the States parties. Since 1977 they have been available unless States parties request otherwise. The summary records of public meetings have also been made available to the public since 1974.[15]

Casual vacancies

To fill a casual vacancy the State party whose expert has ceased to function as a member of the Committee appoints "another expert from among its nationals subject to the approval of the Committee".[16] When the question of a casual vacancy arose for the first time, the Secretary-General informed the Committee of Communications he had received from the expert country's Permanent Mission to the United Nations about his transfer to other work and his inability to continue as a member, as well as the nomination of another person to take his place.

Thereupon, the Committee adopted a revised Rule 13 of its provisional rules of procedure.[17] The main changes were to provide for the name of the expert appointed to be submitted to the Committee for approval "by secret ballot" and, except in the case of a vacancy arising from a member's death or disability, the Secretary-General and the Committee act in accordance with the procedure laid down "only after receiving from the member concerned, written notification of his decision to cease to function as a member of the Committee".[18] What is required is a personal act consisting of a notification in writing which should come from the member concerned and express his personal decision. On this basis of agreement, the proposer of the revised rule withdrew the word "directly" before the words "from the member concerned".[19] This procedure was followed in the filling of a vacancy in 1976.

Possibility of appointing alternates or temporary substitutes for members

Proposals whereby a member of the Committee might, in certain circumstances, be enabled to designate an alternate have been made but withdrawn;[20] they were opposed mainly as being inconsistent with the nature of the membership provided for in the Convention.

Scope of material utilisable by members

A new rule was proposed to provide that, in the consideration of reports and information under Article 9 or of copies of petitions and reports received under Article 15, members of the Committee might raise any matter relevant to the situation described in the documents before the Committee or related to the implementation of the Convention in the territory of the State party concerned.[21] The members of the Committee, it was pointed out, were experts, as provided in the Convention, and should not be expected to ignore or put aside their expertise and merely confine themselves to a discussion of information placed before them. They could and should use any relevant information in order to discharge properly and adequately their functions under the Convention, which did not prohibit recourse to such information. This was also said to be borne out by the practice of the Committee.

On the other hand it was argued that the Convention restricted the sources of information available to the Committee to reports and information submitted under Articles 9 and 15. At the conclusion of the debate the Chairman stated that "it appeared from the discussion that the Committee would continue the practice it had followed to date allowing members to use any information they might have as experts".[22]

ii) REPORTS AND INFORMATION FROM STATES PARTIES

Types of reports and information and their purpose

Article 9 specifies three types of reports from States parties: initial reports, biennial reports and additional reports; the first two are called "periodic reports" by the Committee. Initial reports are due one year after the entry into force of the Convention for the State concerned. Thereafter, reports are due every two years. Additional reports are due whenever the Committee so requests.

The Committee "may request further information from the States parties".[23] The words "if necessary" at the end of the text were excluded in order to avoid differences of opinion arising between members of the Committee and the States parties on whether the necessity for the request existed or not.

The purpose of the reports is to ascertain the legislative, judicial, administrative or other measures which States parties have adopted and which give effect to the provisions of the Convention.[24] The Committee's Rules 64 and 65 specify that the Committee "may, through the Secretary-General, inform the States parties of its wishes regarding the form and contents of the periodic reports and for additional reports or further information, it may indicate the manner as well as the time within which either is to be supplied".

At its first session in 1970, the Committee adopted a set of guidelines concerning the form and contents of States reports under Article 9. These were replaced by a revised set adopted at the Committee's 21st session, in 1980.[25]

Non-submission of reports and information

Rule 66 of the Committee provides that, in the event of the non-receipt of reports or non-compliance with requests for further information, the Committee may transmit a reminder to the State party concerned. If that is unproductive the Committee includes a reference to that effect in its annual report. In 1981, the Committee reported that it had received 425 of the 483 reports due under Article 9(I) as of August 1981. In addition 61 supplementary reports had been received from States Parties. In one case the Committee had sent 12 reminders to a State and in another it had sent 10.[26]

Consideration of reports and information from States parties

The examination of the reports and other information furnished by States parties has been held in full Committee and in public meetings. The Committee has, during its various sessions, provided new rules or adopted general recommendations and followed certain practices, procedures and methods for its examination of the reports and concerning their contents, but these are constantly evolving.

At first, the Committee made general requests for supplementary rather than additional reports and called for additional information to fill the missing information in the Committee's guidelines, but usually refrained from making any direct request to a State party for further information of a specific nature. These general requests were sent with the relevant records of discussion to the States parties concerned.

As a consequence of paragraph 5 of Resolution 2783 (XXVI) of 6 December 1971 of the General Assembly where the Assembly expressed the view that the work of the Committee would be facilitated if the reports submitted by States parties conformed to the guidelines laid down by the Committee for that purpose and if the Committee invited representatives of States parties to be present at its meetings when their reports were examined, the Committee adopted Rule 64A.

Under Rule 64A the Committee, through the Secretary-General, notifies the States parties (as early as possible) of the opening date, duration and place of the session at which their respective reports are to be examined. Representatives of the States parties may be present at the meeting when their reports are examined. The Committee may also inform the State party from which it decides to seek further information that it may authorize its representative to be present at a specified meeting. Such a representative should be able to answer questions which may be put to him by the Committee and make statements on reports already submitted by his State and may also submit additional information from his State.

In practice, with few exceptions, States parties have been represented at the Committee when their reports were examined and have made statements and answered questions or said that their next report would deal with them. The few exceptions may be ascribed to many reasons but not, it would appear, from any desire on the part of a State party not to co-operate. The rule is also couched in non-mandatory terms and the Committee has retained its freedom to proceed with its consideration of a report whether a representative of the State concerned is present or not. In 1980 the General Assembly (Res 35/40) urged all States parties to extend full co-operation to the Committee and noted with regret that on one occasion such co-operation was withheld by one State party.

Also in response to GA res.2783 (XXVI)(1971), the Committee adopted Rule 66A in which three paragraphs give an indication of how the Committee views its mandate under Article 9 when examining reports of States parties. The Committee, first, is to "determine whether the report provides the information referred to in the relevant communications of the Committee".

Second, if a report of the State party, "in the opinion of the Committee, does not contain sufficient information", in practice, specific decisions may or may not be taken in this regard in the case of each report, but usually States have been asked to submit their next reports in the light of the discussions held in the Committee, as reflected in the summary records of the meetings. Sometimes, of course, such information is given at the meetings of the Committee by the representative of the State party concerned, invited under Rule 64A.

Third, "if, on the basis of its examination of the reports and information supplied by the State party, the Committee determines that some of the obligations of that State under the Convention have not been discharged, it may make suggestions and general recommendations in accordance with Article 9(2) of the Convention". The Committee has so far adopted five general recommendations and a subsequent request for specific information which was related to one of them.

A further suggestion, that the Committee determine to be unsatisfactory any report which, in its opinion, indicated that a State party had not discharged all its obligations under the Convention, and request that State party to submit information on the manner in which it proposed to discharge its undischarged obligations, was considered as being too rigid and as applying the same criteria to every report, which would prevent the Committee from taking into account the special circumstances of each country and not leave the Committee the required flexibility.

It may be recalled that, from the beginning, the classification of reports as "satisfactory" or "unsatisfactory" was intended to indicate the relative completeness or incompleteness of the information contained in the reports and not the degree of fulfillment of the anti-discrimination requirements laid down in Articles 2 to 7 of the Convention. As the reports began to fulfill the reporting requirements more completely and attention in considering them focused on the substantive significance of the information provided, the previous practice became not only less necessary but perhaps less useful and also more likely to mislead. In 1974, the Committee discarded the previous practice and the summary of the deliberations in the Committee in its annual report to the General Assembly began to reflect on a country by country basis the evaluation made by the Committee of the various features of the reports of States parties as such, as well as the views expressed by the Committee or by its members regarding the legislative, judicial, administrative or other measures which give effect to the provisions of Part I of the Convention or failed to do so. Accordingly, with the representatives of the States parties concerned usually being present, the Committee has adopted a variety of opinions based on Rule 66A, generally coupled with an expression of hope for continued co-operation of the governments with the Committee.

Ever since its third session, the Committee has been seized on several occasions with information from reporting States to the effect that racial discrimination was being practised on parts of their national territory outside their effective control as a result of occupation or other forms of *de facto* control by States not Parties to the Convention.

On two aspects of such situations there has never been disagreement among members of the Committee: that the political or other disputes leading to, or deriving from, the occupation or *de facto* control of the territories in question lay outside the competence of the Committee; and that the Committee could not be indifferent to reported practices of racial discrimination on the territory of States parties to the Convention.

Differences of opinion have arisen among members of the Committee, however, over such questions as the receivability of the information concerned under article 9 of the Convention and the competence of the Committee to take any action at all—or, if competent, the kind of action it could take—with regard to the information before it, in discharge of its obligations under article 9. The fact that all States occupying or controlling the territories under consideration had not ratified or acceded to the Convention created other problems; the Committee lacked the competence to request them to provide information and was prohibited by the Convention from inviting, or permitting, their representatives to participate in its examination of the reports before it. Since the tenth session, all the decisions adopted by the Committee on these issues have been taken by consensus. The cases in question have involved the Panama Canal Zone, the Golan Heights, Cyprus, the West Bank of the River Jordan and the Sinai Peninsula.

In the decisions it adopted regarding the reports on those territories, the Committee has: requested further information; asked the reporting State to keep it informed on future developments; taken note of the information before it; taken note of relevant resolutions, adopted by competent organs of the United Nations; taken note of relevant reports of United Nations bodies; expressed its concern; expressed its hope for the restoration of certain basic human rights; drawn the attention of the General Assembly to the information at hand; asked the General Assembly to take certain specified steps; and/or asked the General Assembly to ensure that no changes which have the effect of establishing racial discrimination are brought about in the territories concerned.[27] In 1980 the Assembly (Res 35/40) expressed its grave concern that some States parties owing to reasons beyond their control, were being prevented from fulfilling their obligations under the Convention in parts of their respective territories.

A proposal that the Committee should inform a reporting State that the procedure under Article 11 was applicable in cases where the State submitted a report or information under Article 9 concerning measures affecting its territory but which had been taken by another State party was rejected by the Committee in 1972.[28]

Suggestions and general recommendations of the Committee and comments thereon by States parties

The Committee may make suggestions and general recommendations based on the examination of the reports and information received from the States parties. Such suggestions and general recommendations, according to Article 9(2), "shall be reported to the General Assembly together with comments, if any, from States parties".

An amendment in the Third Committee of the General Assembly to omit "general" before "recommendations" was rejected. Another amendment to delete the reference to "suggestions", since it "implied that the Committee would make specific proposals", was also rejected. An amendment was adopted to omit the words "the" and "concerned" from the second sentence of paragraph 2 of Art. 9, which had provided that the suggestions and general recommendations of the Committee should be reported to the General Assembly together with comments, if any, "from the States parties concerned".

At the second session, the Committee, taking account of the General Assembly discussion, decided in Rule 67 that such suggestions and general recommendations as the Committee may make under Article 9 of the Convention "shall be communicated by the Committee through the Secretary-General to the States parties for their comments and that the Committee may, when necessary, indicate a time limit within which those comments are to be received. It was agreed that the Committee shall report its suggestions and general recommendations to the General Assembly together with comments from States parties, if any were received".

The Committee has made no suggestions but has adopted five general recommendations, which are described hereafter. The comments of the States parties on these general recommendations so far have been submitted in full to the General Assembly in the Committee's annual reports. The Committee has not undertaken any general analysis of these comments; some analysis of comments on General Recommendation III were, however, forwarded to the General Assembly.[29]

In its General Recommendation II, the Committee considered some reports from States parties which expressed or implied the belief that the information mentioned in the Committee's guidelines need not be supplied by States parties on whose territories racial discrimination did not exist. The Committee stated, however, that since all the categories of information listed referred to obligations undertaken by the States parties under the Convention, communication is addressed to all States parties without distinction, whether or not racial discrimination exists in their respective territories.

In its General Recommendation III, the Committee stated that it had considered some reports from States parties containing information about measures taken to implement resolutions of the United Nations organs concerning relations with the racist regimes in southern Africa. The Committee noted the provisions of the tenth preambular paragraph and Article 3 of the Convention and General Assembly Resolution 2784 (XXVI) relating to trade with South Africa. It expressed the view that measures adopted on the national level to give effect to the provisions of the Convention are interrelated with measures taken on the international level to encourage respect everywhere for the principles of the Convention. The Committee welcomed the inclusion in the reports submitted under Article 9 by any State party which chooses to do so, of information regarding the status of its diplomatic, economic and other relations with the racist regime in South Africa. The practice of the Committee inaugurated in its adoption of this general recommendation was commended by the General Assembly in Resolution 3266 (XXIX) of 10 December 1974. Further views of the Committee on this recommendation were set out in its Decision 2 (XI) of 7 April 1975. In 1980 the Assembly (Res 35/40) commended the Committee for paying greater attention to the question of the elimination of the policy of apartheid in South Africa and Namibia and invited States parties when submitting information under the revised guidelines to include information on their relations with the racist regime of South Africa.

In General Recommendation IV, the Committee, having considered reports submitted by States parties and bearing in mind the need for the
reports to be as informative as possible, invited States parties to endeavour
to include in their reports relevant information on the demographic composition of the population referred to in the provisions of Article 1 of the Convention.

General Recommendation I was adopted on the basis of the consideration
at its fifth session of reports submitted by States parties when the Committee found that the legislation of a number of States did not include the
provisions envisaged in Article 4 (a) and (b) of the Convention, the implementation of which (with due regard to the principles embodied in the Universal
Declaration of Human Rights and the rights expressly set forth in Article 5 of
the Convention) was obligatory under the Convention for all States parties.
The Committee accordingly recommended that the States parties whose legislation was deficient in this respect should consider, in accordance with their
national legislative procedures, the question of supplementing their legislation with provisions conforming to the requirements of Article 4 (a) and (b) of
the Convention.

The subject matter of General Recommendation I was followed later by a
request by the Committee for information from States parties concerning
their obligations under Article 4 of the Convention. The Committee requested
States parties: a) to indicate what specific penal legislation designed to
implement the provisions of Article 4 (a) and (b) had been enacted in their
respective countries and to transmit to the Secretary-General the texts
concerned as well as such provisions of general penal law as must be taken
into account when applying such specific legislation; and b) where no such
specific legislation had been enacted, to inform the Committee of the manner and the extent to which the provisions of the existing penal laws, as
applied by the Courts, effectively implemented their obligations under Article 4 (a) and (b).

In the Committee's 1945 annual report the need for information on "administrative and other measures was noted".[30] In Recommendation V of 13 April
1977 the Committee requested every State Party to provide "adequate information on the measures which it has adopted and which give effect to the
provisions of article 7..." (relating to teaching, education, culture and
information).

iii) INTER-STATE COMMUNICATIONS ON NOT GIVING EFFECT TO THE CONVENTION
    AND GOOD OFFICES AND CONCILIATION PROCEDURES RELATING THERETO

Initiation of inter-state communications (article 11, paragraph 3)

Under Article 11 of the Convention, if a State party considers that another
State party is not giving effect to the provisions of the Convention, it may
bring the matter to the attention of the Committee. The Committee is then to
transmit the communication to the State party concerned. Within three months,
the State which receives the communication is to submit to the Committee

written explanations or statements clarifying the matter and the remedy, if any, that it may have adopted.

According to Rule 68 of the rules of procedure of the Committee, when a matter is brought to the attention of the Committee in accordance with Article 11, the Committee "shall examine it at a private meeting and then transmit it to the State party concerned through the Secretary-General. The Committee, in examining the communication, shall not consider its substance. Any action at this stage by the Committee in respect of the communication shall in no way be construed as an expression of its views on the substance of the communication".

"After several attempts to achieve unanimity failed" as regards the action to be taken while the Committee is not in session, the Committee adopted the following procedure: the Chairman brings the matter to the attention of the members of the Committee, if it is not in session, by transmitting copies of the communication on behalf of the Committee, specifying that they have three weeks for their replies. Upon receipt of the consent of the majority of the Committee or if, within the time limit, no replies are received, the Chairman is to transmit the communication to the State party concerned through the Secretary-General "without delay". In the event of any replies being received which represent the views of the majority of the members of the Committee, the Chairman, "while acting in accordance with such replies", is to bear in mind the requirement of urgency in transmitting, on behalf of the Committee, the communication to the State party concerned. The Committee or the Chairman, on behalf of the Committee, is to remind the receiving State of the time limit of three months for its reply. When the reply has been received, the procedure laid down above is to be followed in transmitting it to the State party initiating the communication.

Referral to the Committee of a matter not adjusted to the satisfaction of the States parties (Article 11, paragraph 2)

If the matter raised in the initial communication by a State party is not adjusted to the satisfaction of both parties, either by bilateral negotiation or by any procedure open to them within six months after the receipt by the receiving State of the initial communication, either State has the right to refer the matter again to the Committee by notifying it and also the other State.

The reference to the matter being adjusted "to the satisfaction of both parties" in no way diminishes the fact that such satisfaction must relate to adjustment concerning the provisions of the Convention to which effect is not being given, since that is the only ground on which an initial communication is submitted, although there is no reference, as in Article 12, paragraph 1 (a) of the Convention, to "an amicable solution of the matter on the basis of respect for the Convention".

The Committee has in Rule 70 provided that the Chairman, through the Secretary-General, is to inform the States parties concerned of the forthcoming consideration of the matter not later than thirty days in advance of the first meeting of the Committee, in the case of a regular session, and at least eighteen days in advance of the first meeting, in the case of a special session.

Consideration of a matter referred to the Committee, including exhaustion of domestic remedies (Article 11, paras. 3 to 5)

When a matter has been referred to the Committee, it shall deal with it "after it has ascertained that all available domestic remedies have been invoked and exhausted in the case, in conformity with generally recognized principles of international law. This shall not be the rule where the application of the remedies is unreasonably prolonged."

According to paragraphs 4 and 5 of Article 11, in any matter referred to the Committee, it may call upon the States parties concerned to supply any other relevant information, and they have the right to send representatives to take part in the proceedings of the Committee, without voting rights, while the matter is under consideration.

Rule 69 of the rules of Procedure of the Committee perhaps states these purposes better in providing that the Committee may call upon the States parties concerned "to supply information relevant to the application of Article 11 of the Convention"; the Committee may indicate the manner as well as the time within which such information is to be supplied, while Rule 70 requires proper notifications of the meetings of the Committee to be conveyed to the States parties.

While providing for various sources of information, written and oral, to be made available to the Committee, there is no guidance to it on how it is to ascertain whether all available domestic remedies have been exhausted and on whom the burden of proof lies in this respect. Such difficulties and the possibility of abusing the provision on exhaustion of remedies led, in the General Assembly, to a proposal for its deletion, but it was rejected. The Assembly also rejected that the reply of the State receiving the initial communication should be the basis for ascertaining the exhaustion of domestic remedies.

Objections were voiced in the Committee on the Elimination of Racial Discrimination to a proposal made by a member to provide that "the Committee may also invite any person whose rights under the Convention are alleged by a State party to have been violated by another State party to appear before the Committee or otherwise submit a written statement". The proponent withdrew the proposal stating that he might raise the issue again when the Committee dealt with a specific case under Article 11 of the violation of Article 5 of the Convention.

Establishment of a conciliation commission and its purpose (Article 12)

Once the Committee has ascertained that all available domestic remedies have been invoked and exhausted or, if it considers the application of remedies to be unreasonably prolonged, and after it has obtained and collated all the information it deems necessary, its chairman appoints an *ad hoc* conciliation commission whose good offices are to be made available to the States parties concerned, with a view to an amicable solution of the matter on the basis of respect for the Convention. States parties to the dispute are to share equally all the expenses of the members of the Commission.

Nature of the Commission, its appointment and its composition (Article 12, paras. 1 and 2)

The Chairman of the Committee appoints five persons as members of an *ad hoc* Commission with the unanimous consent of the parties to the dispute. If the States parties to the dispute fail to reach agreement within three months on all or part of the composition of the Commission, its members not agreed upon by the States parties to the dispute are to be elected by secret ballot, by a two-thirds majority vote of the Committee from among its own members. The members of the Commission are to serve in their personal capacity. They are not to be nationals of the States parties to the dispute or of a State not party to the Convention.

As one of the sponsors of the proposal stated, it was natural to let the parties to the dispute, who were directly concerned, decide on the members of the Commission and it was reasonable to hope that States concerned would always manage to reach agreement on persons of such standing that neither State could object to them. In order to prevent the conciliation procedure from being paralyzed by lack of such agreement, the sponsors had provided for those members of the Commission not agreed upon by the parties to the dispute to be elected by a two-thirds majority vote of the Committee from among its own members. If that was deleted, the only remedy for failure of agreement would be to refer the dispute to the International Court of Justice, which was provided for in the final clauses, but that was not part of any compulsory procedure and it also gave rise to many reservations.

The full and unanimous consent of the States parties to the dispute to the composition of the Commission was, however, a pre-condition for a number of delegations. Such consent was claimed as a primary requirement for an amicable settlement and for full confidence in the conciliation procedure, as well as the only effective method to ensure that the decision of a Commission was carried out; there was also no reason to believe that States parties would be unable to find five conciliators within the period of three months, if they really wished to do so, whereas members to be elected to the Commission under the proposed text might be precisely those not agreed upon by the States parties concerned, which would be "utterly paradoxical".

The Third Committee rejected an amendment to delete the provision empowering the Committee to elect those members of the Conciliation Commission on which States parties could not agree from among the Committee's membership.

Rule 71 of the rules of procedure of the Committee provides for the Chairman's notifying States parties to the dispute and undertaking consultations with them concerning the composition of an *ad hoc* commission, and Rule 72 provides that, upon receiving the unanimous consent of the States parties, the Chairman is to proceed to appoint the members of the Commission and to inform the States parties to the dispute of the composition. Rule 73 provides that if, within three months of the Chairman's notification, States parties to the dispute fail to reach agreement on all or part of the composition of the Commission, the Chairman is to bring the situation to the attention of the Committee. The Committee then proceeds to elect by secret ballot, by a two-thirds majority vote, the members of the Commission concerned from among its own members, and the Chairman informs the States parties to the dispute of the composition of the Commission.

Rule 74 provides that upon assuming his duties, each member of the Commission is to make the following solemn declaration at the first meeting of the Commission: "I solemnly declare that I will perform my duties and exercise my powers as a member of the *ad hoc* Conciliation Commission honourably, faithfully, impartially and conscientiously."

Whenever a vacancy arises in the Commission, according to Rule 75, the Chairman fills it as soon as possible in accordance with the procedures laid down in Rules 71 to 73, upon receipt of a report from the Commission or upon notification by the Secretary-General.

The Committee reported to the General Assembly that one member "expressed the view that a vacancy would arise if one of the parties to a dispute, having originally consented to the composition of an *ad hoc* Conciliation Commission, subsequently withdraws that consent with respect to a member of the Commission. Other members of the Committee questioned the view that subsequent withdrawal of consent by a party to a dispute would create a vacancy in the Commission. No action was taken on this matter".[31]

Rules of procedure, officers, meeting place and secretariat (Article 12, paras. 3-5 and 8)

The Commission elects its Chairman and adopts its own rules of procedure. Its meetings are normally held at Headquarters or any other convenient place determined by the Commission. The secretariat of the Committee also serves the Commission.

Proceedings and report of an ad hoc Commission (Article 12, para. 8, and Article 13)

When the Commission has fully considered the matter, it prepares and submits to the Chairman of the Committee a report embodying its findings on all questions of fact relevant to the issue between the parties and containing such recommendation as it may think proper for the amicable solution of the dispute. This provision of Article 13(1) differs from that of paragraph 1 (a) of

Article 12 under which the good offices of the Commission are to be made available to the States concerned with a view to an amicable solution of the matter "on the basis of respect for this Convention". This difference probably is unintentional because the purpose of setting up an *ad hoc* Conciliation Commission is stated in the provision of Article 12(1)(a), whereas Article 13(1) concerns the report which the Commission is to draw up, and any recommendations which the Commission may make for an amicable solution to the dispute can only be on the basis of respect for the Convention. It may also be recalled that the Commission will have before it, under Article 12(8), the information obtained and collated by the Committee, and the Commission may call upon the State concerned to supply any relevant information.

The report of the Commission is communicated by the Chairman of the Committee to each of the States parties to the dispute. These States, within three months, inform the Chairman whether or not they accept the recommendations contained in the report of the Commission. Rule 77 of the rules of procedure provides for both the report of the Commission and the information received from the States parties to the dispute concerning the recommendations contained in the report to be transmitted to the members of the Committee.

After the expiration of the time limit of three months, the Chairman of the Committee communicates the report of the Commission and the declarations of the States parties concerned to the other States parties to the Convention. With this step the conciliation procedure comes to an end. An amendment by El Salvador, submitted to the Third Committee of the Assembly, to provide that "if they [the States parties to the dispute] do not accept the recommendations, the Committee shall reconsider the problem until a satisfactory solution is reached", was not discussed and it was rejected by eleven votes to ten, with 62 abstentions.

As of January 1982 no disputes had been referred to the Committee under Article II and the procedures described above have thus not been further developed in practice.

iv) COMMUNICATIONS FROM INDIVIDUALS AND GROUPS OF INDIVIDUALS
   (ARTICLE 14)

Optional nature of the provisions

Paragraphs 1, 3 and 9 of Article 14 make clear the optional nature of the article. A State party may at any time declare that it recognizes the competence of the Committee on the Elimination of Racial Discrimination to receive and consider communications from individuals or groups of individuals within its jurisdiction claiming to be victims of a violation by that State party of any of the rights set forth in the Convention. No communication is received by the Committee if it concerns a State party which has not made such a declaration. A declaration is deposited with the Secretary-General and may be withdrawn at any time by notification to the Secretary-General, but such with-drawal does affect communications pending before the Committee. The Committee can exercise the functions provided for in the article only when at least ten States parties have made the declarations.

As of 1 January 1982 only seven States parties had made declarations: Costa Rica, Ecuador, Italy, Netherlands, Norway, Sweden and Uruguay. On several occasions the General Assembly has appealed to States parties to study the possibility of making declarations under Article 14.

Optional prior recourse to a body within a State party's legal order and its functions and powers

After an initial proposal for a purely national machinery for considering individual claims of violation of any of the rights enumerated in the Convention had been withdrawn in favour of a complex text which would have provided for an in-between procedure for individual communications, problems still arose concerning the effect of any such machinery on the constitutional, legal and political systems of various countries.[32]

What was adopted by the General Assembly is in the nature of an optional clause for a national machinery. It still poses many problems, as will become evident and, in the light of Article 6 of the Convention on national protection, remedies and reparation, it may be wondered whether it will play any significant part in the implementation of the Convention, since it can hardly be used by States parties to evade their obligations under Article 6.

The text adopted provides that any State party may establish or indicate a body within its national legal order (hereafter referred to as the national body) which is to be competent to receive and consider petitions from individuals and groups of individuals within its jurisdiction who claim to be victims of a violation of any of the rights set forth in the Convention and who have exhausted other available local remedies.

The national body keeps a register of petitions and certified copies of the register are filed annually through appropriate channels with the Secretary-General on the understanding that the contents shall not be publicly disclosed. Paragraph 5 of Article 14 stipulates that in the event of failure to obtain satisfaction from the national body, the petitioner has the right to communicate the matter to the Committee within six months.

In the absence of a national body whose name has been deposited with the Secretary-General and transmitted to the other States parties, communications to the Committee on the Elimination of Racial Discrimination may be sent directly to it without any pre-condition such as that set out in paragraph 5. None of the States parties who have so far made declarations under paragraph 1 of Article 14 have mentioned anything about a national body.

Source of communication and its subject matter

Individuals or groups of individuals within a State party's jurisdiction claiming to be victims of a violation by that State party of any of the rights set forth in the Convention may send communications, provided that State party has made the required declaration previously.[33]

When a body within its national legal order has been established or indicated by the State party concerned, the same persons as mentioned above may communicate to it, provided they have exhausted other available local remedies[34] and, only in the event of failure to obtain satisfaction from the national body within six months, may the Committee be seized of it.[35]

The use of the term "individual or groups of individuals" appears wide enough to cover all individuals, whether nationals, non-nationals or persons without nationality; and non-governmental organizations are not *qua* organizations but as groups of individuals, so long as they are within the jurisdiction of the State party concerned. According to paragraph 6 (a), the Committee is not to receive anonymous communications.

Further texts providing that the Committee shall act on a communication "if it considers it to be receivable" were moved but withdrawn on grounds that they may be open to abuse, especially if no criteria were laid down concerning receivability of a petition or its rejection. It was thought best to leave to the Committee, which is empowered to adopt its own rules of procedure, to decide whether and how it will deal, if at all, with the question of receivability going beyond those specified in the Convention.

Functions and powers of the Committee

The Committee brings any communication referred to it, to the attention of the State party alleged to be violating any provision of the Convention without divulging the identity of the author unless he expressly consents. Within three months, the receiving State submits to the Committee written explanations or statements clarifying the matter and the remedy, if any, that may have been taken by that State. The Committee considers communications in the light of all information made available to it by the State party concerned and by the petitioner, so long as it has ascertained that the petitioner has exhausted all available domestic remedies, unless the application of the remedies is unreasonably prolonged. The Committee forwards its suggestions and recommendations, if any, to the State party concerned and to the petitioner. It includes in its annual report to the General Assembly, submitted under Article 9(2) of the Convention a summary of such communications and, where appropriate, a summary of the explanations and statements of States parties concerned and of its own suggestions and recommendations.[36]

v) CONSIDERATION OF COPIES OF PETITIONS AND REPORTS REGARDING DEPENDENT
   TERRITORIES (ARTICLE 15)

The article starts with a statement that, pending the achievement of the objectives of the Declaration on the Granting of Independence to Colonial Countries and Peoples (GA res. 1514(XV) of 1960), the provisions of the

Convention are in no way to limit the right of petition granted to those peoples by other international instruments or by the United Nations and its specialized agencies.[37]

The Committee receives copies of the petitions and submits expressions of opinion and recommendations on these petitions to the bodies of the United Nations which deal with matters directly related to the principles and objectives of the Convention in their consideration of petitions from the inhabitants of Trust and Non-Self-Governing Territories and all other territories to which General Assembly Resolution 1514 (XV) applies, relating to matters covered by the Convention which are before those bodies.

The Committee also receives from competent UN bodies copies of the reports concerning the legislative, judicial, administrative or other measures directly related to the principles and objectives of the Convention applied by the administering Powers within the Territories and expresses opinions and makes recommendations to those bodies. The Committee includes in its annual report to the General Assembly a summary of the petitions and reports it has received from United Nations bodies and the expressions of its opinion and recommendations relating to them. Under paragraph 4, the Committee may request from the Secretary-General all information relevant to the objectives of the Convention which is available to him regarding the territories.

Resolution 2106 B (XX), adopted by the General Assembly at the same time as the Convention, called upon the Secretary-General to make available to the Committee, periodically or at its request, all information in his possession relevant to Article 15 and requested the Special Committee of Twenty-Four and all other bodies of the United Nations authorized to receive and examine petitions from the peoples of colonial countries, to transmit to the Committee periodically or at its request, copies of petitions from those people relevant to the Convention for the comments and recommendations of the Committee. These United Nations bodies were requested to include in their annual reports to the General Assembly a summary of the action taken by them under the terms of the resolution.

These provisions and the Assembly resolution were agreed upon after much discussion and controversy surrounding the aim and purpose of the article. Many of the texts proposed were considered by some to go beyond the law of treaties by imposing obligations on States not parties to the Convention. Among the proposals made were: to apply the provisions of the Convention in full to the inhabitants of the dependent territories; to have the Committee on the Elimination of Racial Discrimination receive directly petitions regarding legislative, judicial, administrative or other measures adopted by administering Powers to give effect to the provisions of the Convention, or concerning violation of human rights stemming from racial discrimination; to have the Committee examine such petitions, in consultation with the administering Power concerned, with power to make appropriate recommendations; to omit reference to consultation with administering Powers but still to provide for direct petition right to the Committee, which would then send its expression of opinions and recommendations to the United Nations bodies concerned; to have the Committee express itself and make recommendations on the legislative, judicial, administrative or other measures applied by the administering Powers within the territories to give effect to the provisions of the Convention.

Disquietude was not dissipated by the new approach to the text of the article, and it led the United Kingdom government to make the following reservation to the Convention, which was not objected to under Article 20 of it:

"The United Kingdom maintains its position in regard to Article 15. In its view this article is discriminatory in that it establishes a procedure for the receipt of petitions relating to dependent territories while making no comparable provisions for States without such territories. Moreover, the article purports to establish a procedure applicable to the dependent territories of States whether or not those States have become parties to the Convention."

On 29 January 1970 the Committee on the Elimination of Racial Discrimination adopted a Statement of its Responsibilities under Article 15. This referred to such matters as territories to which the article applied and the sources and channels of information and stated that, in expressing its opinions and recommendations to the United Nations bodies concerned, it would "endeavour to avoid, as far as possible, duplicating the work of other competent bodies of the United Nations".[38]

Consideration of copies of petitions and reports and expressions of opinion and recommendations thereon by the Committee

The Committee has so far received copies of reports from the Trusteeship Council and the Special Committee of Twenty-Four; it has also received certain copies of petitions from the Special Committee but none so far from the Trusteeship Council.

The present procedure followed for considering this material is for the Chairman to appoint three working groups relating to various groups of territories. The working groups hold meetings and consultations in private and submit draft reports for examination in public meetings by the Committee as a whole.

In lieu of summaries of petitions and reports received by the Committee from United Nations bodies, the Committee has listed the documents received in annexes to its annual reports to the General Assembly. The Committee has also adopted decisions addressed directly, or through the General Assembly, to the bodies of the United Nations concerned, to obtain as full information as possible pertaining to racial discrimination and the achievement of the principles and objectives of the Convention in all the territories. However, it may be noted that the Committee has consistently complained, in its annual reports, of the inadequacy of the information available to it in accordance with Article 15 and of the irrelevance of much of the material forwarded to it.[39]

The expression of opinions and recommendations agreed upon by the Committee are included not in separate texts but in one integrated text and submitted to the General Assembly and the United Nations bodies concerned in the annual reports of the Committee to the Assembly. The opinions and recommendations have been adopted without a formal vote, and sometimes reservations made by members have been mentioned. These texts of the Committee are wide ranging and an analysis of the opinions and recommendations they contain cannot be attempted here.

Action by the General Assembly

Actions by the General Assembly on the Committee's texts have been either to note them generally as part of noting the report of the Committee as a whole, to commend its efforts to obtain the required information or to endorse them specifically, and to draw the attention of the United Nations bodies concerned to them. (See, for example, General Assembly res. 35/40 (1980).

Actions taken by the United Nations bodies concerned

As regards the United Nations bodies concerned, they have decided to take note of the Committee's recommendations and sometimes to adopt specific decisions; they have also reported to the General Assembly on their actions as requested by the Assembly in its Resolution 2106 B (XX).

Both the Trusteeship Council and the Special Committee of Twenty-Four have directed the attention of the administering Powers to the requests of the Committee and, where appropriate, requested the Secretary-General to include the required information in the working papers prepared on the various territories.[40]

vi) USE OF OTHER MACHINERY OR PROCEDURES OF IMPLEMENTATION
    (ARTICLE 16)

The provisions of the Convention concerning the settlement of disputes or complaints are to be applied without prejudice to other procedures for settling disputes or complaints in the field of discrimination laid down in the constituent instruments of, or in conventions adopted by, the United Nations and the specialized agencies. Nor should they prevent the States parties from having recourse to other procedures for settling a dispute in accordance with general or special international agreements in force between them.

It could be that the purpose of Article 16 is to safeguard other procedures containing elements of racial discrimination going beyond its own definition and other provisions in the Convention.

There was nothing said in the General Assembly to elucidate the full scope of Article 16 and especially whether it covered individual communications. However, Italy, Norway and Sweden, in making a declaration under Article 14(1), have made the reservation that "the Committee shall not consider any communication from an individual or a group of individuals unless the Committee has ascertained that the same matter is not being examined or has not been examined under another procedure of international investigation or settlement".

vii) CO-OPERATION WITH THE INTERNATIONAL LABOUR ORGANISATION AND UNESCO

In the second year of its existence, the Committee received communications from the ILO and Unesco in which those organizations expressed a desire to co-ordinate their work as closely as possible with that of the Committee with regard to the implementation of the Convention in their respective spheres of competence. After considerable debate the Committee decided to authorize the Secretary-General to distribute written statements, relating to Article 9 and submitted by those organizations to the members of the Committee, and to invite representatives of those organizations to "attend the meetings of the Committee", thus withholding consent to the idea of participation by those representatives in the Committee's consideration of reports from States parties under Article 9 as well as the idea of distributing to the Committee as such written statements from those organizations relevant to Article 9.[41] Since those debates, Committee members have asked questions of the representatives of both ILO and Unesco and have heard statements by those representatives on matters of common concern.

At the Committee's 19th session, held in 1979 at Unesco Headquarters in Paris, the Committee undertook, in the context of its consideration of the implementation of Article 7 of the Convention (relating to measures in the fields of teaching, education, culture and information), a thorough discussion of the Unesco Declaration on Race and Racial Prejudice and the resolution on its implementation adopted by the Unesco General Conference in 1978.[42] In its decision (2(XIX)) the Committee invited Unesco to transmit to it suggestions for the preparation of general guidelines with a view to assisting States parties to implement Article 7. In 1980, the Committee discussed a Unesco document submitted to it in accordance with its decision.[43]

viii) JURISDICTION OF THE INTERNATIONAL COURT OF JUSTICE (ARTICLE 22)

Any dispute between two or more States parties with respect to the interpretation or application of the Convention, which is not settled by negotiation or by the procedures expressly provided in the Convention, at the request of any of the parties to the dispute, is to be referred to the International Court of Justice for decision, unless the disputants agree to another mode of settlement.

An amendment to make recourse to the Court subject to the agreement of all parties to a dispute was rejected, though it was contended that this was in line with current practice. Nevertheless, some 24 reservations to the article were made, and they were not usually objected to under Article 20 of the Convention.

ix) ANNUAL REPORT OF THE COMMITTEE ON ITS ACTIVITIES TO THE GENERAL ASSEMBLY (ARTICLES 9, 14 AND 15)

Article 9 requires the Committee to submit annually to the General Assembly a report on its activities. Suggestions and recommendations of the Committee based on its examination of the reports and information from States parties under the same article are also to be reported to the General Assembly with comments of States parties on them, if any. These comments, as mentioned earlier, have so far been included in the annual reports of the Committee, but they need not be. The annual report is to include a summary of communications from individuals or groups of individuals considered by the Committee under Article 14 (not yet in force) and, where appropriate, a summary of the explanations and statements of the States parties concerned and of its own suggestions and recommendations. Also to be included in the annual report is a summary of the copies of petitions and reports from United Nations bodies received under Article 15 of the Convention concerning Trust, Non-Self-Governing and other Territories, to which General Assembly Resolution 1514 (XV) applies, and the expression of opinions and recommendations of the Committee relating to the said petitions and reports. Moreover, the annual report concerned with activities of the Committee is likely to include some information on any inter-State communication (there have been none so far) and the role of the Committee and, if it is set up, of any *ad hoc* conciliation commission in regard to it.

The Committee had submitted twelve annual reports to the General Assembly as of January 1982 (see bibliography). The reports so far submitted have been discussed in the Third Committee of the Assembly, usually in general terms, though from 1973 onwards, at the behest of the Committee,[44] the Assembly has discussed the report separately from other sub-items relating to elimination of racial discrimination. Some of the specific actions taken by the General Assembly have been mentioned earlier, in particular in relation to consideration by the Committee of reports under Article 9 and of material under Article 15. The General Assembly has taken note of the reports of the Committee, usually with appreciation.

The Committee itself takes the deliberations and decisions of the General Assembly seriously and discusses them annually. In its Decision 3 (XII) of 1975[45] it recommended to the Assembly that a member appointed by the Committee should be invited to participate in meetings of the Third Commit-

tee, at which the annual report of the Committee is considered. However, the
Assembly took no action in response to the recommendation.

Moreover, both the Assembly and the Committee are co-operating in the
programme relating to the Decade for Action to Combat Racism and Racial
Discrimination (1973-1983). Much of that programme derives directly from
the provisions, purposes and objectives of the Convention.

At each of its sessions since 1974 the Decade has been an item on the
Committee's agenda. Attaching great importance to the programme for the
Decade and with the aim of implementing the purposes of the Convention,
the Committee indicated ways of co-operating in the programme and suggested or recommended certain essential goals to be achieved under it. In
1975, the General Assembly endorsed the Committee's decision to make its
contribution to the total and unconditional elimination of racism and racial
discrimination, especially by concentrating its efforts under Articles 3, 9 and
15 of the Convention, by proposing recommendations with regard to the most
flagrant and large-scale manifestations of racial discrimination, particularly
in areas still under domination of racist or colonial regimes and foreign occupation. In making an urgent appeal to States which are not yet parties to
become so, the Assembly asked them, pending such action, to be guided by
the basic provisions of the Convention in their internal and foreign policies.
Specifically, the Assembly has reaffirmed its conviction that the acceptance
and implementation of the Convention on a universal basis are necessary for
the realization of the objectives of the Decade.[46] In 1979, the General Assembly (res. 34/24) invited the Committee to monitor the implementation of the
provisions of Articles 4 and 7 of the Convention "in order to prevent any
incitement to racism and racial discrimination and to promote understanding,
tolerance and friendship among nations and racial or ethnic groups".[47]

*(b). International Covenants on Human Rights and Optional Protocol to
the International Covenant on Civil and Political Rights*

Institutions and procedures for implementation became a matter of serious
concern from the very beginning of the discussion on the preparation of an
International Bill of Rights.[48]

At first, the machinery discussed mainly related to civil and political rights.
A great variety of schemes was presented, ranging from giving special responsibilities to United Nations organs (those proposed included the General
Assembly, the Security Council, the Economic and Social Council, the International Court of Justice and the Commission on Human Rights) to setting up
special permanent or *ad hoc* bodies of governmental or expert representation, to establishing an International Court of Human Rights or a High
Commissioner (Attorney General) for Human Rights, to not including any
international measures at all. As far as economic, social and cultural rights
are concerned, the machinery for their implementation which was agreed to
by the Commission was left largely unchanged by the General Assembly. The

same fate did not await the Commission on Human Rights' proposals on civil and political rights.

The General Assembly's Third Committee held a general discussion on measures of implementation of the Covenants in 1963, and detailed discussion and adoption of such measures took place at its 1966 session. As adopted, the measures of implementation of the Covenant on Economic, Social and Cultural Rights consist in a system of reporting by States parties and specialized agencies concerned to the Economic and Social Council, which may transmit them to the Commission on Human Rights. The Council considers them in collaboration with the specialized agencies and reports to the General Assembly. States parties agree that international action for the progressive achievement of the rights includes all the methods available to the United Nations and the specialized agencies, particularly as regards technical assistance. The Covenant on Civil and Political Rights also provides a reporting system as the primary and only obligatory method of international implementation, though the system differs from the other Covenant and the reports are to be submitted to a Human Rights Committee of experts. In addition to reporting, the Covenant provides for an optional system of State to State communication on the application of the provisions of the Covenant leading to possible conciliation by *ad hoc* commissions, appointed with their consent. The task of the Human Rights Committee, as regards the reports, is to transmit its reports and general comments to States parties and to the Council. Under the Optional Protocol to the Covenant on Civil and Political Rights, those who become parties to it (provided they are also parties to the Covenant) subscribe to the Human Rights Committee considering an individual's communication claiming violation of any of his rights enumerated in the Covenant, under certain conditions, and the Committee forwards its views to the State party concerned and to the individual. The Committee submits an annual report on its activities under the Covenant and the Optional Protocol to the General Assembly through the Economic and Social Council. There are no provisions involving the International Court of Justice. The Covenants and the Optional Protocol came into effect in 1976 and the description of the institutions and procedures which follows can hardly indicate the practice relating to them.

i) INTERNATIONAL COVENANT ON ECONOMIC, SOCIAL AND CULTURAL RIGHTS

The Reporting System

Purpose of the reports of States parties, their destination and frequency

The purpose of the reports from States parties is to ascertain the measures which they have adopted and the progress made in achieving the observance of the rights recognized in the Covenant.[48a] Reports may indicate factors and difficulties affecting the degree of fulfillment of obligations under the Covenant.[49] Where relevant information has previously been furnished to the United Nations or to any specialized agency by any State party, reproduction of that information is not necessary and a precise reference to it suffices.[50] All reports are to be submitted to the Secretary-General who is to transmit them to the Economic and Social Council.[51]

The reports of States parties are to be submitted in stages, in accordance with a programme to be established by the Economic and Social Council within one year of the entry into force of the Covenant, after consultations with the States parties and the specialized agencies concerned.[52] Under Council resolution 1988 (LX) (1976) States parties are to furnish biennially their reports beginning September 1977: first stage, rights covered by Articles 6 to 9; second stage, rights covered by Article 10 to 12; third stage, rights covered by Articles 13 to 15. States parties were requested in reporting to give full attention to the principles contained in Articles 1 to 5 of the Covenant and to indicate factors and difficulties affecting the degree of fulfillment of their obligations "when necessary".

Role of the specialized agencies and their reports

Many of the economic, social and cultural rights in the Covenants fall within the purview of the specialized agencies such as the ILO, Unesco, WHO and FAO. All of them have their own forms of reporting and other methods of ascertaining the achievement of the objectives of their organizations or conventions and recommendations concluded under their auspices.[53] The role assigned to these agencies under the Covenant is not what many of them had desired during the preparation of the Covenant, and the exact nature of it will become evident only as the decisions of the Council come into play.

The specialized agencies receive from the Secretary-General copies of the reports or any relevant parts therefrom from States parties which are also members of the agencies insofar as these reports or parts therefrom relate to any matters which fall within the responsibilities of the agencies in accordance with their constitutional instruments.[54] The Secretary-General was asked to do this by the Council in paragraph 5 of its Resolution 1988 (LX) (1976).

The Council also makes arrangements with the specialized agencies in respect of their reporting to it on the progress made in achieving the observance of the provisions of the Covenant, falling within the scope of their activities. These reports may include particulars of decisions and recommendations on their implementation by the competent organs.[55]

Guidelines for reports

In accordance with paragraph 8 of Council resolution 1988 (LX) the Secretary-General, in co-operation with the specialized agencies concerned, drew up general guidelines for the reports to be submitted by States parties and by specialized agencies.[56] The Council also decided that States parties submitting reports under the Covenant need not submit reports on similar questions under the general reporting procedure established by Council Res. 1074 C (XXXIX)(1965). The Council later (decision 1978/9) requested the Secretary-General to prepare an analytical summary, based on the general guidelines, of the reports submitted by States parties to facilitate the work of a sessional working group on implementation of the Covenant established by the Council.

Action on reports and reports by the Economic and Social Council

All reports from States parties are submitted to the Secretary-General, who transmits copies to the Economic and Social Council for consideration.[57] The Council may transmit them, as well as the reports from specialized agencies, to the Commission on Human Rights for study and general recommendation or, as appropriate, for information. States parties and specialized agencies concerned may submit comments to the Council on any general recommendation made by the Commission or reference to such general recommendation in any report of the Commission or any documentation referred to therein.[58]

The Council may submit from time to time to the General Assembly reports with recommendations of a general nature and a summary of the information received from the States parties and the specialized agencies on the measures taken and the progress made in achieving general observance of the rights recognized in the Covenant.[59] The Council may also bring to the attention of other organs of the United Nations, their subsidiary organs and specialized agencies concerned with furnishing technical assistance any matters arising out of the reports which may assist such bodies in deciding, each within its field of competence, on the advisability of international measures likely to contribute to the effective progressive implementation of the Covenant.[60] States parties agree that international action for the achievement of the rights, recognized in the Covenant, includes such methods as the conclusion of conventions, the adoption of recommendations, the furnishing of technical assistance and the holding of regional meetings and technical meetings for the purpose of consultation and study organized in conjunction with the Governments concerned.[61]

Both under the draft of the Commission on Human Rights and the provisions described above, the task of considering the reports and taking action thereon is entrusted to the Economic and Social Council, assisted by other United Nations bodies, and acting in co-operation with the specialized agencies. The question arose in the General Assembly as to whether the system of reporting would not function better if entrusted to a body of experts based, in varying degrees, on Articles 8 and 9 of the Convention on the Elimination of All Forms of Racial Discrimination. Two sets of proposals were submitted, but opposition to them led to their withdrawal.

In fact, the Council decided by its Resolution 1988 (LX) of 11 May 1976 that a sessional working group of the Council, with appropriate representation of States and with due regard to equitable geographical distribution, should be established by it, to assist whenever reports are due for consideration. Representatives of specialized agencies concerned may take part in the proceedings of the working group when matters falling within their field of competence are considered. An appeal has been addressed to States to include, if possible, in their delegations to the relevant sessions of the Council, members competent in the subject matters to be considered. The procedures initiated by the Council in 1976 and 1978 (res. 1988 (LX) and decision 1978/10) led to the first session of the sessional working group of the Council in April-May 1979 after protracted consultations and negotiations concerning its composition. That session was confined mainly to formulating the group's methods of work, which were approved by the Council (E/1979/64 and res. 1979/43). At its second session in 1980 the group did consider some of the reports of the States parties concerning Articles 6 to 9 of the Covenant, but the Council, after noting that the group had encountered certain difficulties in discharging its responsibilities, decided to review early in 1981 its composition, organization and administrative arrangements, and solicited through the Secretary-General the views of members of the Council and all States parties on these arrangements (E/1980/60 and res. 1980/24). Thus, the implementation measures provided for the Covenant may be said to be still at a preliminary stage.

The report of the Third Committee mentions that "it was generally agreed that the Council's own reports and recommendations to the Assembly should be of a 'general' character in more than one sense: they should, if necessary, deal with the application everywhere of all the rights recognized in the Covenant, but they should not refer to any particular State. One opinion was, however, that Article 62 of the Charter seemed to place no such restriction on the competence of the Council to make recommendations."[62] It was also remarked that Article 24 could not impair the provisions of the Charter.

Relationship between the United Nations and the specialized agencies; responsibilities of their organs

According to Article 24, nothing in the Covenant is to be interpreted as impairing the provisions of the Charter and of the constitutions of the specialized agencies, which define the respective responsibilities of the various organs of the United Nations and of the specialized agencies in regard to the matters dealt with in the Covenant.[63]

ii) INTERNATIONAL COVENANT ON CIVIL AND POLITICAL RIGHTS

The Human Rights Committee[64]

Composition and election of the members of the Human Rights Committee and their emoluments

A Human Rights Committee (hereafter referred to as the Committee) is established to carry out the functions provided for it in the Covenant.[65] The

Committee consists of eighteen members, nationals of the States parties, of high moral character and recognized competence in the field of human rights, consideration being given to the usefulness of the participation of some persons having legal experience, who are to serve in their personal capacity[66] and who, before taking up their duties, must make solemn declarations in open Committee that they will perform their functions impartially and conscientiously.[67]

The members of the Committee are elected by secret ballot by the States parties from among their nationals; each State party may nominate not more than two persons, who are eligible for renomination for later elections.[68] In the election by the States parties consideration is given to equitable geographical distribution of membership and to the representation of the "different forms of civilization and of the principal legal systems"; no more than one national of the same State may be elected to the Committee.[69]

Members serve for four years and are eligible for re-election if re-nominated. There is an election for half the membership every two years.[70] The geographical distribution of the membership of the Committee for 1981-82 is 5 from Western European and other countries, 4 from Eastern Europe and 3 each from Africa, Asia and Latin America. Members receive emoluments from United Nations resources on such terms and conditions as the Assembly may decide, having regard to the importance of the Committee's responsibilities.[71]

Vacancies are filled by elections by States parties, in the same way as for the ordinary elections; a member elected to fill a vacancy holds office for the remainder of the term of office of the member who vacated the seat.[72] A vacancy arises in the event of the death or the resignation of a member of the Committee, or when, in the unanimous opinion of the other members, a member has ceased to carry out his functions for any cause other than absence of a temporary character.[73]

Although the Covenant stipulates that members of the Committee must be nationals of States parties, nationals of States parties which have not accepted the provisions of optional Article 41 on inter-State communications or the provisions of the Optional Protocol on individual communications are not precluded from acting under Article 41 or the Protocol, though only nationals of the States parties accepting the optional provision of Article 41 can be members of an *ad hoc* conciliation commission established under Article 42.

Meetings, officers and rules of procedure of the Committee and its secretariat (Articles 36, 37 and 39)

Most of the Committee's meetings have been held in Geneva. The Committee elects its officers for a term of two years; they may be re-elected. It was to establish its own rules of procedure, but these rules were to provide that twelve members should constitute a quorum and that decisions of the Committee were to be made by a majority vote of the members present. The Committee has adopted provisional rules of procedure based upon those of

the United Nations organs and of the Committee on the Elimination of Racial
Discrimination, as well as certain rules relating to reports from States parties (including participation of representatives of States parties in the Committee when their reports are considered), rules relating to communications
received from States parties under Article 41 of the Covenant, and rules
concerning communications received under the Optional Protocol, bearing in
mind the relevant provisions of the Covenant.[74]

The Secretary-General is to provide the necessary staff and facilities for
the effective performance of the functions of the Committee.[75]

The reporting system (Article 40)

Purpose of reports

From the discussions in both the Commission and the Third Committee of
the General Assembly, it appears that the aim is, by and large, to impose
obligations under the Covenant of an immediate and not an indefinite nature.
In line with this, the proposal for States parties to submit to the Committee
reports on the measures "they have adopted and the progress made in giving
effect to the rights recognized" in the Covenant was changed to "measures
they have adopted which give effect to the rights recognized" in the Covenant and, in addition, "on the progress made in the enjoyment of those
rights." Reports are to indicate also the factors and difficulties, if any, affecting the implementation of the Covenant.[76]

Frequency and destination of reports

Reports are to be submitted within one year of the entry into force of the
Covenant for the State party concerned and thereafter whenever the Committee so requests.[77] All reports are to be submitted to the Secretary-General
who is to transmit them to the Committee for consideration.[78] The Secretary-
General may, after consultation with the Committee, transmit to the specialized agencies concerned copies of such parts of the reports as may fall within
their field of competence.[79] The question of co-operation between the Committee and the agencies has been the subject of considerable discussion by
the Committee. In 1978, it decided that the specialized agencies should not be
invited to submit any comments on the reports of States parties since the
Covenant contained no provision to that effect.[80] While reiterating that position in 1980 the Committee also stated that it was "convinced of the need for
all possible information from the specialized agencies that was relevant to its
work, in a relationship of mutual co-operation with those agencies; accordingly and to that end, the Committee agreed that information, mainly on the
specialized agencies interpretation of, and practice in relation to, the corresponding provisions of their instruments, should be made available to members of the Committee on a regular basis, and that information of any other
kind may be made available to them on request during meetings of the

Committee which were attended by representatives of the specialized agencies".[81]

Action on reports

The Committee is to study the reports submitted by the States parties and to transmit its reports and such general comments as it may consider appropriate to the States parties.[82] The States parties may submit to the Committee observations on any comments that may be made by it.[83] The Committee may also transmit to the Economic and Social Council its general comments along with copies of the reports it has received from States parties.[84] The Committee is further required to submit to the General Assembly, through the Council, an annual report on its activities.[85]

As of the end of 1980 the Committee had not forwarded any "general comments" to States parties whose reports it had examined, nor had any such comments been contained in its annual reports to the General Assembly. However, the annual reports do contain descriptions of the Committee's consideration of each State's report including the questions posed by members and the additional information requested by them. At its eleventh session, in 1980, the Committee adopted a ten-point consensus relating to its subsequent examination of States parties reports (see CCPR/C/SR.260 (1980)). It decided that it would begin to formulate general comments based on the consideration of reports for transmission to the States parties. In formulating general comments the Committee will be guided by the following principles: they should be addressed to the States parties, in conformity with article 40, paragraph 4 of the Covenant; they should promote co-operation between States parties in the implementation of the Covenant; they should summarize experience the Committee has gained in considering States reports; they should draw the attention of States parties to matters relating to the improvement of the reporting procedure and the implementation of the Covenant; and, they should stimulate activities of States parties and international organizations in the promotion and protection of human rights.

The general comments could be related, *inter alia*, to the following subjects: the implementation of the obligation to submit reports under article 40 of the Covenant; the implementation of the obligation to guarantee the rights set forth in the Covenant; questions related to the application and the content of individual articles of the Covenant; suggestions concerning the co-operation between States parties in applying and developing the provisions of the Covenant.

The Committee also confirmed its aim of engaging in a constructive dialogue with each reporting State, and for this purpose it established a three or four year periodicity for subsequent States' reports under article 40.

It also decided to develop guidelines for these new reports, the contents of which should concentrate on: the progress made in the meantime; changes made on laws and practices involving the Covenant; difficulties in the implementation of the Covenant; the completion of the initial report, taking into account the questions raised in the Committee; additional information as to questions not answered or not fully answered; information taking into account general comments that the Committee may have made in the meantime; and action taken as a result of the experience gained in co-operation with the Committee.

For their general information and to provide more active assistance to States parties when drawing up both initial and subsequent reports, it was considered useful as a first step to establish a digest or list of questions most frequently asked by members of the Committee, relating to the various subjects under the Covenant. Such a digest or list should be drawn up, and be up-dated from time to time, by the Secretariat on the basis of the summary records of Committee meetings and should be circulated to States parties for their information only after approval by the Committee.

Prior to the meetings with representatives of the reporting States, at which the second report will be considered, a working group of three members the Committee will meet to review the information so far received by the Committee in order to identify those matters which it would seem most helpful to discuss with the representatives of the reporting State. This will be without prejudice to any member of the Committee raising any other matter which appears to him to be important.

The Committee will request the Secretariat to establish after each examination of a State report an analysis of the study of its report. This analysis should set out systematically both the questions asked and the responses given with precise references to the domestic legal sources quoting the main ones.

Optional provisions concerning good offices and conciliation procedures resulting from initiation of inter-State communications (Articles 41-42)

Optional acceptance of provisions concerning inter-State communications and making available the good offices of the Human Rights Committee

Optional acceptance of the provisions

A State party to the Covenant may at any time declare that it recognizes the competence of the Committee to receive and consider communications to the effect that a State party claims that another State party is not fulfilling its obligations under the Covenant.[86] Communications are receivable only if submitted by a State party, which has made a declaration recognizing, in regard to itself, the competence of the Committee and not if it concerns a State party which has not made such a declaration. These declarations are to be deposited with the Secretary-General and may be withdrawn at any time by notification to him, but this will not affect continuance of consideration of a matter which has been the subject of an initial communication by a State party. With this exception, no further communication by any State party is to be received after the notification of withdrawal of the declaration has been received by the Secretary-General, unless the State party concerned has made a new declaration.

Of the 62 States parties to the Covenant as of 1 January 1982, fourteen had made the declaration under Article 41. The provisions of that Article entered into force on 28 March 1979, but as of January 1982 no State had invoked the procedure.

Initial communication between States parties

If a State party considers that another State party is not giving effect to the provisions of the Covenant, it may, by written communication, bring the matter to the attention of that State party. Within three months after the receipt of the communication, the receiving State is to afford the State which sent the communication an explanation or any other statement in writing clarifying the matter, which is to include, to the extent possible and pertinent, reference to domestic procedures and remedies taken, pending or available in the matter.[87]

Submission of a matter to the Human Rights Committee and its functions

If the matter is not adjusted to the satisfaction of both States parties within six months after the receipt by the receiving State of the initial communication, either State has the right to refer the matter to the Committee, by notice given to the Committee and to the other State.

The Committee deals with a matter only after it has ascertained that all available domestic remedies have been invoked and exhausted in the matter in conformity with the generally recognized principles of international law. This is not the rule when the application of the remedies is unreasonably prolonged.

The Committee makes available its good offices to the States parties concerned with a view to a friendly solution of the matter on the basis of respect for human rights and fundamental freedoms as recognized in the Covenant. The Committee holds closed meetings when examining the matter. It may call upon States parties concerned to supply any relevant information. Such States have the right also to be represented when the matter is being considered in the Committee and to make submissions orally and/or in writing.

Action by the Human Rights Committee

Within twelve months after the date of being seized with the matter, the Committee submits a report. If a friendly solution of the matter on the basis of respect for human rights and fundamental freedoms as recognized in the Covenant is reached, the Committee confines its report to a brief statement of the facts and of the solution reached.[88] If such a solution is not reached, the Committee confines its report to a brief statement of the facts; the written submissions and record of the oral submissions made by the States parties concerned are attached to the report.[89] In every matter the report is communicated to the States parties concerned. The Committee has laid down the procedure for the consideration of communications received under Article 41 of the Covenant (A/34/40, Chapter III and annex III).

Possible further action on inter-State communications by ad hoc conciliation commissions

Establishment and composition of an ad hoc commission

If the Committee is not able to resolve a matter referred to it under Article 41 to the satisfaction of the States parties concerned it has the option, subject to the prior consent of the States parties concerned, to appoint an *ad hoc* conciliation commission (hereinafter referred to as the Commission).[90] The good offices of the Commission are made available to the States parties concerned with a view to an amicable solution of the matter on the basis of respect for the Covenant.

Any such Commission consists of five persons acceptable to the States parties concerned. If the States parties fail to reach agreement within three months on all or part of the composition of the Commission, its members concerning whom no agreement has been reached are elected by secret ballot by a two-thirds majority vote of the Committee from among its members.[91] The members serve in their personal capacity; they cannot be nationals of the States parties concerned, or of a State not party to the Covenant, or of a State party which has not made a declaration under Article 41.[92] It is likely that in practice the Committee will rely heavily upon consent of the States concerned to the membership until at least there are large numbers of declarations under Article 41.

Officers, meeting, secretariat and rules of procedure of a commission

The Commission elects its own Chairman and adopts its own rules of procedure. Its meetings are normally held at Headquarters or in Geneva. However, they may be held at such other convenient places as the Commission may determine in consultation with the Secretary-General and the States parties concerned. The Secretariat provided by the United Nations for the Committee also serves the Commission.

Consideration of a matter by a commission

The Covenant provides for the Commission to consider the matter fully.[93] In considering the matter, the information received and collated by the Committee is made available to the Commission and the Commission may call upon the States parties concerned to supply any other relevant information.[94] Unlike Article 41, there is no provision entitling the States parties concerned to be represented when the matter is being considered in the Commission and to make submissions orally and/or in writing.[95] It is hardly likely, however, that the Commission, which will have come into being with the prior consent of the States parties concerned, will not allow for such participation and submissions, especially as it is specifically provided that, when a solution is not reached, the Commission's report is to contain the written submissions and a record of the oral submissions made by the States parties concerned.[96]

Report of an ad hoc conciliation commission

When the Commission has fully considered the matter, but in any event not later than twelve months after having been seized of it, it submits to the Chairman of the Committee a report for communication to the States parties concerned. If the Commission is unable to complete the consideration of the matter within twelve months, it confines its report to a brief statement of the status of its consideration of the matter.

If an amicable solution to the matter on the basis of respect for human rights as recognized in the Covenant is reached, the Commission confines its report to a brief statement of the facts and of the solution reached.

If an amicable solution is not reached, the Commission's report presents its findings on all questions of fact relevant to the issues between the States parties concerned, and its views on the possibilities of an amicable solution of the matter. The report also contains the written submissions and a record of the oral submissions made by the States parties concerned.[97] The States parties, within three months of the receipt of the report, notify the Chairman of the Committee whether or not they accept the contents of the report of the Commission.

The initial proposal incorporated similar provisions to those of the International Convention on the Elimination of All Forms of Racial Discrimination according to which the Commission would submit a report containing its findings on all questions of fact relevant to the issues between the parties and such recommendations as it may consider proper for the amicable solution of the matter.[98] Changes were introduced, in particular to insert the words "and containing its views on the possibilities of an amicable solution to the matter," instead of referring to recommendations in case of failure to reach an amicable solution, and the replacement of acceptance of "recommendations" contained in the report of the Commission by the States parties concerned by acceptance of "the contents of the report of the Commission". These provisions of paragraph 7 of Article 42 were adopted by narrow majorities. Questions may be raised as to whether the term "contestations" in French is the same as "views" in English (as well as "observaciones" in Spanish), which was the contention of the representative of France, the mover of the change.

Privileges and immunities of the members of the Human Rights Committee and of an ad hoc conciliation commission

Unlike the International Convention on the Elimination of All Forms of Racial Discrimination, the Covenant provides that members of the Commit-

tee and of an *ad hoc* conciliation commission which may be appointed under
the Covenant are entitled to the facilities, privileges and immunities of experts on mission for the United Nations as laid down in the relevant sections
of the Convention on the Privileges and Immunities of the United Nations.

Relations and division of responsibilities between the United Nations and
the specialized agencies; relationship between the implementation provisions
of the Covenant and other procedures prescribed in the field of human rights

In the first place, the Covenant establishes as a general rule applying to
the whole of it in Article 46 that nothing in the Covenant is to be interpreted
as impairing the provisions of the Charter and of the Constitutions of the
specialized agencies which define the respective responsibilities of the various organs of the United Nations and of the specialized agencies in regard to
the matters dealt with in the Covenant. The same provision is included in
Article 23 of the Covenant on Economic, Social and Cultural Rights.

In the second place, Article 44 provides that the provisions for the implementation of the Covenant are to apply without prejudice to the procedures
prescribed in the field of human rights by or under the constituent instruments and the conventions of the United Nations and of the specialized
agencies and is not to prevent the States parties to the Covenant from having
recourse to other procedures for settling a dispute in accordance with general
or special agreements in force between them.

Article 44 was adopted after prolonged discussion on various texts and
suggestions, and after the latter part of it was voted on separately. Particular objection was taken to a proposal which included a paragraph providing
that the Human Rights Committee was to take no action under Articles 41
and 42 of the Covenant with regard to any matter in respect of which any of
the procedures referred to had been invoked. It is impossible to give any
exact indication of the scope of Article 44 which might not be challenged on
some ground or other.

Provisions on implementation and the International Court of Justice

The proposed articles of the Covenant as drafted by the Commission on
Human Rights concerning the Court were deleted. Under the first of the
articles the Commission had proposed that States parties would agree that
any State party having been complained of or having lodged a complaint
might, if no solution had been reached within the terms of what is now Article
41, para. 1 (b) (ii) and Article 42, para. 7 (c) and (d), bring the case before the
Court, after the reports provided for in those articles had been drawn up.
The second provided that the provisions of the Covenant were not to prevent
States parties from submitting to the Court any dispute arising out of the
interpretation or application of the Covenant in a matter within the competence of the Committee. The third would have provided that the Committee

might recommend to the Economic and Social Council that the Council request the Court to give an advisory opinion on any legal question connected with a matter of which the Committee was seized.

Besides these provisions, the Commission text also envisaged the election of the Human Rights Committee by the International Court of Justice. It may be contended that the attitude in the General Assembly towards the Court was affected by the judgment of 18 July 1966 of the Court on South West Africa Cases (*Ethiopia v. South Africa; Liberia v. South Africa*), Second Phase,[99] even if some sponsors of deletions of the Commission's texts expressed other views. However, it is well to recall certain observations made in the Third Committee to the effect that, even without such specific provisions as those mentioned above, a matter might be brought before the Court if States parties concerned agreed to do so, that recourse to the Court might be possible under the provisions of Article 44 of the Covenant, and the Charter provisions empowering the General Assembly (to which the Human Rights Committee is to submit annual reports) to seek advisory opinions from the Court would remain unimpaired.

Annual report by the Human Rights Committee to the General Assembly through the Economic and Social Council

An annual report on its activities is submitted by the Human Rights Committee to the General Assembly through the Economic and Social Council. Under the Optional Protocol the Committee includes in its annual report a summary of its activities under that Protocol.[100]

Up to 1982 the Committee has submitted five annual reports. So far, the Council has transmitted these reports to the Assembly without discussing their substance. The Committee had expressed the wish that its Chairman be invited to present its annual report to the Assembly (A/32/44, para. 185) but the Assembly took no action on the matter. The resolutions adopted by the Assembly have been similar in content with suitable variations reflecting the contents of the Committee's reports.[101]

iii) OPTIONAL PROTOCOL TO THE COVENANT ON CIVIL AND POLITICAL RIGHTS[102]

All proposals made in the Commission on Human Rights concerning the right of petition, including those in response to the General Assembly's request to draft provisions on it, were either rejected or withdrawn. In 1966, the Assembly's Third Committee discussed an optional article for inclusion in the Covenant on the right of individuals or groups to submit petitions but rejected it.[103] Thereupon an Optional Protocol on the subject was submitted and adopted.[104] The Covenant on Civil and Political Rights and the Optional Protocol are separate instruments, but they are related since only parties to the Covenant can become parties to the Protocol.

The Protocol came into force simultaneously with the Covenant and, as of 1 January 1982, there were 16 States parties to the Covenant which were also parties to the Protocol. A State party may denounce the Protocol at any time by written notification to the Secretary-General, the denunciation becoming effective three months after the receipt of notification. The provisions of the Protocol continue to apply to any communications submitted under it before the effective date of the denunciation.

The body empowered to receive and act on communications under the Protocol is the Human Rights Committee established under the Covenant.

Generally speaking, the various rules of procedure, methods of work and other actions of the Committee made public (documentation and discussions under the Protocol are confidential) appear to bear out what was said in the Third Committee on behalf of the sponsors of the Protocol. When questions were asked concerning the criteria which the Committee would apply in deciding on conditions of admissibility of communications under Article 3 of the Protocol, particularly those to be considered "to be an abuse of the right of submission of such communications", it was stated that in applying those conditions "the line of conduct which the Committee was to follow could not be dictated; rules could be drawn up gradually on the basis of experience".[105] The Committee has regarded the Protocol's provisions as prescribing its duties, but not all its functions which are subject to change as the Committee gains more experience.

Sources of communications, their subject matter and admissibility (Articles 1 to 3)

The Committee is competent to receive communications from individuals subject to the jurisdiction of a State party to the Protocol (but not a party to the Covenant only) who claim to be victims of a violation by that State party of any of the rights set forth in the Covenant and who have exhausted all available domestic remedies. The Committee is to consider inadmissible any communication which is anonymous, or which it considers to be an abuse of the right of submission or to be incompatible with the provisions of the Covenant.

In the Committee's view, a communication should normally be submitted by the alleged victim himself. This does not mean that he must sign the communication himself, as he may also act through a duly appointed representative. Where he is unable to submit the communication himself the Committee may decide to consider a communication submitted on his behalf provided a close link exists between the author(s) and the alleged victim (e.g. a close family connection).[106]

Communications have been declared inadmissible if the alleged violations took place prior to the date of entry into force of the Covenant and the Protocol for the States parties concerned, but a reference to them may be taken into account and considered if the author claims that they have continued after such date or that they have had effects which themselves constitute a violation after that date.[107]

In order to assist the authors of communications, the Committee has authorized the Secretariat to draw up and make use of guidelines and a model form of communication as appropriate, explaining to the authors that the use of the model form is not obligatory but merely intended as a guide to facilitate their task.[108]

Consideration of admissibility and exhaustion of domestic remedies (Articles 1 to 5).

Under rule 84 of the provisional rules of procedure a member of the Committee shall not take part in the examination of a communication if he has any personal interest in the case, or if he has participated in any capacity in the making of any decision on the case covered by the communication: any questions arising on these are to be decided by the Committee.

According to rule 86, the Committee may, at any time prior to forwarding its final views on a communication to a State party concerned, inform that State of its views as to whether interim measures might be desirable to avoid irreparable damage to the victim of the alleged violations, and indicate that such views do not imply a determination on the merits. A working group of the Committee, established under rule 89, makes recommendations to the Committee regarding the fulfillment of the conditions of admissibility of communications. It usually meets for one week immediately before each session of the Committee and, if necessary, during the session.

The Committee may also decide to discontinue consideration of a communication, without taking a decision as to its admissibility. Rules are laid down for assisting the Committee and its working group in carrying out these functions. For instance, under rule 91, the working group may request the State party concerned or the author of the communication to submit additional written information or observations relevant to the question of admissibility.

As recalled earlier, a prior condition which applies under Article 2 of the Protocol is the exhaustion of all available domestic remedies by the victim of an alleged violation. The Committee itself, under Article 5 (2) of the Protocol is not to consider any communication unless it has ascertained (a) that the same matter is not being examined under another procedure of international investigation or settlement, and (b) that the individual has exhausted all available domestic remedies; neither of these is to be the rule where the application of the remedies is unreasonably prolonged.[109]

As regards Article 5 (2) (a) the Committee has recognized that cases considered by the Inter-American Commission on Human Rights constitute matters under examination in accordance with another procedure of international investigation or settlement. On the other hand, the Committee has determined that the procedure set up under Economic and Social Council resolution 1503 (XLVIII) does not constitute a procedure under Article 5 (2) (a), since it is concerned with the examination of situations which appear to reveal a consistent pattern of gross violations of human rights and a situation is not "the same matter" as an individual complaint. The Committee has also determined that Article 5, (2) (a) can only relate to procedures implemented by inter-State or intergovernmental organizations on the basis of inter-State or intergovernmental agreements or arrangements. Procedures established by non-governmental organizations, as for example, the procedure of the Inter-Parliamentary Council of the Inter-Parliamentary Union, cannot, therefore, bar the Committee from considering communications submitted to it under the Protocol.[110]

The Committee has further concluded that a subsequent opening of a case submitted by an unrelated third party under another procedure of international investigation or settlement does not preclude the Committee from considering a communication submitted under the Protocol. The Committee has also determined that it is not precluded from considering a communication, although the same matter has been submitted under another procedure of international investigation or settlement, if it has been withdrawn from or is no longer being examined under the latter procedure at the time that the Committee reaches a decision on the admissibility of the communication submitted to it.[111]

Concerning Article 5 (2) (b), the Committee considers that its provisions should be interpreted and applied in accordance with the generally accepted principles of international law with regard to the exhaustion of domestic remedies as applied in the field of human rights. If the State party concerned disputes the contention of the author of a communication that all available domestic remedies have been exhausted, the State party is required to give details of the effective remedies available to the alleged victim in the particular circumstances of his case. In this connection, the Committee has deemed insufficient a general description of the rights available to accused persons under the law and a general description of the domestic remedies designed to protect and safeguard these rights.[112]

Final action by the Committee and report to the General Assembly (Articles 4 to 6).

According to rule 93 (1) of the provisional rules of procedure, as soon as possible after the Committee has decided that a communication is admissible, that decision and the text of relevant documents are communicated, through the Secretary-General, to the State party concerned. The decision is similarly communicated to the author of the communication. The State party concerned is required, under Article 4, (2) of the Protocol, to submit to the Committee, within six months, written explanations or statements clarifying the matter and the remedy, if any, that may have been taken. The State party's submission is forwarded to the author of the communication who may within such time limits as established by the Committee, submit any additional written information or observations. According to rule 93 (4) the Committee may even at this stage review its decision that a communication is admissible in the light of the submissions of the State party concerned.

Provided the communication is still admissible, the Committee considers the communication in the light of all written information forwarded by both parties. For this purpose, the working group has been assigned the task, in accordance with rule 94 (1), to examine and make recommendations to the Committee in formulating its final views under Article 5, (4) of the Protocol. With regard to certain communications, the Committee has also assigned this latter task to individual members of the Committee, acting as special rapporteurs for that purpose.[113]

The final views of the Committee are forwarded to the State party concerned under Article 5, (4) of the Protocol, and to the individual under rule 94 (2) of the provisional rules of procedure of the Committee. Any member of the Committee may, under rule 94 (3), request that a summary of his individual opinion be appended to the views of the Committee when they are communicated to the individual and to the State party concerned.

The Committee's 1980 report to the General Assembly indicated that 72 communications were placed before the Committee between its second session (1977) and its tenth (1980). The communications related to Canada (17), Colombia (4), Denmark (4), Finland (3), Iceland (1), Italy (1), Madagascar (1), Mauritius (1), Norway (2), Sweden (1), Uruguay (36) and Zaire (1). Of those: 8 were declared suspended or discontinued; 17 were declared inadmissible; 12 were to be examined further, prior to a decision as to their admissibility; and 27 were declared admissible for consideration on their merits. Consideration of a total of six communications had been concluded by the adoption of views under Article 5, paragraph 4 of the Protocol. These latter communications concerned Uruguay and the views on them were given in 1979 and 1980; with one exception, the views referred to breaches of various provisions of the Covenant. These views have been set out in some detail in the Committee's annual reports to the General Assembly.[114]

Relationship to procedures on petitions available to peoples concerning territories to which the Declaration on the Granting of Independence to Colonial Countries and Peoples applies

Pending the achievement of the objectives of the Declaration on the Granting of Independence to Colonial Countries and Peoples as set forth in General Assembly Resolution 1514 (XV) of 14 December 1960, the provisions of the Protocol are in no way to limit the right of petition granted to those people by the Charter of the United Nations and other international conventions and instruments under the United Nations and its specialized agencies.[115] This provision was said to reaffirm, and to avoid overlapping or jurisdictional problems, arising out of the petition rights relating to Trust Territories under Article 87 (b) of the Charter, those provided for the Special Committee of Twenty-Four established following General Assembly Resolution 1514 (XV), as well as the Fourth Committee of the General Assembly among others.

(c). Other Conventions on Human Rights and Fundamental Freedoms

In the present section, consideration is given to the implementation procedures provided for in the major United Nations instruments which have not been dealt with above. As noted in the previous chapter, several other instruments are presently being drafted within the UN system but it is not possible at this stage to review their approach to implementation.[116]

i) WAR CRIMES AND CRIMES AGAINST HUMANITY, INCLUDING GENOCIDE
   AND APARTHEID

Convention on the Prevention and Punishment of the Crime of Genocide

Article VI of the Convention provides that persons charged with genocide or any of the other acts enumerated in Article III of the Convention are to be tried by a competent tribunal of the State in the territory of which the act was committed, or by such international penal tribunal as may have jurisdiction, with respect to those contracting parties which shall have accepted its jurisdiction.

Article VIII provides that any contracting party may call upon the competent organs of the Unitd Nations, as they consider appropriate, for the prevention and suppression of acts of genocide or of any of the other acts enumerated in Article III.

The question of an international criminal jurisdiction is taken up below.

In a recent "study of the question of the prevention and punishment of the crime of genocide" by a special Rapporteur of the Sub-Commission on Prevention of Discrimination and Protection of Minorities (E/CN.4/Sub.2/416 of 1978) detailed consideration has been given to questions of implementation of the Convention.

International Convention on the Suppression and Punishment of the Crime of Apartheid

This Convention entered into force in July 1976. According to Article V of the Convention, persons charged with the acts enumerated in its Article II may be tried by a competent tribunal of any State party to the Convention, which might acquire jurisdiction over the person of the accused, or by an international penal tribunal having jurisdiction with respect to those States parties which shall have accepted its jurisdiction.

Under Article VI of the Convention, States parties undertake to accept and carry out in accordance with the Charter the decisions taken by the Security Council aimed at the prevention, suppression and punishment of the crime of *apartheid*, and to co-operate in the implementation of decisions adopted by other competent organs of the United Nations, with a view to achieving the purposes of the Convention. This provision is not dependent on prior initiative of a State party, as is Article VIII of the Genocide Convention, but the text of Article VIII of the latter is also included as Article VIII in the *Apartheid* Convention. It was explained during the discussion that States could call upon the Special Committee on *Apartheid*, the Commission on Human Rights or any other body.

The Convention contains a system of reporting. Under Article VII the States parties undertake to submit periodic reports to the group established under Article IX on the legislative, judicial, administrative or other measures that they have adopted and that give effect to the provisions of the Convention; copies of such reports are to be transmitted through the Secretary-General to the Special Committee on *Apartheid*. The main function with respect to reports, however, is given to the group appointed by the Chairman of the Commission on Human Rights. Under Article IX the Chairman is to appoint a group consisting of three of its members, who are also representatives of States parties to the Convention, to consider the reports. The group may meet for a period of not more than five days, either before the opening or after the closing of a session of the Commission, to consider the reports.

The Commission is empowered, under Article X, paragraph 1 (a), to request United Nations organs, when transmitting copies of petitions under Article 15 of the International Convention on the Elimination of All Forms of Racial Discrimination, to draw the Commission's attention to complaints concerning acts which are enumerated in Article II of the Convention.

Under Article X, paragraph 1 (c), the Commission is empowered to request information from the competent United Nations organs, concerning measures taken by the authorities responsible for the administration of Trust and Non-Self-Governing Territories, and all other Territories to which General Assembly Resolution 1514 (XV) applies, with regard to such individuals alleged to be responsible for crimes under Article II of the *Apartheid* Convention, who are believed to be under their territorial and administrative jurisdiction.

The Commission, under Article X, paragraph 1 (b), is to prepare, on the basis of reports from the competent organs of the United Nations and periodic reports of the States parties (and presumably the report of the group of the Commission thereon), as well as on the basis of complaints in copies of petitions and information submitted by the competent organs referred to in Article X, paragraph 1 (a) and (c), though these are not clearly specified (they do not appear to be the same as "reports from competent organs"), a list of individuals, organizations, institutions and representatives of States, who are alleged to be responsible for the crimes enumerated in Article II, as well as those against whom legal proceedings have been undertaken by States parties.

Article X states that pending the achievement of the Declaration on the Granting of Independence to Colonial Countries and Peoples, contained in General Assembly Resolution 1514 (XV) of 14 December 1960, the provisions of the *Apartheid* Convention are in no way to limit the right of petition granted to those peoples by other international instruments or by the United Nations and its specialized agencies.

At its first session, in 1978, the Group of Three established under the Convention drew up a set of guidelines to assist States parties in the preparation of their reports. In 1980, the Group examined the reports submitted by States parties in the presence of those States' representatives.[117] It also made a number of recommendations to the Commission in connection with the more effective implementation of the Convention.[118]

The question of an international criminal jurisdiction

The Genocide (Article VI) and *Apartheid* (Article V) Conventions provide for trial of persons charged with either crime by an international penal tribunal, if there is one. Such a possibility was also considered in connection with the 1968 Convention on the Non-Applicability of Statutory Limitations to War Crimes and Crimes against Humanity.

When adopting the Convention on Genocide, the General Assembly adopted a resolution in which, considering that the discussion of the Convention had raised the question of the desirability and possibility of having persons charged with genocide tried by a competent international tribunal, and considering that, in the course of development of the international community, there will be an increasing need for an international judicial organ for the trial of certain crimes under international law, it invited the International Law Commission to study the desirability and possibility of establishing an international judicial organ for the trial of persons charged with genocide or other crimes, over which jurisdiction might be conferred upon that organ by international conventions.[119]

The Commission was requested to pay attention to the possibility of establishing a criminal chamber of the International Court of Justice. The International Law Commission concluded that an international criminal court was both possible and desirable but recommended it to be a separate institution rather than a criminal chamber of the Court. Thereafter two committees appointed by the General Assembly considered the matter and draft statutes for such a separate court were submitted, the last in 1954.[120] However, the General Assembly in 1954 and 1957 decided that the problems raised were closely related to defining aggression and to the draft code of offences against the peace and security of mankind and deferred consideration until the latter were taken up.[121]

In 1974 the Assembly approved (Res. 3341 (XXIX)) the text defining aggression, and in 1978 recommenced discussion of the draft code of offences against the peace and security of mankind, which is continuing. Although it has not resumed discussion of the question of an international criminal jurisdiction, in 1979 it approved, within the context of the implementation of the programme for the Decade for Action to Combat Racism and Racial Discrimination, the undertaking of a study to include the establishment of international jurisdiction envisaged by the International Convention on the Suppression and Punishment of the Crime of *Apartheid* (Res. 34/24, annex. para. 20) by the Commission on Human Rights' *Ad Hoc* Working Group of Experts on southern Africa.[122]

Within the work on the implementation of that Convention enquiries have been directed to States parties to suggest ways and means for the establishment of the international penal tribunal referred to in Article V of the Convention. A report by the Group of Three, containing suggestions concerning such a tribunal, was submitted to the Commission on Human Rights in 1981.[123]

ii) STATELESSNESS AND REFUGEES

Convention on the Reduction of Statelessness

Article 11 of the Convention provides that the States parties are to promote the establishment within the framework of the United Nations, as soon as may be after the deposit of the sixth instrument of ratification or accession, of a body to which a person claiming the benefit of the Convention may apply for the examination of his claim and for assistance in presenting it to the appropriate authority. In 1976, the General Assembly, in Res. 31/36, after noting that the United Nations High Commissioner for Refugees was already carrying out the functions required under the Convention, requested him to continue to so do.

Convention relating to the Status of Stateless Persons

Article 33 provides for States parties to communicate to the Secretary-General the laws and regulations which they may have adopted to ensure the application of the Convention.

Convention and Protocol relating to the Status of Refugees

Both the Convention and the Protocol contain identical provisions concerning co-operation of the national authorities of States parties with the United Nations and communication by them of national legislation and regulations on their application to the Secretary-General.

The States parties undertake to co-operate with the Office of the United Nations High Commissioner for Refugees in the exercise of its functions, and they are in particular to facilitate its duty of supervising the application of the provisions of the Convention and the Protocol. In order to enable the High Commissioner to make reports to the competent organs of the United Nations, the States parties undertake to provide in the appropriate form information and statistical data requested concerning: a) the condition of refugees, b) the implementation of the Convention and the Protocol, and c) laws, regulations and decrees which are, or may hereafter be, in force relating to refugees.[124]

iii) STATUS OF WOMEN

The Convention on the Political Rights of Women,[125] the Convention on the Nationality of Married Women[126] and the Convention on Consent to Marriage, Minimum Age for Marriage and Registration of Marriages do not contain specific international measures of implementation.

Under the International Convention on the Elimination of All Forms of Discrimination Against Women, which was adopted by the General Assembly on 18 December 1979, but which had not entered into force as of 1 January 1982, a Committee on the Elimination of Discrimination against Women is to be established. At the time of entry into force of the Convention (requiring 20 ratifications or accessions) it is to consist of 18 members; it is to be increased to 23 after 35 States parties have ratified or acceded to it. Members are to be experts of high moral standing and competence in the field, will be elected by States parties from among their nations and shall serve in their personal capacity. In the election, by secret ballot, consideration will be given to equitable geographical distribution and to the representation of the "different forms of civilization as well as the principal legal systems" (Art. 17(i)).

Members are elected for a four-year term with half being elected every two years. For the filling of casual vacancies, the State party whose expert has ceased to function as a member of the Committee shall appoint another expert from among its nationals, subject to   the approval of the Committee. As with the Human Rights Committee the U.N. Secretary-General is to provide the necessary staff and facilities for the effective functioning of the Committee. The Committee is to adopt its own rules of procedure and to elect its officers for a two-year term.

Under Article 18 of the Convention, the States parties undertake to submit to the Secretary-General for consideration by the Committee, a report on the legislative, judicial, administrative or other measures which they have adopted to give effect to the provisions of the Convention and on the progress made in this respect:

(a) Within one year after the entry into force for the State concerned;
(b) Thereafter at least every four years and further whenever the Committee so request.

Reports may indicate factors and difficulties affecting the degree of fulfillment of obligations under the present Convention. The Committee will normally meet for a period of not more than two weeks annually in order to consider these reports (Art. 20). The Convention also provides that the Committee shall, through the Economic and Social Council, report annually to the

General Assembly on its activities and may make suggestions and general recommendations based on the examination of reports and information received from the States parties. Such suggestions and general recommendations shall be included in the report of the Committee together with comments, if any, from States parties (Art. 21(i)).

The specialized agencies shall be entitled to be represented at the consideration of the implementation of such provisions of the present Convention as fall within the scope of their activities. The Committee may invite the specialized agencies to submit reports on the implementation of the Convention in areas falling within the scope of their activities (Art. 22).

It is also stated that nothing in the Convention shall affect any provisions that are more conducive to the achievement of equality between men and women which may be contained: (a) In the legislation of a State party; or (b) in any other international convention, treaty or agreement in force for that State (Art. 23). Moreover, under Article 24 States parties undertake to adopt all necessary measures at the national level aimed at achieving the full realization of the rights recognized in the Convention.

Finally, it should be noted that the Convention provides that any dispute between two or more States parties concerning the interpretation or application of the Convention which is not settled by negotiation shall, at the request of one of them, be submitted to arbitration. If, within six months from the date of the request for arbitration, the parties are unable to agree on the organization of the arbitration, any one of those parties may refer the dispute to the International Court of Justice by request in conformity with the Statute of the Court. However, each State party may at the time of signature or ratification of the Convention or accession thereto declare that it does not consider itself bound by this provision in which case any other States parties shall not be bound by it with respect to any State party which has made such a reservation (Art. 29).

iv) TRAFFIC IN PERSONS AND SLAVERY CONVENTIONS

Under Article 21 of the Convention for the Suppression of the Traffic in Persons and of the Exploitation of the Prostitution of Others (1949), the States parties are to communicate to the Secretary-General such laws and regulations as have already been promulgated in their States, and thereafter annually, such laws and regulations as may be promulgated relating to the subject of the Convention, as well as all measures taken by them concerning the application of the Convention. The information received is to be published periodically by the Secretary-General and sent to all Member States of the United Nations and to non-Member States eligible to become parties to the Convention.

At the request of the Social Commission, a report was submitted to it in 1958 primarily based on the policy and principles in the Convention. It included two studies dealing respectively with a programme of action to combat the traffic in persons and the exploitation of the prostitution of others and with measures prerequisite to and in conjunction with the suppression of the regulation of prostitution.[127]

In 1959, the Council drew the attention of Governments of States parties and of those eligible to become parties to the Convention to the report and in particular to the programme of action set out in Chapter IX of it.

The States parties to the Slavery Convention of 1926, as amended by the Protocol of 1953, undertake, under Article 7, to communicate to each other and to the Secretary-General any laws and regulations which they may enact with a view to the application of the provisions of the Convention.[128]

Under Article 8 of the 1956 Supplementary Convention on the Abolition of Slavery, the Slave Trade, the Institutions and Practices Similar to Slavery, the States parties undertake to co-operate with each other and with the United Nations to give effect to the provisions of the Convention. They also undertake to communicate to the Secretary-General copies of any laws, regulations and administrative measures enacted or put into effect to implement the provisions of the Convention. The Secretary-General is to communicate the information received to other parties and to the Economic and Social Council as part of the documentation for any discussion which the Council might undertake with a view to making further recommendations for the abolition of slavery, the slave trade or the institutions and practices which are the subject of the Convention.

Briefly, the efforts which have been undertaken in this connection, and which have not always been confined to States parties to the Convention, have related to: the establishment of the Working Group on Slavery of the Sub-Commission on Prevention of Discrimination and Protection of Minorities, in 1974,[129] the appointment of Rapporteurs on the question, gathering information and making surveys concerning the provisions of the Conventions with increasingly enlarged scope taking in other practices and manifestations, such as slavery-like practices of *apartheid* and colonialism, traffic in persons, transfer and inheritance of women, etc.; seeking active assistance and co-operation of United Nations bodies, specialized agencies, intergovernmental organizations, INTERPOL, and non-governmental organizations; furnishing technical assistance and establishing a list of experts on economic, sociological, legal and other disciplines who advise governments (neither of these have apparently been asked for by governments); making general and specific recommendations for various actions, such as ratification of certain ILO Conventions; providing penal sanctions for certain acts defined in the Conventions.

As authorized by the Economic and Social Council in 1974, and as determined by Resolution 7 (XXVI) of the Sub-Commission on the Prevention of Discrimination and Protection of Minorities, the Sub-Commision appointed a group of five from among its membership to meet for not more than three working days, prior to each of its annual sessions. The group is to review developments in the field of slavery and the slave trade in all their practices and manifestations, including the slavery-like practices of *apartheid* and colonialism, the traffic in persons and the exploitation of the prostitution of others as they are defined in the Convention on Slavery of 1926, the Supplementary Convention of 1956 and the Convention for the Suppression of the Traffic in Persons and of the Exploitation of the Prostitution of Others of 1949. The group is to consider and examine any information from credible sources on the subject of slavery and slavery-like practices with a view to recommending remedial action.

On 21 August 1974, in Resolution 11 (XXVII), the Sub-Commission, *inter alia*, requested Governments, specialized agencies, regional inter-governmental organizations, non-governmental organizations in consultative status and individuals to submit to the Secretary-General for transmission to the Working Group such reliable information on slavery and the slave trade in all their practices and manifestations, the traffic in persons and the exploitation of the prostitution of others as may be available to them. The Group, which had held its first session, was also asked to make proposals for future methods of work.

In 1976, the Sub-Commission, after considering the report of the second session of the Group, decided to have the Working Group meet biennially and to continue with its mandate, and to consider such problems as the sale of children and debt bondage, and requested world-wide publicity to be given to the Group's terms of reference (Res. 5 (XXIX) in doc. E/CN.4/1218). The Sub-Commission also requested States parties to comply with the reporting procedure under Article 21 of the 1949 Convention and asked the Secretary-General to revive the procedure for the publication of the reports received. States parties to the 1956 Supplementary Convention on Slavery were called upon to report annually on the legal, administrative and practical situation within their countries in relation to the abolition of the institutions and practices covered by the Convention. The Sub-Commission also requested close assistance of other United Nations agencies such as the ILO, Unesco, the FAO, the United Nations High Commissioner for Refugees and Unicef, as well as other bodies, such as INTERPOL (which had already been requested by the Council to forward to the Secretary-General and the Sub-Commission annually any information at its disposal with regard to international traffic in persons, including reports received from its national central bureau), and all relevant non-governmental organizations in consultative status, in compiling information and furthering the work of the Group. Wide publicity was requested to be given to slavery-like practices, including in particular those of South Africa and Southern Rhodesia, as set out in the Group's report (doc. E/CN.4/Sub.2/373).

v) CONVENTION ON THE INTERNATIONAL RIGHT OF CORRECTION

Under the Convention, the Contracting States agree that when a Contracting State contends that a news dispatch capable of injuring its relations with other States or its national prestige or dignity, transmitted from one country to another by correspondents or information agencies of a Contracting or non-Contracting State, and published or disseminated abroad, is false or distorted, it may submit its version of the facts (called *communiqué*) to the Contracting States within whose territories the dispatch has been published or disseminated. The *communiqué* must be without comment or expression of opinion and be no longer than is necessary to correct the alleged inaccuracy or distortion. With the least possible delay, a Contracting State receiving such a correction shall release the *communiqué* to correspondents and information agencies through the channels customarily used for the release of news concerning international affairs for publication. In the event that any Contracting State to which a *communiqué* has been transmitted fails to fulfil this obligation, the State exercising the right of correction may submit the *communiqué* to the Secretary-General, together with the text of the dispatch to which it relates, and at the same time notify the State complained against of this act. The latter State may, within five clear days after receiving such notice, submit its comments to the Secretary-General. These should relate only to the allegation that it has not discharged its obligations mentioned above. The Secretary-General, in any event, within ten clear days after receiving the *communiqué*, is to give appropriate publicity to it, together with the dispatch and the comments, if any, submitted to him by the State complained about.

The complaining State has two remedies if the receiving State fails to carry out its obligations: reciprocal treatment of a future *communiqué* from the receiving State and recourse to the Secretary-General as outlined above. As regards the first, Article III (2) provides that, when a receiving State does not discharge its obligations, the other State may accord, on the basis of reciprocity, similar treatment to a *communiqué* thereafter submitted to it by the defaulting State.

With respect to the functions of the Secretary-General, there is little to add except to say the Convention fails to allow for any "margin of appreciation" by the Secretary-General who probably has to carry out his tasks irrespective of irregularities in the procedure or whatever his views on the dispatch concerned being false or distorted or not having been transmitted from one country to another.[130]

NOTES

1. See Chapter 10, *supra*.

2. The conferences to draw up the 1956 Supplementary Convention on Slavery and the 1951 Convention relating to the Status of Refugees.

3. See UN docs. A/35/312 and Add. (1980) concerning a Review of the Multilateral Treaty-Making Process.

4. See E/CN.4/SR.238 (1951) concerning sponsorship by a member of the Commission on Human Rights of proposals originally put forward by the ILO. As regards non-governmental

organizations, the arrangements for consultation with them made by the Economic and Social Council were confined to certain categories of them, at the beginning, but later extended to all those with consultative status and many of them played an important role by submitting written comments or making oral interventions. Even views of other non-governmental bodies and individuals were submitted to certain preparatory bodies, particularly in the non-confidential lists of written communications prepared for them.

5. See documents of the United Nations Conference on International Organizations (UNCIO), 1945, Vol. 3, pp. 271, 383, 602; Vol. 6, pp. 324-325 and 456.

6. The Convention relating to the Status of Refugees and the International Convenants on Human Rights respectively.

7. These principles are set out in Articles 26 and 27 of the Vienna Convention on the Law of Treaties.

8. In the same Resolution, the Assembly asked the Secretary-General in respect of future conventions to act as depository for documents containing reservations or objections thereto without passing on the legal effect of such documents, which are to be communicated to all States concerned, to whom it would be left to draw the legal consequences. In its Resolution 1452 (XIV) of 7 December 1959, the Assembly asked the Secretary-General to follow the same practice with respect to United Nations conventions concluded before, as well as after, its Resolution of 1952. See also Articles 19 to 23 of the 1969 Vienna Convention on the Law of Treaties.

9. A/33/18 (1978), Chapter VI. See also, as regards the International Covenant on Civil and Political Rights, A/32/44, para. 138.

10. As the late Sir Hersch Lauterpacht wrote, "The preoccupation with the enforcement of the Bill of Rights ought not to conceal the fact that the most effective way of giving reality to it is through the normal activity of national courts and other organs applying the law of the land", *International Law and Human Rights*, New York, Praeger, 1950, p. 356.

11. It has been said that in these matters there must be patience; that it was eight years before the Committee of Experts was established by the ILO; that there is a time-lag involved in establishing confidence in a procedure, for instance, the authority of the Committee of Experts was a gradual development; and that there is a third time-lag which involves giving a government time to submit its case, to make a finding thereon, to accept that finding and to implement it fully. Jenks, "The International Protection of Trade Union Rights", *The International Protection of Human Rights*, Luard, D.E.T., New York, Praeger, 1967, pp. 244-246.

12. "It is no longer a law between States only and exclusively but a law which embodies guarantees of individual rights which are simultaneously national and international in character and are enforceable by both national and international procedures". C. W. Jenks, *The Common Law of Mankind*, London, Stevens, 1956, p. 46.

13. The late Mrs. Eleanor Roosevelt said at the United Nations on 27 March 1958: "Where, after all, do universal human rights begin? In small places, close to home—so close and so small that they cannot be seen on any map of the world. Yet they are the world of the individual persons: the neighborhood he lives in; the school or college he attends; the factory, farm or office where he works. Such are the places where every man, woman and child seeks equal justice, equal opportunity, equal dignity without discrimination. Unless these rights have meaning there, they have little meaning anywhere. Without concerted citizen action to uphold them close to home, we shall look in vain for progress in the larger world." See *Teaching Human Rights: A Handbook for Teachers*, United Nations Publication: Sales No. 63.I.34.

14. The current provisional rules of procedure are contained in CERD/C/35 (1978).

15. See rules of procedure 34 and 62; A/9618, paras. 21-30 and decision 1(IX); and A/32/18, paras. 331-333 and decision 2 (XVI).

16. Article 8.5(b).

17. A/8718, paras. 4 and 5; A/9018, paras. 28-30.

18. *Ibid.*, Chapter X, Section A, Decision 2 (VII).

19. *Ibid.*, para. 30.

20. A/8027, para. 14.

21. A/8718, para. 27 and the discussion is summarized in paras. 28-33.

22. *Ibid.*, para. 33.

23. The second sentence of para. 1 of Art. 9 was voted on separately and adopted by 85 votes to none, with seven abstentions (A/6181, para. 114 (a) (iii)). Such a provision is not included in Art. 40 of the Covenant on Civil and Political Rights or, for that matter, in any other international convention on human rights. That is not to say that further information cannot be requested under other systems of reporting.

24. Contrast this detailing of measures with the provisions of Art. 16 of the Covenant on Economic, Social and Cultural Rights and Art. 40 of the Covenant on Civil and Political Rights where the term "measures" was considered broad and wide in meaning to encompass all measures, including legislative, judicial and administrative measures.

25. See A/8027, Annex III for 1970 guidelines and A/35/18, Annex IV for 1980 guidelines.

26. A/35/18, paras. 42-53.

27. See *Committee on the Elimination of Racial Discrimination and the Progress Made Toward the Achievement of the Objectives of the International Convention on the Elimination of All Forms of Racial Discrimination*, UN Sales No. E.79.XIV.4, 1979, paras. 130-139.

28. A/8718, para. 25.

29. A/9018, paras. 317-322.

30. See A/10018, paras. 185-187.

31. See A/8027, para. 34.

32. For various proposals, decisions and discussions, see A/6181, paras. 144-153, and A/C.3/SR.1355-1357 and 1362-1363. An enquiry into the difficulties, problems and feasibility of systems for national bodies is a subject worthy of further study in depth, preferably in a comprehensive manner to cover national, regional and international co-operative efforts.

33. Article 14, paras. 1 and 3.

34. Article 14, para. 2.

35. Article 14, para. 5.

36. Article 14, paras. 6-8.

37. While a brief indication is given in this chapter concerning the working of Art. 15, a deeper analysis concerning its working ought to be undertaken, as should its impact on the inhabitants of the dependent Territories and the Administering Powers in achieving the principles and objectives of the Convention.

38. A/8027, Annex IV, para. 9.

39. E.g. A/10018, para. 197; A/31/18, para. 259; A/32/18, para. 343; A/34/18, para. 494; and A/35/18, para. 476. For the response of the Committee of Twenty-four (now 25) see A/35/18, Annex V.

40. A/8718, paras. 109-110, A/9018, para. 326, and Decision 2 (VIII); see also A/9618, paras. 256-257.

41. A/8718, paras. 122-132, and decision 2(VI).

42. A/34/18, Chap. III. See also General Assembly resolution 35/40 on the Committee expanding its cooperation with Unesco and ILO.

43. A/35/18, chap. III.

44. A/9018, letter of transmittal of the report by the Chairman of the Committee.

45. A/10018, Chapter II C and Chapter VII B.

46. General Assembly Resolutions 3134 (XXVIII) (1973), 3223 (XXIX) and 3225 (XXIX) (1974), 3266 (XXIX) (1974), 3377 (XXX) and 3381 (XXX) of 1975.

47. During 1980 the Committee considered undertaking the preparation of a study on these two Articles but deferred a decision until 1981. A/35/18, para. 510.

48. A comprehensive documentary reference to United Nations material on this subject

does not exist. Considerable material and documentary references before 1954 may be found in the annotations to the Covenants, prepared by the Secretary-General (doc. A/2929). Thereafter, see the documents of the General Assembly and ECOSOC, the UN *Yearbooks on Human Rights* the UN *Juridical Yearbooks* since 1963, which include some bibliographical material of outside publications, and the bibliography to the present textbook. A full commentary and bibliographical material on the Covenants and the Optional Protocol are badly needed.

48a. Article 16, para. 1.

49. Article 17, para. 2.

50. Article 17, para. 3.

51. Article 16, para. 2 (a).

52. Article 17, para. 1.

53. See, for example, Chapters 12 and 13 *infra*.

54. Article 16, para. 2 (b).

55. Article 18.

56. The general guidelines for Articles 6 to 9 of the Covenant are contained in E/1978/8, annex, and those for Articles 10 to 12 in E/1980/6, annex.

57. Article 16, para. 2 (a) and Council resolution 1988 (LX), para. 4.

58. Articles 19 and 20. The Council has not, as of 1981, decided to involve the Commission in this or in any other way in the implementation of the Covenant. Some indication of the role envisaged for the Commission in the preparatory work is given in A/2929, Chap. IX, para. 12.

59. Article 21.

60. Article 22.

61. Article 23.

62. A/6546, para. 74.

63. The possibility of providing for inter-State and individual communications was discussed in the Commission on Human Rights, but proposals relating to them were not adopted. See A/2929, paras. 42-48.

64. See A/32/44; A/33/40; A/34/40; and A/35/40; A/32/333; A/33/472; A/34/687; and A/35/637.

65. Article 28, para. 1.

66. Article 28, paras. 2 and 3.

67. Article 38.

68. Article 29.

69. Article 31.

70. Article 32.

71. Article 35. From 1981, besides receiving travel and daily subsistence allowances for meetings of the Committee, its members are paid honoraria of $3,000 and its Chairman $5,000 (General Assembly res. 35/218).

72. Articles 33 and 34.

73. These provisions may be contrasted to those on vacancies in the Committee on the Elimination of Racial Discrimination.

74. Article 39. The provisional rules of procedure, as revised, are contained in CCPR/C/3/Rev.1 (1980). See for summaries of discussion: A/32/44, paras. 16-94; A/33/40, para. 587; and A/34/40, paras. 28 to 53. The normal procedure set out in the rules of United Nations organs is that decisions are to be made by a majority vote of the "members present and voting", which is included in the provisional rules of procedure of the Committee on the Elimination of Racial Discrimination in the absence of any specific voting requirements in the Convention establishing that Committee. But the Covenant Article 39, para. 2(b) omits the words "and voting". Accordingly, if a bare quorum of 12 members of the Human Rights Committee are present and a decision is put to a vote it can be adopted only if there are 7 affirmative votes for it. It is immaterial that other votes cast are against or abstentions; there is nothing in the record of discussions on Article 39, para. 2, to suggest that an

abstention is to be regarded as a negative vote as the Committee was informed. See CCPR/C/SR.7, paras. 37 to 40. As the Committee does not appear so far to have taken any votes the question posed here has not actually arisen. It is also to be noted that a footnote to rule 51 of the provisional rules of the Committee sets out the view generally expressed by the members of the Committee that its method of work normally should allow for attempts to reach decisions by consensus before voting, provided that the Covenant and the rules of procedure are observed and that such attempts do not unduly delay the work of the Committee. Members agreed that the Chairman may, at any meeting and at the request of any member, put the proposal to a vote. See A/32/44, paras. 26 to 34.

75. Article 36. For a discussion on the assistance required by the Committee from the Secretariat and on the proper role of the Secretary-General in the performance of his functions under the Covenant see CCPR/C/SR.153 and 174 (1979).

76. Article 40, paras. 1 and 2.

77. Article 40, para. 1 (a) and (b). At its second session, in 1977, the Committee drew up a list of general guidelines regarding the form and contents of reports from States parties under Article 40 of the Covenant. See A/32/44, paras. 136 to 141 and annex IV. See also A/35/40, annexes III and IV concerning status of submission of reports by States parties and their non-receipt.

78. Article 40, para. 2.

79. Article 40, para. 3.

80. A/33/40, para. 605.

81. A/35/40, para. 414.

82. Article 40, para. 4.

83. Article 40, para. 5.

84. Article 40, para. 4.

85. Article 45.

86. Article 41, para. 1.

87. Article 41, para. 1 (a). Although the optional declaration is to be made for inter-State communications in case of "claims that another State party is not fulfilling its obligations" under the Covenant (Art. 41, para. 1), these obligations arise out of the provisions of the Covenant and, therefore, are covered by the broader phrase "not giving effect to the provisions" of the Covenant (Art. 41, para. 1 (a)).

88. Article 41, para. 1 (h), (i).

89. Article 41, para. 1 (h), (ii).

90. Article 42, para. 1 (a). See also A/34/40, paras. 51 and 52, and annex III, rule 77E.

91. Article 42, para. 1 (b).

92. Article 42, para. 2.

93. Article 42, para. 7.

94. Article 42, para. 6.

95. Article 41, para. 1 (g).

96. Article 42, para. 7 (c).

97. Article 42, para. 7 (c).

98. Article 13, para. 1 of that Convention and A/6546, para. 441.

99. *I.C.J. Reports*, 1966, p. 6.

100. Article 6 of the Optional Protocol.

101. By way of example reference may be made to the Assembly resolution of 1980 (35/132) by which the Assembly: noted with appreciation the report of the Committee and expressed satisfaction at the serious and constructive manner in which it was continuing to undertake its functions; appreciated that it continues to strive for uniform standards in the implementation of provisions of the Covenant and the Protocol and emphasized the importance of the strictest compliance by States parties with their obligations; urged States parties which have not yet done so to submit their reports as speedily as possible and those which have been requested to provide additional information to comply, as well as to

consider making declarations under Article 41; took note that the Committee is considering the question of the follow-up to its consideration of the reports; again invited States to become parties to the Covenant and the Optional Protocol; welcomed the measures already taken by the Secretary-General to improve the publicity for the work of the Committee and encouraged the latter to continue its consideration of this question; and requested the Secretary-General to make appropriate arrangements for holding meetings of the Committee in developing countries.

102. See A/32/44, Chapters III and V; A/33/40, Chapter IV; A/34/40, Chapter V and annexes VI and VII; A/35/40, Chapter IV and annexes V to X; CCPR/C/3/Rev.1, rules 78 to 94. On the use of the words "petition" and "communication", see A/C.3/SR.1418, para. 8; A/C.3/SR.1438, para. 44; and A/5411, Part IV.

103. Rejected by 41 votes to 39, with 16 abstentions. A/6546, para. 485.

104. Adopted in the Third Committee by 59 votes to 2, with 32 abstentions. A/6546, para. 597. Adopted in plenary meeting of the Assembly by 66 votes to 2, with 38 abstentions. A/PV.1496.

105. See A/C.3/SR.1440, para. 24.

106. A/35/40, para. 393, and rule 90, para. (1), (b).

107. A/35/40, para. 394.

108. A/33/40, para. 591.

109. It is to be noted that several States parties, in ratifying or acceding to the Protocol, have made reservations to Article 5 (2) in connection with other procedures of international investigation. See UN publication, Sales No. 81.V.10, chapter IV, 5.

110. See A/33/40, paras. 582 to 585, and A/35/40, para. 395.

111. See A/35/40, para. 396.

112. See A/35/40, para. 397.

113. See A/35/40, para. 388.

114. See A/34/40, annex VII; A/35/40, Chapter IV and annexes V to X. See also the statement of the representative of Uruguay to the General Assembly. A/PV.92 (1980), p. 190.

115. Article 7.

116. It may be mentioned that all of the conventions dealt with here except the Convention on the Non-Applicability of Statutory Limitations to War Crimes and Crimes against Humanity include provisions for settlement of disputes by the International Court of Justice.

117. The reports of the Group are contained in E/CN.4/1286 (1978); E/CN.4/1328 (1979); and E/CN.4/1358 (1980). States reports under the Covenant are in documents E/CN.4/1277 and Add.; E/CN.4/1353 and Add.; and E/CN.4/1415 and Add.

118. Resolutions of the Commission relating to the Group's work are: 13 (XXXIII)(1977); 7(XXXIV)(1978); 10(XXXV)(1979); 13(XXXVI)(1980); 6(XXXVII) (1981).

119. Resolution 260 B (III) of 9 December 1948. For a memorandum by the Secretary-General on an early "Historical Survey of the Question of International Criminal Jurisdiction", see United Nations publication: Sales No. 1949.V.8.

120. General Assembly Resolution 489 (V) of 12 December 1950 and Resolution 687 (VIII) of 5 December 1952. For the reports of the Committees, see *ibid.*, Sixth Session, Supplement No. 11 (A/2136), and Ninth Session, Supplement No. 12 (A/2645).

121. Resolution 898 (IX) of 14 December 1954 and Resolution 1187 (XII) of 11 December 1957.

122. The study, including a draft statute for a proposed International Criminal Court, is contained in E/CN.4/1426 (1981).

123. E/CN.4/1417 (1981).

124. Convention, Art. 35; Protocol, Art. II; Convention, Art. 36; Protocol, Art. III.

125. For a brief history and commentary on the Convention, see United Nations publication: Sales No. 1955.IV.17.

126. For a historical background and a commentary on the Convention, see United Nations publication: Sales No. 62.IV.3; and Sales No. 1964.IV.1.

127. *Study on Traffic in Persons and Prostitution*, United Nations publication: Sales No. 59.IV.5.

128. See *The Suppression of Slavery*, UN Sales No. 1951.XIV.2; and *Report on Slavery*, UN Sales No. E.67.XIV.2, which is presently being updated (see Economic and Social Council Decision 1980/123).

129. See Chapter 10, *supra*, n. 29.

130. The Convention falls short of imposing any legal obligations on the media of information and refers in the preamble to the difficulty of providing machinery for verifying the accuracy of corrections which might lead to imposition of penalties.

12 The International Labour Organisation (ILO)

Nicolas Valticos

Introduction: *THE PLACE OF HUMAN RIGHTS IN THE CONSTITUTION AND THE VARIOUS INSTRUMENTS OF THE ILO AND THE LEGAL FRAMEWORK FOR THEIR PROTECTION*

(i). HUMAN RIGHTS AND THE CONSTITUTION OF THE ILO

Both the Constitution and the Conventions and Recommendations of the International Labour Organisation (ILO) have, since 1919, assigned a large place to human rights and have also been a principal inspiration of the universal and regional texts relating to economic and social rights, and to certain civil and political rights.

The initial text of the ILO Constitution formed Part XIII of the Treaty of Versailles of 1919 and it was amended and expanded in 1946. It not only contains provisions relating to the Organisation's procedure, but it also established certain general principles with regard to which René Cassin has written[1] that "the notion of international common law regarding essential individual liberties was provided with a basis in treaty form in Part XIII of the Treaty of Versailles, which constitutes the Charter of the ILO" and that that Constitution "constitutes a genuine declaration of the worker's rights".

The general principles established by the ILO Constitution are contained in the first place in its Preamble, according to which "conditions of labour exist involving such injustice, hardship and privation to large numbers of people as to produce unrest so great that the peace and harmony of the world are imperilled; and an improvement of those conditions is urgently required: as, for example, by the regulation of the hours of work, including the establishment of a maximum working day and week, the regulation of the labour supply, the prevention of unemployment, the provision of an adequate living wage, the protection of the worker against sickness, disease and injury arising out of his employment, the protection of children, young persons and women, provision for old age and injury, protection of the interests of workers when employed in countries other than their own, recognition of the principle of equal remuneration for work of equal value, recognition of the principle of freedom of association, the organization of vocational and technical education and other measures".

Fundamental principles of the Organisation are also contained in the "Declaration concerning the Aims and Purposes of the ILO" adopted by the International Labour Conference at Philadelphia in 1944 and incorporated in the ILO Constitution in 1946. That Declaration states *inter alia*:

I

The Conference reaffirms the fundamental principles on which the Organisation is based and, in particular, that—
(a) labour is not a commodity;
(b) freedom of expression and of association are essential to sustained progress;
(c) poverty anywhere constitutes a danger to prosperity everywhere;...

II

(a) all human beings, irrespective of race, creed or sex, have the right to pursue both their material well-being and their spiritual development in conditions of freedom and dignity, of economic security and equal opportunity.

These constitutional principles have not merely served as guidelines for the organs of the ILO, thus assisting them in the preparation of particular Conventions and Recommendations. They have also constituted fundamental standards which have given rise to certain direct legal consequences. Thus, the fact that the principle of freedom of association was affirmed by the ILO Constitution, into which the Declaration of Philadelphia was incorporated, served as a basis for the establishment, in 1950, of special machinery for the protection of freedom of association, which is dealt with below. It was on a similar basis that the International Labour Conference, "acting as a spokesman for the social conscience of mankind", took the view, in 1964, that the policy of *apartheid* in South Africa was incompatible with the Declaration of Philadelphia, which the Government of South Africa had undertaken to observe in accepting the ILO's Constitution, and it condemned that policy and submitted a detailed programme aimed at eliminating it in the field of labour.[2]

Lastly, the ILO's Constitution established the bases upon which, as will be seen below, were founded the supervision of the implementation of the standards formulated by the Organisation, particularly in respect of human rights.

(ii). HUMAN RIGHTS AND THE CONVENTIONS AND RECOMMENDATIONS
OF THE ILO

As important as is the place occupied by human rights in the ILO's Constitution and as notable as have been the consequences, it is on the Conventions and Recommendations adopted by the Organisation that its action to promote and protect human rights within the sphere of its competence has been based. Conventions are texts intended to create international obligations for the States which ratify them, whereas the purpose of Recommendations is not to create obligations but to define standards designed to provide guidance for governments. It is not necessary to give a detailed account here of the content of these various texts or of their relation to human rights since these matters are dealt with elsewhere in this work. Besides, the question has been covered by numerous studies,[3] as well as by official reports.[4] I shall merely give a very general outline of that body of standards—often described as the "International Labour Code"—by means of which it will be possible to appreciate more exactly the import of the machinery set up for the purposes of their implementation.

Between 1919 and 1981 a total of 156 Conventions and 165 Recommendations were adopted by the ILO, and it may be said[5] that practically all these texts concern the promotion and protection of human rights in the broad sense, since even the most technical of them relate to concrete aspects of the right to just and favourable working conditions provided for in article 7 of the International Covenant on Economic, Social and Cultural Rights.

Some of these texts, however, are more particularly concerned than others with fundamental rights and freedoms: these are, in particular, the Conventions on freedom of association, the main one of which is Convention No. 87 of 1948. In this connection, a resolution adopted by the International Labour Conference in 1970 stressed that trade union rights should be founded on respect for the civil liberties set forth in particular in the Universal Declaration of Human Rights and in the International Covenant on Civil and Political Rights, and that the absence of such civil liberties removes all significance from the concept of trade union rights.[6] Special mention must also be made of the 1930 and 1957 Conventions on forced labour, the second of which provides for the suppression of forced or compulsory labour in five categories of cases and, in particular, "as a means of political coercion or education or as a punishment for holding or expressing political views or views ideologically opposed to the established political, social or economic system". Lastly, in respect of equality of opportunity and treatment, the 1958 Convention and Recommendation (No. 111) concerning Discrimination in Respect of Employment and Occupation, are basic texts which have provided inspiration for the Conventions subsequently adopted by Unesco and the United Nations regarding discrimination. Similarly, the Convention (No. 100) and the Recommendation (No. 90) of 1951 on Equality of Remuneration have had wide repercussions. Furthermore, various Conventions have been adopted for the protection of migrant and foreign workers.

In respect of the right to work, a series of Conventions and Recommendations have dealt successively with unemployment, employment agencies, vocational training and apprentices, employment services and, in 1964, employment policy, designed to promote full, productive and freely chosen employment. The right to fair remuneration has been dealt with in Conventions relating to minimum wages, the protection of wages and social policy as a whole.

The right to satisfactory conditions of work and existence has been the subject of numerous Conventions, in particular in respect of the reduction of hours of work, weekly rest, paid annual holidays and occupational safety and health. The right to social security has been dealt with in several texts relating to particular branches or establishing an overall minimum standard.

The protection of children and young persons has been sought through Conventions relating to questions such as the minimum age for employment, the prohibition of night work, medical inspection and conditions of work.

With respect to work by women, certain Conventions aim at the abolition of all discrimination between men and women workers in respect of remuneration, while others are designed to ensure protection in the event of childbirth or against particularly arduous working conditions, such as night work, work in mines, etc.

(iii). INTERPRETATION OF THE CONSTITUTION AND CONVENTIONS
      OF THE ILO

The Conventions of the ILO, like its Constitution, may present problems of interpretation which may be referred to the International Court of Justice (Article 37 of the ILO Constitution). Opinions in this regard have been requested from the Court only in a small number of cases. The same provision of the ILO Constitution also provides for the possibility of appointing a tribunal for the expeditious determination of any dispute or question referring to the interpretation of a Convention, but recourse has not so far been had to this possibility. On the other hand, the Director-General of the International Labour Office is frequently consulted by governments regarding the interpretation to be given to a particular provision of a Convention, and the opinions which he expresses, while stipulating that he does not have special competence in the matter, are communicated to the Governing Body of the Office and published in the *Official Bulletin*. Such opinions seem to be tacitly accepted, and provide authoritative documentation in this regard.

(iv). CASE-LAW

As is shown below, several quasi-judicial bodies have been set up by the ILO in order to supervise and promote the implementation of international labour Conventions and, more generally, of the standards and principles of the Organisation. In carrying out this task, these bodies have had to define the exact scope of the standards. They have thus gradually established a substantial body of case-law in the broad sense of the term. This is particularly true of the Committee of Experts on the Application of Conventions and Recommendations which, in examining the degree of application of ratified Conventions each year since 1927, has often found it necessary to consider the effect of particular provisions of Conventions. This interpretative role has been especially important in respect of Conventions drafted in general terms, particularly in regard to forced labour, freedom of association and, more recently, discrimination in employment.[7] Another organ which has developed a considerable body of case-law is the Committee on Freedom of Association, which is also discussed below. This case-law, which obviously has to be viewed taking into account the specific context of each case, has clarified and, in certain respects, supplemented and extended the standards expressly enshrined in the Conventions and has been the subject of a special publication.[8]

The ratification of Conventions

An international labour Convention is binding only for those States that have ratified it. The ILO Constitution (Article 19) provides for measures to promote the application and ratification of Conventions. Under this article, all Member States of the Organisation are required to submit each Convention and Recommendation to their competent national authorities (as a general rule, the legislative authority), no later than twelve or eighteen months after it has been adopted, so that those authorities may examine the possibility of giving effect to them.[9] Where those authorities decide in the affirmative, States must communicate to the ILO the ratification of the Convention under consideration. The international labour Conventions have been very widely ratified. In 1980, this number had exceeded 4,800. In addition, some 1,040 declarations of application had been registered on behalf of twenty-nine non-metropolitan territories.

The number of ratifications varies considerably according to the country and the Convention. Thus, forty-five States have each ratified more than forty Conventions and eighteen more than sixty[10] whereas nine States have ratified fewer than ten Conventions. The average number of ratifications for each Member State is fifty-eight for the West European countries, forty-nine for the East European countries, thirty-eight for the American countries, twenty-six for the African countries, nineteen for the Asian countries and thirty-two for Oceania. Sixty per cent of the total number of ratifications are from developing countries. It is to be noted in this connection that by virtue of a practice almost unanimously followed by the new States which become Members of the ILO, those States have confirmed that they would continue to be bound by the obligations previously assumed on their behalf by the States responsible for their international relations. This practice of State succession[11] has resulted in the registration of more than 1,000 ratifications representing the confirmation, by sixty new States, of obligations previously assumed in the name of the territory constituted by those new States prior to their independence. It has been strongly encouraged by the organs of the ILO and, in particular, by the First African Regional Conference, held in 1960. The number of ratifications also differs appreciably according to the Conventions: forty-two Conventions have each received more than forty ratifications, and twenty-one more than sixty. In particular, the six Conventions directly relating to fundamental rights (freedom of association, forced labour and discrimination) have received an average of 104 ratifications each.

The procedures and bodies established by the ILO for the purpose of ensuring the protection of the human rights set forth in the Constitution and in the Conventions and Recommendations of the Organisation[12] have a two-fold objective: on the one hand, to supervise the execution by States of the obligations assumed under the ILO Constitution or by virtue of the ratification of a Convention and, on the other, to promote, irrespective of any formal obligation, the application of the standards established by the instruments of the ILO. This machinery can be divided into two categories: the statutory machinery applicable to all the conventions and Recommendations of the ILO, and that machinery relating more particularly to the international protection of freedom of association. In addition, various supplementary methods are used such as studies and investigations, educational and training measures, and technical co-operation.

(a). Supervisory machinery applicable to all the Conventions and Recommendations

Two major types of machinery have been established to supervise and promote the application of the standards contained in the ILO's Conventions and Recommendations: permanent automatic supervision based on the examination of reports provided by governments, and legal proceedings based on the filing of complaints.

(i). PERMANENT SUPERVISION BASED ON THE EXAMINATION
     OF REPORTS FROM GOVERNMENTS

Three separate functions derive from the three categories of reports that Member States undertake to make to the ILO under the Organisation's Constitution (Articles 19 and 22). The reports relate to:

-information concerning the measures taken to bring the Conventions and Recommendations before the competent authorities, no later than twelve or eighteen months after the adoption of those texts, with particulars of the authorities regarded as competent, and of the action taken by them;[13]

-annual or two-yearly or four-yearly reports on ratified Conventions; the relevant rules are designed to secure more frequent reporting for certain Conventions (particularly those concerning basic human rights) as well as in the initial period following ratification and whenever there exist significant problems of implementation, or comments are received from employers' or workers' organizations.[14] These reports must be drafted on the basis of detailed forms established by the Governing Body of the ILO;

-for non-ratified Conventions and for Recommendations, reports at intervals requested by the Governing Body, concerning national law and practice, showing the extent to which the State concerned has given effect or proposes to give effect to those texts, and stating the difficulties which prevent or delay the ratification of the Convention concerned or the application of the Recommendation in question.[15]

Governments are also obliged (Article 23, para. 2, of the Constitution) to communicate copies of their reports to national employers' and workers' organizations. Any observations made by these organizations must be communicated to the ILO by governments, which may also attach their own comments. A total of some 3,000 reports are supplied each year by governments.

Two bodies are entrusted with the examination of these reports: an independent body, the Committee of Experts on the Application of Conventions and Recommendations; and a body composed of representatives of governments, employers and workers, the Committee on the Application of Conventions and Recommendations set up at the International Labour Conference.

The Committee of Experts on the Application of Conventions and Recommendations, established in 1927, is composed of persons of recognized competence who are completely independent of governments. This independence is marked by the fact that the members of that Committee are appointed by the Governing Body of the ILO on the recommendation of the Director-General and not of the governments of the countries of which they are nationals. They are chosen from among highly qualified persons in the legal and social fields, principally in the judiciary (several have been chief justices of supreme courts), education (professors of international law, labour law, etc), or from among former statesmen. The fundamental principles guiding the Committee have been, in its own terms, that it has always considered that its functions consist in pointing out "in a spirit of complete independence and entire objectivity" the extent to which the situation in each country is in conformity with the terms of the Conventions and with the obligations assumed by that country by virtue of the ILO Constitution. "The members of the Committee must accomplish their task in complete independence as regards all member States".[16]

The Committee of Experts currently consists of twenty members from various regions of the world. The experts are appointed for periods of three years and their term of office is generally renewed since continuity makes it possible to acquire more thorough knowledge of the matters dealt with by the Committee and also ensures the greater independence of its members.

The Committee of Experts is not a court, but its function is of a judicial character in that it is required to assess the extent to which national law and practice are in conformity with the provisions of the ILO Constitution or Conventions. Its power of assessment depends on the terms of the Conventions considered and is necessarily fairly broad in connection with Conventions establishing standards which are set out in general terms (for instance regarding forced labour or freedom of association). In order to give its opinion concerning the conformity of national laws in such cases, the Committee must, of course, assess the scope which should be attributed to such international standards. This sort of case-law developed over the years has acquired considerable weight. The Committee's power of assessment is also broad in the case of Conventions which provide for the gradual application of a principle, taking into account the methods in force in the country concerned (for instance, in respect of equal remuneration, discrimination in employment and employment policy). The Committee's role in such cases is to decide, in successive years, whether the measures taken by each State correspond in good faith to the dynamic character of the Convention and to national conditions.

The Committee allocates among its members—or among working groups composed of a number of its members—the intitial responsibility for the questions which are to be examined. After this preliminary work, the resulting comments are examined and approved by the Committee as a whole. The services of the International Labour Office constitute the secretariat of the Committee. The procedure followed by the Committee is based on documentation, since the Committee assesses situations on the basis of governments' reports, legislation and any other relevant documentation (for instance, such observations as may be made by national employers' and workers' organizations) and on replies of governments to such comments as the Committee may have made.

The comments presented by the Committee take the form either of individual comments or of general surveys. The Committee makes individual comments when it is required to give its opinion concerning the execution, by each State, of its international obligations in regard to the ILO, that is to say the application of ratified Conventions and compliance with the obligation to submit Conventions and Recommendations to the competent authorities. These comments take two different forms: in respect of the most important cases, *observations* are made on any discrepancy it has noted (these observations are included in the printed report of the Committee); in other cases, *requests* are communicated directly to the government concerned so that the latter may reply in its next report (these requests are not published in the printed report of the Committee, which simply mentions cases in which such requests have been made). If, within a reasonable period of time, the government does not reply or does not take the necessary measures, the question may be the subject of a public observation. The purpose of this method is to include in the printed report of the Committee only the most important questions and to provide governments with time to explain or rectify certain situations before the matter becomes public. The direct request procedure is used to a large extent. In 1977, the Committee of Experts formulated some 400 observations and 800 direct requests on the application of ratified Conventions.

In addition to these two types of individual comments, each year the Committee of Experts carries out a general survey relating to a given area, on the basis of the reports requested from all States regarding the relevant Conventions and Recommendations—whether or not those States have ratified the Conventions under consideration. The object of these studies is to describe the situation existing in the various States in this regard, to evaluate the difficulties which may stand in the way of the application of the texts in question and possibly to suggest means of surmounting those difficulties. In recent years several general surveys have concerned the Conventions on fundamental human rights, notably freedom of association (in 1973), forced labour (in 1962, 1968 and 1979), discrimination in employment (in 1963 and

1971), employment policy (in 1972) and equality of opportunity (in 1975 and 1980).

The Committee on the Application of Conventions and Recommendations of the International Labour Conference. At each of its annual sessions, the International Labour Conference appoints a Committee, composed of representatives of governments and national employers' and workers' organizations, which has the task of examining the question of the application of Conventions and Recommendations. For the last few years this Committee has had more than a hundred members. It takes as the basis for its work the report of the Committee of Experts and it invites the governments concerned to provide explanations concerning the discrepancies pointed out by that Committee and the measures which they have taken or which are contemplated to eliminate them. Starting from the governments' written or oral replies, discussions—sometimes of a very vigorous nature—are held and the representatives of workers and employers speak, often with force, about the way in which the Conventions are implemented, either in their own country or in others. The Committee summarizes its discussions and conclusions in a report which it transmits to the Conference and which is discussed in plenary session.

With the ever-increasing number of questions, the Conference, like the Committee of Experts, has had to adopt a more selective method so as to be able to concentrate its attention on the most important cases in the limited amount of time available to it. It thus chooses, from among the observations presented by the Committee of Experts, those which appear to be the most important. It limits its discussions to these cases while requesting governments to reply to the other points in their next annual reports. Of the some 400 observations made by the Committee of Experts, it selects around 120 for discussion. Among the cases thus discussed, the Committee of the Conference has, since 1957, drawn particular attention in its general report, on the basis of certain criteria, to cases in which governments "appeared to encounter serious difficulties in discharging obligations under the ILO Constitution or under Conventions which they have ratified". While the Committee has always stressed that its role is not that of a court and that the inclusion of a country on this list does not constitute a sanction but is intended to bring to light the most serious cases with a view to helping to find positive solutions to the problems encountered, this "special list" is nevertheless often considered by the governments concerned to be a sort of moral sanction, and inclusion on the list sometimes gives rise to lively discussions. The governments included on it generally make a special effort to remedy the situation which led to their inclusion. In addition, the Committee has, during the last few years, also specially drawn the Conference's attention to certain other cases on which it has held detailed discussions.

"Direct contacts" with governments. The fact that the procedure of the Committee of Experts is essentially based on documentation, and the nature

and the limited duration of the discussions in the Committee of the Conference, have sometimes given rise to protracted disputes with governments in which there has been insufficient time to allow thorough examination of the questions involved. A procedure for "direct contacts" with governments was therefore introduced in 1968. This procedure—which follows certain principles established by the supervisory bodies—is initiated on the request or with the agreement of the governments concerned, in cases where special and sufficiently serious difficulties are encountered in the application of ratified Conventions. It involves thorough discussion, in the country concerned, between a representative of the Director-General of the ILO (who may be either an independent person or a qualified official of the ILO), and the government authorities—contacts are also established with national employers' and workers' organizations during these discussions. While this procedure is under way, the supervisory bodies suspend their examination of the case under discussion for a reasonable period (normally no more than a year) so as to be able to take account of its outcome. From 1969 to 1979 this procedure, intended to establish a broader and more fruitful dialogue between the ILO and the governments concerned, was used in some thirty countries, principally in Latin America, but also in Africa, Asia and Europe, with results which, on the whole, were distinctly positive. The procedure has also been useful for the examination of obstacles to the ratification of Conventions and for the supply by governments of the reports and information required by the ILO's Constitution. In any event, these direct contacts, which are essentially aimed at facilitating better application of ratified Conventions, in no way limit the functions and responsibilities of the Committee of Experts and the Conference Committee.

The principal difficulties encountered. The supervisory bodies encounter difficulties at two different stages: that of the evaluation of national situations and that of bringing those situations into conformity with international standards.

A first question which arises for various countries is whether, following the ratification of a Convention, the terms of that Convention are incorporated into national law and, if so, whether the Convention may consequently be considered to be satisfactorily applied. In several countries, the national Constitution provides that ratified treaties become part of municipal law— and even sometimes take precedence over ordinary laws. The consequences of these constitutional systems have sometimes raised problems for the supervisory bodies of the ILO.[17] The first series of problems are of a legal character. Many of the provisions of international labour Conventions—indeed most of them—are not self-executing, that is to say, are not drafted in sufficiently precise terms for them to be directly applicable merely because they have been incorporated in principle in the internal legal system of a country. The situation may be similar when incorporation in the internal legal system does not result from the national constitutional system but from the law approving ratification. In these various cases, the supervisory bodies have on several occasions drawn attention to the fact that such non-self-executing provisions require the adoption of explicit and more concrete measures of application, in the form of laws, regulations, etc. A similar legal problem is that of the possible conflict between a Convention incorporated automatically in the internal system and a more general or more specific ordinary law, adopted previously or subsequently.

Moreover, to the legal problem is added a practical problem. Even assuming that the ratified Convention is self-executing and should take precedence, in a particular case, over a conflicting national law, it may happen that in practice it is not so well known by judges, administrators and legal practitioners, or simply by private individuals, as the national law contained in labour codes or other widely known and accessible collections of laws. Consequently, the supervisory bodies have often pointed out that, even when the ratified Convention is considered to have abrogated tacitly the terms of a conflicting law, it would also be desirable formally to bring the national law into conformity with the Convention (by expressly abrogating or modifying earlier laws or codes in respect of the points dealt with by the Convention), so that there is no doubt or uncertainty as to the state of the law, or to take appropriate measures so that all those concerned may be informed of the incorporation of the Convention into municipal law and of its effect on pre-existing law. Such measures have often been taken by governments.[18]

Another problem relating to the evaluation of national situations is that presented in certain countries by the application of international labour Conventions by means of collective agreements.[19]

However, the greatest difficulty in regard to a system of supervision founded on documents is to be able to assess the effective application of Conventions in practice and not merely legislative conformity. The ILO's permanent supervisory bodies are able to form a certain impression in this connection by indirect means. One of these means consists—and the report forms contain special questions on this subject—in requesting governments to provide data which will at least make it possible to form an idea of the practical application of each Convention (judicial decisions, particulars concerning the authorities responsible for the application of the national provisions giving effect to the Convention, information on methods of inspection and supervision, extracts from reports of the labour inspectorate, various statistics, such as on the number of workers protected, the penalties inflicted, the social security benefits provided, etc.). Another element of information on the practical application of Conventions lies in the opportunity given—as indicated above—to national employers' and workers' organizations to submit observations on the application of Conventions in their country. A special question to this effect is contained in the report forms. An effort to ensure that such organizations are adequately informed has been made in the last few years and a distinct increase has been noted in the number of observations of this kind.

When evaluation of national law and practice reveals discrepancies in respect of the provisions of ratified Conventions, the second series of problems for the supervisory bodies is to ensure that such national situations are brought into conformity with the international standard. The difficulties encountered in this connection derive from very different causes.

Sometimes the economic and social conditions of the country in question prevent it from fully applying a ratified Convention. This occurs, in particular, when the State concerned did not initially appreciate the obligations which would follow from ratification of the Convention, or when a newly independent State invokes the requirements of economic development to explain that effect cannot be given to this or that Convention. In this connection, the supervisory bodies have taken the view that the requirements of Conventions remain constant and uniform for all countries, while the modes of their implementation may be different in different States. "These are international standards and the manner in which their implementation is evaluated must be uniform and must not be affected by concepts derived from any particular social or economic system".[20] A solution to the variety of national situations may, however, be sought within the framework of the very terms of the Conventions. Most of the Conventions contain flexibility clauses making it possible to take account to a certain extent of the unequal degree of development of countries.[21] In other cases, the solution to the problem has been sought in the gradual application of the Convention considered. This type of difficulty often raises the problem of the balance to be found between economic development and social development and involves the danger that concern for economic development may result in its social and human purpose being forgotten.

In other cases, the difficulties encountered are more simply of an administrative nature: slowness of the administration, shortage and inadequacy of staff, lack of co-ordination and sometimes conflicts between the different services. We see here the extent to which the protection of human rights depends more generally on the existence of a competent, conscientious and effective public administration.

Sometimes, again, obstacles of a political kind may prevent or delay the adoption of the measures necessary for national law to be brought into conformity: these sometimes derive from domestic disturbances or difficulty in getting the parliament to adopt the necessary texts, but the greatest problem stems from the fact that sometimes the government concerned undoubtedly considers—generally without wishing to admit it—that the adoption of the measures required by Conventions such as those on freedom of association, forced labour or discrimination, would endanger interests which in its eyes are vital for the country or the established régime.

The difficulties of ensuring conformity may also derive from constitutional problems, particularly in federal countries, when the measures necessary for the application of a Convention fall within the competence of the various constituent units of the federation. Difficulties of this kind may be avoided when the federal government, as in Australia, before ratifying a Convention, obtains the agreement of the authorities of the constituent units. Similarly, certain Conventions, such as that (No. 111) concerning discrimination in employment, of 1958, are drafted in such a way as to enable them to be applied by means of measures taken by the federal authorities of the country. Similar problems to those of federal countries may arise in cases where decentralization results in the various "labour collectivities" of the country having extensive powers in regard to the regulation of working conditions.

Finally, difficulty may arise in cases—which in fact are rare—where the government concerned does not share the opinion of the supervisory bodies as to the existence of a discrepancy between its law and the provisions of a ratified Convention. This has sometimes led to deadlocks. The direct contacts procedure may now help to resolve difficulties of this type.

The results obtained. The results of this supervisory machinery need to be examined from two points of view. First of all, to what extent do governments comply with the obligation to make reports—in particular, on the application of ratified Conventions—which are the basis of the entire system of supervision? In the last few years, the proportion of reports received has become established at around an average of 81 per cent at the time of the meeting of the Committee of Experts, and 87 per cent at the time of the meeting of the Committee of the Conference. As to the content of the reports, it is highly variable. The omissions observed may to a certain extent be made up for by consulting legislative texts and other available public documents. When a government omits to reply to questions raised by the supervisory bodies, the International Labour Office has been instructed by those bodies to contact that government immediately in order to draw its attention to the matter, and this practice has resulted in a notable improvement in the content of the reports. At the subsequent stage of discussions in the Committee of the Conference, almost all of the governments concerned respond to the Committee's invitation to furnish explanations concerning the discrepancies noted.

While a dialogue is the first requirement for this system of supervision, the effectiveness of the supervision depends ultimately on the tangible results which it can achieve. In this connection, neither the serious problems encountered by supervision nor the generally positive results of this activity can be denied.[22] These results must first of all be examined from the point of view of the application of the ratified Conventions, that is of the States' compliance with obligations which they have expressly assumed in ratifying Conventions. A systematic study of the effect of this system of supervision[23] has already provided evidence of the distinctly positive results which it achieved during the first thirty years. Moreover, each year the Committee of Experts points out, alongside the discrepancies detected by it, some of which span a fairly long period, cases where governments have acted on its observations and taken measures to bring their legislation into conformity with ratified Conventions. In 1979, it pointed out that during the previous sixteen years, there had been more than 1,200 cases of progress of this kind, concerning more than 150 States or territories. These cases of progress break down approximately as follows: 23 per cent for Africa, 31 per cent for the Americas (principally Latin America which has furnished the greatest number of ratifications in that hemisphere), 16 per cent for Asia and Oceania and the remaining 30 per cent for Europe. In this connection, the Committee of Experts has stressed the large number of developing countries figuring among those which have furnished concrete proof of their determination fully to discharge their obligations under ILO Conventions.[24] Among the numerous cases of progress noted over the years, around 15 per cent concern the implementation of Conventions relating to fundamental rights. More precisely, during the years 1964 to 1979, there were fifty-eight cases in which discrepancies noted by the Committee of Experts in regard to freedom of association were eliminated, eighty per cent of which were achieved in the last few years. This clearly shows that continuity and perseverance are important aspects of the effectiveness of supervision.

Alongside such easily recognizable measures, the Committee of Experts has often emphasized that there exist numerous cases of "invisible" or less apparent progress which may be directly attributed to the procedures aimed at promoting the application of international labour standards.[25] In addition, the very existence of a system of vigilant supervision has played an important role in that it has encouraged States to take the measures necessary for the application of a ratified Convention so as to guard against comments by the supervisory bodies. Official declarations made, for instance, in the Federal Republic of Germany, Australia and the United Kingdom thus reveal the extent to which, prior to ratification of a Convention, the national authorities take care to examine, in the light of the comments of the supervisory bodies, the measures required to ensure the application of the text whose ratification is being contemplated. The preventive role of supervision is also seen in the fact that, on more than one occasion, governments have declined to make changes in their legislation which would have been incompatible with the terms of a ratified Convention. Such cases have confirmed the function of Conventions as an "international safety lock" against possible backsliding and as a factor contributing to the consolidation of the progress achieved.

Over and above the direct or indirect effects thus resulting from supervision when it concerns the implementation of ratified Conventions, it also fulfils a broader function in that it bears on action taken on non-ratified Conventions and Recommendations. The reports requested each year from States on certain texts or groups of texts naturally lead governments to review the possibilities of giving effect to them and of ratifying the Conventions considered. The particulars provided by the Committee of Experts in its general surveys on the import of those texts are sometimes of assistance to governments in overcoming the difficulties encountered. The discussions of these surveys in the Conference Committee also draw governments' attention to the texts in question. It has been observed that the presentation of reports relating to non-ratified Conventions and the ensuing examination have on various occasions led to an appreciable number of ratifications of the Conventions examined. This has been noted in particular in regard to the Conventions on freedom of association.

Morover, the effect of international labour standards is not limited to cases where the supervisory procedures are used to ensure that they are applied by the States which have ratified ILO Conventions. Irrespective of the formal obligations arising from the ratifications of Conventions, the standards contained in those Conventions have more generally played the role of a sort of international common law in which governments find a customary source of inspiration. Various monographs have revealed the influence exercised by Conventions, ratified or not, in countries whose conditions and state of development are very different.[26] A representative of the Organization of African Unity has said that practically all the Labour Codes of the African States have as a common denominator the Conventions and Recommendations of the ILO. Regional texts, such as the European Social Charter of 1961 and the Arab Convention on Labour Standards of 1967, were established on the model of ILO standards.

(ii). CONTENTIOUS PROCEDURES

The ILO Constitution provides for two forms of complaints which may set in motion contentious procedures relating to the application of a ratified Convention: the complaint proper and the representation.

The *complaint procedure* in the strict sense is provided for in articles 26 to 34 of the Constitution, and is the ILO's most formal procedure for supervision. Such a complaint may be lodged by any Member State "if it is not satisfied that any other Member is securing the effective observance of any Convention which both have ratified". The filing of such complaints is not subject to the complainant State or any of its nationals having suffered any direct prejudice. It has been concluded from this that a State may have a legal interest in ensuring the observance, in the territories of another State, of Conventions relating to the general welfare, irrespective of any effect upon its own nationals or on its direct or concrete interests.[27] The complaint procedure may also be initiated by the Governing Body of the ILO, either of its own motion or on receipt of a complaint from a delegate to the International Labour Conference. When a complaint has been filed, the Governing Body of the ILO may appoint a Commission of Inquiry to make a thorough examination of the matter. Each Member State is obliged to place at the disposal of the Commission of Inquiry all information bearing on the matter. Following its deliberations, the Commission of Inquiry must present a report containing its findings on all questions of fact relevant to determining the issue between the parties, together with its recommendations as to the steps which should be taken to meet the complaint. The governments concerned are required to state, within three months, whether or not they accept the recommendations of the Commission of Inquiry and, if not, whether they wish to refer the complaint to the International Court of Justice. The decision of the latter is final. If a Member does not comply, within the prescribed period, with the recommendations of the Commission of Inquiry or of the International Court of Justice, the Governing Body may recommend to the International Labour Conference such action as it may deem necessary to secure compliance therewith.

The complaint procedure was used for the first time in 1961 on the initiative of a State, with the complaint lodged by the Government of Ghana concerning the application by Portugal of the Abolition of Forced Labour Convention, 1957 (No. 105) in its African territories. Some months later, another complaint was lodged by Portugal concerning the application by Liberia of the Forced Labour Convention, 1930 (No. 29). In 1968, this procedure was initiated by workers' delegates to the International Labour Conference concerning the application of Conventions No. 87 and 98 on freedom of association by the military government which had assumed power in Greece. In 1974, the complaint procedure was also initiated, following a resolution of the Conference, concerning the observance by Chile of the Hours of Work (Industry) Convention, 1919 (No. 1), and the Discrimination (Employment and Occupation) Convention, 1958 (No. 111).

The procedure followed was similar in all cases.[28] The Governing Body set up Commissions of Inquiry composed of three members whom it appointed on the recommendation of the Director-General of the ILO. These were prominent persons appointed in their personal capacity. The Governing Body and the Commissions themselves emphasized their independence and the judicial character of their functions. Their members were called on to make the same solemn declaration, in the same terms, as the judges at the International Court of Justice: "I will honourably, faithfully, impartially and conscientiously perform my duties and exercise my powers".

In establishing the first Commission, the Director-General of the ILO declared to its members, *inter alia*, that the task entrusted to them was that of ascertaining the facts, without fear or favour; that they had but one master and one allegiance—the truth; and that they were responsible to their own consciences alone.

The task of the first Commission was, in particular, to consider whether the complaint submitted was supported by elements sufficiently precise to justify the continuation of the procedure. While not accepting that a government could place responsibility on the ILO for a complete inquiry into the matter, the Commission considered that its role was not limited to consideration of the information that might be provided by the parties, but that it should itself take all the necessary steps to obtain "complete and objective

information on the questions involved", in accordance with the general instructions received from the Governing Body and taking into account the
public interest presented by the questions raised.

The Commissions began by requesting from the complainant detailed information and elements of proof in support of the complaint, and asked the
defendant for its observations. They also provided the governments of the
countries neighbouring the countries or territories in question and those of
countries with considerable economic relations with the said countries with
the opportunity to furnish information on questions of fact. They also gave
the same opportunity to a number of international organizations of employers
and workers and to certain other non-governmental organizations active in
the legal or humanitarian fields.

After examining that documentation, the Commissions proceeded with the
formal hearing of the parties and the witnesses in Geneva. In addition to the
witnesses proposed by the parties, the Commissions themselves established
lists of persons whom they wished to hear and requested the governments in
question to take the necessary steps for those persons to be able to appear.
These different witnesses were heard *in camera* by the Commissions in
Geneva, in the course of a hearing with the parties, and numerous questions
were put to them both by the members of the Commissions and by the agents
of the parties, in the latter case subject to the control of the Commissions.

After hearing the witnesses, the Commission of Inquiry considered it necessary, in the Ghana v. Portugal case, to proceed to Angola and Mozambique to
form a direct impression of the situation. The visits took place on the basis of
a programme established by the Commission and accepted by the Portuguese
Government, which granted the necessary facilities. The Commission covered more than 5,000 miles, gathered information from the authorities and
the directors and staff of enterprises, and established contact with African
workers without representatives of the enterprises or the authorities being
present. The Commission itself decided where it wished to go and chose the
workers whom it wished to question.

In the Chile case, the Commission of Inquiry, which was also fulfilling the
functions of the Fact-Finding and Conciliation Commission on Freedom of
Association, made an on-the-spot examination of the situation, as will be seen
below.

In the Portugal v. Liberia case, the Commission of Inquiry did not consider
it necessary to make an on-the-spot investigation. The reasons for this were,
on the one hand, that the complaint did not involve any sufficiently precise
allegations of fact and, on the other, that in the course of the procedure, the
government in question modified its legislation. In the Greece case, because
the government withdrew its co-operation from the Commission on account
of its objections to the hearing of a witness presented by the complainants,
the Commission decided not to pursue further the question of a possible visit
to Greece, which had been originally contemplated. On the basis of the in-

formation and testimony received, it reached a series of conclusions bearing both on the provisions of trade union legislation and on certain more general civil liberties which were regarded as necessary for the effective exercise of trade union rights.

In their reports, adopted unanimously, the Commissions, after noting that a number of measures had been taken following the filing of the complaints in order to eliminate discrepancies, addressed a number of recommendations to the governments concerned. These recommendations were, in each case, accepted by the two parties who subsequently took various legislative and administrative measures with a view to giving effect to them to a lesser or greater extent.[29]

In these different cases, the Commissions of Inquiry requested that the Committee of Experts on the Application of Conventions and Recommendations be regularly informed, through the governments' annual reports, of the measures taken to give effect to the recommendations which they had made. A link was thus established between the occasional complaint procedure and the regular supervision founded on the examination of reports, the latter following up from the conclusion of the complaint procedure. And in fact, the Committee of Experts has closely followed the extent to which the governments concerned have given effect to the recommendations of the Commissions of Inquiry, and the Conference Committee has regularly discussed the matter with the representatives of those governments.

From these procedures a few major characteristics emerge: the independent character of the body responsible for examining the complaints, the measures taken to ensure the objectivity of the procedure, the thoroughgoing character of the investigations made, the principle according to which such complaints give rise to proceedings in the public interest and by virtue of which the Commissions themselves must take steps to obtain complete and objective information, and lastly the concern to ensure continuity of supervision after the end of the complaint procedure. These bodies are assisted in their functions by a senior official of the Organisation, who is appointed as the representative of the Director-General and recognized as the intermediary between the independent Commissions and the parties. They also have at their disposal a qualified secretariat, made available to them by the Director-General. Finally, as regards the effect of these procedures, it is significant that, in these different cases, legislative or other measures were already being taken by the governments in question when the proceedings were under way and that, subsequently, the parties to the complaints accepted the recommendations of the Commissions of Inquiry, the implementation of which has since been regularly followed by the supervisory bodies.

The complaint proceedings are manifestly of a quasi-judicial nature, their ultimate purpose being to determine whether a situation is in conformity with the international obligations assumed. This is stressed by the membership of the Commissions of Inquiry, the procedure which they follow and the fact that their conclusions may be the subject of an appeal to the International Court of Justice. The conclusions of the Commissions of Inquiry have a binding character, as emerges from the fact that the Conference, on the recommendation of the Governing Body, may recommend such action as it may deem wise and expedient to secure compliance with the recommendations of those Commissions. This being so, the Commissions of Inquiry do not limit themselves to stating the law and to noting the extent to which the State in question is meeting its international obligations. They are also called upon to make recommendations for the purpose of remedying the shortcomings noted in this connection. The detailed and constructive nature of the recommendations made derives from a concern to obtain a positive solution to the problems encountered. In the final analysis, it is through persuasion rather than the imposition of mandatory measures that the Commissions of Inquiry seek, while basing themselves on respect for legal obligations, to obtain the implementation of the standards concerned.

The *representation* procedure is the second type of legal proceedings provided for by the ILO Constitution (articles 24-25). Representations may be made by employers' and workers' organizations against a State which, in their opinion, has failed to secure in any respect the effective observance within its jurisdiction of any Convention to which it is a party. This type of complaint is governed by specific rules of procedure which provide essentially that the representation shall be examined first by a Committee of three members, and then by the Governing Body of the ILO.

It was in connection with a representation of this type that the Governing Body established, in 1938, a principle which has been confirmed since in respect of various other procedures and according to which the fact that the complainant organization withdraws its representation does not give rise to the automatic withdrawal of the case. This principle was inspired by the fear of pressure being applied on the complainant organization and also by the fact that the proceedings are recognized to be of public interest (see also below in connection with the Fact-Finding and Conciliation Commission on Freedom of Association).

Only thirteen representations have been referred to the ILO, of which six were during the last twenty-five years; five of these were made by workers' organizations and one by an employers' organization. This limited number is no doubt due to the existence of other procedures whereby employers' and workers' organizations are able to put forward their points of view (reports on the application of Conventions and special procedures in regard to freedom of association). However, representations relating to the important question of discrimination in employment on the basis of opinion were submitted in 1977 and 1978 and this procedure is therefore still considered useful.

(b). Special machinery for the protection of freedom of association

In view of the importance of freedom of association, a special procedure in this field was established by the ILO in 1950 following an agreement with the

United Nations Economic and Social Council which, by its resolution 277 (X) (1950) on trade union rights (freedom of association) formally accepted, on behalf of the United Nations, the ILO's services in this matter.

This procedure[30] supplements the procedures of general application described above, which of course apply to the Conventions on freedom of association as they do to the other Conventions of the ILO. It is founded on the submission of complaints which may be made either by governments or by employers' or workers' organizations. The latter case is the most frequent. An important characteristic of this procedure is the fact that such complaints can be made even against States which have not ratified the Conventions on freedom of association and which therefore have not assumed any formal undertakings relating to them. As far as such States are concerned, this special machinery is based on the fact that the ILO Constitution, to which those States have subscribed in becoming Members of the Organisation, affirms the principle of freedom of association. It has therefore been considered that this principle, which has even been regarded as a sort of customary rule above the Conventions, should be observed by Member States by virtue of their belonging to the Organisation[31] and that, even if the ILO's more specific standards in the matter of freedom of association cannot be imposed on States that have not ratified the corresponding Conventions, the Organisation may promote the implementation of those constitutional principles by such means as investigation and conciliation.

The machinery thus established comprises two different bodies: the Committee on Freedom of Association and the Fact-Finding and Conciliation Commission on Freedom of Association.

(i). THE COMMITTEE ON FREEDOM OF ASSOCIATION[32]

This Committee, which has acquired world renown, is appointed by the Governing Body of the ILO from among its Members, and comprises nine Members (three Government, three Employers' and three Workers'). Owing to the quasi-judicial nature of its functions, its procedure is accompanied by various measures whose purpose is to ensure its impartiality. Continuity has been ensured, in particular, by the fact that, since it was set up in 1951, it has had but two Chairmen: Paul Ramadier, former Prime Minister of France, during the first ten years; and, since 1961, Roberto Ago, professor of international law at the University of Rome, former Chairman of the Governing Body of the ILO, and more recently, judge at the International Court of Justice. The Committee generally conducts its business on the basis of documents, but in several cases independent persons representing the Director-General of the ILO, accompanied by an official of the ILO, have made on-the-spot investigations, at the request or with the agreement of the government concerned, to establish the facts, meet representatives of the government, the employers and workers concerned (sometimes including trade unionists under detention), and submit a report to the Committee. Thus, the "direct contact" procedure, mentioned above, is tending to be increasingly used in this field, at the request or with the agreement of the governments concerned (Jordan in 1974, Uruguay in 1975 and 1977, Bolivia in 1976 and Argentina, Chile and the Dominican Republic in 1978).

The Committee was originally intended to be a body responsible for making a preliminary examination of complaints and recommending to the Governing Body of the ILO whether some of them merited being referred to the Fact-Finding and Conciliation Commission, which is discussed below. When it was subsequently found that there were difficulties in the way of referring them to that Commission, the Committee on Freedom of Association itself proceeded to examine the substance of complaints and submitted to the Governing Body detailed reports with proposed conclusions and, when necessary, suggested recommendations to be made to the governments concerned. Most of the time, the Governing Body has approved these recommendations without discussion.

Close to 1063 cases have been referred to the Committee since it was created. These have concerned widely varied aspects of freedom of association: legislation alleged by the complainants to be contrary to the principle of freedom of association, measures taken by governments, such as the dissolution of trade unions, the arrest of trade union leaders, interference in trade union affairs, etc. In examining the cases referred to it, the Committee has taken as its basis the general principles of freedom of association and has been guided by the provisions contained in the Conventions adopted in this field. In delivering its opinions in regard to hundreds of cases, it has been led, as was pointed out above, gradually to build up a considerable body of case-law which has often related to various civil liberties on which depend the effective exercise of trade union rights, such as the right of assembly, freedom of expression, the right to personal security, etc. The Committee has thus emphasized on several occasions the importance which, in all cases, including those where trade unionists are accused of political or criminal offences considered by the government to have no relation to their trade union activities, it attaches to the principle of prompt and fair trial of the persons in question by an impartial and independent judicial authority.

The Committee has more generally taken the attitude that, in view of the nature of its responsibilities, it cannot consider itself bound by the rule relating to the exhaustion of domestic remedies which applies, for instance, in cases of international arbitration. However, whenever the case referred to it is pending before an independent national judicial body whose proceedings afford appropriate guarantees and when it considers that the decision to be reached is likely to furnish it with additional elements of information, the Committee suspends examination of the case for a reasonable period pending its being in possession of that decision, if no further prejudice will be caused by such delay to the party whose rights are alleged to have been violated.

The effect of the activity of the Committee on Freedom of Association has been very uneven. In several cases, the States concerned have taken account of the Committee's recommendations by amending legislation, by releasing imprisoned trade union leaders or by taking measures of clemency. In other cases, these recommendations have had no effect. Yet in other cases, while no result has been obtained in the short run, there remains the possibility of an effect being produced in the longer term. As the effectiveness of international procedures hinges to a large extent on the continuity and perseverance of that action, the recommendations of the Committee on Freedom of Association are, in the case of States that have ratified the Conventions on freedom of association, brought to the attention of the Committee of Experts on the Application of Conventions and Recommendations in order that that Committee may take steps to be regularly informed of the matter. For States that have not ratified those Conventions, the procedure of the Committee on Freedom of Association has, for some years, made it possible periodically to ascertain the effect given by governments to the recommendations made to them.

In addition to specific cases where the Commmittee's recommendations have been acted on, this procedure has resulted in the establishment, in the field of freedom of association, of a general accountability for governments— and even a sort of habit for them to report on the measures taken by them in that field. This obligation has also undoubtedly played a preventive role in respect of the action of the public authorities. Finally, the working of the procedure has helped to gain wider recognition for the international value of the principles of freedom of association.

(ii). THE FACT-FINDING AND CONCILIATION COMMISSION

This Commission[33] constitutes the formal body set up in 1950 at the time of the establishment of the machinery for the protection of freedom of association. It is made up of independent persons appointed by the Governing Body of the ILO on the recommendation of the Director-General of the ILO. Entrusted with the task of examining complaints regarding violations of freedom of association, the Commission has essentially a fact-finding role, but it may also examine, in conjunction with the government concerned, the questions referred to it in order to settle difficulties by way of agreement. In principle, a case can be referred to the Commission only with the consent of the government concerned. For several years, this proved to be the stumbling-block of the system. The first governments to which the request was made refused to give their consent, and it was consequently decided to give wide publicity to those cases. In 1964, the Government of Japan, which had not at the time ratified the Freedom of Association Convention, 1948 (No. 87), gave its consent for a case concerning trade union rights in the public sector in Japan to be referred to the Commission. The procedure followed was similar to that for formal complaints described above: three independent members of the Commission were appointed to examine the case; information was requested from the parties and from international and national employers' and workers' organizations; and the Commission heard numerous witnesses in Geneva, some of whom were designated by itself and others by the parties. It then went to Japan where it had private discussions with representatives of the complainant organizations and representatives or members of the government. During these discussions, the Commission submitted certain proposals to the two parties for examination. Before the end of the procedure these proposals were accepted and it was thus that the Government of Japan ratified Convention No. 87 and that exchanges of views began between authorities and trade unions. Following this, the Commission formulated its conclusions and a series of very detailed recommendations in the final report which it submitted in July 1965.[34]

The Governing Body of the ILO took note of that report in November 1965 and the representatives of the Japanese Government and the complainant organization (the Japanese General Council of Trade Unions) indicated that they accepted the report of the Commission as a basis for the progressive settlement of the points at issue. Admittedly, the difficulties have not vanished and the Freedom of Association Committee has again had to examine various subsequent complaints in this field, but the recommendations of the Commission constituted an important stage in the history of industrial relations in the public sector in Japan and provided one of the bases for the dialogue which has been established since, with its ups and downs, between the public authorities and the trade union organizations concerned.

In January 1965, a second case was referred to the Fact-Finding and Conciliation Commission, the Government of Greece at that time having spontaneously given its consent. The procedure began in the same way as in the previous case, but during the consideration of the case the complainant organization (the Greek Confederation of Trade Unions) informed the Commission of its desire to withdraw its complaint. The Commission decided to close the procedure only after making sure, by hearing all the parties concerned, that the withdrawal of the complaint was not the result of pressure being applied.

In 1973, a case involving Lesotho, which is not a member of the ILO, was referred to the Fact-Finding and Conciliation Commission in pursuance of a decision by the United Nations Economic and Social Council, under the terms of the agreement between the United Nations and the ILO. After the negotiations, the Chairman of the Commission, accompanied by a member of the Secretariat, went to the country, with the agreement of the Government, in January 1975, and had conversations with the authorities and trade union leaders, one of whom was under detention. The Commission's report was communicated by the Governing Body to the United Nations in the middle of 1975.

One of the most important cases entrusted to the Commission concerned

Chile. Following the events of September 1973, several complaints from trade union organizations were submitted to the ILO and, on the recommendation of the Committee on Freedom of Association, after a first examination of the case, the Governing Body of the ILO decided, in June 1974, to refer the matter to the Fact-Finding and Conciliation Commission, the government having consented thereto. The Commission was composed of three independent persons under the chairmanship of a former President of the International Court of Justice. It was also constituted as a Commission of Inquiry under article 26 of the ILO's Constitution, with responsibility for the examination of other complaints relating to ratified Conventions. The Commission held a session in Geneva, in October 1974, in the course of which it heard witnesses put forward by the principal complainants (the three major workers' organizations) and by the government. In November-December 1974 it visited Chile, after arrangements had been made to ensure the necessary facilities and guarantees (possibility of meeting freely and privately any person that it might wish to hear with the guarantee that the persons encountered would not be subjected to any coercion, sanction or punishment on that account). In Chile the Commission visited various regions in the country, went to many establishments and had discussions with the authorities, and a variety of other persons including numerous trade union leaders (some of whom were under detention), dismissed workers, teachers, lawyers and priests. At the end of its visit, it transmitted to the government certain preliminary observations and recommendations. The Commission's final report was completed in April-May 1975.[35] This report bore both on trade union matters and on problems of human rights and civil liberties which are closely linked with the effective exercise of trade union rights. During the discussion of the report, in May 1975, the representative of the Government of Chile, while formulating certain observations, declared that the Government accepted the recommendations contained therein. The Governing Body appealed to the Government to give effect to those recommendations and on several occasions since then it has requested it to make detailed reports— which are examined by the Committee on Freedom of Association and by the Governing Body—on the measures taken. In June 1975, the International Labour Conference also adopted a resolution along the same lines. Since then the matter has been followed at regular intervals by the organs of the ILO.

By its nature, the special machinery for the protection of freedom of association just described makes it possible, in several respects, to supplement the general procedures for supervision which apply to all the Conventions. Since it is founded on complaints, it provides a means for investigating issues—in particular questions of fact—which may have escaped supervision founded on the examination of governments' reports. Since it can be brought into play even in regard to countries which have not ratified the Conventions on freedom of association, it makes it possible, as far as such countries are concerned, to deal with questions which could have been examined only with difficulty and in a less thorough and less rapid manner, in the framework of the general procedures. Since it is based on general principles in regard to freedom of association rather than on specific provision of the Conventions in that field, it possesses greater flexibility and may more easily be adapted and even extended to different situations. And because the Committee on Freedom of Association meets three times a year, it enables questions to be examined more rapidly than in the framework of annual or biennial reports from governments.

(c). Special inquiries and studies

Independently of the procedures for supervision as such, more or less far-ranging inquiries and studies have been carried out in various fields relating to human rights.

(i). FREEDOM OF ASSOCIATION

The majority of these investigations and studies have been concerned with *freedom of association*. In certain cases they have been entrusted to missions of ILO officials which have gone to particular countries at the invitation of the government concerned in order to gather complete and impartial information on the trade union situation which had been called into question at the international level (for instance in Hungary, as early as 1920, and in Venezuela in 1949). Sometimes the study, while being concerned with all the labour problems in the country, has to a certain extent been the result of complaints concerning the trade union situation (as in Greece in 1947). In other cases, the study has been of a more general scope, in the sense that it has dealt with all of the Member States or with a given number of them. Thus, in 1955, a Committee composed of independent persons under the chairmanship of Lord McNair, former President of the International Court of Justice, was instructed to examine the *independence of the employers' and workers' organizations* of all Member States of the ILO. After the Committee had submitted its report, the Governing Body set up, from 1958 to 1963, *machinery to establish facts relating to freedom of association* in Member States. In contradistinction with the procedures for the purpose of considering a complaint, the object of these studies was to investigate the *de facto* situation, and they were entrusted to the International Labour Office itself. Missions composed of ILO officials thus went on the invitation of the governments concerned, to the U.S.A., U.S.S.R., United Kingdom, Sweden, Malaya and Burma. They established reports which, without seeking to make a judgment concerning the situations themselves, were intended to provide a comprehensive picture. These investigations made it possible for a clearer view of the situation in the various countries concerned to be obtained.

More recently, in 1967, following a request from the Government of Spain, which had not ratified the Conventions on freedom of association, the Governing Body of the ILO set up a *study group* (composed of independent

persons) *to examine the labour and trade union situation in Spain.*[36] This
was not a procedure based on complaints, although complaints regarding the
trade union situation in Spain had previously been examined by the Committee on Freedom of Association. Instead, the study was concerned with the
situation existing in a country, irrespective of any international obligation
assumed by that country and of any complaint initiating the procedure. It had
been stipulated by the Governing Body of the ILO that the study was to be
carried out in the light of the principles set forth in the ILO Constitution. In
this connection, the group pointed.out in its report that it had been guided in
particular by the principle according to which "freedom of expression and of
association are essential to sustained progress" which, since it is contained in
the Declaration of Philadelphia, forms part of the ILO Constitution. The
study group also pointed out that, while it did not constitute a Commission of
Inquiry or a Fact-Finding and Conciliation Commission and while it did not
possess judicial powers, its responsibilities had to be discharged in a judicial
manner. Its members therefore had the duty to record their findings without
fear or favour and they could not limit themselves to a factual description of
the existing situation but had to assess its relationship with the principles of
the ILO and appraise the possibilities of future evolution.

Mutatis mutandis, the procedure was modelled on that followed by the
Fact-Finding and Conciliation Commission and by the Commissions of Inquiry. A specific preliminary agreement between the Director-General of the
ILO and the government established all the necessary guarantees for the
group to be able to discharge its task in complete independence and objectivity. These conditions provided, *inter alia*, for the group to have complete
freedom of movement, for it to be entitled to undertake private talks and
interviews at which no witness would be present, and for guarantees that no
person who would be in contact with the group might for that reason be
subjected to coercion, sanctions or punishment at any time.

After hearing representatives of the government and of the three major
international workers' organizations in Geneva, the group went to Spain in
March 1969. There it divided its time between, on the one hand, official visits
and consultations, in particular with ministers and senior officials, the highest judicial authorities and employers' and workers' representatives from the
Spanish trade union organization and, on the other hand, private interviews
with persons ranging from ecclesiastical authorities and professors of law to
public figures belonging to the opposition and trade unionists in prison. The
final report of the group[37] contains a detailed description of the situation in
Spain and also certain observations concerning future prospects. It concluded
in particular that Spaniards alone could determine what that situation would
be in the future, but that "Spain's place in the world will be significantly
influenced by her attitude towards world standards". The study group pointed
out in this connection the "unequivocal" universal and regional standards
which exist in labour and trade union matters and in respect of civil liberties—

standards which, it specified, are contained in the International Covenants on Human Rights, in the European Social Charter and in the international labour Conventions and in particular those concerned with freedom of association. These standards, the group added, do not impose contractual obligations on any State, unless it has ratified the appropriate instrument, but "no State can escape comparison with them and evaluation of the measure of freedom which it secures to its people on the basis of the comparison".

The Governing Body of the ILO, which took note of this report in November 1969, also decided to adopt measures to ensure its widespread diffusion, and the report became an important element in the discussions which followed concerning Spanish trade union legislation. More recently, with the change in the political situation in Spain, the principles of the ILO and the Report of the Study Group were clearly taken into consideration when new trade union legislation, following rather closely the standards of Convention No. 87, was adopted in April 1977, and the Convention itself was ratified by Spain a few days later.

(ii). FORCED LABOUR

In respect of *forced labour*, special procedures of inquiry and study have been used, since as early as 1921, in collaboration with the League of Nations, and from 1926 onwards, through the establishment of a Committee of Experts on Indigenous Labour. After the Second World War, the work of a Special Committee on Forced Labour, set up in 1951 by the ILO in conjunction with the United Nations and continued to 1959 by a Committee of Forced Labour set up by the International Labour Office, led *inter alia* to the adoption of the Abolition of Forced Labour Convention, 1957 (No. 105).

(iii). DISCRIMINATION

In respect of *discrimination*, the Governing Body of the ILO approved in 1973, as an experimental measure, a formula for studies of national situations in regard to discrimination in employment in order to facilitate the implementation of the Discrimination (Employment and Occupation) Convention, 1958 (No. 111). Such studies, which would necessitate more or less extensive contacts in the country concerned, could take place either at the request of governments that wish to obtain an impartial, outside opinion, or with the consent of the government concerned and under certain conditions, at the request of employers' or workers' organizations or the government of another country whose interests would be affected. The studies would be carried out by an ILO official or an expert or group of experts, and their organization and the conditions under which they would be carried out would be determined by the Director-General of the ILO in agreement with the government concerned, which should always provide the appropriate guarantees.

Thus, on an *ad hoc* basis, a mission of ILO officials visited Israel and the occupied territories in 1978, 1979 and 1980 to consider the question of equality of opportunity for, and treatment of, the Arab workers of those territories. The mission's findings and suggestions were contained in reports submitted to the International Labour Conference.

(d). Education and training measures

Implementation of the ILO's standards is also sought through various educational and training measures, such as the workers' education programme established some years ago by the ILO. More recently, a programme of practical action was launched in respect of the prevention of discrimination in employment. Finally, the Office organizes, generally each year, regional seminars which bring together national officials and officials of the ILO and make it possible, in particular, to find solutions to the difficulties encountered in the application of international labour standards, in particular in respect of human rights.

(e). Technical co-operation and the World Employment Programme

The ILO Constitution provides, in its article 10, para. 2 (b), that the Office shall "accord to governments at their request all appropriate assistance within its power in connection with the framing of laws and regulations on the basis of the decisions of the conference". Since 1950, the technical co-operation accorded to the different countries by the ILO in conjunction with the United Nations has developed substantially.[38] It may sometimes constitute a means of assisting governments to attain the level of the standards established in various international labour Conventions, thus enabling them either to ratify some of those Conventions or to eliminate the discrepancies noted in the application of ratified Conventions. International labour standards thus serve as guidance to the technical co-operation experts in their task, and are also taken into consideration by the services of the International Labour Office when governments request them—and such cases are numerous and frequent—to assist them in framing or amending their labour and social security legislation.

With regard more especially to the right to work, in 1964 the ILO launched the World Employment Programme, which is based on the standards contained in the Convention and Recommendation (No. 122) on Employment Policy, of 1964, and which is intended to assist countries to attain the highest level of productive employment possible. In the framework of this programme, employment strategy missions organized by the ILO have gone, at the request of the governments concerned, to many countries in Africa, America and Asia[39] and have submitted recommendations to the governments in question.

(i). PRINCIPAL CHARACTERISTICS OF THE SYSTEM OF SUPERVISION

Founded in the main on specific texts of the ILO Constitution—which has provided it with a firm foundation—the ILO's system of supervision has not however been strictly limited by those texts. These have served as starting points for progressive developments. Dynamism is thus the first characteristic of this system which, starting from a solid foundation, has been constantly developing.

This process of change has followed two directions which, although juridically separate from each other, pursue a common aim. Supervision was first of all aimed at ensuring compliance with the obligations assumed by States by virtue of their having ratified Conventions. It also aimed at promoting the implementation of ILO standards irrespective of any formal obligation of this type. In both cases what is involved is the activity of an international organization which, by separate procedures, seeks to attain the objectives assigned to it.

This accounts for another characteristic specific to the ILO's system of supervision, namely its diversity. Seeking maximum effectiveness, this system comprises, as has been seen, a great variety of procedures intended to meet different situations and needs: automatic regular supervision founded on the examination of governments' reports, legal cases founded on the submission of complaints, conciliation procedures, objective studies of situations,[40] etc. In their diversity, these procedures have a complementary character, being supported by each other and often following on from each other.

As different as they may be, the procedures of the ILO present a number of common features, from the point of view both of their constituent elements and of the rules and principles on which they are modelled.

Generally speaking, the ILO's system is composed of four elements. First of all, any system of supervision presupposes the existence of a secretariat capable of assisting its organs in an often complex and arduous task. The organs of the ILO thus have at their disposal a qualified secretariat of officials belonging to the International Labour Office, which carries out an objective and thorough analysis of all the documentation available and assists those organs in their work and in the formulation of their conclusions.[41]

Apart from that, the essential element of supervision is the body responsible for determining whether national law and practice are in conformity with international standards, and sometimes for ascertaining facts. As a general rule it is composed of independent persons. This is a fundamental principle of the ILO's system of supervision. It may even be said that it is the key to success in the matter of international supervision.[42] Only such a guarantee of impartiality is capable of inspiring the confidence of the governments concerned, the complainants, the international organization as a whole and, more generally, public opinion—and of giving to the conclusions of those bodies the authority which may lead to their being accepted.

The members of these bodies are therefore nominated by the Director-General of the ILO (and not by governments) and appointed, in their personal capacity, by the Governing Body of the ILO. The independence which should characterize such persons concerns primarily their functions (they should not hold a national office which links them too closely to the administration of a State). The other qualifications required[43] are, generally, sound

legal training, high-level experience of public affairs and national and international problems and, lastly, more personal qualities of judgment and character, and in particular integrity and authority likely to inspire confidence
and respect.

When the independent body has concluded its examination, a third element
enters into play, namely the policy-making organs of the ILO (Governing
Body and International Labour Conference), within which are represented
the various interests involved. The conclusions of the independent body are
laid before these organs and they examine the measures required by those
conclusions, seek with the representatives of the governments concerned a
solution to the problems encountered and give to the supervision process the
backing of the Organisation's weight. This phase is especially useful in that,
on account of the "tripartite" structure of the ILO, those non-governmental
elements constituted by employers' and workers' organizations participate in
it on an equal footing with governments. Being able, on account of that
structure and the established procedures, to file complaints, furnish elements
of information and comment upon governments' reports, the representatives
of employers' and workers' organizations, through their participation in the
tripartite organs, give a particular dynamism to the ILO's system of supervision.

Finally, a fourth element, less apparent but sometimes decisive, is that
which may be described as diplomacy in the broad sense of the term. In
affairs which are sometimes complex and delicate, it is often useful for there
to be, alongside or in addition to official procedures and the tensions which
accompany them, an effort at persuasion and explanation discreetly directed
at the parties concerned, under the responsibility of the Director-General of
the ILO, with a view to facilitating the search for solutions. It is thus that, in
the procedures for investigation, conciliation or on-the-spot studies, the independent organs have had the constant co-operation of a senior official
responsible not only for advising them in regard to matters concerning the
Organisation, but also for: serving as an intermediary between the independent organ and the parties, or the government concerned; eliminating mis-
understandings; and maintaining the degree of co-operation necessary, without
affecting the quasi-judicial mission of the supervisory body. The "direct contacts" recently introduced stem from a similar concern.

Thorough-going work by the secretariat, objective examination by an independent body, discussion within a representative tripartite body and "discreet diplomacy" are thus the four essential elements of the supervisory
machinery. Each of these elements has a clearly defined function. They complement each other, though without merging.

In the working of this machinery, certain principles and certain rules of
procedure deserve to be noted more specifically. In the first place, in order to
observe complete objectivity and in conformity with the old adage *auditur et
altera pars*, various rules of procedure give to the parties concerned, in

particular the States involved, every opportunity to put forward fully their points of view.

A second feature to be noted is the thorough and precise character of the supervisory operations, essential for not only the effectiveness but also the authenticity of supervision. For genuine supervision cannot be made with a superficial examination and vague conclusions. The reports and other elements of information requested from governments must therefore be established on the basis of precise forms; the supervisory bodies, with the assistance of their secretariats, make an in-depth examination of the situations considered— without limiting themselves solely to the data furnished by governments— and their conclusions and recommendations are formulated with precision and sometimes in detail.

In the third place, an important factor in the effectiveness of the system is its continuity. Thus the Committee of Experts is periodically informed of the state of matters which have not been settled and returns to them at regular intervals so long as they remain outstanding.

A last detail to be noted concerns the private or public character of the various phases of the procedures. Some of these phases (deliberation of quasi-judicial organs, hearings of witnesses, discreet diplomacy) are of a private character, so as to allow of a calm and objective examination, guard against publicity and endeavour more easily to obtain the necessary action by the governments involved. Other phases (reports and conclusions of the various supervisory bodies, discussions within the Governing Body and the International Labour Conference) are, on the contrary, of a public character, and special publicity is sometimes given to particular cases of lack of co-operation on the part of governments and of persistent discrepancies. Publicity at these stages and in such cases is an element of information for the Organisation and its Members, which is normal for such procedures in the public interest, and even a means of pressure upon the governments concerned, when more discreet measures have not produced results.

However, over and above the various rules of procedure, there has emerged from the working of the various supervisory bodies what has been called the "unwritten wisdom" of the ILO, that is to say a general spirit[44] whose dominant features include scrupulous exactitude in the establishment of facts, strict objectivity in the assessment of situations, firmness of the principles and obligations involved, and courage, together with a sense of proportion and reality, and lastly the desire to arrive, by means of constructive dialogue, at positive solutions.

(ii). THE PLACE OF THE ILO SYSTEM IN THE INTERNATIONAL
    PROTECTION OF HUMAN RIGHTS

Having been in the vanguard of efforts to ensure the international protection of human rights,[45] the ILO's system of supervision is not concerned only with the implementation of the standards for which the Organisation has direct responsibility. It also has a more general significance for the protection of human rights as a whole.

This is true first of all on account of the value of the ILO system as a model for other systems for the implementation of human rights.[46] There has often been speculation as to what extent the procedures of the ILO, which have opened up new avenues for international supervision and which are among the most advanced and the most effective in existence, might also be used in the framework of other international organizations. The question has been raised, in the course of the years, by eminent jurists, particularly by some of those who, having been members of the Committee of Experts, have had closer knowledge of that system of supervision, such as Georges Scelle,[47] Lord McNair,[48] who was President of the International Court of Justice, and the former Chief Justice of the United States, Earl Warren.[49] The question continues to be regularly raised, whether in respect of the entire system of supervision of the ILO,[50] or in respect of particular rules such as those relating to the submission of Conventions to the competent authorities or the transmission of reports on non-ratified Conventions. Thus, for example, Professor Roberto Ago has raised the question whether these procedures might not be extended to Conventions adopted under the auspices of the United Nations,[51] or in relation to procedures for the protection of freedom of association.[52]

There is no doubt, however, that the procedures of the ILO have had a greater or lesser influence on the system of supervision established in other organizations, be they organizations belonging to the United Nations family or regional organizations, such as the Council of Europe.[53] Thus, in such organizations is to be found the system of periodic reports and of recourse to bodies composed of independent members or of persons who at least sit in their individual capacity. This approach is being increasingly accepted, albeit in sometimes limited and imperfect form. A place is sometimes accorded to conciliation procedures and a certain role is sometimes granted to employers' and workers' organisations. Nowhere else, however, are to be found combined all the characteristics which give the ILO's system of supervision its force. This stems, at least in part, from the fact that that system was established in the framework of the specific constitutional provisions and structure of the ILO and that these cannot be transposed, as they stand, to organizations which have neither the same rules nor the same traditions. The fact nonetheless remains that some of the techniques and principles of the ILO could still exercise greater influence in the development of other systems of supervision.

In addition to its value as a model, the ILO system also plays a more extensive role by virtue of the co-operation which has been established with other supervisory systems set up by other organizations, which have also adopted instruments relating to human rights. One of the objects of this co-operation is to avoid contradictions between the measures taken by the supervisory bodies responsible for the implementation of different instruments containing similar provisions. Such co-operation is sometimes provided for in the international text itself.

Thus the International Covenant on Economic, Social and Cultural Rights of 1966 provides (articles 16 and 18) that the specialized agencies shall receive copies of the reports of governments bearing on questions within their competence and that arrangements may be concluded in order for these agencies to submit reports bearing *inter alia* on the decisions of their competent bodies concerning the implementation of the provisions of the Covenant falling within the scope of their activities. The specialized agencies may also submit observations on any recommendation made by the Human Rights Commission (article 20). Since the great majority of the provisions of this Covenant concern questions on which the ILO has adopted numerous detailed Conventions, the ILO's supervisory bodies may play a considerable role in the effective implementation of the Covenant. Participation by the specialized agencies is also provided for, though in less precise terms, by the International Covenant on Civil and Political Rights (article 40, para. 3).

In other cases, co-ordination is effected through administrative arrangements for reciprocal representation and exchange of information, as is the case between the ILO and Unesco, regarding the application of parallel conventions by those organizations relating to discrimination in employment and in education. Similar co-ordination has been developed in respect of the implementation of the United Nations' International Convention on the Elimination of All Forms of Racial Discrimination.

Finally, certain texts of regional institutions, such as the Council of Europe, expressly provide for measures of co-ordination. The European Social Charter, which was adopted in 1961 with the technical assistance and on the basis of the standards of the ILO, thus provides for participation, in a consultative capacity, by an ILO representative in the deliberations of the Committee of Independent Experts responsible for supervising its application. Even closer co-ordination has been worked out under the European Code of Social Security (Minimum Standards) Convention, 1952 (No. 102). The Code provides that a competent body of the ILO will be consulted in the first instance concerning the reports of the Contracting Parties and that its conclusions will be communicated to the Council of Europe.

NOTES

1. Cassin, René, "L'homme, sujet de droit international, et la protection des droits de l'homme dans la société universelle", in *La technique et les principes de droit public, mélanges en l'honneur de Georges Scelle*, Vol. 1, Paris, 1959, p. 68.

2. ILO, Geneva, *Apartheid in Labour Matters* (1966), pp. 3-52.

3. See in particular Jenks, C. Wilfred, *Human Rights and International Labour Standards*, Stevens and Sons, London, and Praeger, New York, 1960; Valticos, N., "Les normes

de l'Organisation Internationale du travail en matière de droits de l'homme", *RDH/HRJ*, vol. IV, No. 4, 1971, pp. 691-769; by the same author, *Droit international du travail*, Paris, Dalloz, 1970; and updated edition in English, *International Labour Law*, Deventer (Netherlands), Kluwer, 1979. See also Van der Ven, J.J.M., "La liberte, motif juridique dans l'Organisation internationale du Travail", *RDH/HRJ*, vol. VIII, No. 4, 1975, pp. 869-882.

4. *The ILO and human rights*, Report of the Director-General of the International Labour Office to the International Labour Conference, 52nd session, 1968. "Comparative analysis of the International Covenants on Human Rights and the international labour Conventions and recommendations", *Official Bulletin*, vol. LII, 1969, No. 2, pp. 188-226.

5. Jenks, C. Wilfred, "Human Rights, Social Justice and Peace—The Broader Significance of the ILO Experience". In: *International Protection of Human Rights. Proceedings of the 7th Nobel Symposium* published under the direction of A. Eide and A. Schou, ed., Almquist and Wiksell, Stockholm, 1968, pp. 235-236.

6. Valticos, N., "Un développement du droit international du travail: les droits syndicaux et les libertés publiques". In: *En hommage à Paul Horion*, Liège Faculty of Law, 1972, pp. 263-289.

7. Reference may be made, particularly, to the more detailed information contained in the general studies submitted by the Committee of Experts concerning the Conventions on freedom of association (in 1959 and 1973), forced labour (in 1962 and 1968) and discrimination in employment (in 1963 and 1971).

8. *Freedom of Association. Digest of Decisions of the Freedom of Association Committee*, ILO, Geneva, 2nd edition, 1976.

9. Valticos, N. *International Labour Law, op. cit.* pp. 225-227.

10. The following States: Belgium, Bulgaria, Cuba, Djibouti, Federal Republic of Germany, Finland, France, Italy, Netherlands, Norway, Panama, Peru, Poland, Spain, Sweden, United Kingdom, Uruguay and Yugoslavia.

11. Concerning this practice and its importance, see Jenks, C. Wilfred, "State Succession in Respect of Law-Making Treaties", in *The British Yearbook of International Law*, 1952, pp. 105-144; Wolf, F., "Les Conventions internationales du travail et la succession d'Etat", in *Annuaire français de droit international*, 1961, pp. 742-751. By the same author, "L'Organisation internationale du travail, sa compétence et les transformations étatiques", in *Communizioni e Studi*, Milan, vol. 9, 1957, pp. 47-71; O'Connell, *State Succession in Municipal Law and International Law*, Cambridge, 1967, vol. II, pp. 202-204.

12. Valticos, N., "Un systeme de contrôle international: la mise en oeuvre des conventions internationales du travail", in *RCADI*, vol. 123, 1968-I, pp. 311-407; by the same author: *International Labour Law, op. cit.*, pp. 239-257; and Wolf, F., "Aspects judiciaires de la protection internationale des droits de l'homme par l'OIT", in *RDH/HRJ*, vol. IV-4, 1971, pp. 773-838. See also the reports submitted by the ILO to the United Nations on the matter: docs. E/4144 (1965), A/6699/Add 1 (1967), and E/CN.4/1023/Add. 1 (1971).

13. The Governing Body of the ILO has adopted in this connection a detailed memorandum which provides precise information as to the coverage of the rule and presents governments with a number of questions.

14. The rules governing this selective system for the spacing out of reports on ratified Conventions were approved by the Governing Body at its 201st Session, in November 1976. They are designed to ensure the continuing effectiveness of supervision, while lightening the burden falling on both national administrations and ILO supervisory bodies.

15. Each year the Governing Body of the ILO selects certain Conventions or Recommendations and requests States to make reports of this type, on the basis of forms which are less detailed than in the case of ratified Conventions. As is indicated below, such reports have been requested more especially, and on several occasions, on Conventions concerning fundamental human rights.

16. ILO, Geneva, International Labour Conference: *Report of the Committee of Experts on the Application of Conventions and Recommendations*, Report III (Part IV), 1967, p. 3;

1967, p. 11; 1969, p. 19, 1971, p. 6; 1977, p. 13; (this report will be referred to subsequently as *Rep. Comm. Exp.*).

17. See in particular a study of this question in the Report of the Committee of Experts 1963, pp. 8-12, paras. 21-34, and 1970, p. 8, paras. 18-19. See also in this connection Valticos, "Droit international du travail et droit interne français", *Travaux du Comité français de droit international privé (1973-1975)*, Paris, Dalloz, 1977, pp. 11-28.

18. Thus, in France, under the Labour Code (Act. No. 73-4 of 2 January 1973) the text of provisions of international labour Conventions applicable in French municipal law was published as an Annex to the Code.

19. Jenks, C. Wilfred, "The Application of International Labour Conventions by Means of Collective Agreements", in *Zeitschrift für Ausländisches Öffentliches Recht und Völkerrecht*, Festgabe Makarov, Stuttgart and Cologne, Aug. 1958, pp. 197-224. Wolf, F., "L'application des Conventions internationales du travail par voie de Conventions collectives", *Annuaire français de droit international*, 1974, pp. 103-114.

20. *Rep. Comm. Exp.* 1977, p. 11.

21. See Valticos and Wolf, "L'Organization internationale du Travail et les pays on voie de développement: techniques d'élaboration et mise en oeuvre de normes universelles", in *Pays en voie de développement et transformation du droit international*, Societé française pour le droit international, Colloque d'Aix-en-Provence, Pédone, Paris, 1974, pp. 127-146 and 167-168. Valticos, *International Labour Law, op. cit.*, pp. 51-54.

22. The results of this supervision are dealt with in a more general ILO study on the *Impact of the International Labour Conventions and Recommendations*, ILO, Geneva, 1977.

23. Landy, E.A., *The Effectiveness of International Supervision—Thirty Years of ILO Experience*, London, Stevens and Sons, and Dobbs Ferry, New York, Oceana Publications, 1966. See also, by the same author: "The influence of international labour standards: Possibilities and Performance", in *International Labour Review*, vol. 101, No. 6, June 1970, pp. 55-604.

24. See *Rep. Comm. Exp.* 1972, para. 125.

25. See e.g. *Rep. Comm. Exp.* 1973, para. 103.

26. See in this connection the articles published in the *International Labour Review* on the influence of Conventions in Belgium (Nov. 1968), Colombia (Feb. 1969), the Federal Republic of Germany (Dec. 1974), France (April 1970), Greece (June 1955), India (June 1956), Ireland (July 1972), Italy (June 1961), Nigeria (July 1960), Norway (Sept. 1964), Poland (Nov. 1965), Republic of Cameroon (Aug-Sept. 1973), Switzerland (June 1958), Tunisia (March 1965), United Kingdom (May 1968), and Yugoslavia (Nov. 1967). See also the general study mentioned above, note 22.

27. See the opinion of Judge Philip C. Jessup in the *South-West African* cases, International Court of Justice, Digest, 1962, judgement of 21 December 1962, pp. 428 and 431. Judge Jessup added that this rule reflected the conviction that the well-being of mankind is as indivisible as peace and that it constitutes the application to the international sphere of the well-known lines of the English poet John Donne, written more than three centuries ago: "No man is an Island entire of itself; every man is a piece of the Continent, a part of the main. Any man's death diminishes me, because I am involved in Mankind".

28. See concerning the first two procedures, Vignes, Daniel, "Procédures internationales d'enquête", in *Annuaire français de droit international* 1963, p. 444. See the reports of those two Commissions: ILO, *Official Bulletin*, vol. XLV, No. 2, Supplement II, April 1962, and vol. XLVI, No. 2, Supplement II, April 1963. For the report on Greece, see also *Official Bulletin*, vol. LIV, No. 2, Special Supplement, 1971. For the procedure concerning Chile, it was combined with that concerning freedom of association: see below, note 34.

29. More recently, in 1975, 1976 and 1977, respectively, delegates of workers' organizations to the International Labour Conference lodged complaints against the governments of Uruguay, Bolivia and Argentina concerning the application of the Conventions on freedom

of association. For the time being, the questions raised are dealt with in accordance with the special procedure for the protection of freedom of association which is described further on. "Direct contacts" took place in the first two cases.

30. Jenks, C. Wilfred, *The International Protection of Trade Union Freedom*, London, Stevens and Sons, 1957, and "The International Protection of Trade Union Rights", in *The International Protection of Human Rights*, edited by Evan Luard, London, Thames and Hudson, 1967, pp. 210-247. Von Potobsky, G., "Normas internacionales, libertad sindical y derecho colectivo del trabajo", in *Tratado de derecho del trabajo*, vol. V, Buenos Aires, 1966, pp. 597-699. Cassese A., "Il controllo internazionale sul rispetto della liberta sindacale nel quadro delle attuali tendenze in materia de protezione internazionale dei diritti dell'uomo", extract from: *Communicazioni e Studi,* vol. XII, Milan, 1966, pp. 293-418. Valticos, N., "La protection internationale de la liberté syndicale vingt-cinq ans après", in *RDH/HRJ*, vol. VII-1, 1974, pp. 5-39, Valticos, "Les méthodes de protection intérnationale de la liberté syndicale", in *RCADI*, vol. 144, 1975-I, pp. 77-138.

31. This was affirmed by the Second European Regional Conference of the ILO in a resolution adopted on 23 January 1974. See also the Report on *The Trade Union Situation in Chile*, by the Fact-Finding and Conciliation Committee, ILO, Geneva, 1975, p. 108, paragraph 466.

32. See more particularly: von Potobsky, G., "Protection of trade union rights: Twenty years' work by the Committee on Freedom of Association", in *International Labour Review*, vol. 105, No. 1, January 1972, pp. 69-83.

33. Valticos, N., "La Commission d'investigation et de conciliation en matière de liberté syndicale", in *Annuaire français de droit international* 1967, pp. 445-468.

34. See ILO, *Official Bulletin*, vol. XLIX, No. 1, special supplement, January 1966.

35. *The trade union situation in Chile. Report of the Fact-Finding and Conciliation Commission on Freedom of Association*, ILO, Geneva, 1975. Concerning this procedure, see also Valticos, "Un double type d'enquête de l'OIT au Chili", *Annuaire français de droit international*, 1975, pp. 483-502.

36. Valticos, N., "Une nouvelle expérience de protection des droits de l'homme: le groupe d'étude de l'OIT chargé d'examiner la situation en matière de travail et en matière syndicale en Espagne", in *Annuaire français de droit international*, 1970, pp. 567-590; and "L'OIT et l'évolution de la législation syndicale en Espagne", *Estudios de Derecho Internacional, Homenaje al Profesor Mioja de la Múela*, Madrid, 1979, pp. 793-812.

37. ILO, Geneva, 1969: *The Labour and Trade Union Situation in Spain*, VIII, 298 pp.

38. The ILO's total expenditure for technical co-operation exceeded 78 million dollars in 1979 and involved the use, as of January 1979, of over 700 experts in 125 countries. See for a general survey: Blanchard, F., "L'OIT et la coopération technique", in *Revue française des affaires sociales*, April-June 1969, pp. 37-54.

39. Such missions have been to Colombia, Dominican Republic, Iran, Kenya, Philippines, Sudan and Sri Lanka, and on-the-spot studies have been carried out in Burundi, Chile, Costa Rica, Ethiopia, Jamaica, Laos, Liberia, Madagascar, Morocco, Panama, Pakistan and Zaire.

40. I have endeavoured to identify the part played by international inspection in these procedures in: Valticos, N., "L'inspection internationale dans le droit international du travail", in *L'inspection internationale*, G. Fischer and D. Vignes, eds., Bruylant, Brussels, 1976, pp. 379-437.

41. Concerning the scope and limits of this work by the secretariat, see Jenks in Evan Luard, *op. cit.*, pp. 240-241; Van Asbeck, "Une commission d'experts", in *Symbolae Verzijl*, The Hague, 1958, p. 19; and "Quelques aspects du contrôle international non judiciare de l'application par les gouvernements de Conventions internationales", in *Nederlands Tijdschrift voor Internationaal Recht*, volume in honour of Professor François, Leyden, 1959, p. 33.

42. See in this connection Jenks in Evan Luard, *op. cit.*, pp. 239-240; Van Asbeck, "Une commission d'experts", *op. cit.*, pp. 18-19; Golsong H., "Implementation of International

Protection of Human Rights", in *RCADI*, 1963-III, pp. 24, 34 and 140-141; Juvigny, P., "The Legal Protection of Human Rights at the International Level", in *International Social Science Journal*, vol. XVIII, No. 1, 1966, p. 76; by the same author, "L'OIT et les droits de l'homme", in *Revue française des affaires sociales*, April-June 1969, p. 94, where it is stated *inter alia* that "it is to the honour of the ILO that it has created conditions which have given rise to a genuine tradition of objectivity" within those organs.

43. See Jenks in Evan Luard, *op. cit.*, pp. 239-240.

44. See in this connection Jenks in *Nobel Symposium*, *op. cit.*, pp. 249-256; Valticos, N., "Un systeme de contrôle international: la mise en oeuvre des Conventions internationales du travail", *op. cit.*, pp. 386-388.

45. See also the statement by U Thant, Secretary-General of the United Nations, to the International Labour Conference on 18 June 1969, *Report of Proceedings*, 53rd session, Geneva, 1969, p. 319.

46. Jenks, C. Wilfred, *Social Justice in the Law of Nations. The ILO Impact after Fifty Years*, Oxford University Press, London-Oxford-New York, 1970, pp. 33 *et seq.*

47. Scelle, G. *Précis de droit des gens*, vol. I, Paris, 1932, p. 521.

48. Lord McNair, *The Expansion of International Law*, Jerusalem, 1962, p. 45.

49. See address delivered in Abidjan in August 1973, *American Bar Association Journal*, November 1973, p. 1259.

50. Thus, on 27 March 1974, the Sub-Commission on international organizations and movements of the Commission for Foreign Affairs of the Chamber of Representatives of the United Nations suggested that the ILO's methods in regard to the protection of human rights should be emulated by other international organizations. See also, a similar suggestion by the International Confederation of Free Trade Unions, *Free Labour World* (Brussels) Nov.-Dec. 1979, p. 7.

51. Ago, Robert, "La codification du droit international et les problèmes de sa réalisation", in *Recueil d'études de droit international en hommage à Paul Guggenheim*, Geneva, 1968, pp. 117 *et seq.*

52. Cassese, A., "Il controllo internazionale sul rispetto della libertá sindacale nel quadro delle attuali tendenze in materia di protezione internazionale dei diritti dell'uomo", *op. cit.*, pp. 293-418. Vellas, P., "L'évolution de la compétence de l'OIT et l'affaire de la liberte syndicale au Japon", in *Droit social*, Paris, June 1967, p. 362. See also the report of a commission of the American Society of International Law, in *American Journal of International Law*, vol. 64, no. 4, p. 309.

53. Valticos, N., "Les systèmes de contrôle non judiciare des instruments internationaux relatifs aux droits de l'homme", in *Mélanges offerts à P. Modinos (Problèmes des droits de l'homme et de l'unification européenne)*, Paris, Pédone, 1968, pp. 331-356. By the same author: "Un système de contrôle international: la mise en oeuvre des Conventions ratifiées", *op. cit.*, pp. 389-398, and *Droit international du travail*, *op. cit.*, pp. 600-607.